NEW CONCISE

PROJECT MATHS 2

FOR JUNIOR CERT HIGHER LEVEL

GEORGE HUMPHREY, BRENDAN GUILDEA, GEOFFREY REEVES
LOUISE BOYLAN

GILL & MACMILLAN

Gill & Macmillan
Hume Avenue
Park West
Dublin 12
with associated companies throughout the world
www.gillmacmillan.ie

© George Humphrey, Brendan Guildea, Geoffrey Reeves and
Louise Boylan 2012

978 07171 5357 2

Print origination by MPS Limited

The paper used in this book is made from the wood pulp of managed forests. For every tree felled, at least one tree is planted, thereby renewing natural resources.

Any links to external websites should not be construed as an endorsement by Gill & Macmillan of the content or views of the linked materials.

For permission to reproduce photographs, the authors and publisher gratefully acknowledge the following:

©Alamy: 113, 179T, 179B, 208, 236, 259, 472B, 472T;
© Getty Images: 124, 408, 416, 418R.

The authors and publisher have made every effort to trace all copyright holders, but if any has been inadvertently overlooked we would be pleased to make the necessary arrangement at the first opportunity.

Contents

Preface		v
Acknowledgments		vi
1	Factors	1
2	Algebraic Fractions	13
3	Long Division in Algebra	21
4	Simultaneous Linear Equations	24
5	Irrational Numbers – Surds	30
6	Quadratic Equations	38
7	Linear Inequalities in one Variable	47
8	Changing the Subject of a Formula	54
9	Indices, Index Notation and Reciprocals	59
10	Distance, Speed and Time	74
11	Collecting and Processing Data	85
12	Averages and the Spread of Data	96
13	Representing Data	114
14	Sets	163
15	Coordinate Geometry of the Line	180
16	Trigonometry	213
17	Applied Arithmetic	237
18	Perimeter, Area, Volume and Nets	259
19	Probability	318

20	Functions	360
21	Graphing Functions	369
22	Patterns and Sequences	395
23	Angles, Triangles and Quadrilaterals	419
24	Congruent Triangles	439
25	Circle Theorems	449
26	Similar Triangles	461
27	Pythagoras' Theorem	479
28	Transformations	495
29	Proofs of Theorems	524
30	Constructions	530
31	Using Equations to Solve Problems	550
	Answers	567

Preface

New Concise Project Maths 2 completes the course for Junior Certificate Mathematics, Higher Level. It contains strands 1–4 of the Project Maths syllabus, and strand 5 of the existing syllabus. *New Concise Project Maths 2* with *New Concise Project Maths 1* completes the course for Higher Level students in 2014.

New Concise Project Maths 2 incorporates the approach to the teaching of mathematics envisaged in **Project Maths**. It reflects the greater emphasis on the understanding of mathematical concepts, developing problem-solving skills and relating mathematics to everyday events.

The authors strongly sympathise with the main aims and objectives of the new Project Maths syllabus and examination. In the worked examples, a numbered, step by step approach is used throughout the book to help with problem solving. The constructions are demonstrated with excellent diagrams. There is a comprehensive range of carefully graded exercises to reflect the new exam. Exam style context questions are included to enhance students' understanding of everyday practical applications of mathematics. The emphasis is on a clear and practical presentation of the material. Simple and concise language is used throughout, instead of technical language, which is not required in the exam.

Additional teachers resources, including a **Digital Flipbook**, are provided online at www.gillmacmillan.ie.

An excellent resource for teachers and students is the dynamic software package **GeoGebra**. The package is of particular use for coordinate geometry, geometry and graphing functions. It can be accessed at www.geogebra.org

George Humphrey
Brendan Guildea
Geoffrey Reeves
Louise Boylan
May 2012

Acknowledgments

The authors wish to express their thanks to the staff at Gill and Macmillan, in particular, Neil Ryan and Anthony Murray, and to Kristin Jensen of 'Between the lines Editing' for their advice, guidance and assistance in the preparation and presentation of the text.

The authors would also like to thank Colman Humphrey, Elaine Guildea, Lauren Watson and Sorcha Forde who helped with proof reading, checking answers and making many valuable suggestions that are included in the final text.

Factorising

> Factorising is the reverse procedure to removing brackets.

Expanding removes brackets.
Factorising does the opposite by putting in brackets.
For example:

> Expanding: $5(2a + 3b) = 10a + 15b$ Remove brackets.
> Factorising: $10a + 15b = 5(2a + 3b)$ Put in brackets.

The process of finding the factors of an expression is called **factorisation**.
There are four types of factors that we will meet on our course:

	Type	Example	Factors
1.	Take out the HCF	$12pq - 6q^2$	$6q(2p - q)$
2.	Factors by grouping	$6a^2 - 2ab + 3ac - bc$	$(3a - b)(2a + c)$
3.	Quadratic trinomials	$10x^2 - 3x - 1$	$(5x + 1)(2x - 1)$
4.	Difference of two squares	$16a^2 - 25b^2$	$(4a - 5b)(4a + 5b)$

Note: It is good practice to check your answer by removing the brackets to make sure that the factors give the original expression you were asked to factorise.

Taking out the highest common factor (HCF)

> 1. Find the HCF of all the terms making up the expression.
> 2. Put the HCF outside the brackets.
> 3. Divide each term by the HCF to find the factor inside the brackets.

Notes: 1. To factorise an expression **completely**, the HCF must appear outside the brackets.
2. 1 or −1 is always a common factor.

EXAMPLE

Factorise: **(i)** $15pq + 3q^2$ **(ii)** $4x^2y - 6xy^2$ **(iii)** $ab - ac + a$

Solution:

(i) $15pq + 3q^2$

The HCF is $3q$.

$\therefore 15pq + 3q^2$ (put $3q$ outside the bracket,

$= 3q(5p + q)$ then divide each term by $3q$)

$$\frac{15pq}{3q} = 5p$$
$$\frac{3q^2}{3q} = q$$

(ii) $4x^2y - 6xy^2$

The HCF is $2xy$.

$\therefore 4x^2y - 6xy^2$ (put $2xy$ outside the bracket,

$= 2xy(2x - 3y)$ then divide each term by $2xy$)

$$\frac{4x^2y}{2xy} = 2x$$
$$\frac{-6xy^2}{2xy} = -3y$$

(iii) $ab - ac + a$

The HCF is a.

$\therefore ab - ac + a$ (put a outside the bracket,

$= a(b - c + 1)$ then divide each term by a)

(there must be a 1 here)

$$\frac{ab}{a} = b$$
$$\frac{-ac}{a} = -c$$
$$\frac{a}{a} = 1$$

Notice that the HCF is the same as one of the terms.

Exercise 1.1

Simplify questions 1–15.

1. $\dfrac{10x}{5}$ 2. $\dfrac{8y}{2}$ 3. $\dfrac{15xy}{5y}$ 4. $\dfrac{9pq}{3p}$ 5. $\dfrac{12ab}{4ab}$

6. $\dfrac{8xyz}{4xy}$ 7. $\dfrac{7q}{7q}$ 8. $\dfrac{-2xy}{-2xy}$ 9. $\dfrac{8ab}{-4b}$ 10. $\dfrac{-20xy}{10y}$

11. $\dfrac{-5xy}{5x}$ 12. $\dfrac{6pq}{3pq}$ 13. $\dfrac{12x^2y}{6xy}$ 14. $\dfrac{15pq^2}{15pq}$ 15. $\dfrac{6a^2b}{3ab}$

Copy questions 16–23 and fill in the missing expression in the brackets.

16. $3x + 3y = 3(\qquad)$ 17. $5p - 15q = 5(\qquad)$

18. $x^2 + 2x = x(\qquad)$ 19. $4a^2 - 2a = 2a(\qquad)$

20. $3p^2 - 6pq = 3p(\qquad)$ 21. $-5pq - 10p = -5p(\qquad)$

22. $6x^2y - 4xy^2 = 2xy(\qquad)$ 23. $-2x^2 + 6x = -2x(\qquad)$

Factorise each of the following in questions 24–41.

24. $5x + 10$

25. $pq + pr$

26. $2x + xy$

27. $x^2 + 5x$

28. $4x^2 + 2x$

29. $a^2 - 3a$

30. $2a - 3ab$

31. $3ab - 6ac$

32. $x^2 - x$

33. $8x - 12x^2$

34. $x^2 - 6x$

35. $15bc - 3c^2$

36. $4x^2y - 8xy^2$

37. $ax^2 + ax$

38. $10p - 15pq$

39. $pq + pr + p$

40. $ab - 2a^2b + 3ab^2$

41. $8ab - 12ab^2 + 16a^2b$

42. Several possible factorisations of $36a^2 - 12a$ are shown below.

$4a(9a - 3)$ $6a(6a - 2)$ $12a(3a - 1)$ $36a(a - 1)$ $2a(18a - 6)$

   (i) Which pair of factors is incorrect? Justify your answer.

   (ii) Which pair of factors gives the answer to the question 'factorise $36a^2 - 12a$ completely'?

43. The area of a rectangle is $(4x^2 + 2x)$ cm^2. Its length is $2x$ cm. Find it breadth.

44. The volume of a cuboid is $(5x^3 + 15x^2)$ cm^3. The area of its base is $(x^2 + 3x)$ cm^2. Find its height.

45. Simplify $5(x^2 - 2x + 4) - 2(2x^2 - 3x + 10)$ and then factorise the simplified expression.

46. Simplify $(2p + 3q)(p - 4q) + (p + 6q)(p + 2q)$ and then factorise the simplified expression.

47. (i) Factorise: (a) $12pq - 6p$ (b) $6q - 3$

   (ii) Hence, simplify $\dfrac{12pq - 6p}{6q - 3}$ by dividing the top and bottom by common factors.

Factors by grouping

On our course, an expression consisting of four terms with no common factor can be factorised with the following steps.

> 1. Group into pairs with a common factor.
> 2. Take out the common factor in each pair separately.
> 3. Take out the new common factor.

EXAMPLE 1

Factorise: (i) $2pr - 2ps + qr - qs$ (ii) $6a^2 - 3ab - bx + 2ax$ (iii) $xy + xz - y - z$

Solution:

(i) $2pr - 2ps + qr - qs$ (already in pairs with a common factor)

   $= 2p(r - s) + q(r - s)$ (take out the common factor in each pair)

   $= (r - s)(2p + q)$ (take out the common factor $(r - s)$)

(ii) $\quad 6a^2 - 3ab - bx + 2ax$ $\qquad$ (already in pairs with a common factor)

$\quad = 3a(2a - b) - x(b - 2a)$ $\qquad$ (take out the common factor in each pair)

$\quad = 3a(2a - b) + x(2a - b)$ $\qquad$ $(-x(b - 2a) = +x(2a - b))$

$\quad = (2a - b)(3a + x)$ $\qquad$ (take out the common factor $(2a - b)$)

Note: In this example, the order of the last two terms could have been rearranged to make the factorising easier.

$\qquad 6a^2 - 3ab - bx + 2ax = 6a^2 - 3ab + 2ax - bx$ and then factorise.

(iii) $\;xy + xz - y - z$

We will look at two ways of factorising this expression.

Method 1:

$\qquad xy + xz - y - z$ $\qquad$ (already in pairs with a common factor)

$\quad = x(y + z) - 1(y + z)$ $\qquad$ (take out the common factor in each pair)

$\quad = (y + z)(x - 1)$ $\qquad$ (take out the common factor $(y + z)$)

Note: 1 or −1 is always a common factor.

Method 2:

$\qquad xy + xz - y - z$ $\qquad$ (rearrange order of the terms so that they are still

$\quad = xy - y + xz - z$ $\qquad$ grouped into pairs with a common factor)

$\quad = y(x - 1) + z(x - 1)$ $\qquad$ (take out the common factor in each pair)

$\quad = (x - 1)(y + z)$ $\qquad$ (take out the common factor $(x - 1)$)

Note: $(y + z)(x - 1) = (x - 1)(y + z)$

More difficult factors by grouping

Sometimes rearranging is necessary.

EXAMPLE 2

Factorise $6pq + rs - 2sq - 3rp$.

Solution:

There are no common factors in the first two pairs or in the last two pairs.

Therefore, we have to rearrange the terms.

$\qquad 6pq + rs - 2sq - 3rp$ $\qquad$ (rearrange order of the terms so that they are grouped

$\quad = 6pq - 3rp + rs - 2sq$ $\qquad$ into pairs with a common factor)

$\quad = 3p(2q - r) + s(r - 2q)$ $\qquad$ (take out the common factor in each pair)

$\quad = 3p(2q - r) - s(2q - r)$ $\qquad$ $(s(r - 2q) = -s(2q - r))$

$\quad = (2q - r)(3p - s)$ $\qquad$ (take out the common factor $(2q - r)$)

Note: This expression could also have been rearranged into pairs with common factors in other ways before factorising, such as

$\qquad 6pq - 2sq - 3rp + rs \quad$ or $\quad 6pq - 3rp - 2sq + rs$.

Exercise 1.2

Factorise questions 1–14.

1. $c(a + b) + d(a + b)$

2. $r(p - q) - s(p - q)$

3. $2x(p + 3q) + y(p + 3q)$

4. $3a(x - 2y) - 2b(x - 2y)$

5. $ax + ay + bx + by$

6. $pq + pr + xq + xr$

7. $am - an + 4m - 4n$

8. $pq + pr - 3q - 3r$

9. $x^2 - 3x + xy - 3y$

10. $x^2 - xy + xz - yz$

11. $pq - 2q + p^2 - 2p$

12. $ab - ac + bc - c^2$

13. $6x^2 - 3xz + 2xy - yz$

14. $x^2 - 3xy + 2ax - 6ay$

Copy questions 15–22 and fill in the missing expression in the bracket.

15. $-3p - 3q = -3($ $)$

16. $-5ab - 5ac = -5a($ $)$

17. $-2x^2 - 2x = -2x($ $)$

18. $-2p + 2q = -2($ $)$

19. $-x^2 + 3x = -x($ $)$

20. $-3xy + x^2 = -x($ $)$

21. $a + b = 1($ $)$

22. $x - y = -1($ $)$

Factorise questions 23–52.

23. $ab + ac - 2b - 2c$

24. $x^2 + xy - 3x - 3y$

25. $p^2 + pq - pr - qr$

26. $px + 3p - qx - 3q$

27. $ax + bx + a + b$

28. $px + qx - p - q$

29. $p(x - y) + 2(y - x)$

30. $a(b - c) - (c - b)$

31. $x^2 - 2x - xy + 2y$

32. $3p - p^2 - 3q + pq$

33. $ap - aq - qx + px$

34. $5a - 5b - 2bx + 2ax$

35. $x^2 - 3xy - 2ax + 6ay$

36. $px - py - x + y$

In questions 37–46, rearranging is necessary before factorising.

37. $ac + bd + ad + bc$

38. $pq + 2r + pr + 2q$

39. $xy - zw + yw - xz$

40. $3x + yq - 3y - xq$

41. $2xa - yb + 2xb - ya$

42. $ab + 2 + b + 2a$

43. $3b - 2a^2 - 2ab + 3a$

44. $p^2 - 6q + 3p - 2pq$

45. $an - 5b - 5a + bn$

46. $3ax + 4by - 6bx - 2ay$

In questions 47–52, remove the brackets and rearrange before factorising.

47. $p^2 - p(2q - 1) - 2q$

48. $q^2 - q(2a - b) - 2ab$

49. $x^2 - x(a + b) + ab$

50. $a^2 + 3b - a(3 + b)$

51. $p(10r - q) - 5qr + 2p^2$

52. $a^2 - a(2x + y) + 2xy$

53. The area of a rectangle is $(ax + ay + bx + by)$ cm^2. Its length is $(x + y)$ cm. Find its breadth.

54. The rectangle *ABCD* is made up of four other rectangles with areas ax, ay, bx and by, as shown.

    (i) Find expressions for the lengths of the rectangle *ABCD*.

    (ii) Find the area of the rectangle in two different ways.

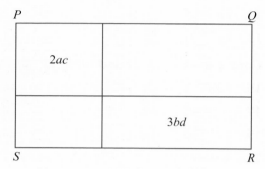

55. The area of the rectangle *PQRS* is $2ac + bc + 6ad + 3bd$.

    PQRS contains four other rectangles, as shown. The areas of two of these rectangles are $2ac$ and $3bd$, as shown.

    Copy the diagram and complete the areas of the two other rectangles.

Quadratic trinomials

An expression of the form $ax^2 + bx + c$, where a, b and c are numbers, is called a **quadratic trinomial**, since in the expression the highest power of x is 2 (quadratic) and it contains three terms (trinomial).

Factorising quadratic trinomials

Quadratic trinomials can be broken up into **two** types.

1. **Final term positive**

   When the final term is positive, the signs inside the middle of the brackets will be the **same** (either two pluses or two minuses). Keep the sign of the middle term given in the question.

Middle term plus:	(number x + number)(number x + number) (two pluses)
Middle term minus:	(number x − number)(number x − number) (two minuses)

2. **Final term negative**

   When the final term is negative, the signs inside the middle of the brackets will be **different**.

   (number x + number)(number x − number)   (different signs)

   or

   (number x − number)(number x + number)   (different signs)

In both cases the factors can be found by trial and improvement. The test is to multiply the inside terms, multiply the outside terms and add the results to see if you get the middle term of the original quadratic trinomial.

EXAMPLE 1

Factorise: (i) $2x^2 + 7x + 3$ (ii) $5x^2 - 7x - 6$

Solution:

(i) $2x^2 + 7x + 3$

The factors of $2x^2$ are $2x$ and x.

Final term + and middle term is +.

Therefore, the factors are $(2x + \text{number})(x + \text{number})$.

Factors of 3
1×3

1. $(2x + 3)(x + 1)$ middle term $= 3x + 2x = 5x$ (no)

2. $(2x + 1)(x + 3)$ middle term $= x + 6x = 7x$ (yes)

$\therefore 2x^2 + 7x + 3 = (2x + 1)(x + 3)$

(ii) $5x^2 - 7x - 6$

The factors of $5x^2$ are $5x$ and x.

Final term $-$.

Therefore, the factors are $(5x + \text{number})(x - \text{number})$

or $(5x - \text{number})(x + \text{number})$

Factors of 6
1×6
2×3

1. $(5x + 1)(x - 6)$ middle term $= x - 30x = -29x$ (no)

2. $(5x + 6)(x - 1)$ middle term $= 6x - 5x = x$ (no)

3. $(5x + 2)(x - 3)$ middle term $= 2x - 15x = -13x$ (no)

4. $(5x + 3)(x - 2)$ middle term $= 3x - 10x = -7x$ (yes)

$\therefore 5x^2 - 7x - 6 = (5x + 3)(x - 2)$

Sometimes the coefficient of x^2 has more than one set of factors. When this happens write out **all** the possible factors of the coefficient of x^2 and the constant term before starting the process of trial and improvement.

7

EXAMPLE 2

Factorise $6x^2 - 5x - 4$.

Solution:

The factors of $6x^2$ are $6x$ and x or $3x$ and $2x$.

Final term $-$ and middle term $-$.

Therefore, the factors are

$(6x + \text{number})(x - \text{number})$ or $(3x + \text{number})(2x - \text{number})$.

Factors of 4
1×4
2×2

Note: The signs inside these brackets could be swapped.

1. $(6x + 1)(x - 4)$ middle term $= x - 24x = -23x$ (no)

2. $(6x + 4)(x - 1)$ middle term $= 4x - 6x = -2x$ (no)

3. $(3x + 1)(2x - 4)$ middle term $= 2x - 12x = -10x$ (no)

4. $(3x + 4)(2x - 1)$ middle term $= 8x - 3x = 5x$ (no, wrong sign)

The fourth attempt has the wrong sign of the coefficient of the middle term.
Therefore, all that is needed is to swap the signs in the middle of the brackets.

5. $(3x - 4)(2x + 1)$ middle term $= -8x + 3x = -5x$ (yes)

$\therefore 6x^2 - 5x - 4 = (3x - 4)(2x + 1)$

Exercise 1.3

Factorise each of following in questions 1–39.

1. $2x^2 + 5x + 3$
2. $3x^2 + 11x + 6$
3. $2x^2 - 7x + 6$
4. $3x^2 + 4x - 7$
5. $2x^2 - 9x - 5$
6. $3x^2 + 8x - 3$
7. $5x^2 + 16x + 3$
8. $5x^2 + 9x - 2$
9. $7x^2 + 5x - 2$
10. $2x^2 - x - 10$
11. $3x^2 - x - 10$
12. $3x^2 - x - 2$
13. $2x^2 - 5x - 3$
14. $x^2 + 3x + 2$
15. $x^2 + 7x + 12$
16. $x^2 - 10x + 21$
17. $x^2 - 2x - 15$
18. $x^2 - 4x - 12$
19. $2x^2 + 11x + 14$
20. $2x^2 + 7x - 15$
21. $3x^2 - 11x - 20$
22. $7x^2 - 23x + 6$
23. $11x^2 - 19x - 6$
24. $13x^2 + 25x - 2$
25. $4x^2 + 8x + 3$
26. $6x^2 + 11x + 3$
27. $4x^2 + 13x + 3$

28. $6x^2 - 13x + 2$

29. $4x^2 - 11x - 3$

30. $6x^2 - x - 2$

31. $8x^2 + 6x - 5$

32. $10x^2 - x - 3$

33. $9x^2 + 2x - 7$

34. $6x^2 - 7x - 10$

35. $4x^2 + 5x - 6$

36. $9x^2 + 6x - 8$

37. $8x^2 - 13x - 6$

38. $24x^2 + x - 3$

39. $15x^2 - 2x - 8$

40. The factors of $x^2 + 9x + 18$ are $(x + p)$ and $(x + q)$. Evaluate **(i)** $p + q$ **(ii)** pq.

41. The factors of $2x^2 + x - 15$ are $(ax + b)$ and $(cx + d)$. Find the values of a, b, c and d.

42. The area of a rectangle is $(3x^2 + 14x - 5)$ cm^2. Its length is $(3x - 1)$ cm.

    (i) Find its breadth.

    (ii) Explain why $x > \frac{1}{3}$.

43. The rectangle $ABCD$ is made up of four other rectangles, as shown. Two of the rectangles have areas of x^2 and 14. The lengths of the sides of the rectangle $ABCD$ are $(x + a)$ and $(x + b)$.

    (i) Find two possible pairs of values of a and b.

    (ii) Copy the diagram and complete the areas of the other two rectangles.

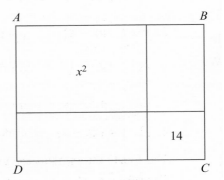

44. The rectangle $PQRS$ is made up of four other rectangles with areas $2x^2$, $8x$, $3x$ and 12, as shown.

    Find expressions for the lengths of the sides of the rectangle $PQRS$.

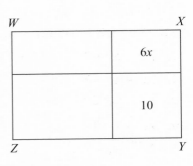

45. The area of rectangle $WXYZ$ is $3x^2 + 11x + 10$.

    $WXYZ$ contains four other rectangles, as shown.

    The area of two of these rectangles are $6x$ and 10.

    Copy the diagram and complete the areas of the other two rectangles.

46. Simplify $(2x - 1)(x + 1) - 2(x + 7)$ and factorise the simplified expression.

47. Simplify $(x - 2)^2 - 2(x - 2) - 15$ and factorise the simplified expression.

48. Simplify $2(x + 1)^2 + 7(x + 1) + 3$ and factorise the simplified expression.

49. Simplify $(3x + 1)^2 - (2x + 1)(x - 5) + 2$ and factorise the simplified expression.

50. **(i)** Find the mean (average) of 2, 3, 5 and 14.

(ii) $A = 6x^2 + 7x - 20$ $B = x^2 + 11x - 31$
$C = 3x^2 - 4x + 10$ $D = -2x^2 + 6x - 7$

Find the mean of A, B, C and D and factorise the result.

Difference of two squares

An expression such as $a^2 - b^2$ is called the **difference of two squares**.

The product $(a - b)(a + b) = a^2 - b^2$.

In reverse, $a^2 - b^2 = (a - b)(a + b)$.

We use this to factorise any expression that can be written as the difference of two squares.

We factorise the difference of two squares with the following steps.

> **1.** Write each term as a perfect square with brackets.
> **2.** Use the rule $a^2 - b^2 = (a - b)(a + b)$.
> In words: $(\text{first})^2 - (\text{second})^2 = (\text{first} - \text{second})(\text{first} + \text{second})$.

EXAMPLE

Factorise: **(i)** $9 - 4y^2$ **(ii)** $25x^2 - 49y^2$ **(iii)** $16a^2 - 1^2$

Solution:

(i) $9 - 4y^2$
$= (3)^2 - (2y)^2$ (write each term as a perfect square in brackets)
$= (3 - 2y)(3 + 2y)$ (apply the rule: (first − second)(first + second))

(ii) $25x^2 - 49y^2$
$= (5x)^2 - (7y)^2$ (write each term as a perfect square in brackets)
$= (5x - 7y)(5x + 7y)$ (apply the rule: (first − second)(first + second))

(iii) $16a^2 - 1^2$
$= (4a)^2 - (1)^2$ (write each term as a perfect square in brackets)
$= (4a - 1)(4a + 1)$ (apply the rule: (first − second)(first + second))

Exercise 1.4

Copy questions 1–9 and fill in the missing term in the brackets.

1. $4a^2 = ($ $)^2$
2. $9p^2 = ($ $)^2$
3. $16b^2 = ($ $)^2$
4. $36q^2 = ($ $)^2$
5. $1 = ($ $)^2$
6. $64x^2 = ($ $)^2$
7. $81y^2 = ($ $)^2$
8. $121p^2 = ($ $)^2$
9. $144q^2 = ($ $)^2$

Factorise each of the following in questions 10–30.

10. $4p^2 - 9q^2$
11. $16a^2 - 25b^2$
12. $36x^2 - 49y^2$
13. $64a^2 - 81b^2$
14. $100 - 9a^2$
15. $1 - 25p^2$
16. $16x^2 - 1$
17. $25x^2 - 4y^2$
18. $64q^2 - 1$
19. $q^2 - 16$
20. $81a^2 - 16b^2$
21. $x^2 - 25$
22. $100 - a^2$
23. $25x^2 - 16y^2$
24. $25a^2 - 4$
25. $49 - 100m^2$
26. $121x^2 - 9y^2$
27. $144p^2 - 25q^2$
28. $1 - 196x^2$
29. $100p^2 - 81q^2$
30. $a^2b^2 - 4c^2$
31. Simplify $(3x - 1)(2x + 5) - 2(x^2 + 6x + 2) - x$ and factorise the simplified expression.
32. Simplify $(3x - 2y)^2 - y(5y - 12x)$ and factorise the simplified expression.
33. Simplify $(7x - 2)(7x + 2) - (5y - 2)(5y + 2)$ and factorise the simplified expression.

Expressions that have three factors

> Always look for a highest common factor first.

Sometimes we have to factorise an expression that has three factors.

Expressions that have three factors are factorised with the following steps.

> 1. Take out the highest common factor first.
> 2. Then factorise the expression inside the brackets, which will be one of:
>   **(a)** Factors by grouping   (four terms)
>   **(b)** Quadratic trinomial   (three terms)
>   **(c)** Difference of two squares   (two terms)

EXAMPLE

(i) Find the three factors of $20a^2 - 45b^2$.

(ii) Factorise $3px^2 - 6px - 45p$.

Solution:

(i) $\quad 20a^2 - 45b^2$

$\quad = 5[4a^2 - 9b^2]$ $\qquad$ (take out the common factor 5)

$\quad = 5[(2a)^2 - (3b)^2]$ $\qquad$ (write the terms inside the brackets as perfect squares)

$\quad = 5(2a - 3b)(2a + 3b)$ $\qquad$ (apply the rule (first − second)(first + second) to the terms inside the brackets)

(ii) $\quad 3px^2 - 6px - 45p$

$\quad = 3p(x^2 - 2x - 15)$ $\qquad$ (take out the common factor $3p$)

$\quad = 3p(x + 3)(x - 5)$ $\qquad$ (factorise the quadratic trinomial inside the bracket)

Exercise 1.5

Find the three factors of each of the following in questions 1–22.

1. $3x^2 - 3y^2$

2. $2x^2 - 8y^2$

3. $12 - 27y^2$

4. $5x^2 + 15x + 10$

5. $3x^2 - 6x - 24$

6. $4a^2 - 8x - 12$

7. $3ax + 6b + 6a + 3bx$

8. $10ax + 10bx - 5ay - 5yb$

9. $6a + 2bq - 6b - 2aq$

10. $18ax^2 - 50ay^2$

11. $12x^2 + 42x + 18$

12. $6qx^2 + 20qx - 16q$

13. $x^3 + x^2y + 4x^2 + 4xy$

14. $20p^2q - 45q^3$

15. $8abp^2 - 2abq^2$

16. $4p^2q - 10pr - 10pq + 4p^2r$

17. $75a^3 - 12ab^2$

18. $4a^3b - 25ab^3$

19. $3x^3 - 12xy^2$

20. $50a^3 - 98ab^2$

21. $2ax^2 + 6ax - 20a$

22. Three students, Ann, Brendan and Colman, were asked to factorise $4x^2 - 4x - 8$. Their answers were:

Ann	Brendan	Colman
$(4x + 4)(x - 2)$	$(2x - 4)(2x + 2)$	$(x - 2)(4x + 4)$

(i) Are all the answers correct? Justify your answer.

(ii) Why can one quadratic trinomial have three different factorisations?

(iii) Which of the following is said to be factorised completely?

$\quad 2(x - 2)(2x + 2) \qquad 4(x - 2)(x + 1) \qquad 2(2x - 4)(x + 1)$

Justify your answer.

23. Simplify $(5x - 3)^2 - 4$ and fully factorise the simplified expression.

24. Simplify $(2x + a)(4x - 2a) - (3y + a)(6y - 2a)$ and fully factorise the simplified expression.

Multiplication and division of algebraic fractions

Operations with algebraic fractions follow the same rules as in arithmetic. Before attempting to simplify when multiplying or dividing algebraic fractions, factorise where possible and divide the top and bottom by common factors. The contents of a bracket should be considered as a single term.

Note: The top of a fraction is called the numerator and the bottom of a fraction is called the denominator.

EXAMPLE 1

Simplify each of the following.

(i) $\dfrac{4abxy + 2axy}{6ax}$ (ii) $\dfrac{8x^2}{14y} \div \dfrac{4x}{7y^2}$ (iii) $\dfrac{4x - 2}{15 - 3x} \div \dfrac{2x - 1}{5 - x}$

Solution:

(i) $\dfrac{4abxy + 2axy}{6ax}$

$= \dfrac{2axy\,(2b + 1)}{6ax}$ (factorise the top (numerator))

$= \dfrac{y(2b + 1)}{3}$ (divide top and bottom by common factors)

(ii) $\dfrac{8x^2}{14y} \div \dfrac{4x}{7y^2}$

$= \dfrac{8x^2}{14y} \times \dfrac{7y^2}{4x}$ (turn the fraction we divide by upside down and multiply)

$= xy$ (divide top and bottom by common factors)

(iii) $\dfrac{4x - 2}{15 - 3x} \div \dfrac{2x - 1}{5 - x}$

$= \dfrac{4x - 2}{15 - 3x} \times \dfrac{5 - x}{2x - 1}$ (turn the fraction we divide by upside down and multiply)

$= \dfrac{2(2x - 1)}{3(5 - x)} \times \dfrac{(5 - x)}{(2x - 1)}$ (factorise top and bottom)

$= \dfrac{2}{3}$ (divide top and bottom by common factors)

EXAMPLE 2

Simplify: (i) $\dfrac{x^2 + 8x + 15}{x^2 - x - 12}$ (ii) $\dfrac{x^2 + x - 20}{4x^2 + 19x - 5}$

Solution:

Factorise top and bottom, then divide by common factor.

(i) $\dfrac{x^2 + 8x + 15}{x^2 - x - 12}$

$= \dfrac{(x + 3)(x + 5)}{(x + 3)(x - 4)}$

$= \dfrac{x + 5}{x - 4}$

(ii) $\dfrac{x^2 + x - 20}{4x^2 + 19x - 5}$

$= \dfrac{(x + 5)(x - 4)}{(4x - 1)(x + 5)}$

$= \dfrac{x - 4}{4x - 1}$

Exercise 2.1

In questions 1–27, simplify the expression.

1. $\dfrac{6xy}{3y}$

2. $\dfrac{15a^3b}{5a^2b}$

3. $\dfrac{24a^2b^2}{3a^2b}$

4. $\dfrac{8x^3y}{4x^3y}$

5. $\dfrac{2xy}{2xy}$

6. $\dfrac{3x + 6}{x + 2}$

7. $\dfrac{8x + 10}{4x + 5}$

8. $\dfrac{3x + 6}{4x + 8}$

9. $\dfrac{5x - 15}{3x - 9}$

10. $\dfrac{-4x - 12}{-2x - 6}$

11. $\dfrac{8x^2}{5y^2} \times \dfrac{10y^2}{8x}$

12. $\dfrac{5a^2}{8b^2} \div \dfrac{5a}{16b^3}$

13. $\dfrac{x^2 + x - 2}{x + 2}$

14. $\dfrac{x^2 - 9}{x - 3}$

15. $\dfrac{3x^2 - 6xy}{x - 2y}$

16. $\dfrac{4x - 12}{x^2 + x - 12}$

17. $\dfrac{x + 2}{x^2 - 4}$

18. $\dfrac{6x - 4}{3x^2 + 10x - 8}$

19. $\dfrac{x^2 - 2x}{x^2 + x - 6}$

20. $\dfrac{x^2 - 2x - 15}{2x^2 - 9x - 5}$

21. $\dfrac{3ab}{a^2b + ab^2}$

22. $\dfrac{2x + 4}{3x - 15} \times \dfrac{x - 5}{x + 2}$

23. $\dfrac{x^2 - 2x}{6x + 9} \times \dfrac{4x + 6}{x - 2}$

24. $\dfrac{8x - 4}{2y + 6} \div \dfrac{2x - 1}{y + 3}$

25. $\dfrac{y + 5}{x} \div \dfrac{2y + 10}{x^2}$

26. $\dfrac{x^2 + 2x}{x^2 + 3x + 2} \div \dfrac{x}{2x + 2}$

27. $\dfrac{x^2 + 8x + 15}{x^2 - 9} \div \dfrac{xy + 5y}{x^2 - 3x}$

Arithmetic fractions

We often encounter fractions when working in algebra. As a first step it is vital that you can understand and handle fractions with numbers only without using a calculator (arithmetic).

> **EXAMPLE**
>
> Find the value of each of the following without using a calculator and write your answer in its simplest form $\frac{a}{b}$ where $a, b \in \mathbb{Z}$.
>
> (i) $\frac{4}{7} + \frac{3}{4}$ (ii) $\frac{2}{3} + \frac{4}{5} - \frac{1}{2}$ (iii) $\frac{3}{x} - \frac{8}{y} + \frac{5}{z}$ where $x = 7$, $y = 9$ and $z = 2$
>
> **Solution:**
>
> (i) The LCM of 7 and 4 is 28.
> $$\therefore \frac{4}{7} + \frac{3}{4} = \frac{(4)(4) + (3)(7)}{28} = \frac{16 + 21}{28} = \frac{37}{28}$$
>
> (ii) The LCM of 3, 5 and 2 is 30.
> $$\therefore \frac{2}{3} + \frac{4}{5} - \frac{1}{2} = \frac{(10)(2) + (6)(4) - (15)(1)}{30} = \frac{20 + 24 - 15}{30} = \frac{29}{30}$$
>
> (iii) $\frac{3}{x} - \frac{8}{y} + \frac{5}{z}$ where $x = 7$, $y = 9$ and $z = 2$ becomes $\frac{3}{7} - \frac{8}{9} + \frac{5}{2}$.
>
> The LCM of 7, 9 and 2 is given by $(7)(9)(2) = 126$.
> $$\frac{3}{7} - \frac{8}{9} + \frac{5}{2} = \frac{(18)(3) - (14)(8) + (63)(5)}{126} = \frac{54 - 112 + 315}{126} = \frac{257}{126}$$

Exercise 2.2

1. Find the value of each of the following without using a calculator and write your answer in the form $\frac{a}{b}$ where $a, b \in \mathbb{Z}$.

   (i) $\frac{3}{2} - \frac{1}{9} - \frac{7}{10}$ (ii) $\frac{5}{6} - \frac{3}{5}$ (iii) $\frac{2}{3} + \frac{3}{4} - \frac{4}{5}$

In questions 2 and 3, substitute the given values and evaluate each expression without using a calculator. Write each answer in its simplest form $\frac{a}{b}$ where $a, b \in \mathbb{Z}$.

2. If $p = 2$ and $q = 9$:

   (i) $\frac{1}{p} + \frac{1}{q}$ (ii) $\frac{1}{q} - \frac{1}{p}$ (iii) $\frac{3}{p} + \frac{2}{q}$ (iv) $\frac{p}{q} + \frac{q}{p}$

3. If $x = 3$, $y = 4$ and $z = 5$:

   (i) $\frac{1}{x} + \frac{1}{y} + \frac{1}{z}$ (ii) $\frac{x + y}{2} - \frac{z}{4}$ (iii) $\frac{x}{y} + \frac{z}{y}$ (iv) $\frac{3}{x} - \frac{3}{y} + \frac{3}{z}$

Addition and subtraction of algebraic fractions

Algebraic fractions that have numbers as denominators can be added or subtracted in exactly the same way as in arithmetic, i.e. we express the fractions with the lowest common denominator (the LCM of the denominators).

Algebraic fractions are added or subtracted with the following steps.

> **1.** Put brackets in where necessary.
>
> **2.** Find the LCM of the expressions on the bottom.
>
> **3.** Proceed in exactly the same way as in arithmetic.
>
> **4.** Simplify the top (add and subtract terms which are the same).

Note: If part of the expression is not a fraction, it can be changed into fraction form by putting it over 1.

For example, $7 = \dfrac{7}{1}$, $3x = \dfrac{3x}{1}$, $2x - 5 = \dfrac{2x - 5}{1}$.

EXAMPLE 1

Express $\dfrac{3x + 2}{8} - \dfrac{x}{4} + \dfrac{x + 1}{2}$ as a single fraction.

Verify your answer by letting $x = 1$.

Solution:

$$\dfrac{3x + 2}{8} - \dfrac{x}{4} + \dfrac{x + 1}{2}$$

$$= \dfrac{(3x + 2)}{8} - \dfrac{x}{4} + \dfrac{(x + 1)}{2} \qquad \text{(put brackets on top)}$$
$$\text{(the LCM is 8)}$$

$$= \dfrac{1(3x + 2) - 2x + 4(x + 1)}{8} \qquad \text{(do the same as in arithmetic)}$$

$$= \dfrac{3x + 2 - 2x + 4x + 4}{8} \qquad \text{(remove the brackets on top)}$$

$$= \dfrac{5x + 6}{8} \qquad \text{(simplify the top)}$$

$$\therefore \dfrac{3x + 2}{8} - \dfrac{x}{4} + \dfrac{x + 1}{2} = \dfrac{5x + 6}{8}$$

LHS $x = 1$ RHS

$\dfrac{3x + 2}{8} - \dfrac{x}{4} + \dfrac{x + 1}{2}$ $\dfrac{5x + 6}{8}$

$= \dfrac{3(1) + 2}{8} - \dfrac{1}{4} + \dfrac{1 + 1}{2}$ $= \dfrac{5(1) + 6}{8}$

$= \dfrac{3 + 2}{8} - \dfrac{1}{4} + \dfrac{2}{2}$ $= \dfrac{5 + 6}{8}$

$= \dfrac{5}{8} - \dfrac{1}{4} + 1$ $= \dfrac{11}{8}$

$= 1\dfrac{5}{8} - \dfrac{1}{4}$ $= 1\dfrac{3}{8}$

$= 1\dfrac{3}{8}$

$$\text{LHS} = \text{RHS}$$

$$\therefore \; \frac{3x + 2}{8} - \frac{x}{4} + \frac{x + 1}{2} = \frac{5x + 6}{8}$$

EXAMPLE 2

If $\dfrac{4}{4x - 1} - \dfrac{3}{3x + 2} = \dfrac{k}{(4x - 1)(3x + 2)}$, find k where $k \in \mathbb{N}$.

Solution:

$$\frac{4}{4x - 1} - \frac{3}{3x + 2}$$

$= \dfrac{4}{(4x - 1)} - \dfrac{3}{(3x + 2)}$ (put brackets on bottom)
                                                  (the LCM is $(4x - 1)(3x + 2)$)

$= \dfrac{4(3x + 2) - 3(4x - 1)}{(4x - 1)(3x + 2)}$ (do the same as in arithmetic)

$= \dfrac{12x + 8 - 12x + 3}{(4x - 1)(3x + 2)}$ (remove the brackets on top)

$= \dfrac{11}{(4x - 1)(3x + 2)}$ (simplify the top)

$\dfrac{11}{(4x - 1)(3x + 2)} = \dfrac{k}{(4x - 1)(3x + 2)}$ (from question)

$$\therefore k = 11 \text{ by comparison.}$$

Note: It is common practice **not** to multiply out the expression on the bottom.

EXAMPLE 3

Write $\dfrac{4}{2x-3} - \dfrac{1}{3-2x}$ as a single fraction in its simplest form.

Solution:

Method 1:

$$\dfrac{4}{2x-3} - \dfrac{1}{3-2x}$$

$$= \dfrac{4}{(2x-3)} - \dfrac{1}{(3-2x)} \qquad \text{(put brackets on the bottom)}$$
$$\text{(the LCM is } (2x-3)(3-2x))$$

$$= \dfrac{4(3-2x) - 1(2x-3)}{(2x-3)(3-2x)} \qquad \text{(do the same as in arithmetic)}$$

$$= \dfrac{12 - 8x - 2x + 3}{(2x-3)(3-2x)} \qquad \text{(remove the brackets on top)}$$

$$= \dfrac{15 - 10x}{(2x-3)(3-2x)} \qquad \text{(simplify the top)}$$

$$= \dfrac{5(3-2x)}{(2x-3)(3-2x)} \qquad \text{(factorise the top)}$$

$$= \dfrac{5}{(2x-3)} \qquad \text{(divide the top and bottom by the common factor } (3-2x))$$

Method 2:

$$\dfrac{4}{2x-3} - \dfrac{1}{3-2x}$$

$$= \dfrac{4}{2x-3} + \dfrac{1}{2x-3} \qquad (-(3-2x) = (2x-3))$$

$$= \dfrac{4+1}{2x-3} \qquad \text{(same denominator)}$$

$$= \dfrac{5}{2x-3}$$

Note: Method 2 works when the only difference between the denominators is the sign. For example, $3x - 4$ and $4 - 3x$ or $5 - 2x$ and $2x - 5$.

$$\dfrac{5}{2x-1} + \dfrac{2}{1-2x} = \dfrac{5}{2x-1} - \dfrac{2}{2x-1} = \dfrac{5-2}{2x-1} = \dfrac{3}{2x-1}$$

Exercise 2.3

In questions 1–27, write the expression as a single fraction.

1. $\dfrac{2x}{3} + \dfrac{3x}{4}$

2. $\dfrac{5x}{3} + \dfrac{x}{2}$

3. $\dfrac{2x}{5} - \dfrac{x}{3}$

4. $\dfrac{x+1}{2} + \dfrac{x+5}{3}$

5. $\dfrac{5x-1}{4} + \dfrac{2x-3}{5}$

6. $\dfrac{2x+3}{7} - \dfrac{x+1}{3}$

7. $\dfrac{5x}{3} - \dfrac{1}{6} + \dfrac{2-3x}{2}$

8. $\dfrac{3x+5}{6} - \dfrac{2x+3}{4}$

9. $\dfrac{4x+3}{6} - \dfrac{6x+4}{9} + \dfrac{x}{3}$

10. $\dfrac{2x+3}{4} + 3x + 2$

11. $\dfrac{5}{4x} + \dfrac{7}{3x}$

12. $\dfrac{6}{5x} - \dfrac{3}{4x}$

13. $\dfrac{2}{x+1} + \dfrac{3}{x+2}$

14. $\dfrac{2}{x+3} + \dfrac{3}{x+5}$

15. $\dfrac{1}{x+2} + \dfrac{2}{x-4}$

16. $\dfrac{3}{2x+1} + \dfrac{2}{3x+4}$

17. $\dfrac{5}{2x+1} + \dfrac{4}{2x-1}$

18. $\dfrac{2}{3x-2} + \dfrac{3}{2x+5}$

19. $\dfrac{5}{3x-1} - \dfrac{3}{2x}$

20. $\dfrac{3}{2x-5} + \dfrac{4}{x-3}$

21. $\dfrac{5}{3x-1} + \dfrac{3}{2-3x}$

22. $\dfrac{2}{x+3} + 3$

23. $\dfrac{5}{3} - \dfrac{2}{x+4}$

24. $\dfrac{2}{3} + \dfrac{5}{2x-1} - \dfrac{1}{2}$

25. $\dfrac{1}{x} - \dfrac{1}{x+3} + \dfrac{1}{4}$

26. $\dfrac{1}{x} + \dfrac{2}{x+1} + \dfrac{1}{3}$

27. $\dfrac{5}{x} - \dfrac{3}{x-2} + \dfrac{1}{3}$

28. Show that each of the following reduces to a constant.

    (i) $\dfrac{8x+1}{4} - \dfrac{6x-1}{3}$ (ii) $\dfrac{4x-1}{2} - \dfrac{14x-5}{7}$

29. Express $\dfrac{2x-3}{10} + \dfrac{x-2}{6} + \dfrac{1}{2}$ as a single fraction and verify your answer by letting $x = 2$.

30. Express $\dfrac{3}{2x+1} + \dfrac{2}{2x-1}$ as a single fraction and verify your answer by letting $x = 1$.

31. If $\dfrac{4}{3x-1} + \dfrac{4}{3x+1} = \dfrac{kx}{(3x-1)(3x+1)}$, find the value of k where $k \in \mathbb{N}$.

32. If $\dfrac{1}{5-4x} + \dfrac{2}{8x-11} = \dfrac{h}{(5-4x)(8x-11)}$, find the value of h where $h \in \mathbb{Z}$.

33. Write down an expression for the perimeter of these shapes. Hence, express the perimeter as a single fraction.

    (i)

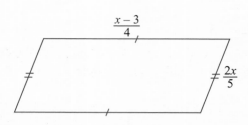

    (ii)

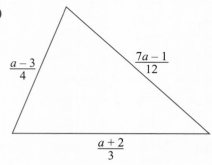

34. (i) $\dfrac{6x + 5}{21} - \dfrac{2x - 3}{7} = \dfrac{p}{q}$, $p, q \in \mathbb{R}$.

    Write down the value of p and q, where $\dfrac{p}{q}$ is in its simplest form.

    (ii) $\dfrac{3}{x + 1} + \dfrac{4}{x - 2} = \dfrac{ax + b}{(x + 1)(x - 2)}$

    Write down the value of a and the value of b.

35. Simplify each of the following.

    (i) $\dfrac{3(x + 1)}{(x + 2)(x + 1)}$　(ii) $\dfrac{10 - 4x}{(2x - 5)(5 - 2x)}$　(iii) $\dfrac{-3 + 9x}{(3x - 1)(1 - 3x)}$　(iv) $\dfrac{1 - x}{(x - 1)(1 - x)}$

36. Write each of the following as a single fraction in its simplest form.

    (i) $\dfrac{3}{x - 1} + \dfrac{1}{1 - x}$　(ii) $\dfrac{5}{x - 2} + \dfrac{2}{2 - x}$　(iii) $\dfrac{3}{x - 5} - \dfrac{7}{5 - x}$

    (iv) $\dfrac{5}{2x - 3} - \dfrac{3}{3 - 2x}$　(v) $\dfrac{4}{3x - 1} - \dfrac{1}{1 - 3x}$　(vi) $\dfrac{2}{2 - 5x} - \dfrac{5}{5x - 2}$

37. Show that each of the following reduce to a constant.

    (i) $\dfrac{1}{x - 1} + \dfrac{1}{1 - x}$　(ii) $\dfrac{10}{4 - x} + \dfrac{10}{x - 4}$　(iii) $\dfrac{x}{x + 1} + \dfrac{1}{x + 1}$　(iv) $\dfrac{x}{x - 3} + \dfrac{3}{3 - x}$

CHAPTER 3

LONG DIVISION IN ALGEBRA

Long division in algebra

Long division in algebra follows the same procedure as long division in arithmetic. The stages in dividing one algebraic expression by another are shown in the following examples.

> ● EXAMPLE

> **(i)** Divide $x^3 - x^2 - 11x + 15$ by $x - 3$.
>
> **(ii)** Divide $4x^3 - 7x + 3$ by $2x - 1$.
>
> **Solution:**
>
> **(i)** $(x^3 - x^2 - 11x + 15) \div (x - 3)$
>
> $$
> \begin{array}{r}
> x^2 + 2x - 5 \\
> x - 3 \overline{\smash{\big)}\, x^3 - x^2 - 11x + 15} \\
> \underline{x^3 - 3x^2} \\
> 2x^2 - 11x \\
> \underline{2x^2 - 6x} \\
> -5x + 15 \\
> \underline{-5x + 15} \\
> 0
> \end{array}
> $$
>
> $\quad(x^3 \div x = x^2,$ put x^2 on top$)$
> $\quad(x^2(x - 3) = x^3 - 3x^2)$
> $\quad$(subtract, bring down $-11x$, $2x^2 \div x = 2x$, put $2x$ on top)
> $\quad(2x(x - 3) = 2x^2 - 6x)$
> $\quad$(subtract, bring down 15, $-5x \div x = -5$, put -5 on top)
> $\quad(-5(x - 3) = -5x + 15)$
> $\quad$(subtract)
>
> $\therefore (x^3 - x^2 - 11x + 15) \div (x - 3) = x^2 + 2x - 5$
>
> **(ii)** $(4x^3 - 7x + 3) \div (2x - 1)$
> $\quad = (4x^3 + 0x^2 - 7x + 3) \div (2x - 1)$
>
> It helps in setting out the division if we put in the **missing term**, $0x^2$.
> All missing terms should be included in this way.
>
> $$
> \begin{array}{r}
> 2x^2 + x - 3 \\
> 2x - 1 \overline{\smash{\big)}\, 4x^3 + 0x^2 - 7x + 3} \\
> \underline{4x^3 - 2x^2} \\
> 2x^2 - 7x \\
> \underline{2x^2 - x} \\
> -6x + 3 \\
> \underline{-6x + 3} \\
> 0
> \end{array}
> $$
>
> $\quad(4x^3 \div 2x = 2x^2,$ put $2x^2$ on top$)$
> $\quad(2x^2(2x - 1) = 4x^3 - 2x^2)$
> $\quad$(subtract, bring down $-7x$, $2x^2 \div 2x = x$, put x on top)
> $\quad(x(2x - 1) = 2x^2 - x)$
> $\quad$(subtract, bring down 3, $-6x \div 2x = -3$, put -3 on top)
> $\quad(-3(2x - 1) = -6x + 3)$
> $\quad$(subtract)
>
> $\therefore (4x^3 - 7x + 3) \div (2x - 1) = 2x^2 + x - 3$

Exercise 3.1

In questions 1–10, simplify the expression.

1. $\dfrac{x^3}{x}$

2. $\dfrac{2x^2}{x}$

3. $\dfrac{6x^3}{3x}$

4. $\dfrac{4x}{4x}$

5. $\dfrac{8x^2}{2x}$

6. $\dfrac{-8x}{4x}$

7. $\dfrac{-10x^2}{5x}$

8. $\dfrac{-3x}{3x}$

9. $\dfrac{-5x}{x}$

10. $\dfrac{-6x^2}{2x}$

11. Divide $x^2 + 3x + 2$ by $x + 2$.   12. Divide $x^2 + 7x + 12$ by $x + 4$.

13. Divide $x^2 + 5x + 6$ by $x + 3$.   14. Divide $x^2 + 9x + 20$ by $x + 5$.

15. Divide $2x^2 + 7x + 6$ by $2x + 3$.   16. Divide $3x^2 + 19x + 20$ by $3x + 4$.

17. Divide $2x^2 - 5x - 3$ by $2x + 1$.   18. Divide $6x^2 + 11x - 10$ by $3x - 2$.

19. Divide $x^3 + 4x^2 + 5x + 2$ by $x + 1$.   20. Divide $x^3 + 6x^2 + 11x + 6$ by $x + 2$.

21. Divide $2x^3 + 7x^2 + 5x + 1$ by $2x + 1$.   22. Divide $6x^3 + 13x^2 + 9x + 2$ by $3x + 2$.

23. Divide $3x^3 + 7x^2 + 5x + 1$ by $3x + 1$.   24. Divide $4x^3 + 12x^2 + 17x + 12$ by $2x + 3$.

25. Divide $2x^3 + x^2 - 16x - 15$ by $2x + 5$.   26. Divide $3x^3 + x^2 - 11x + 6$ by $3x - 2$.

27. Divide $x^3 - 2x^2 - 9x + 18$ by $x + 3$.   28. Divide $x^3 - 7x^2 + 7x + 20$ by $x - 4$.

29. Divide $2x^3 - 3x^2 - 12x + 20$ by $x - 2$.   30. Divide $3x^3 - 2x^2 - 19x - 6$ by $3x + 1$.

31. Divide $2x^3 + 5x^2 - 9x - 18$ by $2x + 3$.   32. Divide $3x^3 - 8x^2 - 41x + 30$ by $3x - 2$.

33. Divide $6x^3 - 17x^2 + 27x - 20$ by $3x - 4$.   34. Divide $8x^3 + 2x^2 - 5x + 1$ by $2x - 1$.

35. Divide $x^3 + x^2 - 12x$ by $x + 4$.   36. Divide $6x^3 + 26x^2 - 20x$ by $3x - 2$.

37. Divide $x^3 + x^2 + 4$ by $x + 2$.   38. Divide $x^3 + 11x - 30$ by $x - 2$.

39. Divide $x^3 - 13x + 12$ by $x + 4$.   40. Divide $2x^3 - 5x^2 + 1$ by $2x - 1$.

41. Divide $4x^3 - 13x - 6$ by $x - 2$.   42. Divide $6x^3 - 13x^2 + 4$ by $2x + 1$.

43. Divide $x^3 + 6x^2 + 11x + 6$ by $x + 3$ and verify your answer by letting $x = 1$.

44. Divide $2x^3 - x^2 - 7x + 6$ by $2x - 3$ and verify your answer by letting $x = 3$.

45. (i) $(x^3 + 2x^2 - 5x - 6) \div (x - 2) = ax^2 + bx + c$. Find the values of a, b and c.

   (ii) (a) Evaluate $\sqrt{bc(b - a)}$.   (b) Factorise $ax^2 + bx + c$.

46. $f(x) = x^3 - 3x^2 - 4x + 12$ and $g(x) = x + 2$.

   $f(x) \div g(x) = ax^2 + bx + c$. Factorise $ax^2 + bx + c$.

47. The area of a rectangle is $(x^3 + 4x^2 + 6x + 3)$ cm^2. Its breadth is $(x + 1)$ cm. Find its length.

48. The volume of a cuboid is $(2x^3 + 5x^2 - 4x - 12)$ cm^3.

The height of the cuboid is $(2x - 3)$ cm and its base is a square.

  (i) Find the area of the base.

  (ii) Find the length of a side of the base.

 (iii) Explain why $x > \frac{3}{2}$.

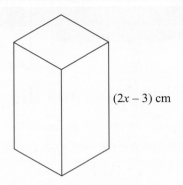

$(2x - 3)$ cm

In questions 49–52 there is no x term in the answer.

49. Divide $x^3 + 3x^2 + 4x + 12$ by $x + 3$.

50. Divide $x^3 + 4x^2 - 5x - 20$ by $x + 4$.

51. Divide $2x^3 + 4x^2 - 7x - 14$ by $x + 2$.

52. Divide $2x^3 + 3x^2 - 8x - 12$ by $2x + 3$.

In questions 53–56 there is no x^2 term and no x term.

53. Divide $x^3 + 8$ by $x + 2$.

54. Divide $x^3 - 1$ by $x - 1$.

55. Divide $x^3 - 27$ by $x - 3$.

56. Divide $8x^3 - 125$ by $2x - 5$.

Simultaneous linear equations

An equation such as $2x + 3y = 19$ is called a linear equation in two unknowns, x and y. Simultaneous linear equations are a pair of such equations. Two equations are necessary if we are to be able to find the values of x and y that satisfy both equations.

For example, consider the following pair of simultaneous linear equations:

$$5x + 2y = 20 \quad ①$$
$$4x + 3y = 23 \quad ②$$

The solution of this pair of simultaneous linear equations is $x = 2$ and $y = 5$.

This pair of values satisfies both equations simultaneously (at the same time).

We can check this by substituting $x = 2$ and $y = 5$ in both equations and showing that the left-hand side is equal to the right-hand side in each equation.

Check:

$5x + 2y$	20 ①	$4x + 3y$	23 ②
$5(2) + 2(5)$		$4(2) + 3(5)$	
$10 + 10$		$8 + 15$	
LHS = RHS		LHS = RHS	

$\therefore$ Our solution $x = 2$ and $y = 5$ is correct.

Equations that are solved together are called simultaneous equations.

Solving a pair of simultaneous linear equations means finding the values of x and y that make both equations true at the same time.

Consider the following pair of simultaneous linear equations:

$$p - 2q = 10 \quad \text{and} \quad 3p + 5q = -22.$$

Is $p = 0$ and $q = -5$ the correct solution for both?

To check, we proceed as in the previous example and substitute $p = 0$ and $q = -5$ into **both** equations.

Check:

$p - 2q$	10	$3p + 5q$	-22
$(0) - 2(-5)$		$3(0) + 5(-5)$	
$0 + 10$		$0 - 25$	
LHS = RHS		LHS $\neq$ RHS	

$\therefore$ $p = 0$ and $q = -5$ is not the correct solution for both equations.

Exercise 4.1

Check if the given solution in each case is correct for the simultaneous (both) linear equations.

1. $x - 4y = 3$
   $x + y = 13$
   Solution: $x = 11, y = 8$

2. $x + 3y = 2$
   $3x + y = 14$
   Solution: $x = 5, y = -1$

3. $3p - 3q = 48$
   $p + 2q = -5$
   Solution: $p = 9, q = -7$

4. $5a + 4b = 24$
   $a - 2b = 4$
   Solution: $a = 4, b = 1$

5. $p + q = 8$
   $4p - 3q = 11$
   Solution: $p = 5, q = -3$

6. $m + 9n = 14$
   $-2m + n = 10$
   Solution: $m = -4, n = 2$

7. $6x - y = 17$
   $3y + x = 1$
   Solution: $x = 2, y = -5$

8. $2x + 4y + 9 = 0$
   $x - 2y + 5 = 0$
   Solution: $x = 7, y = 6$

9. $x - 3y - 14 = 0$
   $y + 2x + 7 = 0$
   Solution: $x = -1, y = -5$

Simultaneous linear equations in two variables are solved with the following steps.

1. Write both equations in the form $ax + by = k$ and label the equations ① and ②, where a, b and k are whole numbers.

2. Multiply one or both of the equations by a number in order to make the coefficients of x or y the same, but of opposite sign.

3. Add to remove the variable with equal coefficients but of opposite sign.

4. Solve the resultant equation to find the value of the remaining unknown (x or y).

5. Substitute this value in equation ① or ② to find the value of the other unknown.

EXAMPLE 1

Solve the following simultaneous equations:

$$p = -\frac{1}{2}q - 2$$
$$3q = 4p - 17$$

Solution:

1. Write both equations in the form $ap + bq = k$ where a, b and k are whole numbers and label the equations ① and ②.

$$p = -\frac{1}{2}q - 2$$
$$2p = -q - 4 \quad \text{(multiply each part by 2)}$$
$$2p + q = -4 \quad ① \quad \text{(in the form } ap + bq = k\text{: label the equation ①)}$$
$$3q = 4p - 17$$
$$-4p + 3q = -17 \quad ② \quad \text{(in the form } ap + bq = k\text{: label the equation ②)}$$

2. Make the coefficients q the same but of opposite sign.
   Multiply ① by -3.

$$-6p - 3q = 12 \quad ① \times -3$$
$$-4p + 3q = -17 \quad ②$$

3. Add these new equations.

$$-10p = -5$$
$$10p = 5 \qquad \text{(multiply both sides by } -1)$$

4. Divide both sides by 10.

$$p = \frac{5}{10} = \frac{1}{2}$$

5. Substitute $p = \frac{1}{2}$ into ① or ②.

$$2p + q = -4 \quad ①$$
$$\downarrow$$
$$2\left(\frac{1}{2}\right) + q = -4$$
$$1 + q = -4 \qquad \text{(subtract 1 from both sides)}$$
$$q = -5$$

∴ The solution is $p = \frac{1}{2}$ and $q = -5$.

EXAMPLE 2

Solve the simultaneous equations $2x + y = 3(y - x) + 7$ and $\frac{x}{3} = 2 - \frac{y}{4}$.

Solution:

1. First write both equations in the form $ax + by = k$ and number the equations ① and ②.

$$2x + y = 3(y - x) + 7$$
$$2x + y = 3y - 3x + 7 \qquad \text{(remove the brackets)}$$
$$2x + y - 3y + 3x = 7 \qquad \text{(letters to the left, number to the right)}$$
$$5x - 2y = 7 \quad ① \qquad \text{(in the form } ax + by = k \text{, number the equation ①)}$$

$$\frac{x}{3} = 2 - \frac{y}{4}$$
$$12\left(\frac{x}{3}\right) = 12(2) - 12\left(\frac{y}{4}\right) \qquad \text{(multiply each part by 12)}$$
$$4x = 24 - 3y \qquad \text{(simplify)}$$
$$4x + 3y = 24 \quad ② \qquad \text{(in the form } ax + by = k \text{, number the equation ②)}$$

$$5x - 2y = 7 \quad ①$$
$$4x + 3y = 24 \quad ②$$

2. Make coefficients of y the same.
Multiply ① by 3 and ② by 2.

3. Add these new equations.

4. Divide both sides by 23.

5. Substitute $x = 3$ into ① or ②.

$$15x - 6y = 21 \quad ① \times 3$$
$$8x + 6y = 48 \quad ② \times 2$$
$$23x = 69$$
$$x = 3$$
$$5x - 2y = 7 \quad ①$$
$$\downarrow$$
$$5(3) - 2y = 7$$
$$15 - 2y = 7$$

(subtract 15 from both sides)

(multiply both sides by −1)

(divide both sides by 2)

∴ The solution is $x = 3$ and $y = 4$.

$$-2y = -8$$
$$2y = 8$$
$$y = 4$$

Solution containing fractions

If the solution contains fractions, the substitution can be difficult.

In such cases, the following method is useful:

> 1. Eliminate y and find x.   2. Eliminate x and find y.

EXAMPLE 3

Solve the simultaneous equations $2x + 3y = -2$ and $3x + 7y = -6$.

Solution:

Both equations are in the form $ax + by = k$. Number the equations ① and ②.

1. Eliminate y and find x.

$$2x + 3y = -2 \quad ①$$
$$3x + 7y = -6 \quad ②$$
$$14x + 21y = -14 \quad ① \times 7$$
$$9x + 21y = -18 \quad ② \times 3$$
$$5x = 4 \text{ (subtract)}$$
$$x = \frac{4}{5}$$

2. Eliminate x and find y.

$$2x + 3y = -2 \quad ①$$
$$3x + 7y = -6 \quad ②$$
$$6x + 9y = -6 \quad ① \times 3$$
$$6x + 14y = -12 \quad ② \times 2$$
$$-5y = 6 \text{ (subtract)}$$
$$5y = -6$$
$$y = -\frac{6}{5}$$

Therefore, the solution is $x = \frac{4}{5}$ and $y = -\frac{6}{5}$.

Note: This method can also be used if the solution does not contain fractions.

Exercise 4.2

In questions 1–9, solve the pair of simultaneous equations.

1. $x + y = 7$
   $x - y = 1$

2. $p + q = 11$
   $p - q = 1$

3. $2x + y = 14$
   $x + y = 9$

4. $3x + y = 13$
   $2x - y = 7$

5. $x + y = 3$
   $6x - 5y = 7$

6. $x - y = 4$
   $x + 2y = 1$

7. $3x + 2y = 13$
   $4x - 3y = 6$

8. $3p + 5q = 19$
   $7p = -14$

9. $3y = -12$
   $5x - 2y = 13$

In questions 10–15, write both equations in the form $ax + by = k$ before attempting to solve.

10. $x = y + 5$
    $3y = 15 - 2x$

11. $g = -3f + 13$
    $2f - g - 7 = 0$

12. $x = y$
    $2x + 3y = 25$

13. $x = -2y$
    $y + 9 - x = 0$

14. $3x + 2y - 7 = 0$
    $x - 3y + 5 = 0$

15. $2x = 5 - 3y$
    $x + 14 = 4y$

In questions 16–27, solve the pair of simultaneous equations.

16. $x + 2y = 7$
    $3x - 5y = -34$

17. $2x - y = -3$
    $x - 2y = -3$

18. $\frac{1}{3}f + \frac{1}{2}g = 0$
    $-\frac{11}{6}f + \frac{1}{4}g = -6$

19. $2x - 5y = 19$
    $\frac{3x}{2} + \frac{4y}{3} = -1$

20. $2x + 5y = 40$
    $\frac{2x}{5} - \frac{5y}{2} = -6$

21. $3x - 4y = -3$
    $\frac{x}{2} + \frac{y}{3} = \frac{5}{2}$

22. $\frac{3x}{5} - \frac{y}{4} = 8$
    $\frac{2x}{3} + \frac{3y}{4} = 13$

23. $\frac{x}{3} + \frac{y}{4} = 2$
    $0.3x + 0.4y = 2.5$

24. $x = 2y$
    $2(x + 3) = 5 + 3y$

25. $p = \frac{1}{2}q + 3$
    $q = \frac{1}{2}p - 3$

26. $2(m - 5) = 3n$
    $\frac{2m + 1}{5} + \frac{m + n}{2} = 1$

27. $3g - f = 2 = g + f$

The simultaneous equations in questions 28–33 have solutions containing fractions. Solve these equations.

28. $5p + q = 10$
    $3p - q = 2$

29. $7f - 3g = 6$
    $3f - 6g = 1$

30. $5x + 10y = 11$
    $2x + y = 2$

31. $2x - 5 = 0$
    $3x + 5y + 5 = 0$

32. $x + 6y = 4$
    $\frac{1}{2}x + y = \frac{10}{3}$

33. $\frac{p}{2} + \frac{q}{3} = \frac{1}{5}$
    $p - q = \frac{7}{5}$

34. Three lines with equations $5x + 2y = 9$, $2x + 7y = 16$ and $7x + 9y = k$ meet at a single point. Find the value of k.

35. The system of simultaneous equations

$$3a + 2b = 10$$
$$4a - kb = -5, k \in \mathbb{R}$$

has a solution with $a = 3$. Find k.

36. Ciana has two types of candles, labelled x and y. The candles labelled x are in the shape of a cone and the candles labelled y are in the shape of a cylinder. She finds that the following combinations balance.

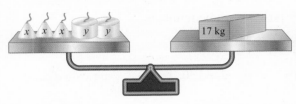

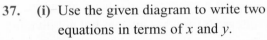

    (i) Find the values of x and y.

    (ii) Ciana also has some spherical candles labelled z. She finds the following combinations balance. Find the value of z.

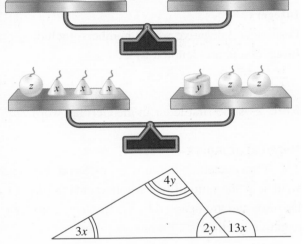

37.   **(i)** Use the given diagram to write two equations in terms of x and y.

    (ii) Hence solve for x and y.

CHAPTER 5

IRRATIONAL NUMBERS – SURDS

Types of numbers

Numbers are classified according to type.

Natural numbers

The whole numbers 1, 2, 3, 4, 5, … are called the **natural** numbers and are denoted by $\mathbb{N}$.

$$\mathbb{N} = \{1, 2, 3, 4, 5, 6, \cdots\} = \text{positive whole numbers.}$$

Integers

Positive and negative **whole** numbers, including zero, … −3, −2, −1, 0, 1, 2, 3, … are called the **integers** and are denoted by $\mathbb{Z}$.

$$\mathbb{Z} = \{\cdots -3, -2, -1, 0, 1, 2, 3, \cdots\} = \text{positive or negative whole numbers.}$$

Note: $\mathbb{Z}$ is the first letter in the German word *Zallen*, which means numbers.

Rational numbers

The first five letters in the word **rational** spell **ratio**. A rational number is a number that can be written as the ratio of two whole numbers (dividing one integer by another integer, but not dividing by zero) and are denoted by $\mathbb{Q}$. In other words, any number that can be written as a simple positive or negative fraction is a rational number.

$$\text{Examples are } \frac{1}{3}, \ -\frac{8}{7}, \frac{1}{5}, \ 4, \ -6, \ 0, \ 3\cdot 1, \sqrt{23}.$$

$$\left(4 = \frac{4}{1}, \ -6 = -\frac{6}{1}, \ 0 = \frac{0}{1}, \ 3\cdot 1 = \frac{31}{10}, \ \sqrt{25} = 5 = \frac{5}{1} \right)$$

$$\mathbb{Q} = \left\{ \frac{p}{q} \middle| p \in \mathbb{Z}, q \in \mathbb{Z}, q \neq 0 \right\} = \text{positive or negative fractions.}$$

Note: $\mathbb{Q}$ is the first letter in the German word *Quotient*, which means ratio.

Irrational numbers

The word **irrational** literally means **no ratio**. Numbers which cannot be written as simple fractions are called irrational numbers (cannot be written as one integer divided by another integer). As decimals they never repeat or terminate.

Using your calculator to evaluate $\sqrt{2}$ and π gives:

$$\sqrt{2} = 1\cdot414213562\ldots \qquad \text{(irrational, never repeats or terminates)}$$
$$\pi = 3\cdot141592654\ldots \qquad \text{(irrational, never repeats or terminates)}$$

The popular approximation of $\pi = \dfrac{22}{7} = 3\cdot142857143\ldots$ is close but **not accurate**.

Note: There is no agreed international symbol for irrational numbers. Some authors use I or $\overline{\mathbb{Q}}$.
On our course, we use $\mathbb{R}\backslash\mathbb{Q}$.

Real numbers

The natural numbers are a subset of the integers. The integers are a subset of the rational numbers. In other words, all natural numbers and integers are also rational numbers. Rational numbers and irrational numbers are two totally separate number types. They have no numbers in common. When the rational and irrational numbers are joined together, they form a set of numbers called the **real** numbers and are denoted by $\mathbb{R}$.

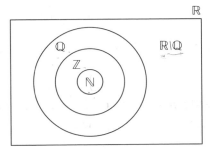

Exercise 5.1

1. For each number in the table below, either show that it is rational by writing it as a whole number or a fraction, or place a tick in the 'Irrational' column.

Number	2·3	$\sqrt{3}$	$\sqrt{16}$	$3\frac{2}{5}$	32%	π	$\dfrac{-\sqrt{16}}{8}$	$\dfrac{\pi}{3}$	−0·625	$\sqrt{7+9}$
Rational, $\mathbb{Q}$										
Irrational, $\mathbb{R}\backslash\mathbb{Q}$										

2. Is $-2\frac{1}{4}$ a rational number? Justify your answer.

3. All natural numbers are rational numbers. True or false? Justify your answer.

4. A rational number is an integer. True or false? Justify your answer with an example.

Surds

Irrational numbers such as $\sqrt{2}$, $\sqrt{3}$, $\sqrt{5}$ and $\sqrt{7}$ are called **surds**.

Properties of surds

Property	Example
1. $\sqrt{ab} = \sqrt{a}\sqrt{b}$	$\sqrt{20} = \sqrt{4 \times 5} = \sqrt{4}\sqrt{5} = 2\sqrt{5}$
2. $\sqrt{\dfrac{a}{b}} = \dfrac{\sqrt{a}}{\sqrt{b}}$	$\sqrt{\dfrac{9}{16}} = \dfrac{\sqrt{9}}{\sqrt{16}} = \dfrac{3}{4}$
3. $\sqrt{a}\sqrt{a} = a$	$\sqrt{3}\sqrt{3} = 3$

When simplifying surds, the key idea is to find the largest possible square number bigger than 1 that will divide evenly into the number under the square root symbol.

The square numbers greater than 1 are 4, 9, 16, 25, 36, 49, 64, 81, 100, 121, 144, etc. You can use your calculator to help you find the largest possible square number that will divide exactly into the number under the square root symbol. Try 4, then try 9, then try 16 and so on until you find the largest possible square number that will divide exactly.

EXAMPLE 1

Express (i) $\sqrt{18}$ (ii) $\sqrt{75}$ (iii) $\sqrt{80}$ in the form $a\sqrt{b}$, where $a \neq 1$.

Solution:

(i) $\sqrt{18} = \sqrt{9 \times 2} = \sqrt{9}\sqrt{2} = 3\sqrt{2}$

(ii) $\sqrt{75} = \sqrt{25 \times 3} = \sqrt{25}\sqrt{3} = 5\sqrt{3}$

(iii) $\sqrt{80} = \sqrt{16 \times 5} = \sqrt{16}\sqrt{5} = 4\sqrt{5}$

EXAMPLE 2

Express (i) $\sqrt{\dfrac{4}{25}}$ (ii) $\sqrt{1\dfrac{7}{9}}$ in the form $\dfrac{a}{b}$, where $a, b \in \mathbb{N}$.

Solution:

(i) $\sqrt{\dfrac{4}{25}} = \dfrac{\sqrt{4}}{\sqrt{25}} = \dfrac{2}{5}$ (ii) $\sqrt{1\dfrac{7}{9}} = \sqrt{\dfrac{16}{9}} = \dfrac{\sqrt{16}}{\sqrt{9}} = \dfrac{4}{3}$

Addition and subtraction of surds

> Like surds can be added or subtracted.

Method: Express each surd in its simplest form and add or subtract like surds.

● EXAMPLE 3

Express $\sqrt{75} + \sqrt{48} - \sqrt{12}$ in the form $a\sqrt{b}$, where $a, b \in \mathbb{N}$.

Solution:

$\sqrt{75} + \sqrt{48} - \sqrt{12}$

$\sqrt{75}$	$\sqrt{48}$	$\sqrt{12}$
$= \sqrt{25 \times 3}$	$= \sqrt{16 \times 3}$	$= \sqrt{4 \times 3}$
$= \sqrt{25}\sqrt{3}$	$= \sqrt{16}\sqrt{3}$	$= \sqrt{4}\sqrt{3}$
$= 5\sqrt{3}$	$= 4\sqrt{3}$	$= 2\sqrt{3}$

$\therefore \ \sqrt{75} + \sqrt{48} - \sqrt{12} = 5\sqrt{3} + 4\sqrt{3} - 2\sqrt{3} = 9\sqrt{3} - 2\sqrt{3} = 7\sqrt{3}$

Exercise 5.2

Note: All questions in this exercise need to be done without a calculator.

Write questions 1–15 in the form $a\sqrt{b}$, where $a \neq 1$.

1. $\sqrt{8}$
2. $\sqrt{20}$
3. $\sqrt{27}$
4. $\sqrt{32}$
5. $\sqrt{12}$

6. $\sqrt{50}$
7. $\sqrt{200}$
8. $\sqrt{45}$
9. $\sqrt{125}$
10. $\sqrt{28}$

11. $\sqrt{72}$
12. $\sqrt{98}$
13. $\sqrt{24}$
14. $\sqrt{128}$
15. $\sqrt{63}$

16. Express $3\sqrt{20}$ in the form $k\sqrt{5}$, where $k \in \mathbb{N}$.

17. Express $\frac{1}{3}\sqrt{72}$ in the form $k\sqrt{k}$, where $k \in \mathbb{N}$.

18. Verify $\frac{2}{3}\sqrt{108} = \sqrt{48}$.

Write questions 19–28 in the form $\frac{a}{b}$, where $a, b \in \mathbb{N}$.

19. $\sqrt{\dfrac{4}{9}}$
20. $\sqrt{\dfrac{16}{25}}$
21. $\sqrt{\dfrac{81}{100}}$
22. $\sqrt{\dfrac{64}{49}}$
23. $\sqrt{\dfrac{121}{81}}$

24. $\sqrt{\dfrac{1}{9}}$
25. $\sqrt{\dfrac{1}{25}}$
26. $\sqrt{2\dfrac{1}{4}}$
27. $\sqrt{1\dfrac{9}{16}}$
28. $\sqrt{7\dfrac{1}{9}}$

Write questions 29–40 in the form $a\sqrt{b}$, where $a, b \in \mathbb{N}$.

29. $5\sqrt{2} + 4\sqrt{2}$

30. $4\sqrt{3} + 2\sqrt{3}$

31. $7\sqrt{5} - 4\sqrt{5}$

32. $5\sqrt{3} - \sqrt{3}$

33. $10\sqrt{2} - 7\sqrt{2} + \sqrt{2}$

34. $8\sqrt{5} - 10\sqrt{5}$

35. $\sqrt{18} + \sqrt{8}$

36. $\sqrt{27} + \sqrt{12} + \sqrt{3}$

37. $\sqrt{32} + \sqrt{2}$

38. $\sqrt{20} + \sqrt{45} + \sqrt{80}$

39. $\sqrt{75} + \sqrt{12} - \sqrt{48}$

40. $\sqrt{200} - \sqrt{50} - \sqrt{18}$

41. If $5\sqrt{3} + \sqrt{48} - \sqrt{27} = k\sqrt{3}$, find the value of k.

42. If $\sqrt{200} + \sqrt{72} - \sqrt{32} = k\sqrt{2}$, express $\sqrt{k}$ in the form $a\sqrt{3}$.

43. Express $\sqrt{72} + \sqrt{48} + \sqrt{8} - \sqrt{12}$ in the form $a\sqrt{2} + b\sqrt{3}$.

44. Express $\sqrt{20} + \sqrt{45} + \sqrt{18} - \sqrt{50}$ in the form $p\sqrt{p} - q\sqrt{q}$, $p, q \in \mathbb{N}$.

45. Is $\sqrt{\dfrac{49}{64}}$ rational? Justify your answer.

Multiplication

EXAMPLE 1

Simplify each of the following.

(i) $\sqrt{5}\,\sqrt{5}$ (ii) $\sqrt{3}\,\sqrt{12}$ (iii) $3\sqrt{2} \times 4\sqrt{2}$ (iv) $4(1 + \sqrt{3}) - \sqrt{3}(2 + \sqrt{3})$

Solution:

(i) $\sqrt{5}\,\sqrt{5} = 5$ or $\sqrt{5}\,\sqrt{5} = \sqrt{5 \times 5} = \sqrt{25} = 5$

(ii) $\sqrt{3}\,\sqrt{12} = \sqrt{3 \times 12} = \sqrt{36} = 6$

(iii) $3\sqrt{2} \times 4\sqrt{2} = 3 \times 4 \times \sqrt{2} \times \sqrt{2} = 12 \times 2 = 24$

(iv) $4(1 + \sqrt{3}) - \sqrt{3}(2 + \sqrt{3})$

$= 4 + 4\sqrt{3} - 2\sqrt{3} - 3$ (remove brackets)

$= 1 + 2\sqrt{3}$ (simplify like terms)

Note: $\sqrt{a}\,\sqrt{a} = a$ and numbers such as $(1 + \sqrt{3})$ and $(\sqrt{2} - 5)$ are irrational numbers.

EXAMPLE 2

(i) Show that $(2 + \sqrt{3})(2 - \sqrt{3}) = 1$.

(ii) If $k(5 - \sqrt{2})(5 + \sqrt{2}) = 46$, find the value of k.

Solution:

(i) $(2 + \sqrt{3})(2 - \sqrt{3})$

$= 2(2 - \sqrt{3}) + \sqrt{3}(2 - \sqrt{3})$

$= 4 - 2\sqrt{3} + 2\sqrt{3} - 3$

$= 4 - 3$

$= 1$

(ii)

$$k(5 - \sqrt{2})(5 + \sqrt{2}) = 46$$

$$k[5(5 + \sqrt{2}) - \sqrt{2}(5 + \sqrt{2})] = 46$$

$$k[25 + 5\sqrt{2} - 5\sqrt{2} - 2] = 46$$

$$k(23) = 46$$

$$23k = 46$$

$$k = 2$$

EXAMPLE 3

(i) Express $\dfrac{15}{\sqrt{5}}$ in the form $a\sqrt{b}$, where $a, b \in \mathbb{N}$.

(ii) Express $\dfrac{6 - \sqrt{8}}{2}$ in the form $p - \sqrt{q}$, where $p, q \in \mathbb{N}$.

Solution:

(i) $\dfrac{15}{\sqrt{5}}$

$= \dfrac{15}{\sqrt{5}} \times \dfrac{\sqrt{5}}{\sqrt{5}}$

(multiply top and bottom by $\sqrt{5}$)

$= \dfrac{15\sqrt{5}}{5}$

$= 3\sqrt{5}$

(divide top and bottom by 5)

(ii) $\dfrac{6 - \sqrt{8}}{2}$

$= \dfrac{6 - 2\sqrt{2}}{2}$ $\qquad (\sqrt{8} = 2\sqrt{2})$

$= \dfrac{6}{2} - \dfrac{2\sqrt{2}}{2}$

(divide both parts on top by 2)

$= 3 - \sqrt{2}$

Note: $\dfrac{\sqrt{5}}{\sqrt{5}} = 1$. Thus, we are effectively multiplying by 1, which does not change the value of $\dfrac{15}{\sqrt{5}}$.

Exercise 5.3

Note: All questions in this exercise need to be done without a calculator.

Express questions 1–22 in the form a, where $a \in \mathbb{Z}$.

1. $\sqrt{2}\,\sqrt{2}$
2. $\sqrt{3}\,\sqrt{3}$
3. $\left(\sqrt{5}\right)^2$
4. $\left(\sqrt{8}\right)^2$
5. $\sqrt{2}\,\sqrt{8}$
6. $\sqrt{12}\,\sqrt{3}$
7. $2\sqrt{3}\,\sqrt{3}$
8. $4\sqrt{5}\,\sqrt{5}$
9. $2\sqrt{5}\,2\sqrt{5}$
10. $3\sqrt{2}\,5\sqrt{2}$
11. $4\sqrt{3}\,5\sqrt{3}$
12. $\left(3\sqrt{2}\right)^2$
13. $\left(\sqrt{2}+1\right)\left(\sqrt{2}-1\right)$
14. $\left(5+\sqrt{3}\right)\left(5-\sqrt{3}\right)$
15. $\left(3+\sqrt{2}\right)\left(3-\sqrt{2}\right)$
16. $\left(\sqrt{7}+4\right)\left(\sqrt{7}-4\right)$
17. $\left(3-\sqrt{7}\right)\left(3+\sqrt{7}\right)$
18. $\left(\sqrt{6}+\sqrt{2}\right)\left(\sqrt{6}-\sqrt{2}\right)$
19. $\left(3\sqrt{5}+2\right)\left(3\sqrt{5}-2\right)$
20. $\left(3\sqrt{2}+2\sqrt{3}\right)\left(3\sqrt{2}-2\sqrt{3}\right)$
21. $3\left(2-\sqrt{3}\right)\left(4+2\sqrt{3}\right)$
22. **(i)** Evaluate $\left(5-\sqrt{7}\right)\left(5+\sqrt{7}\right)$. **(ii)** Hence, solve for k: $k\left(5-\sqrt{7}\right)\left(5+\sqrt{7}\right)=54$.
23. Find the value of $k \in \mathbb{N}$ for which:

    (i) $k\left(5+\sqrt{3}\right)\left(5-\sqrt{3}\right)=66$ **(ii)** $k\left(2\sqrt{2}-3\right)\left(2\sqrt{2}+3\right)=-4$
24. $\sqrt{2}\,\sqrt{6}=k\sqrt{3}$. Find the value of k, where $k \in \mathbb{N}$.
25. $\sqrt{5}\,\sqrt{10}=a\sqrt{2}$. Find the value of a, where $a \in \mathbb{N}$.
26. Express $\sqrt{8}$ in the form $k\sqrt{k}$. Hence, show that $2\left(3-\sqrt{2}\right)-\left(4-\sqrt{8}\right)=2$.

Express questions 27–36 in the form $a+b\sqrt{c}$, where $a, b \in \mathbb{Z}$ and $c \in \mathbb{N}$.

27. $3\left(3+\sqrt{2}\right)+2\left(4+\sqrt{2}\right)$
28. $\sqrt{3}\left(\sqrt{3}+5\right)-2\left(1+2\sqrt{3}\right)$
29. $4\left(2-\sqrt{5}\right)-2\left(1-\sqrt{5}\right)$
30. $\left(2+\sqrt{3}\right)^2$
31. $\left(3+\sqrt{5}\right)^2$
32. $\left(5-\sqrt{2}\right)^2$
33. $\dfrac{6+3\sqrt{2}}{3}$
34. $\dfrac{20+15\sqrt{2}}{5}$
35. $\dfrac{8+\sqrt{20}}{2}$
36. $\dfrac{4-\sqrt{80}}{4}$

Simplify questions 37–41.

37. $2 \times \dfrac{1}{2}$
38. $\dfrac{1}{3} \times 3$
39. $\sqrt{2} \times \dfrac{1}{\sqrt{2}}$
40. $\dfrac{1}{\sqrt{5}} \times \sqrt{5}$
41. $\dfrac{2}{\sqrt{7}} \times \sqrt{7}$

42. Is $\left(\sqrt{2}+\dfrac{1}{\sqrt{2}}\right)\left(\sqrt{2}-\dfrac{1}{\sqrt{2}}\right)$ a rational number? Justify your answer.

43. Express $\left(3+\dfrac{1}{\sqrt{3}}\right)\left(3-\dfrac{1}{\sqrt{3}}\right)$ in the form $\dfrac{a}{b}$, where $a, b \in \mathbb{N}$.

44. Express $\left(\sqrt{6}-2\sqrt{3}\right)\left(5\sqrt{3}-3\sqrt{6}\right)$ in the form $a\sqrt{2}+b$, where $a, b \in \mathbb{Z}$.

45. Express $\sqrt{3}\left(2\sqrt{6}-4\sqrt{3}\right)-\sqrt{10}\left(3\sqrt{5}-2\sqrt{10}\right)$ in the form $a+b\sqrt{2}$, where $a, b \in \mathbb{Z}$.

Express questions 46–51 in the form $a\sqrt{b}$, where $a \neq 1$.

46. $\dfrac{8}{\sqrt{2}}$ 47. $\dfrac{6}{\sqrt{3}}$ 48. $\dfrac{20}{\sqrt{5}}$ 49. $\dfrac{4}{\sqrt{2}}$ 50. $\dfrac{9}{\sqrt{3}}$ 51. $\dfrac{16}{\sqrt{8}}$

52. Express (i) $\dfrac{\sqrt{700} - \sqrt{7}}{3}$ (ii) $\dfrac{\sqrt{3} + \sqrt{27}}{2}$ in the form $a\sqrt{b}$, where $a, b \in \mathbb{N}$.

53. Express $\dfrac{2}{3\sqrt{8}}$ in the form $\dfrac{\sqrt{2}}{k}$, where $k \in \mathbb{N}$.

54. Verify that $\left(2 + \sqrt{\dfrac{3}{2}}\right)\left(2 - \sqrt{\dfrac{3}{2}}\right)$ is rational.

55. Write down two unequal irrational numbers whose:

    (i) Product is rational   (ii) Sum is rational

Quadratic equations

An equation such as $3x^2 - 5x - 12 = 0$ is called a quadratic equation in x.

A quadratic equation has x^2 as its highest power. In general, a quadratic equation has two different solutions (often called roots), but with some quadratic equations the two solutions are the same.

For example, consider the quadratic equation $2x^2 + 5x - 3 = 0$.

The two solutions of the equation $2x^2 + 5x - 3 = 0$ are $x = -3$ and $x = \frac{1}{2}$.

We can check this by substituting $x = -3$ or $x = \frac{1}{2}$ in the equation and showing in each case that the left-hand side is equal to the right-hand side.

Check $x = -3$:

LHS	RHS
$2x^2 + 5x - 3$	0
$2(-3)^2 + 5(-3) - 3$	
$2(9) - 15 - 3$	
$18 - 18$	
0	

LHS = RHS ✓

Check $x = \frac{1}{2}$:

LHS	RHS
$2x^2 + 5x - 3$	0
$2(\frac{1}{2})^2 + 5(\frac{1}{2}) - 3$	
$2(\frac{1}{4}) + \frac{5}{2} - 3$	
$\frac{1}{2} + \frac{5}{2} - 3$	
0	

LHS = RHS ✓

Therefore, our solutions $x = -3$ or $x = \frac{1}{2}$ are correct.

There are three types of quadratic equations we will meet on our course:

> 1. $3x^2 - 13x - 10 = 0$ (three terms)
> 2. $2x^2 + 3x = 0$ (no constant term)
> 3. $x^2 - 16 = 0$ (no x term)

Solving a quadratic equation means finding the values of x that make the equation true.

Quadratic equations are solved with the following steps.

> 1. Bring every term to the left-hand side.
>   (If necessary, multiply both sides by -1 to make the coefficient of x^2 positive.)
> 2. Factorise the left-hand side.
> 3. Let each factor $= 0$.
> 4. Solve each simple equation.

Type 1

 EXAMPLE 1

Solve for x: $3x^2 - 12 = 5x$.

Solution:

$$3x^2 - 12 = 5x$$
$$3x^2 - 5x - 12 = 0 \qquad \text{(every term on the left-hand side)}$$
$$(3x + 4)(x - 3) = 0 \qquad \text{(factorise the left-hand side)}$$
$$3x + 4 = 0 \text{ or } x - 3 = 0 \qquad \text{(let each factor } = 0)$$
$$3x = -4 \text{ or } x = 3$$
$$x = -\frac{4}{3} \text{ or } x = 3 \qquad \text{(solve each simple equation)}$$

Type 2

 EXAMPLE 2

Solve for x: $5x = 2x^2$.

Solution:

$$5x = 2x^2$$
$$-2x^2 + 5x = 0 \qquad \text{(every term on the left-hand side)}$$
$$2x^2 - 5x = 0 \qquad \text{(multiply both sides by } -1)$$
$$x(2x - 5) = 0 \qquad \text{(factorise the left-hand side)}$$
$$x = 0 \text{ or } 2x - 5 = 0 \qquad \text{(let each factor } = 0)$$
$$x = 0 \text{ or } 2x = 5$$
$$x = 0 \text{ or } x = \frac{5}{2} \qquad \text{(solve each simple equation)}$$

Note: It is important not to divide both sides by x, otherwise the root $x = 0$ is lost.

Type 3

 EXAMPLE 3

Solve for x: $4x^2 - 9 = 0$.

Solution:
There are two methods to solve this quadratic equation.

Method 1:

$$4x^2 - 9 = 0 \quad \text{(every term is on the left-hand side)}$$
$$(2x)^2 - (3)^2 = 0 \quad \text{(difference of two squares)}$$
$$(2x - 3)(2x + 3) = 0 \quad \text{(factorise the left-hand side)}$$
$$2x - 3 = 0 \text{ or } 2x + 3 = 0 \quad \text{(let each factor = 0)}$$
$$2x = 3 \text{ or } 2x = -3$$
$$x = \frac{3}{2} \text{ or } x = -\frac{3}{2} \quad \text{(solve each simple equation)}$$

Method 2:

$$4x^2 - 9 = 0$$
$$4x^2 = 9 \quad \text{(add 9 to both sides)}$$
$$x^2 = \frac{9}{4} \quad \text{(divide both sides by 4)}$$
$$x = \pm\sqrt{\frac{9}{4}} \quad \text{(take the square root of both sides)}$$
$$= \pm\frac{\sqrt{9}}{\sqrt{4}} = \pm\frac{3}{2}$$
$$x = \frac{3}{2} \text{ or } -\frac{3}{2}$$

Exercise 6.1

In questions 1–49, solve the equation.

1. $(x - 3)(x + 4) = 0$
2. $(2x - 3)(x + 5) = 0$
3. $(3x - 2)(2x + 5) = 0$
4. $x(2x - 3) = 0$
5. $x(x + 2) = 0$
6. $(3x - 2)(3x + 2) = 0$
7. $2x^2 - 11x + 5 = 0$
8. $2x^2 + 7x + 3 = 0$
9. $3x^2 + 2x - 5 = 0$
10. $5x^2 + 4x - 1 = 0$
11. $3x^2 + 5x - 12 = 0$
12. $2x^2 + x - 3 = 0$
13. $7x^2 + 29x + 4 = 0$
14. $3x^2 + 10x = 8$
15. $5x^2 + 3x = 2$
16. $x(x - 4) = 21$
17. $x(x - 6) = 16$
18. $(x + 3)(x - 5) = 9$
19. $x^2 + 3x = 0$
20. $x^2 - 2x = 0$
21. $x^2 - 5x = 0$
22. $2x^2 + 5x = 0$
23. $3x^2 = 2x$
24. $5x^2 = 4x$
25. $x^2 - 4 = 0$
26. $x^2 - 16 = 0$
27. $x^2 - 1 = 0$
28. $9x^2 - 4 = 0$
29. $4x^2 - 25 = 0$
30. $4x^2 - 1 = 0$

31. $\dfrac{4x^2 - 3}{11} = x$

32. $\dfrac{6x^2 - 5}{13} = -x$

33. $\dfrac{8x^2 + 3}{14} = x$

34. $x^2 - 2x + 1 = 0$

35. $4x^2 - 4x + 1 = 0$

36. $9x^2 - 12x + 4 = 0$

37. $4x^2 - 29x + 7 = 0$

38. $6x^2 + 20 = 29x$

39. $4x^2 + 5 = 12x$

40. $x(2x + 7) + 6 = 0$

41. $6x(x - 1) + 2 = x(3 - 4x)$

42. $x^2 + 3 = (2x + 1)(x + 3)$

43. $(2x - 3)^2 = 4$

44. $(x + 1)^2 + (x - 2)^2 = 9$

45. $(3x - 1)^2 = (x + 2)^2$

46. $(5x - 2)(3x + 1) = (3x + 1)(2x - 3)$

47. $(2x + 3)(x + 1) = (x + 3)^2$

48. $(x + 1)^2 + (x + 2)^2 = (x + 3)^2$

49. $(x - 1)^2 + (x + 6)^2 = (x + 7)^2$

Quadratic formula

In many quadratic equations, $ax^2 + bx + c$ cannot be resolved into factors. When this happens the formula **must** be used. To save time trying to look for factors, a clue that you must use the formula is often given in the question. When the question requires an approximate answer, e.g. 'correct to two decimal places', 'correct to three significant figures', 'correct to the nearest integer' or 'express your answer in surd form', then the formula must be used.

The roots of the quadratic equation $ax^2 + bx + c = 0$ are given by the formula:

$$x = \frac{-b \pm \sqrt{b^2 - 4ac}}{2a}$$

Notes: 1. The whole of the top of the right-hand side, including $-b$, is divided by $2a$.

2. It is often called the $-b$ or quadratic formula.

3. Before using the formula, make sure every term is on the left-hand side, i.e. write the equation in the form $ax^2 + bx + c = 0$.

Note: If $\sqrt{b^2 - 4ac}$ is a whole number, then $ax^2 + bx + c$ can be factorised.
The formula can still be used even if $ax^2 + bx + c$ can be factorised.

EXAMPLE

Solve the equation $3x^2 - 8x - 2 = 0$, giving your solutions correct to two decimal places.

Solution:

$3x^2 - 8x - 2 = 0$ (two decimal places ∴ use formula)

$a = 3, b = -8, c = -2$

$$x = \frac{-b \pm \sqrt{b^2 - 4ac}}{2a}$$

$$= \frac{8 \pm \sqrt{(-8)^2 - 4(3)(-2)}}{2(3)}$$

$$= \frac{8 \pm \sqrt{64 + 24}}{6}$$

$$= \frac{8 \pm \sqrt{88}}{6}$$

$$= \frac{8 + \sqrt{88}}{6} \text{ or } x = \frac{8 - \sqrt{88}}{6}$$

$$= 2.896805253 \text{ or } x = -0.2301385866$$

∴ $x = 2.90$ or $x = -0.23$, correct to two decimal places.

Note: Show the full answers from your calculator before rounding off.

Exercise 6.2

In questions 1–6, solve by (i) resolving into factors (ii) using the formula.

1. $x^2 - 5x + 4 = 0$
2. $x^2 + 8x + 12 = 0$
3. $2x^2 - 3x - 2 = 0$
4. $3x^2 + 5x - 12 = 0$
5. $3x^2 - 10x - 8 = 0$
6. $5x^2 + 7x - 6 = 0$

In questions 7–18, solve the equation, correct to two decimal places.

7. $2x^2 - 3x - 7 = 0$
8. $x^2 + 7x - 3 = 0$
9. $2x^2 + 3x - 4 = 0$
10. $3x^2 - 7x - 2 = 0$
11. $3x^2 + 5x - 7 = 0$
12. $5x^2 + 6x - 3 = 0$
13. $4x^2 + x - 1 = 0$
14. $5x^2 + 7x - 4 = 0$
15. $7x^2 + 8x - 2 = 0$
16. $2x^2 - 11x + 4 = 0$
17. $3x^2 + 10x + 4 = 0$
18. $4x^2 + 2x - 5 = 0$

Solving quadratic equations exactly

Sometimes we are asked to give the solutions in surd form. This means that we can leave the answers with a square root part rather than approximating the solution with decimal places. Such solutions are considered **exact** as they have not been rounded off or approximated in any way.

EXAMPLE

Solve the equation $x^2 - 6x + 1 = 0$, giving your solutions in surd form.

Solution:

$x^2 - 6x + 1 = 0$ (surd form $\therefore$ use formula)

$a = 1, b = -6, c = 1$

$$x = \frac{-b \pm \sqrt{b^2 - 4ac}}{2a}$$

$$= \frac{6 + \sqrt{(-6)^2 - 4(1)(1)}}{2(1)}$$

$$= \frac{6 \pm \sqrt{36 - 4}}{2}$$

$$= \frac{6 \pm \sqrt{32}}{2}$$

$$= \frac{6 \pm 4\sqrt{2}}{2} \qquad\qquad (\sqrt{32} = \sqrt{16 \times 2} = 4\sqrt{2})$$

$$= 3 \pm 2\sqrt{2} \qquad\qquad \text{(divide both parts on top by 2)}$$

$\therefore$ The roots are $3 + 2\sqrt{2}$ and $3 - 2\sqrt{2}$.

Note: $x^2 = 1x^2$ and therefore $a = 1$.

Exercise 6.3

In questions 1–6, express the surd in the form $a\sqrt{b}$, where b is a prime number.

1. $\sqrt{12}$ 2. $\sqrt{18}$ 3. $\sqrt{32}$ 4. $\sqrt{50}$ 5. $\sqrt{27}$ 6. $\sqrt{80}$

In questions 7–15, solve the equation, giving your solutions in surd form.

7. $x^2 - 2x - 4 = 0$ 8. $x^2 - 2x - 2 = 0$ 9. $x^2 - 4x + 1 = 0$

10. $x^2 + 6x + 7 = 0$ 11. $x^2 + 4x - 8 = 0$ 12. $x^2 - 4x - 14 = 0$

13. $x^2 - 8x - 4 = 0$ 14. $2x^2 - 2x - 1 = 0$ 15. $4x^2 + 2x - 1 = 0$

16. Solve $x^2 - 4x - 8 = 0$, giving your solutions in the form $a \pm a\sqrt{b}$.

17. Verify that $1 + \sqrt{7}$ is a solution of the equation $x^2 - 2x - 6 = 0$.

18. Verify that $-2 + \sqrt{5}$ is a solution of the equation $x^2 + 4x - 1 = 0$.

19. Verify that $-5 + \sqrt{2}$ is a solution of the equation $x^2 + 10x + 23 = 0$.

20. Verify that $2 - \sqrt{3}$ is a solution of the equation $x^2 - 4x + 1 = 0$.

Quadratic equations solved by substitution

In some questions we can use the roots of one quadratic equation to help us solve another quadratic equation by using a substitution.

EXAMPLE

Solve $x^2 - 12x + 35 = 0$ and hence solve $(2t + 1)^2 - 12(2t + 1) + 35 = 0$.

Solution:

$$x^2 - 12x + 35 = 0$$
$$(x - 5)(x - 7) = 0$$
$$x - 5 = 0 \text{ or } x - 7 = 0$$
$$x = 5 \text{ or } x = 7$$

If we substituted (replaced) the x in the first equation with $(2t + 1)$, then we would have the second equation.

We can quickly derive the answers by the same substitution: substitute $(2t + 1)$ for x.

or

$x = 5$		$x = 7$
$2t + 1 = 5$ (substitution)		$2t + 1 = 7$ (substitution)
$2t = 4$		$2t = 6$
$t = 2$		$t = 3$

$$\therefore t = 2 \text{ or } 3.$$

Note: Sometimes the substitution produces more quadratic equations, leading to four solutions.

Exercise 6.4

1. (i) Solve the equation $x^2 - 2x - 8 = 0$.
    (ii) Hence or otherwise, find the values of y for which $(y - 3)^2 - 2(y - 3) - 8 = 0$.

2. (i) Solve the equation $x^2 - 8x + 15 = 0$.
    (ii) Hence or otherwise, find the values of t for which $(2t - 1)^2 - 8(2t - 1) + 15 = 0$.

3. (i) Solve the equation $x^2 - 4x - 21 = 0$.
    (ii) Hence or otherwise, solve $(5t + 2)^2 - 4(5t + 2) - 21 = 0$.

4. (i) Solve the equation $4x^2 - 12x + 5 = 0$.

    (ii) Hence or otherwise, solve $4\left(\dfrac{t}{2} - 1\right)^2 - 12\left(\dfrac{t}{2} - 1\right) + 5 = 0$.

5. **(i)** Solve the equation $2x^2 - 5x - 12 = 0$.

   (ii) Hence or otherwise, solve $2\left(\dfrac{h}{2} + 1\right)^2 - 5\left(\dfrac{h}{2} + 1\right) - 12 = 0$.

6. **(i)** Solve the equation $x^2 - 8x + 12 = 0$.

   (ii) Hence, use your solutions to find the four values of y for which $(y^2 + y)^2 - 8(y^2 + y) + 12 = 0$.

7. **(i)** Solve the equation $x^2 - 8x - 84 = 0$.

   (ii) Hence, solve $(t^2 - 5t)^2 - 8(t^2 - 5t) - 84 = 0$.

8. **(i)** Solve the equation $y^2 - 7y + 10 = 0$.

   (ii) Hence, solve $(x^2 + 1)^2 - 7(x^2 + 1) + 10 = 0$.

9. **(i)** Solve the equation $20 + 8x - x^2 = 0$.

   (ii) Hence, solve $(x^2 - 3x)^2 - 8(x^2 - 3x) - 20 = 0$.

10. **(i)** Solve, correct to one decimal place, the equation $x^2 + 3x - 5 = 0$.

   (ii) Using your answers to part **(i)** or otherwise, find, correct to one decimal place, the values of y for which $(2y + 1)^2 + 3(2y + 1) - 5 = 0$.

11. **(i)** Solve, correct to two decimal places, the equation $3x^2 - 2x - 2 = 0$.

   (ii) Hence or otherwise, find, correct to one decimal place, the values of x for which
$3(2x - 1)^2 - 2(2x - 1) - 2 = 0$.

12. **(i)** Solve, correct to one decimal place, the equation $5x^2 - 7x - 10 = 0$.

   (ii) Hence or otherwise, find the values of y for which $5(3y - 2)^2 - 7(3y - 2) - 10 = 0$ and give your answers correct to one decimal place.

13. **(i)** Solve the equation $x^2 - 11x + 24 = 0$.

   (ii) Hence, solve $(x^2 - 2x)^2 - 11(x^2 - 2x) + 24 = 0$.

14. By using a suitable substitution or otherwise, simplify and solve $3(x - 1)^2 - 2(x - 1) - 1 = 0$.

15. By using a suitable substitution or otherwise, simplify and solve $2(3x - 1)^2 - 5(3x - 1) - 2 = 0$, giving your answer correct to one decimal place.

Constructing a quadratic equation when given its roots

This is the reverse process to solving a quadratic equation by using factors.

 EXAMPLE

Find a quadratic equation with roots -2 and 3.

Write your answers in the form $ax^2 + bx + c = 0$, $a, b, c \in \mathbb{Z}$.

Solution:

Roots -2 and 3.

$x = -2$ or $x = 3$

$x + 2 = 0$ or $x - 3 = 0$

$(x + 2)(x - 3) = 0$

$x^2 - x - 6 = 0$

Exercise 6.5

In questions 1–15, construct a quadratic equation with the given roots. In each case, write your answer in the form $ax^2 + bx + c = 0$, $a, b, c \in \mathbb{Z}$.

1. 2, 3
2. -1, 2
3. -2, 5
4. -1, 4
5. -3, -2
6. 4, 5
7. -3, 4
8. -8, 3
9. -3, 3
10. 2, 2
11. -2, 0
12. 0, 5
13. -1, 1
14. -1, 8
15. -7, 5
16. The equation $x^2 + mx + n = 0$ has roots -3 and 5. Find the values of m and n.
17. If $x = 2$ is one root of the equation $2x^2 + kx + 2 = 0$, find:
    (i) The value of k (ii) The other root

The four inequality symbols are:

1.	$>$	means	greater than
2.	$\geq$	means	greater than or equal to
3.	$<$	means	less than
4.	$\leq$	means	less than or equal to

Algebraic expressions that are linked by one of the four inequality symbols are called **inequalities**.

For example, $2x + 1 \geq 11$ and $-3 < 2x - 1 \leq 7$ are inequalities.

Solving inequalities is exactly the same as solving equations, with the following exception:

> Multiplying or dividing both sides of an inequality by a negative number reverses the direction of the inequality.
>
> That is:
>
> | $>$ | changes to | $<$ | $\geq$ | changes to | $\leq$ |
> |---|---|---|---|---|---|
> | $<$ | changes to | $>$ | $\leq$ | changes to | $\geq$ |

For example, $4 > -7$ is true. If we multiply both sides by -1, it gives $-4 > 7$, which is **not** true.

However, $-4 < 7$ is true. Multiplying both sides by -1 and reversing the direction of the inequality keeps the inequality true.

Note: Inequalities can be reversed. For example:

$$5 \leq x \text{ means the same as } x \geq 5.$$

$$8 \geq x \geq 3 \text{ means the same as } 3 \leq x \leq 8.$$

Solving an inequality means finding the values of x that make the inequality true.

The following rules apply to graphing inequalities on a number line.

> Number line for $x \in \mathbb{N}$ or $x \in \mathbb{Z}$, use dots.
>
> Number line for $x \in \mathbb{R}$, use a full heavy line.

Simple inequalities

  EXAMPLE 1

Find the range of values of x for which $7x - 11 \leq 2x + 9$, $x \in \mathbb{N}$.
Graph your solution on the number line.

Solution:

$$7x - 11 \leq 2x + 9$$
$$7x - 2x \leq 9 + 11 \qquad \text{(rearrange)}$$
$$5x \leq 20 \qquad \text{(simplify both sides)}$$
$$x \leq 4 \qquad \text{(divide both sides by 5)}$$

As $x \in \mathbb{N}$, this is the set of natural numbers less than or equal to 4.
Thus, the values of x are 1, 2, 3 and 4.
Number line:

Note: As $x \in \mathbb{N}$, dots are used on the number line.

  EXAMPLE 2

Find the range of values of $x \in \mathbb{R}$ for which $4(x - 2) > 5(2x - 1) - 9$ and graph your
solution on the number line.

Solution:

$$4(x - 2) > 5(2x - 1) - 9$$
$$4x - 8 > 10x - 5 - 9 \qquad \text{(remove the brackets)}$$
$$4x - 10x > -5 - 9 + 8 \qquad \text{(rearrange)}$$
$$-6x > -6 \qquad \text{(simplify both sides)}$$
$$6x < 6 \qquad \text{(multiply both sides by } -1 \text{ and reverse the}$$
$$\text{inequality, i.e. turn } > \text{ into } <)$$
$$x < 1 \qquad \text{(divide both sides by 6)}$$

Number line:

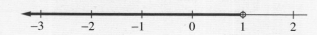

Note: 1. As $x \in \mathbb{R}$, we use full heavy shading on the number line.
     2. A circle is put around 1 to indicate that it is **not** included in the solution.

Sometimes we have to combine two simple inequalities. Consider the next example.

EXAMPLE 3

  (i) Find the solution set E of $2x + 7 \le 11$, $x \in \mathbb{Z}$.

  (ii) Find the solution set H of $4 - 2x < 10$, $x \in \mathbb{Z}$.

  (iii) Find $E \cap H$ and graph your solution on the number line.

Solution:

We solve each inequality separately and then combine the solutions.

  (i) $E : 2x + 7 \le 11$ **(ii)** $H : 4 - 2x < 10$

           $2x \le 11 - 7$ $-2x < 10 - 4$

           $2x \le 4$ $-2x < 6$

            $x \le 2$ $2x > -6$

                                      $x > -3$

(iii) Combining the two inequalities gives:

$$E \cap H : \quad -3 < x \le 2, \quad x \in \mathbb{Z}$$

This is the set of positive and negative whole numbers between -3 and 2, including 2 but not including -3.

Number line:

Note: As $x \in \mathbb{Z}$, dots are used on the number line.

Double inequalities

A double inequality is one like $-3 \le 5x + 2 \le 7$.

There are two methods for solving double inequalities.

Method 1:

> Whatever we do to one part, we do the same to all three parts.

Method 2:

> **1.** Write the double inequality as two separate simple inequalities.
>
> **2.** Solve each simple inequality and combine their solutions.

EXAMPLE

Solve $-4 \le 3x + 2 < 11$, $x \in \mathbb{R}$.

Solution:

Method 1: Do the same to all three parts.
$$-4 \le 3x + 2 < 11$$
$$-6 \le 3x < 9 \qquad \text{(subtract 2 from each part)}$$
$$-2 \le x < 3 \qquad \text{(divide each part by 3)}$$

Method 2: Write the double inequality as two separate simple inequalities.

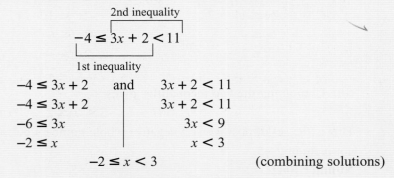

$$-4 \le 3x + 2 \qquad \text{and} \qquad 3x + 2 < 11$$
$$-4 \le 3x + 2 \qquad\qquad\qquad 3x + 2 < 11$$
$$-6 \le 3x \qquad\qquad\qquad\qquad 3x < 9$$
$$-2 \le x \qquad\qquad\qquad\qquad x < 3$$
$$-2 \le x < 3 \qquad\qquad \text{(combining solutions)}$$

Number line:

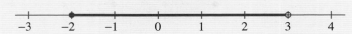

Note: 1. As $x \in \mathbb{R}$, we use full heavy shading on the number line.
2. A circle is put around 3 to indicate that 3 is **not** included in the solution.

Exercise 7.1

Solve each of the inequalities in questions 1–22. In each case, graph your solution on a number line.

1. $x + 3 < 7$, $x \in \mathbb{N}$
2. $5x - 7 > 3$, $x \in \mathbb{N}$
3. $2x + 5 < x + 11$, $x \in \mathbb{Z}$
4. $7x + 1 \le 3x - 15$, $x \in \mathbb{R}$
5. $3y - 1 \ge 4y + 3$, $y \in \mathbb{R}$
6. $4x - 2 \le 5x - 6$, $x \in \mathbb{Z}$
7. $2(x + 4) < 2 - x$, $x \in \mathbb{R}$
8. $5(x + 2) \ge 2(x - 1)$, $x \in \mathbb{R}$
9. $3(x - 4) \le 2(x - 3)$, $x \in \mathbb{N}$
10. $2(t + 3) < 6(t + 2)$, $t \in \mathbb{R}$
11. $5(x - 2) - 7 \ge 3(x - 4)$, $x \in \mathbb{R}$
12. $9(x + 1) - 1 \ge 2(5x + 6)$, $x \in \mathbb{Z}$
13. $-12 \le 4x \le 4$, $x \in \mathbb{R}$
14. $-13 < 4x - 1 < 19$, $x \in \mathbb{R}$

15. $-1 \le 2k + 1 < 9,\ k \in \mathbb{R}$

16. $-5 \le 2p - 3 \le -1,\ p \in \mathbb{R}$

17. $-13 \le 4x - 1 \le 3,\ x \in \mathbb{R}$

18. $-33 \le 7x - 5 < -12,\ x \in \mathbb{R}$

19. $-1 < 6x + 5 \le 17,\ x \in \mathbb{R}$

20. $2 > -2m > -8,\ m \in \mathbb{Z}$

21. $3 > 2b - 7 \ge -5,\ b \in \mathbb{R}$

22. $-9 < 1 - 5x < 6,\ x \in \mathbb{R}$

23. Write down the values of $x \in \mathbb{Z}$ for which $-3 \le 2x + 5 < 11$.

24. **(i)** The solution of the inequality $-10 < 4x - 2 < 10,\ x \in \mathbb{R}$, is given as $a < x < b$. Find the values of a and b.

    (ii) Hence, evaluate $\sqrt{3a^2 + 8b}$.

25. **(i)** The solution of the inequality $4 \ge 1 - 3x \ge -5,\ x \in \mathbb{R}$, is given as $p \le x \le q$. Find the values of p and q.

    (ii) Hence, evaluate $\sqrt{\dfrac{1}{q^2} - 6p}$.

26. **(i)** The solution of the inequality $-7 \le 5 - 3x,\ x \in \mathbb{N}$, is given as $\{a, b, c, d\}$. Write down the values of a, b, c and d where $a < b < c < d$.

    (ii) Hence, evaluate $\sqrt{\dfrac{a}{0 \cdot b} + cd - 1}$.

27. **(i)** Find the solution set of   **(a)** $A : x + 2 \ge 5,\ x \in \mathbb{R}$ **(b)** $B : x + 2 \le 7,\ x \in \mathbb{R}$

    (ii) Find $A \cap B$ and graph your solution on the number line.

28. **(i)** Find the solution set of   **(a)** $H : 2x - 3 \le 5,\ x \in \mathbb{R}$ **(b)** $K : 3x + 2 \ge -1,\ x \in \mathbb{R}$

    (ii) Find $H \cap K$ and graph your solution on the number line.

29. **(i)** Find the solution set P of $4t - 1 \le 3,\ t \in \mathbb{R}$.

    (ii) Find the solution set Q of $5 - t \le 8,\ t \in \mathbb{R}$.

    (iii) Find $P \cap Q$ and graph your solution on the number line.

30. **(i)** Find the solution set G of $3x - 1 \le 9 - 2x,\ x \in \mathbb{R}$.

    (ii) Find the solution set H of $1 - 3x \le 8 - x,\ x \in \mathbb{R}$.

    (iii) Find $G \cap H$ and graph your solution on the number line.

31. **(i)** Find the solution set M of $4 - x \le 6,\ x \in \mathbb{R}$.

    (ii) Find the solution set N of $3x - 1 \le x + 9,\ x \in \mathbb{R}$.

    (iii) Find $M \cap N = a \le x \le b$. Write down the value of a and the value of b.

32. Write an inequality to represent each of the following shaded sections of the number line.

(i)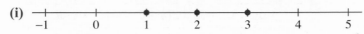

(ii)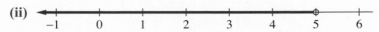

(iii)

(iv)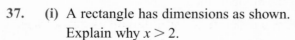

33. Write down the values of x that satisfy each of the following.

   (i) $x + 1 \leq 6$, where x is a positive even number.

  (ii) $x + 4 < 7$, where x is a positive odd number.

(iii) $2x - 13 < 37$, where x is a square number.

(iv) $2x + 5 < 27$, where x is a prime number.

34. The lengths of the sides of a triangle are $(2p + 3)$ cm, $(2p + 2)$ cm and p cm. Find the range of values of p for which this triangle exists.

35. The lengths of the sides of a triangle are $(2x - 3)$ cm, $(2x - 1)$ cm and x cm. Find the range of values of x for which this triangle exists.

36. The width of a rectangle is x cm and its length is $(2x - 3)$ cm, where $x \in \mathbb{N}$.

  (i) If the perimeter of the rectangle must be greater than 21 cm, find the smallest possible value of x.

 (ii) Hence, find the area of the rectangle for this value of x.

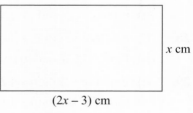

x cm

$(2x - 3)$ cm

37. (i) A rectangle has dimensions as shown. Explain why $x > 2$.

 (ii) The number of centimetres in its perimeter is greater than the number of square centimetres in its area. Write an inequality to represent this information and solve it to find the range of values of x.

$(x - 2)$ cm

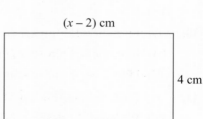

4 cm

38. The following table shows the ages of four brothers.

Name	Alan	Brian	Colm	David
Age in years	9	n	21	$2n + 3$

    (i) David is older than Alan but younger than Colm. Write an inequality to represent this information.

    (ii) Simplify this inequality to find an inequality which represents Brian's age.

    (iii) What are the youngest and oldest possible ages that Brian can be?

    (iv) Hence, find the youngest and oldest possible ages that David can be.

    (v) Is it possible that any of the brothers are twins? Explain your answer.

39. The diagram shows a map of an island. A treasure is buried at a place where the x and y coordinates are positive whole numbers. Use the clues to work out the coordinates of where the treasure is buried.

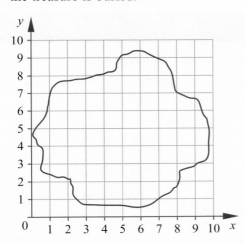

Clues:

    (i) $x > 4$

    (ii) $y > 7$

    (iii) $x + y = 15$

    (iv) One of x and y is prime and the other is not.

40. Kevin needs to buy a new car and must trade in his old car. A car dealer offers him a trade in amount of €4,500 for his old car, but only if he spends at least €10,000 on a new car. Kevin has a maximum of €12,500 cash.

    (i) Write an inequality in x to show the range of money he could spend in the dealership.

    (ii) Write an inequality in y to show the price range of the cars that he could buy.

41. Saoirse is in a clothes shop and has a voucher which she **must** use. The voucher gives an €8 reduction when more than €30 is spent. She also has €55 cash.

    (i) Write an inequality in x to show the range of money she could spend in the shop.

    (ii) Write an inequality in y to show the price range of article she could buy.

Changing the subject of a formula

When we rearrange a formula so that one of the variables is given in terms of the others, we are **changing the subject of the formula**.

Changing the subject of a formula is solved with the following method.

> Whatever you do to one side, you must do **exactly the same** to the other side.

Note: Keep balance in mind. Whatever letter comes after the word 'express' is to be on its own.

EXAMPLE 1

(i) Given that $px - q = r$, express x in terms of p, q and r, where $p \neq 0$.

(ii) Given that $u^2 + 2as = v^2$, express s in terms of v, u and a.

(iii) Express t in terms of p and q when $p = \dfrac{q - t}{3t}$, $t \neq 0$.

Solution:

(i) $px - q = r$

$\quad\quad px = r + q$ (add q to both sides)

$\quad\quad \dfrac{px}{p} = \dfrac{r + q}{p}$ (divide both sides by p)

$\quad\quad x = \dfrac{r + q}{p}$ (simplify the left-hand side)

(ii) $u^2 + 2as = v^2$

$\quad\quad 2as = v^2 - u^2$ (subtract u^2 from both sides)

$\quad\quad \dfrac{2as}{2a} = \dfrac{v^2 - u^2}{2a}$ (divide both sides by $2a$)

$\quad\quad s = \dfrac{v^2 - u^2}{2a}$ (simplify the left-hand side)

(iii) $\quad\quad p = \dfrac{q - t}{3t}$

$\quad\quad 3tp = \dfrac{3t(q - t)}{3t}$ (multiply both sides by $3t$)

$\quad\quad 3tp = q - t$ (simplify the right-hand side)

$\quad\quad 3tp + t = q$ (add t to both sides)

$$t(3p + 1) = q \qquad \text{(take out the common factor } t \text{ on the left-hand side)}$$

$$\frac{t(3p + 1)}{3p + 1} = \frac{q}{3p + 1} \qquad \text{(divide both sides by } (3p + 1))$$

$$t = \frac{q}{3p + 1} \qquad \text{(simplify the left-hand side)}$$

EXAMPLE 2

If $3p = \dfrac{2}{q} - \dfrac{1}{r}$, express q in terms of p and r.

Solution:

$$3p = \frac{2}{q} - \frac{1}{r}$$

$$qr(3p) = qr\left(\frac{2}{q}\right) - qr\left(\frac{1}{r}\right) \qquad \text{(multiply both sides by } qr)$$

$$3pqr = 2r - q \qquad \text{(simplify the left-hand side)}$$

$$3pqr + q = 2r \qquad \text{(add } q \text{ to both sides)}$$

$$q(3pr + 1) = 2r \qquad \text{(take out common factor } q \text{ on the left-hand side)}$$

$$\frac{q(3pr + 1)}{3pr + 1} = \frac{2r}{3pr + 1} \qquad \text{(divide both sides by } (3pr + 1))$$

$$q = \frac{2r}{3pr + 1} \qquad \text{(simplify the left-hand side)}$$

EXAMPLE 3

If $v = \sqrt{\dfrac{u - s}{ut}}$, express t in terms of u, v and s.

Solution:

$$v = \sqrt{\frac{u - s}{ut}}$$

$$(v)^2 = \left(\sqrt{\frac{u - s}{ut}}\right)^2 \qquad \text{(square both sides)}$$

$$v^2 = \frac{u - s}{ut} \qquad \text{(removes square root symbol)}$$

$$v^2 ut = u - s \qquad \text{(multiply both sides by } ut)$$

$$\frac{v^2 ut}{v^2 u} = \frac{u - s}{v^2 u} \qquad \text{(divide both sides by } v^2 u)$$

$$t = \frac{u - s}{v^2 u} \qquad \text{(simplify the left-hand side)}$$

EXAMPLE 4

If $r = \dfrac{p-q}{2a^2}$, express a in terms of p, q and r.

Solution:

$$r = \frac{p-q}{2a^2}$$

$$2a^2(r) = 2a^2\left(\frac{p-q}{2a^2}\right) \quad \text{(multiply both sides by } 2a^2\text{)}$$

$$2a^2r = p - q \quad \text{(simplify)}$$

$$a^2 = \frac{p-q}{2r} \quad \text{(divide both sides by } 2r\text{)}$$

$$a = \pm\sqrt{\frac{p-q}{2r}} \quad \text{(take the square root of both sides)}$$

Note: If $x^2 = k$, then $x = \pm\sqrt{k}$. Always include both the positive and negative solutions.

Exercise 8.1

Change each of the formulae in questions 1–33 to express the letter in square brackets in terms of the others.

1. $2x + y = z$ $[x]$
2. $3a - b = c$ $[a]$
3. $pq + r = s$ $[p]$
4. $u + at = v$ $[t]$
5. $2b - 3a = 5c$ $[b]$
6. $3r - 4p = 2q$ $[r]$
7. $2(p - q) = r$ $[p]$
8. $a(b - c) = d$ $[b]$
9. $x(y + z) = w$ $[y]$
10. $\frac{1}{2}p = q$ $[p]$
11. $\frac{x}{2} + y = z$ $[x]$
12. $s + \frac{t}{3} = r$ $[t]$
13. $\frac{a}{2} + \frac{b}{3} = c$ $[a]$
14. $\frac{p+q}{2} = r$ $[q]$
15. $w = \frac{1}{3}(r + s)$ $[r]$
16. $x = \frac{y - 2z}{3}$ $[z]$
17. $a + \frac{c}{d} = b$ $[c]$
18. $2p + \frac{3q}{r} = s$ $[q]$
19. $\frac{a - 3b}{c} = 5$ $[a]$
20. $s = \frac{p}{q} + \frac{r}{q}$ $[q]$
21. $\frac{3a}{b} - \frac{2c}{b} = d$ $[b]$
22. $\frac{1}{2}(3a + b) = \frac{1}{3}c$ $[a]$
23. $u^2 + 2as = v^2$ $[a]$
24. $p = \frac{q}{4} - 2c$ $[c]$
25. $\frac{1}{2}at^2 = s$ $[a]$
26. $v = \frac{1}{3}\pi r^2 h$ $[h]$
27. $s = ut + \frac{1}{2}at^2$ $[a]$
28. $r = \frac{1}{s} + t$ $[s]$
29. $p - \frac{t}{q} = r$ $[q]$
30. $x + \frac{y}{z} = w$ $[z]$
31. $\frac{a}{b} = \frac{b}{c} + d$ $[c]$
32. $\frac{1}{u} + \frac{1}{v} = \frac{1}{f}$ $[f]$
33. $\frac{3}{a} = \frac{4}{b} - \frac{1}{c}$ $[c]$

34. Given that $2(2q - 7p) = q(3p - q)$, express p in terms of q.

35. If $p = \dfrac{q}{r - s}$, express s in terms of p, q and r.

36. (i) If $c = \dfrac{2ab}{a + b}$, express b in terms of a and c.

    (ii) Hence or otherwise, find the value of b when $a = 4$ and $c = 6$.

37. If $p^2q = r$, express p in terms of q and r.

38. If $\frac{1}{2}at^2 = s$, express t in terms of a and s.

39. If $c = \dfrac{b}{a^2}$, express a in terms of b and c.

40. If $\sqrt{x} = y$, express x in terms of y.

41. If $\sqrt{pq} = r$, express p in terms of q and r.

42. If $a = \sqrt{\dfrac{p}{q}}$, express q in terms of a and p.

43. If $3\sqrt{xy} = z$, express y in terms of x and z.

44. If $\frac{1}{2}\sqrt{ut} = s$, express u in terms of t and s.

45. If $\sqrt{2x - 3} = y$, express x in terms of y.

46. If $\sqrt{pq - r} = s$, express p in terms of q, r and s.

47. If $t = k\sqrt{\dfrac{l}{g}}$, express l in terms of t, k and g.

48. (i) If $t = \sqrt{\dfrac{x}{y - 2}}$, express y in terms of t and x.

    (ii) Hence, determine the value of y if $x = 25$ and $t = 5$.

49. (i) The area of a trapezium is given by

    $A = \left(\dfrac{a + b}{2}\right)h$. Express h in terms of A, a and b.

    (ii) Find the value of h when $A = 150$, $a = 10$ and $b = 15$.

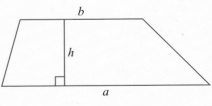

50. The diagram shows a rectangle of length l and width w. Its perimeter is P and its area is A. Express:

    (i) P in terms of l and w (ii) w in terms of P and l

    (iii) A in terms of l and w (iv) w in terms of A and l

    (v) Hence, express A in terms of P and l.

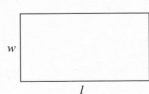

51. (i) If $m^2 = \dfrac{1}{h^2} - 8p$, express h in terms of p and m.

    (ii) Hence, determine the values of h when $m = 9$ and $p = -7$.

52. (i) Given that $x = 2t - 1$ and $y = \frac{2}{3}t + 2$, express $3x - y + 2$ in terms of t, in its simplest form.

    (ii) Hence, find the value of t when $3x - y + 2 = 0$.

53. $z + 3 = 2x, \ y = 2z - 3(x - 2)$

    (i) Express z in terms of x.   (ii) Express y in terms of x.

54. $y = ax + a^3, \ x = 3 - 2a^2$

    (i) Express y in terms of a.   (ii) Evaluate y when $a = 1$.

55. $y = ax - 2a^2, \ x = 2 + 3a$

    (i) Express y in terms of a.   (ii) Evaluate a when $y = 0$.

INDICES, INDEX NOTATION AND RECIPROCALS

Notation for indices

We use a shorthand called **index notation** to indicate repeated multiplication.

For example, $(\text{number})^3 = (\text{number}) \times (\text{number}) \times (\text{number})$.

Thus, $4^3 = 4 \times 4 \times 4 = 64$

$4^3 \leftarrow$ power or index

The power or index simply tells you how many times a number is multiplied by itself.

For example, 3^5 means 3 is to be multiplied by itself five times.

$$3^5 = 3 \times 3 \times 3 \times 3 \times 3 = 243$$
$$2 \times 2 = 2^2 \quad \text{read as '2 squared'}$$
$$2 \times 2 \times 2 = 2^3 \quad \text{read as '2 cubed'}$$
$$2 \times 2 \times 2 \times 2 = 2^4 \quad \text{read as '2 to the power of 4'}$$
$$2 \times 2 \times 2 \times 2 \times 2 = 2^5 \quad \text{read as '2 to the power of 5' and so on.}$$

Note: The first power, or 'to the power of one', of a number is the number itself.

For example, $2^1 = 2$, $3^1 = 3$, $4^1 = 4$.

Rules of indices

1. $a^p \times a^q = a^{p+q}$ Example: $2^4 \times 2^3 = 2^{4+3} = 2^7$
   Multiplying powers of the same number: **add** the indices.

2. $\dfrac{a^p}{a^q} = a^{p-q}$ Example: $\dfrac{3^9}{3^5} = 3^{9-5} = 3^4$

   Dividing powers of the same number: **subtract** the index on the bottom from the index on top.

3. $(a^p)^q = a^{pq}$ Example: $(4^5)^3 = 4^{5\times3} = 4^{15}$
   Raising the power of a number to a power, multiply the indices.

4. $(ab)^p = a^p b^p$ Example: $(2 \times 3)^5 = 2^5 \times 3^5$
   Raising a product to a power, every factor is raised to the power.

5. $\left(\dfrac{a}{b}\right)^p = \dfrac{a^p}{b^p}$ Example: $\left(\dfrac{2}{5}\right)^3 = \dfrac{2^3}{5^3}$
   Raising a fraction to a power, **both** top and bottom are raised to the power.

6. $a^0 = 1$ Example: $4^0 = 1$
   Any number to the power of zero is 1.

7. $a^{-p} = \dfrac{1}{a^p}$ 　　　　Example: $5^{-2} = \dfrac{1}{5^2}$

A number with a negative index is equal to its reciprocal with a positive index.

Note: If a term is brought from the top to the bottom of a fraction (or vice versa), the sign of its index is changed.

8. $a^{\frac{p}{q}} = (a^{\frac{1}{q}})^p$ 　　　Example: $32^{\frac{3}{5}} = (32^{\frac{1}{5}})^3$

Take the root first and then raise to the power (or vice versa).

$8^{\frac{1}{3}}$ means, what number multiplied by itself three times will equal 8?

Thus, $8^{\frac{1}{3}} = 2$, as $2 \times 2 \times 2 = 8$.

Similarly, $25^{\frac{1}{2}} = 5$, as $5 \times 5 = 25$ 　and　 $81^{\frac{1}{4}} = 3$, as $3 \times 3 \times 3 \times 3 = 81$.

Note: $\sqrt{a} = a^{\frac{1}{2}}$. For example, $\sqrt{16} = 16^{\frac{1}{2}} = 4$.

Also, $\sqrt{a}\sqrt{a} = a^{\frac{1}{2}}, a^{\frac{1}{2}} = a^{\frac{1}{2}+\frac{1}{2}} = a^1 = a$.

Alternative notation: $a^{\frac{1}{n}} = \sqrt[n]{a},$ 　　　example $8^{\frac{1}{3}} = \sqrt[3]{8}$

$a^{\frac{m}{n}} = \sqrt[n]{a^m},$ 　　　example $32^{\frac{2}{5}} = \sqrt[5]{32^2}$

When dealing with fractional indices, the calculations are simpler if the root is taken first and the result is raised to the power.

For example, $16^{\frac{3}{4}} = \left(16^{\frac{1}{4}}\right)^3 = (2)^3 = 8$.

(root first)　(power next)

EXAMPLE 1

Simplify each of the following.

(i) $32^{\frac{3}{5}}$ 　(ii) $64^{-\frac{2}{3}}$ 　(iii) $16^{\frac{3}{4}} \times 27^{-\frac{2}{3}}$ 　(iv) $\left(2\dfrac{1}{4}\right)^{1\frac{1}{2}}$ 　(v) $\left(\dfrac{25}{16}\right)^{-\frac{3}{2}}$

Solution:

(i) $32^{\frac{3}{5}} = \left(32^{\frac{1}{5}}\right)^3 = (2)^3 = 8$

(ii) $64^{-\frac{2}{3}} = \dfrac{1}{64^{\frac{2}{3}}} = \dfrac{1}{\left(64^{\frac{1}{3}}\right)^2} = \dfrac{1}{(4)^2} = \dfrac{1}{16}$

(iii) $16^{\frac{3}{4}} \times 27^{-\frac{2}{3}} = \dfrac{16^{\frac{3}{4}}}{27^{\frac{2}{3}}} = \dfrac{\left(16^{\frac{1}{4}}\right)^3}{\left(27^{\frac{1}{3}}\right)^2} = \dfrac{(2)^3}{(3)^2} = \dfrac{8}{9}$.

(iv) $\left(2\dfrac{1}{4}\right)^{1\frac{1}{2}} = \left(\dfrac{9}{4}\right)^{\frac{3}{2}} = \dfrac{9^{\frac{3}{2}}}{4^{\frac{3}{2}}} = \dfrac{\left(9^{\frac{1}{2}}\right)^3}{\left(4^{\frac{1}{2}}\right)^3} = \dfrac{(3)^3}{(2)^3} = \dfrac{27}{8}$

(v) $\left(\dfrac{25}{16}\right)^{-\frac{3}{2}} = \dfrac{25^{-\frac{3}{2}}}{16^{-\frac{3}{2}}} = \dfrac{16^{\frac{3}{2}}}{25^{\frac{3}{2}}} = \dfrac{\left(16^{\frac{1}{2}}\right)^3}{\left(25^{\frac{1}{2}}\right)^3} = \dfrac{(4)^3}{(5)^3} = \dfrac{64}{125}$

EXAMPLE 2

(i) Express   (a) 243   (b) $\sqrt{27}$ in the form 3^n.

(ii) Express $\dfrac{\sqrt{3} \times \sqrt{27}}{3 \times 243}$ in the form 3^n.

Solution:

(i) (a) $243 = 3 \times 3 \times 3 \times 3 \times 3 = 3^5$

   (b) $\sqrt{27} = (27)^{\frac{1}{2}} = (3^3)^{\frac{1}{2}} = 3^{3 \times \frac{1}{2}} = 3^{\frac{3}{2}}$

(ii) $\dfrac{\sqrt{3} \times \sqrt{27}}{3 \times 243} = \dfrac{3^{\frac{1}{2}} \times 3^{\frac{3}{2}}}{3^1 \times 3^5} = \dfrac{3^{\frac{1}{2}+\frac{3}{2}}}{3^{1+5}} = \dfrac{3^2}{3^6} = 3^{2-6} = 3^{-4}$

Exercise 9.1

For questions 1–16, express each as a single power.

1. $2^3 \times 2^4$
2. $3^2 \times 3^6$
3. 3×3^5
4. $4^3 \times 4^2$
5. $4^{\frac{1}{2}} \times 4^{\frac{1}{2}}$
6. $2 \times 2^2 \times 2^4$
7. $7^{\frac{3}{2}} \times 7^{\frac{1}{2}}$
8. $\dfrac{2^8}{2^5}$
9. $\dfrac{3^5}{3^2}$
10. $\dfrac{4^7}{4^3}$
11. $\dfrac{-9^6}{9^4}$
12. $\dfrac{5^{10}}{-5^6}$
13. $(2^2)^3$
14. $(5^4)^2$
15. $(8^2)^5$
16. $(6^4)^5$

In questions 17–24, calculate the value of a.

17. $3^5 \times 3^2 = 3^a$
18. $\dfrac{5^7}{5^4} = 5^a$
19. $\dfrac{7^6}{7^2} = 7^a$
20. $(5^2)^3 = 5^a$
21. $3^a = \dfrac{1}{3^6}$
22. $\left(\sqrt{5}\right)^4 = 5^a$
23. $\left(\sqrt{7}\right)^5 = 7^a$
24. $6^{-3} = \dfrac{1}{6^a}$

Evaluate the expressions in questions 25–44.

25. $25^{\frac{1}{2}}$

26. $8^{\frac{1}{3}}$

27. $121^{\frac{1}{2}}$

28. $64^{\frac{1}{3}}$

29. $125^{\frac{1}{3}}$

30. $32^{\frac{1}{5}}$

31. $81^{\frac{1}{4}}$

32. $16^{\frac{3}{4}}$

33. $(20 \cdot 25)^{\frac{1}{2}}$

34. $\sqrt{121} \times \sqrt{49}$

35. $32^{\frac{3}{5}}$

36. $4^{\frac{3}{2}}$

37. $8^{\frac{2}{3}}$

38. $25^{\frac{3}{2}}$

39. $(\sqrt{8})^4$

40. $125^{\frac{2}{3}}$

41. $64^{\frac{2}{3}}$

42. $\sqrt{100} \div \sqrt{6 \cdot 25}$

43. $9^{\frac{5}{2}}$

44. $16^{\frac{5}{4}}$

Express questions 45–56 in the form $\dfrac{a}{b}$, $a, b \in \mathbb{N}$.

45. $4^{-\frac{1}{2}}$

46. $9^{-\frac{1}{2}}$

47. $27^{-\frac{2}{3}}$

48. $32^{-\frac{4}{5}}$

49. $\left(\dfrac{8}{27}\right)^{\frac{1}{3}}$

50. $\left(\dfrac{8}{125}\right)^{\frac{2}{3}}$

51. $\left(\dfrac{27}{64}\right)^{-\frac{2}{3}}$

52. $\left(\dfrac{16}{9}\right)^{-\frac{3}{2}}$

53. $\left(27^{-\frac{1}{3}}\right)^2$

54. $\dfrac{16^{-\frac{3}{4}}}{81^{-\frac{1}{2}}}$

55. $\dfrac{27^{-\frac{1}{3}}}{8^{-\frac{2}{3}}}$

56. $\dfrac{4^{-\frac{1}{2}}}{64^{\frac{2}{3}}}$

57. If $2^{-3} + 3^{-2} = \dfrac{p}{q}$, $p, q \in \mathbb{N}$, find the value of p and the value of q.

58. If $9^{-\frac{1}{2}} + 8^{-\frac{2}{3}} = \dfrac{a}{b}$, $a, b \in \mathbb{N}$, find the value of a and the value of b.

59. Simplify $\dfrac{4^6 \times 4^3}{4^2 \times 4^5}$, giving your answer in the form 4^n.

60. Simplify $\dfrac{3^5 \times 3^3}{3^2 \times 3^2}$, giving your answer in the form 3^n.

61. Simplify $\dfrac{2 \times 2^3 \times 2^7}{(2^2)^4}$, giving your answer in the form 2^n.

62. Express $\dfrac{4}{\sqrt{2}}$ in the form 2^n.

63. Express $\dfrac{125}{\sqrt{5}}$ in the form 5^n.

64. Express $\dfrac{\sqrt{2}}{8}$ in the form 2^n.

65. Show that **(i)** $\left(\dfrac{\sqrt{a}}{a^2}\right)^2 = a^{-3}$ **(ii)** $\dfrac{(a\sqrt{a})^3}{a^4} = \sqrt{a}$.

66. **(i)** Express **(a)** $25^{\frac{1}{2}}$ **(b)** 125 in the form 5^n.

    (ii) Hence or otherwise, express $\dfrac{5^2 \times 25^{\frac{1}{2}}}{125 \times 5^3}$ in the form 5^n.

67. Express $\dfrac{\sqrt{3} \times 81^{\frac{3}{4}}}{9}$ in the form 3^n.

68. Express $\dfrac{8^{\frac{2}{3}} \times 32^{\frac{4}{5}}}{2 \times 16^{\frac{1}{2}}}$ in the form 2^n.

69. (i) Simplify $(x + \sqrt{x})(x - \sqrt{x})$ when $x > 0$.

   (ii) Hence or otherwise, find the value of x for which $(x + \sqrt{x})(x - \sqrt{x}) = 6$.

70. (i) Simplify: (a) $\sqrt{a^2}$ (b) $\sqrt{b^2}$ (c) $\sqrt{x^2}$ (d) $\sqrt{(x+3)^2}$

   (ii) Factorise: (a) $x^2 + 2x + 1$ (b) $x^2 + 4x + 4$

   (iii) Simplify $\sqrt{x^2 + 4x + 4} + \sqrt{x^2 + 2x + 1}$, given that $x \geq 0$.

   (iv) Given that $x \geq 0$, solve for x: $\sqrt{x^2 + 4x + 4} + \sqrt{x^2 + 2x + 1} = x^2$.

71. Two of the numbers $9^{1/2}$, 9^{-1}, 27^0, $(-3)^2$ and 3^{-2} are equal. Write down these two values. Justify your answer.

72. The foundation for a building is in the shape of the letter L, as shown. The shape is formed from two squares of dimensions x m and $\sqrt{x}$ m.

   (i) Write down an expression in terms of x of the area of the foundation.

   (ii) If the area of the foundation is 42 m^2, write a quadratic equation in terms of x and calculate the value of x.

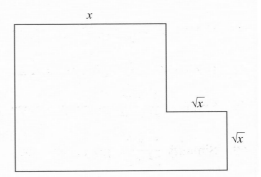

Exponential equations

Exponent is another name for power or index.

An equation involving the variable in the power is called an **exponential equation**.

For example, $3^{2x+3} = 9$ is an exponential equation.

Exponential equations are solved with the following steps.

> 1. Write all the numbers as powers of the same number (usually a prime number).
> 2. Write both sides as one power of the same number using the laws of indices.
> 3. Equate these powers and solve the equation.

EXAMPLE

Find the value of x if: (i) $4^{x+1} = 128$ (ii) $5^{3x+1} = \dfrac{125}{\sqrt{5}}$

Solution:

(i) 1. $\quad 4^{x+1} = 128$ (both 4 and 128 can be written as powers of 2)

$\quad (2^2)^{x+1} = 2^7$ $(4 = 2^2$ and $128 = 2^7)$

2. $\quad 2^{2(x+1)} = 2^7$ (multiply the indices on the left-hand side)

$\quad 2^{2x+2} = 2^7$ $(2(x+1) = 2x+2)$

3. $\quad 2x + 2 = 7$ (equate the powers)

$\quad 2x = 5$

$\quad x = \dfrac{5}{2}$

(ii) 1. $\quad 5^{3x+1} = \dfrac{125}{\sqrt{5}}$ (both 125 and $\sqrt{5}$ can be written as powers of 5)

$\quad 5^{3x+1} = \dfrac{5^3}{5^{\frac{1}{2}}}$ $\left(125 = 5^3 \text{ and } \sqrt{5} = 5^{\frac{1}{2}}\right)$

2. $\quad 5^{3x+1} = 5^{3-\frac{1}{2}}$ (subtract the index on the bottom from the index on top)

$\quad 5^{3x+1} = 5^{2\frac{1}{2}}$ $\left(3 - \frac{1}{2} = 2\frac{1}{2}\right)$

3. $\quad 3x + 1 = 2\frac{1}{2}$ (equate the powers)

$\quad 6x + 2 = 5$ (multiply both sides by 2)

$\quad 6x = 3$

$\quad x = \dfrac{1}{2}$

Exercise 9.2

Express questions 1–16 in the form a^n, where a is a prime number.

1. 8 2. 9 3. 32 4. 27

5. 125 6. 81 7. 49 8. 64

9. 243 10. 128 11. 343 12. $\dfrac{1}{16}$ $\dfrac{1}{2^4} = 2^{-4}$

13. $\dfrac{1}{243}$ 14. $\dfrac{27}{\sqrt{3}}$ 15. $\dfrac{\sqrt{5}}{25}$ 16. $32^{\frac{3}{5}}$

In questions 17–32, solve for x.

17. $5^{2x} = 5^{10}$
18. $7^{2x+1} = 7^7$
19. $3^{3x-1} = 3^5$
20. $2^x = 8$

21. $2^{x-1} = 16$
22. $3^{2x-1} = 27$
23. $9^{x+1} = 81$
24. $4^{x-1} = 32$

25. $16^{x+1} = 32$
26. $2^{2x-2} = \dfrac{1}{16}$
27. $3^{x-1} = \dfrac{1}{81}$
28. $25^{x-2} = \dfrac{1}{125}$

29. $2^{2x+1} = \dfrac{4}{\sqrt{2}}$
30. $\dfrac{2^{2x+3}}{2^{x+1}} = 32$
31. $\dfrac{3^{3x-1}}{3^{x+1}} = 9$
32. $\dfrac{5^{4x-1}}{25} = 5$

33. (i) Express $32^{\frac{4}{5}}$ in the form 4^n. (ii) Hence or otherwise, solve $4^{2x-1} = 32^{\frac{4}{5}}$.

34. (i) Express $2^5 - 2^4$ in the form 2^n. (ii) Hence, solve $2^{3x-5} = 2^5 - 2^4$.

35. Find the two values of x for which $\dfrac{2^{x^2}}{2^x} = 4$.

36. (i) Write each of the following as a power of 2.

    (a) $\sqrt{2}$ (b) 8 (c) $8^{\frac{4}{3}}$ (d) $8\sqrt{2}$

  (ii) Hence, solve for x.

    (a) $2^{5x-1} = 8^{\frac{4}{3}}$ (b) $2^{5x-4} = 8\sqrt{2}$ (c) $2^{3x+1} = \left(8\sqrt{2}\right)^2$

37. (i) Write each of the following as a power of 3.

    (a) $\sqrt{3}$ (b) $\dfrac{1}{\sqrt{3}}$ (c) 81 (d) $\dfrac{81}{\sqrt{3}}$

  (ii) Hence, solve for x.

    (a) $3^{2x} = \sqrt{3}$ (b) $3^{2x-1} = \dfrac{1}{\sqrt{3}}$ (c) $3^{x-2} = \dfrac{81}{\sqrt{3}}$

38. (i) Write each of the following as a power of 5.

    (a) 125 (b) $\sqrt{5}$ (c) $\dfrac{125}{\sqrt{5}}$ (d) $\left(\dfrac{125}{\sqrt{5}}\right)^2$

  (ii) Hence, solve for x.

    (a) $5^{3x+1} = \sqrt{5}$ (b) $5^{2x+3} = \dfrac{125}{\sqrt{5}}$ (c) $5^{2x-1} = \left(\dfrac{125}{\sqrt{5}}\right)^2$

39. (i) Use the following exponential equations to form two simultaneous equations: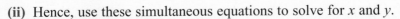
$3^{2x+y} = 3^4$ and $4^{x-y} = 4^{-1}$.

  (ii) Hence, use these simultaneous equations to solve for x and y.

40. (i) Use the following exponential equations to form two simultaneous equations:
$5^{3x} \times 5^{2y} = 5^{-10}$ and $7^x \times 7^{4y} = 7^0$.

  (ii) Hence, use these simultaneous equations to solve for x and y.

41. (i) Simplify $\sqrt{x}\left(\sqrt{x} + \dfrac{1}{\sqrt{x}}\right)$, where $x > 0$.

(ii) Hence or otherwise, solve for x: $\sqrt{x}\left(\sqrt{x} + \dfrac{1}{\sqrt{x}}\right) = 5$. Verify your answer.

42. (i) Write down the formula for the area of a triangle.

(ii) The triangle shown has a base length of $2x\sqrt{x}$ cm and perpendicular height of $\sqrt{x}$ cm.

(a) Express its area, A, in terms of x.

(b) If $A = 81$ cm^2, calculate the value of x and verify your answer.

43. The rectangle shown has a length of 4 m and a width of 2^k m.

(i) Express its area, A, in the form 2^{k+p} m^2.

(ii) Calculate k if:

(a) $A = 32$ m^2

(b) $A = 4\sqrt{2}$ m^2

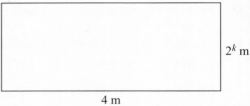

2^k m

4 m

Index notation

Index notation is a shorthand way of writing very large or very small numbers. For example, try this multiplication on your calculator: $8{,}000{,}000 \times 7{,}000{,}000$.

The answer is $56{,}000{,}000{,}000{,}000$.

It has 14 digits, which is too many to show on most calculator displays.

Your calculator will display your answer as (5·6 E 13)   or   ($5·6 \times 10^{13}$)   or   ($5·6^{13}$)

This tells you that the 5·6 is multiplied by 10^{13}.

This is written as:

$$5·6 \times 10^{13}$$

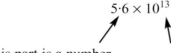

This part is a number between 1 and 10 (but not including 10).

This part is written as a power of 10 (the power is always a whole number).

Another example to try on your calculator is $0 \cdot 00000023 \times 0 \cdot 00000004$.

The answer is $0 \cdot 0000000000000092$.

Your calculator will display your answer as $\boxed{9 \cdot 2 \text{ E} -15}$ or $\boxed{9 \cdot 2 \times 10^{-15}}$ or $\boxed{9 \cdot 2^{-15}}$

This tells you that the $9 \cdot 2$ is multiplied by 10^{-15}.

This is written as:

$$9 \cdot 2 \times 10^{-15}$$

This way of writing a number is called **index notation** or **exponential notation**, or sometimes **standard form**. (It was formerly called **scientific notation**.)

Index notation gives a number in two parts:

$$\boxed{\begin{array}{c} \text{Number between 1 and 10} \\ \text{(but not 10)} \end{array}} \quad \times \quad \boxed{\text{Power of 10}}$$

This is often written as $a \times 10^n$, where $1 \leq a < 10$ and $n \in \mathbb{Z}$.

EXAMPLE 1

Express 3,700,000 in the form $a \times 10^n$, where $1 \leq a < 10$, $n \in \mathbb{Z}$.

Solution:

$$3,700,000 \quad \text{(put in the decimal point)}$$
$$3 \cdot 700000 \quad \text{(move the decimal point six places to the \textbf{left}}$$
$$\text{to give a number between 1 and 10)}$$
$$\therefore 3,700,000 = 3 \cdot 7 \times 10^6$$

EXAMPLE 2

Express the number $0 \cdot 000846$ in the form $a \times 10^n$, where $1 \leq a < 10$, $n \in \mathbb{Z}$.

Solution:

$$0 \cdot 000846 \quad \text{(decimal point already there)}$$
$$8 \cdot 46 \quad \text{(move the decimal point four places to the \textbf{right}}$$
$$\text{to give a number between 1 and 10)}$$
$$\therefore 0 \cdot 000846 = 8 \cdot 46 \times 10^{-4}$$

EXAMPLE 3

(i) Express $\dfrac{1{,}456}{0 \cdot 28}$ in the form $a \times 10^n$, where $1 \le a < 10$, $n \in \mathbb{Z}$.

(ii) Find n if $\dfrac{441}{0 \cdot 007} = 6 \cdot 3 \times 10^n$.

Solution:

(i) $\dfrac{1{,}456}{0 \cdot 28} = 5{,}200 = 5 \cdot 2 \times 10^3$

(ii) $\dfrac{441}{0 \cdot 007} = 63{,}000 = 6 \cdot 3 \times 10^4$

By comparing $6 \cdot 3 \times 10^n$ to $6 \cdot 3 \times 10^4$,

$n = 4$.

Exercise 9.3

In questions 1–16, evaluate and express the result in the form $a \times 10^n$, where $1 \le a < 10$ and $n \in \mathbb{Z}$.

1. 7,000	2. 85,000	3. 431,000	4. 540
5. 6,800	6. 3,700,000	7. 486	8. 41
9. 0·004	10. 0·0007	11. 0·089	12. 0·000283

13. $\dfrac{896}{0 \cdot 32}$ 14. $\dfrac{51{,}300}{0 \cdot 09}$ 15. $\dfrac{0 \cdot 00525}{0 \cdot 15}$ 16. $\dfrac{0 \cdot 01752}{2 \cdot 4}$

In questions 17–19 calculate the value of n.

17. $\dfrac{4{,}482}{5 \cdot 4} = 8 \cdot 3 \times 10^n$ 18. $\dfrac{36{,}540}{0 \cdot 87} = 4 \cdot 2 \times 10^n$ 19. $\dfrac{0 \cdot 01764}{4 \cdot 9} = 3 \cdot 6 \times 10^n$

20. $55{,}000 \times 0 \cdot 6 = a \times 10^n$, where $1 \le a < 10$ and $n \in \mathbb{Z}$. Write down the value of a and n.

21. $1{,}200 \times 1 \cdot 5^2 = a \times 10^n$, where $1 \le a < 10$ and $n \in \mathbb{Z}$. Write down the value of a and n.

Using a calculator

Most scientific calculators can be set to **display all answers** in index (scientific) notation. The procedure varies with different models and different manufacturers, so you are advised to read your calculator's manual. Furthermore, you will need to be able to return your calculator to its normal display settings.

Calculators that have a $\boxed{\text{SET UP}}$ button (which may need to be preceded with $\boxed{\text{SHIFT}}$) may offer you either an option **FSE** or take you to a list of display options. Selecting the **FSE** option may also take you to a list of display options.

The usual display options include **FIX**ed decimal place, **SCI**entific notation and **NORM**al. Using the **SCI** option will cause all answers to be displayed in index notation and the calculator screen should show **SCI** to confirm the display mode. You may continue to enter numbers in the usual manner.

To return your display to its usual state, you will need to go through the procedure again, this time choosing **NORM**al display. Most calculators have two versions of **NORM**al, so you may have to select **1** or **2**. The calculator screen will no longer show the **SCI** indicator.

Calculators that do not have a $\boxed{\text{SET UP}}$ button should have a $\boxed{\text{MODE}}$ button, which if pressed repeatedly will provide display options.

Notes: 1. The display modes only refer to how the **answer** is displayed. You may enter numbers in any format at all times.
2. Very large and very small numbers are always displayed in index notation.
3. Remember to set your calculator back to **NORM**al display mode.

Addition and subtraction

Numbers given in index notation can be keyed into your calculator by using the **exponent key**. It is marked $\boxed{\text{EXP}}$ or $\boxed{\text{EE}}$ or $\boxed{\times 10^x}$.

To key in a number in index notation, do the following.

> 1. Key in 'a', the 'number part', first.
> 2. Press the exponent key next.
> 3. Key in the index of the power of 10.

To enter $3·4 \times 10^6$, for example, you key in $3·4$ $\boxed{\text{EXP}}$ 6.

To enter negative powers, you need to find the **negative** button on your calculator. It is usually marked $\boxed{(-)}$ or $\boxed{+/-}$ and is used to enter negative numbers.

To enter $7·1 \times 10^{-3}$, for example, you key in $7·1$ $\boxed{\text{EXP}}$ $\boxed{(-)}$ 3.

Note: If you press $\boxed{=}$ at the end, the calculator will write the number as a decimal number, provided the index of the power of 10 is not too large.

To add or subtract two numbers in index notation, do the following.

> 1. Write each number as a simple number.
> 2. Add or subtract these numbers.
> 3. Write your answer in index notation.
> Alternatively, you can use your calculator by keying in the numbers in index notation and adding or subtracting as required.

EXAMPLE

Calculate **(i)** $2\cdot32 \times 10^4 + 3\cdot8 \times 10^3$ **(ii)** $8\cdot72 \times 10^3 - 5\cdot2 \times 10^2$

Write your answers in the form $a \times 10^n$, where $1 \leq a < 10$ and $n \in \mathbb{N}$.

Solution:

(i) $2\cdot32 \times 10^4 = 23{,}200$
$$3\cdot8 \times 10^3 = \underline{3{,}800}$$
$$27{,}000 \quad \text{(add)}$$
$$= 2\cdot7 \times 10^4$$

🖩 $2\cdot32$ EXP 4 $+$ $3\cdot8$ EXP 3 $=$

27,000 (on the display)
$= 2\cdot7 \times 10^4$

(ii) $8\cdot72 \times 10^3 = 8{,}720$
$$5\cdot2 \times 10^2 = \underline{520}$$
$$8{,}200 \quad \text{(subtract)}$$
$$= 8\cdot2 \times 10^3$$

🖩 $8\cdot72$ EXP 3 $-$ $5\cdot2$ EXP 2 $=$

8,200 (on the display)
$= 8\cdot2 \times 10^3$

Multiplication and division

To multiply or divide two numbers in index notation, do the following.

1. Multiply or divide the 'a' parts (the number parts).
2. Multiply or divide the powers of 10 (add or subtract the indices).
3. Write your answer in index notation.

Alternatively, you can use your calculator by keying in the numbers in index notation and multiplying or dividing as required.

EXAMPLE

Express **(i)** $(3\cdot5 \times 10^2) \times (4\cdot8 \times 10^3)$ **(ii)** $(4\cdot86 \times 10^4) \div (1\cdot8 \times 10^7)$ in the form $a \times 10^n$, where $1 \leq a < 10$ and $n \in \mathbb{Z}$.

Solution:

(i) $(3\cdot5 \times 10^2) \times (4\cdot8 \times 10^3)$
$$= 3\cdot5 \times 10^2 \times 4\cdot8 \times 10^3$$
$$= 3\cdot5 \times 4\cdot8 \times 10^2 \times 10^3$$
$$= 16\cdot8 \times 10^{2+3} \quad \text{(add the indices)}$$
$$= 16\cdot8 \times 10^5$$
$$= 1{,}680{,}000$$
$$= 1\cdot68 \times 10^6$$

🖩 $3\cdot5$ EXP 2 $\times$ $4\cdot8$ EXP 3 $=$

$= 1{,}680{,}000$ (on the display)
$= 1\cdot68 \times 10^6$

(ii) $(4\cdot86 \times 10^4) \div (1\cdot8 \times 10^7)$
$$= \frac{4\cdot86 \times 10^4}{1\cdot8 \times 10^7}$$
$$= \frac{4\cdot86}{1\cdot8} \times \frac{10^4}{10^7}$$
$$= 2\cdot7 \times 10^{4-7} \quad \text{(subtract the indices)}$$
$$= 2\cdot7 \times 10^{-3}$$

🖩 $4\cdot86$ EXP 2 $\div$ $1\cdot8$ EXP 7 $=$

$= 0\cdot0027$ (on the display)
$= 2\cdot7 \times 10^3$

Exercise 9.4

In questions 1–22, simplify and express your answer in the form $a \times 10^n$, where $1 \leq a < 10$ and $n \in \mathbb{Z}$.

1. $2 \cdot 5 \times 10^3 + 9 \times 10^2$
2. $2 \cdot 54 \times 10^5 + 2 \cdot 7 \times 10^4$
3. $7 \cdot 2 \times 10^4 - 2 \cdot 8 \times 10^3$
4. $4 \cdot 83 \times 10^3 - 2 \cdot 32 \times 10^4$
5. $6 \cdot 2 \times 10^{-3} - 2 \times 10^{-4}$
6. $3 \cdot 48 \times 10^{-4} - 5 \cdot 4 \times 10^{-5}$
7. $(1 \cdot 75 \times 10^3) \times (4 \times 10^4)$
8. $(2 \cdot 3 \times 10^3) \times (1 \cdot 5 \times 10^3)$
9. $(2 \cdot 4 \times 10^3) \times (3 \cdot 6 \times 10^2)$
10. $(5 \cdot 3 \times 10^2) \times (1 \cdot 8 \times 10^4)$
11. $(3 \cdot 8 \times 10^5) \div (2 \times 10^2)$
12. $(4 \cdot 5 \times 10^8) \div (1 \cdot 5 \times 10^5)$
13. $(4 \cdot 3 \times 10^3) \times (2 \cdot 25 \times 10^5)$
14. $(5 \cdot 02 \times 10^6) \div (3 \times 10^2)$
15. $(1 \cdot 6 \times 10^5) \times (4 \cdot 8 \times 10^3)$
16. $(8 \times 10^8) \div (3 \cdot 2 \times 10^5)$
17. $(9 \cdot 86 \times 10^5) \div (1 \cdot 7 \times 10^2)$
18. $(3 \cdot 8 \times 10^4) \times (2 \cdot 5 \times 10^2)$
19. $\dfrac{(2 \cdot 4 \times 10^4) \times (1 \cdot 5 \times 10^3)}{1 \cdot 2 \times 10^3}$
20. $\dfrac{(3 \cdot 2 \times 10^5) + (8 \cdot 5 \times 10^4)}{8 \cdot 1 \times 10^2}$
21. $\dfrac{2 \cdot 45 \times 10^5 - 1 \cdot 8 \times 10^3}{1 \cdot 6 \times 10^3}$
22. $\dfrac{1 \cdot 4 \times 10^3 + 5 \cdot 6 \times 10^2}{7 \times 10^{-1}}$

23. Calculate the value of $7 \cdot 95 \times 10^{-2} - 7 \cdot 2 \times 10^{-3}$. Write your answer as a decimal number. Say whether this number is greater than or less than $0 \cdot 08$.

24. Calculate the value of $\dfrac{2 \cdot 8 \times 10^4 + 4 \cdot 2 \times 10^5}{2 \cdot 24 \times 10^6}$. Write your answer as a decimal number.

    Say whether this number is greater than or less than $0 \cdot 19$.

25. $\sqrt{\dfrac{3 \cdot 64 \times 10^5 - 1 \cdot 7 \times 10^3}{9 \cdot 0575 \times 10^2}} = k$. Find the value of k.

26. A certain kind of bacteria moves very slowly, taking steps that have a distance of 0.00000025 metres each. If this bacteria takes 4,250,000,000 steps, how far does it travel?

27. The mass of the moon is $7 \cdot 3 \times 10^{22}$ kg. If the mass of the Earth is 82 times the mass of the moon, calculate the mass of the Earth. Express your answer in the form $a \times 10^n$, where $n \in \mathbb{Z}$ and $1 \leq a \leq 10$.

28. The human eye blinks about $6 \cdot 25 \times 10^6$ times each year. How many times has a teenager's eye blinked by their 14th birthday? Express your answer in the form $a \times 10^n$, where $n \in \mathbb{Z}$ and $1 \leq a \leq 10$.

29. The speed of light is 3×10^8 metres/second. If the sun is $1\cdot5 \times 10^{11}$ metres from Earth, how many seconds does it take light from the sun to reach the Earth? Express your answer in the form $a \times 10^n$, where $n \in \mathbb{Z}$ and $1 \leq a \leq 10$.

30. Approximately $1\cdot3 \times 10^5$ serious crimes are reported to Gardaí every year. How many serious crimes are reported every hour? Give your answer to the nearest whole number.

31. 6,800 identical bricks are in a crate. If the total mass of the bricks is $8\cdot5 \times 10^3$ kg, calculate the mass of each brick.

32. A swimming pool contains $2\cdot45 \times 10^3$ m³ of water. Before cleaning the pool the water must be drained. The water drains out of the pool at a rate of 175 m³ every 10 minutes.
    (i) How much water is left in the swimming pool after one hour? (Give your answer in scientific notation.)
    (ii) How many minutes does it take until the pool is completely empty?

Reciprocals

If the product of two numbers is 1, then each number is the reciprocal of the other.

The reciprocal of 5 is $\dfrac{1}{5}$ and the reciprocal of $\dfrac{1}{5}$ is 5.

> Examples of reciprocals:
> $$5 \times \frac{1}{5} = 1 \qquad \frac{2}{3} \times \frac{3}{2} = 1 \qquad -\frac{7}{9} \times -\frac{9}{7} = 1$$

To find the reciprocal of a number, do the following.

> **Method 1:** Write the given number as a single fraction and turn it upside down.
> **Method 2:** Use the reciprocal button, $\boxed{x^{-1}}$ or $\boxed{1/x}$, on your calculator.

EXAMPLE 1

Write the reciprocal of each of the following numbers.

(i) 6   (ii) $-\dfrac{1}{8}$ (iii) $\dfrac{5}{7}$ (iv) $3\dfrac{1}{2}$

Solution:

(i) The reciprocal of 6 is $\dfrac{1}{6}$, since $6 \times \dfrac{1}{6} = 1$.

(ii) The reciprocal of $-\dfrac{1}{8}$ is $-\dfrac{8}{1}$, since $-\dfrac{1}{8} \times -\dfrac{8}{1} = 1$.

(iii) The reciprocal of $\frac{5}{7}$ is $\frac{7}{5}$, since $\frac{5}{7} \times \frac{7}{5} = 1$.

(iv) Write $3\frac{1}{2}$ as a single fraction: $\frac{7}{2}$.

The reciprocal of $\frac{7}{2}$ is $\frac{2}{7}$, since $\frac{7}{2} \times \frac{2}{7} = 1$.

EXAMPLE 2

Use the reciprocal button on your calculator, $\boxed{x^{-1}}$ or $\boxed{1/x}$, to find the reciprocal of each of the following.

(i) 2·5   (ii) 1·4   (iii) −3·8

Solution:

(i) The reciprocal of 2·5:   2·5 $\boxed{x^{-1}}$ = 0·4

(ii) The reciprocal of 1·4:   1·4 $\boxed{x^{-1}}$ = 0·714

(iii) The reciprocal of −3·8:   −3·8 $\boxed{x^{-1}}$ = −0·263

Exercise 9.5

In questions 1–12, write the reciprocal as a fraction.

1. 2

2. −8

3. 7

4. −6

5. $\frac{2}{3}$

6. $\frac{5}{8}$

7. $-\frac{1}{9}$

8. $-\frac{4}{7}$

9. $\frac{1}{37}$

10. $-\frac{7}{13}$

11. $\frac{12}{11}$

12. $-\frac{10}{7}$

In questions 13–16, express the number as a single fraction and hence find the reciprocal as a fraction.

13. $2\frac{1}{3}$

14. $3\frac{1}{4}$

15. $5\frac{2}{7}$

16. $3\frac{5}{9}$

In questions 17–20, use your calculator to find the reciprocal correct to three decimal places.

17. 2·55

18. −3·21

19. 0·52

20. 1·49

CHAPTER 10 — DISTANCE, SPEED AND TIME

Distance, speed and time

There are three formulas to remember when dealing with problems involving distance (D), speed (S) and time (T). It can be difficult to remember these formulas; however, the work can be made easier using a triangle and the memory aid 'Dad's Silly Triangle'.

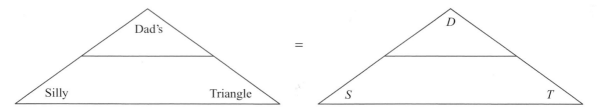

$$1. \ \text{Speed} = \frac{\text{Distance}}{\text{Time}} \qquad 2. \ \text{Time} = \frac{\text{Distance}}{\text{Speed}} \qquad 3. \ \text{Distance} = \text{Speed} \times \text{Time}$$

Consider the triangle on the right. By covering the quantity required, D, S or T, any of the three formulas above can be found by inspection.

Note: It is important to be able to change minutes into hours and vice versa. For example:

$$40 \text{ minutes} = \frac{40}{60} \text{ hour} = \frac{2}{3} \text{ hour}$$

$$12 \text{ minutes} = \frac{12}{60} \text{ hour} = \frac{1}{5} \text{ hour}$$

$$0 \cdot 25 \text{ hours} = \frac{25}{100} \text{ hour} = \frac{1}{4} \text{ hour} = 15 \text{ mins}$$

$$0 \cdot 8 \text{ hour} = \frac{80}{100} \text{ hour} = \frac{4}{5} \text{ hour} = 48 \text{ mins}$$

EXAMPLE 1

(i) A journey of 18 km took 40 minutes. Find the average speed in metres per second.

(ii) A journey of 276 km began at 10:40 and ended on the same day at 14:30. Find the average speed in km/h.

Solution:

(i)   18 km = 18,000 m

40 minutes = 40 × 60 = 2,400 seconds

$$\text{Speed} = \frac{\text{Distance}}{\text{Time}}$$

$$= \frac{18,000}{2,400}$$

$$= 7\frac{1}{2} \text{ m/s}$$

(ii)   Time = 14:30 hrs − 10:40 hrs

= 3 hours 50 minutes = $3\frac{5}{6}$ hours

$$\text{Speed} = \frac{\text{Distance}}{\text{Time}}$$

$$= \frac{276}{3\frac{5}{6}}$$

$$= 72 \text{ km/h}$$

Note: Metres per second can be written as m/s or ms^{-1}.

Two-part problems

Two-part questions on distance, speed and time involve two separate journeys. In these questions we need the total distance travelled for both journeys and the total time for both journeys. We then use the formula:

$$\frac{\text{Overall average speed}}{\text{for both journeys}} = \frac{\text{Total distance for both journeys}}{\text{Total time for both journeys}}$$

 EXAMPLE 2

A lorry travels 140 km at an average speed of 56 km/h. It then travels for 2 hours at an average speed of 65 km/h. What is the average speed for the whole journey?

Solution:

In the first journey the time is required

$$\text{Time} = \frac{\text{Distance}}{\text{Speed}}$$

$$= \frac{140}{56}$$

$$= 2\frac{1}{2} \text{ hours}$$

In the second journey the distance is required

$$\text{Distance} = \text{Speed} \times \text{Time}$$

$$= 65 \times 2$$

$$= 130 \text{ km}$$

$$\frac{\text{Average speed for}}{\text{the whole journey}} = \frac{\text{Total distance travelled}}{\text{Total time taken}}$$

$$= \frac{140 + 130}{2\frac{1}{2} + 2} = \frac{270}{4\frac{1}{2}} = 60 \text{ km/h}$$

EXAMPLE 3

A recipe for cooking a turkey states:

'For the first 5 kg, allow 30 minutes per kg; for each kilogram over 5 kg, allow 20 minutes; finally, add an extra 15 minutes cooking time.'

The graph opposite represents the position.

Use the graph to estimate:

  (i) The cooking time for a turkey weighing
     (a) 4 kg **(b)** 7 kg.

 (ii) The weight of a turkey that requires a cooking time of
     (a) 125 minutes **(b)** 225 minutes.

(iii) Write a formula for the cooking time, y minutes, in the form $y = mx + c$ required for a turkey weighing x kg where
     (a) $x \leq 5$ **(b)** $x > 5$.

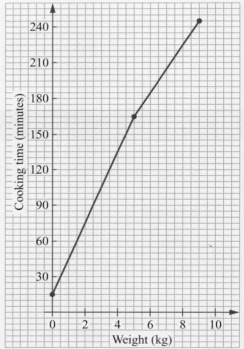

Solution:

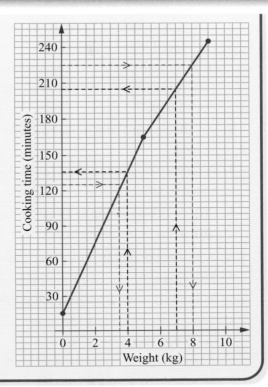

(i) From the graph (via black lines)

    (a) 4 kg → 136 mins

    (b) 7 kg → 205 mins

(ii) From the graph (via red lines)

    (a) 125 mins → $3\frac{1}{2}$ kg

    (b) 225 mins → 8 kg

(iii) **(a)** for $x \leq 5$

        $y = 30x + 15$

    (b) for $x > 5$

        $y = 30(5) + 20(x - 5) + 15$

        $y = 150 + 20x - 100 + 15$

        $y = 20x + 65$

Exercise 10.1

1. Which of these four supermarket queues should Sheldon join in order to get to a checkout in the shortest possible time?

    Woman (W)   Couple (C)   Man (M)   Adult with child (A)

Key: Average checkout times for

M = man takes 90 secs

W = woman takes $2\frac{1}{2}$ mins

C = couple takes 2·25 mins

A = adult with child takes 2 mins 50 secs

Queue 1 : M, M, W, M, M, M, M   Queue 3 : W, W, C, W, C

Queue 2 : A, W, A, W, M   Queue 4 : A, W, C, W, M

2. **(i)** A train takes 3 hours 30 minutes to travel a distance of 315 km. Calculate the average speed of the train in km/h.

   (ii) A cyclist travels $6\frac{3}{4}$ km at an average speed of 5 m/s. How long does the journey take?

   (iii) A car travels for 2 hours 20 minutes at an average speed of 81 km/h. How far does it travel?

3. An athlete ran 1,500 m in 4 minutes. Find the average speed of the athlete in metres per second.

4. A journey of 170 km began at 11:45 and ended on the same day at 14:35. Find the average speed in km/h.

5. **(i)** A girl is cycling at 18 km per hour. Convert her speed to m/s.

   (ii) A car is travelling at 27·5 m/s. Convert its speed to km/h.

6. A journey of 900 m took 40 seconds. Find the average speed in km/h.

7. The distance between two railway stations is 253 km. If the train leaves one station at 08:40 and travels at an average speed of 69 km/h, calculate the arrival time at the other station.

8. The speed of sound is 330 m per second. This speed is referred to as Mach 1. Mach 2 is twice that speed and so on.

   A new military jet can fly at an average speed of Mach 5. Find how long it takes in hours and minutes to fly across the Pacific Ocean from Sydney to Los Angeles, a distance of 11,583 km.

9. **(i)** A man travels from Arklow to Blanchardstown, a distance of 90 km. He leaves Arklow at 09:25 and arrives in Blanchardstown at 10:55. Calculate his average speed for the journey.

   (ii) He continues from Blanchardstown to Cootehill, a distance of 112 km. He increases his average speed by 4 km/h for this section of his journey. At what time does he arrive in Cootehill?

10. The main runway at Monsignor Horan Airport is $2\frac{1}{4}$ km long.

    (i) An Airbus 380 taking off starts its takeoff at A and becomes airborne at the point P. The Airbus takes 52 seconds at an average speed of 126 km/h to become airborne. Estimate, in metres, $|AP|$.

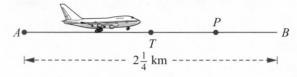

Not to scale

    (ii) A smaller aircraft, a Cessna 510, becomes airborne at T when starting from A. T is 1,575 m from A. The average speed of the Cessna during takeoff was 90 km/h how long did the Cessna take to travel from A to T?

    (iii) Comment on the accuracy, or otherwise, of your answers to **(i)** and **(ii)**.

11. The lengths of the sides of a right-angled triangle *ABC* are as shown in the diagram.

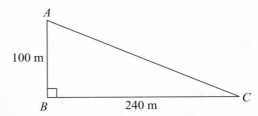

(i) Simon travels from *A* to *C* on his quad bike. He can travel on the road from *A* through *B* to *C* at an average speed of 72 km/h. How long will the journey take?

(ii) Using the theorem of Pythagoras, find the length of [*AC*].

(iii) Simon can travel in a straight line from *A* to *C* on his quad bike over rough ground. On rough ground his average speed is 48 km/h. Which of the two routes is quicker? Justify your answer.

12. (i) A motorist travels a journey of 185 km. The motorist travels the first 80 km at an average speed of 75 km/h. How many hours and minutes does it take the motorist to travel the first 80 km?

(ii) The remainder of the journey takes 1 hour 45 minutes. Calculate the average speed for this part of the journey in km/h.

13. Anne walks a distance of 1·7 km to school from home. She walks at an average speed of 5·1 km/h. What is the latest time she can leave home to be in school at 08:55?

14. It takes 4 hours 20 minutes to travel a journey at an average speed of 120 km/h. How many hours and minutes will it take to travel the same journey if the average speed is reduced to 100 km/h?

15. In a journey of 235 km a man drives for 2 hours at an average speed of 80 km/h. How long does the journey take if he travels the remainder of the journey at an average speed of 50 km/h?

16. The time taken by Jack to travel from Derry to Waterford, a distance of 378 km, is 6 hours. His return journey from Waterford to Derry, by the same route, takes an extra 45 mins. By how many km/h is his average speed slower on the return journey?

17. Hugh can swim, with the flow of the river, from *P* to *Q*, a distance of 300 m, in 200 seconds. He can swim against the flow of the river from *Q* to *P* in 4 minutes 10 seconds. Find:

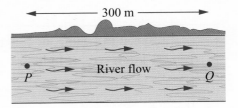

(i) His speed swimming from *P* to *Q* in m/s.

(ii) His speed swimming from *Q* to *P* in m/s.

Hence or otherwise, calculate the following in m/s.

(iii) The difference between the speeds in (i) and (ii).

(iv) Hugh's speed when swimming in still water.

(v) The average speed of the river flow.

18. Rebecca and Bren plan a walking holiday in Scotland.
    To help plan the holiday they use a map of the
    section of the country with a scale of 1:1,000,000.

    (i) Bren measures the straight line distance between
        Inverness (Q) and Fort William (P). Find the distance
        on the map, to the nearest mm.

    (ii) Convert this distance on the map to the real
         distance in km.

    (iii) Rebecca knows the maximum distance
          they can walk in one day is 34 km. Is it
          reasonable for her to conclude they can
          make this journey in 3 days? Justify
          your answer.

19. Light travels at a speed of approximately ($2 \cdot 9 \times 10^5$) km/sec. How many kilometres will
    light travel in 8 minutes? Express your answer in the form $a \times 10^n$, where $n \in \mathbb{N}$ and
    $1 \leq a < 10$.

20. Four drivers complete a 540 km journey
    by car. The bar chart shows the fuel
    consumption of each driver. Copy and
    complete the following table.

    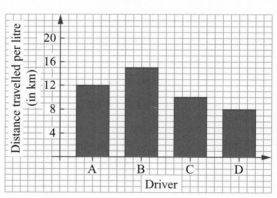

Driver	Speed in km/h	Time for journey in hours	Fuel consumption km per l	Quantity of fuel required in l	Cost € to nearest cent
A		9			
B	80			36	57·06
C	100				
D		$4\frac{1}{2}$			

21. A train travelled 168 km at an average speed of 112 km/h. It then travelled for 45 minutes at an average speed of 100 km/h. Calculate the following.

  (i) The total distance travelled

  (ii) The total time taken

  (iii) The average speed for the whole journey

22. **(i)** In a 160 km road race, a cyclist cycled the first 120 km at a steady speed of 30 km/h and completed the race at a steady speed of 40 km/h. Calculate the time taken by the cyclist for:

  (a) the first 120 km **(b)** the rest of the race.

  (ii) A second cyclist started the race at the same time as the first cyclist. At what steady speed must the second cyclist travel the 160 km so as to finish level with the first cyclist?

23. A taxi company k, charges an initial fee plus a metered amount charged at €$\frac{5}{6}$ per minute. Taxi company h charges an initial fee plus a metered amount charged at €$\frac{8}{15}$ per minute. From the graph, estimate the following.

  (i) The initial fee charged by

  (a) company k **(b)** company h.

  (ii) The fare for a journey of 24 minutes' duration for

  (a) company k **(b)** company h.

  (iii) The time for which both companies charge the same fare. Write down your estimate of that fare.

  (iv) You plan to make a journey that will take 15–18 minutes. Which company would you use? Justify your answer.

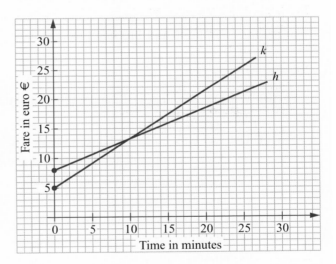

24. On a journey, Jack cycles his bike in the following manner.
   For the first half hour he cycles at an average
   speed of 20 km/h. For the remainder of the
   journey he cycles at an average speed of 15 km/h.
   From the graph, estimate the following.

   (i) Jack's time to complete a journey of
       (a) 8 km   (b) 12 km.
   (ii) The distance Jack will cycle in
       (a) 17 minutes   (b) 51 minutes.
   (iii) Write a formula for the distance travelled,
       y km, required for a journey taking x minutes
       where (a) $x \leq 30$ (b) $x > 30$.

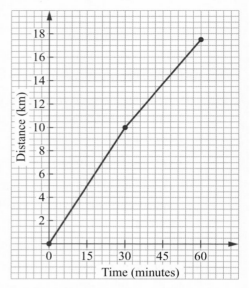

25. The graphs show the relationship between distances travelled and fuel consumption for
   Carol's jeep. The line segments l and k represent the fuel consumption at average (steady)
   speeds of 70 km/h and 110 km/h respectively.

   (i) Find the slope of l.
   (ii) Find the slope of k.
   (iii) What do the slopes of l and k tell you about the fuel consumption of the jeep at
       these speeds?
   (iv) The fuel tank holds 40 l. From the graph, estimate the total distance the jeep can
       travel with a full tank at an average speed of   (a) 70 km/h   (b) 110 km/h.
   (v) Carol drives the jeep non-stop a distance of 308 km. Calculate how long the drive
       will take at an average speed of   (a) 70 km/h   (b) 110 km/h.
   (vi) Fuel costs 193·5 cent per litre. Carol is paid €16 per hour for driving. On a journey
       of 308 km at a steady speed, which is cheaper, the journey at 70 km/h or at 110 km/h?
       Explain your answer.

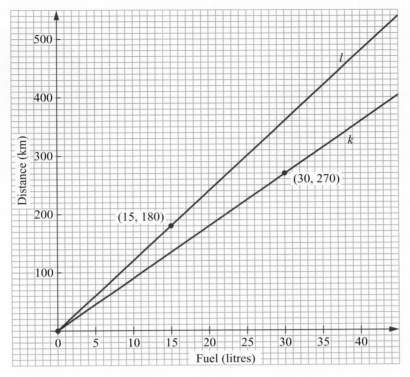

26. **(i)** A mill wheel with centre O rotates in a clockwise direction, as represented in the diagram. On average, the wheel rotates once every 18 seconds. Find the average number of rotations per hour.

(ii) The miller knows from experience a particular task takes 8 hours 45 minutes. On average, how many rotations will the wheel make performing such a task?

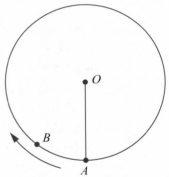

27. The sweep of the arm on the radar imaging screen is one revolution every 2 seconds. K represents the location of the radar observation post. The position of a ship is traced by the collinear points A, B, C and D, as shown. Each position was recorded as indicated at intervals of 100 revolutions. The distance from A to D is 3 km. Find the average speed of the ship in km/h.

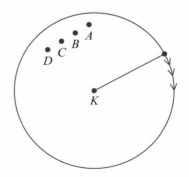

28. A satellite travels around the Earth in a circle
500 km above the Earth's surface.

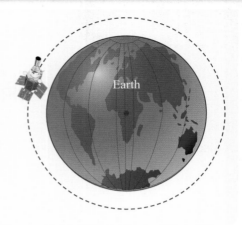

Earth

(i) Assuming that the radius of the Earth is
6,400 km, find the distance travelled by the
satellite in one orbit, where the length of
one orbit is given by $2\pi r$. (Assume $\pi = 3\cdot 14$.)

(ii) The satellite takes 1 hour 30 minutes to complete
one orbit. Find the average speed of the satellite.

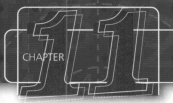

Types of data

Data is a collection of facts. It can be numbers, measurements, descriptions or observations. On our course we consider **two** types of data.

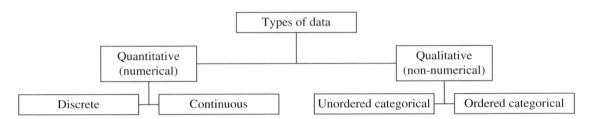

Quantitative data (numerical)

Discrete numerical data	Continuous numerical data
Discrete numerical data are data which can only have certain values.	Continuous data are data which can take any numerical value within a certain range.
Examples are number of students in a school, number of goals scored in a match and shoe sizes (including half-sizes).	Examples are time, weight, height, temperature, pressure and area. (Accuracy depends on the measuring device used.)

Qualitative data (non-numerical)

Unordered categorical data	Ordered categorical data
Unordered categorical data are data that can be sorted according to a category but have **no** order or ranking (rating scale). It can be counted but not measured.	Ordered categorical data are data that can be sorted according to a category and have an order or ranking. It can be counted and ordered but not measured.
Examples are colours, blood groups and gender (male or female).	Examples are examination grades, football divisions and opinion scales.

Note: Ordered categorical data are sometimes called **ordinal data**.

If a code is used to put data into a category, the data is called **nominal data**. The data are assigned a code in the form of a number or letter. The numbers or letters are simply labels. For example, males could be coded as 1 and females as 2. Marital status can be coded as M if married or S if single. Nominal data can be counted but not measured or ordered.

Exercise 11.1

In questions 1–24, classify the data as either discrete numerical, continuous numerical, unordered categorical or ordered categorical.

1. Number of cars in a car park
2. Temperatures of patients in a hospital
3. Colour of balloons
4. Subject grades A, B, C, D, E, F and NG
5. Gender (male or female)
6. Year groups in a school
7. Height of a plant
8. Number of rooms in a house
9. Tyre pressure
10. School subjects
11. Number of socks in a drawer
12. Position in a race
13. Age in complete years
14. Area of a field
15. Crops grown on a farm
16. Number of doors on a car
17. Cost of posting a parcel
18. Distance from Cork to Dublin
19. Speed of cars in a race
20. Dress sizes
21. Country of birth
22. Time taken to complete a task
23. Weight of a potato
24. Blood group

25. The illustration shows a red car.
    State a variable about the car that is:

    (i) Categorical

    (ii) Discrete numerical

    (iii) Continuous numerical

26. Mary collects stamps and records information about each stamp in her collection. Write down a variable that she could record as:

    (i) Categorical   (ii) Continuous numerical   (iii) Discrete numerical

27. Apartments are advertised as 1 bedroomed, 2 bedroomed or 3 bedroomed.
    What type of data is this? Justify your answer.

28. A lecturer in statistics said, 'Shoe size cannot be discrete numerical data because you can buy half sizes.' Explain why the lecturer is wrong.

29. Write a short question where the answer given will contain data that is:

    (i) Discrete numerical data
    (ii) Continuous numerical data
    (iii) Unordered categorical data
    (iv) Ordered categorical data

Collecting data

Data is collected for many reasons. For example, a company may do some market research to find out if people like their new products or the Department of Education may collect information on the number of children in a certain area to see if they need to build more schools in that area. **Raw data** are the data as they were collected before any processing has been done. **Data logging** usually involves just counting. For example, if a shop owner wanted to record the number of customers that entered their shop, they can use a data logger which would count customers as they enter. **Electronic data capture** is the process by which data are transferred from a paper copy, for example a questionnaire, to an electronic file, usually on a computer.

Primary data
Primary data (first-hand data) are data that you collect yourself or are collected by someone under your direct supervision.

Secondary data
Secondary data (second-hand data) are data that have already been collected and made available from an external source such as newspapers, government departments, organisations or the internet.

Primary and secondary data have advantages and disadvantages.

Data	Advantages	Disadvantages
Primary	Know how it was obtained. Accuracy is also known.	Time consuming. Can be expensive.
Secondary	Easy and cheap to obtain.	Could be out of date. May have mistakes and be biased. Unknown source of collection.

Note: 'Data' is a plural word, so we should really say 'data are . . .', not 'data is . . .'. However, in everyday speech, most people use 'data' as a singular word. In this book we use data as a plural word.

Census
The **population** is the complete set of data under consideration. For example, a population may be all the females in Ireland between the ages of 12 and 18, all the sixth year students in your school or the number of red cars in Ireland. A **census** is a collection of data relating to a population. A list of every item in a population is called a **sampling frame**.

Sample
A **sample** is a small part of the population selected. A **random sample** is a sample in which every member of the population has an equal chance of being selected. Data gathered from a sample are called **statistics**. Conclusions drawn from a sample can then be applied to the whole population (this is called **statistical inference**). However, it is very important that the sample chosen is representative of that population to avoid bias.

Bias

Bias (unfairness) is anything that distorts the data so that they will not give a representative sample. Bias can occur in sampling due to:

1. Failing to identify the correct population.
2. Choosing a sample that is not representative of the population.
3. A sample size that is too small (larger samples are usually more accurate).
4. Careless or dishonest answers to questions.
5. Using questions that are misleading or ambiguous.
6. Failure to respond to a survey.
7. Errors in recording the data, for example recording 23 as 32.
8. The data can go out of date, for example conclusions drawn from an opinion poll can change over a period of time.

Reasons for using samples:

1. They are quick and cheap.
2. It is essential when the sampling units are destroyed (called destructive sampling). For example, we cannot test the lifetimes of every light bulb manufactured until they fail.
3. Quality of information gained is more manageable and better controlled, leading to better accuracy. (More time and money can be spent on the sample.)
4. It is often very difficult to gather data on a whole population.

Sample survey

A survey collects data (information). A **sample survey** is a survey that collects data from a sample of the population, usually using a questionnaire. Questionnaires are well-designed forms that are used to conduct sample surveys.

Note: It is good practice to do a **pilot survey**. A pilot survey is a small-scale survey carried out before the main survey. This helps to test your questions and the data collection method. It also helps to check if the survey will produce the information required.

The main survey methods are:

- **Personal interview:** People are asked questions directly. This is regularly used in market research.
- **Telephone survey:** Often used for a personal interview.
- **Postal survey:** A survey is sent to someone's address.
- **Online questionnaires:** People fill out the questionnaire online.

Advantages and disadvantages of surveys are as follows.

Method	Advantages	Disadvantages
Personal interview (face to face)	• High response rate. • Can ask many questions. • Can ask more personal questions.	• Can be expensive. • Interviewer can influence response.
Telephone survey	• High response rate. • Can ask many questions. • Can ask more personal questions.	• Can be expensive. • Interviewer can influence response. • Easier to tell lies.
Postal survey	• Relatively cheap. • Can ask many questions. • Can ask more personal questions.	• Poor response rate. • Partly completed. • Limited in the type of data collected. • No way of clarifying any questions.
Online questionnaires	• Cheap and fast to collect large volumes of data. • More flexible design. • Ease of editing. • Can be sent directly to a database such as Microsoft Excel. • No interviewer bias. • Anonymity. • No geographical problems.	• Limited to those with access to an online computer. This leads to sample bias. • Technical problems (crashes, freezes). • Protecting privacy is an ethical issue.

Questionnaires

Designing a questionnaire

Always have a clear aim for your survey and ask questions in a logical order.

A **questionnaire** is a set of questions used to obtain data from a population. Anyone who answers a questionnaire is called a **respondent**. The part where you give your answer is called the **response section**.

The questionnaire should:

Be clear about who is to complete it.	Be as brief as possible.
Start with simple questions.	Be able to be answered quickly.
Be clear how the answers are to be recorded.	Be clear where the answers are to be recorded.

The questions should:

Be short and use simple language.	Not be leading in any way, as this can influence the answer.
Provide tick boxes.	Not cause embarrassment or offend (avoid personal questions).
Be clear about what is asked.	Be relevant to the survey.
Allow a 'yes' or 'no' answer, a number or a response from a choice of answers.	Not be open-ended, which might produce long or rambling answers that are difficult to analyse.

Other methods for collecting data

Observational studies

Data obtained by making observations are called **observational studies**. The data is collected by counting, measuring or noting things that happen. For example, a traffic survey might be done in this way to reveal the number of vehicles passing over a bridge. Important factors are place, time of day and the amount of time spent collecting the data. Observational studies can be laborious and time consuming.

Designed experiments

The purpose of an experiment is to discover information. A **designed experiment** is a controlled study in which the researcher understands the cause-and-effect relationships. The study is controlled. This method of collecting data is very popular with drug companies testing a new drug to see if has any effect on those who take it. The experiment can usually measure the effects, if any, that result from changes in the situation. The experiment must be designed so that it will collect a sufficient amount of the right kind of information and does not mix up the information with something else. If the experiment is not well designed, any data you collect may be biased. An example of a good experiment is throwing a die many times to see if it is biased. The key things to remember are that the experiment must be repeated a number of times and that the experiment must be capable of being replicated by other people.

Single-response questions

Question	Comment
Gender: Male ☐ Female ☐	Good clear question.

Multiple-response questions

Question	Comment
How old are you?	Personal question, as people may be embarrassed to give their age. No indication of accuracy.
A better question would be: Which is your age group, in years? Under 18 18–40 41–60 Over 60 ☐ ☐ ☐ ☐	Only one response required. No gaps and no overlapping of boxes.
You prefer to go out on Saturdays, don't you?	A leading question. It forces an opinion on the person being surveyed.
A better question is: On which day do you prefer to go out? Please tick one box. Mon Tue Wed Thu Fri Sat Sun ☐ ☐ ☐ ☐ ☐ ☐ ☐	A much better question. Respondents have a choice. Better accuracy for the survey.
How much TV do you watch on a school weeknight? A lot ☐ A bit ☐ Very little ☐	This question is too vague.
A better question is: How many hours of TV, to the nearest hour, do you watch on a school weeknight? Please tick one box. 0 1 2 3 4 or more ☐ ☐ ☐ ☐ ☐	This is more precise. Better accuracy for the survey.

Opinion scale

In some questions the response uses an opinion scale to measure attitudes and reactions. For example:

The local shops sell high-quality goods. Please tick one box.

☐   ☐   ☐   ☐   ☐

Strongly disagree   Disagree   No opinion   Agree   Strongly agree

Exercise 11.2

1. What is the difference between primary data and secondary data?

2. Write down which of the following is primary data or secondary data.

    (i) Tom counted the number of red cars that passed through a road junction in his area.

    (ii) Jane looked on the internet to find the number of babies born in Ireland in 2010.

    (iii) For his homework, Ian used a table of statistics on the ages of footballers from a newspaper.

    (iv) Gillian threw a die 100 times and recorded the results to investigate if the die is biased.

3. Give one difference between a census and a sample.

4. A company that makes batteries wishes to carry out a study to see how long their batteries last. Should they use a census or a sample? Justify your answer.

5. Make **one** criticism of why each question is unsuitable for a questionnaire.

    (i) Saturday is the best day to have a disco, wouldn't you agree?

    (ii) How many emails did you send today? 0–5 ☐ 0–10 ☐ 10 or more ☐

    (iii) The waiter service in this restaurant is: Excellent ☐ Very good ☐

    (iv) What do you think of our new and improved apple juice?

    (v) Sweets are bad for your teeth. Do you eat many sweets?

    (vi) Have you stolen goods from a shop?

6. The owner of a local cinema wants to find out how often teenagers attend the cinema. As teenagers left the cinema the owner gave them a questionnaire containing the following question.

    > How often do you attend the cinema?
    > Tick one box.
    >
    > ☐ Sometimes   ☐ Occasionally   ☐ Regularly

    (i) Write down **two** criticisms of the response section.

    (ii) Write a better question for this questionnaire. Include tick boxes.

7. A teacher is investigating the number of hours her pupils spend on the internet in a month. One of her questions is shown on the right.

    > How many hours do you spend on the internet?
    > Tick one box.
    >
    > ☐   ☐   ☐   ☐   ☐
    > 0–10   10–20   20–30   30–40   40+

    (i) (a) Write one criticism of the question.

        (b) Write one criticism of the response.

    (ii) Write a better question. Include tick boxes.

8. Alex is taking a survey about how far, to the nearest km, people have to travel to their workplace. Here is his response section.

   Tick one box.

   ☐ 1–2   ☐ 2–3   ☐ 5–6   ☐ Over 6

   State three **criticisms** from his response section.

9. As each customer left a shop the owner gave them a questionnaire containing the following question.

How much money did you spend in the shop today?
Tick one box.

Less than €20	Less than €40	Less than €60	€60 or more
☐	☐	☐	☐

   Write down one reason why the response section of this question is unsuitable.

10. A builder used the following question in a survey: 'How much do you pay each month on your mortage?' (Tick one box.)

    Under €400 ☐   €400–€600 ☐   €600–€1,000 ☐

    (i) Give two criticisms of the response section.

    (ii) Give one criticism of the question asked.

11. A market research company wishes to interview a sample of 50 adults in a large town in order to obtain their views on the proposed construction of a bypass around the town. The company interviewed the first 50 adults leaving the local train station on a Friday in June.

    (i) List two reasons why this method of sample selection is not suitable.

    (ii) Suggest how a random sample of 50 adults could be selected from the town.

    (iii) One question the company used was:

    'Do you think we should have a bypass to make our village safer?'

    What is wrong with this question?

12. Maura is carrying out an investigation into the cost of food in the school canteen. She asks students in the queue for the school canteen: *Do you agree that the food in the school canteen is overpriced?*

    (i) (a) Why is her sample likely to be biased?   (b) Why is her question biased?

    (ii) Suggest two reasons for her to carry out a sample survey.

    (iii) For a different investigation, Maura selects a sample of 60 students from the 800 students in her school. Describe how she could select a simple random sample.

13. A company produces compost for germinating seeds. It develops Better Grow, a new compost, which the company claims helps seeds germinate much more quickly than its competitors' compost. Design a simple statistical experiment that could be carried out to test the company's claim.

14. The table shows the numbers of each type of male and female employees at a large store.

	Shop assistants	Warehouse	Management	Security
Male	50	39	19	12
Female	150	71	11	8

The owner wishes to choose some employees to form a committee to represent the views of all employees.

  (i) He decided to take of sample of 10 male shop assistants. Give **two** reasons why this sample would be biased.

 (ii) How many people work in this store?

(iii) As an alternative, the owner is advised to take a representative sample of 36 employees based on work area and gender.
Complete the table below to show how many of each type of employee the owner should choose.

	Shop assistants	Warehouse	Management	Security
Male				
Female				

15. Mary goes to an all-girls school. She decided to do a sample survey to find out the time students spent studying per week in her area. Mary chose 40 students randomly from her own school register and asked each of these students the time, to the nearest hour, they spent studying per week. The raw data were recorded as follows.

    7   9   14   6   1   10   2   6   7   11   10   1   10   2   6   3   5   3   0   5
    11   7   13   10   1   9   5   2   15   6   6   11   6   4   0   12   9   13   4   8

Complete the following grouped frequency table.

Time spent studying, in hours	0–3	4–7	8–11	12–15
Tally				
Number of students				

  (i) Is this primary or secondary data? Give a reason for your answer.
 (ii) Is the data discrete or continuous? Explain your answer.
(iii) Give two reasons why this may be a biased sample.
(iv) Suggest two ways Mary could improve her sample to make it more representative.

16. A company that makes toothpaste says the new brand is better than the old brand. A dentist wants to investigate this claim. He chooses 40 boys and 40 girls at random from his patients. The boys are given the new brand and the girls are given the old brand. After four months the dentist compares the boys' and girls' teeth.

   (i) Write down two reasons why this is not a reliable experiment.
   (ii) Give two ways in which this experiment could be improved.

17. Helen is collecting data about the speed of cars in her town. She decides to collect data during the rush hour. Comment on Helen's choice of sample.

18. John carried out a survey to find out people's opinion on attending sports events in his local area. He stood outside the local sport stadium and asked a random sample of people their opinions on attending sport events as they entered the stadium.

   (i) Is the data that John collects primary or secondary? Justify your answer.
   (ii) Give two reasons why this sample may be biased.
   (iii) Make two suggestions to John to improve the accuracy of his survey.

19. Staff at a tourist site wish to undertake a survey to find out how long visitors spend at the site. They decided to use face-to-face interviews to collect the information. Give one advantage and one disadvantage in using this method of data collection. Suggest a better method to collect this information.

20. Brian wants to use a questionnaire to find out what kind of music the students at his school like. He also wants to find out if the boys and girls in his school like the same type of music and if there is a difference between year groups. Write down three questions that Brian might include in his questionnaire.

21. Prepare a data capture sheet for surveys to find out the following by observation.

   (i) The colours of cars at a road intersection
   (ii) The gender and approximate age of people entering a supermarket

22. A company wants to find out what the public thinks of their products and services. To collect the data, they intend to use a questionnaire.

   (i) Write down three important points that should be remembered when designing the questionnaire.
   (ii) The company is going to post the questionnaire to people's homes. Give one
      (a) advantage and (b) disadvantage of using the postal system.

AVERAGES AND THE SPREAD OF DATA

Averages

Much of our work in analysing data is concerned with finding a value that in some way is typical or representative of all the values in a distribution. The three most widely used are:

1. The mode **2. The median** **3. The mean**

They are often called **measures of central tendency**.

Mode | The mode is the value that occurs most often.

In other words, the mode is the value with the highest frequency or the most popular value.

Median | The median is the middle value when the values are arranged in order of size.

Half the values lie below and half above the median. For an even number of values, the median is halfway between the two middle values (the mean of the two middle values).

Mean | The mean of a set of values is the sum of all the values divided by the number of values.

That is:

$$\text{Mean} = \frac{\text{Sum of all the values}}{\text{Number of values}}$$

Note: The 'mean' is the proper name for what most people call the 'average'.

This table will help you to decide which average to use.

Averages	Advantages	Disadvantages
Mode	Easy to find. Will be one of the data values. Not affected by extreme values. Can be used with (qualitative and quantitative) any type of data.	Sometimes there is no mode. Sometimes there is more than one mode. No further useful mathematical applications.
Median	Easy to calculate. Not affected by extreme values.	Not always one of the given data. No further mathematical applications. Cannot be used with qualitative data, only with numerical data.
Mean	Uses all the data values. Has further mathematical applications.	Not always one of the given data. Always affected by extreme values. Cannot be used with qualitative data, only with numerical data.

96

Range | The range is the difference between the highest and lowest value.

That is: | Range = (Highest value) − (Lowest value)

This gives a measure of how spread out the data are (it is not an average). Sometimes it is called a 'measure of variability'.

Mathematical shorthand for the mean

μ, pronounced 'mu', is the symbol for the mean.

Σ, pronounced 'sigma', means the sum of (add up).

Σx, pronounced 'sigma x', means add up all the x values.

The formula is often written: | Mean $= \mu = \dfrac{\Sigma x}{n}$ | where n is the number of values.

 EXAMPLE 1

The ages of the seven dwarfs are as follows.

Name	Happy	Doc	Sleepy	Sneezy	Dopey	Grumpy	Bashful
Age	685	702	498	539	402	685	619

(i) Find the mean age.

(ii) Find the (mode) modal age.

(iii) Find the median age.

(iv) Find the range of these ages.

Solution:

(i) Mean age $= \dfrac{\text{Sum of all their ages}}{\text{Number of dwarfs}} = \dfrac{\Sigma x}{n}$

Mean $= \dfrac{685 + 702 + 498 + 539 + 402 + 685 + 619}{7}$

$\mu = \text{Mean} = \dfrac{4{,}130}{7} = 590$

(ii) Mode = 685   The number that occurs most often.

(Happy and Grumpy are twins!)

Note: Sometimes we say the modal age is 685 years.

(iii) Median = Middle value in ascending or descending order

= 702, 685, 685, **619**, 539, 498, 402

Median = 619

(iv) Range = (Highest age) − (Lowest age)

= 702 − 402 = 300 years

EXAMPLE 2

Cormac counted the number of books on different shelves in a library. He recorded the following numbers: 41, 43, 29, 52, 40, 46.

Find the median of the number of books on each shelf.

Solution:

Median: First write the numbers in ascending order.

$$29, 40, (41, 43), 46, 52$$

There is an even number of numbers.

∴ The median is the mean of the two middle values $= \dfrac{41 + 43}{2} = \dfrac{84}{2} = 42$ books.

Given the mean

Sometimes we are given the mean and we need to find one of the values. Essentially, we are given an equation in disguise and by solving this equation we calculate the missing value.

EXAMPLE 1

The mean of the five numbers 10, 5, 4, 8 and x is 6. Calculate the value of x.

Solution:

Method 1

Mean = 6

∴ $\dfrac{10 + 5 + 4 + 8 + x}{5} = 6$

$\dfrac{27 + x}{5} = 6$

$27 + x = 30$

(multiply both sides by 5)

$x = 3$

Method 2

The mean of the five numbers is 6

∴ The numbers must add up to 30

$\left(\text{because } 5 \times 6 = 30 \quad \text{or} \quad \dfrac{30}{5} = 6\right)$

∴ $10 + 5 + 4 + 8 + x = 30$

$27 + x = 30$

$x = 3$

Sometimes we are given questions that require some strategic thinking.

 EXAMPLE 2

Set $A = \{p, q, r, r, r\}$ where $p, q, r \in N$. Given that set A has a mode of 8 and a mean of 12, write down a set for A that satisfies these conditions.

Solution:

Since 8 is the mode, $A = \{p, q, 8, 8, 8\}$.

$$\text{Mean} = \mu = 12 = \frac{p + q + 8 + 8 + 8}{5}$$

$$60 = p + q + 24$$
$$36 = p + q$$

One possible solution, $p = 2$ and $q = 34$, gives $A = \{2, 34, 8, 8, 8\}$.

Some other possible solutions are $\{18, 18, 8, 8, 8\}$, $\{20, 16, 8, 8, 8\}$.

Exercise 12.1

Find the mean, mode, median and range for questions 1–4.

1. 3, 7, 2, 5, 3

2. 10, 4, 5, 4, 12, 2, 8, 5, 4

3. $\frac{1}{3}, \frac{1}{2}, \frac{1}{3}, \frac{3}{4}, \frac{1}{3}, \frac{3}{4}$

4. 2·8, 3·1, 6·7, 1·4, 5·6, 8·6

5. A waitress kept a record of her tips given to her each day for seven days.
   The record read: €3·68, €10·11, €2·93, €5·42, €1·94, €6·19, €5·15.
   Calculate **(i)** the mean and **(ii)** the median amount of tips given to her per day.
   Give a reason why there is no mode in the record.

6. The mean of five numbers is 9. Find the sum of the numbers.

7. The mean of the six numbers 10, 7, 3, 4, 9, x is 7. Find x and, hence, the median.

8. The mean of eight numbers is 9. When one of the numbers is taken away, the mean is increased by 1. Find the number that is taken away.

9. The table shows the number of compact discs sold per day in a shop from Monday to Friday of a particular week.

Day	Monday	Tuesday	Wednesday	Thursday	Friday
No. of compact discs sold	32	17	48	42	61

(i) Calculate the mean number of compact discs sold per day from Monday to Friday.

(ii) The shop was also open on the Saturday of that particular week. The mean number of compact discs sold per day from Monday to Saturday was 50. Calculate the number of compact discs sold on that Saturday.

10. Four people have a meal in a restaurant. The average cost of the meal per person is €37·50. What is the total bill for the four people if a 12% service charge is added?

11. Consider the array of numbers 8, 5, 7, 2, 5, 8, 9, 2, 8.

If a = the mean, b = the median and c = the mode, calculate the value of $\dfrac{a + b + c}{3}$.

12. (i) Calculate the mean, in terms of x, of each of the following.

   (a) $x, 2x, 3x, 4x, 5x$

   (b) $x + 3, 2x - 5, 3x + 1, 2x + 1$

   (c) $4x + 1, 2x - 3, 6x + 5$

   (d) $4x + 6, x - 3, 7x + 12, 3 - x, 4x + 7$

(ii) The median of 10, p, 3, 5, 9, 4 is 6. Calculate p.

13. (i) The mean of the three numbers 7, 9 and x is 10. Calculate the value of x.

(ii) The mean of the four numbers 5, x, 7 and 10 is 6. Calculate the value of x.

(iii) The mean of the five numbers $2x$, 5, x, 7 and 10 is 8. Calculate the value of x.

(iv) The mean of the six numbers 7, $2x + 1$, $3x$, 8, 4 and 2 is 7. Calculate the value of x.

14. (i) The mode of the nine numbers 2, 3, 7, 4, 9, 2, x, 3, 5 is x. How many different values of x are possible?

(ii) Given that x is also the median of the nine values, what is the exact value of x?

15. A basketball player had an average of eight points per game in her last seven games. How many points must she score in her next game if she is to increase her average to nine points per game?

16. A set of four odd numbers has a mode of 5, a median of 6 and a mean of $6\frac{1}{2}$. What are these four numbers?

17. The mean of p, q and r is 4. Find the mean of $p + 2$, $q + 2$ and $r + 2$.

18. The mean of x, y and z is 9. Find the mean of $5x$, $5y$ and $5z$.

19. The mean of g, e, f is 6. Find the mean of $2g - 1$, $2e - 1$ and $2f - 1$.

20. B is a set with five elements $\{x, x, x, y, z\}$ where x, y and $z \in N$. B has a median of 11 and a range of 20. Write down a possible set that satisfies these conditions.

21.   (i) The mean of seven numbers is 8. The mean of four of these numbers is 5. What is the mean of the remaining three numbers?

  (ii) The mean of 15 numbers is 4. The mean of 10 of these numbers is 2. What is the mean of the remaining five numbers?

22. The size and mean of three different data sets are given in the table below.

	P	Q	R
Size (N)	6	24	10
Mean (μ)	10	6	24
Total (Nμ)	x	y	240

  (i) Write down the value of x and the value of y.

Complete the sentences below by inserting the relevant letter in each space.

  (ii) The set that contains more numbers than any other is _____ and the set that contains fewer numbers than any other is _____.

  (iii) On average the data in set _____ are the biggest numbers and the data in set _____ are the smallest numbers.

  (iv) If the three sets are combined, the median is most likely to be a value in set _____.

  (v) Calculate the value of the mean when the three sets are combined.

23.   (i) Write down a list of seven numbers whose mean is zero.

  (ii) Write down a list of eight numbers whose mean is *not* zero.

  (iii) Elaine writes down a list of nine numbers whose mean is zero.

      Tick the correct box for each statement about Elaine's list of numbers.

Statement	Must be true	Could be true	Cannot be true
All of the numbers are zero			
Some of the numbers are zero			
There are as many negative numbers as positive numbers			
The sum of *all* the numbers is zero			
All of the numbers are positive numbers			
Some of the numbers are positive numbers			

24. The mean of p, q and r is r. Express the mean of p and q in terms of r.

25. The table below shows the distances travelled by seven paper airplanes after they were thrown.

Airplane	A	B	C	D	E	F	G
Distance (cm)	188	200	250	30	380	330	302

    (i) Find the median of the data.

   (ii) Find the mean of the data.

  (iii) Airplane D is thrown again and the distance it travels is measured and recorded in place of the original measurement. The median of the data remains unchanged and the mean is now equal to the median. How far did airplane D travel the second time?

  (iv) What is the minimum distance that airplane D would need to have travelled in order for the median to have changed?

Comparison of two sets of data

We usually compare sets of data in two parts:

> **1.** How the ranges compare.
>
> **2.** How one or more of the averages, mean, median or mode, compare.

Note: The higher the range, the greater the spread of the values (less consistent).

The lower the range, the smaller the spread of the values (more consistent).

EXAMPLE

A maths teacher gave a maths test to a third year class. The marks for the boys and the girls were recorded in the following table.

Boys	59	71	58	94	18	92	14	78	72	64
Girls	53	73	59	62	40	52	76	62	50	63

Calculate the mean and range for each group. Comment briefly on how the two groups compare.

Solution:
Boys

$$\text{Mean} = \frac{59 + 71 + 58 + 94 + 18 + 92 + 14 + 78 + 72 + 64}{10}$$

$$= \frac{620}{10} = 62 \text{ marks}$$

Range = (Highest mark) − (Lowest mark)
= 94 − 14 = 80 marks

Girls

$$\text{Mean} = \frac{53 + 73 + 59 + 62 + 40 + 52 + 76 + 62 + 50 + 63}{10}$$

$$= \frac{590}{10} = 59 \text{ marks}$$

Range = (Highest mark) − (Lowest mark)
= 76 − 40 = 36 marks

Comment: The boys have a slightly higher mean mark than the girls. However, the girls have a much lower range of marks. Their marks are **less spread out**, which shows the girls are more consistent.

Exercise 12.2

1. The following table shows the results for Eileen and Sean in four language tests.

Student	Test 1	Test 2	Test 3	Test 4
Eileen	64	73	54	61
Sean	69	10	88	84

   (i) Calculate the mean mark and the range of marks for Eileen.

   (ii) Calculate the mean mark and the range of marks for Sean.

   (iii) Using the means and ranges, comment briefly on how Eileen's and Sean's results compare.

2. The battery life, to the nearest hour, of seven mobile phones from each of two companies, A and B, were recorded as follows.

   A: 53   48   36   58   52   54   49
   B: 54   42   53   40   41   54   52

   (i) Complete the following two-way table.

	Mean	Median	Range
Company A			
Company B			

   (ii) Which brand would you buy? Explain your answer.

3. There is one place left on the boy's senior netball team. Two boys, Brendan and Colm, are trying out for this last place. Their scores for each of their last 10 games were recorded as follows.

Brendan: 4 8 3 5 5 2 2 1 3 2
Colm: 4 5 3 4 4 2 3 3 5 3

  (i) Calculate the mean number of goals per match for each boy.
 (ii) Calculate the range for each boy.
(iii) Calculate the median number of goals per match for each boy.
(iv) Which boy should be picked for the team? Justify your selection.

4. On the first day of every second month at noon, the temperature in degrees centigrade (°C) was measured in Cairo and Sydney. The graph below shows six readings over a year.

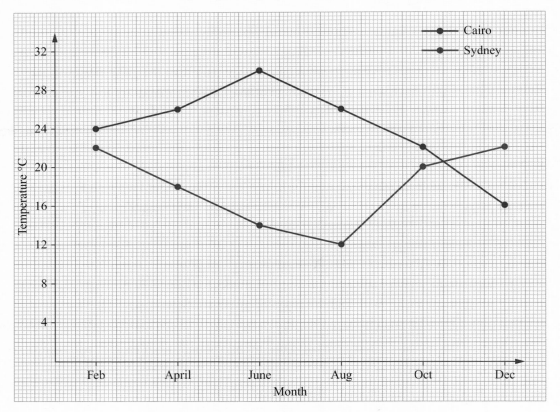

For example, on 1 April the temperature in Cairo was 26°C and in Sydney it was 18°C.
  (i) Find the average temperature for Cairo.
 (ii) Find the average temperature for Sydney.
(iii) Find the yearly temperature range for Cairo.
(iv) Find the yearly temperature range for Sydney.

5. In an interview, an employer looked for five qualities in the candidates:

Punctuality (P)

Dress sense (D)

Ability to speak clearly (S)

Information about the job (I)

Qualifications (Q)

There were 10 marks for each quality. There were three outstanding candidates: Yousef, Lily and Stephen. The marks they got are given below.

	P	D	S	I	Q
Yousef	10	7	5	7	8
Lily	9	7	7	6	8
Stephen	10	8	8	8	3

   (i) Calculate the mean (μ) score for each candidate.

   (ii) Calculate the range for each candidate.

   (iii) Which candidate would you choose to employ? Justify your choice.

6. Data on the type of broadband connection used by enterprises in Ireland for 2008 and 2009 is contained in the table below.

	2008	2009
	%	%
Broadband connection	84	84
By type of connection		
DSL (<2Mb/S)	31	29
DSL (>2Mb/S)	41	45
Other fixed connection	31	20
Mobile broadband	24	27

Source: Central Statistics Office

   (i) Display the data in a way that allows you to compare the data for the two years.

   (ii) Identify any trends that you think are shown by the data.

Frequency distribution

Data are often summarised using a frequency distribution. This section shows you how to calculate the range, mode, median and mean when the data is given in a frequency table.

The range, mode and median can be found from the table.

However, to calculate the mean we do the following.

1. Multiply each value by its corresponding frequency.

2. Sum all these products.

3. Divide this sum by the total number of frequencies.

Mathematical shorthand for the mean

$$\text{Mean} = \mu = \frac{\Sigma fx}{\Sigma f}$$

(i) x is the value of each measurement.

(ii) f is the frequency of each measurement.

(iii) Σfx is the sum of all the fx values.

(iv) Σf is the sum of all the frequencies.

EXAMPLE 1

A survey of the number of people per car in 21 cars passing an intersection was recorded in the following table.

Number of people per car	1	2	3	4	5
Number of cars	2	7	4	5	3

Calculate the **(i)** range **(ii)** mode **(iii)** median **(iv)** mean of the number of people per car.

Solution:

(i) Range = (highest value) − (lowest value) = 5 − 1 = 4 people.

(ii) The mode is the value which occurs most often. In a frequency table the mode is the value with the highest frequency.

(mode = 2 people, occurs most often)

Number of people per car	1	2	3	4	5
Number of cars	2	7	4	5	3

(highest frequency)

From the table, we can see that 2 occurs more often than any other value. Therefore, the mode is 2 people per car.

Note: Remember that the mode is the value, **not** the frequency.

(iii) In a frequency table the values are already arranged in order of size. The median is the middle value. There are 21 values (2 + 7 + 4 + 5 + 3 = 21). Thus, the median is the 11th value.

Number of people per car	1	2	3	4	5
Number of cars	2	7	4	5	3

2 cars to here

9 cars to here
(2 + 7 = 9)

13 cars to here, 11th value
is here (2 + 7 + 4 = 13)

The first 2 cars contain 1 person. The next 7 cars contain 2 people. The next 4 cars contain 3 people. This contains the 11th value.

Thus, the median = 3 people per car.

(iv) Mean = $\dfrac{\text{Sum of the values}}{\text{Number of values}}$

$$= \frac{2(1) + 7(2) + 4(3) + 5(4) + 3(5)}{2 + 7 + 4 + 5 + 3} \qquad \boxed{\mu = \frac{\Sigma fx}{\Sigma f}}$$

$$= \frac{2 + 14 + 12 + 20 + 15}{21} = \frac{63}{21} = 3 \text{ people per car.}$$

EXAMPLE 2

A casino owner tested a new six-sided die by throwing it 36 times and recording the results.

$$\begin{array}{cccccccccccc}
4 & 3 & 2 & 6 & 3 & 1 & 2 & 5 & 6 & 1 & 1 & 3 \\
2 & 2 & 5 & 6 & 4 & 5 & 1 & 5 & 5 & 3 & 6 & 2 \\
1 & 1 & 6 & 4 & 5 & 3 & 2 & 2 & 3 & 5 & 6 & 1
\end{array}$$

  (i) Show these results on a frequency distribution table.

  (ii) What conclusions, if any, might the casino owner draw from the results?

(iii) What further action, if any, might the casino owner take?

Justify your statements.

Solution:

  (i) Frequency distribution table

Score on die	1	2	3	4	5	6
Tally	‖‖ ‖	‖‖ ‖	‖‖ ‖	‖‖‖	‖‖ ‖	‖‖ ‖
Frequency	7	7	6	3	7	6

(ii) In making 36 throws of the die, the casino owner might expect each score to appear six times (36 throws ÷ 6 numbers = 6 times each). Since the score of 4 appears only three times, it might be concluded the die is not fair (**biased**). Hence, the new six-sided die would be rejected.

(iii) However, the casino owner might decide that 36 throws is not enough. The experiment might be repeated with another 36 (or more) throws. This course of action would give a more accurate description of the situation.

Exercise 12.3

For each of the following frequency distributions in questions 1–3, calculate the
(i) range **(ii)** mode **(iii)** median **(iv)** mean.

1.

Value	1	2	3	4
Frequency	4	3	2	1

2.

Value	0	2	4	6	8
Frequency	4	3	5	7	2

3.

Value	5	6	7	8	9
Frequency	6	5	4	3	2

4. 35 students hire skates at the ice-rink. Their sizes are recorded in the following table.

Skate size	3	4	5	6	7	8	9	10
Frequency	1	3	5	5	7	9	3	2

   (i) Write down the modal skate size.

   (ii) Calculate **(a)** the range and **(b)** the mean skate size.

   (iii) Is the mean or the mode the best average to use for this group of skaters? Justify your answer.

5. In a street with 24 houses, a postman recorded the number of letters delivered to each house. The results were:

1 2 5 3 2 3 0 1 1 4 3 0

2 1 1 4 0 2 2 1 4 1 2 3

Complete the following table.

Number of letters	0	1	2	3	4	5
Tally						
Frequency					3	

    (i) State the modal number of letters per house.

    (ii) Calculate the mean number of letters per house.

6. A machine is designed to pack pins into boxes containing 20 pins in each box. To check the machine's accuracy, a random sample of boxes is taken at regular intervals and the number of pins per box is counted (this is called **quality control**). The results are shown below.

Number of pins	18	19	20	21	22
Number of boxes	10	9	3	2	1

    (i) How many boxes were sampled?

    (ii) Write down the modal number of pins per box.

    (iii) Calculate **(a)** the range **(b)** the mean number of pins per box.

    (iv) Describe briefly the machine's performance.

7. The mass, to the nearest kilogram, of 21 parcels was recorded in the following table.

Mass, in kg	1	2	3	4	5
Number of parcels	2	7	4	5	3

    (i) Write down **(a)** the mode and **(b)** the median.

    (ii) Calculate **(a)** the range and **(b)** the mean.

    (iii) Explain briefly why none of these answers can be exact.

8. A test consisting of eight questions was given to 40 pupils. One mark was awarded per question for a correct solution and no marks for an incorrect solution. The results were as follows.

```
3   2   5   6   1   3   5   7   1   4
2   4   3   7   4   8   6   3   2   3
6   5   6   1   5   5   2   4   5   4
5   4   2   3   4   3   4   5   3   5
```

    (i) Represent the information in a frequency distribution table.

    (ii) Calculate the mean mark per pupil.

    (iii) Calculate the median mark.

    (iv) What is the mode?

    (v) If the pass mark was 4, what percentage of the pupils failed the test?

    (vi) Ten other pupils did the same test. The mean mark then for the 50 pupils was unchanged. Calculate the sum of the marks for the 50 pupils.

    (vii) A second set of 50 pupils did the same test and the mean for the 100 pupils was increased by one mark. Calculate the mean mark for the second set of 50 pupils.

Discrete or continuous grouped frequency distributions

Sometimes the range of the values is very wide and it is not suitable to show all the values individually. When this happens, we arrange the values into suitable groups called **class intervals**, such as 0–10, 10–20, etc. When the information is arranged in class intervals, it is not possible to calculate the exact value of the mean. However, it is possible to estimate it by using the **mid-interval value** of each class interval. The easiest way to find the mid-interval value is to add the two extreme values and divide by 2.

For example, in the class interval 30–50, add 30 and 50 and divide by 2,

i.e. $\dfrac{30 + 50}{2} = \dfrac{80}{2} = 40.$ ∴ 40 is the mid-interval value.

Otherwise, the procedure for estimating the mean is the same as in the previous section.

> Use the formula $\mu = \dfrac{\Sigma fx}{\Sigma f}$, taking x as the mid-interval value.

EXAMPLE

Twenty pupils were given a problem to solve. The following grouped frequency distribution table gives the number of pupils who solved the problem in the given time interval.

Time (minutes)	0–4	4–12	12–24	24–40
Frequency	3	8	7	2

(i) By taking the data at mid-interval values, calculate the mean number of minutes taken per pupil to solve the problem.

(ii) In which class interval does the median lie?

Solution:

(i) The table can be rewritten using the mid-interval values.

Time (minutes)	2	8	18	32
Frequency	3	8	7	2

$$\text{Mean} = \mu = \frac{\Sigma fx}{\Sigma f} = \frac{3(2) + 8(8) + 7(18) + 2(32)}{3 + 8 + 7 + 2}$$

$$= \frac{6 + 64 + 126 + 64}{20} = \frac{260}{20} = 13 \text{ minutes}$$

(ii) There are 20 pupils altogether. The two middle values are the 10th and 11th. We require the class interval in which the 10th and 11th values lie.

By looking at the grouped frequency distribution table, the 10th and 11th values lie in the 4–12 minutes class interval.

∴ The median lies in the 4–12 minutes class interval.

Exercise 12.4

Assuming that the data can be taken at mid-interval values, estimate the mean of each of the following grouped frequency distributions in questions 1–5. In each case, state in which class interval the median lies. Also write down the modal class.

   Note: 5–15 means 5 is included but 15 is not, etc.

1.

Value	5–15	15–25	25–35
Frequency	5	8	2

2.

Value	0–2	2–4	4–6	6–8
Frequency	12	9	6	3

3.

Value	100–120	120–140	140–160	160–180	180–200
Frequency	2	5	8	6	4

4.

Value	0–5	5–10	10–20	20–35	35–40	40–50
Frequency	3	5	8	9	3	2

5.

Value	0–5	5–15	15–25	25–50
Frequency	10	21	47	22

6. A survey of 80 students gave the amount of money spent per month in the school canteen.

Amount in €	0–8	8–16	16–24	24–32	32–40
Number of students	8	12	20	24	16

   Note: 0–8 means 0 is included but 8 is not, etc.

   (i) Taking the amounts at the mid-interval values, show that the mean amount of money spent per student was €22·80.

   (ii) 'The money amount in euro is a continuous variable.' Do you agree or disagree with this statement? Justify your answer.

7. The following table shows the sizes, in hectares, of 20 farms in a particular area.

Number of hectares	15–45	45–75	75–105	105–195
Number of farms	1	4	8	7

   Note: 15–45 means that 15 is included but 45 is not and so on.

   (i) Taking 30, 60, etc. as mid-interval values, estimate the mean number of hectares per farm.

   (ii) 'The area amount in hectares is a continuous variable.' Do you agree or disagree with this statement? Justify your answer.

8. The braking distance in metres, i.e. the distance travelled from when the brakes are applied to when a car stops, is recorded for 50 drivers. The results were as follows.

18	18	29	33	15	14	18	13	14	20
7	15	29	21	15	23	34	24	25	17
17	27	19	11	21	17	17	18	32	17
18	38	19	36	20	33	31	20	16	14
9	15	18	25	35	12	11	12	13	19

(i) Copy and complete the following tally and frequency table.

Braking distance (m)	0–10	10–20	20–28	28–34	34–40
Tally				卌I	
Number of drivers		28			

Note: 0–10 means 0 is included but 10 is not, etc.

(ii) Taking mid-interval values, estimate the mean braking distance, giving your answer correct to the nearest metre.

9. A survey of 100 people is conducted to find out how long people spend travelling to work. The following results were recorded.

Travelling time (mins)	5–25	25–35	35–45	45–55	55–75
Frequency	12	18	33	23	14

Note: 5–25 means 5 or more but less than 25, etc.

(i) Is this primary or secondary data? Give a reason for your answer.
(ii) Is the data discrete or continuous? Explain your answer.
(iii) Taking the mid-interval values for the travelling time, calculate the mean (μ).
(iv) Write down the modal class (mode).
(v) What is the greatest number of people who could have spent more than 60 minutes travelling to work?
(vi) What is the greatest number of people who could have spent less than 30 minutes travelling to work?

10. The duration of each log-on to the internet in a public library was recorded over a certain period. The results are summarised in the following table.

Duration (mins)	0–4	4–8	8–12	12–16	16–20	20–24
Number of log-ons	3	5	9	20	21	12

Note: 4–8 means 4 minutes or more but less than 8 minutes, etc.

   (i) What was the total number of log-ons made?
  (ii) In which class interval does the median lie?
 (iii) Write down the modal class (mode).
 (iv) Taking mid-interval values, estimate the total amount of time spent online.
  (v) Hence, verify the mean log-on time was 15 minutes, correct to the nearest minute.

11. A department store carried out a survey on the length of time a number of people spent shopping in their store. The table shows the length of time spent shopping in 10-minute intervals.

Time interval in minutes	0–10	10–20	20–30	30–40	40–50	50–60	60–70
Number of shoppers	30	x	24	30	40	20	10

Note: 0–10 means 0 is included but 10 is not, etc.

   (i) If the average number of shoppers for the first, second and third intervals was 30, calculate the value of x.
  (ii) Using mid-interval values, estimate the average shopping time in the store.
 (iii) What is the least number of shoppers who completed their shopping within 35 minutes?
 (iv) In which class interval does the median lie?
  (v) Name the modal class.
 (vi) Comment on the mean, mode and median values you found. Do you think that any one of the three averages is better or worse than the others to help describe the situation? Explain your reasoning.
(vii) Describe two difficulties the store may have encountered when carrying out this survey.

CHAPTER 13

REPRESENTING DATA

Diagrams

Many people find numerical data easier to understand if it is presented in a diagram. On our course there are five ways of representing data in a diagram.

1. **Bar charts**
2. **Line plots**
3. **Pie charts**
4. **Histograms**
5. **Stem and leaf diagrams**

When drawing a statistical diagram, the following is important:

1. Label both axes (where necessary) and include a title.
2. Use scales that are easy to read and give a clear overall impression.

Bar charts

Bar charts are a simple and effective way of displaying categorical and discrete numerical data. The bars can be drawn vertically or horizontally. The height, or length, of each bar represents the frequency. Each bar must be the same width and leave the same space between the bars. The bar with the greatest height, or longest length, represents the mode.

Note: A bar chart **cannot** be used to represent continuous data. This is the reason a gap is left between the bars.

EXAMPLE

A survey was taken of a number of students to find out the number of text messages that they sent on a particular day. The frequency table shows the results of the survey.

Number of text messages	0	1	2	3	4	5
Number of students	1	3	6	8	5	2

(i) Draw a bar chart of the data.

(ii) How many students took part in the survey?

(iii) What percentage of the students sent three or more text messages on that particular day?

Solution:

(i) Bar chart

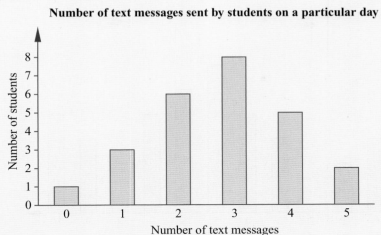

Number of text messages sent by students on a particular day

(ii) Total number of students in the survey $= 1 + 3 + 6 + 8 + 5 + 2 = 25$.

(iii) Number of students who sent 3 or more text messages $= 8 + 5 + 2 = 15$.

Percentage of students who sent 3 or more text messages

$$= \frac{\text{Number of students who sent 3 or more text messages}}{\text{Total number of students in the survey}} \times 100\%$$

$$= \frac{15}{25} \times 100\% = 60\%$$

Exercise 13.1

1. The spreadsheet below shows the number of different drinks purchased from a vending machine on a particular day.

	A	B
1	**Drink**	**Number of drinks**
2	Tea	11
3	Coffee	12
4	Chocolate	10
5	Soup	8
6	Other	9

(i) Represent the data with a bar chart.

(ii) What was the total number of drinks sold on the day?

(iii) Express the most popular drink as a percentage of the total number of drinks sold on the day.

2. A maths test consisted of 10 questions. 1 mark was given for a correct solution and 0 marks were given for an incorrect solution. The following bar chart represents the marks obtained by a class in the test.

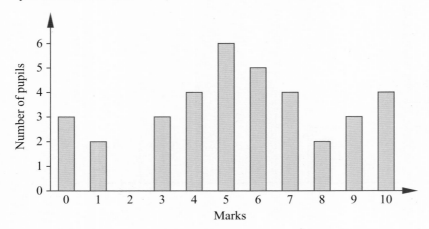

(i) Complete the following table.

Marks	0	1	2	3	4	5	6	7	8	9	10
Number of pupils	3								2		

(ii) How many pupils scored 2 marks?

(iii) How many pupils scored 8 marks or more?

(iv) Write down the modal mark.

(v) How many pupils took the test?

(vi) Calculate the mean mark.

(vii) If the pass mark is 5 or more, calculate the percentage of pupils that passed the test.

3. Here are some areas (in 1,000,000 km^2) for Earth's oceans and seas.

Ocean/sea	Pacific	Atlantic	Indian	Remainder
Area	160	80	70	30

(i) Represent the data on a bar chart.

(ii) Write down the area of the Indian Ocean in km^2.

(iii) Express the area of the Pacific as a percentage of the total area of Earth covered by oceans and seas. Give your answer correct to the nearest whole number.

4. George tossed a fair six-sided die 50 times. His scores are listed below.

$$6 \quad 4 \quad 4 \quad 4 \quad 6 \quad 2 \quad 3 \quad 6 \quad 2 \quad 6$$
$$2 \quad 4 \quad 4 \quad 1 \quad 5 \quad 1 \quad 2 \quad 3 \quad 2 \quad 2$$
$$3 \quad 1 \quad 3 \quad 6 \quad 3 \quad 4 \quad 5 \quad 5 \quad 1 \quad 1$$
$$2 \quad 1 \quad 6 \quad 1 \quad 4 \quad 5 \quad 3 \quad 3 \quad 6 \quad 3$$
$$5 \quad 1 \quad 6 \quad 2 \quad 3 \quad 1 \quad 2 \quad 2 \quad 3 \quad 3$$

(i) Complete the following table that includes a tally row.

Score	1	2	3	4	5	6
Tally		卌 卌				
Frequency						8

(ii) Represent the data with a bar chart.

(iii) How many times did George throw an even number?

(iv) What percentage of the throws were fours or higher?

5. This bar chart shows the number of passengers travelling on a coach each weekday from Urlingford to Dublin.

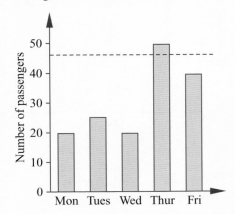

Homer says, 'The dotted line shows the mean for the five days.' Use the bar chart to explain why Homer cannot be correct.

6. These bar charts show the amount saved per month by four members of a credit union during a six-month period.

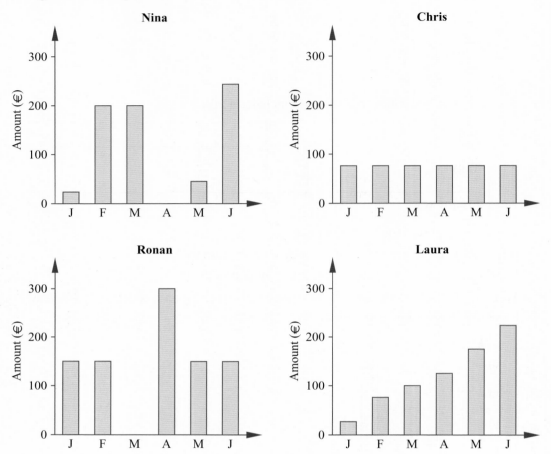

Whose graph matches these comments?

 (i) Each month I saved more than the month before.
 (ii) I never know how much I am going to save in any month.
(iii) Each month I saved the same amount. I am a very dependable, consistent saver.
(iv) I am a fairly consistent saver and reached my target to save of €900 in six months.

7. The following dual bar chart compares time spent watching TV by Rebecca and Bren during one particular week.

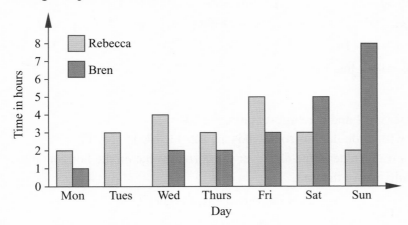

(i) Complete the following two-way table.

Day	Mon	Tues	Wed	Thurs	Fri	Sat	Sun
Rebecca number of hours							
Bren number of hours							

(ii) Who watched the most TV? Explain your answer.

(iii) Find the range for (a) Rebecca (b) Bren.

(iv) Find the mean time spent watching TV by Bren.

(v) Write down the mode for (a) Rebecca (b) Bren.

Line plots

For categorical and discrete numerical data, a line plot is similar to a bar chart, with the bars replaced with dots. A line plot is often called a **dot plot**. It is used for small sets of data, usually fewer than 50 values. It consists of a horizontal axis on which the values (or categories) are evenly marked, from the smallest value to the largest value, including any value in between that does not occur. Each value is indicated with a dot over the corresponding value on the horizontal axis. Each dot represents **one** value. The number of dots above each value indicates how many times each value occurs. Dots must be equally spaced over each value. Each dot is similar to a tally mark used in a frequency distribution. The main advantage of a line plot is that it can be created very quickly, even while collecting the data.

EXAMPLE

The data shows the ages of students in a youth club.

14 13 15 14 13 15 14 15 17 12 17 16 13 16
16 14 14 15 12 16 15 13 17 14 13 17 15 14

Represent this data with a line plot.

Solution:
The smallest number is 12 and the largest number is 17.
The numbers that will go on the horizontal axis are 12, 13, 14, 15, 16, 17.
Put a single dot for each value in the data over the correct value on the horizontal axis.
Space all dots equally above the line.

Ages of students in a youth club

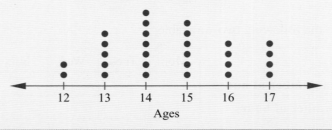

Ages

Note: Sometimes Xs are used instead of dots.

Exercise 13.2

1. Ciara collects data from a group of students on the number of siblings (brothers or sisters) each student has. Her results are shown below.

2 0 1 4 3 1 0 2
1 3 0 3 2 5 4 1
3 4 3 1 5 0 2 3

 (i) Construct a line plot to represent this data.
(ii) How many of these students have no siblings?

2. In a survey, 30 people were asked how much money they spent each week on the National Lottery. The results, in €, are shown below.

4 0 8 4 6 0 4 2 4 0 2 4 0 6 2
10 4 8 6 4 6 8 4 8 10 4 2 6 0 6

(i) Complete the following data capture sheet.

Amount, in €	0	2	4	6	8	10
Tally						
Number of people						

(ii) Represent the data with a line plot.

(iii) Write down the modal amount of money spent per week on the lottery for these 30 people.

(iv) Calculate the mean amount of money spent on the lottery for these 30 people.

3. Colin surveyed some students on the number of movies they watched on their holidays. His results are shown on the line plot below.

Number of movies watched by students on holidays

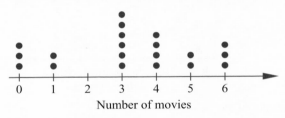

Number of movies

Complete the following frequency distribution table.

Number of movies watched	0	1	2	3	4	5	6
Number of students							

(i) What does each dot represent?

(ii) Write down the modal number of movies watched.

(iii) How many students did Colin survey?

(iv) Calculate the mean number of movies watched.

4. The line plot below illustrates the number of cars sold by a dealer over a six-month period.

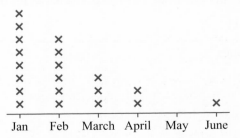

(i) How many cars were sold in February?

(ii) How many cars were sold during the six months?

(iii) What is the percentage of cars sold in January?

(iv) Why do you think more cars were sold in January than in any other month?

(v) To cover the monthly expenses, the dealer must sell at least two cars. Name the months the dealer does not cover the monthly expenses.

5. The hair colours of all the students in a class are recorded. The line plot below shows the results.

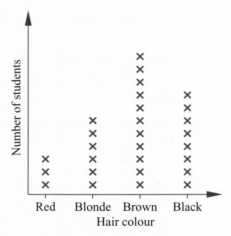

(i) How many students are in this class?

(ii) What type of data does this line plot contain?

(iii) What average (mean, mode or median) are you using when you refer to the most common hair colour?

Pie charts

A pie chart is a circle divided into sectors in proportion to the frequency of the data. It displays the proportions as angles measured from the centre of the circle (but not the actual frequencies). The largest sector represents the mode. It is a good way of representing data when you want to show how things are shared or divided. In addition, pie charts are particularly suitable for displaying categorical data.

Steps in drawing a pie chart

1. Add up all the frequencies.
2. Divide this into 360°.
3. Multiply the answer in step 2 by each individual frequency.
   (This gives the size of the angle for each sector.)
4. Draw the pie chart, label each sector and give it a title.
   (It is a good idea to write the size of each angle on the pie chart.)

Note: It is good practice to check that all your angles add up to 360° before drawing the pie chart.

EXAMPLE

The favourite colours of a number of students are shown in the frequency table.

Favourite colour	Purple	Red	Blue	Yellow	Black
Number of students	15	18	9	6	24

(i) State the type of data presented in the table.

(ii) Represent this information with a pie chart.

Solution:

(i) The data presented in the table is categorical data.

(ii) $15 + 18 + 9 + 6 + 24 = 72$, therefore there are 72 pupils altogether.

In a circle there are 360°. The whole circle has to include all 72 pupils, so it is first necessary to find out how many degrees one pupil will represent on the pie chart. This is then multiplied by the number of pupils in each category.

So we have: 72 pupils = 360°.

Therefore, 1 pupil = 5° (divide both sides by 72).

In other words, one pupil will take up 5° on the pie chart. We make up a table to work out the angle for each sector.

Sector	Number of pupils	Angle
Purple	15	$15 \times 5° = 75°$
Red	18	$18 \times 5° = 90°$
Blue	9	$9 \times 5° = 45°$
Yellow	6	$6 \times 5° = 30°$
Black	24	$24 \times 5° = 120°$
Total	72 pupils	360°

Make sure your total is 360°

Students' favourite colour

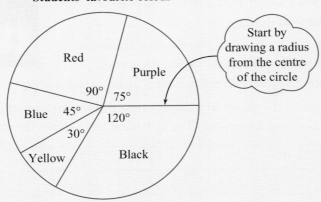

Start by drawing a radius from the centre of the circle

Note: An alternative method to calculate the angles is to use fractions.

Sector	Number of pupils	Fraction	Angle
Purple	15	$\frac{15}{72}$	$\frac{15}{72} \times 360° = 75°$
Red	18	$\frac{18}{72}$	$\frac{18}{72} \times 360° = 90°$
Blue	9	$\frac{9}{72}$	$\frac{9}{72} \times 360° = 45°$
Yellow	6	$\frac{6}{72}$	$\frac{6}{72} \times 360° = 30°$
Black	24	$\frac{24}{72}$	$\frac{24}{72} \times 360° = 120°$
Total	72 pupils	$\frac{72}{72}$	360°

Exercise 13.3

1. The languages taken by first year students and the angle in each sector in the pie chart are shown in the table below. Represent the data with a pie chart.

Language	German	French	Italian	Spanish
Angle in sector	60°	150°	30°	120°

2. In a recent Olympic Games, the number of medals and the type of medal won by a certain country were:

Type of medal	Gold	Silver	Bronze
Number of medals	9	21	24

   (i) Find the total number of medals won.
  (ii) Represent the information on a pie chart.
 (iii) Write down the mode of the data.
 (iv) The country's Minister for Sport expressed disappointment with the overall level of gold medals won in the games.
       Would you agree or disagree with the minister? Justify your answer.

3. Over a period of one month, the owner of a factory recorded the number of days that each of his 45 employees was absent from work. The following table shows the results.

No. of days absent	0	1	2	3	4	5
No. of employees	7	8	10	11	6	3

(i) Illustrate the information on a pie chart.

(ii) Write down the mode.

(iii) Find the percentage of the employees who were absent for more than the (mode) modal number of days.

4. Draw a pie chart to indicate how a lottery prize could be divided in the ratio of 1 : 2 : 3 : 4. Show clearly how you calculate the size of each angle.

5. 82,440 people attended a concert. The following table is a summary of admission ticket types.

Type of ticket	VIP	Complimentary	General Admission
No. of people	6,870	W	59,540

(i) Find the value of W.

(ii) Illustrate this information on a pie chart.

(iii) Write the number of complimentary tickets as a percentage of the total attendance. Give your answer correct to the nearest whole number.

6. The annual salaries of the employees in a manufacturing firm were recorded. The following were the results.

Salary (in 1,000s €)	0–20	20–40	40–60	60–80	80–100
Number of employees	10	15	20	25	5

Note: 20–40 means 20 or more but less than 40, etc.

(i) Find the total number of employees.

(ii) Draw a pie chart to illustrate the data in the frequency table.

(iii) Write down the (mode) modal class.

(iv) Multiplying the total number of employees by the mid-interval value of the modal class gives €5,250,000 as an estimated value for the total annual salaries of the employees. Do you think this estimate is:

(a) Too low

(b) Too high

(c) Just about correct?

Justify your answer.

Given the pie chart

In some questions we are given the pie chart, or the angles in a pie chart, and we have to work backwards to calculate the numbers in each category.

In each question we are given an equation in disguise, and from this we can work out the number represented by $1°$.

EXAMPLE

An election for a leader is held between four candidates, A, B, C and D.

The pie chart represents the number of people who voted in the election for each candidate.

If 180 people voted for candidate A, how many people voted for candidates B, C and D?

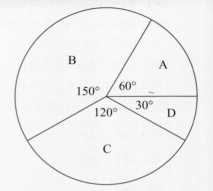

Solution:

In this example we work in reverse. So we have:

$60° = 180$ people   (equation given in disguise)

$1° = 3$ people   (divide both sides by 60)

In other words, $1°$ represents 3 people on the pie chart.

B: Angle $= 150°$ Number of people $= 3 \times 150 = 450$

C: Angle $= 120°$ Number of people $= 3 \times 120 = 360$

D: Angle $= 30°$ Number of people $= 3 \times 30\ \ = 90$

450 voted for B, 360 voted for C and 90 voted for D.

Exercise 13.4

1. A survey was taken of the people entering a supermarket during a certain day. The results are shown in the pie chart.

    (i) What angle size represents the number of men?

    (ii) 180 children were counted in the survey. What was the total number of people counted entering the supermarket?

    (iii) How many men were counted entering the supermarket?

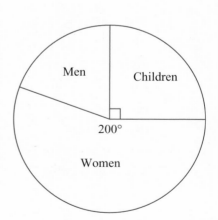

2. The pie chart on the right shows the means of transport used by all the pupils in a school.

   (i) What angle size represents the bicycle as a means of transport?

   (ii) Complete the following table.

Mode of transport	Bus	Walking	Train	Bicycle
Number of pupils	240			

   (iii) How many pupils are in the school?

3. An examination was taken by a number of pupils and each obtained a grade of A, B, C, D or E. The pie chart illustrates the grades obtained.

   (i) What is the angle size representing grade E?

   (ii) Complete the following table.

Grade	A	B	C	D	E
Number of pupils	40				

4. The pie chart illustrates the results of an opinion poll on government policy.

   (i) What is the size of the angle that represents those that disagree with the government?

   (ii) Given that 891 of the respondents had no opinion, find:

      (a) The number of respondents who disagree with the government

      (b) The total number of respondents in the opinion poll

5. A pie chart is drawn to represent the numbers $x + 2$, 7, 11. Calculate the value of x.

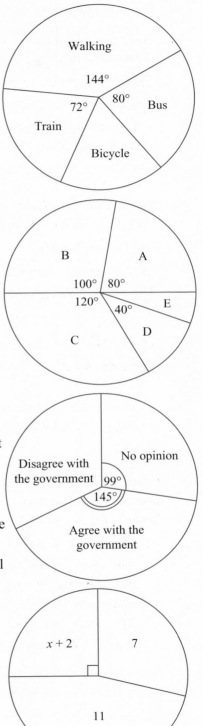

6. The incomplete table and pie chart show the number of seats in a theatre and their respective cost.

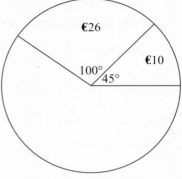

Price per seat, €	10	26	30	40
Number of seats	135	x	390	y

   (i) Calculate the value of x and the value of y.

   (ii) Calculate the total number of seats sold.

   (iii) Calculate the mean price per seat.

   (iv) Complete the pie chart.

7. The pie chart illustrates the type of supporters at a football match with an attendance of 64,440.

Find the number of:

   (i) Away team supporters

   (ii) Home team supporters at the match

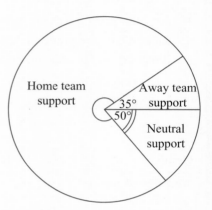

8. In a survey, 420 students in St Bridget's Secondary School and 780 students in St Joseph's Secondary School were asked to state the level of Mathematics they were studying.

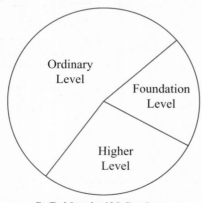

St Bridget's 420 Students

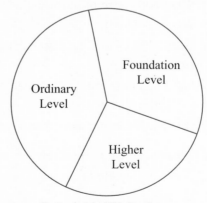

St Joseph's 780 Students

Emily looked at the pie charts and said, 'There are about the same number of students taking Higher Level Mathematics in St Bridget's and St Joseph's.'

Do you agree or disagree with Emily? Justify your answer.

9. There are 24 students in a class. On a Friday each student present in class is asked for the number of days they had been absent that week. The results are recorded in the table below.

Number of days absent	None	One	Two	Three	Four	Five
Number of students	9	2	3	4	1	0

(i) How many students were absent on that Friday?

(ii) On the following Monday all of the students were present in class and the table was updated to include the entire class. Which number from the above table could not have changed? Give a reason for your answer.

(iii) The total number of days that were missed during the week will depend on the answers given by the students who were absent on Friday. Complete the tables below to show how the largest possible and smallest possible number of days missed would arise.

Smallest possible number of days missed						
Number of days absent	None	One	Two	Three	Four	Five
Number of students						

Largest possible number of days missed						
Number of days absent	None	One	Two	Three	Four	Five
Number of students						

(iv) Cathal decides to draw a pie chart of the actual data collected on Monday. He calculates the number of degrees for each sector of the pie chart. Use this data to calculate the mean number of absences per pupil for the previous week correct to one decimal place.

Number of days absent	None	One	Two	Three	Four	Five
Number of students						
Number of degrees	135°	30°	75°	60°	45°	15°

Histograms

Histograms are used to represent discrete or continuous data, usually contained in grouped frequency distributions. A histogram uses rectangles to represent frequency. The area of each rectangle represents the frequency. On our course the class intervals will have equal widths. If the widths are equal, then the vertical axis can represent frequency. In a histogram, the rectangles representing the data **must** touch. This is because the numbers on the horizontal axis form a **continuous range from left to right**. In other words, there are no gaps in the numbers along the horizontal axis.

For the sake of drawing a histogram or using a histogram to work out frequencies, we say that the area of each rectangle represents the frequency. However, in a histogram with equal widths, the heights of the rectangles are proportional to the frequencies. In other words, if one class interval has a frequency twice that of another, then the height of the rectangle representing this class will be twice the height of the rectangle representing the other class. Also, all the heights in a histogram can be doubled, trebled or halved and still represent the same distribution. In other words, the vertical axis can be measured in **frequency density**.

Note: Bar charts and histograms are often confused with each other. The differences are that bar charts **cannot** represent continuous data and in a histogram the rectangles **must** touch.

EXAMPLE

The duration of each log-on to the internet in a public library was recorded over a certain period. The results are summarised in the following table.

Duration (minutes)	0–5	5–10	10–15	15–20	20–25	25–30
Number of log-ons	2	4	7	10	8	5

Note: 5–10 means 5 minutes or more but less than 10 minutes, etc.

(i) Draw a histogram to illustrate the data in the table.
(ii) Write down the total number of log-ons over the period.
(iii) Write down the modal class (mode).
(iv) Write down the mid-interval of the modal class.
(v) To get an estimate for the total number of minutes spent online in the period, the librarian multiplied the total number of log-ons by the mid-interval of the modal class. In your view, was this estimate too high, too low or just about correct? Explain your answer.

Solution:

(i)

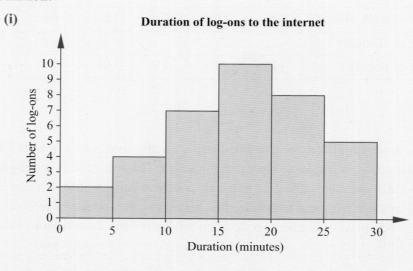

Duration of log-ons to the internet

(ii) Total number of log-ons

$2 + 4 + 7 + 10 + 8 + 5 = 36$

(iii) Modal class = most common number of log-ons.

Identified by tallest box = 15–20 minutes.

(iv) Mid-interval of 15–20 = $17\frac{1}{2}$ minutes.

(v) $17\frac{1}{2} \times 36 = 630$ minutes.

As the mode is an average, I conclude that the mode × number of log-ons gives a good estimate of the total minutes online.

Note: Using mid-intervals for the original data gives

$(2)(2\frac{1}{2}) + (4)(7\frac{1}{2}) + (7)(12\frac{1}{2}) + (10)(17\frac{1}{2}) + (8)(22\frac{1}{2}) + (5)(27\frac{1}{2}) = 615$ minutes.

You might conclude 630 is a bit high.

Exercise 13.5

Construct a histogram to represent each of the following grouped frequency distributions in questions 1 and 2.

1.

Interval	0–2	2–4	4–6	6–8
Frequency	3	5	4	2

Note: 0–2 means 0 is included but 2 is not, etc.

2.

Interval	0–4	4–8	8–12	12–16	16–20	20–24
Frequency	2	4	8	7	5	1

Note: 8–12 means 8 is included but 12 is not, etc.

3. 42 first year students were asked how much pocket money they spent in a certain week. The results are shown in the frequency distribution table below.

Amount of pocket money in €	0–5	5–10	10–15	15–20	20–25
Number of students	8	10	12	x	5

Note: 5–10 means €5 or more but less than €10, etc.

(i) Find the value of x.

(ii) Represent the data with a histogram.

(iii) Could this data be represented by a bar chart? Justify your answer.

(iv) Write down the modal class.

(v) Write down the mid-interval of the modal class.

(vi) Hence or otherwise, estimate the total amount of pocket money spent.

4. The number of hours spent studying, per week, by 40 students in a certain school was recorded as follows.

7	9	14	6	1	10	2	6	7	11
10	1	10	2	6	3	5	3	0	5
11	7	13	10	1	9	5	2	15	6
6	11	6	4	0	12	9	13	4	8

(i) Complete the following table.

Time in hours	0–4	4–8	8–12	12–16
Tally				
Number of students				

Note: 4–8 means 4 or more but less than 8, etc.

(ii) Write down the modal class.

(iii) Represent the data with a (a) histogram (b) pie chart.

(iv) Discuss the differences, advantages and disadvantages of using either diagram to represent this data.

5. A survey of a group of 167 people who own mobile phones was used to collect data on the amount of time they spent per day using their phones. The results are displayed in the table below.

Time spent per day (t minutes)	$0 \leq t < 15$	$15 \leq t < 30$	$30 \leq t < 45$	$45 \leq t < 60$	$60 \leq t < 75$	$75 \leq t < 90$
Number of people	21	32	35	41	27	11

(i) State the modal group.

(ii) Draw a fully labelled histogram to represent the data.

(iii) Use the mid-interval values to estimate the mean time spent per day on these mobile phones. Give your answer correct to the nearest minute.

(iv) Given the charge per minute is 2·5 cents, estimate the income per day for the service provider generated by 1·35 million users of such mobile phones with owners using their phones the same amount of time per day as the surveyed group.

6. The table shows the number and the weight (kg) of fish delivered to a local fish market one morning.

(i) Draw a histogram for this data. Use a scale of 1 cm to represent 0·1 kg on the horizontal axis and 1 cm to represent 100 units on the vertical axis. Label the axes clearly.

Answer the follow questions using the relevant mid-interval values.

Weight (kg)	Frequency (number)
$0.50 \leq w < 0.70$	160
$0.70 \leq w < 0.90$	360
$0.90 \leq w < 1.10$	440
$1.10 \leq w < 1.30$	240
$1.30 \leq w < 1.50$	100

(ii) A pet food company buys all the fish of weight <0·90 kg and pays €1·20 per kg. Find how much the pet food company pays for its fish that day.

(iii) A zoo buys all the fish of weight ≥1·30 kg and pays €2·25 per kg. Find how much the zoo pays for its fish that day.

(iv) A restaurant buys all the remaining fish at €4·80 per kg. Find how much the restaurant pays for its fish that day.

(v) Hence, find the total amount paid for the fish that day and calculate the average price paid per fish correct to the nearest euro.

Given the histogram

Sometimes we are given the histogram already drawn and we need to calculate the frequencies represented by the rectangles. We are usually given the area of one of the rectangles (which represents the frequency) and its height (read directly from the diagram). We can then work out the remaining frequencies from the information given.

In histograms, it is useful to know that

> Frequency = area of rectangle = base × height

EXAMPLE

The claims made against an insurance company for a certain year are shown in the histogram.

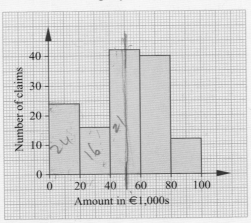

133

(i) Complete the corresponding frequency distribution table.

Amount (€1,000s)	0–20	20–40	40–60	60–80	80–100
Number of claims			42		

(ii) Write down the total number of claims for the year.

(iii) In which interval does the median lie?

(iv) By taking the mid-interval of the median score in euro, find an estimate for the total amount paid out by the company in the year.

Solution:

(i)

Amount (€1,000s)	0–20	20–40	40–60	60–80	80–100
Number of claims	24	16	42	40	12

(ii) Total number of claims = 24 + 16 + 42 + 40 + 12 = 134.

(iii) Median ⇒ middle claim when claim amounts are arranged in ascending (or descending) order.

Mid-point of 126 claims ⇒ claim 63.

Amount (€1,000s)	0–20	20–40	40–60	60–80	80–100
Number of claims	24	16	42		

24 claims to here

24 + 16 = 40 claims to here

24 + 16 + 42 = 82 claims to here, including claim 63

Thus, 40–60 is the interval where the median lies.

(iv) Mid-interval value of 40–60 is 50 in €1,000s.

∴ Estimate for yearly claim payout = €50,000 × 134 claims = €6,700,000.

Exercise 13.6

1. The information is displayed in the frequency table below.

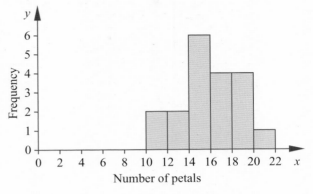

Number of petals (x)	Frequency
$10 < x \le 12$	2
$12 < x \le 14$	a
$14 < x \le 16$	6
$16 < x \le 18$	b
$18 < x \le 20$	4
$20 < x \le 22$	1

   (i) Find the values of a and b.

   (ii) State the modal group.

   (iii) Calculate an estimate of the mean number of petals.

2. A supermarket opens at 08:00. The histogram shows the distribution of the times employees arrive for work.

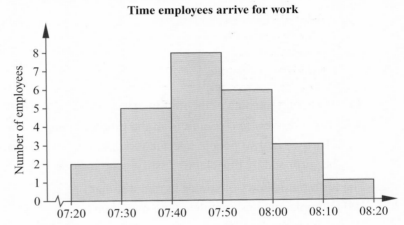

Time employees arrive for work

   (i) Complete the following frequency distribution.

Time	07:20–07:30	07:30–07:40	07:40–07:50	07:50–08:00	08:00–08:10	08:10–08:20
No. of employees						

   (ii) How many employees arrived for work that day?

   (iii) How many employees arrived before 07:50?

   (iv) How many employees were definitely late for work? Explain your answer.

   (v) What is the modal class?

   (vi) What percentage of the employees arrived before 07:40?

   (vii) What is the maximum number of employees that could have arrived before 07:45?

   (viii) Could this data be represented with a bar chart? Give a reason for your answer.

3. The distribution of contributions, in euro, given to a charity by a number of people is shown in the histogram below.

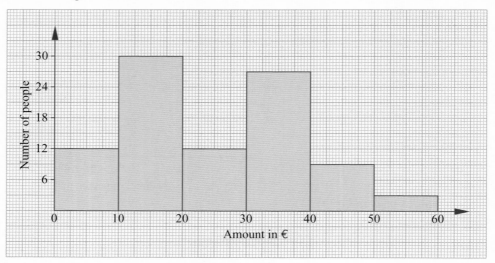

(i) Complete the corresponding frequency distribution table.

Amount in €	0–10	10–20	20–30	30–40	40–50	50–60
Number of people		30				

(ii) By taking the data at the mid-interval values, calculate the mean contribution.

(iii) You interview two people from the group of people who made a contribution to the charity. The two people interviewed claim to have donated a total of €100. Would you be surprised by this claim? Justify your answer.

4. The histogram shows the times in minutes that 100 Olympic athletes completed the marathon after the winner crossed the line.

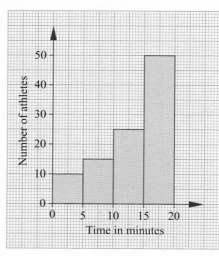

(i) Complete the following frequency table.

Time in minutes	0–5	5–10	10–15	15–20
Number of athletes				

(ii) In which class interval does the 30th athlete to finish lie?

(iii) Write down the maximum number of athletes that could have finished less than 12 minutes behind the winner.

(iv) From the histogram or otherwise, estimate how many athletes could have finished between 3 and 16 minutes after the winner. Justify your estimate.

5. At a Garda checkpoint, the speed of 200 vehicles was recorded in the histogram.

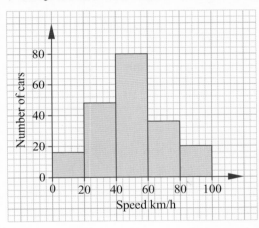

(i) Complete the following table.

Speed in km/h	0–20	20–40	40–60	60–80	80–100
No. of cars					20

(ii) Estimate the number of vehicles with a speed less than or equal to the modal speed.

(iii) Write down **(a)** the minimum number of vehicles with a speed of at least 70 km/h
(b) the maximum number of vehicles with a speed of at least 70 km/h.

6. An airline recorded the weight of each passenger's baggage on a particular flight. The results are shown in the histogram.

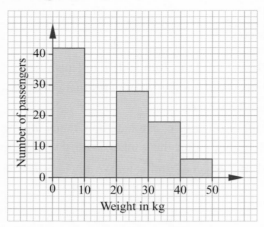

(i) Copy and complete the following frequency table.

Weight in kg	0–10	10–20	20–30	30–40	40–50
No. of passengers	42				

Note: 0–10 means 0 or more but less than 10, etc.

(ii) How many passengers were on the plane?

(iii) The airline charged an excess baggage fee of €12 for every kg over 25 kg. The airline collected €1,728 from passengers in the 30–40 kg group.

(a) Find the average excess baggage fee paid per passenger in the 30–40 kg group.

(b) Find the average baggage weight per passenger in the 30–40 kg group.

(iv) Estimate the total amount in excess baggage fees paid by the passengers in the 40–50 kg group.

Stem and leaf diagrams

Stemplots are sometimes referred to as **stem and leaf diagrams**. They can be useful ways of presenting data. However, they are generally only useful for small amounts (e.g. a maximum of 30) of data. Stemplots can be used to compare two samples by showing the results together on a back-to-back stemplot.

The **stems** represent the first part of each number and are written on the left-hand side.

The **leaves** represent the remaining part of each number and are written on the right-hand side.

Consider the numbers 50, 52, 57, 61, 65, 68, 69, 73, 77.

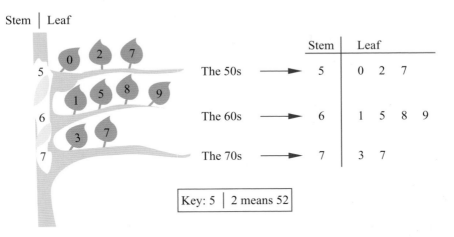

Stem	Leaf
5	0 2 7
6	1 5 8 9
7	3 7

Key: 5 | 2 means 52

In the above stem and leaf plots, the tens digits are the **stems** and the ones digits are the **leaves**.

Note: A stem and leaf plot is often called a stemplot.

When constructing a stem and leaf plot, do the following.

1. Write down the smallest and largest values.
2. Write the stems in a vertical line from the smallest to the largest. (Keep equal intervals and include any missing stems in between.)
3. Draw a vertical line to the right of the stems.
4. Write the leaves next to their corresponding stems.
5. Always include a **key** to show the place value that is meant.
6. Give your stem and leaf plot a heading.

The leaf always consists of **one digit**.

52 has stem 5 and leaf 2   674 has stem 67 and leaf 4

1·3 has stem 1 and leaf 3   2,839 has stem 283 and leaf 9

Usually, a stem and leaf plot is **ordered**. This simply means that the leaves are arranged in increasing order from left to right. There is no need to separate the leaves with commas since each leaf is always a single digit (number).

EXAMPLE 1

The number of minutes taken to complete an exercise was recorded for 24 students in a class. The results were as follows.

> 20   9   36   24   17   32   25   21   14   8   26   38
> 18   15   21   8   11   23   6   37   25   32   17   36

   (i) Represent the data with a stem and leaf plot.

Calculate:

   (ii) The range

   (iii) The median

   (iv) The lower quartile

   (v) The upper quartile

   (vi) The interquartile range

Solution:

   (i) The smallest value is 6 and the largest value is 38.

   Let the intervals be 0–9, 10–19, 20–29, 30–39.

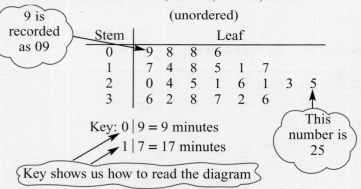

9 is recorded as 09

(unordered)

Stem	Leaf
0	9 8 8 6
1	7 4 8 5 1 7
2	0 4 5 1 6 1 3 5
3	6 2 8 7 2 6

This number is 25

Key: 0 | 9 = 9 minutes
     1 | 7 = 17 minutes

Key shows us how to read the diagram

Number of minutes taken to complete an exercise.

(ordered)

Stem	Leaf
0	6 8 8 9
1	1 4 5 7 7 8
2	0 1 1 3 4 5 5 6
3	2 2 6 6 7 8

Key: 0 | 9 = 9 minutes
     1 | 7 = 17 minutes

Enter the leaves, crossing out the values as you record them. This is called an **unordered** stem and leaf plot. Then create a new stem and leaf plot so that the leaves are in increasing order. This is called an **ordered** stem and leaf plot.

Note: A stem and leaf plot is like a histogram, but it shows the individual values.

Turn the stem and leaf plot on its side (or turn your head to the right) and it should look like a backward histogram of the same data.

(ii) Range = largest value − smallest value = 38 − 6 = 32 minutes.

(iii) The median mark (Q_2) is the time value halfway through the distribution.

The halfway value is between the 12th and 13th values

$$= \tfrac{1}{2}[21 + 21] = 21$$

∴ The median = 21 minutes.

(iv) The lower quartile (Q_1) is the value one-quarter of the way through the distribution.

This one-quarter value is between the 6th and 7th values

$$= \tfrac{1}{2}[14 + 15] = 14\tfrac{1}{2}$$

∴ The lower quartile (Q_1) = $14\tfrac{1}{2}$ minutes.

(v) The upper quartile (Q_3) is the value three-quarters of the way through the distribution.

This three-quarters value is between the 18th and 19th values

$$= \tfrac{1}{2}[26 + 32] = 29$$

∴ The upper quartile (Q_3) = 29 minutes.

(vi) The interquartile range

$$= Q_3 - Q_1$$
$$= 29 - 14\tfrac{1}{2}$$
$$= 14\tfrac{1}{2} \text{ minutes}$$

Note: The interquartile range is more useful than the range.

Here is a diagram to help clarify the situation.

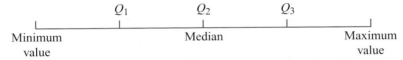

The median (Q_2) is the value that subdivides the ordered data into two halves.

The quartiles (Q_1 and Q_3) subdivide the data into quarters.

The interquartile range = the upper quarter − the lower quarter

$$= Q_3 - Q_1$$

EXAMPLE 2

Use a stem and leaf diagram (stemplot) to compare the examination marks in History and Geography for a class of 20 primary school students.

History	75	69	58	58	46	44	32	50	57	77
	81	61	61	45	31	44	53	66	48	53
Geography	52	58	68	77	38	85	43	44	55	66
	65	79	44	71	84	72	63	69	79	72

Use the stemplots to find the median mark of History and the median mark of Geography.

Solution:

The first four entries for History (75, 69, 58, 58) and for Geography (52, 58, 68, 77) are entered onto a back-to-back stemplot, as follows.

Key: History 9|6 means 69				

```
                          3
                          4
            8 8     5    2 8
              9     6    8
              5     7    7
                    8
```

Key: Geography 5|2 means 52

The completed diagram before rearranging:

```
            1 2     3    8
        8 4 5 4 6   4    3 4 4
      7 3 3 0 8 8   5    2 8 5
          6 1 1 9   6    8 6 5 3 9
              7 5   7    7 9 1 2 2 9
                1   8    5 4
```

The final diagram, arranged in order:

Key: History 8|5 means 58				

```
              History         Geography
            2 1     3    8
        8 6 5 4 4   4    3 4 4
      8 8 7 3 3 0   5    2 5 8
          9 6 1 1   6    3 5 6 8 9
              7 5   7    1 2 2 7 9 9
                1   8    4 5
```

Key: Geography 6|3 means 63

From the diagram, it is clear that the class had higher marks in Geography than in History and it appears that they performed better in Geography. This would, however, depend on the standard of marking used in the two examinations. It would also depend on the standards of questions used in the two examinations.

The median for both subjects is associated with the middle result when the results are written in order.

The median for both subjects is the average of the 10th and 11th results in the final diagram.

History	Geography
53 and 57	66 and 68
are the relevant results.	are the relevant results.
$\therefore$ Median for History	$\therefore$ Median for Geography
$= \dfrac{53 + 57}{2}$	$= \dfrac{66 + 68}{2}$
$= 55$ marks	$= 67$ marks

A comparison of the medians reinforces our belief that the marks for Geography are greater than the marks for History.

Given a stem and leaf plot

Sometimes we are given a stem and leaf plot already drawn and we are required to interpret, draw conclusions or make numerical summaries based on what we are given. In addition, we may be required to recognise the limitations of the given plot, recognise the assumptions in what we are given and perhaps correct errors presented in the stemplot.

EXAMPLE

The back-to-back stem and leaf diagram shows how much time in a week selected adults spent watching television (in minutes).

Key: 3 | 7 = 73	Men		Women	Key: 7 | 0 = 70
	2 2 0	4		
	8 6 3 1	5	1 5 7	
	9 7 5 3	6	4 6 9 9	
	3 1	7	0 5 6 8	
	8 2	8	2 8 8	
		9	5	

(i) What is the total number of adults represented in this stem and leaf plot?

(ii) What is the median time for (a) men (b) women?

(iii) What is the range of times for (a) men (b) women?

(iv) Do these facts show that women spend more time watching television than men do? Explain your answer.

Solution:

(i) 15 men + 15 women = 30 adults

(ii) (a) 63 (b) 70

(iii) (a) 88 − 40 = 48 (b) 95 − 51 = 44

(iv) One possible answer is that the sample is too small to draw conclusions. Another answer could be yes, women watch more TV from (ii) and (iii) above.

Exercise 13.7

1. Using a suitable key in each case, construct a stem and leaf diagram to represent the following data.

    (i) The times in seconds for the nine contestants in a race.

    $$7·5, 8·1, 6·2, 6·4, 7·3, 5, 5·3, 6·2, 7·7$$

    (ii) The length of time in minutes spent by a man over a two-week period watching television each day.

    $$48, 53, 69, 75, 84, 82, 78, 68, 56, 45, 64, 73, 88, 70$$

    (iii) The number of CDs a group of 24 students had in their collection.

2	23	4	2	7	28	14	8	5	0	26	13
28	16	2	17	19	18	24	9	10	2	22	21

    (iv) The heights of 30 adults were recorded in cm.

153	182	159	194	154	179	186	174	167	185
164	185	209	185	165	203	180	205	177	172
172	195	205	186	173	198	164	199	179	175

2. The number of guests in a hotel over a period was recorded as follows:

    $$36 \quad 43 \quad 39 \quad 53 \quad 29 \quad 43 \quad 33 \quad 47 \quad 51 \quad 27 \quad 42 \quad 31 \quad 34 \quad 22 \quad 28$$

    (i) Represent this data on a stem and leaf diagram.

    (ii) Calculate the range.

    (iii) Calculate the median.

    (iv) How many recordings showed less than 30 guests in the hotel?

3. The number of litres of diesel bought by 20 motorists was recorded as follows.

$$17 \quad 22 \quad 28 \quad 11 \quad 35 \quad 43 \quad 23 \quad 26 \quad 18 \quad 15$$
$$25 \quad 45 \quad 37 \quad 35 \quad 27 \quad 16 \quad 41 \quad 34 \quad 13 \quad 29$$

   (i) Construct a stem and leaf plot to represent the data.
   (ii) Calculate the (a) range and (b) the mean number of litres of diesel bought per motorist.
   (iii) Does this data contain a mode? Justify your answer.
   (iv) Calculate the median.
   (v) How many motorists purchased more than the median amount of diesel?

4. Below is a stem and leaf plot of the heights of a group of students, in cm.

Key: 13 | 3 means 133 cm

```
13 | 3
13 | 5  6
14 | 0  0  1
14 | 6  6  7  8
15 | 0  1  2  2  3  3
15 | 5  5  6  7
```

   (i) How many students are in the group?
   (ii) What is the range of heights in the group?
   (iii) What percentage of the students are between 145 cm and 154 cm in height?

5. A stemplot is given below, but it does not have a key.

```
Stem |        Leaf
  4  | 9
  5  | 1  4
  5  | 7  8  (9)
  6  | 2  3  3  4
  6  | 5  6  6  6  7  7
  7  | 0  3  4
  7  | 6
```

   State the value ringed and the width of the interval that it is in when the diagram illustrates the following.
   (i) The time taken for a race, where 7 | 3 represents 7·3 minutes.
   (ii) The lengths, in metres (m) to two decimal places, of components where 7 | 3 represents 0·73 m.
   (iii) The masses, in grams (g) to three decimal places, of components where 7 | 3 represents 0·073 g.

6. The time, in seconds, taken to answer 18 mobile phone calls was recorded as follows.

| 2·5 | 3·5 | 5·6 | 3·6 | 2·4 | 4·5 | 3·3 | 4·2 | 3·2 |
| 5·9 | 1·9 | 3·3 | 2·9 | 3·3 | 5·8 | 3·7 | 3·2 | 2·9 |

(i) Copy and complete the stem and leaf diagram to represent this data.

Time, in seconds, taken to answer a mobile call

Stem	Leaf
1	
2	4
3	
4	2
5	

Key: 2 | 4 means 2·4 seconds

(ii) What was the **(a)** shortest time and **(b)** the longest time taken to answer the calls?

(iii) Calculate the range.

(iv) Write down the modal time taken to answer a call.

(v) Calculate the mean time taken to answer a call.

(vi) The time 3·5 seconds was incorrectly recorded as 5·3 seconds. Would this error increase or decrease the mean? Justify your answer.

(vii) Calculate the change in the mean due to this error.

(viii) Somebody suggested that the data should have been represented with a pie chart. Do you agree? Explain your answer.

7. A class group of 30 sat an examination in either French or Spanish. The back-to-back stem and leaf plot below shows the results for the class.

| *Key:* 3 | 6 = 63 marks | French | | Spanish | *Key:* 4 | 9 = 49 marks |

French		Spanish
	3	8 8
8 7 2	4	4 9
5	5	0 1 1 1 6 7
8 7 3	6	6 7 8 8
2 2	7	3 4 4 5 8
	8	1 3

(i) How many students took **(a)** French **(b)** Spanish?

(ii) Write down the median mark for **(a)** French **(b)** Spanish.

(iii) What is the upper quartile mark for **(a)** French **(b)** Spanish?

(iv) If a distinction is awarded for a score above 65 marks, how many students were awarded a distinction in (a) French (b) Spanish?

(v) Which, if any, set of results, French or Spanish, is better? Explain your answer.

8. The ordered stem and leaf diagram shows the pulse rates for a group of 16 runners before and after a mini marathon.

```
Key: 2|9 = 92

          7   9   2 |  6 |
      8   8   4   0 |  7 |
      5   3   3   3 |  8 | 0
          8   4   2 |  9 | 6   8
                  3 | 10 | 3   3   4   5
                    | 11 | 2   2   5   5   5   8
                    | 12 | 0   1   1   9
                    | 13 | 3
```

Describe five errors in the stem and leaf plot above.

9. The pulse rates of 30 workers in a factory were measured before and after taking exercise.

Before: 110, 93, 81, 75, 73, 73, 48, 53, 69, 69, 66, 111, 100, 93, 90, 50, 57, 64, 90, 111, 91, 70, 70, 51, 79, 93, 105, 51, 66, 98.

After: 117, 84, 77, 108, 130, 69, 77, 84, 84, 86, 95, 125, 96, 104, 104, 137, 143, 70, 80, 131, 145, 106, 130, 109, 137, 75, 104, 72, 97, 80.

(i) Display the data in a back-to-back stemplot. (Use class intervals 40–49, 50–59, 60–69, etc.)

(ii) Calculate the median value for (a) before and (b) after taking exercise.

(iii) Calculate the range of values of pulse rates for (a) before and (b) after taking exercise.

(iv) By analysing your answers to (i), (ii) and (iii), what conclusions can you draw?

(v) This investigation of the factory workers' pulse rates arose from comments that these workers were unusually athletic. State **one** additional piece of information that you would need in order to decide whether that is true.

10. A teacher recorded the times taken by 20 boys to swim one length of the pool. The times are given to the nearest second.

(i) Using the intervals 24–25, 26–27, etc., draw a stem and leaf diagram to illustrate the results.

32	31	26	27	27	32	29	26	25	25
29	31	32	26	30	24	32	27	26	31

(ii) The teacher later recorded the times taken by 20 girls to swim one length of the pool. The times are given to the nearest second. Display the data for boys and girls in a back-to-back stemplot. (Use the intervals 24–25, 26–27, etc.)

25	34	29	26	27	27	33	28	26	24
30	31	33	25	29	25	33	26	26	32

(iii) By considering two statistical terms, e.g. range, median, mean, mode, what conclusions can you draw when comparing the times for the two groups?

11. John's third year Physical Education class did a fitness test. The number of sit-ups that each student did in one minute is recorded below.

59	48	27	53	36	29	52	46	45	37	49	51
33	45	38	52	40	51	37	44	47	45	60	41

The students practised this exercise for the next three weeks and then repeated the test in the same order. The data for the second test are as follows.

61	52	33	51	39	40	50	49	46	37	59	49
38	48	39	58	44	52	38	44	49	51	62	44

(i) Represent the data from the two tests on a back-to-back stem and leaf diagram.

(ii) How many students are in the class?

(iii) What is the *range* of sit-ups for the class?   Test 1 _____ Test 2 _____

(iv) Based on the data and the diagram, do you think that practice improves the ability to do sit-ups? Give a reason for your answer.

(v) John did 41 sit-ups in Test 1 and 44 in Test 2. How did his performance compare with that of the rest of the class?

Misuses of statistics

Misleading graphs and diagrams

Many advertisements frequently use graphs and diagrams to present information. In most cases the graphs and diagrams are well presented and give an honest and fair representation of the facts. However, some are deliberately drawn to mislead. The most common methods to present correct information in misleading graphs and diagrams is to use a false origin, insert no scale or a non-uniform scale on the vertical axis or drawing graphs with unequal widths and dimensions. Other misleading methods to watch out for are using a biased sample or a sample that is too small; deliberate omissions, errors and exaggerations; misleading comparisons; and using unreliable sources.

Consumers should try to spot misleading graphs and diagrams, errors, omissions and exaggerations when presented with information (statistics).

EXAMPLE 1

Sometimes averages can be misleading. Sometimes they just don't make sense at all. Be careful when averaging different variables that the quantities you're averaging are comparable. Remember Ballybrigs!

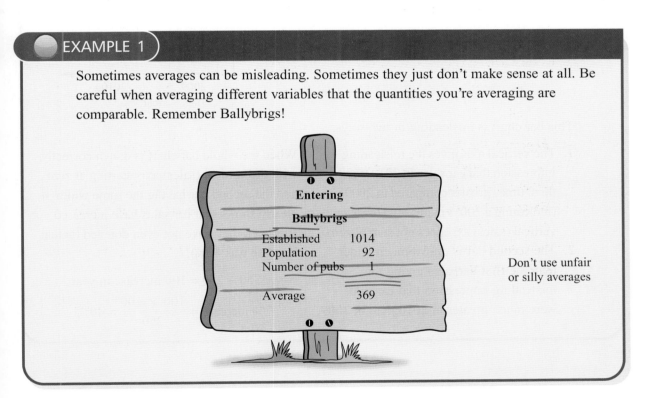

Entering
Ballybrigs

Established	1014
Population	92
Number of pubs	1
Average	369

Don't use unfair or silly averages

EXAMPLE 2

Briefly comment on these bar charts, which represent the number of cars sold over two years on a garage forecourt.

Solution:

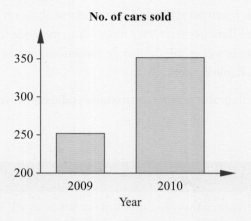

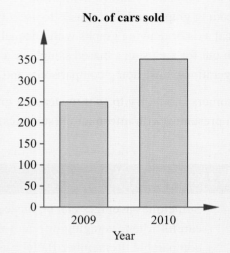

This bar chart is misleading in two ways.

1. The vertical axis gives the misleading impression that car sales in 2010 were three times greater compared to 2009 (indicating a 200% increase). However, the vertical (sales) axis does not start at zero.

2. The second bar is drawn much wider than the first bar, also giving the misleading impression that car sales were much greater in 2010 than in 2009.

When the whole bar chart is drawn correctly, with the vertical (sales) axis starting at zero and the second bar having the same width, it clearly shows that car sales have increased. However, they have not even doubled (actual increase was 40%).

Note: $350 - 250 = 100$ increase in year

$$\% \text{ increase} = \frac{100 \times 100}{250} = 40\%$$

Exercise 13.8

1. In each case, give two reasons why the graphs are misleading.

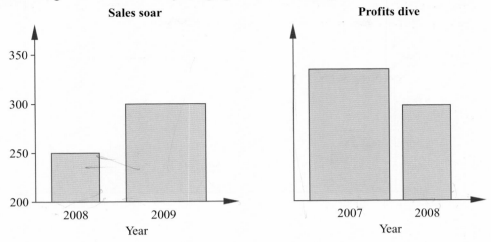

2. This bar chart is drawn to compare the amount of money, in euro, raised for charity by two classes. Give three reasons why the bar chart is misleading.

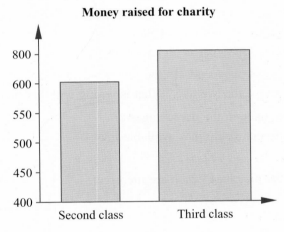

3. A car manufacturer produces two makes of car, A and B. They sell twice as much of B as A. The following diagram has been drawn to represent this information. Explain why the diagram is misleading.

4. The diagram has been drawn to represent the number of trucks sold over a 10-year period. Give two reasons why this diagram is misleading.

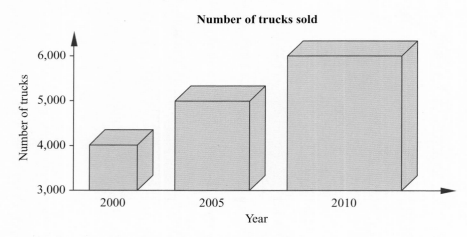

Number of trucks sold

5. Seven people work for a company. Their annual salaries, in euro, are as follows.

   180,000   40,000   40,000   40,000   40,000   40,000   40,000

   The company decides to advertise for another employee. The company claims in the advertisement that the average salary is €60,000 per year. Is the company trying to mislead with this advertisement? Give reasons for your answer.

6. A professor of economics once said, 'In the future we hope that economic growth rates in all countries will be above the average.' What is wrong with his statement?

7. The pie chart displays data on the percentages of students studying different disciplines available in a university.

   Find two aspects of the pie chart which are incorrect.

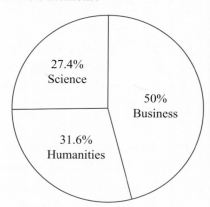

8. The bar chart below summarises the results of 420 throws of a die. A person says that this graph indicates that the die is biased in favour of six. Do you think that the die is biased? Justify your answer.

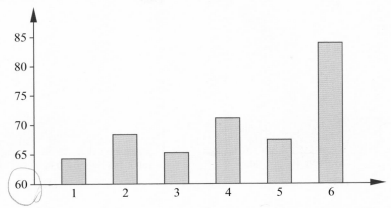

9. A cat food manufacturer makes a cat food called KATT food. The manufacturer claims eight out of 10 owners said that their cats preferred KATT food. Comment on how this claim could be misleading.

10. **The shrinking world**

Time period	1600–1850	1850–1930	1950–1970	2000 →
Transport vehicle	Horse-drawn coach	Steam train	Propeller aircraft	Jet aircraft
Best average speed in km/h	18	90	450	900

The development of the speed of generally available transport vehicles since the nineteenth century has been spectacular. The three bar charts (P), (Q) and (R) attempt to show the information given in the table above. Only one of the bar charts (P), Q), (R) is correct. Which one is correct? Explain your choice.

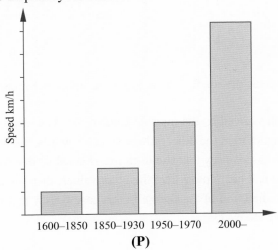

(P)

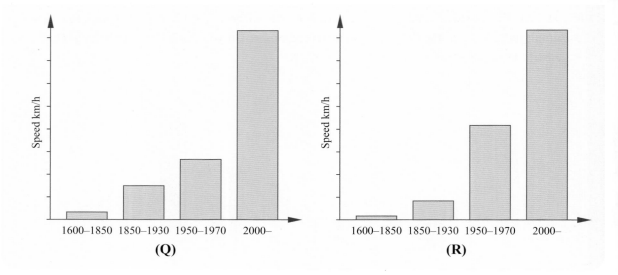

(Q)   (R)

Shape of a distribution

In some distributions, certain values look unusual or are not typical. Consider the values 2, 3, 4, 4, 5, 6, 7, 9 and 41. The value 41 is not typical of the rest of the values. It is often called an **outlier**. In this case, it has a small effect on the median (this is one of the reasons why the median value is used in horse sales). However, it does have a big effect on the mean.

Consider the 8 values without the value 41:

2, 3, 4, 4, 5, 6, 7, 9

$$\text{Median} = \frac{4 + 5}{2} = 4 \cdot 5$$

(average of the two middle values)

$$\text{Mean} = \mu = \frac{2 + 3 + 4 + 4 + 5 + 6 + 7 + 9}{8}$$

$$= \frac{40}{8} = 5$$

Consider the 9 values including the value 41:

2, 3, 4, 4, 5, 6, 7, 9, 41

Median = 5

(middle value)

$$\text{Mean} = \mu = \frac{2 + 3 + 4 + 4 + 5 + 6 + 7 + 9 + 41}{9}$$

$$= \frac{81}{9} = 9$$

The value 41, outlier, increases the median by 0·5 and increases the mean by 4.

We say that the data has been **skewed** by the unusual value of 41. The mean has been increased because the unusual value of 41 is higher than the other values. In other words, the mean has been pulled in the direction of the skew. In this case we say that **the data are skewed to the right** or the data are **positively skewed**. If the unusual value had been lower than the other values, then the mean would have been lowered (again, pulled in the direction of the skew). In this case we say that **the data are skewed to the left** or the data are **negatively skewed**.

Note: Skewness only applies to distributions that contain discrete or continuous data.

Symmetrical distribution

If all of the values in a distribution are evenly spread (or roughly evenly spread) around the mean, the distribution is said to be **symmetrical**. The diagram shows a symmetrical distribution. The mean and the median coincide.

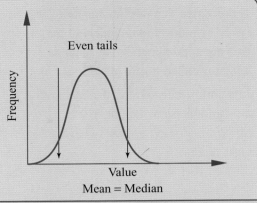

Skewed right distribution

If most of the values in a distribution are low, then the tail is on the right-hand side. The distribution is said to be **skewed to the right** (right-hand tail). It is also said to be **positively skewed**. The diagram shows a distribution that is **skewed to the right**. In this case the mean of the data is **greater** than the median. The mean is pulled right (increased) by the right-hand skew.

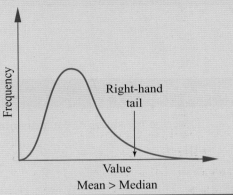

Skewed left distribution

If most of the values in a distribution are high, then the tail is on the left-hand side. The distribution is said to be **skewed to the left** (left-hand tail). It is also said to be **negatively skewed**. The diagram shows a distribution that is **skewed to the left**. In this case the mean of the data is **less** than the median. The mean is pulled left (lowered) by the left-hand skew.

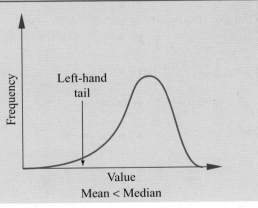

A histogram that doesn't appear to have any mode and in which all the bars are approximately the same height is called **uniform**.

In a uniform histogram, the bars are all about the same height. The histogram doesn't appear to have a clear mode.

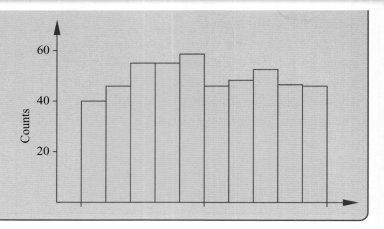

EXAMPLE

Describe the shape of each distribution. Are there any outliers?

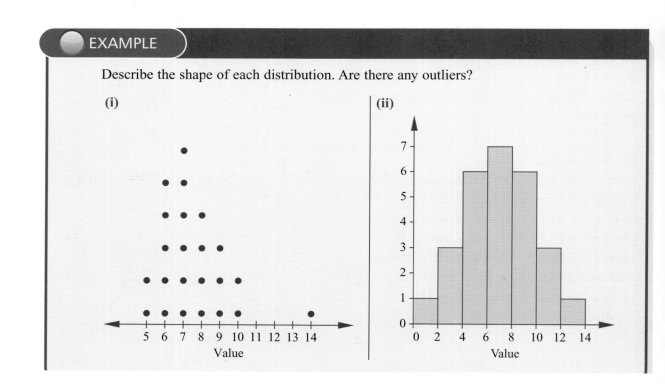

(i)

(ii)

Solution:

(i)

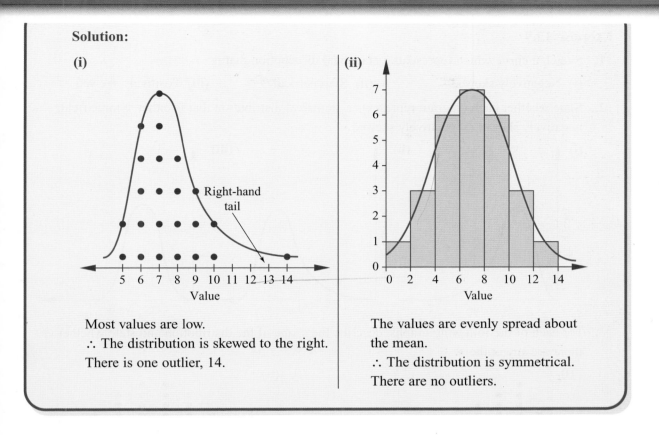

Most values are low.

∴ The distribution is skewed to the right.

There is one outlier, 14.

(ii)

The values are evenly spread about the mean.

∴ The distribution is symmetrical.

There are no outliers.

When we talk about the direction of skewness, we are talking about the direction of the tail of the distribution. The tail indicates the area where there are fewer values.

Values **evenly** spread around the mean gives two even tails, which is called **symmetrical**.

Fewer values to the **left** gives a left-hand tail, which is called **skewed to the left** or **negatively skewed**.

Fewer values to the **right** gives a right-hand tail, which is called **skewed to the right** or **positively skewed**.

Exercise 13.9

1. Sketch a curve which represents a statistical distribution that is:

   (i) Negatively skewed   **(ii)** Symmetrical   **(iii)** Positively skewed

2. State whether each diagram represents a statistical distribution that is either symmetrical, negatively skewed or positively skewed.

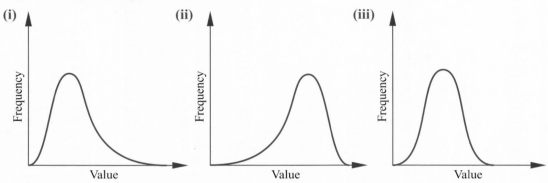

3. For each of the following graphs, describe the shape of the distribution and state whether there are any outliers.

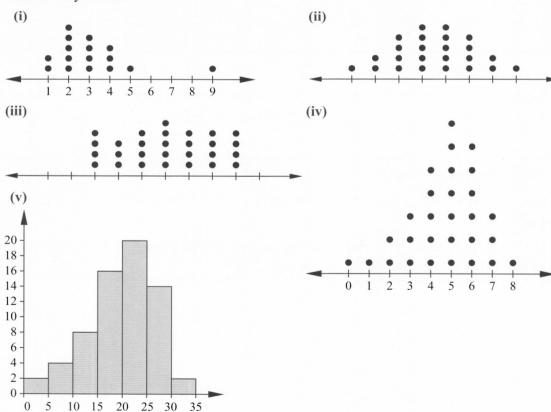

(vi)

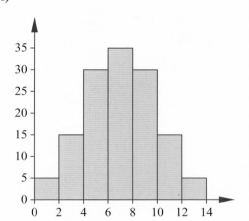

(vii)

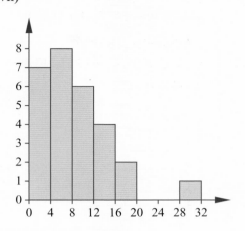

When dealing with stem and leaf diagrams, it may help to rotate the page by 90°.

(viii)

Stem	Leaf					
1	1	3				
2	0	2	5			
3	1	3	4	7		
4	0	4	5	6	7	8
5	1	3	6	6	7	8	9
6	2	4	7	8	9	
7	0	1	3			

(ix)

Stem	Leaf				
10	5				
11	1	4			
12	0	1	2	5	
13	0	3	4	7	8
14	1	3	6	8	
15	2	5			
16	3				

(x)

Stem	Leaf			
200	3			
201				
202	8	8	8	9
203	3	4	5	6
204	2	2	2	7
205	1	3	5	

4. The following two histograms show the number of people in their seats at Croke Park before and after a major championship match.

    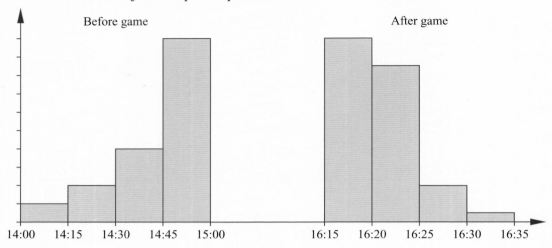

    (i) Describe the shape of each distribution.

    (ii) Describe an additional difference between the two sets of data.

5. The students in a Leaving Cert class decided to investigate their heights. They measured the heights of each boy and girl, in cm, and the results were as follows.

Boys			Girls		
173	180	174	167	161	160
175	178	176	159	164	172
180	171	170	168	149	161
182	176	166	167	167	171

    (i) Construct a back-to-back stem and leaf plot of the above data.

    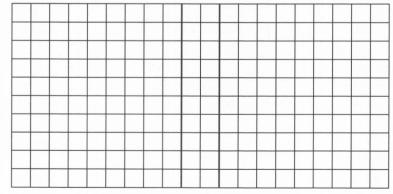

    (ii) State one difference and one similarity between the two distributions.

    (iii) There is one outlier in the data. Describe the outlier.

6. **(i)** Here are the marks, in percentages, achieved by a class of 22 students.

$$58 \quad 25 \quad 20 \quad 24 \quad 40 \quad 40 \quad 57 \quad 61 \quad 85 \quad 82 \quad 90$$
$$63 \quad 64 \quad 72 \quad 70 \quad 95 \quad 88 \quad 83 \quad 81 \quad 82 \quad 78 \quad 91$$

Complete the following frequency distribution table.

% score	0–20	20–40	40–60	60–80	80–100
No. of students					

Note: 0–20 means 0 is included, 20 is excluded, etc.

(ii) By drawing a histogram or otherwise, describe the distribution of the data.

(iii) The same group of students wrote down the distance they travelled (to the nearest km) to school each day. The distances were:

$$2 \quad 5 \quad 3 \quad 2 \quad 5 \quad 4 \quad 3 \quad 4 \quad 3 \quad 2 \quad 4$$
$$3 \quad 2 \quad 2 \quad 3 \quad 3 \quad 4 \quad 2 \quad 5 \quad 6 \quad 2 \quad 2$$

By analysing the above information, classify the distribution as either symmetrical, negatively skewed or positively skewed.

(iv) The ages of the 22 students were recorded (in years) as:

$$14 \quad 15 \quad 16 \quad 14 \quad 15 \quad 15 \quad 14 \quad 15 \quad 16 \quad 15 \quad 15$$
$$14 \quad 16 \quad 15 \quad 15 \quad 16 \quad 15 \quad 15 \quad 15 \quad 16 \quad 16 \quad 14$$

Classify the age distribution using the terms from part **(iii)**.

7. Students in two schools – one in County Kerry and the other in County Offaly – were arguing about which county had the nicest weather in the summer. They agreed to record the highest temperature at each school on 10 randomly selected days during the summer of 2012. The results were as follows.

Temperature at Kerry school (°C)			Temperature at Offaly school (°C)		
18·5	17·2	17·8	22·1	18·0	19·1
17·6	17·5	17·2	17·2	18·4	18·6
17·1	16·9	16·9	19·8	19·0	17·6
17·1			17·0		

(i) Construct a back-to-back stem and leaf plot of the above data.

(ii) State two differences between the two distributions.

(iii) Comment on the shape of both distributions.

(iv) Are there any outliers in either data set? Justify your answer.

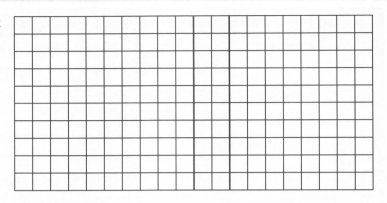

8. Using Excel, a teacher generates some random numbers between 1 and 60. The teacher represents the results generated in the histogram below.

   Note: 0–10 means 0 is excluded, 10 is included, etc.

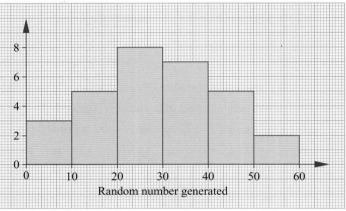

(i) Construct the frequency table.

(ii) How many numbers were generated?

(iii) Describe the distribution.

(iv) Did you expect this distribution? Explain your answer.

9. By constructing two separate histograms or otherwise, from the information contained in the two pie charts describe the shape of the distribution in both sets of data.

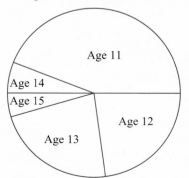

Age (in years) of a group of students at scout camp

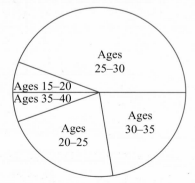

Age (in years) of a group of people at a party

Revision

Symbol	Definition	Example
$\in$	is an element of	$5 \in \{1, 2, 4, 5, 9\}$
$\notin$	is not an element of	$8 \notin \{1, 2, 4, 5, 9\}$
#	the number of elements in	#{cat, dog, fish} = 3
=	is equal to	$\{t, e, a\} = \{e, a, t\}$
$\varnothing$	the empty (or null) set	$\varnothing$ or {}
$\subset$	is a subset of	$\{1, 3\} \subset \{1, 2, 3, 4, 5\}$
$\not\subset$	is not a subset of	$\{p, e, n\} \not\subset \{c, a, s, e\}$
U	the universal set	all the elements
$\cap$	intersection	$\{1, 2, 3\} \cap \{2, 4, 6\} = \{2\}$
$\cup$	union	$\{1, 2, 3\} \cup \{2, 4, 6\} = \{1, 2, 3, 4, 6\}$
\	set difference	$\{2, 3, 5, 7\} \setminus \{1, 2, 3, 6\} = \{5, 7\}$
$'$	complement	$U = \{1, 2, 3, 4\}, S = \{2, 3\}$ $\therefore S' = U \setminus S = \{1, 4\}$

Exercise 14.1

1. $A = \{2, 4, 6, 8\}$, $B = \{1, 2, 3, 6\}$ and $C = \{1, 3, 5\}$.

   State whether each of the following is true or false.

   (i) $2 \in A$ (ii) $3 \in B$ (iii) $4 \notin C$

   (iv) $A \cap B = \{2\}$ (v) $B \cap C = \{3\}$ (vi) $A \setminus B = \{4, 8\}$

   (vii) $\#(A \cap B) = \#A - \#B$ (viii) $(B \setminus A) \subset C$ (ix) $\#A = \#B$

   (x) $\#(A \cup C) = \#A + \#C$ (xi) $A \cup B = B \cup C$ (xii) $A \cap C = \varnothing$

2. In general, for two sets S and T, $\#(S \cup T) \neq \#S + \#T$.

   (i) Using a Venn diagram or otherwise, explain the reason for this.

   (ii) Under what circumstances would $\#(S \cup T) = \#S + \#T$?

Numerical problems for two sets

Four regions for two sets

The diagram below indicates the four regions when dealing with the sets U, A and B.

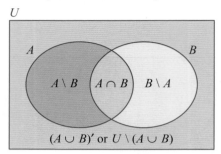

Note: If the universal set, U, is not involved, there are only three regions.

Symbol	Meaning
#A	the number of elements in A
$\cap$	and
$A \cap B$	in A and B
$\cup$	or
$A \cup B$	in A or B
$\backslash$	but not in
$A \backslash B$	in A but not in B
U	universal set
$A' = U \backslash A$	in U but not in A

When putting values into a Venn diagram, always work from the centre outwards. In many problems we introduce a variable x to represent the number of elements in a region. Then we express the number of elements in other regions in terms of x. From the question we link the number of elements in the regions to form an equation and solve this equation.

EXAMPLE 1

A sports club has 69 members. 37 members play tennis and 25 play squash. Some members play tennis and squash. Twice as many members play neither of these games as play both.

How many members play **(i)** tennis and squash? **(ii)** only one of these games?

Solution:

Draw a Venn diagram showing U for all the members of the club, T for the members who play tennis and S for the members who play squash.

Let the number of members that play both $= x$.

Thus $\qquad$ $\#(T \cap S) = x$

$\therefore$ $\qquad$ $\#(T \setminus S) = 37 - x$

and $\qquad$ $\#(S \setminus T) = 25 - x$

and $\qquad$ $\#[U \setminus (S \cup T)] = 2x$

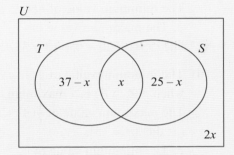

Given: $\qquad$ $\#U = 69$

$(37 - x) + x + (25 - x) + 2x = 69$

$37 - x + x + 25 - x + 2x = 69$

$x + 62 = 69$

$x = 7$

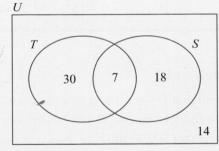

(i) The number of members who play tennis and squash $= 7$.

(ii) The number of members who play only one of these games $= 30 + 18 = 48$.

Maximising and minimising

The following is very useful when dealing with maximum and minimum problems on two sets.

> **1.** To maximise $\#(A \cup B)$, we minimise $\#(A \cap B)$.
>
> **2.** To minimise $\#(A \cup B)$, we maximise $\#(A \cap B)$.

EXAMPLE 2

A and *B* are two sets such that #*A* = 20 and #*B* = 15.
Using a Venn diagram in each case, calculate:
  (i) The possible maximum value of #(*A* ∪ *B*)
  (ii) The possible minimum value of #(*A* ∪ *B*)

Solution:
  (i) The maximum value of #(*A* ∪ *B*) occurs
  when #(*A* ∩ *B*) is a minimum.
  The minimum value of #(*A* ∩ *B*) = 0.
  ∴ The maximum value of
  #(*A* ∪ *B*) = 20 + 0 + 15 = 35.

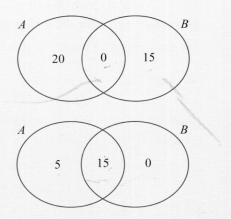

  (ii) The minimum value of #(*A* ∪ *B*) occurs
  when #(*A* ∩ *B*) is a maximum.
  The maximum value of #(*A* ∩ *B*) = 15
  (as the #*B* = 15).
  ∴ The minimum value of
  #(*A* ∪ *B*) = 5 + 15 + 0 = 20.

Exercise 14.2

1. 80 pupils were asked in a survey whether they
   liked rock music, *R*, or classical music, *C*, or
   neither. The results are shown in the Venn diagram.

   How many said they liked:
   (i) Both **(ii)** Rock music
   (iii) Classical music **(iv)** Neither
   (v) Only one of these types of music

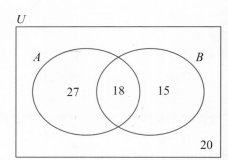

2. In a class of 34 pupils, 20 play basketball (*B*),
   17 play football (*F*) and 2 play neither.

   (i) Copy the Venn diagram and complete it.
   (ii) How many pupils in the class play:
     (a) Both games
     (b) Only one of these games
     (c) At least one of these games

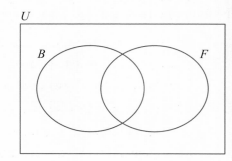

3. A school sports day was attended by 250 pupils. 70 pupils took part in the long jump event. 40 pupils took part in the high jump event. 160 pupils did not take part in either of the two jump events. Using a Venn diagram or otherwise, find the number of pupils who took part in the long jump event only.

In questions 4–6, use a Venn diagram to find the solution.

4. $\#(A) = 13$, $\#(B) = 14$ and $\#(A \cap B) = 6$. Find: **(i)** $\#(A \setminus B)$ **(ii)** $\#(A \cup B)$

5. $\#X = 15$, $\#Y = 9$ and $\#(X \cup Y) = 19$. Find: **(i)** $\#(X \cap Y)$ **(ii)** $\#(Y \setminus X)$

6. $\#U = 57$, $\#P = 31$, $\#Q = 28$ and $\#(P \cap Q) = 10$.
   Find: **(i)** $\#(P \setminus Q)$ **(ii)** $\#[U \setminus (P \cup Q)]$ **(iii)** $\#[(P \cap Q)']$

7. The Venn diagram represents the number of girls in a class of 30 who study French, F, Spanish, S, or both.

   (i) If each girl in the class must study French or Spanish, calculate x.

   (ii) How many girls study:
   (a) French only **(b)** Spanish only **(c)** Only one of these subjects

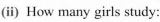

8. The Venn diagram shows the number of elements, in terms of x, in the sets U, A and B.
   (i) If $\#B = 41$, calculate x.
   Hence, calculate:
   (ii) $\#(A \cap B)$ **(iii)** $\#(A \setminus B)$
   (iv) $\#[U \setminus (A \cup B)]$ **(v)** $(A \cup B) \setminus (A \cap B)$

9. A and B are two sets such that $\#(A \cap B) = 5$ and $\#(A \setminus B) = 3[\#(B \setminus A)]$.
   If $\#(A \cup B) = 21$, calculate $\#(A \setminus B)$.
   (Hint: Let $\#(B \setminus A) = x$.)

   $4x + 5 = 21$
   $4x = 16$
   $x = 4$.

10. P and Q are two sets such that $\#(P \cap Q) = 2$ and $\#(P \cup Q) = 32$.
    If $\#(Q \setminus P) = \frac{1}{2}[\#(P \setminus Q)]$, calculate $\#P$. 22

    $P \setminus Q = X$
    $Q \setminus P = \frac{1}{2}X$ $\frac{3}{2}X + 2 =$
    $X = 20$

11. A club has 47 members. 18 members play chess and 13 play tennis. Some members play chess and tennis. Three times as many members play neither of these games as play both.
    How many members play **(i)** chess and tennis? 8 **(ii)** Only one of these games? 15

    $3(1 + 2x = 47)$
    $x = 8$

12. A group of 63 people was asked whether they had a television and/or a computer. Four times as many had a television only as had both and 3 people had neither.

    If 24 people said they had a computer, calculate the number who said they had:

    (i) A television and a computer 9

    (ii) A television or a computer but not both 81

    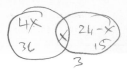
    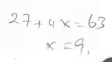

    $27 + 4x = 63$
    $x = 9$.

13. A and B are two sets such that $\#A = 20$ and $\#B = 12$.
    (i) Calculate the maximum possible value of $\#(A \cup B)$.
    (ii) Calculate the minimum possible value of $\#(A \cup B)$.
    (iii) If $\#(A \cup B) > 3$, calculate the maximum possible value of $\#(A \cup B)$.

14. P and Q are two sets such that $\#(P) = 10$, $\#(Q) = 11$ and $\#(P \cap Q) \geq 2$.
    (i) Calculate the maximum possible value of $\#(P \cup Q)$.
    (ii) Calculate the minimum possible value of $\#(P \cup Q)$.

15. U is the universal set and P and Q are two subsets of U.
    $\#U = 40$, $\#P = 28$ and $\#Q = 11$.

    (i) Using a Venn diagram, find the minimum value of $\#(P \cup Q)'$.
    (ii) Using a Venn diagram, find the maximum value of $\#(P \cup Q)'$.

16. U is the universal set and G and H are two subsets of U.
    $\#U = u$, $\#G = g$, $\#H = h$ and $\#(G \cup H)' = x$.

    Using a Venn diagram, show that if $g > h$ and x is a maximum, then $u = g + x$.

17. U, P and Q are sets such that $\#U = 43$, $\#P = 20$ and $\#Q = 15$.
    $\#(P \cup Q) = x$ and $\#(P \cap Q) = y$.

    (i) If $a < x < b$ and $c < y < d$ where $a, b, c, d \in \mathbb{N}$, find the value of a, b, c and d.
    (ii) Calculate the maximum possible value of $\#[U \setminus (P \cup Q)]$.

Numerical problems for three sets

Eight regions for three sets
The diagram below indicates the eight regions when dealing with the sets U, A, B and C.

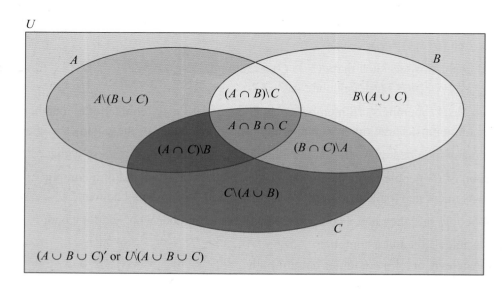

Symbol	Meaning
$A \cup B \cup C$	in A or B or C
$A \cap B \cap C$	in A and B and C
$(A \cup B) \setminus C$	in A or B but not in C
$(A \cap B) \setminus C$	in A and B but not in C
$A \setminus (B \cup C)$	in A but not in B or C (A only)
$(A \cup B \cup C)'$ or $U \setminus (A \cup B \cup C)$	in U but not in A or B or C

EXAMPLE 1

Three problems, A, B and C, were given to a set of students. 31 solved A, 20 solved B and 22 solved C. 4 solved A and B but not C, 10 solved A and C but not B and 5 solved all three problems. Each student solved at least one problem.

  (i) How many students solved A only?

 (ii) Find the maximum possible number of students that could have solved A or B or C.

(iii) If there were 46 students in all, how many solved C only?

Solution:

  (i) Draw a Venn diagram showing A for the set of students who solved problem A, B for the set of students who solved problem B and C for the set of students who solved problem C.

    Given: $\#A = 31$, $\#B = 20$, $\#C = 22$,
    $\#[(A \cap B) \setminus C] = 4$, $\#(A \cap C) \setminus B] = 10$,
    $\#(A \cap B \cap C) = 5$ and $\#(A \cup B \cup C)' = 0$.
    Number who solved A only
    $= 31 - (4 + 5 + 10) = 31 - 19 = 12$.

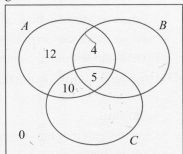

 (ii) Maximum possible number of students that could have solved A or B or C, i.e. maximise $\#(A \cup B \cup C)$.

    The maximum value of $\#(A \cup B \cup C)$ occurs when $\#[(B \cap C) \setminus A]$ is a minimum.
    The minimum value of $\#[(B \cap C) \setminus A] = 0$.
    The number who solved B only $= 20 - 4 - 5 = 11$.
    The number who solved C only $= 22 - 10 - 5 = 7$.
    The maximum number that could have solved A or B or $C = 12 + 4 + 11 + 10 + 5 + 0 + 7 = 49$.

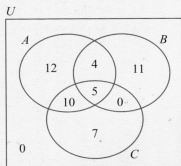

(iii) If there were 46 students in all, how many solved C only?

Let x = the number who solved B and C but not A,

i.e. let $\#[(B \cap C) \setminus A] = x$.

$\therefore$ The number who solved B only $= 20 - 4 - 5 - x = 11 - x$.

$\therefore$ The number who solved C only $= 22 - 10 - 5 - x = 7 - x$.

Given: 46 students in all.

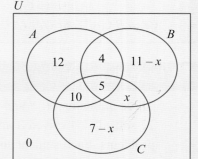

$$\#(A \cup B \cup C) = 46$$
$$12 + 4 + (11 - x) + 10 + 5 + x + (7 - x) = 46$$
$$12 + 4 + 11 - x + 10 + 5 + x + 7 - x = 46$$
$$49 - x = 46$$
$$-x = -3$$
$$x = 3$$

The number who solved C only $= 7 - x = 7 - 3 = 4$.

EXAMPLE 2

After a two-hour study period, 160 pupils were asked whether they had studied Mathematics, Science or French. The results were as follows.

13 studied Mathematics only, 7 studied Science only and 10 studied French only. 11 studied none of these subjects. 12 studied Mathematics and Science, 9 studied Mathematics and French and 6 studied Science and French.

How many pupils studied Mathematics and Science and French?

Solution:

Draw a Venn diagram showing U for all 60 pupils, M for Mathematics, S for Science and F for French.

Put in the numbers for Mathematics only, Science only and French only.

Let x = the number of pupils who studied Mathematics and Science and French,

i.e. let $\#(M \cap S \cap F) = x$.

Therefore, the number who studied
Mathematics and Science but not French = $12 - x$
Mathematics and French but not Science = $9 - x$
Science and French but not Mathematics = $6 - x$
Given: 60 pupils surveyed altogether.

$$\#U = 60$$
$$13 + (12 - x) + 7 + (9 - x) + x + (6 - x) + 10 + 11 = 60$$
$$68 - 2x = 60$$
$$-2x = -8$$
$$x = 4$$

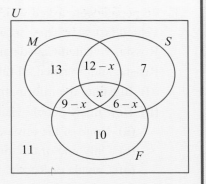

4 pupils studied Mathematics and Science and French.

Exercise 14.3

1. All 62 members in a youth club were asked in a survey if they played Soccer (S), Tennis (T) or Hockey (H). The results are shown in the Venn diagram. Using the Venn diagram, find the number of members of the youth club who play:

   (i) All three sports
   (ii) Soccer and tennis
   (iii) Soccer or tennis
   (iv) None of these sports
   (v) Tennis and hockey but not soccer
   (vi) Tennis or hockey but not soccer
   (vii) Soccer
   (viii) Tennis but not soccer or hockey
   (ix) Only one of these sports
   (x) Only two of these sports
   (xi) At least two of these sports

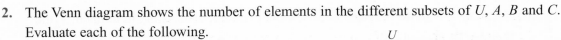

2. The Venn diagram shows the number of elements in the different subsets of U, A, B and C. Evaluate each of the following.

   (i) $\#U$
   (ii) $\#A$
   (iii) $\#B$
   (iv) $\#C$
   (v) $\#(A \cap B \cap C)$
   (vi) $\#(B \cup C)$
   (vii) $\#(A \cup B \cup C)$
   (viii) $\#[(A \cup B \cup C)']$
   (ix) $\#[(A \cap B)\backslash C]$
   (x) $\#[(B \cup C)\backslash A]$
   (xi) $\#[B \backslash (A \cup C)]$
   (xii) $\#(A \cup B) - \#(A \cap B)$

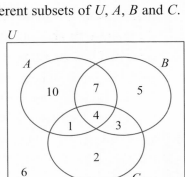

3. 46 people were asked which of the three countries Canada, France or Russia they had visited last year. They answered as follows: 26 visited Canada, 18 visited France, 17 visited Russia, 9 visited Canada and France, 12 visited Canada and Russia, 8 visited France and Russia, and 5 visited all three countries.

   (i) Illustrate the information on a Venn diagram.

   (ii) How many people visited:

       (a) None of the three countries   (b) Russia but not Canada or France

       (c) Only one of the three countries   (d) At least one of these countries

       (e) Canada or Russia   (f) Canada and France but not Russia

4. A survey was taken of a group of 44 students, each of whom was studying one or more of the three subjects History, Geography and Art. 28 students studied History. 30 students studied Geography. 22 students studied Art. 6 students studied History only. 15 students studied both History and Geography. 3 students studied all three subjects.

   (i) Use a Venn diagram to find the number of students who studied History and Geography but not Art.

   (ii) How many students studied History and Art but not Geography?

   (iii) Let x represent the number of students who studied Geography and Art but not History. Express, in terms of x, the number of students who studied:

       (a) Geography only   (b) Art only

       (c) Put these expressions for x into your Venn diagram.

       (d) Calculate the value of x.

5. 52 fifth year students were asked whether they had chosen Accounting, Biology or Chemistry as one of their subjects in school. The results were as follows.

   30 chose Accounting, 28 chose Biology and 29 chose Chemistry.
   19 chose Accounting and Biology, 3 chose Accounting and Chemistry but not Biology.
   12 chose all three subjects and 4 chose not to take any of these subjects.

   Let x represent the number of students who chose Biology and Chemistry but not Accounting.

   (i) Illustrate the above information in a Venn diagram, expressing, in terms of x, the number of students who chose   (a) Biology only   (b) Chemistry only.

   (ii) Calculate the value of x.

   (iii) How many students chose:

       (a) Biology only   (b) Chemistry only   (c) Two of these subjects

       (d) At least two of these subjects

6. An auctioneer has 60 houses for sale. 6 of these houses have a garage and a conservatory and gas central heating, 10 have a conservatory and gas central heating, 5 have a garage and a conservatory but no gas central heating, 13 have a garage and gas central heating.

11 have none of these three features. Equal numbers of these houses have only one of the three features.

   (i) Using x to represent the number of these houses that have only one of these features, illustrate the above information in a Venn diagram.

  (ii) Calculate the value of x.

 (iii) How many of these houses do not have a garage or gas central heating?

7.   A survey was taken of a group of 33 people, each of whom read one or more of the magazines P, Q and R. The results are shown in the Venn diagram.

   (i) Calculate the value of x.

  (ii) How many of this group read only one of these magazines?

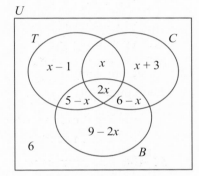

8.   All 30 students in a class were asked which of the three modes of transport they used to travel to school, train, T, car, C, or bus, B, in the past year. The results are shown in the Venn diagram.

   (i) Calculate the value of x.

  (ii) How many of these pupils used two of these modes of transport to travel to school?

9.   Three tasks, A, B and C, were given to a group of people. Each person completed at least one task. The number who completed A and B and C was x. 23 completed A, 22 completed B and 16 completed C.

9 completed A and B, 6 completed A and C, 1 completed B and C.

   (i) Express, in terms of x, the number of people who completed:

     (a) A and B but not C

     (b) A and C but not B

     (c) B and C but not A

     (d) A only, B only and C only

  (ii) Hence, complete, in terms of x, the Venn diagram.

 (iii) If there were 43 people in the group, calculate the value of x.

10. As 55 people left a fruit market they were asked if they had bought apples or bananas or clementines. The results were as follows.

29 bought apples, 34 bought bananas and 27 bought clementines.
15 bought apples and bananas, 16 bought apples and clementines, 17 bought bananas and clementines. 3 bought none of these fruits.

   (i) Using x to represent those people who bought all three fruits, illustrate the above information in a Venn diagram.

   (ii) Calculate the value of x.

11. In a club of 46 people, 21 played darts, 22 played chess and 27 played snooker. 11 played both darts and chess, 10 played both darts and snooker, 13 played chess and snooker. 6 did not play any of these three games.

   (i) Using x to represent the number of people in the club who played all three games, illustrate the above information in a Venn diagram.

   (ii) Calculate the value of x.

   (iii) Calculate the number of people in the club who played (a) only one of these games (b) at least two of these games.

12. Three problems, P, Q and R, were given to a set of pupils. Each pupil solved at least one problem. 25 solved P,, 24 solved Q and 18 solved R. 8 solved P and Q and R. 12 solved P and Q, 3 solved P and R but not Q.

   (i) How many pupils solved P and Q but not R?

   (ii) How many pupils solved P only?

   (iii) Find the (a) maximum (b) minimum number of pupils that could have solved P or Q or R.

   (iv) If there were 39 pupils in all, how many pupils solved Q and R but not P?

   (Hint: Let $\#[(Q \cap R \setminus P] = x$.)

13. A survey was taken of a number of people as to which of the three forms of exercise, running (R), walking (W) or cycling (C), they did to keep fit. Each person used one or more of these exercises. The results were as follows. 25 run, 16 walk and 22 cycle. 10 run and walk, 11 run and cycle, 8 walk and cycle. Let x be the number that take all three forms of exercise.

   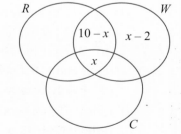

   (i) Complete, in terms of x, the Venn diagram.

   (ii) Show that the number of people that use at least one of these forms of exercise is $x + 34$.

   (iii) Find (a) the greatest and (b) the least value of x.

   (iv) Hence or otherwise, find the greatest number of people that were in the survey.

   (v) If a total of 40 people took part in the survey, calculate the value of x.

14. A survey was taken of 54 students, each of whom was studying one or more of the three subjects A, B and C.

6 students studied B and C.

5 students studied A and C.

3 times as many students studied A and B as studied all 3 subjects.

20 students altogether studied B.

17 students studied C only and 14 students studied A only.

Using x to represent those students who studied all three subjects, illustrate the above information in a Venn diagram. Calculate the value of x.

15. A group of people were asked which of the games football, F, badminton, B, and tennis, T, they play. The results are shown in the Venn diagram.

11 played badminton and tennis. 23 played badminton.

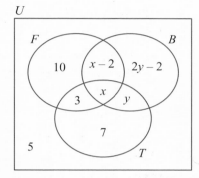

  (i) Write down two equations in x and y.

 (ii) Solve your two equations simultaneously.

(iii) How many people play:

    (a) All three games **(b)** Football **(c)** Tennis

    (d) Badminton and tennis but not football

    (e) Football and badminton but not tennis

(iv) Calculate the total number of people in the group.

Investigating sets

Sets and the number of regions on a Venn diagram

There are many relationships between the number of regions on a Venn diagram, the number of sets and the number of statements needed to numerically complete a Venn diagram. By investigation, we may be able to find a pattern of results which suggest a relationship.

EXAMPLE

  (i) Draw a Venn diagram showing sets A and B.

 (ii) How many regions are there?

(iii) Show that it is not possible to complete the diagram using **only two** of the following statements:

    (a) $\#A = 10$ **(b)** $\#(A \cap B) = 4$ **(c)** $\#(A \cup B) = 21$

(iv) Suggest a connection between the number of regions and the number of statements needed to complete the diagram.

Solution:

(i)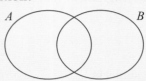

(ii) 3 regions

(iii) There are three possibilities.

(a) and (b):	(a) and (c):	(b) and (c):
4 in the centre	21 altogether	4 in the centre
10 in A, 6 in A only	10 in A ∴ 11 in B only	17 remaining

A 6 4 ? B	A ? ? 11 B	A ? 4 ? B

Thus, it is not possible to complete the diagram with any two of the given statements.

(iv) Using the **three** statements, it **is** possible to complete the diagram.

Perhaps the connection is that to complete **three** regions, we need **three** statements.

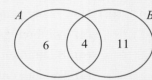

The associative property

We have met a number of arithmetical operations such as addition (+) and multiplication (×). Most of the arithmetical operations that we are familiar with need **two** numbers. The associative property of an operation concerns the outcome when we are handling **three** numbers.

Suppose a, b and c are three numbers and we are asked to calculate $a + b + c$. Because we only add two numbers at a time, should we calculate

$$(a + b) + c \quad \text{or} \quad a + (b + c)?$$

Fortunately, addition is associative (the different grouping does not affect the answer) and we can calculate it either way. It is best if you follow the **BEMDAS** rule, which tells us to work from left to right when we have operations (such as addition) of similar importance.

Subtraction is not associative as $a - b - c$ cannot be written as both $(a - b) - c$ and $a - (b - c)$. One of them is correct but the other is wrong.

Sets also have a number of operations that we can perform on them. If we can write $A \cup B \cup C$ as either $(A \cup B) \cup C$ or $A \cup (B \cup C)$, then we can say set union is associative.

The distributive property

In algebra, we often meet expressions with brackets and multiply them out, as in

$$6(a + 2b)$$
$$= 6a + 12b$$

If we look at this in detail, we can see that we begin with **one** multiplication and spread it over the adding part of the expression to create **two** multiplications.

$$6 \times (a + 2b)$$
$$= (6 \times a) + (12 \times b)$$

We can see this when we break up a bar of chocolate:

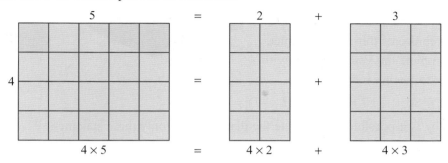

$$20 = 4 \times 5 = 4 \times (2 + 3) = (4 \times 2) + (4 \times 3) = 8 + 12$$

Thus, we can say that multiplication is distributive over addition.

However, the converse is not true because we know that $4 + (a \times b) \neq (4 + a) \times (4 + b)$. Thus, addition is not distributive over multiplication.

In general, we can say that $*$ is distributive over $\Box$ if $x * (y \Box z) = (x * y) \Box (x * z)$.

Exercise 14.4

1. (i)   Draw separate Venn diagrams with a universal set containing:
    (a) A set A
    (b) Sets A and B
    (c) Sets A, B and C
    How many regions are there in each diagram?   *2, 4, 8*   *2*

    (ii) Can you predict the number of regions for a universal set with four sets?   *4*

    (iii) Does the pattern work if the universal set does not contain a set?

    (iv) Would a universal set containing 10 sets have **(i)** less than or **(ii)** greater than 1,000 regions?   *2^{10} greater*

2. (i)   Draw a Venn diagram with a universal set and two sets P and Q.

    (ii) How many regions are there on the diagram?   *4*

    (iii) Select three of the following statements and try to complete the diagram.
    $$\#P = 14, \quad \#Q = 18, \quad \#(P \cup Q) = 24, \quad \#P' = 22$$

    (iv) Use the four statements to complete the diagram.

    (v)   Can you draw a conclusion from parts **(iii)** and **(iv)** as to how many statements are needed to complete a diagram as described in part **(i)**?

3. (i) Draw a Venn diagram with a universal set and two sets L and T.

    (ii) A survey was taken on the proportion of people who had a laptop or a tablet computer. If L represents those with a laptop and T represents those with a tablet, complete the Venn diagram with the following information:

$$\#L = 80\%, \quad \#T = 25\%, \quad \#(L \cup T)' = 11\%.$$

    (iii) Why is it possible to complete the diagram with only three statements?

    (iv) If there were 75 people surveyed, how many had a laptop and a tablet computer?

4. $A = \{s, p, i, e, r\}$, $B = \{i, d, r, m, a\}$ and $C = \{e, r, m, a, n\}$.

    (i) Show this information on a Venn diagram.

    (ii) List the elements of (a) $A \cup B$ (b) $B \cup C$.

    (iii) Hence, find (a) $(A \cup B) \cup C$ (b) $A \cup (B \cup C)$.

    (iv) Does this prove that set union is associative?

5. (i) Draw two Venn diagrams, each with a universal set and three sets X, Y and Z.

    (ii) On one diagram, shade the part represented by $X \cup Y$.
    Hence, shade the part represented by $(X \cup Y) \cup Z$.

    (iii) On the other diagram, shade the part represented by $Y \cup Z$.
    Hence, shade the part represented by $X \cup (Y \cup Z)$.

    (iv) Compare the two diagrams. Does this prove that set union is associative?

6. $E = \{f, r, a, t, i\}$, $F = \{a, c, i, o\}$ and $G = \{t, i, o, n\}$.

    (i) Show this information on a Venn diagram.

    (ii) List the elements of (a) $E \cap F$ (b) $F \cap G$.

    (iii) Hence, find (a) $(E \cap F) \cap G$ (b) $E \cap (F \cap G)$.

    (iv) Does this prove that set intersection is associative?

7. (i) Draw two Venn diagrams, each with a universal set and three sets X, Y and Z.

    (ii) On one diagram, shade the part represented by $X \cap Y$.
    Hence, indicate the part represented by $(X \cap Y) \cap Z$.

    (iii) On the other diagram, shade the part represented by $Y \cap Z$.
    Hence, indicate the part represented by $X \cap (Y \cap Z)$.

    (iv) Compare the two diagrams. Does this prove that set intersection is associative?

8. $L = \{t, r, a, n\}$, $M = \{r, i, n, g\}$ and $N = \{a, n, g, l, e\}$.

    (i) Show this information on a Venn diagram.

    (ii) List the elements of (a) $L \setminus M$ (b) $M \setminus N$.

    (iii) Hence, find **(a)** $(L \setminus M) \setminus N$ **(b)** $L \setminus (M \setminus N)$.

    (iv) Does this prove that set difference is associative?

9. $P = \{p, l, a, r, o\}$, $Q = \{a, y, g, o, u, n\}$ and $R = \{r, o, u, n, d\}$.

    (i) Show this information on a Venn diagram.

    (ii) List the elements of $Q \cap R$.

    (iii) Hence, find $P \cup (Q \cap R)$.

    (iv) List the elements of **(a)** $P \cup Q$ **(b)** $P \cup R$.

    (v) Hence, find $(P \cup Q) \cap (P \cup R)$.

    (vi) Compare the results from **(iii)** and **(v)**.
        What property seems to be true?

10.   **(i)** Draw a Venn diagram with sets X, Y and Z.
        Shade $Y \cap Z$ and hence shade $X \cup (Y \cap Z)$.

    (ii) Draw separate Venn diagrams with sets X, Y and Z showing:
        (a) $X \cup Y$ **(b)** $X \cup Z$ **(c)** $(X \cup Y) \cap (X \cup Z)$.

    (iii) Which distributive property have you proved?

11. $R = \{t, r, a, p, o\}$, $S = \{a, m, o, l\}$ and $T = \{p, o, l, i, n, e\}$.

    (i) Show this information on a Venn diagram.

    (ii) List the elements of $S \cup T$.

    (iii) Hence, find $R \cap (S \cup T)$.

    (iv) List the elements of **(a)** $R \cap S$ **(b)** $R \cap T$.

    (v) Hence, find $(R \cap S) \cup (R \cap T)$.

    (vi) Compare the results from **(iii)** and **(v)**.
        What property seems to be true?

12.   **(i)** Draw two Venn diagrams, each with sets X, Y and Z.
        Shade $Y \cup Z$ on the first and hence shade $X \cap (Y \cup Z)$ on the second.

    (ii) Draw a Venn diagram with sets X, Y and Z showing $(X \cap Y) \cup (X \cap Z)$.

    (iii) Which distributive property have you proved?

Midpoint of a line segment

If (x_1, y_1) and (x_2, y_2) are two points, their midpoint is given by the formula:

$$\text{Midpoint} = \left(\frac{x_1 + x_2}{2}, \frac{y_1 + y_2}{2} \right)$$

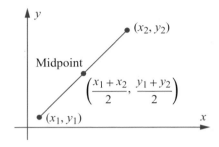

In words:

$$\left(\frac{\text{add the } x \text{ coordinates}}{2}, \frac{\text{add the } y \text{ coordinates}}{2} \right)$$

EXAMPLE 1

$P(5, 6)$ and $Q(7, -4)$ are two points. Find the coordinates of R, the midpoint of $[PQ]$.

Solution:

$P(5, 6)$ $Q(7, -4)$

(x_1, y_1) (x_2, y_2)

$x_1 = 5, y_1 = 6$ $x_2 = 7, y_2 = -4$

$$\text{Midpoint } R = \left(\frac{x_1 + x_2}{2}, \frac{y_1 + y_2}{2} \right)$$

$$= \left(\frac{5 + 7}{2}, \frac{-4 + 6}{2} \right)$$

$$= \left(\frac{12}{2}, \frac{2}{2} \right) = (6, 1)$$

An alternative approach is to consider the midpoint of a line segment as the **average** of its end points.

EXAMPLE 2

$A(-1, 7)$ and $B(9, 3)$ are two points. Find the coordinates of C, the midpoint of $[AB]$.

Solution:

Add points

A	$(-1,$	$7)$
B	$(9,$	$3)$
	$(-1 + 9,$	$7 + 3)$
	$(8,$	$10)$
Midpoint C	$(4,$	$5)$

Divide each coordinate by 2

Given the midpoint

In some questions we will be given the midpoint and one end point of a line segment and be asked to find the other end point.

To find the other end point, use the following method.

1. Make a rough diagram.
2. Find the translation that maps (moves) the given end point to the midpoint.
3. Apply the same translation to the midpoint to find the other end point.

EXAMPLE 3

If $M(6, 5)$ is the midpoint of $[PQ]$ and $P = (3, 7)$, find the coordinates of Q.

Solution:

Step 1: Rough diagram.

$P(3, 7)$ $M(6, 5)$ $Q(\ ,\ )$ [missing coordinates]

Step 2: Translation from P to M. Rule: Add 3 to x, subtract 2 from y.

Step 3: Apply this translation to M.

$$M(6, 5) \rightarrow (6 + 3, 5 - 2) = (9, 3)$$

$\therefore$ The coordinates of Q are $(9, 3)$.

Exercise 15.1

In questions 1–12, find the midpoint of the line segment whose end points are given.

1. $(3, 2)$ and $(5, 4)$
2. $(6, 8)$ and $(4, -2)$
3. $(10, 0)$ and $(8, -6)$
4. $(-3, 7)$ and $(-9, 3)$
5. $(-6, -5)$ and $(-10, -1)$
6. $(-8, 7)$ and $(4, -3)$
7. $(8, 8)$ and $(-2, -2)$
8. $(-7, 5)$ and $(9, -7)$
9. $(5, -1)$ and $(2, -3)$
10. $\left(3\frac{1}{2}, 1\frac{1}{4}\right)$ and $\left(2\frac{1}{2}, \frac{3}{4}\right)$
11. $\left(2\frac{1}{2}, -1\frac{1}{2}\right)$ and $\left(1\frac{1}{2}, \frac{1}{2}\right)$
12. $\left(5\frac{1}{2}, 7\frac{1}{4}\right)$ and $\left(-2\frac{1}{2}, -2\frac{1}{4}\right)$

13. If $M(3, 1)$ is the midpoint of $[PQ]$ and $P = (1, 0)$, find the coordinates of Q.

14. If $M(-3, -3)$ is the midpoint of $[AB]$ and $A = (-1, -5)$, find the coordinates of B.

15. The point $(4, -2)$ is the midpoint of the line segment joining $(-2, 1)$ and (p, q). Find the value of p and the value of q.

16. The point (1, 6) is the midpoint of the line segment joining (a, b) and (4, 7). Find the value of a and the value of b.

17. If the midpoint of (p, q) and (−4, 7) is the same as the midpoint of (4, −3) and (−2, 7), find the value of p and the value of q.

18. Five streetlights are to be placed in a line and evenly spaced. If the first light is placed at (2, 3) and the last is at (10, 15), where should the others be placed?

Distance between two points

If (x_1, y_1) and (x_2, y_2) are two points, the distance, d, between them is given by the formula:

$$d = \sqrt{(x_2 - x_1)^2 + (y_2 - y_1)^2}$$

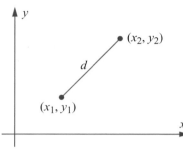

Note: Always decide which point is (x_1, y_1) and which point is (x_2, y_2) before you use the formula. The distance between the points A and B is written $|AB|$.

EXAMPLE

$A(5, 2)$, $B(8, 6)$, $C(6, −1)$ and $D(5, 7)$ are four points.

Calculate: (i) $|AB|$ (ii) $|CD|$

Solution:

(i) $A(5, 2)$ and $B(8, 6)$
(x_1, y_1) (x_2, y_2)
$x_1 = 5, y_1 = 2$ $x_2 = 8, y_2 = 6$

$|AB| = \sqrt{(x_2 - x_1)^2 + (y_2 - y_1)^2}$

$= \sqrt{(8 - 5)^2 + (6 - 2)^2}$

$= \sqrt{(3)^2 + (4)^2}$

$= \sqrt{9 + 16}$

$= \sqrt{25} = 5$

(ii) $C(6, −1)$ and $D(5, 7)$
(x_1, y_1) (x_2, y_2)
$x_1 = 6, y_1 = −1$ $x_2 = 5, y_2 = 7$

$|CD| = \sqrt{(x_2 - x_1)^2 + (y_2 - y_1)^2}$

$= \sqrt{(5 - 6)^2 + (7 + 1)^2}$

$= \sqrt{(-1)^2 + (8)^2}$

$= \sqrt{1 + 64}$

$= \sqrt{65}$

Exercise 15.2

In questions 1–12, find the distance between the pair of points.

1. (5, 2) and (8, 6)
2. (1, 1) and (7, 9)
3. (3, 4) and (5, 5)

4. (1, −3) and (2, 5)
5. (2, 0) and (5, 0)
6. (3, −4) and (3, 2)

7. (3, −6) and (−3, −4)
8. (−2, 2) and (−7, −3)
9. (−7, −2) and (−1, −4)

10. (2, −4) and (−4, 2)
11. $\left(\frac{1}{2}, \frac{1}{2}\right)$ and $\left(2\frac{1}{2}, 1\frac{1}{2}\right)$
12. $\left(\frac{3}{2}, -\frac{1}{2}\right)$ and $\left(\frac{9}{2}, \frac{1}{2}\right)$

13. Verify that the triangle with vertices $A(3, -2)$, $B(-2, 1)$ and $C(1, 6)$ is isosceles. (An isosceles triangle has two sides of equal length.)

14. Find the radius of a circle with centre (2, 2) and containing the point (5, 6).

15. $A(3, 2)$, $B(-1, 5)$ and $C(6, 0)$ are three points.

    (i) Which point is nearest to (2, 1)?

    (ii) Which point is furthest from (2, 1)?

16. $X(2, 3)$, $Y(-1, 6)$ and $Z(1, 8)$ are three points. Show that $|XY|^2 + |YZ|^2 = |XZ|^2$.

17. Find the coordinates of M, the midpoint of the line segment joining $P(7, 4)$ and $Q(-1, -2)$. Show that $|PM| = |QM|$.

18. $A(6, 2)$, $B(-4, -4)$ and $C(4, -10)$ are the coordinates of the triangle ABC.

    (i) Find the coordinates of P, the midpoint of $[AB]$.

    (ii) Find the coordinates of Q, the midpoint of $[AC]$.

    (iii) Verify that $|PQ| = \frac{1}{2}|BC|$.

19. $A(1, 0)$, $B(6, 1)$, $C(9, 4)$ and $D(4, 3)$ form a quadrilateral $ABCD$.

    (i) Draw these points on a coordinated diagram.

    (ii) What type of quadrilateral is $ABCD$?

    (iii) Find the length of each side. Are each pair of opposite sides equal in measure?

    (iv) Find the midpoint of the diagonal $[AC]$.

    (v) How could you show that the diagonals bisect each other?

20. $A(-6, 3)$, $B(14, 18)$ and $C(50, -30)$ form a triangle. Show that the length of each side is less than the sum of the other two.

21. A map of a shopping centre is shown here.

    (i) Why is it easier to calculate $|AP|$ than $|PQ|$?

    (ii) Which is the shorter path from A to B?

    (iii) Would it be possible to reduce the distance on either path?

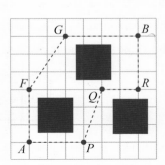

22. A group of nine houses is situated at $(2, 2)$, $(2, 6)$, $(-1, 10)$, $(-1, 14)$, $(6, 18)$, $(7, 14)$, $(7, 10)$, $(10, 6)$ and $(10, 2)$.

Each house is to be connected to a new fibre optic cable for TV and internet and each house is already wired to a suitable connecting point near it. Each of the connecting points is 2 units from its corresponding house.

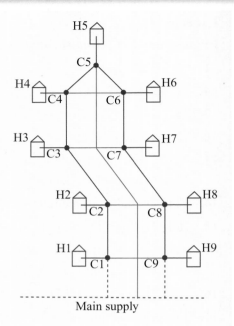

Two options are available:

A. Create a ring from the main supply to connecting points C1 to C9. This is shown in blue on the diagram. C1 and C9 are each 3 units from the main supply.

B. Put a single cable down the centre of the road and use longer connections to each of C1 to C9. This is shown in red.

(i) What are the coordinates of each of the connecting points?

(ii) If option A is used, what is the total length of fibre optic cable needed?

(iii) If option B is used, what is the total length of fibre optic cable needed?

(iv) Why would the service supplier choose the option requiring the greater amount of cable?

Slope of a line

All mathematical graphs are read from **left to right**.

The measure of the steepness of a line is called the **slope**.

The vertical distance (up or down) is called the **rise**.

The horizontal distance (left or right) is called the **run**.

The slope of a line is defined as:

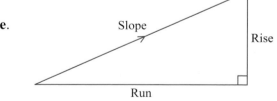

$$\boxed{\text{Slope} = \frac{\text{Rise}}{\text{Run}}}$$

Note: This is also equal to the tangent ratio in trigonometry.

The rise can be negative, and in this case it is often called the **fall** or **drop**.

If the rise is zero, then the slope is also zero.

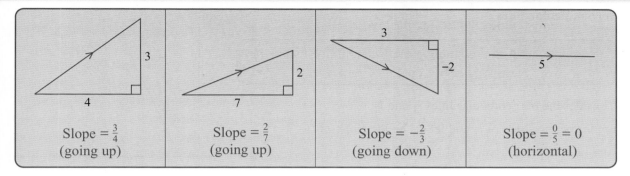

| Slope $= \frac{3}{4}$ (going up) | Slope $= \frac{2}{7}$ (going up) | Slope $= -\frac{2}{3}$ (going down) | Slope $= \frac{0}{5} = 0$ (horizontal) |

Slope of a line when given two points on the line

If a line contains two points (x_1, y_1) and (x_2, y_2), then the slope of the line is given by the formula:

$$m = \frac{y_2 - y_1}{x_2 - x_1}$$

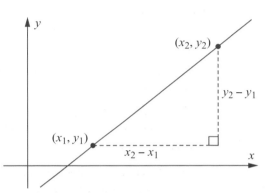

EXAMPLE 1

Find the slope of a line containing the points $(-2, 5)$ and $(3, 8)$.

Solution:

$(-2, 5)$ $(3, 8)$

(x_1, y_1) (x_2, y_2)

$x_1 = -2, y_1 = 5$ $x_2 = 3, y_2 = 8$

$\text{Slope} = \dfrac{y_2 - y_1}{x_2 - x_1}$

$= \dfrac{8 - 5}{3 + 2}$

$= \dfrac{3}{5}$

Parallel lines

> If two lines are **parallel**, they have equal slopes (and vice versa).

Consider the parallel lines l_1 and l_2.

In each case, the line makes the same angle with the x-axis.

Let m_1 be the slope of l_1 and let m_2 be the slope of l_2.

As $l_1 \| l_2$, then $m_1 = m_2$.

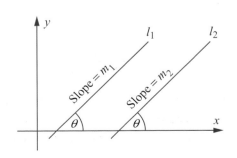

Perpendicular lines

> If two lines are **perpendicular**, when we multiply their slopes we always get -1 (and vice versa).

Consider the perpendicular lines l_1 and l_2.

Let m_1 be the slope of l_1 and let m_2 be the slope of l_2.

As $l_1 \perp l_2$, then $m_1 \times m_2 = -1$.

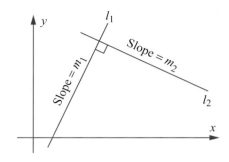

Note: If we know the slope of a line and we need to find the slope of a line perpendicular to it, simply do the following:

> Turn the known slope upside down and change its sign.

For example, if a line has a slope of $-\frac{3}{4}$, then the slope of a line perpendicular to it has a slope of $\frac{4}{3}$ (turn upside down and change its sign), because $-\frac{3}{4} \times \frac{4}{3} = -1$.

EXAMPLE 2

$A(2, 4)$, $B(7, 8)$, $C(2, 0)$ and $D(7, 4)$ are four points. Show that $AB \parallel CD$.

Solution:

Let $m_1 =$ the slope of AB and $m_2 =$ the slope of CD.

$A(2, 4)$	$B(7, 8)$	$C(2, 0)$	$D(7, 4)$
(x_1, y_1)	(x_2, y_2)	(x_1, y_1)	(x_2, y_2)
$x_1 = 2, y_1 = 4$	$x_2 = 7, y_2 = 8$	$x_1 = 2, y_1 = 0$	$x_2 = 7, y_2 = 4$

$$m_1 = \frac{y_2 - y_1}{x_2 - x_1} \qquad\qquad m_2 = \frac{y_2 - y_1}{x_2 - x_1}$$

$$= \frac{8 - 4}{7 - 2} \qquad\qquad\qquad = \frac{4 - 0}{7 - 2}$$

$$= \frac{4}{5} \qquad\qquad\qquad\qquad = \frac{4}{5}$$

$$m_1 = m_2$$
$$\therefore AB \parallel CD$$

EXAMPLE 3

$P(2, 5)$, $Q(6, 3)$ and $R(0, 1)$ are three points. Verify that $PQ \perp PR$.

Solution:

Let m_1 = the slope of PQ and m_2 = the slope of PR.

$P(2, 5)$	$Q(6, 3)$	$P(2, 5)$	$R(0, 1)$
(x_1, y_1)	(x_2, y_2)	(x_1, y_1)	(x_2, y_2)
$x_1 = 2, y_1 = 5$	$x_2 = 6, y_2 = 3$	$x_1 = 2, y_1 = 5$	$x_2 = 0, y_2 = 1$

$$m_1 = \frac{y_2 - y_1}{x_2 - x_1}$$

$$= \frac{3 - 5}{6 - 2}$$

$$= \frac{-2}{4}$$

$$= -\frac{1}{2}$$

$$m_2 = \frac{y_2 - y_1}{x_2 - x_1}$$

$$= \frac{1 - 5}{0 - 2}$$

$$= \frac{-4}{-2}$$

$$= 2$$

$$m_1 \times m_2 = -\frac{1}{2} \times 2 = -1$$

$$\therefore PQ \perp PR$$

Exercise 15.3

1. Write down the slope of the line t in each of the following.

(i)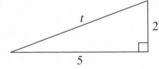

(ii)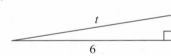

(iii)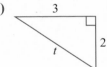

2. The diagram shows lines a, b, c, d, e and f.

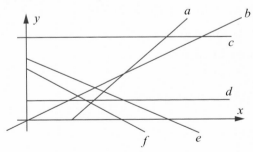

  (i)   Which lines have a negative slope?

 (ii)   Which lines have a zero slope?

(iii)   Which lines have a positive slope?

In questions 3–12, find the slope of the line containing the given pair of points.

3. (1, 2) and (4, 5)

4. (2, 2) and (6, 8)

5. (2, 0) and (10, 8)

6. (0, 0) and (3, 5)

7. (5, 7) and (8, 4)

8. (−4, 6) and (7, −2)

9. (−3, −6) and (−5, −4)

10. (−2, 3) and (−3, −7)

11. $\left(\frac{3}{2}, \frac{1}{2}\right)$ and $\left(\frac{7}{2}, -\frac{3}{2}\right)$

12. $\left(-\frac{1}{4}, \frac{7}{2}\right)$ and $\left(\frac{3}{4}, \frac{3}{2}\right)$

13. $A(-4, -3)$, $B(-1, 1)$, $C(2, 2)$ and $D(5, 6)$ are four points. Verify that $AB \parallel CD$.

14. $P(4, 3)$, $Q(-2, 0)$, $R(-1, 1)$ and $S(-2, 3)$ are four points. Show that $PQ \perp RS$.

15. $X(8, -4)$, $Y(7, -1)$ and $Z(1, -3)$ are three points. Prove that $XY \perp ZY$.

16. $A(-6, 2)$, $B(-2, 1)$ and $C(0, 9)$ are the vertices of triangle ABC. Prove that $|\angle ABC| = 90°$.

17. Show that the points $A(6, -4)$, $B(5, -1)$, $C(-1, -3)$ and $D(0, -6)$ are the vertices of a rectangle.

18. The line k has a slope of $-\frac{3}{4}$. Find the slope of l if $k \perp l$.

19. The line m has a slope of $\frac{5}{3}$. Find the slope of l if $m \perp l$.

20. The line t has a slope of $-\frac{1}{3}$. Find the slope of k if $t \parallel k$.

21. The line l has a slope of $\frac{1}{4}$. Find the slope of m if $l \perp m$.

22. The line k has a slope of -3. Find the slope of l if $l \perp k$.

23. The height of a tree in 2007 was 6·5 m tall. By 2010, its height was 8 m.

   (i) By finding the slope, find the rate of growth of the tree per year.

   (ii) If the tree continues to grow at this rate, what should its height be in 2020?

24. A mountain has ski stations at the following points:
(0, 0), (10, 5), (24, 7), (30, 9), (40, 12), (30, 15),
(15, 17), (35, 22) and (25, 30).

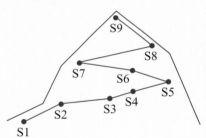

   The skiing sections are graded Beginners, Experienced and Expert. Beginners sections must have a slope below $\frac{1}{3}$, while Expert sections have slopes greater than $\frac{3}{4}$.

   (i) Show this on a coordinated graph.

   (ii) Calculate the slope of each section.

   (iii) Why are some of the slopes negative?

   (iv) How would each section be graded?

25. The brakes on a car are tested on a hill as shown on the diagram. It is considered unsafe to park a car on steeper hills. A road follows the following path over a mountain:

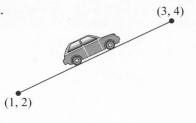

(0, 0), (2, 5), (4, 7), (6, 8), (10, 11), (13, 7), (16, 5), (20, 3) and (25, 0).

  (i) Show this on a coordinated graph.
  (ii) Calculate the slope of each section.
  (iii) Why are some of the slopes negative?
  (iv) Which sections are safe for parking?

26. Would a plane flying in a straight line from Dublin (−6, 53·5) to Luxembourg (6, 49·5) fly directly over either Birmingham (−2, 52·5) or London (0, 51·5)?

Equation of a line 1

Plot the points (−1, 8), (0, 6), (1, 4), (2, 2), (3, 0) and (4, −2).

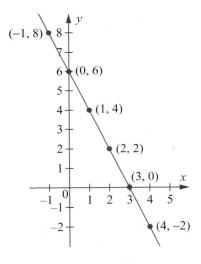

The points all lie on the same straight line.
In this set of points there is the same relationship (connection, link) between the x coordinate and the y coordinate for each point.

If we double the x coordinate and add the y coordinate, the result is always 6.

That is:

$$2x + y = 6$$

This result will hold for every other point on the line.
We say '$2x + y = 6$' is the equation of the line.

Note: $2x + y - 6 = 0$ is also the equation of the line.

To verify that a point belongs to a line

Once we have the equation of a line, we can determine if a point is on the line or not on the line. If a point belongs to a line, its coordinates will satisfy the equation of the line. We substitute the coordinates of the point into the equation of the line. If they satisfy the equation, then the point is **on** the line. Otherwise, the point is **not** on the line.

EXAMPLE 1

Investigate if the points $(2, -1)$ and $(5, -4)$ are on the line $5x + 3y - 7 = 0$.

Solution:

$(2, -1)$ $\quad 5x + 3y - 1 = 0$
Substitute $x = 2$ and $y = -1$.
$$5(2) + 3(-1) - 7$$
$$= 10 - 3 - 7$$
$$= 10 - 10$$
$$= 0$$

Satisfies equation.
$\therefore (2, -1)$ is on the line.

$(5, -4)$ $\quad 5x + 3y - 1 = 0$
Substitute $x = 5$ and $y = -4$.
$$5(5) + 3(-4) - 7$$
$$= 25 - 12 - 7$$
$$= 25 - 19$$
$$= 6 \neq 0$$

Does not satisfy equation.
$\therefore (5, -4)$ is not on the line.

EXAMPLE 2

The equation of the line l is $5x + 4y + 3 = 0$ and the equation of the line m is $3x + ty - 8 = 0$.

The point $(-3, k)$ is on the line l and the point $(2, -1)$ is on the line m.

Find the value of k and the value of t.

Solution:

$$5x + 4y + 3 = 0$$
Substitute $x = -3$ and $y = k$.
$(-3, k)$: $\quad 5(-3) + 4(k) + 3 = 0$
$$-15 + 4k + 3 = 0$$
$$4k - 12 = 0$$
$$4k = 12$$
$$k = 3$$

$$3x + ty - 8 = 0$$
Substitute $x = 2$ and $y = -1$.
$(2, -1)$: $\quad 3(2) + t(-1) - 8 = 0$
$$6 - t - 8 = 0$$
$$-t - 2 = 0$$
$$-t = 2$$
$$t = -2$$

Exercise 15.4

In questions 1–10, investigate whether the point is on the line.

1. $(4, 1)$; $x + y - 5 = 0$

2. $(3, -1)$; $2x + 3y - 3 = 0$

3. $(2, 2)$; $5x - 4y - 1 = 0$

4. $(-3, -2)$; $6x - 7y + 4 = 0$

5. $(-4, 3)$; $3x + 2y - 8 = 0$

6. $(5, 2)$; $3x - 7y - 1 = 0$

7. $(-3, -1)$; $4x + y - 15 = 0$ 8. $(2, 1)$; $x - 4y = 0$

9. $\left(\frac{5}{2}, \frac{3}{2}\right)$; $6x - 2y - 12 = 0$ 10. $\left(\frac{2}{3}, \frac{1}{3}\right)$; $3x - 6y + 3 = 0$

11. l is the line $x - 4y - 5 = 0$. Verify that the point $P(1, -1)$ is on l.

12. The point $(1, 2)$ is on the line $3x + 2y = k$. Find the value of k.

13. The point $(t, 3)$ is on the line $4x - 3y + 1 = 0$. Find the value of t.

14. The point $(-3, k)$ is on the line $5x + 4y + 3 = 0$. Find the value of k.

15. The point $(1, -2)$ is on the line $4x + ky - 14 = 0$. Find the value of k.

16. The point $(-3, -4)$ is on the line $ax - 5y - 8 = 0$. Find the value of a.

Equation of a line 2

To find the equation of a line, we need:

1. The slope of the line, m.   2. A point on the line, (x_1, y_1).

Then use the formula: $\boxed{(y - y_1) = m\,(x - x_1)}$

In short, we need the **slope** and a **point** on the line.

Note: The formula given in the mathematical tables is $y - y_1 = m(x - x_1)$.

The extra brackets will make it easier to use when the value of m is a fraction.

 EXAMPLE

Find the equation of the following lines.

  (i) Containing the point $(2, -3)$ with slope 3
 (ii) Containing the point $(-4, 2)$ with slope $-\frac{2}{3}$

Solution:

Containing $(2, -3)$ with slope 3:

$$x_1 = 2, \quad y_1 = -3, \quad m = 3$$
$$(y - y_1) = m(x - x_1)$$
$$(y + 3) = 3(x - 2)$$
$$y + 3 = 3x - 6$$
$$-3x + y + 3 + 6 = 0$$
$$-3x + y + 9 = 0$$
$$3x - y - 9 = 0$$

Containing $(-4, 2)$ with slope $-\frac{2}{3}$:

$$x_1 = -4, \quad y_1 = 2, \quad m = -\frac{2}{3}$$
$$(y - y_1) = m(x - x_1)$$
$$(y - 2) = -\frac{2}{3}(x + 4)$$
(multiply both sides by 3)
$$3(y - 2) = -2(x + 4)$$
$$3y - 6 = -2x - 8$$
$$2x + 3y - 6 + 8 = 0$$
$$2x + 3y + 2 = 0$$

Exercise 15.5

In questions 1–10, find the equation of the line.

1. Containing (4, 1) with slope 2

2. Containing (−1, −1) with slope 3

3. Containing (0, −2) with slope −1

4. Containing (5, −3) with slope −5

5. Containing (0, 0) with slope 4

6. Containing (4, −7) with slope $\frac{3}{5}$

7. Containing (−3, −1) with slope $-\frac{4}{3}$

8. Containing (2, −5) with slope $\frac{5}{4}$

9. Containing (3, −3) with slope $-\frac{1}{6}$

10. Containing (−2, −1) with slope $-\frac{5}{7}$

11. Find the equation of the line k through (2, −1), the slope of k being $\frac{2}{5}$.

12. Find the equation of the line l through (3, −2), the slope of l being $-\frac{1}{2}$.

13. The time required to cook a particular food is 30 minutes plus 20 minutes per kilogram.

    (i) How long would it take to cook 2 kilograms?

    (ii) How long would it take to cook 5 kilograms?

    (iii) Find the equation of the line containing the point (0, 30) with slope 20.

    (iv) Using a suitable scale, graph this line and describe the axes as *Time (mins)* and *Kilograms*, as appropriate.

    (v) Use your graph to find:

       (a) The time needed to cook 3 kilograms

       (b) The time needed to cook 4 kilograms

       (c) How much food can be safely cooked in 2 hours

Equation of a line 3

To find the equation of a line, we need the **slope** and **one point** on the line.

However, in many questions one or both of these are missing.

 EXAMPLE

Find the equation of the line that contains the points $(-4, 7)$ and $(1, 3)$.

Solution:
The slope is missing. We first find the slope and use **either one** of the two points to find the equation.

$(-4, 7) \quad (1, 3)$	Containing $(-4, 7)$ with slope $-\frac{4}{5}$:
$(x_1, y_1) \quad (x_2, y_2)$	
$x_1 = -4, y_1 = 7 \quad x_2 = 1, y_2 = 3$	$x_1 = -4, \quad y_1 = 7, \quad m = -\frac{4}{5}$
$m = \dfrac{y_2 - y_1}{x_2 - x_1}$	$(y - y_1) = m(x - x_1)$
$= \dfrac{3 - 7}{1 + 4}$	$(y - 7) = -\frac{4}{5}(x + 4)$
$= \dfrac{-4}{5}$	$5(y - 7) = -4(x + 4)$
	(multiply both sides by 5)
$m = -\dfrac{4}{5}$	$5y - 35 = -4x - 16$
	$4x + 5y - 35 + 16 = 0$
	$4x + 5y - 19 = 0$

Exercise 15.6

In questions 1–9, find the equation of the line containing the given pair of points.

1. $(2, 5)$ and $(6, 9)$
2. $(1, 8)$ and $(3, 4)$
3. $(4, -6)$ and $(5, -3)$
4. $(1, 1)$ and $(5, 3)$
5. $(8, -3)$ and $(-6, 7)$
6. $(-6, -1)$ and $(-1, 2)$
7. $(1, -5)$ and $(3, -6)$
8. $(2, -2)$ and $(4, 3)$
9. $\left(\frac{1}{2}, -\frac{5}{2}\right)$ and $\left(-\frac{3}{2}, \frac{3}{2}\right)$

10. $A(3, -2)$, $B(2, 3)$ and $C(5, 7)$ are three points. Find the equation of the line containing A if it is:

    (i) Parallel to BC
    (ii) Perpendicular to BC

11. Find the equation of the perpendicular bisectors of the line segments joining:

    (i) $(2, 3)$ and $(6, 1)$
    (ii) $(-1, 2)$ and $(-3, -2)$

12. Find the equation of the line l containing $(5, -1)$ and passing through the midpoint of $(6, 3)$ and $(-2, -1)$.

13. The line l contains the points (2, 2) and (−1, 4). The line k contains the point (−4, 1) and $k \perp l$. Find the equation of k.

14. At age 12, a boy was 140 cm tall. When he reached 16, his height was 170 cm.

   (i) Using an appropriate scale, show these points on a coordinated graph.
   (ii) Use your graph to estimate the height of the boy when:
      (a) He was nine years old
      (b) He will be 20 years old
   (iii) Form an equation that describes the boy's growth.
   (iv) Why is this not a good method of predicting height?
   (v) If growth occurs in stages, could height be described by linking sections of different lines? Explain your answer.
   (vi) Show a possible graph on the same page, making sure it shows the correct heights at ages 12 and 16.

15. A taxi journey is charged as a fixed amount plus an amount per kilometre. A journey of 4 km cost €8 and a journey of 12 km cost €12.

   (i) Express the costs as points in the form (journey, cost).
   (ii) Find the equation of the line passing through these points.
   (iii) Plot the points and construct a line showing the cost of a taxi journey.
   (iv) From your graph or otherwise, find the fixed charge and the charge per kilometre.

Equation of a line 4

The equation of a line is usually written in one of two ways. The first is:

$$ax + by + c = 0$$

In this format, all the terms are on the left side of the equation and it is usual to write the term involving x first, followed by the y term and then the constant. The line $3x - 6y + 11 = 0$ is in this format.

The second way is:

$$y = mx + c$$

This time, the terms are arranged so that the y is on its own on the left and the other terms are on the right (the x term followed by the constant). The line $y = -4x + 3$ is an example.

EXAMPLE

(i) Write $2x - 3y - 6 = 0$ in the form $y = mx + c$.

(ii) Write $y = \frac{3}{4}x - 3$ in the form $ax + by + c = 0$.

Solution:

(i)

$$2x - 3y - 6 = 0$$
$$-3y = -2x + 6$$
$$3y = 2x - 6$$
$$y = \frac{2}{3}x - 2$$

(ii)

$$y = \frac{3}{4}x - 3$$
$$4y = 3x - 12$$
$$-3x + 4y + 12 = 0$$
$$3x - 4y - 12 = 0$$

Exercise 15.7

In questions 1–9, write the equation of the line in the form $y = mx + c$.

1. $2x + 3y - 9 = 0$
2. $5x - 2y - 12 = 0$
3. $3x - 2y - 8 = 0$

4. $4x - 3y + 21 = 0$
5. $3x - y + 8 = 0$
6. $2x - 3y - 15 = 0$

7. $x + 2y - 16 = 0$
8. $x + 2y - 4 = 0$
9. $5x + 2y + 10 = 0$

In questions 10–18, write the equation of the line in the form $ax + by + c = 0$.

10. $y = 3x + 7$
11. $y = -2x + 11$
12. $y = -8x - 5$

13. $y = \frac{2}{3}x + 1$
14. $y = \frac{3}{5}x - 6$
15. $y = \frac{1}{3}x + 3$

16. $y = -\frac{3}{4}x - 9$
17. $y = -\frac{2}{3}x - 2$
18. $y = -\frac{5}{6}x + 4$

Slope of a line when given its equation

To find the slope of a line when given its equation, do the following.

Method 1:

> Get y on its own, and the number in front of x is the slope.

Note: The number in front of x is called the **coefficient** of x.

The number on its own is called the y **intercept**.

In short, write the line in the form:

$$y \quad = \quad mx \quad + \quad c$$

$$y \quad = \quad \text{(slope)}x \quad + \quad \text{(where the line cuts the } y\text{-axis)}$$

Method 2:

> If the line is in the form $ax + by + c = 0$, then $-\dfrac{a}{b}$ is the slope.

In words: Slope $= -\dfrac{\text{Number in front of } x}{\text{Number in front of } y}$

Note: When using this method, make sure every term is on the left-hand side in the given equation of the line.

EXAMPLE 1

Find the slope of the following lines.   (i) $3x - y - 5 = 0$ (ii) $5x + 4y - 12 = 0$

Solution:

Method 1:

(i) $$3x - y - 5 = 0$$
$$-y = -3x + 5$$
$$y = 3x - 5$$

Compare to $y = mx + c$
$\therefore$ Slope $= 3$

(ii) $$5x + 4y - 12 = 0$$
$$4y = -5x + 12$$
$$y = -\tfrac{5}{4}x + 3$$

Compare to $y = mx + c$
$\therefore$ Slope $= -\tfrac{5}{4}$

Method 2:

(i) $a = 3, \quad b = -1$
$$\text{slope} = -\frac{a}{b}$$
$$= -\frac{3}{-1}$$
$$= 3$$

(ii) $$5x + 4y - 12 = 0$$
$$a = 5, \quad b = 4$$
$$\text{slope} = -\frac{a}{b}$$
$$= -\frac{5}{4}$$

To prove whether or not two lines are parallel, do the following.

1. Find the slope of each line.
2. (i) If the slopes are the same, the lines are parallel.
   (ii) If the slopes are different, the lines are **not** parallel.

To prove whether or not two lines are perpendicular, do the following.

1. Find the slope of each line.

2. Multiply both slopes.

3. **(i)** If the answer in step 2 is −1, the lines are perpendicular.

   (ii) If the answer in step 2 is **not** −1, the lines are **not** perpendicular.

EXAMPLE 2

$l : 3x + 4y − 8 = 0$ and $k : 4x − 3y + 6 = 0$ are two lines. Prove that $l \perp k$.

Solution:

(i)
$$3x + 4y − 8 = 0$$
$$4y = −3x + 8$$
$$y = −\tfrac{3}{4}x + 4$$
$$\text{slope of } l = −\tfrac{3}{4}$$

(ii)
$$4x − 3y + 6 = 0$$
$$−3y = −4x − 6$$
$$3y = 4x + 6$$
$$y = \tfrac{4}{3}x + 2$$
$$\text{slope of } k = \tfrac{4}{3}$$

$$(\text{slope of } l) \times (\text{slope of } k) = −\tfrac{3}{4} \times \tfrac{4}{3} = −1$$
$$\therefore l \perp k$$

Note: To get the slopes, we could have used $m = −\dfrac{a}{b}$ in each case.

Exercise 15.8

In questions 1–12, find the slope of the line.

1. $2x + y + 7 = 0$

2. $3x − y − 2 = 0$

3. $4x − 2y − 7 = 0$

4. $9x + 3y − 11 = 0$

5. $2x + 3y − 15 = 0$

6. $4x − 3y − 12 = 0$

7. $x + 4y − 3 = 0$

8. $x − 3y + 2 = 0$

9. $4x − 3y = 0$

10. $5x − 7y = 8$

11. $3x − 2y − 3 = 0$

12. $7x − 10y − 11 = 0$

13. $l : 5x − 2y − 10 = 0$ and $k : 2x + 5y − 15 = 0$ are two lines. Prove that $l \perp k$.

14. $l : 3x + 2y − 2 = 0$ and $k : 2x − 3y + 6 = 0$ are two lines. Prove that $l \perp k$.

15. $l : 3x + 4y − 11 = 0$ and $k : 6x + 8y − 5 = 0$ are two lines. Prove that $l \parallel k$.

16. If the line $3x + 2y − 10 = 0$ is parallel to the line $tx + 4y − 8 = 0$, find the value of t.

17. If the lines $5x − 4y − 20 = 0$ and $4x + ty − 6 = 0$ are perpendicular, find the value of t.

Equation of a line, parallel or perpendicular to a given line

In some questions we need to find the equation of a line containing a particular point that is parallel to, or perpendicular to, a given line.

When this happens, do the following.

1. Find the slope of the given line.
2. (i) If parallel, use the slope in step 1.
   (ii) If perpendicular, turn the slope in step 1 upside down and change the sign.
3. Use the slope in step 2 with the point in the formula:

$$(y - y_1) = m(x - x_1)$$

Remember: To find the equation of a line, we need:

1. Slope, m.　　　　**2.** One point, (x_1, y_1).　　　　**3.** Formula, $(y - y_1) = m(x - x_1)$.

EXAMPLE

l is the line $5x - 3y - 2 = 0$. The line k contains the point $(3, -1)$ and $k \perp l$.
Find the equation of k.

Solution:
We have a point, $(3, -1)$. The slope is missing.

Step 1: Find the slope of l.

$$5x - 3y - 2 = 0$$
$$-3y = -5x + 2$$
$$3y = 5x - 2$$
$$y = \tfrac{5}{3}x - \tfrac{2}{3}$$
$$\therefore \text{ Slope of } l = \tfrac{5}{3}$$

Step 2: Find the slope of k perpendicular to l.
$\therefore$ Slope of $k = -\tfrac{3}{5}$
(turn upside down and change sign)

Step 3: Containing $(3, -1)$ with slope $-\tfrac{3}{5}$.

$$x_1 = 3, \quad y_1 = -1, \quad m = -\tfrac{3}{5}$$
$$(y - y_1) = m(x - x_1)$$
$$(y + 1) = -\tfrac{3}{5}(x - 3)$$
$$5(y + 1) = -3(x - 3)$$

(multiply both sides by 5)

$$5y + 5 = -3x + 9$$
$$3x + 5y + 5 - 9 = 0$$
$$3x + 5y - 4 = 0$$

The equation of the line k is $3x + 5y - 4 = 0$.

Exercise 15.9

1. Find the equation of the line containing $(2, 1)$ and parallel to $2x - y + 6 = 0$.

2. Find the equation of the line containing $(3, -2)$ and perpendicular to $3x - 2y + 8 = 0$.

3. Find the equation of the line containing $(-1, -4)$ and parallel to $5x + 4y - 3 = 0$.

4. Find the equation of the line containing $(-2, 5)$ and perpendicular to $4x - 3y - 1 = 0$.

5. l is the line $3x + 5y - 10 = 0$. The line k contains the point $(-2, 0)$ and $k \perp l$. Find the equation of k.

6. m is the line $x + 2y - 6 = 0$. The line l contains the point $(-3, -1)$ and $m \parallel l$. Find the equation of the line l.

7. $A(3, -6)$ and $B(-1, -2)$ are two points. C is the midpoint of $[AB]$ and k is the line $2x + 5y - 5 = 0$. The line l contains the point C and $l \perp k$. Find the equation of l.

Point of intersection of two lines

Use the method of solving simultaneous equations to find the point of intersection of two lines.

When the point of intersection contains whole numbers only

EXAMPLE 1

l is the line $2x - 5y - 9 = 0$ and k is the line $3x - 2y - 8 = 0$.
Find the coordinates of Q, the point of intersection of l and k.

Solution:
Write both equations in the form $ax + by = n$.

$$2x - 5y = 9 \qquad (l)$$
$$3x - 2y = 8 \qquad (k)$$

$$6x - 15y = 27 \qquad (l) \times 3$$
$$-6x + 4y = -16 \qquad (k) \times -2$$

$$-11y = 11 \qquad \text{(add)}$$
$$11y = -11$$
$$y = -1$$

Put $y = -1$ into (l) or (k).

$$2x - 5y = 9 \qquad (l)$$
$$2x - 5(-1) = 9$$
$$2x + 5 = 9$$
$$2x = 4$$
$$x = 2$$

∴ The coordinates of Q are $(2, -1)$.

When the point of intersection contains fractions

If the point of intersection contains fractions, the following is a very useful method.

> **Step 1:** Remove the y terms and get a value for x.
> **Step 2:** Remove the x terms and get a value for y.

Note: This method can be used even if the point of intersection contains whole numbers only.

EXAMPLE 2

$l : 6x + 3y - 11 = 0$ and $k : 5x + 2y - 8 = 0$ are two lines. $l \cap k = \{P\}$. Find the coordinates of P.

Solution:

Write both equations in the form $ax + by = n$.

Remove the y terms:

$$6x + 3y = 11 \qquad (l)$$
$$5x + 2y = 8 \qquad (k)$$

$$\overline{}$$

$$12x + 6y = 22 \qquad (l) \times 2$$
$$-15x - 6y = -24 \qquad (k) \times -3$$

$$\overline{}$$

$$-3x = -2 \qquad \text{(add)}$$
$$3x = 2$$
$$x = \tfrac{2}{3}$$

Remove the x terms:

$$6x + 3y = 11 \qquad (l)$$
$$5x + 2y = 8 \qquad (k)$$

$$\overline{}$$

$$30x + 15y = 55 \qquad (l) \times 5$$
$$-30x - 12y = -48 \qquad (k) \times -6$$

$$\overline{}$$

$$3y = 7 \qquad \text{(add)}$$
$$y = \tfrac{7}{3}$$

$\therefore$ The coordinates of P are $\left(\tfrac{2}{3}, \tfrac{7}{3}\right)$.

Exercise 15.10

In questions 1–15, find the point of intersection of the pair of lines.

Note: Questions 10–15 have solutions that contain fractions.

1. $2x + 3y - 7 = 0$
   $5x - 2y - 8 = 0$

2. $5x - 2y - 11 = 0$
   $3x - 4y - 1 = 0$

3. $3x - 2y - 3 = 0$
   $x + 4y - 1 = 0$

4. $4x - 3y + 25 = 0$
   $3x + 5y - 3 = 0$

5. $3x - y + 8 = 0$
   $x - 7y - 4 = 0$

6. $2x - 3y - 15 = 0$
   $5x - y - 5 = 0$

7. $x + 2y - 5 = 0$
$2x - y = 0$

8. $x + 2y - 4 = 0$
$4x - 5y - 29 = 0$

9. $5x + 2y + 1 = 0$
$2x + 5y - 29 = 0$

10. $5x + 10y - 11 = 0$
$2x + y - 2 = 0$

11. $3x - y - 6 = 0$
$x - 7y - 12 = 0$

12. $x + 2y - 2 = 0$
$2x - y - 2 = 0$

13. $2x - 3y + 2 = 0$
$4x - y - 2 = 0$

14. $4x + 2y - 11 = 0$
$3x - y - 7 = 0$

15. $3x + 3y - 20 = 0$
$x + 2y - 10 = 0$

16. $l : x + 3y + 12 = 0$ and $k : 3x - 2y + 3 = 0$ are two lines. $l \cap k = \{P\}$.
Find the coordinates of P.

17. $l : 5x - 4y - 6 = 0$ and $m : 2x - 3y - 8 = 0$ are two lines. $l \cap m = \{Q\}$.
Find the coordinates of Q.

18. $l : 3x - 2y - 4 = 0$ and $k : 5x + 2y - 12 = 0$ are two lines. $l \cap k = \{A\}$.
$m : x + 3y + 8 = 0$ and $n : 3x + 4y + 9 = 0$ are also two lines. $m \cap n = \{B\}$.
Find the equation of the line AB.

Graphing lines

Lines in the form $ax + by = d$
To draw a line, only two points are needed. The easiest points to find are those where a line cuts the x- and y-axes.

This is known as the **intercept method**. We use the following facts.

On the x-axis, $y = 0$.   On the y-axis, $x = 0$.

To draw a line, do the following.

1. Let $y = 0$ and find x.
2. Let $x = 0$ and find y.
3. Plot these two points.
4. Draw the line through these points.

Note: Any two points on the line will do; it is not necessary to use the points where the line cuts the x- and y-axes.

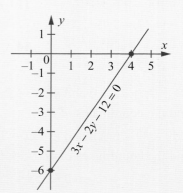

EXAMPLE 1

Graph the line $3x - 2y - 12 = 0$.

Solution:

1. and 2. $\qquad 3x - 2y = 12$

$y = 0$	$x = 0$
$3x = 12$	$-2y = 12$
$x = 4$	$2y = -12$
	$y = -6$
$(4, 0)$	$(0, -6)$

3. Plot the points $(4, 0)$ and $(0, -6)$.

4. Draw the line through these points.

Lines in the form $ax + by + c = 0$
Arrange the equation into the form $ax + by = d$ and use the intercept method.

Lines in the form $y = mx + c$

Method 1: Arrange the equation in the form $ax + by = d$ and use the intercept method.

Method 2: Find two points by using two different values of x. One of these values should be zero. The other value will depend on the coefficient of x.

To draw a line, do the following.

1. Let $x = 0$ and find y.
2. Let $x = $ a different value and find y.
3. Plot these two points.
4. Draw the line through these points.

EXAMPLE 2

Graph the line $y = 2x - 1$.

Solution:
The coefficient of x is 2. As this is a whole number, you may choose **any** other value of x.

1. and 2.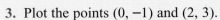

$$y = 2x - 1$$

$x = 0$	$x = 2$
$y = 2(0) - 1$	$y = 2(2) - 1$
$y = -1$	$y = 3$
$(0, -1)$	$(2, 3)$

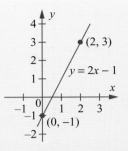

3. Plot the points $(0, -1)$ and $(2, 3)$.

4. Draw the line through these points.

EXAMPLE 3

Graph the line $y = -\frac{2}{3}x + 4$.

Solution:

The coefficient of x is $-\frac{2}{3}$. As this is a fraction, choose a **multiple** of its denominator. As the denominator is 3, the x value should be selected from 3, 6, 9, etc.

1. and 2.

$$y = -\frac{2}{3}x + 4$$

$x = 0$	$x = 3$
$y = -\frac{2}{3}(0) + 4$	$y = -\frac{2}{3}(3) + 4$
$y = -0 + 4$	$y = -2 + 4$
$y = 4$	$y = 2$
$(0, 4)$	$(3, 2)$

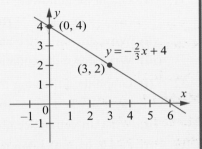

3. Plot the points $(0, 4)$ and $(3, 2)$.

4. Draw the line through these points.

Exercise 15.11

In questions 1–24, graph the following line.

1. $2x + 3y - 6 = 0$
2. $x + y - 5 = 0$
3. $3x - 5y + 15 = 0$

4. $4x - y - 8 = 0$
5. $x - y - 3 = 0$
6. $2x - 5y - 10 = 0$

7. $4x + 3y - 24 = 0$
8. $x - 3y - 12 = 0$
9. $4x - 5y - 10 = 0$

10. $x - y - 6 = 0$
11. $3x - 2y + 12 = 0$
12. $x + 4y - 6 = 0$

13. $y = 3x + 2$
14. $y = x - 1$
15. $y = 5x - 2$

16. $y = -4x + 3$
17. $y = -2x + 5$
18. $y = -3x + 4$

19. $y = \frac{2}{3}x + 2$ **20.** $y = \frac{3}{4}x - 1$ **21.** $y = \frac{5}{3}x - 2$

22. $y = -\frac{4}{3}x + 3$ **23.** $y = -\frac{2}{5}x + 1$ **24.** $y = -\frac{5}{6}x + 3$

25. Draw the line $2x + 3y - 12 = 0$. Show **(i)** graphically and **(ii)** algebraically that the point (3, 2) is on the line.

26. Where does the line $y = 4x - 7$ cross the y-axis?

27. If the line $y = -2x + c$ cuts the y-axis at (0, 3), find the value of c.

28. Write down the equation of a line with slope 3 and which crosses the y-axis at (0, 2).

29. Write down the equation of a line with slope $-\frac{2}{3}$ and which intercepts the y-axis at (0, −3).

30. **(i)** Graph the following lines on the same axes and scales.
   (a) $2x + 3y = 6$ **(b)** $2x + 3y = 12$
   (ii) What do you notice about the lines?

31. **(i)** Graph the following lines on the same axes and scales.
   (a) $y = 2x - 2$ **(b)** $y = 2x + 1$ **(c)** $y = 2x + 3$
   (ii) What do you notice about the lines?
   (iii) Write down the equation of two other lines that match the others.

32. **(i)** Graph the following lines on the same axes and scales.
   (a) $y = -3x + 2$ **(b)** $y = x + 2$ **(c)** $y = 2x + 2$
   (ii) What do you notice about the lines?

33. **(i)** Graph the following lines on the same axes and scales.
   (a) $y = x + 3$ **(b)** $y = x + 1$ **(c)** $y = x + 5$
   (ii) What do you notice about the lines?
   (iii) Mark on your diagram where you think $y = x + 7$ should be.
   (iv) How could you check your answer?

Lines that contain the origin

If the constant in the equation of a line is zero, e.g. $3x - 5y = 0$ or $4x = 3y$, then the line will pass through the origin, (0, 0). In this case the **intercept method** will not work.

To draw a line that contains the origin, (0, 0), do the following.

1. Choose a suitable value for x and find the corresponding value for y (or vice versa).
2. Plot this point.
3. A line drawn through this point and the origin is the required line.

Note: A suitable value is to let x equal the number in front of y and then find the corresponding value for x (or vice versa).

EXAMPLE

Graph the line $3x + 4y = 0$.

Solution:

1. Let $x = 4$ (number in front of y).
$$3x + 4y = 0$$
$$3(4) + 4y = 0$$
$$12 + 4y = 0$$
$$4y = -12$$
$$y = -3$$

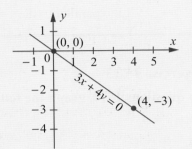

2. Plot the point $(4, -3)$.

3. Draw the line through the points $(4, -3)$ and $(0, 0)$.

Exercise 15.12

Graph each of the following lines.

1. $3x - 2y = 0$
2. $x + y = 0$
3. $3x - y = 0$
4. $5x = 3y$
5. $2x - 5y = 0$
6. $x = 4y$
7. $y = 3x$
8. $4x - y = 0$
9. $3x - 4y = 0$
10. $6x - 5y = 0$
11. $x - y = 0$
12. $2y = 3x$

Lines parallel to the axes

Some lines are parallel to the x- or y-axis.

$x = 5$ is a line parallel to the y-axis through 5 on the x-axis.

$y = -3$ is a line parallel to the x-axis through -3 on the y-axis.

Note:

$y = 0$ is the equation of the x-axis.
$x = 0$ is the equation of the y-axis.

EXAMPLE

On the same axes and scales, graph the lines $x = 2$ and $y = -1$.

Solution:

(i) $x = 2$

Line parallel to the y-axis through 2 on the x-axis.

(ii) $y = -1$

Line parallel to the x-axis through -1 on the y-axis.

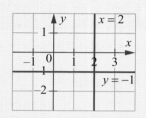

Exercise 15.13

In questions 1–12, graph the following line.

1. $x = 4$
2. $y = 3$
3. $x = -2$
4. $y = -1$
5. $x + 3 = 0$
6. $y - 5 = 0$
7. $x = -5$
8. $y - 4 = 0$
9. $x - 7 = 0$
10. $x = -4$
11. $2x = 1$
12. $2y = 3$

13. $x - 4 = 0$ is the equation of the line l and $y + 2 = 0$ is the equation of the line k.

(i) On the same axes and scales, graph the lines l and k.

(ii) Write down the coordinates of Q, the point of intersection of l and k.

Practical applications

EXAMPLE

The graph shows part of the conversion from °F (degrees Fahrenheit) to °C (degrees Celsius).

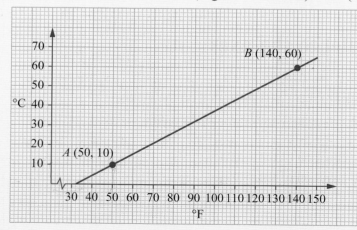

(i) Interpret the points A and B.

(ii) Freezing point is $0°C$. What is this in $°F$?

(iii) Find the slope of the line and hence its equation.

(iv) The boiling point of water is $100°C$.

Convert this to degrees Fahrenheit without extending the graph.

Solution:

We note that points on this graph are of the form (F, C).

(i) (50, 10): $50°F = 10°C$.   (140, 60): $140°F = 60°C$.

(ii) The line passes through at (32, 0), so $0°C = 32°F$.

(iii) (50, 10)   (140, 60)

(x_1, y_1) (x_2, y_2)

$$m = \frac{y_2 - y_1}{x_2 - x_1}$$

$$= \frac{60 - 10}{140 - 50} = \frac{5}{9}$$

$(x_1, y_1) = (50, 10)$ $m = \frac{5}{9}$

$$y - y_1 = m(x - x_1)$$

$$y - 10 = \frac{5}{10}(x - 50)$$

$$9y - 90 = 5x - 250$$

$$-5x + 9y + 160 = 0$$

$$5x - 9y - 160 = 0$$

(iv) We are looking for a point (?, 100), so let $y = 100$ and use the equation from part (iii).

$$5x - 9y - 160 = 0$$

$$5x - 9(100) - 160 = 0$$

$$5x - 1,060 = 0$$

$$5x = 1,060$$

$$x = 212$$

Thus, $100°C = 212°F$.

Exercise 15.14

1. A bank converts euro (EUR) to Swiss francs (CHF) at the rate of €1 = CHF1·20.

(i) Why does the line pass through (100, 120)?

(ii) Use the graph to estimate the value of €40 in Swiss francs.

(iii) Use the graph to estimate the value of 100 Swiss francs in euro.

(iv) Convert CHF90 to EUR.

(v) Find the equation of the conversion line.

(vi) The bank decides to introduce a €3 fee for converting euro into Swiss francs. Tom says just raise the line 3 units, while Jerry says the graph should be moved 3 units to the right. Who is correct?

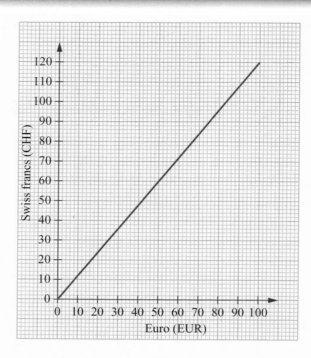

2. The photograph shows some spring-loaded devices used to calculate the mass of a variety of objects such as fish, luggage and babies.

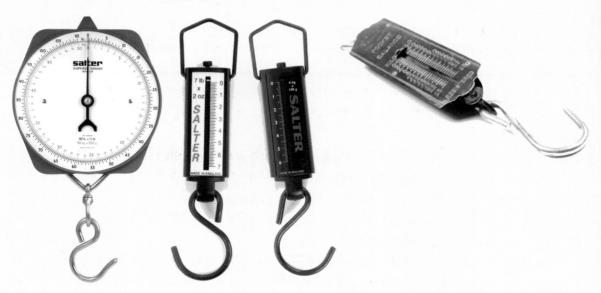

The graph shows the length of the spring compared to the mass attached to it.

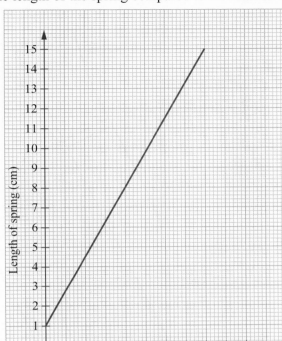

(i) How long is the spring when there is nothing attached to it?

(ii) How would the graph be used to calculate the mass of an object?

(iii) Find the slope of the line.

(iv) How much longer is the spring each time an extra kilogram is attached?

(v) From the graph, estimate the length of the spring using a 5 kg mass.

(vi) Find the equation of the line.

(vii) Use the equation to find the exact length of the spring when 5 kg is attached.

(viii) Using two suitable values, show that if the mass is doubled, then the length of the spring is *not* doubled.

(ix) Why would this type of device be limited to a certain range of masses?

3. A mathematics test is marked out of 250.

(i) Draw a graph showing the marks on the horizontal axis (up to 250 marks) and the percentage on the vertical axis (up to 100%).

(ii) Use your graph to calculate the marks required to achieve a grade B (70%).

(iii) Find the slope of the line.

(iv) Find the equation of this line.

(v) A student sees a score of 100 on his test and mistakenly assumes he got full marks. Explain how your answers to parts (ii) and (iv) can each be used to find his percentage mark.

4. The map shows a section of New York City where many of the streets run parallel or perpendicular to the other.

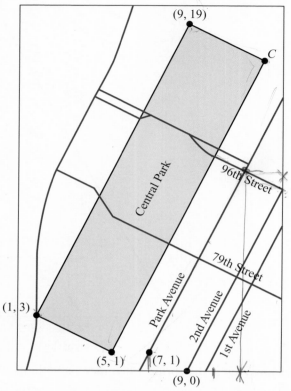

(i) Find the coordinates of the fourth corner, *C*, of Central Park, given that it is a parallelogram.

(ii) A parallelogram that contains one right-angled corner must be a rectangle.

   (a) Confirm that Central Park is a rectangle.

   (b) Explain why a parallelogram with one right-angled corner **must** have right angles in all four corners.

(iii) Find the equation of Park Avenue, given that it passes through (7, 1).

(iv) Find the equation of 96th Street, given that it passes through (14, 10).

(v) Mac and Stella agree to meet on the corner of Park Avenue and 96th. What are the coordinates of that corner?

(vi) Mac travelled from (7, 1) for the meeting. How far was this in map units?

(vii) If each map unit represents 180 metres, how far did Mac actually travel?

(viii) Calculate the area of Central Park to the nearest m^2.

5. The graph shows the cost of using a conference room which is dependent on the number of attendees.

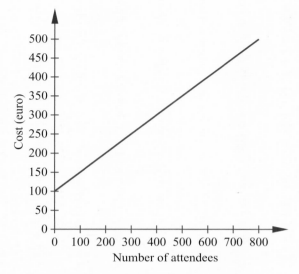

(i) What is the cost of a conference room for 500 people?

(ii) What is the slope of the line?

(iii) How does the slope help to calculate the extra cost if the number of attendees increases by 200?

(iv) Find the equation of the line.

(v) The graph does not start at the origin, (0, 0). Explain why this is to be expected.

6. The map shows a section of the Eixample district in Barcelona, Spain. The point P represents the origin (0, 0).

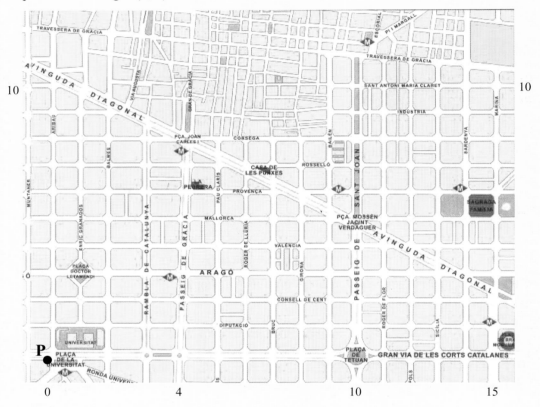

(i) Write down the coordinates of the Plaça de Tetuan (near the bottom of the map).

(ii) Write down the coordinates of the Plaça de Mossèn Jacint Verdaguer.

(iii) If each map unit represents 200 metres, how far is it to travel north from the Plaça de Tetuan to the Plaça de Mossèn Jacint Verdaguer?

(iv) Write down the coordinates of the Plaça Juan Charles, at the junction of the Avinguda Diagonal and Passeio de Gracia.

(v) Find the slope of the line along the Avinguda Diagonal.

(vi) Find the equation of the Avinguda Diagonal.

(vii) Felipe is at the Plaça de Mossèn Jacint Verdaguer. Miguel is at the Plaça Juan Charles. Starting at the same time and travelling at the same speed, they walk toward each other.

    (a) How far apart are they when they start, to the nearest metre?

    (b) Where will they meet?

    (c) Explain why this point is not on a horizontal street.

(viii) Investigate whether a line drawn from P to the Plaça Juan Charles is perpendicular to the Avinguda Diagonal.

Introduction

Trigonometry deals with the relationships between the sides and angles of triangles. Just as a triangle has three sides and three angles, there are three relationships to be considered.

1. **The angles in a triangle**
   In any triangle, the angles always add up to 180°.

   $$A + B + C = 180°$$

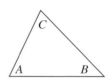

2. **The sides in a triangle**
   In a right-angled triangle, the theorem of Pythagoras applies.

   $$a^2 = b^2 + c^2$$

   Note: We do not have to study the relationship between the sides of a non-right-angled triangle.

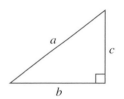

3. **The sides and angles in a right-angled triangle**
   In a right-angled triangle with acute angle θ, we name the sides as:

   Hypotenuse: The side opposite the right angle.
   It is also the longest side.
   Opposite: The side opposite the angle θ.
   Adjacent: The side beside (adjacent to) θ.

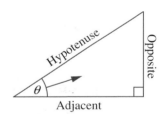

   There are three trigonometrical ratios called sine, cosine and tangent. They are usually abbreviated to sin, cos and tan.

   Note: These definitions only apply when θ is an acute angle. A more comprehensive definition may be given as part of the Leaving Certificate course.

$$\sin \theta = \frac{\text{Opposite}}{\text{Hypotenuse}} = \frac{O}{H}$$

$$\cos \theta = \frac{\text{Adjacent}}{\text{Hypotenuse}} = \frac{A}{H}$$

$$\tan \theta = \frac{\text{Opposite}}{\text{Adjacent}} = \frac{O}{A}$$

   Memory aids

   1. **O** Hell, **A**nother **H**our **O**f **A**lgebra: **s**enior **c**up **t**eam

   2. Silly $= \dfrac{\text{Old}}{\text{Harry}}$ Caught $= \dfrac{\text{A}}{\text{Herring}}$ Trawling $= \dfrac{\text{Off}}{\text{America}}$

   3. SOHCAHTOA

Notes:

1. θ is Greek letter, pronounced 'theta', often used to denote an angle.

2. It might be helpful to point an arrow from the angle to the **opposite** side.

3. We do not have to study the relationship between the sides and angles of a non-right-angled triangle.

EXAMPLE 1

$\sin \theta = \dfrac{5}{13}$ where $0° < \theta < 90°$.

  (i) Find, as fractions, the value of $\cos \theta$ and the value of $\tan \theta$.

  (ii) Show that $\cos^2 \theta + \sin^2 \theta = 1$.

Solution:

  (i) From the trigonometric ratio given, sketch a right-angled triangle to represent the situation and use Pythagoras' theorem to find the missing side.

Given: $\sin \theta = \dfrac{5}{13}$ $\therefore$ Opposite $= 5$ and hypotenuse $= 13$.

Let the length of the adjacent $= x$.

$x^2 + 5^2 = 13^2$ (Pythagoras' theorem)

$x^2 + 25 = 169$

$ x^2 = 144$

$ x = \sqrt{144} = 12$

$\cos \theta = \dfrac{A}{H} = \dfrac{12}{13}$

$\tan \theta = \dfrac{O}{A} = \dfrac{5}{12}$

  (ii) $\cos^2 \theta + \sin^2 \theta$

$= \left(\dfrac{12}{13}\right)^2 + \left(\dfrac{5}{13}\right)^2$

$= \dfrac{144}{169} + \dfrac{25}{169} = \dfrac{169}{169} = 1$

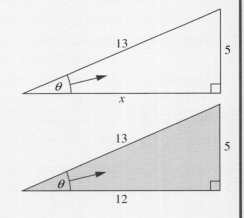

Note: $\cos^2 \theta = (\cos \theta)^2$, $\sin^2 \theta = (\sin \theta)^2$ and $\tan^2 \theta = (\tan \theta)^2$

EXAMPLE 2

(i) By using Pythagoras'
theorem, investigate if the
angle marked B in the
diagram is a right angle.

(ii) Can you conclude whether
$B > 90°$ or $B < 90°$ from
your work? Justify your
conclusion.

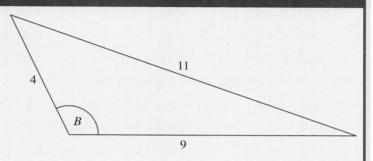

Solution:

(i) Pythagoras' theorem: $z^2 = x^2 + y^2$, where z is the hypotenuse (the longest side).
Check:

LHS	RHS
z^2	$x^2 + y^2$
11^2	$9^2 + 4^2$
121	$81 + 16$
	97

As Pythagoras' theorem does not apply ($121 \neq 97$), the angle B is not a right angle.

(ii) Because $121 > 97$, we can conclude that angle $B > 90°$.

Exercise 16.1

1. In each of the right-angled triangles **(i)**, **(ii)** and **(iii)**, the lengths of the sides are shown in
the diagram and the angles are labelled.

Complete the tables below, writing the answers as fractions, where necessary.

(i) 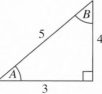 (ii) 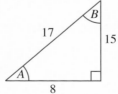 (iii)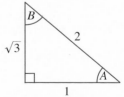

	sin A	cos A	tan A
(i)	$\frac{4}{5}$		
(ii)			$\frac{15}{8}$
(iii)		$\frac{1}{2}$	

	sin B	cos B	tan B
(i)	$\frac{3}{5}$		
(ii)		$\frac{15}{17}$	
(iii)			$\frac{1}{\sqrt{3}}$

2. Evaluate each of the following.

   (i) $3^2 + 4^2$ (ii) $5^2 + 12^2$ (iii) $8^2 + 6^2$ (iv) $20^2 + 21^2$

   (v) $1^2 + 3^2$ (vi) $1^2 + (\sqrt{3})^2$ (vii) $5^2 - 3^2$ (viii) $13^2 - 12^2$

   (ix) $4^2 - 3^2$ (x) $2^2 - (\sqrt{3})^2$ (xi) $(\sqrt{13})^2 - 2^2$ (xii) $(\sqrt{5})^2 - 1^2$

3. Give two examples of right-angled triangles with:

   (i) All three sides of integer length, e.g. 5, 12, 13

   (ii) Two sides integer lengths and one side surd length, e.g. 4, 5, $\sqrt{41}$

4. Use Pythagoras' theorem to find x, the length of the missing side, in surd form where necessary. Express $\sin\theta$, $\cos\theta$ and $\tan\theta$ as simple fractions or as surd fractions in each of the following.

   (i)
   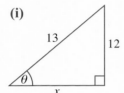

   (ii)
   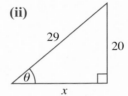

   (iii)
   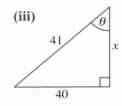

   (iv)
   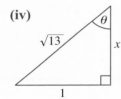

   (v)
   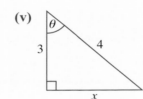

   (vi)
   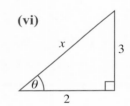

5. (i) From the diagram, if $\cos B = \frac{3}{5}$, label the angle B.

   (ii) Find the value of x.

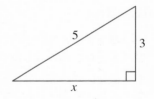

6. (i) Given that $\tan Q = \frac{c}{d}$, label angle Q in the diagram.

   (ii) Hence, express $\cos Q$ and $\sin Q$ as simple fractions.

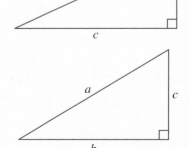

7. By Pythagoras' theorem, $a^2 = b^2 + c^2$ in the right-angled triangle.

Hence or otherwise, in the triangle below, where angle A is obtuse, is $a^2 > b^2 + c^2$ or is $a^2 < b^2 + c^2$? Justify your answer.

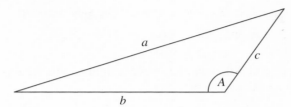

8. Using Pythagoras' theorem, investigate if the angle marked θ in each of the following diagrams equals 90°, is less than 90° or is greater than 90°. Justify your answers.

(i)

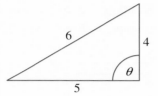

(ii)

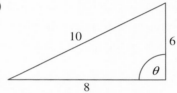

(iii)

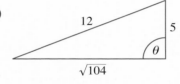

(iv)

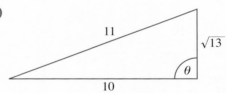

9. $\sin \theta = \frac{7}{25}$, where $0° < \theta < 90°$.

   (i) Find, as fractions, the value of $\cos \theta$ and the value of $\tan \theta$.

   (ii) Show that $\cos^2 \theta + \sin^2 \theta = 1$.

10. $29 \sin \theta = 21$, where $0° < \theta < 90°$.

    If $\tan \theta = \frac{21}{k}$, find the value of k, $k \in \mathbb{N}$.

11. The diagram shows a triangle with lengths of sides 3, 4 and 5.

    (i) Verify that $\dfrac{\sin \theta}{\cos \theta} = \tan \theta$.

    (ii) Evaluate $\sqrt{\dfrac{\sin \theta \tan \theta}{\cos \theta}}$.

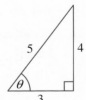

12. If $a^2 < b^2 + c^2$ in this triangle, which of the following statements are true?

    (i) $A = 90°$ **(ii)** $A > 90°$ **(iii)** $A < 90°$

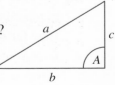

13. (i) If $a = 10$, $b = 6$ and $c = 3$, explain why this does not form a triangle.

   (ii) Assign values to a, b and c, the lengths of the sides, so that:

   (a) $A = 90°$ (b) $A < 90°$ (c) $A > 90°$

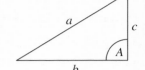

14. What is the longest pencil that can be stored within a cylinder of height 15 cm and base radius 4 cm?

15. A vertical building on horizontal ground is 5 m tall. The building requires an outside support beam to prevent it from collapsing. The maximum amount of space to erect a support beam is 12 m to the left of the building.

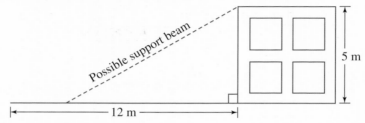

   (i) Using the diagram, calculate the maximum length the support beam can be.

   (ii) An engineer calculates that a support beam reaching up a height of 4 m on the building would be more effective. Find, correct to the nearest cm, the maximum length of this support beam.

   (iii) Further analysis indicates that the optimum (best) angle for the support beam is at 45° to the ground. Find the length of this support beam, correct to the nearest cm, if the point of support is at 4 m high, as in (ii).

   (iv) Give one reason why you think this mathematical model would be suitable or not in practice.

16. An oil rig is 20 km east and 15 km north of Inisoil.

   (i) Calculate the direct distance, x, from Inisoil to the oil rig.

   (ii) A safety inspector flew directly from Enye to the oil rig, which is 12 km west of Enye. How far south, y, is the oil rig from Enye? Give your answer correct to one decimal place.

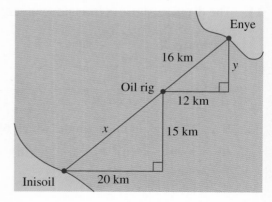

Using a calculator

You can find values of sin, cos and tan for angles measured in degrees using a calculator. Before entering angles in degrees you must make sure that the calculator is in 'degree mode'. You will usually see **DEG** or **D** at the top of the display.

Find the buttons marked $\boxed{\sin}$, $\boxed{\cos}$ and $\boxed{\tan}$.

You will also need a button marked $\boxed{\circ\,'\,''}$ or $\boxed{\text{DMS}}$, which is used to:

(a) Enter parts of a degree called minutes ($60' = 1°$).
(b) Convert decimal degrees to degrees, minutes and seconds or vice versa.

Note: Some calculators put in an opening parenthesis (bracket) when you press sin, cos or tan. If so, you will need to remember to type a closing parenthesis.

sin 19°24′	📱 $\boxed{\sin}$ 19 $\boxed{\circ\,'\,''}$ 24 $\boxed{\circ\,'\,''}$ $\boxed{=}$	0·3321611319
cos 108°32′	📱 $\boxed{\cos}$ 108 $\boxed{\text{DMS}}$ 32 $\boxed{\text{DMS}}$ $\boxed{=}$	−0·317856315
tan 23·51°	📱 $\boxed{\tan}$ 23·51 $\boxed{=}$	0·4350199211

The $\boxed{\sin}$, $\boxed{\cos}$ and $\boxed{\tan}$ keys

EXAMPLE

Use your calculator to evaluate the following, correct to four decimal places where necessary.
(i) cos 120° (ii) tan 1,035° (iii) sin 35°24′ (iv) tan 72·16°

Solution:

(i) cos 120°
  $= -0·5$

(ii) tan 1,035°
  $= -1$

(iii) sin 35°24′
  $= 0·579281172$
  $= 0·5793$ (correct to four decimal places)

(iv) tan 72·16°
  $= 3·107180849$
  $= 3·1072$ (correct to four decimal places)

Exercise 16.2

In questions 1–23, use your calculator to evaluate the expression, correct to four decimal places.

1. $\sin 51°$
2. $\cos 73°$
3. $\tan 47°$

4. $\cos 10°30'$
5. $\sin 59°15'$
6. $\tan 31°54'$

7. $\sin 47{\cdot}4°$
8. $\sin 26{\cdot}8°$
9. $\tan 31{\cdot}9°$

10. $\cos 75{\cdot}1°$
11. $\sin 83{\cdot}3°$
12. $\tan 25{\cdot}8°$

13. $10 \sin 28°$
14. $40 \cos 37°36'$
15. $45 \tan 75°26'$

16. $120 \sin 40°54'$
17. $\dfrac{30}{\sin 50°}$
18. $\dfrac{120}{\sin 53°8'}$

19. $\dfrac{20 \sin 42°18'}{\sin 48°40'}$
20. $\dfrac{18 \sin 16°28'}{\sin 24°54'}$
21. $\frac{1}{2}(5)(8) \sin 80°$

22. $\left(\frac{1}{2}\right)(20)(40) \sin 40°28'$
23. $\left(\frac{1}{2}\right)(7)(3) \sin 18°30'$

In questions 24–30, find the exact value of the expression.

24. $\tan 45°$
25. $\tan 135°$
26. $\cos 60°$

27. $\sin 330°$
28. $\cos^2 120°$
29. $\left(\frac{1}{2}\right)(10)(6) \sin 30°$

30. $\left(\frac{1}{2}\right)(20)(7) \sin 150°$

In questions 31–32, verify the statement.

31. $2 \sin 30° \neq \sin 60°$
32. $\cos 30° + \cos 60° \neq \cos 90°$

The $\boxed{\sin^{-1}}$, $\boxed{\cos^{-1}}$ and $\boxed{\tan^{-1}}$ keys

Given a value of $\sin \theta$, $\cos \theta$ or $\tan \theta$, we can find the value of the angle θ using the inverse trigonometric functions $\sin^{-1}$, $\cos^{-1}$ and $\tan^{-1}$, respectively.

On most calculators, $\sin^{-1}$, $\cos^{-1}$ and $\tan^{-1}$ are obtained by first pressing a button marked $\boxed{\text{SHIFT}}$ or $\boxed{\text{2nd F}}$ and then pressing $\boxed{\sin}$, $\boxed{\cos}$ or $\boxed{\tan}$ as required.

Notes:

1. Some calculators put in an opening parenthesis (bracket) when you press sin, cos or tan. If so, you will need to type a closing parenthesis.

2. The method of entering fractions differs between calculators.

3. When entering a negative value, use the $\boxed{(-)}$ button. The $\boxed{-}$ is used for subtraction.

4. If you choose to use $\boxed{\div}$ (division) to enter a fraction, then you **must** use parentheses.

$\sin^{-1} 0{\cdot}456$	▦ SHIFT sin ·456 =	$27{\cdot}12929446$
$\cos^{-1}(-0{\cdot}296)$	▦ SHIFT cos ((−) ·296) =	$107{\cdot}2175114$
$\tan^{-1} 14{\cdot}92$	▦ SHIFT tan 14·92 =	$86{\cdot}16553521$

Converting decimal angles to degrees, minutes and seconds

To convert a decimal angle to degrees, minutes and seconds, press SHIFT ○′″ or SHIFT DMS .

$\sin^{-1} \frac{5}{7}$	▦ SHIFT sin $\frac{5}{7}$ = SHIFT ○′″	$45{\cdot}5846914$	$45°35'4{\cdot}889''$
$\cos^{-1}\left(-\frac{7}{11}\right)$	▦ SHIFT cos ((−) $\frac{7}{11}$) = SHIFT ○′″	$129{\cdot}5211964$	$129°31'16{\cdot}3''$
$\tan^{-1} \sqrt{5}$	▦ SHIFT tan $\sqrt{5}$ =	$65{\cdot}90515745$	$65°54'18{\cdot}57''$

EXAMPLE 1

(i) Find the value of A, $0° < A < 90°$, to the nearest degree if $\cos A = 0{\cdot}5678$.
(ii) Solve $\tan B = 9{\cdot}6541$ where $0° < B < 90°$.
   Give your answer in degrees correct to two decimal places.

Solution:

(i) $\cos A = 0{\cdot}579$

$\quad A = \cos^{-1} 0{\cdot}579$

$\quad\quad = 54{\cdot}61976134°$

$\quad\quad = 55°$ (nearest degree)

(ii) $\tan B = 9{\cdot}6541$

$\quad B = \tan^{-1} 9{\cdot}6541$

$\quad\quad = 84{\cdot}08622536°$

$\quad\quad = 84{\cdot}09°$ (two decimal places)

EXAMPLE 2

Find the value of θ, $0° < \theta < 90°$, to the nearest minute, given that:
(i) $\sin \theta = 0{\cdot}38$ (ii) $\cos \theta = \frac{3}{5}$ (iii) $4 \tan 2\theta = 1$

Solution:

(i) $\sin \theta = 0{\cdot}38$

$\quad \theta = \sin^{-1} 0{\cdot}38$

$\quad\quad = 22{\cdot}33368266°$

$\quad\quad = 22°20'1{\cdot}258''$

$\quad \theta = 22°20'$ (nearest minute)

(ii) $\cos \theta = \frac{3}{5}$

$\quad \theta = \cos^{-1} \frac{3}{5}$

$\quad\quad = 53{\cdot}13010235°$

$\quad\quad = 53°07'48{\cdot}37''$

$\quad \theta = 53°8'$ (nearest minute)

(iii) $4 \tan 2\theta = 1$

$\tan 2\theta = \frac{1}{4}$ (divide both sides by 4)

$2\theta = \tan^{-1} \frac{1}{4}$

$2\theta = 14.03624347°$

$\theta = 7.018121734°$ (divide both sides by 2)

$\theta = 7°01'05.24''$

$\theta = 7°1'$ (nearest minute)

Note: We use the fact that $1' = 60''$ (1 minute = 60 seconds, like the clock) to round off the answer to the nearest minute.

Exercise 16.3

In questions 1–8, find the measure of the angle θ, where $0° < \theta < 90°$, correct to the nearest degree.

1. $\sin \theta = \frac{2}{3}$ 2. $\cos \theta = \frac{4}{7}$ 3. $\tan \theta = \frac{1}{8}$ 4. $\sin \theta = 0.3$

5. $\tan \theta = 2$ 6. $\cos \theta = \frac{3}{5}$ 7. $\sin \theta = \frac{7}{10}$ 8. $\tan \theta = \frac{1}{\sqrt{10}}$

In questions 9–20, use your calculator to find the angle in degrees, correct to two decimal places, where the angle is between $0°$ and $90°$.

9. $\cos \theta = 0.7835$ 10. $\tan P = 2.4532$ 11. $\sin Q = 0.6528$

12. $\sin \angle ABC = \frac{1}{3}$ 13. $\cos \angle QPR = \frac{2}{5}$ 14. $\tan \angle ZXY = 5$

15. $4 \tan A = 3$ 16. $5 \sin B = 1$ 17. $3 \cos C = 2$

18. $\sin A = \frac{1}{\sqrt{10}}$ 19. $\cos B = \frac{2}{\sqrt{7}}$ 20. $\tan C = \frac{\sqrt{3}}{5}$

In questions 21–26, use your calculator to find the angle, correct to the nearest minute, where the angle is between $0°$ and $90°$.

21. $\sin A = 0.3$ 22. $\cos B = 0.35$ 23. $\tan C = 1.5$

24. $\cos D = 0.762$ 25. $\tan E = 6.491$ 26. $\sin F = 0.209$

In questions 27–29, find the exact angle.

27. $\cos Q = \frac{1}{2}$ 28. $\tan A = \frac{1}{\sqrt{3}}$ 29. $\sin B = \frac{1}{\sqrt{2}}$

In questions 30–32, use your calculator to find the angle, correct to the nearest degree, where the angle is between $0°$ and $90°$.

30. $\tan 2A = \frac{1}{3}$ 31. $\cos 2A = \frac{1}{10}$ 32. $\sin 5A = \frac{5}{7}$

33. $\cos \theta = \frac{4}{5}$, where $0° < \theta < 90°$.

    (i) Find, as fractions, the value of $\sin \theta$ and the value of $\tan \theta$.

    (ii) Show that **(a)** $\cos^2 \theta + \sin^2 \theta = 1$ **(b)** $\cos \theta + \sin \theta > \tan \theta$.

    (iii) Find the measure of the angle θ, correct to the nearest degree.

34. $\tan A = \frac{8}{15}$, where $0° < A < 90°$.

    (i) Find, as fractions, the value of $\sin A$ and the value of $\cos A$.

    (ii) Show that $\cos A + \sin A > \tan A$.

    (iii) Find the measure of the angle A, correct to the nearest degree.

Notation

The diagram shows the usual notation for a triangle in trigonometry.

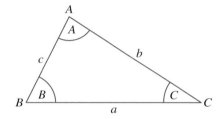

- Vertices: A, B, C.
- Angles: A, B, C.
- Length of sides: a, b, c.

> The lengths of the sides are denoted by a lower case letter and named after the angle they are opposite, i.e. a is opposite angle A, b is opposite angle B and c is opposite angle C.

Using the terminology, we also have the following:

$$A = |\angle BAC| \qquad B = |\angle ABC| \qquad C = |\angle ACB|$$
$$a = |BC| \qquad b = |AC| \qquad c = |AB|$$

Solving right-angled triangles

We can use a trigonometric ratio to calculate the length of a side in a right-angled triangle if we know the length of one side and one angle (other than the right angle). We can also find the size of an angle in a right-angled triangle if we know the lengths of two of its sides.

Summary of which trigonometric ratio to choose linking the given sides and angles

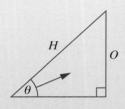

$$\sin \theta = \frac{O}{H}$$

$$\theta = \sin^{-1}\frac{O}{H}$$

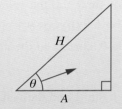

$$\cos \theta = \frac{A}{H}$$

$$\theta = \cos^{-1}\frac{A}{H}$$

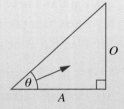

$$\tan \theta = \frac{O}{A}$$

$$\theta = \tan^{-1}\frac{O}{A}$$

EXAMPLE

In the diagram, $PR \perp QS$, $|\angle PQR| = 34°$, $|QR| = 15$ and $|RS| = 8$.

(i) Calculate $|PR|$, correct to two decimal places.

(ii) Hence, calculate $|\angle PSR|$, correct to the nearest degree.

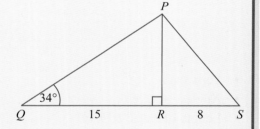

Solution:

Split the diagram into two right-angled triangles.

(i) We require the opposite and know the adjacent. Therefore, use the tan ratio.

$$\tan \theta = \frac{\text{Opposite}}{\text{Adjacent}}$$

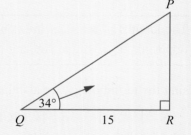

$$\tan 34° = \frac{|PR|}{15} \quad \text{(put in known values)}$$

$$15 \tan 34° = |PR| \quad \text{(multiply both sides by 15)}$$

$$10 \cdot 11762775 = |PR|$$

$$|PR| = 10 \cdot 12 \quad \text{(correct to two decimal places)}$$

(ii) We know the opposite, from part **(i)**, and the adjacent.

Therefore, use the tan ratio.

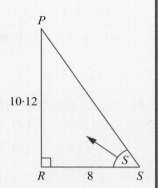

$$S = |\angle PSR|$$

$$\tan \theta = \frac{\text{Opposite}}{\text{Adjacent}}$$

$$\tan S = \left(\frac{10 \cdot 12}{8}\right) \qquad \text{(put in known values)}$$

$$S = \tan^{-1}\left(\frac{10 \cdot 12}{8}\right)$$

$$= 51 \cdot 67314168°$$

$$\therefore |\angle PSR| = 52° \qquad \text{(correct to the nearest degree)}$$

Note: In part **(ii)**, the question uses the word **hence**. Therefore, we must use the value $|PR| = 10 \cdot 12$.

Exercise 16.4

In questions 1–6, calculate, to the nearest degree, the angle marked with a letter.

1.

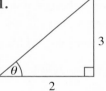

2.

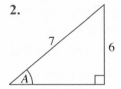

3.

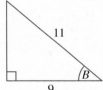

4.

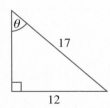

5.

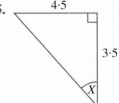

6.

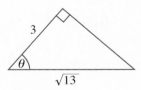

In questions 7–9, calculate the length of the side marked with a letter, correct to two decimal places.

7.

8.

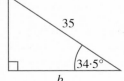

9.

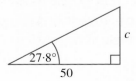

225

10. In triangle ABC, $|\angle ABC| = 90°$, $|AB| = 2$ and $|BC| = 1.5$. Find:

    (i) $|AC|$

    (ii) $|\angle BAC|$, correct to the nearest degree

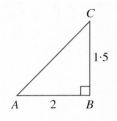

11. In the diagram, $XW \perp YZ$, $|XY| = 10$, $|\angle XYW| = 30°$ and $|WZ| = \frac{2}{5}|XY|$. Calculate:

    (i) $|XW|$ (ii) $|\angle WXZ|$, correct to the nearest degree

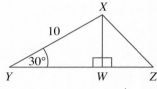

12. In the diagram, $|AB| = 16$ cm and $|\angle ABC| = 90°$. The point D is on $[BC]$. $|BD| = 30$ cm and $|AD| = |DC|$. Find:

    (i) $|AD|$ (ii) $|BC|$

    (iii) $|\angle ACB|$, correct to the nearest degree

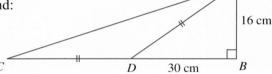

Practical applications

Many practical problems in navigation, surveying, engineering and geography involve solving a triangle. In this section we will restrict the problems to those that involve right-angled triangles. When solving practical problems using trigonometry in this section, represent each situation with a right-angled triangle.

Mark on your triangle the angles and lengths you know and label what you need to calculate, using the correct ratio to link the angle or length required with the known angle or length.

Angles of elevation, depression and compass directions

Angle of elevation

The **angle of elevation** of an object as seen by an observer is the angle between the horizontal line from the object to the observer's eye (upwards from the horizontal).

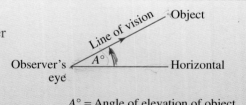

$A°$ = Angle of elevation of object

Angle of depression

If the object is below the level of the observer, the angle between the horizontal and the observer's line of vision is called the **angle of depression** (downwards from the horizontal).

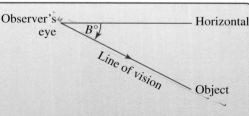

$B°$ = Angle of depression of object

Note: An angle of elevation has an equal angle of depression. The angle of elevation from *A* to *B* is equal to the angle of depression from *B* to *A*. The angles are alternate angles, as the horizontal lines are parallel.

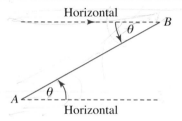

A note on clinometers:

A clinometer is a device used to measure angles of elevation and/or angles of depression.

Q. Who might use a clinometer?

A. Motorway construction engineers, movie production engineers, forestry engineers and secondary school maths students in Ireland!

There are many different types of clinometer. A very simple type looks like this:

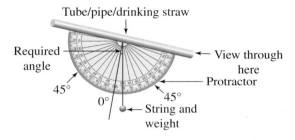

Compass directions

The direction of a point is stated as a number of degrees east or west of north and south.

- *A* is N 60° E
- *B* is N 40° W
- *C* is S 45° W (or SW)
- *D* is S 70° E

Note: N 60° E means start at north and turn 60° towards east.

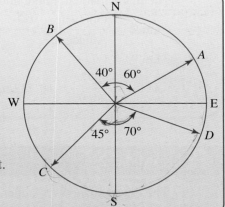

Mathematical modelling

When solving a problem, factors that have a negligible effect are often ignored. This has the advantage of simplifying the problem without sacrificing too much accuracy. This simplified problem is referred to as a **mathematical model** for the real situation.

EXAMPLE 1

On the seafront at Bray, the beach slopes down at a constant angle of 9° to the horizontal. Ciara is 1·7 m tall. How far can she walk out to sea before the water just covers her head?

Solution:

Represent Ciara and her height by a straight line.

Consider that as Ciara walks out to sea, her body (and head!) is at a right angle to the surface of the water.

'The beach slopes down at a constant angle' allows us to ignore rocks, etc. underfoot.

Can you think of any other physical issues the mathematical model eliminates?

The mathematical model allows us to arrive at the diagram:

$$\tan 9° = \frac{\text{Opposite}}{\text{Adjacent}} = \frac{1·7}{y}$$

$$y \tan 9° = 1·7$$

$$y = \frac{1·7}{\tan 9°} = 10·733 \text{ m}$$

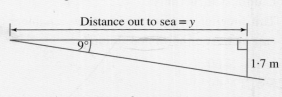

EXAMPLE 2

The diagram shows a ladder, 8 m in length, which leans against a vertical wall on level ground. The ladder makes an angle of 58° with the ground. Calculate the distance from the point where the ladder meets the ground to the wall, correct to two decimal places.

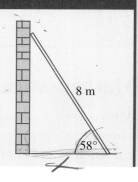

Solution:

Represent the situation with a right-angled triangle. Let d represent the distance from the point where the ladder meets the ground to the wall.

We know the hypotenuse and require the adjacent. Therefore, use the cos ratio.

$$\cos \theta = \frac{\text{Adjacent}}{\text{Hypotenuse}}$$

$\cos 58° = \dfrac{d}{8}$ (put in known values)

$8 \cos 58° = d$ (multiply both sides by 8)

$4{\cdot}239354114 = d$

$4{\cdot}24 = d$ (correct to two decimal places)

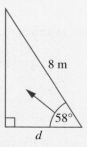

Therefore, the distance from the point where the ladder meets the ground to the wall is 4·24 m (correct to two decimal places).

EXAMPLE 3

Lisa wishes to measure the height of a particular tree in her local park. She brings a tape, a homemade clinometer and her brother Bart.

a = Distance from ground to eye
b = Distance from Bart to tree

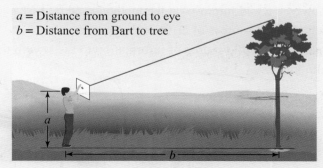

With Bart operating the clinometer by looking through the straw/tube at the top of the tree, Lisa reads the angle of elevation, E.

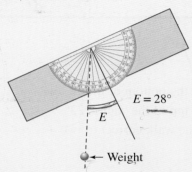

$E = 28°$

E

← Weight

Using the tape, she measures the distance from Bart to the tree, $b = 27.4$ m, and Bart's height to eye level, $a = 1.32$ m. How does she calculate the approximate height of the tree?

Solution:

Lisa uses a mathematical model to describe the situation.

Lisa assumes the tree is at right angles to the ground.

$$\tan 28 = \frac{\text{Opposite}}{\text{Adjacent}} = \frac{x}{27.4}$$

$$27.4 \tan 28 = x$$
$$14.5688 = x$$

Height of the tree $= 14.5688 + 1.32 = 15.8888$

Lisa might claim the height of the tree is approximately 15.89 m $\boxed{\text{or}}$ 15.9 m $\boxed{\text{or}}$ 16 m. Which do you think is best and why?

Exercise

1. Select a suitable tree, pole or high building in your area and find its height using the method followed by Lisa and Bart.

   Note: Be very mindful of motorised traffic if doing this project near a road. It is best to work in teams of two.

2. Suggest how you could improve on the method used by Lisa and Bart.

3. Name three possible sources of error in your work.

4. The internet is a valuable source of information to assist with the construction of a suitable clinometer.

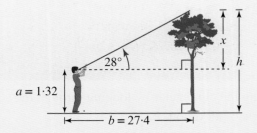

Exercise 16.5

1. From a point 12 m from the bottom of a wall, the angle of elevation to the top of the wall is 22°. Calculate the height of the wall, correct to two decimal places.

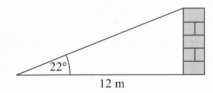

2. When the angle of elevation of the sun is 15°, an upright flagpole casts a shadow of length 18 m. Calculate the height of the pole, correct to one decimal place.

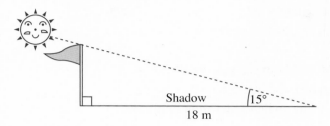

Shadow
18 m

3. The distance of the point P, the top of a wall, from the point Q on level ground is 24 m. The angle of elevation of the point P from the point Q is 29°.

Calculate the height, h, of the wall, correct to two decimal places.

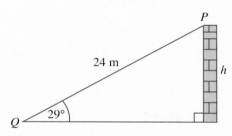

4. A ladder of length 3·7 m rests against a vertical wall so that the base of the ladder is 1·2 m from the wall.
   (i) Find the vertical height that the ladder reaches on the wall.
   (ii) Find the measure of the angle, θ, that the ladder makes with the horizontal, correct to the nearest degree.

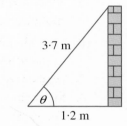

5. The diagram shows a farmyard gate. Its height is 1·6 m. The diagonal bar makes an angle of 30° with the horizontal ground. Calculate the length of the diagonal bar.

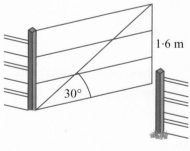

6. A see-saw is 3·8 metres long and when one end is touching the ground, the see-saw is at an angle of 30° to the horizontal ground.

How high is the other end above the ground?

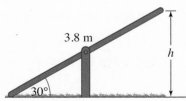

7. A girl is flying a kite. The length of string from her hand to the top of the kite is 60 m.

   The string, which is being held 1 m above the ground, makes an angle of elevation of 50° with the horizontal.

   (i) Calculate the height of the kite above the ground, correct to the nearest metre.

   (ii) Describe how the angle of elevation might be measured.

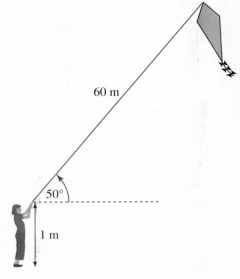

8. A girl is surfing the internet.

   (i) What height are her eyes above the centre of the screen?

   (ii) Find the horizontal distance from her eyes to the centre of the screen.
   (Give each answer correct to one decimal place.)

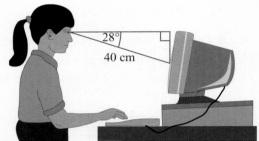

9. A passenger in a plane is told that he is flying at 4,000 m and is 15 km from the airport.

   What is the angle of depression from the plane to the airport? Give your answer to the nearest degree.

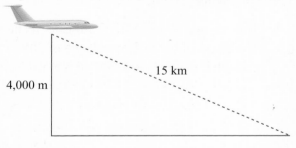

10. A rectangular garden measuring 45 m by 24 m has a tree on one of its corners.

    (i) Find the length of the diagonal [*BC*].

    (ii) If the angle of elevation of the top of the tree from *C* is 21°, find the height of the tree to the nearest metre.

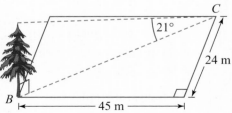

11. Sophie stands 5 m from a tree. From her eye level, the angle of depression of the base of the tree is 19° and the angle of elevation is 64°.

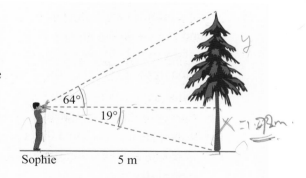

    (i) How tall is the tree? Give your answer to the nearest metre.

    (ii) Use the information to estimate Sophie's height, giving your answer to the nearest centimetre.

   (iii) What further information is needed to accurately calculate Sophie's height?

12. A ski lift connects B to T passing through M on its way. The lift travels 45 m from B to M at an angle of 54° off the vertical and a further 22 m from M to T at an angle of 72° off the vertical.

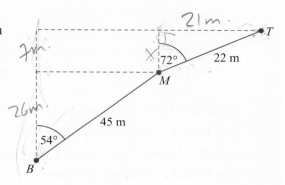

    (i) How far does the ski lift rise vertically going from B to M?

    (ii) Calculate the horizontal distance between M and T.

   (iii) How much higher is T than B?

Give your answers correct to the nearest metre.

13. While trying to swim across a river, Gerry was swept downstream. The river is $150\sqrt{3}$ m wide, but Gerry had to swim 300 m to cross the river.

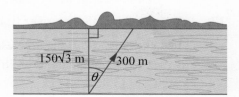

    (i) At what angle was he dragged downstream?

    (ii) Gerry took 2 minutes to cross the river. What was his average speed in m/s?

   (iii) How far downstream was Gerry dragged?

   (iv) Calculate the average speed of the river in m/s.

14. From a boat at sea, the angle of elevation to the top of a vertical cliff 200 m above sea level is 14°. After the boat has sailed directly towards the cliff, the angle of elevation of the cliff is found to be 28°. How far did the boat sail towards the cliff, correct to the nearest metre?

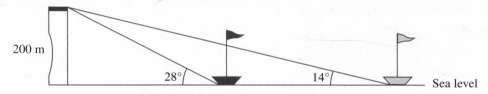

15. When a person stands on level ground at a point 100 m from the foot of a vertical cliff, the angle of elevation of the top of the cliff is 40°.

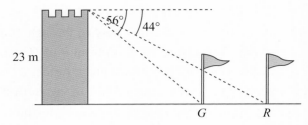

144 m · · · 100 m · · · 40°

(i) Calculate the height of the cliff, correct to the nearest metre.

(ii) If the person moves to a different point on level ground, 244 m from the foot of the cliff, what will the measure of the angle of elevation be then? Give your answer correct to the nearest degree.

16. King George is standing on a tower in his castle and looking towards a river. On one side is his army and on the other a gang of raiders.

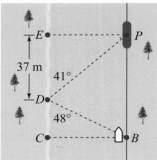

23 m · 56° / 44° · G · R

The angle of depression of his army is 56° while the angle of depression of the raiders is 44°. The tower is 23 m high.

(i) How far is King George's army from the tower?

(ii) How far is the raiders' army from the tower?

(iii) Find the width of the river.

Give your answers correct to the nearest metre.

17. Lulu is walking along a river from *C* toward *E*.

When she reaches *D*, she notices that a boat, *B*, is on the far side behind her at an angle of 48°, while its destination, a pier, *P*, is at 41° in front of her.

She measures the distance from *D* to *E* to be 37 m.

(i) Find the width of the river to the nearest metre.

(ii) Calculate the distance, to the nearest metre, that the boat travelled from *B* to *P*.

(iii) If the boat was moving at an average speed of 6 km/h, how long (to the nearest second) did it take to get from *B* to *P*?

18. Anne is swinging on a wooden garden swing. The seat, S, is held in position by two ropes, all of length 3 m. Her total angle of swing is 110° (55° each way).

  (i) What is the difference in height of the seat at the lowest and highest point in her swing? Give your answer to the nearest cm.

  (ii) In your solution, explain how you think the mathematical model below is arrived at.

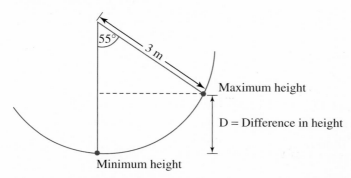

Do you think the mathematical model is accurate? Justify your answer.

19. Copy the diagram and indicate the following directions on it.

    (i) N 20° E
   (ii) S 60° W
  (iii) S 50° E
  (iv) N 70° W

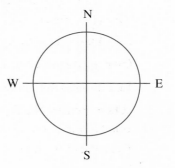

20. Two ships, P and Q, leave a harbour H at the same time. P, the faster ship, sails in a direction S 70° E at 31 km/h. Q sails in the direction S 20° W at x km/h. After two hours' sailing, the ships are 61 km apart. Calculate the distance travelled by ship Q.

21. Two ships, X and Y, left a harbour o at the same time. X travelled due north at 20 km/h while Y travelled in the direction N 60° E. After one hour, Y was directly east of X. Calculate:

  (i) The distance travelled by Y
  (ii) The distance between the ships, correct to the nearest km

22. (i) On leaving a port P, a fishing boat sails in the direction S 30° E for 3 hours at 10 km/h, as shown. What distance has the boat then sailed?

(ii) The boat next sails in the direction
N 60° E at 10 km/h until it is due
east of the port *P*. Calculate how far
the boat is from the port *P*.

(iii) Write a note on the mathematical
model used here. Do you think the
length of the boat is important?
Justify your answer.

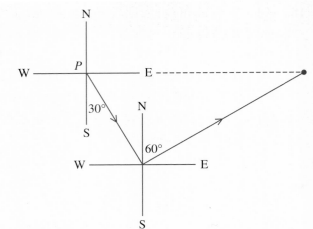

23. An aeroplane is flying from Clifden to Lisdoonvarna. To
avoid flying over water, it must travel 150 km in the
direction S 42° E towards Galway. It then turns 90° and
flies 80 km to Lisdoonvarna.

   (i) Explain why the angle *A* = 48°.

   (ii) Write down the direction to Lisdoonvarna from
   Galway.

   (iii) How much further is it to fly via Galway than flying
   directly?

   (iv) Find *B* to the nearest degree.

   (v) Calculate the direction to Lisdoonvarna from Clifden.

24. Jeff wants to calculate the height of the Eiffel Tower
without climbing to its top. He notices that both he and
the tower cast a shadow on the ground.

Jeff is 1·65 m tall and casts a shadow 0·7 m long.

   (i) What is the angle of elevation of the sun? Give your
   answer to the nearest degree.

   (ii) From a point directly under the centre of the tower,
   Jeff measures the tower's shadow to be 137·2 m.
   Calculate the height of the tower, to the nearest metre,
   using your answer from part **(i)**.

Later on, Jeff realised he could have calculated the
height of the tower without using trigonometry
(see Chapter 26).

Ratio and proportion

The following exercise is a revision of material covered in Chapter 16: Applied Arithmetic from *New Concise Project Maths 1*.

Exercise 17.1

1. €40 is divided between two people in the ratio 7 : 3. How much does each person get?

2. €58·50 is divided between Jane and Robert in the ratio of 8 : 5. How much does each receive?

3. Divide 238 in the ratio 2 : 5 : 7.

4. A prize fund of €18,000 is divided as follows.
   The first prize is half the fund, the second prize is two-thirds
   the first prize and the third prize is what remains. How much
   is the third prize?

5. Express each of the following ratios in their simplest form.

   (i) $1\frac{1}{2} : 2$ **(ii)** $1\frac{1}{4} : 1$ **(iii)** $\frac{1}{3} : 1$ **(iv)** $\frac{1}{2} : \frac{1}{4} : \frac{1}{3}$ **(v)** $\frac{3}{4} : \frac{1}{2} : 1$

6. Divide 462 g in the ratio $\frac{1}{2} : \frac{3}{5} : 1$.

7. €546 was shared among three people in the ratio $1 : \frac{2}{3} : \frac{1}{2}$. How much did each person receive?

8. €140 is divided between A, B and C so that A gets twice as much as B and C gets twice as much as A.

    (i) Who receives the smallest share?

   (ii) How much does each receive?

9. A, B, C and D shared €493. B and C each received twice as much as A while D received 350% of what A received. Calculate how much each received.

10. €450 is divided between A, B and C such that A's share is twice that of B, and C's share is 50% of A and B's share together. Calculate A's share.

11. If $a : b = 2 : 3$ and $b : c = 6 : 7$, find the ratio of $a : b : c$.

12. If $p : q = 1 : 2$ and $q : r = 5 : 7$, find the ratio $p : q : r$.

13. If $a : b = 4 : 5$ and $b : c = 3 : 2$, find the ratio of $a : c$.

14. $x : y : z = 2 : 4 : 5$. If $z = 15$, evaluate $x + y + z$.

15. $a : b : c = 3 : 5 : 6$. If $a = 21$, evaluate $3a + 2b + 5c$.

16. The ratio of the speeds of two cars is 4 : 5. If the faster car is travelling at 85 km/h, calculate the speed of the slower car.

17. The speeds of a train and a motorbike are in the ratio $1\frac{1}{2}$: 2, respectively. If the speed of the train is 84 km/h, find the speed of the motorbike in km/h.

18. A woman gave some money to her four children in the ratio 2 : 3 : 5 : 9. If the difference between the largest and the smallest share is €87·50, how much money did she give altogether?

19. Peter and Anne share a lotto prize in the ratio $3\frac{1}{2}$: $2\frac{1}{2}$. If Peter's share is €35,000, what is the total prize fund?

20. Two brands of blackcurrant squash drinks contain concentrated juice and sugar. In brand *A*, the ratio of concentrated juice to sugar is 19 : 1. In brand *B*, the ratio of concentrated juice to sugar is 9 : 1.

   (i) What is the volume of concentrated juice in 500 ml of brand *A*?
   (ii) What is the volume of sugar in 300 ml of brand *B*?
   (iii) 500 ml of brand *A* is mixed with 300 ml of brand *B*. What is the ratio of the concentrated juice to the sugar in the mixture?

21. Two baby snakes are measured in the zoo. One measures 8 cm and the other measures 12 cm. Two weeks later they are measured again and the first one now measures 11 cm while the second one measures 15 cm. Did the snakes grow in proportion? Explain your answer.

22. Two containers, one large and one small, contain a total of 4 kilograms of bath salts. One quarter of the bath salts from the large container is transferred to the small container so that the ratio of bath salts in the large container to that in the small one becomes 3 : 2. How many kilograms of bath salts were originally in each container?

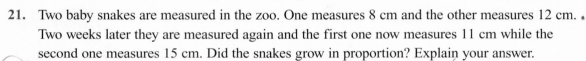

23. A chef can make 3 apple tarts in an hour. His assistant can make 3 apple tarts in 2 hours. They need to make 27 apple tarts. How long will this take them working together?

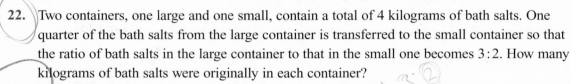

24. One combine harvester can harvest a field of corn in 4·5 hours. Another harvester can harvest the same field in 3 hours. If the farmer uses the two harvesters at the same time how long will it take to harvest the entire field?

25. Two taps are filling a bath. It takes one tap 4 minutes to fill the bath and the other tap 5 minutes. How long will it take to fill the bath with both taps filling at the given rates?

26. 12 men can build a wall in 10 days.

   (i) How many days would it take one man to build the same wall?
   (ii) How many days would it take 15 men to build the same wall?
   (iii) How many men are required to build the wall in five days?

27. 20 people take 15 hours to count the votes after an election.

   (i) How long would it take if 25 people were used to do the counting?

   (ii) How many people would be required to count the votes in six hours?

28. 14 girls can set up a tent in 30 minutes. How long would it take 20 girls to set up the same tent?

29. Five men can complete a certain task in 16 days. If the conditions change and the task must be completed in 10 days, how many extra men are required?

30. Eight workers can build a cabin in 60 hours. How many workers are needed if the cabin is to be built in 32 hours?

Percentages

The following exercise is a revision of material covered in Chapter 16: Applied Arithmetic from *New Concise Project Maths 1*.

Exercise 17.2

1. Find: **(i)** 15% of 200   **(ii)** 21% of 310   **(iii)** 6·5% of €370   **(iv)** $2\frac{1}{4}$% of €164.

2. Find: **(i)** 80% of 90% of 200   **(ii)** The sum of 50% of 20 and 60% of 30.

3. The price of a DVD player is €80 + VAT. If VAT is charged at a rate of 23%, calculate the total cost of the DVD player.

4. A mechanic services a car and the bill comes to €320 + VAT. If he charges VAT at a rate of 13%, calculate the total bill.

5. A TV was priced at €190 + VAT. If a person paid €229·90 for the TV, calculate the rate of VAT.

6. A washing machine was priced at €250 + VAT. If a person paid €297·50 for the washing machine, calculate the rate of VAT.

7. A bill for a family dinner in a restaurant came to €86·25. If this includes VAT at a rate of 15%, calculate the bill before the VAT was added.

8. In a school library, 28% of the books are classified as fiction and the remainder as non-fiction. There are 3,240 non-fiction books in the library. Find the number of books which are classified as fiction.

9. A bill for €96·76 includes VAT at 18%. Calculate the amount of the bill before VAT is added.

10. A bill for €60·75 includes VAT at $12\frac{1}{2}$%. Calculate the amount of VAT in the bill.

11. A girl bought a video game for €73·80, which included VAT at 23%. Find the price of the video game if VAT was reduced to 15%.

12. When the rate of VAT was increased from 18% to 23%, the price of a guitar increased by €60. Calculate the price of the guitar, inclusive of VAT at 23%.

13. When a woman bought a television in a shop, VAT at 23% was added on. If the VAT on the cost of the set was €195·50:

    (i) What was the price of the television set before VAT was added?
    (ii) What was the price including VAT?

14. When 9% of the pupils in a school are absent, 637 are present. How many pupils are on the school roll?

15. A salesperson's income for a year was €70,000. This was made up of a basic pay of €40,000 plus a commission of 5% of sales. Calculate the amount of the sales for the year.

16. A computer salesperson is paid an annual salary of €30,000. He is also paid a commission of 4% on sales. Last year the salesperson earned €38,000. Calculate the value of the sales.

17. A fuel mixture consists of 94% petrol and 6% oil. If the mixture contains 37·6 litres of petrol, calculate the volume of oil.

18. In a sale, the price of a piece of furniture was reduced by 10%. The sale price was €1,125. What was the price before the sale?

19. A salesperson's commission for selling a car is $1\frac{1}{4}$% of the selling price. If the commission for selling a car was €350, calculate the selling price.

20. An auctioneer sells a house for €830,000. The auctioneer's fee is 1·5% on the first €500,000 and 2·5% on the remainder. Calculate the auctioneer's fee.

21. Derek processed 390 passport applications during the month of July. He processed 10% fewer applications during the month of August. How many applications did he process in August?

22. There are 25,000 fish in a fish farm. The number of fish in the farm increases by 40% each year. How many fish will be in the farm at the end of three years?

23. 15% of a number is 96. Calculate 25% of the number.

24. When a number is reduced by 35% the result is 41·6. What is the number?

25. 27% of a number is 24. Calculate 18% of this number.

26. 20% of a number is x. Find, in terms of x, 60% of this number.

27. 15% of a number is y. Find, in terms of y, 12% of this number.

28. k% of a number is 86·4, while 5% of the same number is 18. Calculate k.

29. Three business partners, Aideen, Brian and Caroline, invest €30,000, €40,000 and €70,000, respectively. At the end of each year, 22·5% of the profit made is placed in reserve and the remainder is divided among the partners in proportion to their investments.

   (i) Given that in 2011 the profit amounted to €12,880, calculate the amount placed in reserve.

   (ii) In 2012, Caroline's portion of the profit was €9,331. Calculate how much Aideen and Brian each received in 2012.

   (iii) Calculate the amount placed in reserve in 2012.

30. A meal in a restaurant cost Niamh €70·68. The price included VAT at 14%. Niamh wished to know the price of the meal before the VAT was included. She calculated 14% of €70·68 and subtracted it from the cost of the meal.

   (i) Explain why Niamh will not get the correct answer using this method.

   (ii) Calculate the actual cost of the meal, before the VAT was added.

   (iii) If the rate of VAT was reduced to 11%, how much would Niamh have paid for the meal, inclusive of VAT?

31. Tickets for a concert cost Daniel €152·46. The price included a credit card booking charge of 5%

   (i) Calculate the cost of the tickets, before the credit card charge was added.

   (ii) The cost *before* the credit card charge, includes VAT at 21%. Calculate the cost of the tickets before the VAT was added.

   (iii) If the rate of VAT was increased to 23·5% and the credit card charge was reduced to 4%, how much extra would Daniel pay for the tickets, to the nearest cent?

Foreign exchange

The following exercise is a revision of material covered in Chapter 16: Applied Arithmetic from *New Concise Project Maths 1*.

Exercise 17.3

1. If €1 = $1·08, find the value of **(i)** €150 in dollars **(ii)** $918 in euro.

2. An airline ticket costs $598. If €1 = $1·15, calculate the cost of the ticket in euro.

3. €1 = ¥280 (Japanese yen).
   (i) How many yen would you receive for €110?
   (ii) How many euro would you receive for ¥126,000?

4. A part for a tractor costs €400 in France and the same part costs R912 in South Africa.

   If €1 = R2·4, in which country is it cheaper and by how much (in euro)?

5. When the exchange rate is €1 = $1·18, a person buys 2,950 dollars from a bank. If the bank charges a commission of $2\frac{1}{4}$%, calculate the total cost in euro.

6. A person buys 2,640 Canadian dollars when the exchange rate is €1 = $2·2. A charge (commission) is made for this service.

   (i) How much, in euro, is this charge if the person pays €1,221?
   (ii) Calculate the percentage commission on the transaction.

7. If €1 = $1·20 and €1 = R2·25, how many dollars can be exchanged for 480 rand?

8. **(i)** A tourist changed €2,000 on board ship into South African rand, at a rate of €1 = R2·4. How many rand did she receive?
   (ii) When she came ashore she found that the rate was €1 = R2·48. How much did she lose, in rand, by not changing her money ashore?

9. Dollars were bought for €800 when the exchange rate was €1 = $1·20. A commission is charged for this service. If the person received $936, calculate the percentage commission charged.

10. Una and Conor were travelling to South Africa. They bought 5,760 rand in the bank. The bank charged them €630, which included a 5% service charge. What was the value of the euro in rand (the exchange rate) on that day?

11. A tourist paid $4,620 to a travel agent for a holiday in Ireland, where €1 = $1·32. The cost to the travel agent of organising the holiday was €2,985. Calculate, in euro, the profit made by the travel agent.

12. The Thailand Baht (THB) is at a low of 0·38 Mexican Pesos (MXN). How many THB can be purchased for 1,000,000 MXN?

13. €1 will buy 57 Indian Rupees (INR). €1 will buy US$1·25 (USD). How many INR will one USD buy?

14. €1 will buy 39 Russian Roubles (RUB). €1 will buy 7·5 Norwegian Kroner (NOK). How many RUB will one NOK buy?

Household bills

The following exercise is a revision of material covered in Chapter 16: Applied Arithmetic from *New Concise Project Maths 1*.

Exercise 17.4

1. The monthly line rental on Paula's mobile phone amounts to €12·70. During May, the duration of her calls is 1 hr 41 mins and 50 secs. Calls are charged at 0·6 cent per second. Calculate Paula's total bill for May.

2. Paul has the following pay plan on his mobile phone.

   For €25 (excluding VAT) a month, he gets 150 free minutes and 100 free texts. All additional calls are charged at 22c per minute and all additional texts are charged at 7c per text. VAT of 20% is then added to all charges.

   (i) In March, Paul makes 180 minutes of calls and sends 230 texts. Calculate the total of Paul's bill in March.

   (ii) In April, Paul makes 210 minutes of calls and sends 270 texts. Calculate the total of Paul's bill in April.

3. A family rents a house for a period of 18 months. The refuse charges are €12·60 per month. The electricity bill amounts to €126 every two months. The heating bill amounts to €114 every two months. The television and broadband charges are €55 per month. How much does the family pay in total for these charges for the 18-month period?

4. Three students rent a house for a period of eight months. The refuse charges are €16·80 per month. The electricity bill amounts to €84 every two months. The television and broadband charges are €324 for the period of the rental. How much should each of the three students pay monthly for these charges?

5. Jack has the following pay plan on his mobile phone.

    For €32 (excluding VAT) a month, he gets 200 free minutes and 200 free texts. All additional calls are charged at 28c per minute and all additional texts are charged at 8·5c per text. VAT of 23% is then added to all charges.

    (i) In August, Jack makes 225 minutes of calls and sends 231 texts. Calculate the total of Jack's bill in August.

    (ii) In September, Jack makes 273 minutes of calls and sends 262 texts. Calculate the total of Jack's bill in September.

6. Three students rent a house for a period of 12 months. The television and broadband charges are €564 for the period of the rental. The refuse charges are €13·50 per month. The electricity bill amounts to €96 every two months. How much should each of the three students pay monthly for these charges?

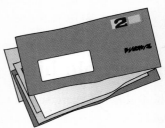

7. The Carey family has used 1,100 units of electricity during the months of April and May. The electricity supply company charges 9 cent per unit of electricity used plus a standing charge of €11·20 per month. VAT of 23% is then added to the total. Calculate how much the Careys' electricity bill will be for the two-month period.

8. Find the values of A, B, C, D and E on the following bill.

Electricity Supply Company					
Bill no. 2731					
Meter reading					
Present	**Previous**	**Units used**	**Rate per unit**	**Description**	**Amount**
42,382	39,815	A	€0·08	Cost of units used	B
				Standing charge	€13·05
				Total before VAT	C
				VAT at 14%	D
				Total due	E

9. Find the values of A, B, C, D, E, F and G on the following bill.

Gas Supply Company					
Bill no. 2731					
Meter reading		**Units used**	**Rate per unit**	**Description**	**Amount**
Present	**Previous**				
81,457	74,905	A	€0·075	Cost of units used	B
Discount of 5% if paid within 30 days				Standing charge	€17·97
				Total before VAT	C
				VAT at 14%	D
				Total due	E
				Discount	F
				Total due after discount	G

Loss and discounts

The following exercise is a revision of material covered in Chapter 16: Applied Arithmetic from *New Concise Project Maths 1*.

Exercise 17.5

1. Jason bought a bicycle for €320. 18 months later he sold it for €280.

    (i) Calculate the loss Jason made on the sale of the bicycle.

    (ii) Find the percentage loss (i.e. the loss as a percentage of the cost price).

2. Janet bought a mobile phone for €140. A year later she sold it for €115.
    (i) Calculate the loss Janet made on the sale of the mobile phone.
    (ii) Find the percentage loss to two decimal places.

3. Sharon bought a car for €15,000. She sold it three years later, making a loss of 32%. Calculate the price she sold the car for.

4. A retailer offers a €90 discount on an armchair costing €450. Calculate the percentage discount.

5. A shop offers a €12 discount on a coat costing €150. Calculate the percentage discount.

6. The price of a litre of petrol on the 1st of August was €1·20. The price on the 1st of September was €1·17. Calculate the percentage decrease over this period.

7. The price of a computer game is €59·99. In a sale the price of this computer game is reduced to €49·99. What is the percentage reduction on the original price of the game in the sale? Give your answer correct to the nearest per cent.

8. A dealer is selling a car for €18,500. She offers a 7% discount if the buyer can pay with cash. How much would the car cost after the discount?

9. A company bought a photocopier and sold it three years later for €2,470, making a loss of 35%. Calculate how much the company paid for the photocopier.

10. A shop sold a laptop for €1,068. This included an 11% discount. Calculate the price of the laptop before the discount was applied.

11. Kevin bought a car and sold it two years later for €15,210, making a loss of 22%. Calculate how much Kevin paid for the car originally.

12. Molly bought an MP3 player and sold it a year later for €111·60, making a loss of 48%. Calculate how much Molly paid for the MP3 player originally, to the nearest cent.

Percentage profit

The percentage profit can be measured as a percentage of the cost price (mark-up) or the selling price (margin).

> Mark-up is the profit as a percentage of the cost price.
> $$\text{Mark-up} = \frac{\text{Profit}}{\text{Cost price}} \times 100$$

> Margin is the profit as a percentage of the selling price.
> $$\text{Margin} = \frac{\text{Profit}}{\text{Selling price}} \times 100$$

EXAMPLE

A shop bought a suite of furniture for €900.

(i) If they sold it for a 32% mark-up, find the sale price.

(ii) If they sold it for a 32% margin, find the sale price to the nearest cent.

Solution:

(i) Mark-up $= \dfrac{\text{Profit}}{\text{Cost price}} \times 100$

$32 = \dfrac{\text{Profit}}{900} \times 100$

$32(900) = 100(\text{profit})$

$28{,}800 = 100(\text{profit})$

$288 = \text{Profit}$

$\therefore$ Sale price $= 900 + 288$

Sale price $= €1{,}188$

(ii) Margin $= \dfrac{\text{Profit}}{\text{Selling price}} \times 100$

$32 = \dfrac{\text{Profit}}{900 + \text{profit}} \times 100$

$32(900 + \text{profit}) = \text{profit} \times 100$

$28{,}800 + 32(\text{profit}) = 100(\text{profit})$

$28{,}800 = 100(\text{profit}) - 32(\text{profit})$

$28{,}800 = 68(\text{profit})$

$423 \cdot 53 = \text{profit}$

$\therefore$ Sale price $= 900 + 423 \cdot 53$

Sale price $= €1{,}323 \cdot 53$

Exercise 17.6

1. A shop bought a coat for €100 and sold it for €120. Calculate:

   (i) The mark-up on the coat

   (ii) The margin on the coat

2. A retailer bought a laptop for €800 and sold it for €950. Calculate:

   (i) The mark-up on the laptop

   (ii) The margin on the laptop

3. A car dealer bought a car for €7,500 and sold it for a 15% mark-up. Calculate the selling price of the car.

4. A retailer bought a mobile phone for €80 and sold it for a 12% mark-up. Calculate the selling price of the mobile phone.

5. An investor bought an apartment for €180,000 and sold it for a 10% margin. Calculate the selling price of the apartment.

6. A jeweller bought a diamond ring at an auction for €6,000 and sold it for a 40% margin. Calculate the selling price of the ring.

7. A retailer bought a suite of furniture for €850.

   (i) If they sold it for a 45% mark-up, find the sale price.

   (ii) If they sold it for a 45% margin, find the sale price to the nearest cent.

8. A retailer bought a refrigerator for €350.

   (i) If they sold it for an 18% mark-up, find the sale price.

   (ii) If they sold it for an 18% margin, find the sale price to the nearest cent.

9. A retailer bought a shipment of games consoles for €4,200.

   (i) If they sold half of the consoles at an 18% mark-up, find the sale price of this half.

   (ii) If they sold the other half of the consoles at a 26% margin, find the sale price to the nearest cent, of this half.

   (iii) Find the total profit, in euro, made on the sale of the entire shipment.

10. A retailer bought a consignment of DVD players for €12,000. He sold half of them at a 14% mark-up and the other half at a 20% margin. Calculate the total selling price and hence the total profit made.

11. A retailer bought a shipment of MP3 players for €8,500. She sold a quarter of them at a 16% mark-up and the remaining three-quarters at a 36·25% margin. Calculate the total selling price and hence the total profit made.

12. (i) A merchant buys tea for €3·29 per kg and then sells it at a profit of 60% of the cost price to a customer in England. The exchange rate is £1 (sterling) = €1·46. Calculate the selling price of the tea in £ sterling, correct to two decimal places.

   (ii) The exchange rate changes to £1 (sterling) = €1·50. The selling price, in sterling, remains the same. Calculate the merchant's margin in this case, correct to the nearest whole number.

Compound interest

The following exercise is a revision of material covered in Chapter 16: Applied Arithmetic from *New Concise Project Maths 1*.

Exercise 17.7

Calculate the compound interest on each of the following investments in questions 1–8.

1. €15,000 for 2 years at 8% per annum
2. €12,000 for 2 years at 7% per annum
3. €18,000 for 3 years at 5% per annum
4. €25,000 for 3 years at 6% per annum
5. €10,000 for 3 years at 3% per annum
6. €20,000 for 3 years at 4% per annum
7. €750 for 3 years at 10% per annum
8. €5,000 for 3 years at 2% per annum

9. €8,000 was invested for two years at compound interest. The interest rate for the first year was 4% and for the second was 5%. Calculate the total interest earned.

10. €6,500 was invested for three years at compound interest. The interest rate for the first year was 5%, for the second year was 8% and for the third year 12%. Calculate the total interest earned.

11. €2,500 was invested for three years at compound interest. The interest rate for the first year was 4%, for the second year was 3% and for the third year 2·5%. Calculate the amount after three years.

12. A woman borrowed €35,000 at 6% per annum compound interest. She agreed to repay €5,000 at the end of the first year, €5,000 at the end of the second year and to clear the debt at the end of the third year. How much was paid to clear the debt?

13. A man borrowed €10,000. He agreed to repay €2,000 after one year, €3,000 after two years and the balance at the end of the third year. If interest was charged at 8% in the first year, 5% in the second year and 6% in the third year, how much was paid at the end of the third year to clear the debt?

14. Tony has €5,000 and would like to invest it for two years. A special savings account is offering a rate of 2·5% for the first year and 3% for the second year, if the money is retained in the account. Tax of 20% will be deducted each year from the interest earned.

    (i) How much will the investment be worth at the end of one year, after tax is deducted?
    (ii) How much will the investment be worth at the end of the second year, after tax is deducted?

15. Margaret has €2,000 and would like to invest it for three years. A special savings account is offering a rate of 2·5% for the first year, 3% for the second year and 4% for the third year, if the money is retained in the account. Tax of 22% will be deducted each year from the interest earned. Calculate the amount of the investment, to the nearest euro, after the three years.

16. €7,500 amounts to €8,100 after one year. Calculate the interest rate.

17. €8,000 was invested for two years at compound interest.

    (i) The interest at the end of the first year was €320. Calculate the rate for the first year.

    (ii) At the end of the second year the investment was worth €8,819·20. Calculate the rate of interest for the second year.

18. €20,000 is borrowed for two years. Interest for the first year is charged at 6% per annum.

    (i) Calculate the amount owed at the end of first year.
    €5,600 is then repaid.

    (ii) Interest is charged at x% per annum for the second year. The amount owed at the end of the second year is €16,146. Calculate the value of x.

19. €50,000 was invested for three years at compound interest. The rate of interest was 4% per annum for the first year and 3% per annum for the second year.

    (i) Calculate the amount of the investment after two years.

    (ii) Then a further €6,440 was invested. If the investment amounted to €61,500 at the end of the third year, calculate the rate of interest for the third year.

20. A person invested €25,000 in a building society. The rate of interest for the first year was $3\frac{1}{2}$%. At the end of the first year the person invested a further €4,125. The rate of interest for the second year was 3%.

    (i) Calculate the value of the investment at the end of the second year.

    (ii) At the end of the second year, a further sum of €2,100 was invested. At the end of the third year, the total value of the investment was €34,485. Calculate the rate of interest for the third year.

21. €2,000 was invested at r% for two years at compound interest. A tax of 25% was deducted each year from the interest gained. At the end of the first year the investment amounted to €2,030 after tax was deducted.

    (i) Calculate the rate of interest, r%.

    (ii) Find the amount of the investment at the end of two years after tax has been deducted.

22. (i) Walter borrows €5,000 for three years at 4% per annum compound interest. He repays €1,800 at the end of each of the first two years. How much must he repay at the end of the third year to clear his loan?

    (ii) Walter wishes to pay off his loan in equal instalments at the end of the first and second year. The rate remains at 4% per annum compound interest. How much would he need to repay at the end of each year to clear his loan after two years? Give your answer correct to the nearest cent.

Given the final amount

Sometimes we are given the final amount and asked to find the original principal. We will use two methods to solve this type of problem.

 EXAMPLE

A sum of money was invested at compound interest. The interest rate for the first year was 10%, for the second year the rate was 8% and the rate was 5% for the third year. After three years this sum amounted to €24,948. Find the sum invested.

Solution:

Year 3	Year 2	Year 1
← 5%	← 8%	← 10%
End of year 3	End of year 2	End of year 1
$A_3 = 24{,}948$	$A_2 = 23{,}760$	$A_1 = 22{,}000$
$105\% = 24{,}948$	$108\% = 23{,}760$	$110\% = 22{,}000$
$1\% = 237 \cdot 60$	$1\% = 220$	$1\% = 200$
$100\% = 23{,}760$	$100\% = 22{,}000$	$100\% = 20{,}000$

Thus, the original sum invested was €20,000.

Method 2:

Calculate what €1,000 (or €100, €10,000, etc.) will amount to and divide this into €24,948 and multiply this answer by €1,000.

$P_1 = 1{,}000$

$A_1 = 1{,}000 \times 1 \cdot 1 = 1{,}100$

$A_2 = 1{,}100 \times 1 \cdot 08 = 1{,}188$

$A_3 = 1{,}188 \times 1 \cdot 05 = 1{,}247 \cdot 40$

$$\frac{A_3}{P_1} = \frac{24{,}948}{1{,}247 \cdot 40} = 20$$

Therefore, the original sum invested = €1,000 × 20 = €20,000.

Exercise 17.8

1. €6,000 was invested at compound interest. The rate for the first year was 4% per annum.
   (i) Calculate the amount of the investment at the end of the first year.
   (ii) At the end of the second year the investment amounted to €6,520·80. Calculate the rate per annum for the second year.

2. A sum of money invested at compound interest amounts to €2,809 at 6% per annum for two years. Calculate the sum invested.

3. A sum of money invested at compound interest amounts to €12,597·12 at 8% per annum for three years. Calculate the sum invested.

4. A sum of money was invested at compound interest. The interest rate for the first year was 8% per annum, for the second year the interest rate was 5% per annum and the interest rate was 4% per annum for the third year. After three years this sum amounted to €53,071·20. Find the sum invested.

5. A sum of money was invested at compound interest. The interest rate for the first year was 10% per annum, for the second year the interest rate was 8% per annum and the interest rate was 5% per annum for the third year. After three years this sum amounted to €27,442·80. Find the sum invested.

In questions 6–14 it may make the working easier to calculate the amount after two years then work backwards from the end of the third year and equate these amounts to find the sum of money withdrawn.

6. (i) A person invested €20,000 for three years at 6% per annum compound interest. Calculate the amount after two years.
   (ii) After two years a sum of money was withdrawn. The money which remained amounted to €22,260 at the end of the third year. Calculate the amount of money withdrawn after two years.

7. A person invested €50,000 for three years at 8% per annum compound interest.
   At the end of the first year, €9,000 was withdrawn.
   At the end of the second year, another sum of money was withdrawn.
   At the end of the third year the person's investment was worth €39,960.
   Calculate the amount of money withdrawn after two years.

8. €42,000 was invested for three years at compound interest. The interest rate for the first year was 6% per annum, the interest rate for the second year was 4% per annum and the interest rate for the third year was 3% per annum. At the end of the first year €1,520 was withdrawn. At the end of the second year €w was withdrawn. At the end of the third year the investment was worth €41,200. Find the value of w.

9. Dermot has €5,000 and would like to invest it for two years. A special savings account is offering a rate of 3% for the first year and a higher rate for the second year, if the money is retained in the account. Tax of 27% will be deducted each year from the interest earned.
   (i) How much will the investment be worth at the end of one year, after tax is deducted?
   (ii) Dermot calculates that, after tax has been deducted, his investment will be worth about €5,296 at the end of the second year. Calculate the rate of interest for the second year.

10. Joanne has €9,000 and would like to invest it for two years. A special savings account is offering a rate of 2·5% for the first year and a higher rate for the second year, if the money is retained in the account. Tax of 25% will be deducted each year from the interest earned.

(i) How much will the investment be worth at the end of one year, after tax is deducted?

(ii) Joanne calculates that, after tax has been deducted, her investment will be worth about €9,444 at the end of the second year. Calculate the rate of interest for the second year.

11. What sum of money invested at 2% per annum compound interest would produce interest of €306·04 after three years?

12. A sum of money was invested at compound interest for two years. The interest rate for each year was 5%. After the two years the sum amounted to €5,512·50. Calculate the original sum of money invested.

13. €6,000 was invested at compound interest. The rate for the first year was 4% per annum.
   (i) Calculate the amount of the investment at the end of the first year.
   (ii) At the end of the second year the investment amounted to €6,520·80. Calculate the rate per annum for the second year.

14. (i) €12,000 was invested for one year. It earned interest at the rate of 8% per annum. Calculate the amount of the investment at the end of the year.
   (ii) A charge of €x was then deducted from this amount. The money which remained was converted into dollars, $, and the dollars were invested for a year at a rate of interest of 5% per annum. At the end of the year, the invested dollars amounted to $16,128. If the exchange rate was €1 = $1·20 on the day the euro were exchanged for dollars, calculate the value of x.

Income tax

The following is called the **income tax equation**:

$$\text{gross tax} - \text{tax credits} = \text{tax payable}$$

Gross tax is calculated as follows:

Standard rate on all income up to the standard rate cut-off point
+
A higher rate on all income above the standard rate cut-off point

EXAMPLE 1

A woman has a gross yearly income of €48,000. She has a standard rate cut-off point of €27,500 and a tax credit of €3,852. The standard rate of tax is 18% of income up to the standard rate cut-off point and 37% on all income above the standard rate cut-off point. Calculate:
   (i) The amount of gross tax for the year
   (ii) The amount of tax paid for the year

Solution:

(i) Gross tax = 18% of €27,500 + 37% of €20,500

$$= €27,500 \times 0 \cdot 18 + €20,500 \times 0 \cdot 37$$
$$= €4,950 + €7,585$$
$$= €12,535$$

Income above the standard rate cut-off point
$$= €48,000 - €27,500$$
$$= €20,500$$

(ii) Income tax equation:

Gross tax − tax credit = tax payable
$$€12,535 - €3,852 = €8,683$$

Therefore, she paid €8,683 in tax.

Note: If a person earns less than their standard rate cut-off point, then they pay tax only at the standard rate on all their income.

EXAMPLE 2

A man paid €10,160 in tax for the year. He had a tax credit of €3,980 and a standard rate cut-off point of €26,000. The standard rate of tax is 17% of income up to the standard rate cut-off point and 36% on all income above the standard rate cut-off point.

Calculate:

(i) The amount of income taxed at the rate of 36%

(ii) The man's gross income for the year

Solution:

(i) Income tax equation:

Gross tax − tax credit = tax payable

17% of €26,000 + 36% of (income above cut-off point) − €3,980 = €10,160

€4,420 + 36% of (income above cut-off point) − €3,980 = €10,160

36% of (income above cut-off point) + €440 = €10,160

36% of (income above cut-off point) = €9,720

1% of (income above cut-off point) = €270

100% of (income above cut-off point) = €27,000

Therefore, the amount of income taxed at the higher rate of 36% was €27,000.

(ii) Gross income = standard rate cut-off point + income above the standard rate cut-off point = €26,000 + €27,000 = €53,000

Exercise 17.9

1. A man has a gross yearly income of €37,000. He has a standard rate cut-off point of €20,500 and a tax credit of €2,490. The standard rate of tax is 18% of income up to the standard rate cut-off point and 38% on all income above the standard rate cut-off point. Calculate:

   (i) The amount of gross tax for the year

   (ii) The amount of tax paid for the year

2. A woman has a gross yearly income of €39,500. She has a standard rate cut-off point of €23,600 and a tax credit of €3,950. The standard rate of tax is 20% of income up to the standard rate cut-off point and 42% on all income above the standard rate cut-off point. Calculate:

   (i) The amount of gross tax for the year

   (ii) The amount of tax paid for the year

3. Howard has a gross yearly income of €43,000. He has a standard rate cut-off point of €28,400 and a tax credit of €3,240. The standard rate of tax is 15% of income up to the standard rate cut-off point and 35% on all income above the standard rate cut-off point. Calculate:

   (i) The amount of gross tax for the year

   (ii) Howard has to pay a Universal Social Charge (USC) of 3% of his gross salary. Calculate how much his USC will be.

   (iii) Calculate Howard's net salary after tax and USC have been deducted.

4. Robyn has a gross yearly income of €47,500. She has a standard rate cut-off point of €28,750 and a tax credit of €4,150. The standard rate of tax is 21% of income up to the standard rate cut-off point and 41% on all income above the standard rate cut-off point. Calculate:

   (i) The amount of gross tax for the year

   (ii) The amount of tax paid for the year

5. James has a gross yearly income of €35,750. He has a standard rate cut-off point of €22,350 and a tax credit of €2,850. The standard rate of tax is 16% of income up to the standard rate cut-off point and 32% on all income above the standard rate cut-off point. Calculate:

   (i) The amount of gross tax for the year

   (ii) James has to pay a USC of 2% of his gross salary. Calculate how much his USC will be.

   (iii) Calculate James' net salary after tax and USC have been deducted.

6. John has a gross income per fortnight of €1,750. The standard rate of income tax is 20% and the higher rate is 42%. He has tax credits of €105 per fortnight and his standard rate cut-off point is €1,295 per fortnight. After tax is paid, what is John's net income per fortnight?

7. Aoife is single and earned €40,000 last year. Aoife's tax credits are listed below.

Single Person Tax Credit	€1,830
PAYE Tax Credit	€1,830
Rent Allowance Tax Credit	€400
Trade Union Payment Tax Credit	€70

    (i) Calculate Aoife's total tax credits.

  (ii) The standard rate cut-off point for a single person was €36,400.
The standard rate of income tax was 20% and the higher rate was 41%. Calculate the tax paid by Aoife on her income.

 (iii) Aoife also had to pay a 2% income levy on her gross income. Calculate Aoife's net income after all deductions had been made.

8. Ciaran is married and earned €52,500 last year. Ciaran's tax credits are listed below.

Married Person Tax Credit	€3,250
PAYE Tax Credit	€1,830
Trade Union Payment Tax Credit	€850

    (i) Calculate Ciaran's total tax credits.

  (ii) The standard rate cut-off point for a married person was €38,500.
The standard rate of income tax was 18% and the higher rate was 39%. Calculate the tax paid by Ciaran on his income.

 (iii) Ciaran also has to pay a $2\frac{1}{2}$% income levy on his gross income, USC of 2% on the first €15,000 of his salary and 3·5% on any income above €15,000, an annual health insurance payment of €900, an annual pension contribution of €3,200 and an annual trade union subscription of €350. Calculate Ciaran's net income after all deductions have been made.

9. Frank is married and earned €46,800 last year. The standard rate cut-off point for a married person was €35,300. The standard rate of income tax was 21% and the higher rate was 42%. Frank has tax credits of €3,600.

    (i) Calculate the tax paid by Frank on his income.

  (ii) Frank also has to pay a 3% income levy on his gross income, USC of 2% on the first €12,500 of his salary and 4% on any income above €12,500, a monthly health insurance payment of €90, a monthly pension contribution of €280 and a weekly trade union subscription of €8. Calculate Frank's annual net income after all deductions have been made.

10. Gustav is single and earned €51,000 last year. The standard rate cut-off point was €37,200. The standard rate of income tax was 19% and the higher rate was 40%. Gustav has tax credits of €4,150.

    (i) Calculate the tax paid by Gustav on his income.

    (ii) Gustav also has to pay a 2% income levy on his gross income, USC of $2\frac{1}{2}$% on the first €10,000 of his salary and 4% on any income above €10,000, a weekly PRSI contribution of €35, a monthly health insurance payment of €65, a monthly pension contribution of €340 and a weekly trade union subscription of €7·50. Calculate Gustav's annual net income after all deductions have been made.

11. A man has a gross yearly income of €26,000. He has a standard rate cut-off point of €28,000 and a tax credit of €1,800. If he pays tax of €3,400, calculate the standard rate of tax.

12. A woman has a gross yearly income of €27,500. She has a standard rate cut-off point of €29,300 and a tax credit of €2,115. If she pays tax of €2,835, calculate the standard rate of tax.

13. Jill has a gross income of €50,000. Her total income tax payable amounts to €10,460. The standard rate cut-off point is €32,000. The standard rate of tax is 20% and the higher rate is 42%. What are Jill's tax credits for the year?

14. A woman paid €10,280 in tax for the year. She had a tax credit of €2,540 and a standard rate cut-off point of €29,000. The standard rate of tax is 18% of income up to the standard rate cut-off point and 40% on all income above the standard rate cut-off point. Calculate:

    (i) The amount of income taxed at the rate of 40%

    (ii) The gross income for the year

15. A man paid €10,775 in tax for the year. He had a tax credit of €1,960 and a standard rate cut-off point of €28,500. The standard rate of tax is 15% of income up to the standard rate cut-off point and 36% on all income above the standard rate cut-off point. Calculate:

    (i) The amount of income taxed at the rate of 40%

    (ii) The gross income for the year

16. The standard rate of income tax is 20% and the higher rate is 42%. Fiona has tax credits of €1,493 for the year and a standard rate cut-off point of €30,000.
    She has a gross income of €31,650 for the year.

    (i) After tax is paid, what is Fiona's income for the year?

    (ii) What would Fiona's gross income for the year need to be in order for her to have an after-tax income of €29,379?

17. (i) The standard rate of income tax is 20% and the higher rate is 42%. Sheila has tax credits of €2,700 for the year and a standard rate cut-off point of €22,000. Sheila has a gross income of €45,000 for the year. Calculate the total tax payable by Sheila for the year.

    (ii) Tony pays tax at the same rates as Sheila. Tony has tax credits of €2,900 for the year and has the same standard rate cut-off point as Sheila. His total tax payable amounts to €13,680 for the year. Calculate Tony's gross income for the year.

18. **(i)** The standard rate of income tax is 20% and the higher rate is 41%. The standard rate cut-off point is €36,500. Aisling has a gross income of €47,500 and total tax credits of €1,830. Calculate Aisling's net income.

    (ii) The following year, Aisling's gross income increases. The tax rates, cut-off point and tax credits remain unchanged. Her net tax now amounts to €15,105. What is her new gross income?

PERIMETER, AREA, VOLUME AND NETS

CHAPTER 18

Revision of perimeter and area

It is recommended that students be familiar with the chapter on perimeter, area, volume and nets from *New Concise Project Maths 1* before starting this chapter.

> The perimeter, P, of a figure is the distance around its edges.

The perimeter is found by adding together the lengths of all the sides. It is measured in length units such as metres (m) or centimetres (cm).

> The area, A, of a figure is the amount of flat surface it contains.

Area is measured in square units such as square metres (m^2) or square centimetres (cm^2).

> When calculating perimeters or areas, make sure that all distances are in the same unit.

Area and perimeter are vital concepts to understand and apply in a wide variety of situations and careers, e.g. planning and designing a new shopping complex.

Formulae required (see the booklet of formulae and tables)

1. Rectangle

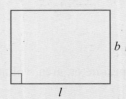

Area = lb
Perimeter = $2l + 2b = 2(l + b)$

2. Square

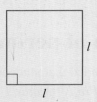

Area = l^2
Perimeter = $4l$

3. Triangle

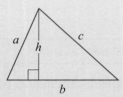

Area = $\frac{1}{2} bh$

Perimeter = $a + b + c$

4. Parallelogram

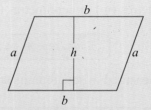

Area = bh
Perimeter = $2a + 2b$
$= 2(a + b)$

5. Circle (disc)

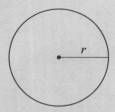

Area = πr^2
Circumference = $2\pi r$ = perimeter

6. Sector of a circle

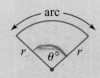

Area = $\dfrac{\theta}{360} \times \pi r^2$

Length of arc = $\dfrac{\theta}{360} \times 2\pi r$

$\left(\text{similar to circle with } \dfrac{\theta}{360} \text{ in front of formulae}\right)$

Perimeter = $r + \dfrac{\theta}{360}(2\pi r) + r$

$= 2r + \dfrac{\theta}{360}(2\pi r)$

EXAMPLE 1

The right-angled triangle shown in the diagram has sides of length 10 cm and 24 cm.

(i) Find the length of the third side.

(ii) Find the length of the perimeter of the triangle.

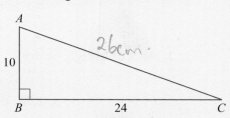

Solution:

(i) Using Pythagoras' theorem:

$|AC|^2 = |AB|^2 + |BC|^2$

$|AC|^2 = 10^2 + 24^2$

$|AC|^2 = 100 + 576 = 676$

$|AC| = \sqrt{676} = 26$ cm

(ii) Perimeter $= |AB| + |BC| + |CA| = 10 + 24 + 26 = 60$ cm

EXAMPLE 2

A shopkeeper has a new metal ice cream cone sign to display on the shop front. The sign is made up of a semicircle and a triangle. (All dimensions are in cm.)

(i) Find the height of the sign.

(ii) Find the area of the sign in cm^2. $\left(\text{Assume } \pi = \dfrac{22}{7}.\right)$

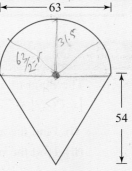

(iii) In order to increase the lifespan of the sign, the shopkeeper decides to apply a galvanized steel coat to both sides of the sign. The cost of galvanizing is €185 per square metre. Find the cost of galvanizing the sign correct to the nearest euro. (In this case, the thickness of the sign is negligible and can be ignored.)

Solution:

(i) The height $= 54 + \text{radius} = 54 + \frac{1}{2}(63) = 54 + 31\frac{1}{2} = 85\frac{1}{2}$ cm.

(ii) Split the figure up into regular shapes, for which we have formulae to calculate the area. Find the area of each shape separately and add these results together.

1. Area of semicircle $= \frac{1}{2}\pi r^2$

$= \frac{1}{2} \times \frac{22}{7} \times \frac{63}{2} \times \frac{63}{2}$

$= 1{,}559 \cdot 25 \text{ cm}^2$

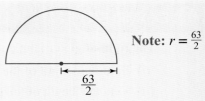

Note: $r = \frac{63}{2}$

2. Area of triangle $= \frac{1}{2}bh$

$= \frac{1}{2} \times 63 \times 54$

$= 1{,}701 \text{ cm}^2$

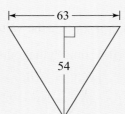

Area of figure = Area of semicircle + Area of triangle

$= 1{,}559 \cdot 25 + 1{,}701$

$= 3{,}260 \cdot 25 \text{ cm}^2$

(iii) Cost of galvanizing = €185 per m²

$3{,}260 \cdot 25 \times 2$ = Area both sides in cm²

$6{,}520 \cdot 5$ = Area both sides in cm²

$\dfrac{6{,}520 \cdot 5}{100 \times 100}$ = Area both sides in m²

Cost $= 0 \cdot 65205 \text{ m}^2 \times 185$

$= €120 \cdot 6295$

$= €121$ (correct to the nearest euro)

EXAMPLE 3

The diagram represents a sector of a circle of radius 15 cm.
$|\angle POQ| = 72°$.

(i) Find the area of the sector OPQ in terms of π.

(ii) Find the perimeter of the sector (assume $\pi = 3 \cdot 14$).

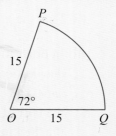

Solution:

(i) Area of sector

$= \dfrac{\theta}{360} \times \pi r^2$

$= \dfrac{72}{360} \times \pi \times 15 \times 15$

$= \frac{1}{5} \times \pi \times 15 \times 15$

$= 45\pi \text{ cm}^2$

(ii) Length of arc PQ

$= \dfrac{\theta}{360} \times 2\pi r$

$= \dfrac{72}{360} \times 2 \times 3 \cdot 14 \times 15$

$= \frac{1}{5} \times 2 \times 3 \cdot 14 \times 15$

Perimeter $= 15 + 15 + 18 \cdot 84 = 48 \cdot 84 \text{ cm}$

Notes: **1.** When using $\pi = \frac{22}{7}$, it is good practice to write the radius as a fraction.

For example, $21 = \frac{21}{1}$ or $4 \cdot 5 = \frac{9}{2}$.

2. If a question says 'give your answer in terms of π', then leave π in the answer: do not use $3 \cdot 14$ or $\frac{22}{7}$ or your calculator for π.

3. If a diagram is not given, drawing a rough diagram can be vital to help see and solve the problem.

4. Always use the value of π from your calculator unless told otherwise in the question.

Given the perimeter or area

In some equations we are given the perimeter, the circumference or the area and asked to find missing lengths. Basically we are given **an equation in disguise** and we solve this equation to find the missing length.

EXAMPLE 1

The perimeter of a rectangle is 180 m. If length : breadth = 2 : 1, find the area of the rectangle.

Solution:

Let the length $= 2x$ and the breadth $= x$.

Equation given in disguise:

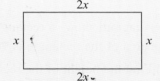

$$\text{Perimeter} = 180$$
$$\therefore \quad 2x + x + 2x + x = 180$$
$$6x = 180$$
$$x = 30$$
$$\therefore \quad \text{Breadth} = 30 \text{ m}$$
$$\text{and length} = 2x = 2(30) = 60 \text{ m}$$

$$\text{Area} = l \times b$$
$$= 60 \times 30$$
$$= 1{,}800$$
$$\therefore \quad \text{Area} = 1{,}800 \text{ m}^2$$

EXAMPLE 2

The circumference of a circle is $37 \cdot 68$ cm. Calculate its area (assume $\pi = 3 \cdot 14$).

Solution:

Equation given in disguise:

$$\text{Circumference} = 37 \cdot 68 \text{ cm}$$
$$\therefore \quad 2\pi r = 37 \cdot 68$$
$$2(3 \cdot 14)r = 37 \cdot 68$$
$$6 \cdot 28r = 37 \cdot 68$$
$$r = \frac{37 \cdot 68}{6 \cdot 28} = 6 \text{ cm}$$

$$\text{Area} = \pi r^2$$
$$= 3 \cdot 14 \times 6 \times 6$$
$$= 113 \cdot 04$$
$$\therefore \quad \text{Area of circle} = 113 \cdot 04 \text{ cm}^2$$

Exercise 18.1

Unless otherwise stated, all dimensions are in cm and assume $\pi = 3\cdot14$. All curved lines represent the circumference, or parts of the circumference, of a circle.

Find (i) the perimeter (ii) the area of each of the following shapes in questions 1–6.

1.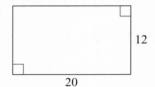

2.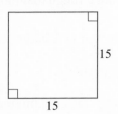

3.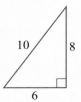

4.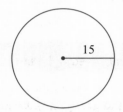

5.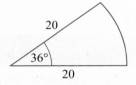

6.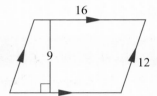

7. The diagram shows a rectangle of length 42 cm. The area of the rectangle is 966 cm^2.

  (i) Find the height of the rectangle.

  (ii) Find the area of the shaded triangle.

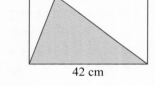

8. The area of the triangle is 80 cm^2. The length of the base is 20 cm. Calculate its perpendicular height, h cm.

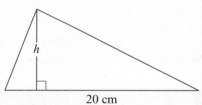

9. The triangle and the rectangle have equal area. Find h.

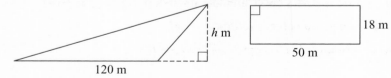

10. Which shape, A, B, C, or D, has:

    (i) The largest area
    (ii) The longest perimeter

    Justify your answers.

(A)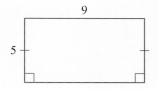

(B)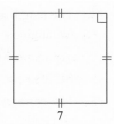

(C)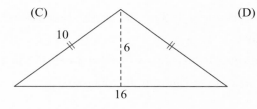

(D)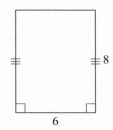

11. A diagram of a circular patio laid inside a square is shown. The scale used is 1 : 80.

    (i) Measure $|AB|$ and calculate its length, using the given scale.

    (ii) Find the total area of gravel. Assume π from your calculator and give your answer in m^2 correct to one decimal place.

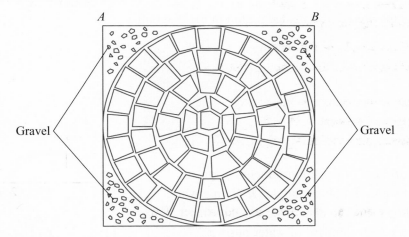

Drawing a rough diagram may help to solve questions 12–17.

12. The area of a rectangle is 320 cm^2. If its length is 40 cm, calculate:

    (i) Its breadth
    (ii) Its perimeter

13. (i) The perimeter of a square is 36 cm. Calculate its area.
    (ii) The area of a square is 25 cm^2. Calculate its perimeter.

14. The length and breadth of a rectangle are in the ratio 3 : 2, respectively. The length of the rectangle is 12 cm. Find:

   (i) its breadth and

   (ii) its area.

15. The perimeter of a rectangle is 120 m. If length : breadth = 3 : 1, find the area of the rectangle.

16. The area of a rectangle is 128 m². If length : breadth = 2 : 1, find the length and the breadth of the rectangle.

17. A right-angled triangle has sides of length 8 cm, 15 cm and 17 cm. Find its area.

18. Calculate the area of the figure in the diagram.

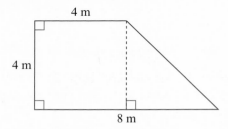

19. Calculate the area of the shaded region in the diagram.

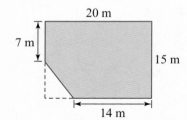

20. The Department of the Environment designs a flag consisting of a blue triangle *OPQ* on a white background *OCBA* to display on beaches that have a very high standard of water purity.

   The flag *OABC* is a rectangle with
   |*OA*| = 1 m and |*OC*| = 80 cm.

   P is the midpoint of [*CB*] and *Q* is the midpoint of [*AB*]. Calculate the area of the blue section of the flag.

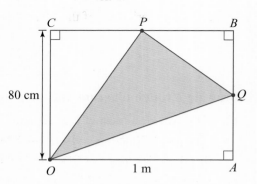

21. Using the theorem of Pythagoras, find $|BC|$ in the diagram. Hence, calculate:

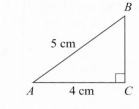

    (i) The perimeter of $\triangle ABC$

    (ii) The area of $\triangle ABC$

22. *ABCD* is a square piece of card from which four equal shaded squares are cut.

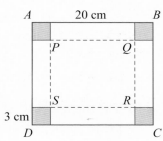

The length of *AB* is 20 cm. Each shaded square has side of length 3 cm. When the four shaded squares are removed, calculate:

    (i) The area remaining

    (ii) The perimeter remaining

23. The area of the circle in this flag covers $\frac{1}{5}$ of the total area of the flag. The other two areas are equal. Calculate:

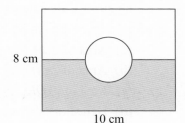

    (i) The area of the flag

    (ii) The area of the circle

    (iii) The area of the shaded section

24. The given hexagon is made up of six equilateral triangles, each of side 8 cm and with perpendicular height $4\sqrt{3}$ cm. Find:

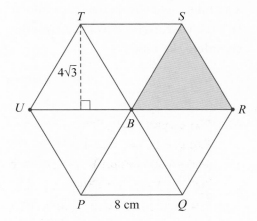

    (i) Area $\triangle BSR$ in surd form

    (ii) Area of the hexagon *PQRSTU* in surd form

    (iii) The perimeter of the hexagon *PQRSTU*

25. The diagram shows a rectangle measuring 15 cm by 8 cm. The lines on the diagram divide the rectangle into four regions of equal area. The lengths of the sides of one of the rectangles are *x* cm and *y* cm, as shown.

    (i) Find the area of the rectangle *ABCD*. Hence, write down the area of each region.

    (ii) Write an expression for $|BQ|$ in terms of *x*. Hence, using the formula for area of a rectangle, solve for *x*.

(iii) Calculate the value of y.

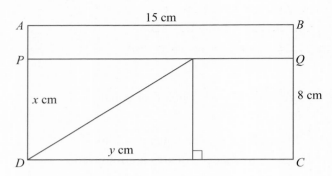

26. **(i)** The triangle ABC is right angled and has $|AB| = 2$ cm and $|BC| = 4$ cm, as shown in the diagram. $PQRB$ is a square with side length x. Calculate the area of $\triangle ABC$.

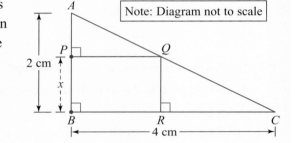

Note: Diagram not to scale

(ii) Find the following in terms of x.

    (a) Area of the square $PQRB$

    (b) Area of $\triangle APQ$

    (c) Area of $\triangle QRC$

    (d) Hence or otherwise, find the value of x.

The table below shows certain information on circles, including the value of π to be used. In each case, write down the equation given in disguise and use this to find the radius and complete the table.

	π	Circumference	Area	Radius
27.	π	10π		
28.	π		$9\,\pi$ m^2	
29.	$3{\cdot}14$		$1{,}256$ m^2	
30.	π		$30{\cdot}25\,\pi$ cm^2	
31.	$\frac{22}{7}$	264 cm		

32. A piece of wire of length 66 cm is in the shape of a semicircle, as shown.
Find the radius length of the semicircle.
(Assume $\pi = \frac{22}{7}$.)

66 cm

33. The diagram shows a small circle drawn inside a larger circle. The small circle has an area of 25π cm². The larger circle has a circumference of 16π cm. Calculate the area of the shaded region in terms of π.

34. The area of the sector shown is $31\cdot4$ cm². Calculate the value of r. (Assume $\pi = 3\cdot14$.)

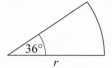

35. The area of the sector shown is $12\cdot56$ cm². Calculate the value of r. (Assume $\pi = 3\cdot14$.)

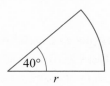

36. C is the centre of the circle with diameter 28 cm. Assume $\pi = \frac{22}{7}$ and calculate the following.

   (i) Area of the circle
   (ii) Perimeter of circle
   (iii) Area of $\triangle ABC$
   (iv) Area of the shaded region
   (v) Perimeter of the quarter-circle ABC

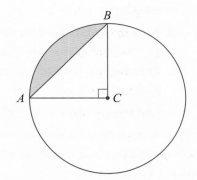

37. The diagram shows a metal strip 10 cm long and $2x$ cm wide, with two semicircular ends. A circular hole x cm in diameter has been drilled in the centre.

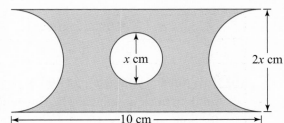

   (i) Given that the area of the rectangular strip is 80 cm², find the value of x.
   (ii) Use the value of x to find the area of the circular hole in terms of π.
   (iii) Hence, show that the area of the shaded region is given by $A = 80 - 20\pi$ cm².

38. Which has the largest area: a square of side 10 cm or a circle of diameter 10 cm? (Assume $\pi = 3\cdot14$.) Justify your answer.

39. Which has the longest perimeter: a circle of diameter 14 cm or a square of side 14 cm? (Assume $\pi = \frac{22}{7}$.) Justify your answer.

40. The diagram shows the earth centre O and a great circle of longitude linking the North Pole and the South Pole. Calculate the distance between the North Pole and the South Pole measured along the circle of longitude. Take the radius of the earth to be 6,400 km. Give your answer to the nearest thousand km.

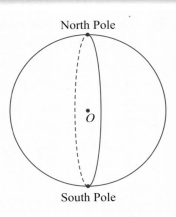

41. A rectangular piece of metal has a width of 16π cm. Two circular pieces, each of radius 8 cm, are cut from the rectangular piece, as shown.

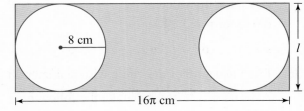

  (i) Find the length, l, of the rectangular piece of metal.

  (ii) Calculate the area of the metal not used (i.e. the shaded section), giving your answer in terms of π.

  (iii) Express the area of the metal not used as a percentage of the total area.

42. **(i)** A running track is in the shape of a rectangle with semicircular ends, as shown. Calculate the length of the track. Assume $\pi = \frac{22}{7}$.

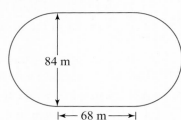

  (ii) Two runners compete in a 400 m race around a running track as shown. The finishing line for both runners is AP.
  The runner on the inside track ($ABCD$) starts at A and runs anticlockwise, as indicated in the diagram. The runner on the outside track also runs anticlockwise. How far from P should the outside track runner start the race in order that the outside track runner covers the same distance as a lap of the inside track? Assume $\pi = \frac{22}{7}$.

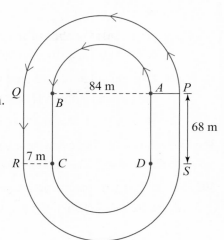

43. The rectangle encloses two touching circles, A and B, as shown in the diagram.

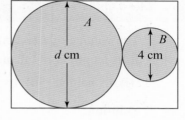

(i) Write down the area of the circle B in terms of π.

(ii) Write down the area of the circle A in terms of π and d.

(iii) Write down an expression for the area of the rectangle in terms of d.

(iv) Hence, show that the unshaded area in the diagram can be written as

$$\tfrac{1}{4}[4d^2 + 16d - 16\pi - d^2\pi].$$

Volume and surface area

The **volume** of a solid is the amount of space it occupies.

Volume is measured in cubic units, such as cubic metres (m^3) or cubic centimetres (cm^3).

Capacity is the volume of a liquid or gas and is usually measured in litres.

Note: 1 litre = 1,000 cm^3 = 1,000 ml

The **surface area** of a solid is the **total area of its outer surface**. It is measured in square units such as square metres or square centimetres.

To calculate the surface area of a solid you have to find the area of each face and add them together (often called the total surface area). With some objects, such as a sphere, the surface area is called the curved surface area.

Note: It is usual to denote volume by V and surface area by SA.

Rectangular solids

Formulae required

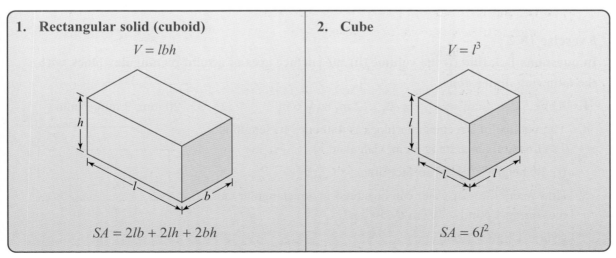

1. **Rectangular solid (cuboid)**

$$V = lbh$$

$$SA = 2lb + 2lh + 2bh$$

2. **Cube**

$$V = l^3$$

$$SA = 6l^2$$

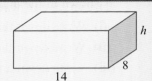

EXAMPLE 1

The volume of a rectangular block is 560 cm^3.
If its length is 14 cm and its breadth is 8 cm, find:

(i) Its height   (ii) Its surface area

Solution:

(i) Equation given in disguise:

Volume = 560 cm^3

$(14)(8)h = 560$

$112h = 560$

$h = \frac{560}{112} = 5$ cm

(ii) Surface area

$= 2lb + 2lh + 2bh$

$= 2(14)(8) + 2(14)(5) + 2(8)(5)$

$= 224 + 140 + 80$

$= 444$ cm^2

EXAMPLE 2

The surface area of a cube is 96 cm^2.
Calculate its volume.

Solution:

Let the length of one side of the cube be l cm.
Equation given in disguise:

Surface area = 96 cm^2

$6l^2 = 96$

$l^2 = 16$

$l = 4$ cm

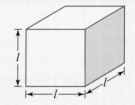

Volume = l^3

$= 4^3$

$= 64$ cm^3

Thus, the volume of the cube is 64 cm^3.

Exercise 18.2

In questions 1–3, find (i) the volume (ii) the surface area of a solid rectangular block with the following dimensions.

1. 6 cm, 5 cm, 4 cm   2. 12 m, 8 m, 6 m   3. 20 mm, 9 mm, 7 mm

4. The volume of a rectangular block is 480 cm^3. Its length is 12 cm and its breadth is 8 cm. Calculate:

(i) Its height   (ii) Its surface area

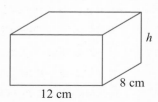

5. How many litres of water can be stored in a rectangular tank measuring 1·5 m by 70 cm by 50 cm?

(Note: 1 litre = 1,000 cm^3)

6. An open rectangular tank (no top) is full of water. The volume of water in the tank is 2·4 litres. If its length is 20 cm and its breadth is 15 cm, find:

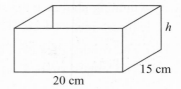

   (i) Its height   (ii) Its surface area

   (**Note:** 1 litre = 1,000 cm^3)

7. How many rectangular packets of tea measuring 12 cm by 4 cm by 4 cm can be packed into a cardboard box measuring 96 cm by 36 cm by 32 cm?

8. The volume of a cube is 27 cm^3. Calculate its surface area.

9. The volume of a cube is 64 cm^3. Calculate its surface area.

10. The surface area of a cube is 24 cm^2. Calculate its volume.

11. The surface area of a cube is 150 cm^2. Calculate its volume.

12. The sides of a rectangular block are in the ratio 2 : 3 : 7. If its volume is 2,688 cm^3, find its dimensions and hence its surface area.

13. The surface area of a solid rectangular block is 258 cm^2. If its breadth is 6 cm and height is 5 cm, calculate (i) its length   (ii) its volume.

14. A jeweller buys a rectangular block of gold of length 4 cm, width 3 cm and height 2 cm. 1 cm^3 of gold costs €500.

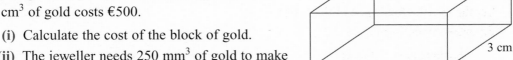

   (i) Calculate the cost of the block of gold.
   (ii) The jeweller needs 250 mm^3 of gold to make a gold ring. How many rings can be made from the block?
   (iii) Each ring is sold for €150. Calculate the amount of profit the jeweller makes on each ring.

15. A solid rectangular metal block has length 12 cm and width 5 cm. The volume of the block is 90 cm^3.

   (i) Find the height of the block in cm.
   (ii) Find the total surface area of the block in cm^2.
   (iii) Each cm^3 of the metal has a mass of 8·4 g. The total mass of a number of these metal blocks is 113·4 kg. How many blocks are there?

16. A quantity of uncooked dough is placed in a baking tray with a square base of 40 cm, as shown in the diagram.

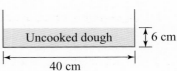

   (i) Find the volume of uncooked dough in the tray.
   (ii) The dough expands to a height of $7\frac{1}{2}$ cm. Find the expansion in percentage terms.
   (iii) Calculate the height of dough in the tray if the dough expands its volume by 16%.

273

17. A swimming pool is in the shape of a cuboid with dimensions 50 metres long by 25 metres wide by 2·5 metres deep. If the pool is completely filled with water, calculate:

   (i) The volume of water in the pool in litres

   (ii) The longest straight surface distance a swimmer could swim in the pool

18. Oil is leaking from this tank at a speed of 0·2 litres per minute. How many days would it take for a full tank of oil to leak away?

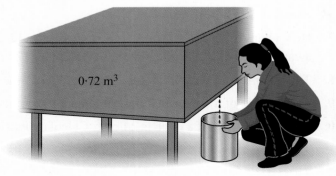

0·72 m³

Uniform cross-section

Many solid objects have the same cross-section throughout their length. Here are some examples.

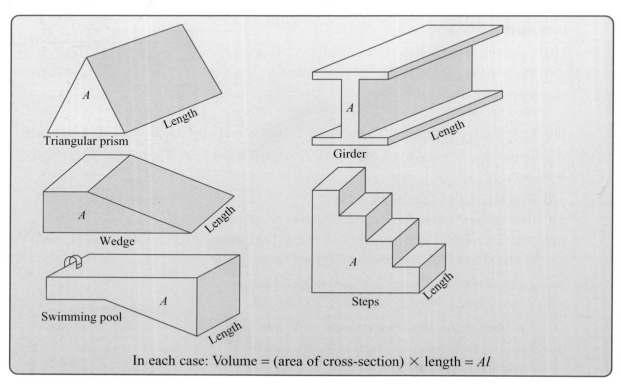

Triangular prism

Wedge

Swimming pool

Girder

Steps

In each case: Volume = (area of cross-section) × length = Al

The above objects are called prisms. A prism is a solid object which has the same cross-section throughout its length and its sides are parallelograms.

A solid cylinder has a uniform cross-section, but it is not a prism.

To find the volume of a solid object with a uniform cross-section, find the area of the cross-section and multiply this by its length.

From the book of formulae and tables

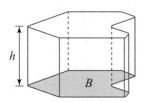

$$V = Bh$$

Solid of uniform cross-section (prism)
taking B as the area of the base

EXAMPLE

The diagram shows the design of a swimming pool.
Calculate the capacity of the pool in m^3.

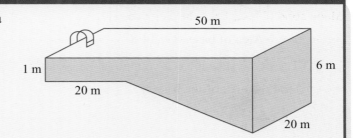

Solution:

The uniform cross-section is a combination of a rectangle and a triangle.

Area of cross-section

$$= l \times b + \tfrac{1}{2}bh$$

$$= 50 \times 1 + \tfrac{1}{2} \times 5 \times 30$$

$$= 50 + 75 = 125 \text{ m}^2$$

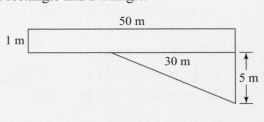

Volume = (area of cross-section) × width

$$= 125 \times 20 = 2{,}500 \text{ m}^3$$

∴ The capacity of the pool is 2,500 m^3.

Exercise 18.3

Calculate the volume of each of the following solids in questions 1–3 (all dimensions are in cm).

1.
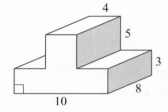

2.
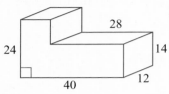

3.
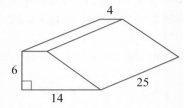

Questions 4 and 5 each show a prism with one of the bases shaded. Calculate the volume of each prism. (All dimensions are in cm.)

4.
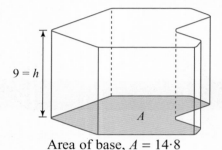

Area of base, $A = 14 \cdot 8$

5.
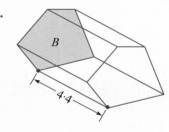

Area of base, $B = 27 \cdot 5$

6. The prism shown has a volume of 1,119 cm^3.
    Find the area of the base W.

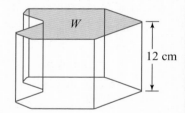

7. The length of a Toblerone packet is 25 cm. The length of the base is 6 cm. The perpendicular height is 4 cm. Find:

    (i) Its volume in cm^3

    (ii) Its capacity in litres

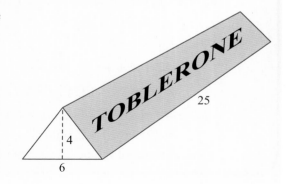

8. The diagram shows a steel girder.
   (i) Calculate the area of its cross-section (shaded region).
   (ii) Calculate the volume, in cm^3, of steel used to manufacture it.

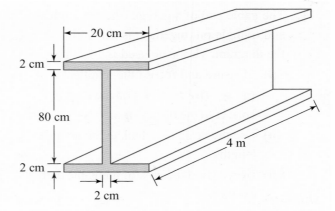

9. Five rectangular-shaped concrete steps are constructed as shown. Each step measures 1·2 m by 0·4 m and the total height is 1 m, with each step having the same height of 0·2 m. Calculate the volume of the solid concrete construction.

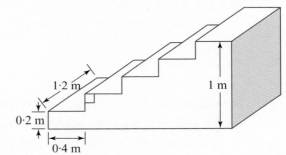

10. The diagram shows the design of a swimming pool.
    (i) Calculate the capacity of the pool in m^3.
    (ii) Calculate the time, in hours and minutes, taken to fill the pool with water if the water is delivered by a pipe at the rate of 10 m^3/min.
    (iii) Calculate the cost of heating the water for 15 hours if the average cost per cubic metre per hour is 0·08 c.

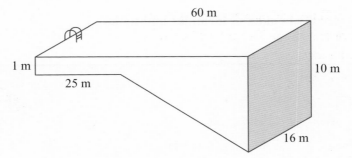

11. The gable end of a garage (the rectangle and triangle put together) is shown in the diagram. The scale used is 1 : 70.
    (i) Measure and record the lengths
        (a) g (b) h (c) f on the diagram correct to the nearest mm.
    (ii) Use the scale to calculate the actual lengths.
    (iii) Hence, find the area of the gable end exterior.
    (iv) The length of the garage is 8·25 m. Find its volume correct to the nearest m^3.

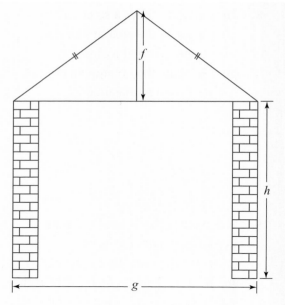

12. The diagram shows a triangular prism which has sloping sides that are perpendicular to each other.
    (i) Calculate the area of its cross-section (shaded region).
    (ii) If its volume is 120 cm^3, find x.

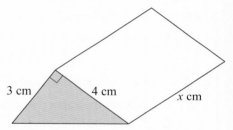

Cylinder, sphere and hemisphere

Formulae required (see the booklet of formulae and tables)

Cylinder:

Volume: $V = \pi r^2 h$

Curved surface area: $CSA = 2\pi rh$

Total surface area: $TSA = 2\pi rh + 2\pi r^2$

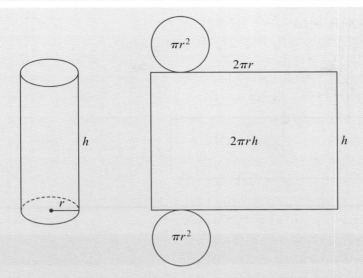

Sphere:

Volume: $$V = \frac{4}{3}\pi r^3$$

Curved surface area: $$CSA = 4\pi r^2$$

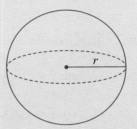

Hemisphere:

Volume: $$V = \frac{2}{3}\pi r^3$$

Curved surface area: $$CSA = 2\pi r^2$$

Total surface area: $$TSA = 2\pi r^2 + \pi r^2 = 3\pi r^2$$

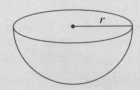

EXAMPLE 1

Find **(i)** the volume **(ii)** the total surface area of a closed cylindrical can of radius 14 cm and height 10 cm (assume $\pi = \frac{22}{7}$).

Solution:

(i) $V = \pi r^2 h$

$V = \frac{22}{7} \times \frac{14}{1} \times \frac{14}{1} \times \frac{10}{1}$

$V = 6{,}160 \text{ cm}^3$

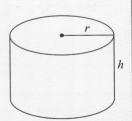

(ii) $TSA = 2\pi rh + 2\pi r^2$

$\quad = \frac{2}{1} \times \frac{22}{7} \times \frac{14}{1} \times \frac{10}{1} + \frac{2}{1} \times \frac{22}{7} \times \frac{14}{1} \times \frac{14}{1}$

$\quad = 880 + 1{,}232$

$\quad = 2{,}112 \text{ cm}^2$

EXAMPLE 2

A solid sphere has a radius of 6 cm. Calculate **(i)** its volume **(ii)** its curved surface area. (Assume $\pi = 3\cdot14$.)

Solution:

(i) $V = \frac{4}{3}\pi r^3$

$\quad = \frac{4}{3} \times 3\cdot14 \times 6 \times 6 \times 6$

$\quad = 904\cdot32 \text{ cm}^3$

(ii) $CSA = 4\pi r^2$

$\quad = 4 \times 3\cdot14 \times 6 \times 6$

$\quad = 452\cdot16 \text{ cm}^2$

Exercise 18.4

Complete the following table, which gives certain information about various closed cylinders.

	π	Radius	Height	Volume	Curved surface area	Total surface area
1.	$\frac{22}{7}$	7 cm	12 cm			
2.	$3\cdot14$	15 cm	40 cm			
3.	π	8 mm	11 mm			

Complete the following table, which gives certain information about various spheres.

	π	Radius	Volume	Curved surface area
4.	$\frac{22}{7}$	21 cm		
5.	$3\cdot14$	9 m		
6.	π	6 mm		

Complete the following table, which gives certain information about various hemispheres.

	π	Radius	Volume	Curved surface area	Total surface area
7.	π	15 mm			
8.	π	$1\frac{1}{2}$ cm			
9.	$\frac{22}{7}$	42 cm			
10.	3·14	12 m			

11. A hollow plastic pipe has an external diameter of 16 cm and an internal diameter of 10 cm. Calculate the volume of plastic in 2 m of pipe.
(Assume $\pi = 3·14$.)

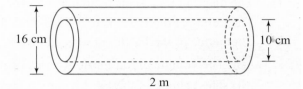

12. (i) The perimeter of a square lawn is 96 m. Find the area of the lawn in m^2.

(ii) A garden roller in the shape of a cylinder has a diameter of 75 cm and is 1 m wide, as shown in the diagram. Calculate the curved surface area of the roller in m^2, correct to one decimal place.

(iii) What percentage of the lawn will be rolled when the roller has completed nine revolutions?

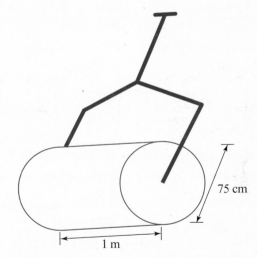

13. A cylindrical jug has a radius of 6 cm and a height of 40 cm. If the jug is full of lemonade, how many cylindrical tumblers, each with a radius of 4 cm and a height of 10 cm, can be filled from the jug?

14. A machine part consists of a hollow sphere floating in a closed cylinder full of oil. The height of the cylinder is 28 cm, the radius of the cylinder is 15 cm and the radius of the sphere is $\frac{21}{2}$ cm. Taking π to be $\frac{22}{7}$, find the volume of:

   (i) The cylinder
   (ii) The sphere
   (iii) The oil

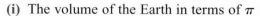

15. The diagram represents a circular cross-section of the Earth. The radius of the Earth is 6,400 km. O is the centre of the Earth. The radius of the Earth's core is 3,200 km. Find:

   (i) The volume of the Earth in terms of π
   (ii) The volume of the Earth's core in terms of π
   (iii) Hence or otherwise, write down the following ratio:

   $$\frac{\text{Volume of the Earth's core}}{\text{Volume of the Earth}}$$

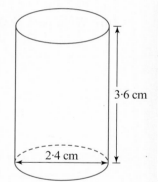

16. Using the given scale, calculate:

   (i) The volume
   (ii) The curved surface area of the cylindrical tin of beans. Assume $\pi = 3.14$ and give answers correct to one decimal place.

   Scale 1 : 3

17. (i) A golf ball has a diameter of 3 cm. Find its volume in terms of π.
   (ii) Four golf balls fit exactly into a cylindrical tube, as shown.

      (a) Find the radius and height of the tube.
      (b) Find the volume of the tube in terms of π.
      (c) Find the fraction of the volume of the cylinder that is taken up by the four golf balls.

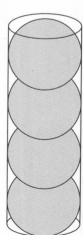

18. A straight tunnel has semicircular ends, as shown. The diameter of the tunnel is 14 m; the length is 60 m.

Find the volume of the tunnel:

(i) In m^3 **(ii)** In litres

Assume $\pi = \frac{22}{7}$.

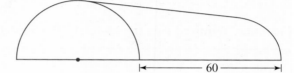

19. A hemispherical dome placed over a playing pitch, as shown in the diagram, below. The rectangular area covered is 56 m long and 42 m wide.

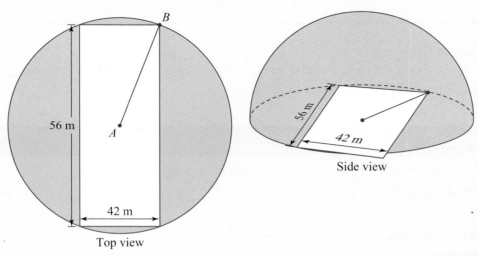

Top view

Side view

(i) Show that $|AB| = 35$ m.

(ii) Hence, if fabric costs €8/m^2, how much does the fabric to cover the dome cost? Assume $\pi = \frac{22}{7}$.

20. **(i)** A water storage tank is in the shape of a hemisphere, radius 120 cm. Find the volume of the tank in terms of π.

(ii) Water flows into the tank at a rate of 320π cm^3 per second. The water flows into the empty tank, as shown in the diagram. Find how long it takes to fill the tank.

Cone

Formulae required (see the booklet of formulae and tables)

Volume: $V = \frac{1}{3}\pi r^2 h$

Curved surface area: $CSA = \pi r l$

Total surface area: $TSA = \pi r l + \pi r^2$

Pythagoras' theorem: $l^2 = r^2 + h^2$

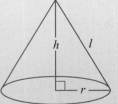

Notes: l is called the slant height.

A cone is often called a **right circular cone**, as its vertex is directly above the centre of the base and its height is at right angles to the base.

EXAMPLE 1

A right circular cone has a height of 12 cm and a base radius of 5 cm. Find:

(i) Its volume   **(ii)** Its curved surface area (assume $\pi = 3\cdot14$)

Solution:

(i) Volume of cone

$= \frac{1}{3}\pi r^2 h$

$= \frac{1}{3} \times 3\cdot14 \times 5 \times 5 \times 12$

$= 314 \text{ cm}^3$

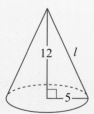

(ii) Slant height is missing

$l^2 = r^2 + h^2$

$l^2 = 5^2 + 12^2$

$l^2 = 25 + 144$

$l^2 = 169$

$l = 13 \text{ cm}$

Curved surface area

$= \pi r l$

$= 3\cdot14 \times 5 \times 13$

$= 204\cdot1 \text{ cm}^2$

EXAMPLE 2

A cone has a radius of 14 cm and a height of $17\frac{1}{2}$ cm.
From the top of this cone, a smaller cone of height 5 cm
is cut. Find the volume of the small cone in terms of π.

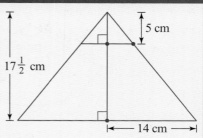

Solution:
We draw two separate diagrams and let r be the radius of the small cone.
We require the radius, r, of the small cone before we can find its volume.
Using the theorem from geometry on similar triangles:

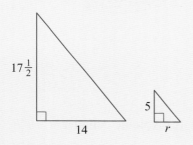

$$\frac{r}{14} = \frac{5}{17\frac{1}{2}}$$

$$\frac{r}{14} = \frac{10}{35}$$

$$35r = 140$$

$$r = \frac{140}{35} = 4 \text{ cm}$$

Hence, the volume of the small cone $= \frac{1}{3}\pi r^2 h = \frac{1}{3}\pi(4)^2(5) = \frac{1}{3}\pi(16)(5) = \frac{80}{3}\pi \text{ cm}^3$.

EXAMPLE 3

(i) The diagram shows a sector of a circle centre O with
$\angle POQ = 116 \cdot 75°$. Calculate the area of the sector and
write your answer in the form $a\pi$ where $a \in \mathbb{N}$.

(ii) The shape OPQ is cut out and folded to make a cone
with slant height 37 cm and curved surface area
$444\pi \text{ cm}^2$. The edges do not overlap. Find:

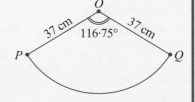

(a) The radius of the cone

(b) The height, h, of the cone

(c) The volume of the cone in terms of π

Solution:

(i)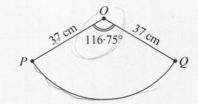

$$\text{Area sector} = \pi r^2 \frac{\theta}{360} \quad \text{(See tables)}$$

$$= \pi (37)^2 \left[\frac{116\cdot 75}{360} \right]$$

$$= \pi (443\cdot 9743056)$$

$$= 444\pi$$

(ii)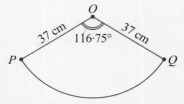

Folded becomes $\Rightarrow$

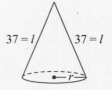

(a) Curved surface area of cone $= \pi r l$

$$444\pi = \pi r(37)$$

$$444 = 37r$$

$$12 \text{ cm} = r$$

(b)

$$l^2 = h^2 + r^2$$

$$(37)^2 = h^2 + (12)^2$$

$$1{,}369 = h^2 + 144$$

$$1{,}225 = h^2$$

$$35 \text{ cm} = h$$

(c) Volume cylinder $= \frac{1}{3}\pi r^2 h$

$$= \frac{1}{3}\pi (12)^2 35$$

$$= 1{,}680\pi \text{ cm}^3$$

Exercise 18.5

Complete the following table, which gives certain information about various cones.

	π	Radius	Height	Slant height	Volume	Curved surface area
1.	π	8 cm	6 cm			
2.	$\frac{22}{7}$		20 mm	29 mm		
3.	3·14	3 cm		5 cm		
4.	3·14		9 cm	41 cm		
5.	$\frac{22}{7}$	2·8 cm	4·5 cm			
6.	3·14	11 cm		61 cm		

7. A cone has a vertical height of 80 cm. The radius of its base is 20 cm. Find, in terms of π, the volume of the cone.

8. A solid cone has a vertical height of 6 cm. The slant height is 7·5 cm.

   (i) Find the radius of its base.

   (ii) Find the total surface area in cm^2.

   Give your answer correct to three significant figures.

9. A cone has a base radius of 8 cm and a slant height of 17 cm.

   (i) Find h, the perpendicular height of the cone.

   (ii) Find the volume of the cone in terms of π.

   (iii) Find the area of the base in terms of π.

   (iv) Find the curved surface area in terms of π.

   (v) The cone is electroplated (coated with a special metal using electricity). Find the cost of electroplating the cone if it costs €12 per cm^2. Assume $\pi = 3\cdot14$.

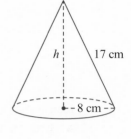

10. A diagram of a space module in the shape of a cone is shown. The scale indicates one cm on the diagram equals 75 cm in reality. Using the given scale, calculate:

    (i) The length of the radius, r

    (ii) The height, h

    (iii) l, the slant height

    (iv) The volume to the nearest m^3

    (v) The total surface area to the nearest m^2

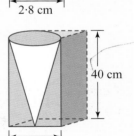

11. A rectangular box with a square base has dimensions as given in the diagram. A cone fits exactly into the box.

    (i) Write down the radius of the cone.

    (ii) Write down the height of the cone.

    (iii) Calculate the value of l, the slant height of the cone.

    (iv) Hence calculate the curved surface area of the cone in terms of π.

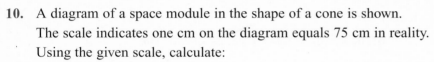

12. (i) A cone has a radius of x and a height of $3x$. Find its volume in terms of π and x.

    (ii) A second cone has twice the radius and half the height of the first cone. Find the ratio of the volume of the second cone to the volume of the first.

13. An egg timer consists of two identical cones of height 6 cm and base radius 4 cm. Sand occupies half the volume of one cone and flows from one to the other at a rate of $\frac{4\pi}{45}$ cm³ per second.

   (i) Calculate the volume of each cone in terms of π.

   (ii) Calculate the length of time it takes for the sand to flow from one cone into the other.

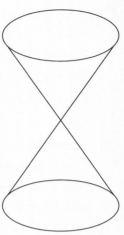

14. Aideen wants to make a paper hat for her little sister. She starts with a sector of a circle, as shown. Answer the following questions correct to one decimal place.

   (i) Calculate the arc length GH.

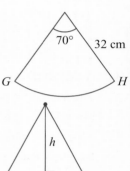

   She joins the straight edges of the sector to form a hat, as shown. The edges do not overlap.

   (ii) Calculate the diameter of the base of the hat.

   (iii) Calculate the height h of the point of the hat above the base.

15. (i) The diagram shows a sector of a circle centre O with $\angle AOB = 288°$. Calculate the area of the sector in terms of π.

   (ii) The shape AOB is cut out and folded to make a cone with slant height 12·5 cm and curved surface area as in (a). Find:

   (a) The radius of the cone

   (b) The height of the cone

   (c) The volume of the cone in terms of π

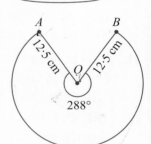

16. A cone has a radius of 9 cm and a height of 36 cm. From the top of this cone, a smaller cone of height h and radius 7·75 cm is cut. Find:

   (i) The height, h, of the smaller cone

   (ii) The volume of the smaller cone to the nearest integer

17. The top of the cone is removed, as shown in the diagram.

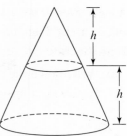

What fraction of the volume of the original cone is left? Justify your answer.

18. In the following table, r, h, l and x all represent lengths. Copy and complete the table. Mark each expression as length, area or volume.

Expression	$r + 2x$	$2xhl$	$\pi r(x + h)$	$\dfrac{r^2h}{xl}$	$\dfrac{3xh}{7}$
Length, area or volume					

19. The expression $\pi a r^n$ represents a volume, where a and r are lengths. What is the value of n, where $n \in \mathbb{N}$?

20. The surface area of a compound shape is given by $S = 2\pi r^2 + \pi r^2$ by considering dimensions. Explain why this is incorrect.

21. Sanjee has copied some formulae from a textbook. State whether each is a formula for length, area, volume or whether Sanjee has made a mistake in copying it.

   (i) $P = arh + r^2$ **(ii)** $Q = 2\pi(r + h)$

(iii) $R = \pi r^2 h$ **(iv)** $S = \dfrac{6r^2a}{h}$

22. **(i)** At one time, Native Americans constructed tipis to live in. A typical tipi was in the shape of a cone. Calculate the curved surface area of the following tipi. Assume $\pi = 3 \cdot 14$ and give your answer correct to the nearest whole number.

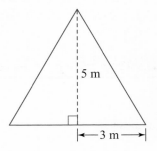

(ii) The area of an average buffalo skin is $2 \cdot 15 \text{m}^2$. To cover the curved surface area of the tipi with buffalo skin, an additional 20% of area was added to allow for overlap when sewing the skins together. Hence, find the least number of adult buffalo skins required to cover the tipi.

23. A right circular cone M has dimensions given in cm, as in the diagram. M is divided horizontally to its base into two sections, J and K.

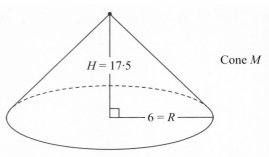

   (i) Write down the radius, r, of the cone J. Justify your answer for r.

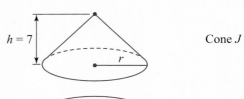

   (ii) Find the volume of J, assume $\pi = \frac{22}{7}$.

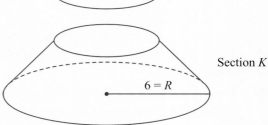

   (iii) Find the volume of the (frustum) section K, assume $\pi = \frac{22}{7}$.

Compound volumes

Many of the objects we need to find the volume of will be made up of different shapes.

When this happens, do the following.

1. Split the solid up into regular shapes for which we have formulae to calculate the volume or surface area.
2. Add these results together (sometimes we subtract these results).

EXAMPLE 1

A solid object consists of three parts: a cone of height 8 cm, A, a cylinder, B, and a hemisphere, C, each having a radius of 6 cm, as shown. If the height of the object is 26 cm, calculate its volume in terms of π.

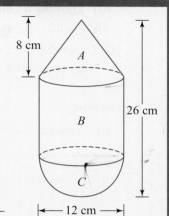

Solution:

A: Volume of cone $= \frac{1}{3}\pi r^2 h$

$\qquad = \frac{1}{3}\pi \times 6 \times 6 \times 8$

$\qquad = 96\pi \text{ cm}^3$

B: Volume of cylinder $= \pi r^2 h$

$\qquad = \pi \times 6 \times 6 \times 12$

$\qquad = 432\pi \text{ cm}^3$

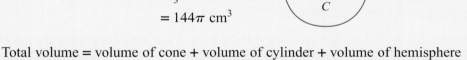

C: Volume of hemisphere $= \frac{2}{3}\pi r^3$

$\qquad = \frac{2}{3}\pi \times 6 \times 6 \times 6$

$\qquad = 144\pi \text{ cm}^3$

Total volume = volume of cone + volume of cylinder + volume of hemisphere
$$= (96\pi + 432\pi + 144\pi) \text{ cm}^3 = 672\pi \text{ cm}^3$$

EXAMPLE 2

An ashtray consists of a solid block with a cone excavated to contain the ash. The radius of the cone is 10 cm with a depth of 6 cm. The sides of the block touch the base circle of the cone, as in the diagram.

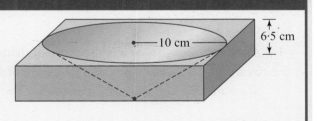

(i) Find the volume of the cone (assume $\pi = 3\cdot14$).

(ii) Find the volume of the block.

(iii) Hence, find the volume of material that makes up the ashtray.

(iv) Comment on the effectiveness or otherwise of this ashtray design. Suggest an alternative design from the shapes covered in this chapter.

Solution:

(i) Volume of cone $= \frac{1}{3}\pi r^2 h$

$$= \frac{1}{3}(3\cdot14)(10)^2(6) = 628\,\text{cm}^3$$

(ii) Volume of block $= lbh$

$$= (20)(20)(6\cdot5) = 2{,}600\,\text{cm}^3$$

(iii) Volume of ashtray material $= 2{,}600 - 628 = 1{,}972\,\text{cm}^3$

(iv) The useful space in this ashtray is $628\,\text{cm}^3$.

$$\Rightarrow \frac{628}{2{,}600} \times 100 \approx 24\% \text{ of the total volume}$$

It follows that 76% (100% − 24%) of this ashtray consists of material. In my opinion, this is too much material from both a practical and cost viewpoint. A good ashtray design should have more space than material.

In addition, the extremely pointed vertex at the base is not very effective and might be a safety issue (ash not properly crushed to extinguish the spark). My suggestion for a more efficient design would be a cylindrical space inside a solid cylinder, as in the diagram. You can suggest your own design.

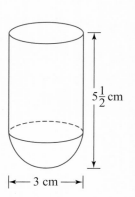

Exercise 18.6

1. A test tube consists of a hemisphere of diameter 3 cm surmounted by a cylinder, as shown. The total height of the test tube is $5\frac{1}{2}$ cm. Show that the volume of the test tube is $\frac{45}{4}\pi\,\text{cm}^3$.

$5\frac{1}{2}$ cm

3 cm

2. The diagram shows a steel nail with a cylindrical flat head surmounted on a cylindrical column ending in a point in the shape of a cone. Calculate the volume of the nail in terms of π.

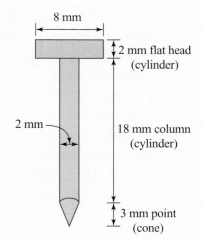

8 mm

2 mm flat head (cylinder)

2 mm

18 mm column (cylinder)

3 mm point (cone)

3. An ice cream dessert consists of an ice cream-filled wafer cone with a hemisphere of extra ice cream on top. The dimensions of the dessert are shown.
   (i) If the wafer cone is exactly covered with a paper wrapper, find the surface area of the paper, correct to one decimal place.
   (ii) Find the total volume of the ice cream, correct to the nearest integer.

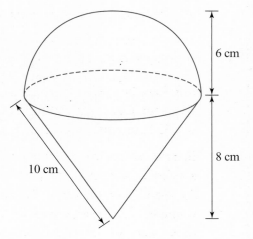

6 cm

8 cm

10 cm

4. A 12 cm by 12 cm ice cube tray is in the shape of a cuboid with 12 hemispheres inset as shown below. The depth of each hemisphere is 1 cm. Give all answers in terms of π.

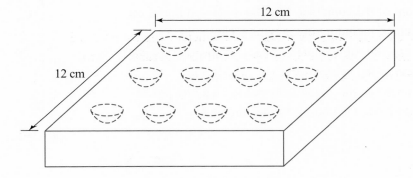

12 cm

12 cm

   (i) If all the hemispheres were filled with water, calculate the total volume of water that the ice cube tray could hold.

293

(ii) Calculate the total surface area of one ice cube from the tray.

(iii) Calculate the total surface area of the top of the ice cube tray, excluding the sections covered by water.

5. A buoy consists of an inverted cone surmounted by a hemisphere, as shown. If the radius of the hemisphere is 6 cm and the height of the cone is 9·1 cm, calculate, assuming $\pi = 3\cdot14$:

(i) The volume of the buoy

(ii) l, the slant height of the cone

(iii) The surface area of the buoy

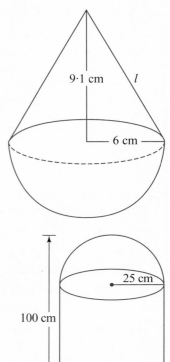

6. (i) A hot water container is in the shape of a hemisphere on top of a cylinder, as shown. The hemisphere has a radius of 25 cm and the container has a height of 100 cm. Find the internal volume of the container in litres, giving your answer correct to the nearest litre.

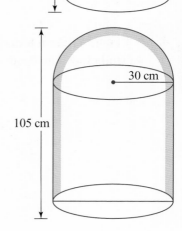

(ii) An external solid plastic lagging jacket 5 cm thick is constructed to fit exactly around the hot water container and in the same shape. The jacket does not cover the bottom of the container. Find the total volume of the container, including the lagging jacket.

(iii) Hence, find the volume of plastic in the lagging jacket correct to the nearest litre.

(iv) Comment on the suggestion that the lagging jacket should cover the bottom of the container.

7. A solid sphere with a radius of 21 cm has a vertical cylindrical shaft with a radius of 1 cm drilled through its centre, c.

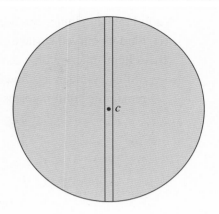

    (i) Calculate the volume remaining when the shaft is drilled. Assume $\pi = \frac{22}{7}$.

   (ii) Show that Volume cylinder : Volume sphere $= 1 : 294$.

Note: The shaft is not an absolute cylinder – it has a slight bulge at each end. However, at the scale involved here it is not significant.

8.

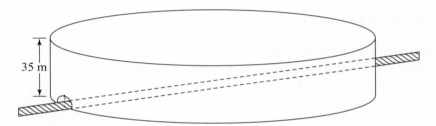

35 m

A stadium is designed in the shape of a cylinder in the diagram above. The stadium has a height of 35 m and a radius of 100 m. A light rail line is constructed in a tunnel which passes directly through the centre, c, of the stadium on a ground-level track. The face of the tunnel is a semicircle. The tunnel is half cylindrical in shape with a radius of 5 m.

    (i) Find the volume of the stadium including the rail line in terms of π.

   (ii) Find the volume of the rail tunnel in terms of π.

  (iii) Hence, express the volume of the rail tunnel as a percentage of the volume of the stadium in the form $\frac{a}{b}\%$, where $a, b \in \mathbb{N}$.

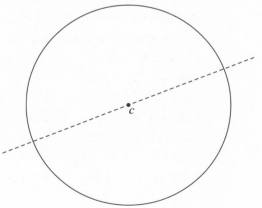

9. A solid metal cylinder has a height of 20 cm and a diameter of 14 cm.
   (i) Find its curved surface area in terms of π.
   (ii) A hemisphere with a diameter of 14 cm is removed from the top
        of this cylinder, as shown. Find the total surface area of the
        remaining solid in terms of π.

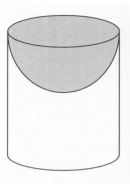

Given the volume or surface area

In some questions we are given the volume or surface area and asked to find a missing dimension. As before, write down the **equation given in disguise** and solve this equation to find the missing dimension.

 EXAMPLE

(i) A cylinder has a volume of 192π cm^3. If its radius is 4 cm, calculate its height.
(ii) The volume of a sphere is $\frac{32}{3}\pi$ cm^3. Calculate its radius.

Solution:

(i) Equation given in disguise:

$$\text{Volume of cylinder} = 192\pi \text{ cm}^3$$
$$\pi r^2 h = 192\pi$$
$$r^2 h = 192 \qquad \text{(divide both sides by } \pi\text{)}$$
$$16h = 192 \qquad \text{(put in } r = 4\text{)}$$
$$h = 12 \text{ cm} \qquad \text{(divide both sides by 16)}$$

(ii) Equation given in disguise:

$$\text{Volume of sphere} = \frac{32}{3}\pi \text{cm}^3$$

$$\frac{4}{3}\pi r^3 = \frac{32}{3}\pi$$

$$4\pi r^3 = 32\pi \qquad \text{(multiply both sides by 3)}$$

$$4r^3 = 32 \qquad \text{(divide both sides by } \pi\text{)}$$

$$r^3 = 8 \qquad \text{(divide both sides by 4)}$$

$$r = 2 \text{ cm} \qquad \text{(take the cube root of both sides)}$$

Exercise 18.7

1. A cylinder has a volume of 720π cm^3. If its radius is 6 cm, calculate:
    (i) Its height   **(ii)** Its curved surface area in terms of π

2. The curved surface area of a sphere is 144π cm^2. Calculate:
    (i) Its radius   **(ii)** Its volume in terms of π

3. The volume of a cone is 320π cm^3. If the radius of the base is 8 cm, calculate its height.

4. The volume of a solid sphere is 36π cm^3. Calculate:
    (i) Its radius   **(ii)** Its total surface area in terms of π

5. A solid cylinder has a volume of 96π cm^3. If its height is 6 cm, calculate:
    (i) Its radius   **(ii)** Its total surface area in terms of π

6. The curved surface area of a cylinder is 628 cm^2 and its radius is 5 cm. Calculate:
    (i) Its height   **(ii)** Its volume (assume $\pi = 3\cdot14$)

7. A solid cylinder has a volume of 462 m^3. If the height is 12 m, assuming $\pi = \frac{22}{7}$, calculate:
    (i) Its radius   **(ii)** Its total surface area

8. The curved surface area of a cone is 60π cm^2. If the radius of its base is 6 cm, calculate:
    (i) Its slant height   **(ii)** Its volume in terms of π

9. A cone has a volume of $\frac{160}{3}\pi$ cm^3. If the radius of the base is 4 cm, find its height.

10. The radius of a cylinder is $2\cdot8$ cm and its volume is $49\cdot28$ cm^3. Calculate, assuming $\pi = \frac{22}{7}$:
    (i) Its height   **(ii)** Its curved surface area

11. The volume of a solid cylinder is 401·92 m³. If its height is 8 m, calculate, assuming $\pi = 3·14$:
    (i) Its radius   (ii) Its total surface area

12. The volume of a cone is $1,215\pi$ cm³. If the height is five times the radius of the base, calculate the height of the cone.

13. A buoy at sea is in the shape of a hemisphere with a cone on top, as in the diagram. The radius of the base of the cone is 0·9 m and its vertical height is 1·2 m.
    (i) Find the vertical height of the buoy.
    (ii) Find the volume of the buoy in terms of π.
    (iii) When the buoy floats, 0·8 m of its height is above water. Find, in terms of π, the volume of that part of the buoy that is above the water.

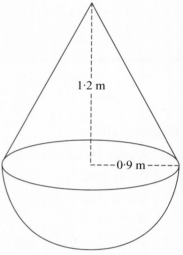

14. A rectangular box has dimensions as shown in the diagram. The length of the box is twice the width. The volume of the box is 810 cm³. Calculate the length of the box.

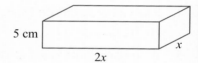

15. An open cylindrical container is to hold 15·7 m³ of grain. If the radius of the cylinder is 1·25 m, find h, the height of the grain in the cylinder. Assume $\pi = 3·14$.

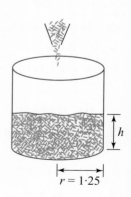

16. The volume of a cylinder is 384π cm^3. The height of the cylinder is $6x$ cm and the radius is x cm. Calculate the value of x.

17. A fishing float consists of a hemisphere of radius length 4 cm surmounted by a solid cone.
    (i) Find, in terms of π, the volume of the hemisphere.
    (ii) Find the volume of the cone in terms of π and h.
    (iii) The volume of the cone is twice the volume of the hemisphere. Find h, the height of the cone.
    (iv) Hence, write down the height of the fishing float.

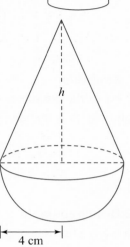

18. A team trophy for the winner of a football match is in the shape of a sphere supported on a cylindrical base, as shown. The diameter of the sphere and of the cylinder is 21 cm.
    (i) Find the volume of the sphere in terms of π.
    (ii) The volume of the trophy is $6,174\pi$ cm^3. Find the height of the cylinder.

Equal volumes

Many questions involve equal volumes with a missing dimension. As before, write down the **equation given in disguise** and solve this equation to find the missing dimension.

Notes:

1. Moving liquid

In many questions we have to deal with moving liquid from one container to another container of different dimensions or shape. To help us solve the problem, we use the following fact:

> The volume of the moved liquid does not change.

2. Recasting

Many of the questions we meet require us to solve a recasting problem. What happens is that a certain solid object is melted down and its shape is changed. We use the following fact:

> The volume remains the same after it is melted down.

3. Displaced liquid

In many questions we have to deal with situations where liquid is displaced by immersing or removing a solid object. In all cases the following principle of Archimedes helps us to solve these problems:

> Volume of displaced liquid = volume of immersed or removed solid object

In problems on moving liquid or recasting or displaced liquid, it is good practice not to put in a value for π (i.e. do **not** put in $\pi = \frac{22}{7}$ or $\pi = 3 \cdot 14$), as the πs normally cancel when you write down the equation given in disguise.

EXAMPLE 1

A sphere of radius 15 cm is made of lead. The sphere is melted down. Some of the lead is used to form a solid cone of radius 10 cm and height 27 cm. The rest of the lead is used to form a cylinder of height 25 cm. Calculate the length of the radius of the cylinder.

Solution:

Equation given in disguise:

Volume of cylinder + volume of cone = volume of sphere

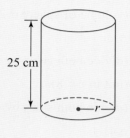 + 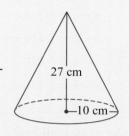 = 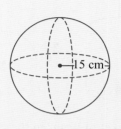   (diagram of the situation)

$$\pi r^2 h + \tfrac{1}{3}\pi r^2 h = \tfrac{4}{3}\pi r^3$$

$$r^2 h + \tfrac{1}{3}r^2 h = \tfrac{4}{3}r^3 \qquad \text{(divide each part by } \pi \text{)}$$

$$25r^2 + \tfrac{1}{3}(10)(10)(27) = \tfrac{4}{3}(15)(15)(15) \qquad \text{(put in given values)}$$

$$25r^2 + 900 = 4{,}500 \qquad \text{(simplify)}$$

$$25r^2 = 3{,}600 \qquad \text{(subtract 900 from both sides)}$$

$$r^2 = 144 \qquad \text{(divide both sides by 25)}$$

$$r = 12 \text{ cm} \qquad \text{(take the square root of both sides)}$$

Therefore, the radius of the cylinder is 12 cm.

EXAMPLE 2

(i) Find, in terms of π, the volume of a solid metal sphere of radius 6 cm.

(ii) Five such identical spheres are completely submerged in a cylinder containing water. If the radius of the cylinder is 8 cm, by how much will the level of the water drop if the spheres are removed from the cylinder?

Solution:

(i) Volume of sphere $= \tfrac{4}{3}\pi r^3 = \tfrac{4}{3}\pi(6)(6)(6) = 288\pi \text{ cm}^3$

(ii) Diagram:

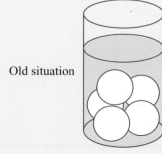

Old situation

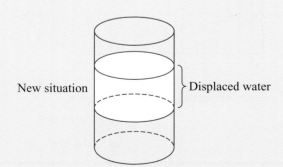

New situation   Displaced water

Equation given in disguise:

Volume of displaced water = volume of five spheres

Diagram:

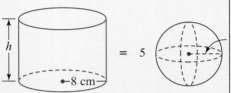

$$\pi r^2 h = 5(288\pi) \quad \text{(volume of sphere} = 288\pi)$$
$$\pi r^2 h = 1{,}440\pi$$
$$r^2 h = 1{,}440 \quad \text{(divide both sides by } \pi)$$
$$64h = 1{,}440 \quad \text{(put in } r = 8)$$
$$h = 22.5 \quad \text{(divide both sides by 64)}$$

Thus, the level of water in the cylinder would fall by 22·5 cm.

EXAMPLE 3

(i) The volume of a hemisphere is 486π cm^3. Find the radius of the hemisphere.

(ii) Find the volume of the smallest rectangular box that the hemisphere will fit into.

Solution:

(i) Volume $\frac{1}{2}$ sphere $= \frac{1}{2}\left[\frac{4}{3}\pi r^3\right]$

$$486\pi = \frac{2}{3}\pi r^3$$
$$486 = \frac{2}{3}r^3$$
$$1{,}458 = 2r^3$$
$$729 = r^3$$
$$9 \text{ cm} = r$$

(ii)

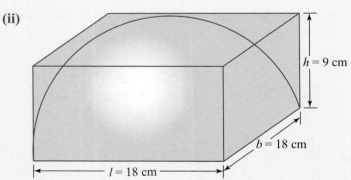

Volume rectangular box $= l \times b \times h$

$$= 18 \times 18 \times 9$$
$$= 2{,}916 \text{ cm}^3$$

Exercise 18.8

Find the missing dimensions in questions 1–6. In each case, the volumes are equal (all dimensions are in centimetres).

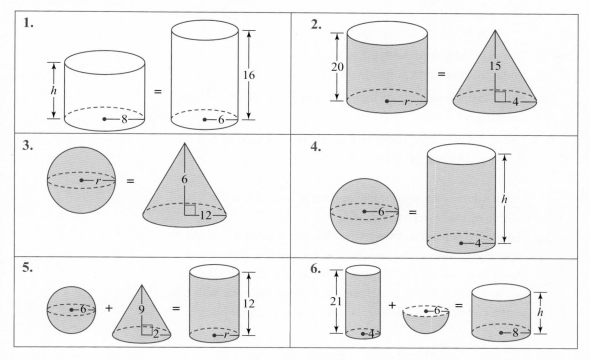

7. A solid lead cylinder of base radius 2 cm and height 15 cm is melted down and recast as a solid cone of base radius 3 cm. Calculate the height of the cone.

8. (i) A solid cylinder made of lead has a radius of length 15 cm and a height of 135 cm. Find its volume in terms of π.

    (ii) The solid cylinder is melted down and recast to make four identical right circular solid cones. The height of each cone is equal to twice the length of its base radius. Calculate the base radius length of the cones.

9. A cylinder of internal diameter 8 cm and height 18 cm is full of liquid. The liquid is poured into a second cylinder of internal diameter 12 cm. Calculate the depth of the liquid in this second cylinder.

10. A spherical golf ball has a diameter of 4 cm.

    (i) Find the volume of the golf ball in terms of π.

    (ii) A cylindrical hole on a golf course is 10 cm in diameter and 12 cm deep. The hole is half full of water. Calculate the volume of water in the hole in terms of π.

    (iii) The golf ball is dropped into the hole. Find the rise in the level of the water, correct to two decimal places.

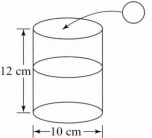

11. A solid metal rectangular block 30 cm by 24 cm by 15 cm is melted down and recast into cubes of side 3 cm. How many such cubes are made?

12. A solid is in the shape of a hemisphere surmounted by a cone, as shown in the diagram.

    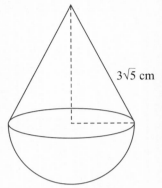

    (i) The volume of the hemisphere is 18π cm^3.
    Find the radius of the hemisphere.

    (ii) The slant height of the cone is $3\sqrt{5}$ cm.
    Show that the vertical height of the cone is 6 cm.

    $3\sqrt{5}$ cm

    (iii) Show that the volume of the cone equals the volume of the hemisphere.

    (iv) This solid is melted down and recast in the shape of a solid cylinder. The height of the cylinder is 9 cm. Calculate its radius.

13. (i) The diameter of a solid metal sphere is 9 cm. Find the volume of the sphere in terms of π.

    (ii) The sphere is melted down. All of the metal is used to make a solid shape which consists of a cone on top of a cylinder, as shown in the diagram. The cone and the cylinder both have a height of 8 cm. The cylinder and the base of the cone both have a radius of r cm. Calculate r, correct to one decimal place.

    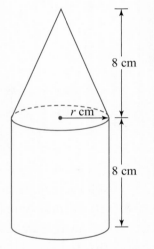

    8 cm

    r cm

    8 cm

14. (i) A steelworks buys steel in the form of solid cylindrical rods of radius 10 cm and length 30 m. The steel rods are melted to produce solid spherical ball bearings. No steel is wasted in the process. Find the volume of steel in one cylindrical rod in terms of π.

    (ii) The radius of a ball bearing is 2 cm. How many such ball bearings are made from one steel rod?

    (iii) Ball bearings of a different size are also produced. One steel rod makes 225,000 of these new ball bearings. Find the radius of the new ball bearings.

15. A vitamin capsule is in the shape of a cylinder with hemispherical ends. The length of the capsule is 20 mm and the diameter is 6 mm.

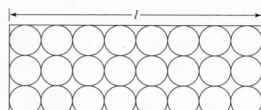

    (i) Calculate the volume of the capsule, giving your answer correct to the nearest mm^3, assume $\pi = 3.14$.

    (ii) A course of these vitamins consists of 24 capsules. The capsules are stacked in three rows of eight in a box, as shown in the diagram. Write down:

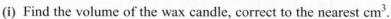
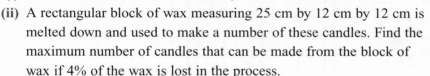

       (a) The length, l

       (b) The height, h

       (c) The width of the box

    (iii) Hence, calculate the volume of the box in mm^3.

    (iv) How much of the internal volume of the box is not occupied by the capsules?

16. A wax candle is in the shape of a right circular cone. The height of the candle is 7 cm and the diameter of the base is 6 cm.

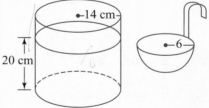

    (i) Find the volume of the wax candle, correct to the nearest cm^3.

    (ii) A rectangular block of wax measuring 25 cm by 12 cm by 12 cm is melted down and used to make a number of these candles. Find the maximum number of candles that can be made from the block of wax if 4% of the wax is lost in the process.

17. (i) Soup is contained in a cylindrical saucepan which has an internal radius of 14 cm. The depth of the soup is 20 cm. Calculate, in terms of π, the volume of soup in the saucepan.

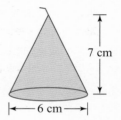

    (ii) A ladle in the shape of a hemisphere with an internal radius of length 6 cm is used to serve the soup. Calculate, in terms of π, the volume of soup contained in one full ladle.

    (iii) The soup is served into cylindrical cups, each with an internal radius of length 4 cm. One ladleful is placed in each cup. Calculate the depth of the soup in each cup.

18. Water flows through a cylindrical pipe at the rate of 12 cm per second. The diameter of the pipe is 8 cm. The water flows into an empty cylindrical tank of radius 24 cm. What is the depth of the water after one minute?

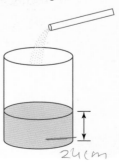

305

19. The diagram below is a scale drawing of a hopper tank used to store grain. An estimate is needed of the capacity (volume) of the tank. The figure of the man standing beside the tank allows the scale of the drawing to be estimated.

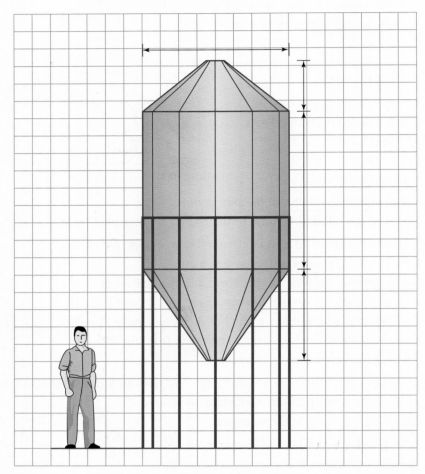

(i) Give an estimate, in metres, of the height of an average adult man.

(ii) Using your answer to part (i), estimate the dimensions of the hopper tank. Write your answers in the spaces provided on the diagram in metres.

(iii) Taking the tank to be a cylinder with a cone above and below, find an estimate for the capacity of the tank in cubic metres.

Nets of 3D shapes

A line has only one **dimension** – length (1D).

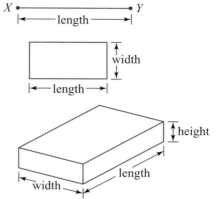

A flat shape has two dimensions – length and width (2D).

A **solid** shape has three dimensions – length, width and height (3D).

When a 3D shape is opened out, the flat shape is called the **net**.

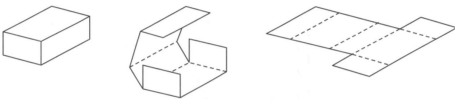

EXAMPLE

(i) This is a **net** of a solid cube.

This is how it folds up to make the cube.

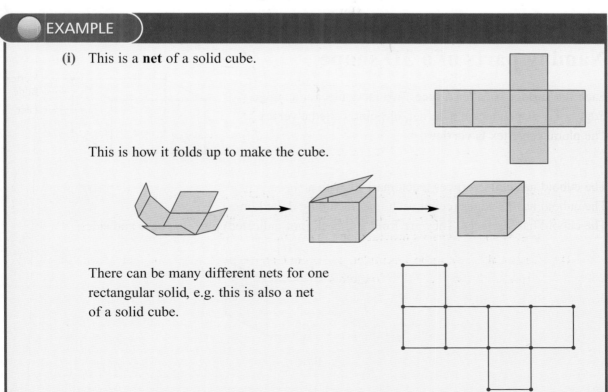

There can be many different nets for one rectangular solid, e.g. this is also a net of a solid cube.

(ii) This is a net for a cuboid that is 4 cm by 2 cm
by 2 cm.
When you draw a net, you have to draw the
lengths accurately.
You may have to use a scale for your drawing.
Choose a scale so that the net fits on your page
and it's not too small.

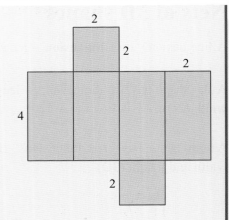

This is how the net folds up to make a cuboid.

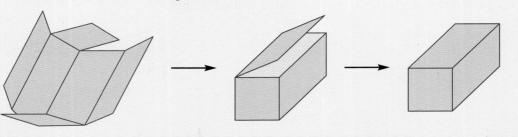

Naming parts of a 3D shape

Each flat surface is called a **face**. Two faces meet at an **edge**.
Edges of a shape meet at a corner, or point, called a **vertex**.
The plural of vertex is **vertices**.

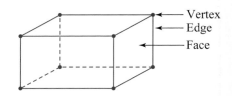

The cuboid has eight vertices (each marked with a •).
The cuboid has 12 edges (count each line, including dotted lines).
The cuboid has six faces. They are front and back (not indicated) plus top, base and sides.

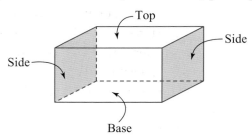

A net diagram indicates the faces clearly.

	Top	
	Back	
Side	Base	Side
	Front	

EXAMPLE

Using a net to determine the surface area of a 3D shape, find the surface area of the cuboid with dimensions height 7 cm, length 10 cm and width 6 cm.

Solution:

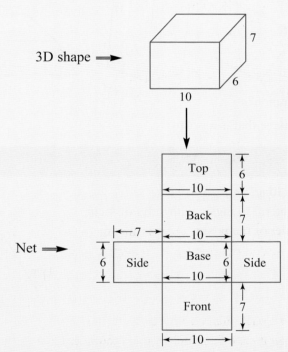

Surface area of a cuboid = The sum of the area of all six faces

$\qquad$ = Sum of the area of all six faces of the net

$\qquad$ = Area of (top + back + base + front + side + side)

$\qquad$ = Area of ((top + base) + (back + front) + (side + side))

$\qquad$ = 2(top) + 2(back) + 2(side)

$\qquad$ = $2(10 \times 6) + 2(10 \times 7) + 2(6 \times 7)$

$\qquad$ = 120 + 140 + 84

$\qquad$ = 344 cm^2

Note: We can write a formula for the surface area of a cuboid as $2lb + 2lh + 2bh$.

Examples of 3D shapes (or solids)

These are all examples of 3D shapes.

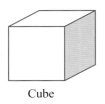

Cube

Cylinder

Pyramid with square base

Sphere

Can you name some other 3D shapes?

These 3D shapes are called prisms.

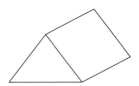 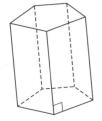 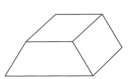

What do prisms have in common?

Can you draw another 3D shape that is a prism?

EXAMPLE 1

This prism is 8 cm long.
The ends are equilateral triangles with sides of 4 cm.
Draw an accurate net of the prism.

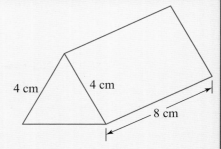

Solution:

Step 1: Draw the rectangular faces of the prism.
Each rectangle is 8 cm long and 4 cm wide.

Step 2: The ends of the prism are equilateral
triangles.
The length of each side of the triangles
is 4 cm.
Use your compass to construct the equilateral
triangles.

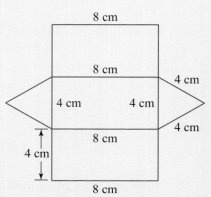

EXAMPLE 2

This is how the net folds up to make a cylinder.

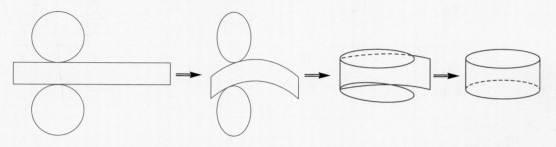

Note: There can be different nets for one solid cylinder.

This is a net for a solid cylinder with radius $\frac{7}{2}$ cm and height 4 cm.

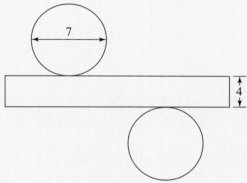

Use the net to find the surface area of the cylinder. Assume $\pi = \frac{22}{7}$.

Solution:

Surface area of a cylinder = area circle + area rectangle + area circle

$$= \pi r^2 \qquad + (l)(b) \qquad + \pi r^2$$

Note: Area of rectangle $= (l)(b) = (2\pi r)(h)$

Because $2\pi r =$ the length of the rectangle = the circumference of the circle and $h =$ the breadth of the rectangle = the height of the cylinder.

Hence, surface area of a cylinder $= 2\pi r^2 + 2\pi rh$

$$= 2\left(\tfrac{22}{7}\right)\left(\tfrac{7}{2}\right)\left(\tfrac{7}{2}\right) + 2\left(\tfrac{22}{7}\right)\left(\tfrac{7}{2}\right)(4)$$

$$= 22\left(\tfrac{7}{2}\right) + (22)(4)$$

$$= 77 + 88$$

$$= 155 \text{ cm}^2$$

Exercise 18.9

1.

	1	2	3	4	5	6
Net						
	A	B	C	D	E	F
3D shape						

The table shows six nets numbered 1, 2, 3, 4, 5, 6 and six 3D shapes labelled A, B, C, D, E, F. Match each net to its correct 3D shape. The first one is done for you: (1, C).

2. Copy each diagram and colour in two extra squares to give you the net of a cube.

(i) 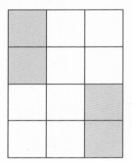 **(ii)** 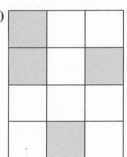 **(iii)**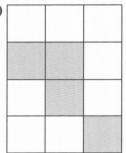

3. Draw an accurate net for each of these 3D shapes.

(i)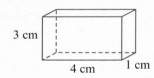
3 cm   4 cm   1 cm

(ii)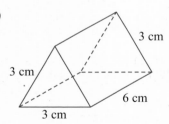
3 cm   3 cm   3 cm   6 cm

(iii)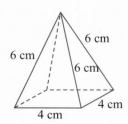
6 cm   6 cm   6 cm   4 cm   4 cm

(iv)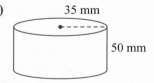
35 mm   50 mm

4. Here is the net of a triangular prism with dimensions in cm.

   (i) State the number of faces for this prism.

   (ii) How many vertices has the prism?

   (iii) Find **(a)** the surface area of the prism **(b)** the volume of the prism.

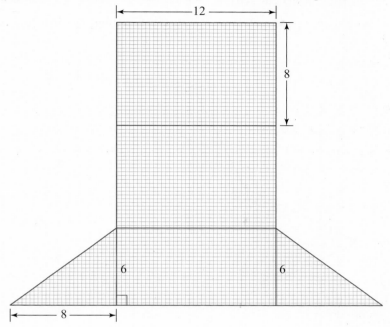

5. A rectangular sheet of metal measures 2 m by $1\frac{1}{2}$ m. A square of side 30 cm is removed from each corner. The remaining piece of metal is folded along the dotted lines to form an open box, as shown.

   (i) Find the surface area of the net used to construct the box.

   (ii) Find the volume of the box in **(a)** cm^3 **(b)** m^3 **(c)** litres.

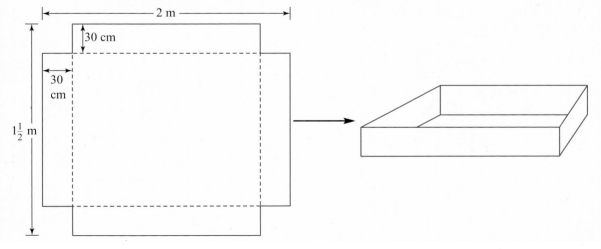

313

6. **(i)** A metal cylindrical tin with no lid is shown.
   Using a scale of 1:10, draw a net of the tin.

   (ii) Hence or otherwise, find the area of the metal required to
   make this tin. Assume $\pi = \frac{22}{7}$.
   Give your answers in **(a)** cm² **(b)** m².

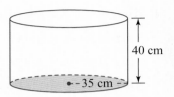

40 cm

35 cm

7. The nets of these shapes have reflection symmetry. Complete the nets and name the two shapes.

   (i)

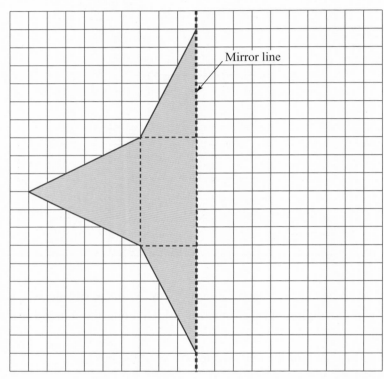

Mirror line

(ii)

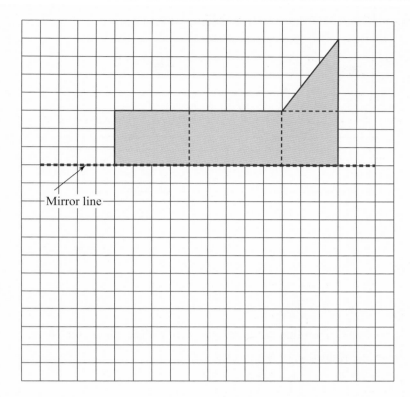

Mirror line

8. Draw the net for each of the following prisms.

(i)

(ii)

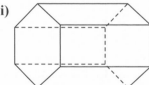

9. The diagram shows a pyramid.
   A model of the pyramid is to be made using straws.
   The straws are each 8 cm long and are joined using pipe cleaners.

   (i) How may edges does the pyramid have?

   (ii) How may vertices does the pyramid have?

   (iii) How may straws are needed to make the pyramid?

   (iv) What is the total length of the edges of the pyramid?

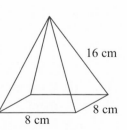

16 cm

8 cm

8 cm

10. This net folds to make a 3-D shape.
    What is the name of the 3-D shape?

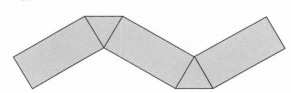

11. The following net has a 3D shape with a volume of 2,512 cm³.

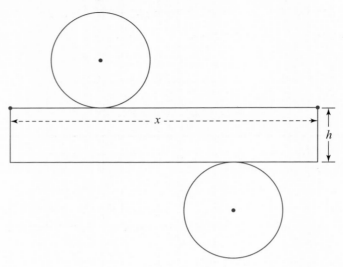

(i) Name the 3D shape.

Assume $\pi = 3\cdot14$ and given that both identical circles have diameter 20 cm:

(ii) Write down the radius, r, of the circles
(iii) Using volume $= \pi r^2 h$, solve for h
(iv) Calculate x, the length of the rectangle
(v) Can a similar 3D solid be made from the given net below? Justify your answer.

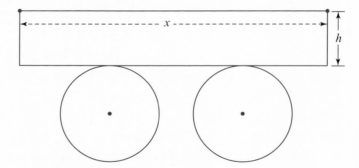

12. (i) Look at buildings in your locality and write the names of four 3D shapes you saw in them.
(ii) Now look at pictures of famous buildings. Did you discover any other 3D shape in them that was not in your part (i)?

13. Discuss the following with a partner or partners. Write down your conclusions in your copy.

    (i) Why are most food tins shaped like a cylinder and not like a cuboid?

    (ii) Why are coins round and not square?

    (iii) Why are traffic cones better than traffic cylinders?

    (iv) Why are roofs usually in the shape of a triangular prism rather than a cuboid?

    (v) Why are most drinks sold in cylindrical shapes?

14. **(i)** Name and sketch a 3D shape that has five vertices.

    (ii) Name and sketch a 3D shape that has seven faces.

Listing outcomes of an experiment

Toss coins

Throw dice

Spin a spinner

Draw a card

If you carry out an operation or experiment, for example using coins, dice, spinners or cards, then each toss, throw, spin or draw is called a **trial**. In other words a trial is **one** go at performing an operation or experiment. If we toss a coin eight times, then we perform eight trials. The possible results that can happen from a trial are called **outcomes**. For example, if we throw a die there are six possible outcomes, 1, 2, 3, 4, 5 and 6.

A list of all possible outcomes is called the **sample space** or **outcome space**. When listing all the possible outcomes, be systematic to make sure you don't miss any possibilities. There are many situations where we have to consider two outcomes. In these situations all the possible outcomes can be listed in a sample space diagram called a **two-way table**.

To help us count the number of possible outcomes we can use the **fundamental principle of counting**.

Fundamental principle of counting

> Suppose one operation has m possible outcomes and that a second operation has n outcomes. The number of possible outcomes when performing the first operation **followed by** the second operation is $m \times n$.

Performing one operation **and** another operation means we **multiply** the number of possible outcomes.

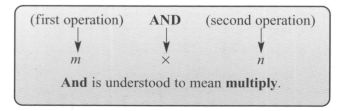

EXAMPLE 1

(i) A die is thrown and a coin is tossed. How many outcomes are possible?

(ii) List all the possible outcomes.

Solution:

(i) Using the fundamental principle of counting:

1. Die There are six possible outcomes for a die: 1, 2, 3, 4, 5, or 6.

2. Coin There are two possible outcomes for a coin: *H* or *T*.

Die   Coin

Hence, the number of different outcomes = $\boxed{6} \times \boxed{2} = 12$.

(ii) Using a two-way table:

	T	•	•	•	•	•	•
Coin	*H*	•	•	•	•	•	•
		1	2	3	4	5	6

Die

A dot indicates an outcome.
There are 12 dots (6 × 2).

List of outcomes

$(1, H), (2, H), (3, H), (4, H), (5, H), (6, H)$

$(1, T), (2, T), (3, T), (4, T), (5, T), (6, T)$

 EXAMPLE 2

In a cinema complex, a customer in the VIP theatre has three choices of snack: popcorn, nachos or candyfloss. The customer also has three choices of drink: water, cola or wine. The customer can choose one snack and one drink.

(i) Write down all the different selections possible.

(ii) How many different selections are possible?

(iii) If your class went on a school trip to that VIP theatre, which selection(s) in your opinion would be **(a)** most popular **(b)** least popular? Justify your opinions.

Solution:

(i) The possible selections are:

Nachos and wine	Popcorn and wine	Candyfloss and wine
Nachos and cola	Popcorn and cola	Candyfloss and cola
Nachos and water	Popcorn and water	Candyfloss and water

Note: We call such a list, with all outcomes, the sample space.

319

(ii) Using the fundamental principle of counting 1

Choices for snack   multiplied by   choices for drink

$$\boxed{3} \qquad \times \qquad \boxed{3} = 9$$

Note: The word 'and' indicates multiply.

An alternative method is to construct a two-way table where we can see all the possible selections.

	Wine	Cola	Water
Nachos			
Popcorn			
Candyfloss			

Note: There are nine blank boxes in the table above. This confirms our previous answer.

(iii) Since popcorn is considered a traditional cinema snack, I think popcorn would be the most popular snack choice. I feel candyfloss would be the least popular snack choice for secondary school students. Candyfloss might be more popular with primary school students.

Given that a majority of secondary students are under 18 years old and that drinking alcohol on a school trip would not be permitted, I think the drinks choice would be split 50:50 between water and cola.

Note: In a justify/discuss type of question, there are no correct or incorrect answers. If you can back up your opinion with a logical statement, you are answering the question correctly.

A note on ordered outcomes or arrangements

Doctor Seamus has to make three house calls, to patients A, B and C, but can choose the order in which he will make these calls. There are six possible ordered outcomes (arrangements). They are

$$ABC \text{ or } ACB \text{ or } BAC \text{ or } BCA \text{ or } CAB \text{ or } CBA$$

where, for example, BCA means that Doctor Seamus visited B first, then C, then A.

Doctor Seamus had three choices for the first visit, two choices for the second visit and one choice for the third visit.

$$\therefore \boxed{3} \times \boxed{2} \times \boxed{1} = 6$$

The boxes are an aid in helping to fill in the number of ways each choice can be made at each position. In an arrangement, the order of the objects is important.

EXAMPLE

Write down all the different arrangements that can be made from these cards, taking two cards at a time if no card can be repeated. Hence or otherwise, how many such arrangements are possible?

Solution:

For questions taking two cards at a time we can use a two-way table.

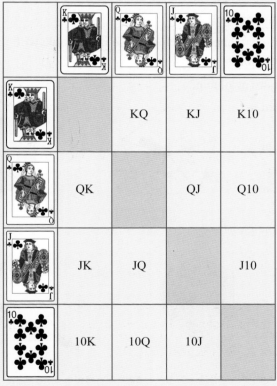

Note 1: We might conclude there are (4 × 4 =) 16 possible arrangements. However, we are not allowed to repeat a card in this question.

Note 2: To answer the question, it's best to complete each box and shade in the boxes that are not allowed.

Note 3: Some candidates would by-pass the two-way table and simply write down all arrangements. That would also be correct.

Finally, how many such arrangements are possible?

Method 1

Count the relevant boxes in the table or count your list. Answer = 12.

Method 2

Use the fundamental principle of counting 1.

We have four choices for the first card and three choices for the second card.

$$\boxed{4} \times \boxed{3} = 12$$

Exercise 19.1

1. A restaurant makes six varieties of pizza. Each of these is available in three different sizes. How many different pizzas can be ordered?

2. A factory makes electric kettles. Kettle sizes are 1 litre, 2 litres and 3 litres. Kettles are silver, cream, brown or black. How many different types of kettle does the factory make?

3. A young person starting a new job needs an outfit consisting of a jacket, trousers and shirt. A local shop has three different types of jacket, two different types of trousers and five different types of shirt. How many different selections of outfit are possible?

4. A student must choose one subject from each of the following subject groups:
   Group A: 3 modern languages
   Group B: 3 science subjects
   Group C: 2 business subjects
   How many different subject selections are possible?

5. A certain car is available as a saloon or a hatchback. Each of these is available with three different engine sizes and five different colours.

   How many different versions of the car are available?

6. A game consists of spinning a five-sided spinner, labelled *P*, *Q*, *R*, *S* and *T*, and tossing a coin. An outcome is a letter and a head or a tail.

   (i) How many outcomes of the game are possible?

   (ii) List all the possible outcomes of the game.

7. A game consists of spinning a fair die and a fair spinner which can land on *A*, *B* or *C*. An outcome is a number and a letter.

    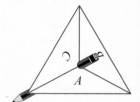

   (i) How many outcomes of the game are possible?

   (ii) List all the possible outcomes of the game.

8. The diagram shows two wheels. The first wheel is divided into four equal segments numbered 1, 2, 3 and 4. The second wheel is divided into three equal segments labelled *A*, *B* and *C*.

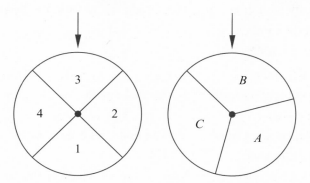

A game consists of spinning the two wheels and noting the segments that stop at the arrows. For example, the outcome shown is (3, *B*).

  (i) Write down all the possible outcomes.

 (ii) How many outcomes contain the letter *D*?

(iii) How many outcomes contain an even number and the letter *C*?

9. Raffle tickets are each labelled with a digit from {1, 2, 3, 4, 5, 6, 7, 8, 9} followed by a letter from the English alphabet {*A, B, C, D, . . . X, Y, Z*} (for example, 1*A*, 2*A*, 3*A*).

  (i) How many different raffle tickets can be formed?

 (ii) Would this amount of tickets be suitable for a raffle in your class? Justify your answer.

10. There are 28 students in a class. 13 of the students are boys. On Monday morning, 3 girls are late. A total of 21 students are not late.

Copy and complete the two-way table to show this information.

	Boys		Total
Late		3	
Total	13		28

11. A new test has been developed for determining whether or not people are carriers of the mozzie virus.

Four hundred people are tested. The results are recorded on a two-way table.

  (i) What is the value of *x*?

 (ii) For how many of the people tested were their test results inaccurate?

	Positive	Negative
Carrier	146	19
Not a carrier	30	*x*

12. Sophie has four cards with numbers on them.

    |2| |3| |4| |9|

    She chooses three cards.

    Write in the spaces which three cards she should use to form the following numbers.

    (i) The smallest odd number   □   □   □

    (ii) The largest even number   □   □   □

13. These are numbered cards. |3| |0| |6| |7| |2|

    (i) Write down the biggest number you can make with
    three of these cards.   □   □   □

    (ii) Write down the smallest number you can make with three of these cards, one of which
    has been placed for you.   □ |0| □

    (iii) Using three of these cards, write down a number which is five times bigger
    than 72.   □   □   □

14. (i) Four points lie on a circle, as in the diagram. How many
    different lines can be drawn by joining any two of the four
    points?

    (ii) Five points lie on a circle, as in the diagram. How many
    different lines can be drawn by joining any two of the five
    points?

15. Four children, Abigail, Barack, Cal and David, are to be seated in a row on a bench.

    (i) If Barack must sit on the left-hand side, write down all six different arrangements.

    (ii) If Barack must sit on the left-hand side and Cal on the right-hand side, write down all
    possible arrangements.

    (iii) How many different arrangements are possible if there are no restrictions on seating?

    (iv) If Cal and David must always sit together, write down at least two such arrangements.
    Hence or otherwise, find the total number of different arrangements where Cal and
    David sit together.

16. The Widget Corporation operates a factory in the Midlands. There are 210 people employed in the factory, 80% of whom drive to work. A new car park, with entrance and exit barriers, is constructed for the exclusive use of the employees. Each employee who drives to work is given a different code to access and leave the car park. The code is made up of three letters from the word 'widget'.

  (i) Find how many different codes can be made:

   (a) If no letter is repeated

   (b) If letter repetition is allowed

  (ii) Which of **(a)** and **(b)** is more suitable for the situation? Justify your opinion.

Theoretical probability

Probability involves the study of the laws of chance. It is a measure of the chance, or likelihood, of something happening. Probability is used throughout the world to predict what is likely to happen in the future. These events can be as simple as throwing a die or as complicated as assessing an insurance risk. At **random** means not knowing in advance what the outcome will be.

If E is an event, then $P(E)$ stands for the probability that that event occurs.

$P(E)$ is read as 'the probability of E'.

Definition

> The measure of the probability of an event, E, is given by:
>
> $$P(E) = \frac{\text{number of successful outcomes}}{\text{number of possible outcomes}}$$

The probability of an event is a number between 0 and 1, including 0 and 1. The chance of an event happening can be shown on a **probability scale**:

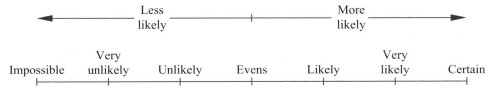

A **probability of 0** means that an event is **impossible**. If E is impossible, then $P(E) = 0$.

A **probability of 1** means an event is **certain**. If E is certain, then $P(E) = 1$.

The probabilities of some events are shown on the probability scale below.

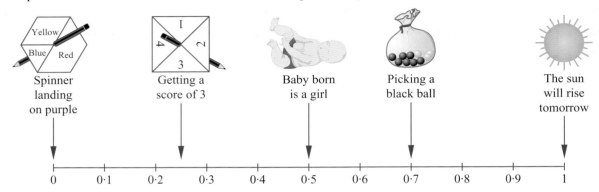

| Spinner landing on purple | Getting a score of 3 | Baby born is a girl | Picking a black ball | The sun will rise tomorrow |

Probabilities should always be written as fractions, decimals or percentages.

A pack of cards consists of 52 cards divided into four suits: clubs (black), diamonds (red), hearts (red) and spades (black). Each suit consists of 13 cards bearing the following values 2, 3, 4, 5, 6, 7, 8, 9, 10, jack, queen, king and ace. The jack, queen and king are called **picture cards**.

The total number of outcomes if one card is picked is 52.

Note: The phrase 'drawn at random' means each object is **equally likely** to be picked. 'Unbiased' means 'fair'.

EXAMPLE 1

A card is drawn at random from a normal pack of 52 playing cards.

What is the probability that the card will be:

  (i) An ace   **(ii)** A spade   **(iii)** Black   **(iv)** Odd numbered

Solution:

  (i) $P(\text{ace}) = \dfrac{\text{number of aces}}{\text{number of cards}} = \dfrac{4}{52} = \dfrac{1}{13}$

  (ii) $P(\text{spade}) = \dfrac{\text{number of spades}}{\text{number of cards}} = \dfrac{13}{52} = \dfrac{1}{4}$

  (iii) $P(\text{black card}) = \dfrac{\text{number of black cards}}{\text{number of cards}} = \dfrac{26}{52} = \dfrac{1}{2}$

  (iv) Each suit has four odd numbers, 3, 5, 7 and 9. There are four suits.
  Therefore, there are 16 cards with an odd number.

$$P(\text{odd-numbered card}) = \dfrac{\text{number of cards with an odd number}}{\text{number of cards}} = \dfrac{16}{52} = \dfrac{4}{13}$$

Probability of an event not happening

If E is any event, then 'not E' is the event that E does not occur. Clearly E and 'not E' cannot occur at the same time. Either E or 'not E' must occur. Thus, we have the following relationship between the probabilities of E and not E:

$$P(E) + P(\text{not } E) = 1$$
$$\text{or}$$
$$P(\text{not } E) = 1 - P(E)$$

Note: $P(\text{not } E)$ is sometimes written as $P(E')$ or $P(\overline{E})$.

EXAMPLE 2

When Richard plays golf, the probability that he will lose a golf ball during a round is $\frac{3}{5}$. During his next round of golf, what is the probability that he will complete a round of golf without losing a golf ball?

Solution:

$P(\text{lose a ball}) = \frac{3}{5}$

$P(\text{will not lose a ball}) = 1 - P(\text{lose a ball})$
$$= 1 - \frac{3}{5} = \frac{2}{5}$$

EXAMPLE 3

Lie detector tests are not always accurate. A lie detector test was administered to 240 people. The results were:

- 40 people lied. Of these, the test indicated 30 had lied.
- 200 people did **not** lie. Of these, the test indicated that 14 had lied.

(i) Complete the given table using the information above.

	Test indicated a lie	Test did not indicate a lie	Total
People who lied			40
People who did NOT lie			200

(ii) For how many of the people tested was the lie detector test accurate?

(iii) For what percentage of the people tested was the test accurate?

(iv) What is the probability that the test indicated a lie for a person who did NOT lie?

Solution:

(i) $40 - 30 = 10$ for whom test did not indicate a lie.

$200 - 14 = 186$ for whom test did not indicate a lie.

	Test indicated a lie	Test did not indicate a lie	Total
People who lied	30	10	40
People who did NOT lie	14	186	200

(ii) For how many of the people tested was the lie detector test accurate?

Test was accurate for the 30 people who lied and test indicated a lie as well as the 186 people who did not lie and test indicated they did not lie.

Answer = $30 + 186 = 216$

(iii) For what percentage of the people tested was the test accurate?

$\dfrac{216}{240} \times 100 = 90\%$

(iv) What is the probability that the test indicated a lie for a person who did NOT lie?

For 14 out of 200 people, the test indicated a lie for a person who did **not** lie.

$\dfrac{14}{200} = \dfrac{7}{100} = 0.07$

Exercise 19.2

1. A bag contains 4 white balls, 3 red balls, 2 green balls and 1 yellow ball. A ball is picked at random from the bag. What is the probability that:

   (i) The ball is red

   (ii) The ball is **not** green

   (iii) The ball is red or white?

2. One letter is chosen at random from the letters of the word JUNIOR.

   (i) Find the probability that the letter chosen is J.

   (ii) Find the probability that the letter chosen is a vowel.

3. A card is selected at random from a full pack of 52 cards (no jokers). What is the probability the card is:

   (i) Black   (ii) A club   (iii) The ace of spades   (iv) A king

4. A bag contains 96 discs, all of the same **shape**. 90 of the discs are **red** and 6 of the discs are **white**.
    One disc is drawn at random from the bag.
    Use the appropriate words from this list:
    likely   or   **unlikely**   or   **impossible**
    to complete **each** of the following sentences.

    (i)   'It is _____ that the
          disc drawn is **blue**.'

    (ii) 'It is _____ that the
          disc drawn is **red**.'

    (iii) 'It is _____ that the
          disc drawn is **white**.'

5. 30% of the surface of Earth is covered by
    land. A comet collides with Earth at random.
    Find the probability that the initial impact of
    the comet is on water.

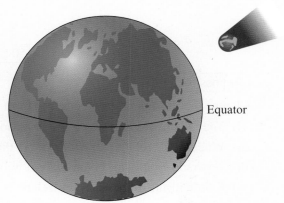

Equator

6. The probability scale shows the
    probabilities of the events A, B, C,
    D, E. Which of the five events:

    (i)   Has an even chance of happening
    (ii) Is impossible
    (iii) Is certain to happen
    (iv) Is unlikely to happen
    (v)   Is very likely to happen

7. To play a game you spin the pointer. You win
    the prize on which the pointer lands. Martin
    has one spin.

    (i)   Which prize is Martin most likely to win?
    (ii) Explain your answer to part **(i)**.
    Copy the scale below.

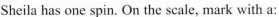

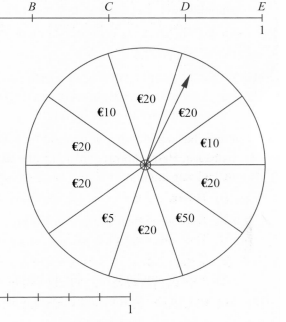

Sheila has one spin. On the scale, mark with a:
(iii) P the probability that Sheila will win €10
(iv) H the probability that Sheila will win €20

8. In a bag there are 10 numbered discs. Claire selects one disc from the bag. What is the probability that Claire selects a disc that has:

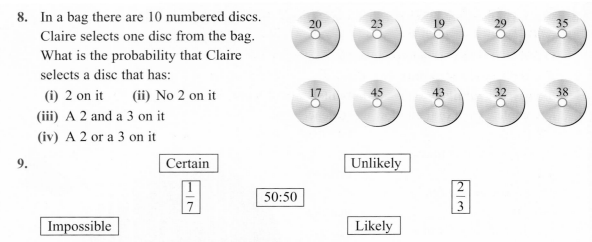

   (i) 2 on it   (ii) No 2 on it

   (iii) A 2 and a 3 on it

   (iv) A 2 or a 3 on it

9.

   | Certain | | Unlikely |

   $\dfrac{1}{7}$ 50:50 $\dfrac{2}{3}$

   | Impossible | | Likely |

   Choose the most appropriate answer from the list above.

   (i) Your Maths teacher was born on a Monday.

   (ii) When a fair regular six-sided die is thrown, the score is greater than 2.

   (iii) A person from your county (area) will win the Lotto tomorrow.

   (iv) Rain will fall somewhere in Ireland in the next 24 hours.

10. Eight students in class 2K do a morning paper round. The number of papers delivered by the students each week are as follows: 147, 125, 170, 168, 95, 180, 170, 118.

    One of the students is chosen at random. What is the probability the student delivers fewer than 150 papers?

11. Of the 35 people working in a firm, 20 walk to work, 10 go by car and the remainder go by bus. One of the people working in the firm is chosen at random. What is the probability that this person goes to work by bus?

12. Frank has accidently put two old batteries back into his bag that also contains eight new batteries. He randomly picks out one battery from the bag. What is the probability that the battery selected is:

    (i) A new battery   (ii) An old battery

    (iii) Represent each answer on the probability scale.

    (iv) How many batteries should he take out to be sure that at least one is new?

13. For each of the following events, say whether it is impossible, very unlikely, unlikely, evens, likely, very likely or certain.

    (i) If you buy a Lotto ticket, you will win the Lotto jackpot.

    (ii) You will get a head when you toss a coin.

(iii) You will pick a vowel at random from the letters of the word 'MOUSE'.

(iv) If you pick a card from a deck of cards it will be a spade.

(v) One day mathematicians will find a whole number between 2 and 3.

(vi) When a fair die is thrown it will land on one of its faces.

(vii) A washing machine that is regularly used will break down during the next 20 years.

14.

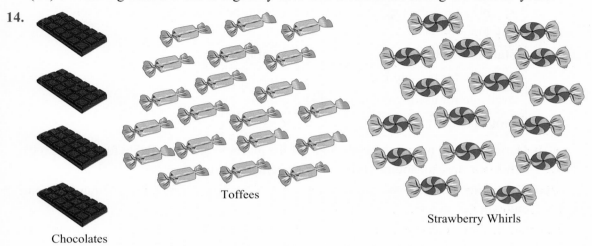

Toffees

Strawberry Whirls

Chocolates

Ngomi has a selection of sweets. He puts them in a bag and chooses one sweet at random.

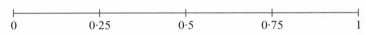

Copy the scale and place the following letters on it.

(i) *A* for the probability of choosing a toffee

(ii) *B* for the probability of choosing a chocolate

(iii) *C* for the probability of choosing a strawberry whirl or a toffee

(iv) *D* for the probability of choosing a Malteser

15. A charity is selling scratch and win cards. You choose one square to scratch and if the square says 'win' you win €20.

On which of these cards are you most likely to get a 'win'?

Justify your answer.

331

16. The lighthouse company makes light bulbs. It has only one machine. The state of the company's machine can be:

Available for use and being used

or   Available for use but not required

or   Broken down.

(i) The table shows the probabilities of the state of the machine in a certain month. Write in the value of k.

State of machine	Probability
Available for use and being used	0·89
Available for use but not required	0·09
Broken down	k

(ii) During another month the probability of the machine being available for use was 0.93. What was the probability of the machine being broken down?

(iii) The lighthouse company calculated the probabilities of a bulb failing within 800 hours and within 1,600 hours.

Copy and complete the table below to show the probabilities of a bulb still working at 800 hours and 1,600 hours.

Time	Failed	Still working
At 800 hours	$\frac{2}{25}$	
At 1,600 hours	$\frac{29}{50}$	

17. A number of sheep were weighed and the results were recorded in the stem and leaf diagram.

Weights (kg)   Key: $5|1 = 51$ kg

4	6 7 8 8 8
5	1 1 5 6 7 9
6	2 3 5 6 6
7	4 6 7
8	0 2

A sheep is selected at random. Find the probability that it weighs:

(i) Less than 50 kg

(ii) Between 50 and 70 kg

(iii) Calculate the probability of selecting

  (a) the model score   **(b)** the median score.

18. Here is a histogram showing the speeds of cars on the M50.

    (i) How many cars were surveyed altogether?

    A car is selected at random. Find the probability that:

    (ii) The speed of the car is between 100–120 km/h.

    (iii) The speed of the car is greater than 120 km/h.

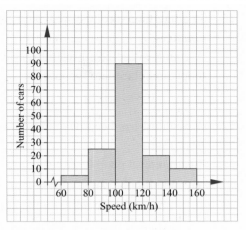

19. The pie chart shows the results of a survey on how people travelled to work. A person is chosen at random. Find the probability of:

    (i) x, the person walked to work

    (ii) y, the person travelled to work by car

    (iii) q, the person travelled to work by public transport

    (iv) Hence, indicate each letter x, y, q on the probability scale.

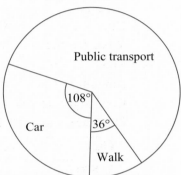

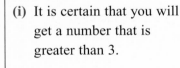

20. On each spinner, write five numbers such that each statement is true.

(i) It is certain that you will get a number that is greater than 3.	(ii) It is more likely that you will get an odd number than an even number.	(iii) It is impossible to get a number divisible by 3.
	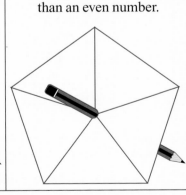	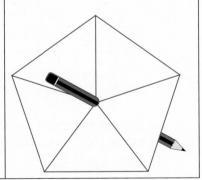

(iv) Copy and complete the spinner so that the probability of getting an even number is $\frac{1}{2}$ and the probability of getting a 2 is $\frac{1}{3}$.

21. In a bag there are only red, blue and yellow counters.
A counter is selected from the bag at random.
Copy and complete the table.

Colour of counters	Number of counters	Probability
Red	9	
Blue		$\frac{1}{4}$
Yellow	9	

22. A new test has been developed for determining whether or not people are carriers of the *Ebola* virus.
Two hundred people are tested. A two-way table is being used to record the results.

  (i) What is the value of *A*?

  (ii) A person selected from the tested group is a carrier of the virus. What is the probability that the test results would show this?

	Positive	Negative
Carrier	78	6
Not a carrier	10	*A*

 (iii) For how many of the people tested were their test results inaccurate?

 (iv) Hence, write down the probability that a person selected at random had an inaccurate result.

23. The percentage distribution of blood groups in the Irish population is given in the table below. The table also gives information about which types of blood can be safely used when people need to be given blood during an operation.

Blood group	Percentage in Irish population	Blood groups to which transfusions can be safely given	Blood groups from which transfusions can be safely received
O−	8	All	O−
O+	47	O+, AB+, A+, B+	O+ and O−
A−	5	A−, A+, AB+, AB−	A− and O−
A+	26	A+ and AB+	A+, O−, O+, A−
B−	2	B−, B+, AB−, AB+	B− and O−
B+	9	B+ and AB+	B+, B−, O−, O+
AB−	1	AB− and AB+	AB−, O−, A−, B−
AB+	2	AB+	all

Source: Irish Blood Transfusion Service

  (i) If an Irish person is chosen at random, what is the probability that person will have blood group AB−?

 (ii) Mary has blood group B−. If a person is chosen at random from the population, what is the probability that Mary could safely receive blood from that person?

(iii) Aaron has blood group O+ and donates blood. What is the probability that his blood can be given to a person randomly chosen from the population?

(iv) The Irish Blood Transfusion Service recently asked that people with blood group O− should give blood as regularly as possible. Give a reason why this might be the case.

Combining two events

There are many situations where we have to consider two outcomes. In these situations all the possible outcomes, called the **sample space** (or **outcome space**), can be listed in a **sample space diagram** (often called a **two-way table** or a **probability space diagram**).

EXAMPLE 1

A fair coin is tossed and a fair die is rolled. List all the outcomes in a sample space diagram. Calculate the probability of obtaining a head and an odd number.

Solution:

Sample space diagram

Coin	T						
	H	•		•		•	
		1	2	3	4	5	6

Die

We indicate each successful outcome with a dot.

P(head and an odd number)

$= \frac{3}{12} = \frac{1}{4}$

EXAMPLE 2

Two unbiased spinners are spun together. Each spinner is divided into equal sectors and numbered as shown. An outcome is achieved by adding the numbers that each arrow lands on.

(i) Represent all the outcomes in a sample space diagram.

(ii) What is the probability that the outcome is 7?

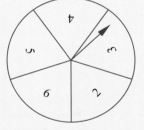
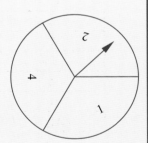

Solution:

(i) Sample space diagram

(ii) There are 15 outcomes.
7 occurs three times.
∴ $P(7) = \frac{3}{15} = \frac{1}{5}$

Second spinner	4	6	7	8	9	10
	2	4	5	6	7	8
	1	3	4	5	6	7
	+	2	3	4	5	6

First spinner

EXAMPLE 3

On Mondays and Tuesdays Sally either goes to the debating club after school or to the homework club. The probability that she goes to the homework club each day is $\frac{3}{5}$.

   (i) Represent the situation with a tree diagram.

Calculate the probability that Sally goes to:

   (ii) The homework club on Monday and Tuesday

   (iii) The debating club on both days

   (iv) The homework club on Monday and the debating club on Tuesday

   (v) The debating club on Monday and the homework club on Tuesday

Solution:

   (i) Let D = the event Sally goes to the debating club

   and H = the event Sally goes to the homework club.

   The probability Sally goes to the homework club

   $= P(H) = \frac{3}{5}$

   and the probability Sally goes to the debating club

   $= P(D) = 1 - \frac{3}{5} = \frac{2}{5}$,   as she goes to one club or the other.

We fill in the probabilities on the tree diagram below.

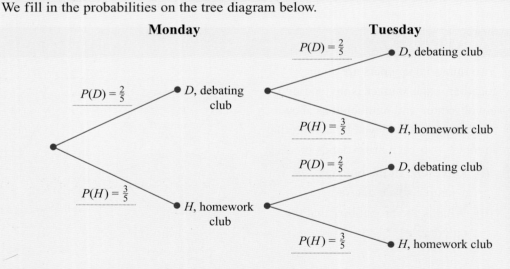

Here, the tree diagram has four branches. They are:

   1. Debating club Monday, debating club Tuesday

   2. Debating club Monday, homework club Tuesday

   3. Homework club Monday, debating club Tuesday

   4. Homework club Monday, homework club Tuesday

(ii) P(homework club on Monday and Tuesday)

$= P(H) \times P(H)$

$= \dfrac{3}{5} \times \dfrac{3}{5}$

$= \dfrac{9}{25}$

(iii) P(the debating club on both days)

$= P(D) \times P(D)$

$= \dfrac{2}{5} \times \dfrac{2}{5}$

$= \dfrac{4}{25}$

(iv) P(homework club Monday and debating club Tuesday)

$= P(H) \times P(D)$

$= \dfrac{3}{5} \times \dfrac{2}{5}$

$= \dfrac{6}{25}$

(v) P(debating club Monday and homework club Tuesday)

$= P(D) \times P(H)$

$= \dfrac{2}{5} \times \dfrac{3}{5}$

$= \dfrac{6}{25}$

Note: The sum of the probabilities on the four branches sum to 1,

i.e. probabilities of $\qquad HH \quad + \quad HD \quad + \quad DH \quad + \quad DD$

$$= \left(\dfrac{3}{5}\right)\left(\dfrac{3}{5}\right) + \left(\dfrac{3}{5}\right)\left(\dfrac{2}{5}\right) + \left(\dfrac{2}{5}\right)\left(\dfrac{3}{5}\right) + \left(\dfrac{2}{5}\right)\left(\dfrac{2}{5}\right)$$

$$= \dfrac{9}{25} \quad + \quad \dfrac{6}{25} \quad + \quad \dfrac{6}{25} \quad + \quad \dfrac{4}{25}$$

$$= \dfrac{25}{25}$$

$$= 1$$

Exercise 19.3

1. **(i)** A fair coin is tossed and a fair five-sided spinner, with sides A, A, B, B, B, is spun. How many outcomes are possible?

T					
H					
	A	A	B	B	B

Find the probability of:

(ii) A head and an A

(iii) A tail and a B

2. For a two-course meal you can choose one main course and dessert from the menu.

Main Course	Dessert
Fish	Ice cream
Steak	
Pizza	Fruit salad

   (i) List all the possible two-course meals that can be chosen.

  (ii) What is the probability that if you choose a two-course meal at random from the menu it will contain steak and ice cream?

3. A fair die is thrown and a fair spinner is spun. The die is numbered 1 to 6 and the spinner is labelled 1 to 4.

 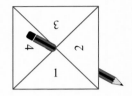

An outcome is achieved by adding the numbers which are face up when the die and spinner come to rest.

   (i) Copy the sample space diagram and data capture sheet. Hence, list all the outcomes in the sample space diagram and complete the data capture sheet.

4						
3						
2						
1						
+	1	2	3	4	5	6

Outcome	2	3	4	5	6	7	8	9	10
Frequency									

  (ii) What is the probability that the outcome is:

    (a) 6   **(b)** 8 or more   **(c)** Prime   **(d)** Divisible by 5

4. **(i)** A game consists of spinning two unbiased spinners, as shown. Using a sample space diagram, or otherwise, list all possible outcomes.

  (ii) Find the probability that in any one game the outcome will be:

    (a) An *A* and an odd number

    (b) A *B* or a *C* and an even number

 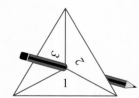

5. Patricia and Derek are playing a game which involves the combined results of spinning a spinner and throwing a die.

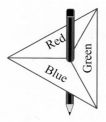 

The table shows all the possible outcomes.

	1	2	3	4	5	6
Red	R1	R2	R3	R4	R5	R6
Blue	B1	B2	B3	B4	B5	B6
Green	G1	G2	G3	G4	G5	G6

(i) What is the probability of throwing a six on the die **and** getting red on the spinner?

(ii) What is the probability of getting an even number on the die, with either blue or green on the spinner?

(iii) Either Patricia or Derek must win this game. A tie is not possible.

The probability of Patricia winning the game is 0·64.

(a) What is the probability of Derek winning the game?

(b) Who is more likely to win the game? Explain your reasoning.

6. A bag contains three red discs and seven blue discs. A disc is taken from the bag, the colour noted, then replaced in the bag. Another disc is then taken.

Using the given tree diagram, find the probability that:

(i) A red disc is drawn first and then a blue disc

(ii) Both discs are blue

(iii) Both discs are different colours

(iv) Both discs are the same colour

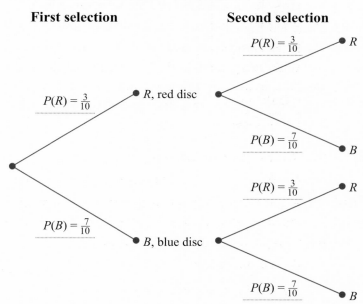

First selection   Second selection

$P(R) = \frac{3}{10}$ ● R, red disc

$P(R) = \frac{3}{10}$ ● R

$P(B) = \frac{7}{10}$ ● B

$P(R) = \frac{3}{10}$ ● R

$P(B) = \frac{7}{10}$ ● B, blue disc

$P(B) = \frac{7}{10}$ ● B

7. A fair coin is tossed twice.

   (i) Copy and complete the tree diagram to show the probability of each possible outcome.

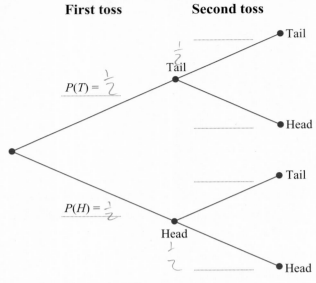

   (ii) Calculate the probability that:
   (a) Both results are heads
   (b) The first is a tail and the second is a head

8. There has been a problem on a car production line and all the cars need to be recalled for a check. The probability that one of these cars has faulty steering is 0·1 and the probability that it has faulty lights is 0·25. These probabilities are independent of each other, i.e. faulty steering has no link with faulty lights or vice versa.

   (i) Copy and complete the tree diagram below.

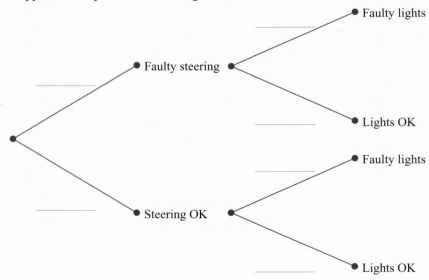

(ii) Using your answer to **(i)** or otherwise, find the probability that a car chosen at random has:

    (a) Both faults

    (b) Neither fault

    (c) Only one fault

9.   **(i)** In a family with three children the sexes of the children is recorded, male (*m*) or female (*f*). The sample space for such families is shown in the diagram. Write down all the possible outcomes.

      For example, *mff* represents the outcome that the oldest child is male and the younger two are female.

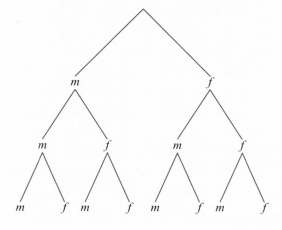

  (ii) Hence, find the probability of a family with three children consisting of:

    (a) Three females

    (b) Two males and one female

10. To play a game, a player spins a wheel. The wheel is fixed to a wall. It spins freely around its centre point. Its rim is divided equally into six regions. Four of the regions are coloured blue (B). Two are coloured white (W).

When the wheel stops, an arrow fixed to the wall points to one of the regions. All the regions are equally likely to stop at the arrow. The colour of this region is the outcome of the game. When the game is played twice, calculate the probability that:

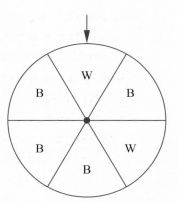

  (i) Both outcomes are blue

 (ii) The first outcome is white and the second is blue

(iii) Both outcomes are the same colour

(iv) One outcome is white and the other is blue

11. Marie and Reg have hired a camper van for a holiday. The picture shows a fair spinner. They used the spinner each day to decide who would drive the camper van. The spinner has six equal-sized sectors.

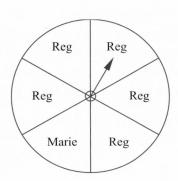

What is the probability that:

  (i) Reg drives the camper van on each of the first two days

 (ii) There are different drivers on each of the first two days

12. Box 1 has four red cones and one blue cone.
    Box 2 has one red cone and three blue cones.
    A cone is chosen at random from box 1 and then
    a cone is chosen at random from box 2.
    Find the probability that:

    (i) Both are red

    (ii) Both are blue

    (iii) The first is red and the second is blue

    (iv) The first is blue and the second is red

    (v) One is red and the other is blue (in any order)

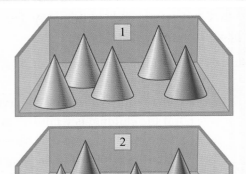

13. In a lottery, 28 numbered balls are used. Seven of the balls are red.

    (i) A ball is drawn at random and replaced. Then a second ball is drawn. Find the
        probability that:

        (a) The first is red

        (b) Both are red

        (c) The first is red and the second is not red

        (d) One is red and the other is not red

    (ii) If the first ball drawn is not replaced, find the probability that:

        (a) Both are red

        (b) One is red and the other is not red, in any order

Experimental probability (relative frequency)

Often a probability can only be found by carrying out a series of experiments and recording the
results. For example, if you drop a drawing pin and you want to find the probability that it lands point
up, there is no obvious method except by dropping a lot of drawing pins and recording the results.
The probability of the event can then be **estimated** from these results. A probability found
in this way is known as **experimental probability** or **relative frequency** of an event. Each separate
experiment carried out is called a **trial**. To find the relative frequency, the experiment has to be
repeated a number of times. It is important to remember that if an experiment is repeated, there will
be different outcomes and that increasing the number of times an experiment is repeated generally
leads to better estimates of probability.

Estimating probabilities using relative frequency

> The relative frequency of an event in an experiment is given by:
>
> $$P(E) = \text{relative frequency of an event} = \frac{\text{number of successful trials}}{\text{number of trials}}$$

Relative frequency can be used to estimate how many times you would **expect** a particular outcome to happen in an experiment.

The expected number of outcomes (or expected value) is calculated as follows.

> Expected number of outcomes = (relative frequency) × (number of trials)
>
> or
>
> Expected number of outcomes = P(event) × (number of trials)

Note: To estimate the probability of some events, it is necessary to carry out a survey or look at historical data (past data).

EXAMPLE 1

The winner of a TV game show spins the spinner shown. Each of the five sections are equally likely to point at the arrow.
Calculate the expected value of one spin.

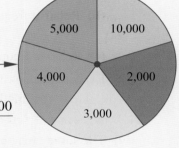

Solution:

The expected value $= \dfrac{2,000 + 3,000 + 4,000 + 5,000 + 10,000}{5}$

$\qquad\qquad\qquad = \dfrac{24,000}{5}$

$\qquad\qquad\qquad = 4,800$

Note: The term 'expected value' can be misleading. The expected value is generally **not** a typical value that the random variable can take. Expected value is similar to the long-run average/relative frequency.

EXAMPLE 2

A traffic survey was carried out at a busy intersection for one hour. The results are recorded in the following data capture sheet.

Direction	Turn right	Turn left	Straight ahead
Number of vehicles	128	108	164

   (i) How many vehicles were recorded in the survey?

 (ii) Calculate the relative frequency of the vehicles in this survey that:

(a) Turned right

(b) Turned left

(c) Went straight ahead

(iii) If 5,400 vehicles used the intersection during the day, estimate the number of vehicles that turned left.

(iv) Give one reason why these figures may not be accurate.

Solution

(i) Total number of vehicles recorded = 128 + 108 + 164

$$= 400$$

(ii) (a) Relative frequency turning right $= \dfrac{128}{400} = 0.32$

(b) Relative frequency turning left $= \dfrac{108}{400} = 0.27$

(c) Relative frequency straight ahead $= \dfrac{164}{400} = 0.41$

(iii) Expected value of those turning left

$$= (5,400)(0.27)$$
$$= 1,458$$

(iv) The survey may have been carried out at a time that was not typical, e.g. school traffic in the morning or road works giving an untypical pattern to traffic flow. Any reasonable suggestion will usually be accepted.

Exercise 19.4

1. Colm found by experiment that he kicked a rugby ball over the post 52 times out of 80 kicks. Estimate the probability that with his next kick he will kick the ball over the post.

2. A light bulb manufacturer tests samples of bulbs to estimate the number that are faulty. From a batch of 10,000 bulbs, 400 were selected at random and it was found that eight were faulty. Based on the sample result, estimate the number of faulty bulbs in the batch.

3. A six-sided die is thrown 120 times. The results of the trials are shown in the table below.

Score	1	2	3	4	5	6
Frequency	23	8	16	22	13	38

Is the die fair? Give a reason for your answer.

4. A fair spinner is labelled as shown.
   The results of the first 10 spins are:

   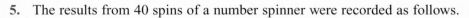

   P   Q   R   R   Q   S   Q   P   R   S

   (i) Write down the experimental probability of the letter Q.
   (ii) As the number of spins increases, what do you expect
        to happen to the experimental probability of Q?

5. The results from 40 spins of a number spinner were recorded as follows.

   1 4 3 2 1 1 2 5 4 4 5 4 3 3 2 1 2 3 3 1
   5 4 3 4 2 1 2 3 5 3 4 3 5 1 4 2 3 4 5 2

   Copy and complete the following table.

Number	1	2	3	4	5
Tally					
Frequency					

   (i) Use these results to estimate the probability of getting a 3 with the next spin.

   (ii) Is the spinner biased? Give a reason for your answer.

6. Catherine made a five-sided spinner. She lettered the sections as shown
   in the diagram. She thought that the spinner wasn't fair, as it seemed to
   land on some letters more than others. She spun the spinner 100 times
   and recorded the results in the table below.

Letter	A	B	C	D	E
Frequency	14	43	8	22	13

   (i) Calculate the experimental probability of each letter.
   (ii) If the spinner was fair, how many times would you expect each letter to occur?
   (iii) Do you think the spinner is fair? Give a reason for your answer.

7. A college has 1,953 students. The probability that a student can drive is $\frac{3}{7}$. Calculate how
   many students at the college can drive.

8. The probability that Susan is late for school is 0·125.
   Her school term lasts 56 days.
   How many days would Susan expect to be late?

9. A spinner with 10 equal sectors is spun 150 times. How often would you expect to spin:

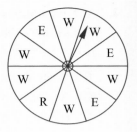

   (i) An E

   (ii) A W

10. Bren does an experiment with a slice of buttered toast. He drops it 18 times and finds that it lands with its buttered side down 15 times. He concludes that the toast is more likely to land butter side down.

   (i) What is the experimental probability of the toast landing butter side down?

   (ii) Based on this probability, how many times would you expect the floor to get buttered if the toast was dropped 90 times?

11. A bag contains seven counters, numbered as follows.

   ① ③ ⑥ ⑩ ⑮ ㉑ ㉘

   (i) One counter is selected at random from the bag. Calculate the expected value of the counter.

   (ii) The counter with number ㉑ is removed. A counter is then selected. Calculate the expected value of the counter.

12. The ratio of heads to tails given by a biased coin is 4:1.

   (i) What is the probability of obtaining a head when this coin is tossed once?

   (ii) What is the expected number of heads if this coin is tossed 360 times?

13. The table below shows the results of a survey of 50 students chosen at random in a school.

   From these 50 students, one is selected at random.

   (i) What is the probability that the student
       (a) is male   (b) has green eyes?

   (ii) A girl is chosen at random. What is the probability that she has brown eyes?

Eye colour	Male	Female
Blue	15	10
Brown	10	8
Green	5	2

   (iii) The school has 800 students. How many students would you expect to be (a) female (b) blue eyed?

14. A biased spinner has sectors marked A, B and C.
    The probability that the spinner will land on each letter is
    given in the table below.

Sector	A	B	C
Probability	0·15	0·5	x

   (i) Work out the value of x.

   (ii) In a game, the spinner was spun 400 times. Estimate the number of times the spinner
        landed on sector C.

15. The back-to-back stem and leaf diagram shows the maths score of students in percentages
    of one class in a school.

Key: Girls 7|6		Girls		Boys		Key: Boys 5|2
Represents 67%						Represents 52%

```
        Girls │   │ Boys
            7 │ 3 │ 6 8
            8 │ 4 │ 1 9 9
          9 2 │ 5 │ 2 2 8 8
            7 │ 6 │ 0 1 2 2 4 7
        4 3 3 │ 7 │ 8
```

   (i) (a) How many boys are in the class?
       (b) How many girls are in the class?

   (ii) How many students scored less than 40%?

   (iii) The class is representative of 744 students in the school. Find the expected number of
         students that would

       (a) Be boys

       (b) Be girls

       (c) Achieve a score less than 40%

16. Red and green spinners were each spun 48 times.
    Each spinner has three sides indicating scores
    of 1, 2 and 3.

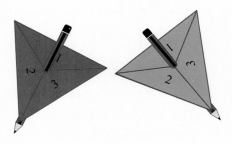

The bar chart shows the results.

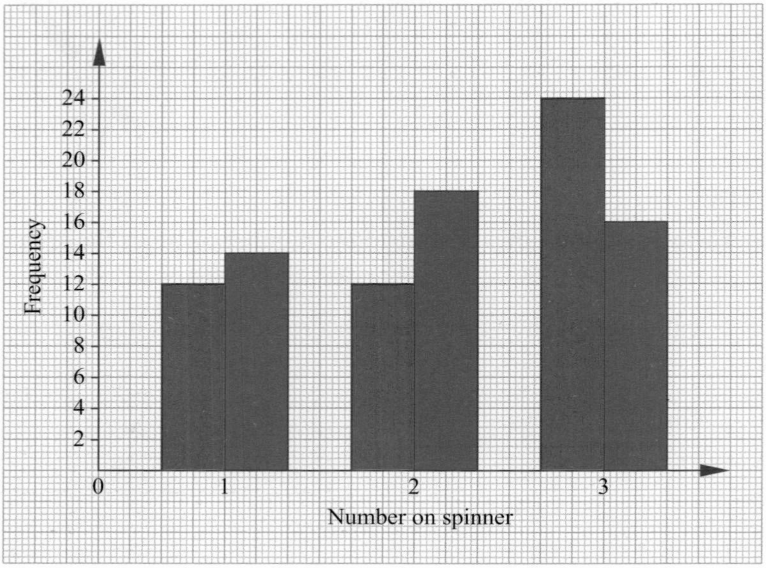

One spinner is fair and the other is unfair. Which spinner do you think is fair? Justify your answer.

17. In a game of 'roll the coin', the rules are as follows:

Roll a 50c coin onto the board (which you don't get back).
If the coin lands inside a square you win **€**5.
If the coin lands on a line you lose.
Neil tested the game by rolling a 50c coin 40 times.
He recorded the results in the table below.

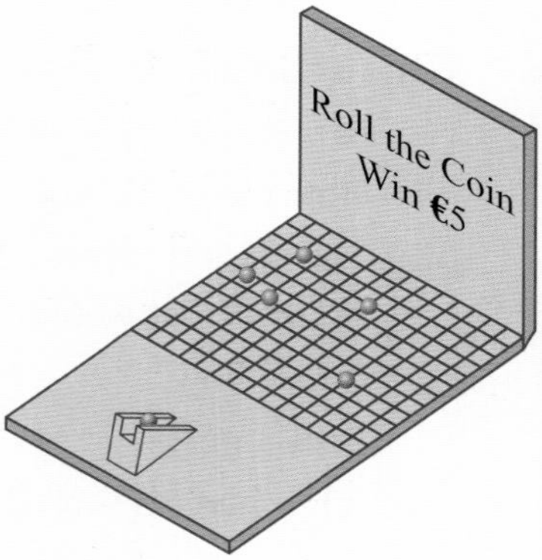

	Tally	Frequency	Probability
Win	卌 ||		
Lose			

(i) Copy and complete the table.

(ii) At a fair, 360 people played this game. How many would you expect to win this game?

(iii) What is misleading in the advertisement for this game?

18. Carol has just bought three dice. She suspects that one of them is biased, landing too frequently on the 1.

Carol asks her sisters to test a die each. To make sure the test is fair, she doesn't say who is testing the suspect die. Each sister rolls their die repeatedly and records how many times they score a 1. Here are their results:

	Number of trails	Number of 1s
Carol	10	3
Siobhan	50	8
Elaina	100	27

(i) Who has the biased die? Give a reason for your answer.

(ii) Use the table above to estimate the probability of scoring a 1 on the biased die.

19. (i) Nima, Nell and Tara each rolled a different die 180 times.
Only one die was fair. Whose was it? Explain your answer.
(ii) Whose die is the most biased? Explain your answer.

Number	Nima	Nell	Tara
1	14	29	60
2	35	31	26
3	39	32	28
4	22	28	27
5	38	27	26
6	32	33	13

20. A die has faces numbered 1 to 6. The die is biased so that the number 6 will appear more often than each of the other numbers. The numbers 1 to 5 are equally likely to occur.

The die was rolled 1,200 times and it was noted that the 6 appeared 450 times.
Which statement is correct?

(i) The probability of rolling the number 5 is expected to be $\frac{1}{7}$.

(ii) The number 6 is expected to appear two times as often as any other number.

(iii) The number 6 is expected to appear three times as often as any other number.

(iv) The probability of rolling an even number is expected to be equal to the probability of rolling an odd number.

21. A TV game show plans to finish with the winner spinning a wheel. The wheel is fixed to a wall. It's divided equally into seven regions and the winning amounts are shown on the wheel in euro. The winner will receive the amount the arrow points to when the wheel stops.

The game show director suspects the wheel is not very fair, as some amounts seem to come more often than others.

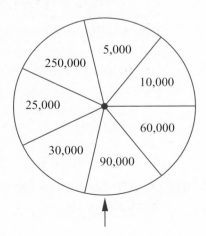

She spun the wheel 140 times and recorded the results. The results are shown in the table.

Amount won, in €1,000s	5	10	25	30	60	90	250
Number of times	7	19	17	8	29	42	18

(i) How many times would the director expect each number to occur if the wheel was fair?

(ii) Work out the experimental probability of spinning:

(a) €5,000 (b) €90,000

(iii) Do you think the director would conclude the wheel was fair? Justify your answer.

22. The colour of 500 cars that pass a particular set of traffic lights during a two-hour period is recorded by a group of students.

Colour	Frequency	Relative frequency	Daily frequency (part (v) below)
Red	70		
Blue	100		
Yellow	45		
White	55		
Black			
Silver	140		
Total	500		

Copy the table and answer the following questions:

(i) Calculate the number of black cars and write it into the table.

(ii) Calculate the relative frequency of each colour and write these into the table.

(iii) Suggest a method to check that your relative frequency calculations are correct. Perform this check.

(iv) What is the probability that the next car to pass the lights is red?

(v) Use the information to estimate the frequency of each colour if 2,400 cars pass the lights in a full day. Write this information into the table.

(vi) The data collected by the students is not a random sample of the cars passing throughout the day. Do you think that this makes your estimates in (v) above unreliable? Give a reason for your answer.

Using set theory in probability

The number of elements in the set A is denoted by $\#A$.

$\#A$ = the number of elements in set A.

EXAMPLE

$A = \{a, b, c, d, e\}$ and $X = \{2, 4, 6, 8\}$.

   (i) Find #A.   **(ii)** Calculate #A − #X.

Solution:

   (i) Since A contains five elements, then #A = 5.

   (ii) Since X contains four elements, then #X = 4.

       Therefore, #A − #X = 5 − 4 = 1.

Universal set

The **universal set** is the set containing all the elements used in a given question. It is denoted by U. In a Venn diagram the universal set is represented by a rectangle. In probability the universal set is often denoted by S, the sample space.

Intersection

> The **intersection** of two sets, A and B, is the set of elements that are in both A and B.

It is written as $A \cap B$, pronounced 'A intersection B'.

Union

> The **union** of two sets, A and B, is the set of elements formed by joining together all the elements of A and B.

It is written as $A \cup B$, pronounced 'A union B'.

Set difference

> $A \setminus B$ is the set of elements that are in A but not in B.

$A \setminus B$ is pronounced 'A less B' or 'A not B' or 'A but not in B'.
In some ways it is like the subtraction of one set from another.

Complement of a set

The **complement** of a set A is the set of elements in the universal set, U, that are **not** elements of A.

> $A' = U \setminus A$
> Every element in the universal set U except those in A.

The complement of a set A is written A' (pronounced 'A complement' or 'A dashed').
It is an extension of set difference.

$$(A \cup B)' = U \setminus (A \cup B) \quad \text{and} \quad (A \cap B)' = U \setminus (A \cap B)$$

The four regions for the three sets U, A and B

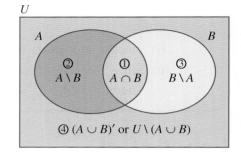

Note: If the universal set, U, is not involved, there are only three regions.

When drawing a Venn diagram, always work from the centre outwards.

Numerical problems on two sets

When using Venn diagrams to solve numerical problems, we put the actual number of elements in a region on the diagram. It is important at this stage that the meanings of the symbols used are considered.

Set notation	Meaning
$\cup$	or
$\cap$	and, both
$A \cup B$	in A or in B
$A \cap B$	in A and in B
$A \setminus B$	in A but not in B, in A only
$B \setminus A$	in B but not in A, in B only
U	universal set
A' or $U \setminus A$	in U but not in A
$(A \cup B)'$ or $U \setminus (A \cup B)$	in U but not in A or B
$(A \cup B)'$ or $U \setminus (A \cap B)$	in U but not in A and B

When putting the values into a Venn diagram, always work from the centre outwards.

EXAMPLE 1

In a class of 34 pupils, 22 study music, 18 study science and eight study both.
Draw a Venn diagram to illustrate the information and use it to find the number of pupils in the class who study **(i)** music only **(ii)** science only **(iii)** neither music nor science.
(iv) A student is chosen at random from the class. Write down the probability that the student studies:

    (a) Music only

    (b) Science only

    (c) Neither music nor science

Solution:

Draw a Venn diagram showing U for the class,
M for music and S for science.

Given: $\#U = 34$, $\#M = 22$, $\#S = 18$ and $\#(M \cap S) = 8$.

Put 8 in the middle intersecting part of the diagram.

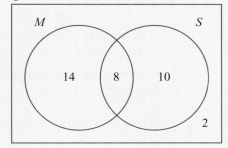

(i) Number who study music only

$= \#(M \setminus S)$

$= 22 - 8$

$= 14$

(ii) Number who study science only

$= \#(S \setminus M)$

$= 18 - 8$

$= 10$

(iii) Number who study neither music nor science

$= \#[U \setminus (M \cup S)]$

$= 34 - (14 + 8 + 10)$

$= 34 - 32 = 2$

Check: $14 + 8 + 10 + 2 = 34$ ✓

(iv) (a) From (i), $P(\text{studies music only}) = \dfrac{14}{34} = \dfrac{7}{17}$

(b) From (ii), $P(\text{studies science only}) = \dfrac{10}{34} = \dfrac{5}{17}$

(c) From (iii), $P(\text{studies neither music nor science}) = \dfrac{2}{34} = \dfrac{1}{17}$

In some questions the number of elements in the intersection of the two sets is not given. This leads to the problem of **double counting**.

EXAMPLE 2

In a survey of 32 people, 20 said they liked rock music, 13 said they liked classical music and four said they liked neither.

(i) Represent the survey with a Venn diagram.

A person is chosen at random from the survey. Find the probability that the person:

(ii) Likes both rock and classical music

(iii) Likes rock music only

(iv) Likes only one of these types of music

Solution:

(i) On the Venn diagram, let U represent the number of people in the survey, R the number who liked rock music and C the number who liked classical music.

The number of people in the survey who liked rock music, classical music or neither
$= 20 + 13 + 4 = 37$.

The number of people in the survey $= 32$.

Therefore, the number of people counted twice $= 37 - 32 = 5$.

Thus, 5 people liked both rock and classical music.

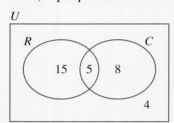

$\#(R \cap C) = 5$

$\#(R \setminus C) = 20 - 5 = 15$

$\#(C \setminus R) = 13 - 5 = 8$

Check: $15 + 5 + 8 + 4 = 32$ ✓

Number of people who only liked rock music $= \#(R \setminus C) = 15$.
Number of people who liked only one of these types of music
$= \#(R \setminus C) + \#(C \setminus R) = 15 + 8 = 23$.

(ii) P(person likes rock and classical music) $= \frac{5}{32}$

(iii) P(person likes rock music only) $= \frac{15}{32}$

(iv) P(person likes only one type of music)
$= \frac{15}{32} + \frac{8}{32} = \frac{23}{32}$

Note: When two sets have no elements in common, then we say B and Q are **mutually exclusive** events. This means they cannot happen at the same time. In probability, this means that $P(B \text{ or } Q) = P(B) + P(Q)$. It also means $P(B \cap Q) = 0$.

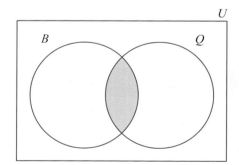

EXAMPLE 3

Eighty passengers on a plane were surveyed as to how they spent their time on the flight. The activities were reading (R), listening to music (M) and watching the in-flight movie (I). The results are shown in the Venn diagram.

$U = 80$

What is the probability of selecting a passenger at random who:

(i) Enjoyed reading, listening to music and watching the movie

(ii) Enjoyed only one activity

(iii) Enjoyed either music or reading

(iv) Write down $P(M \cap R)$ and $P(M \cap I)$. Hence or otherwise, can you identify a pair of sets that are mutually exclusive?

Solution

(i) $P(\text{enjoyed all three activities}) = \frac{0}{80} = 0$

(ii) $P(\text{only one activity}) = \frac{16}{80} + \frac{32}{80} + \frac{8}{80} = \frac{56}{80} = \frac{7}{10}$

(iii) $P(\text{music or reading}) = \frac{16}{80} + \frac{24}{80} + \frac{8}{80} = \frac{48}{80} = \frac{3}{5}$

(iv) $P(M \cap R) = \frac{0}{80} = 0$

∴ M and R are mutually exclusive.

$P(M \cap I) = \frac{24}{80} = \frac{3}{10} \neq 0$

∴ M and I are not mutually exclusive.

Exercise 19.5

1. The Venn diagram shows the number of elements in the sets U, A and B. Write down each of the following probabilities.

(i) $P(U)$

(ii) $P(A \cap B)$

(iii) $P(A')$

(iv) $P(A \cup B)$

(v) $P(B')$

(vi) $P(A \cap B)'$

(vii) $P(A \setminus B)$

(viii) $P(B \setminus A)$

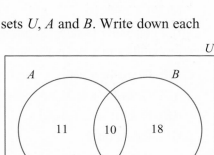

2. There are 240 students in a primary school. The
    Venn diagram shows the numbers of students who
    own a mobile phone (*M*) and who own a computer (*C*).

    If a student is selected at random, find the probability
    that the student owned:

    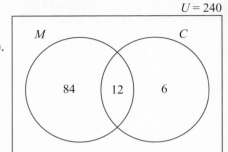

    (i) A mobile phone
    (ii) A computer
    (iii) Neither a mobile phone nor a computer
    (iv) A mobile phone but not a computer
    (v) Both a mobile phone and a computer
    (vi) We are told these 240 primary school students are a representative sample of their
    country. The country has a total of 900,000 primary school students. Find the expected
    number of primary students with a mobile phone in the country.

3. In the given Venn diagram:

    U = the teachers in a school
    S = the teachers teaching Leaving Certificate classes
    J = the teachers teaching Junior Certificate classes

    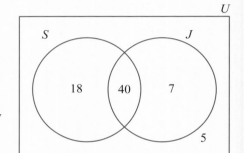

    (i) How many teachers are in the school?
    If a teacher is selected at random, find the probability
    that the teacher:

    (ii) Teaches Leaving Certificate classes
    (iii) Teaches neither Leaving nor Junior Certificate classes
    (iv) Teaches Junior Certificate classes only
    (v) Teaches both Junior and Leaving Certificate classes

4. The Venn diagram shows the numbers of pensioners
    who as a daily pastime read (*R*), watch TV (*T*) and
    go for a walk (*W*).

    If a pensioner is selected at random, find the
    probability that the pensioner:

    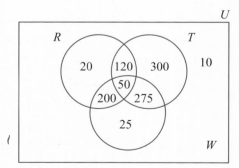

    (i) Goes for a walk
    (ii) Goes for a walk and watches TV
    (iii) Does none of these activities
    (iv) Reads only
    (v) Reads or watches TV
    (vi) Does at least two of the pastimes

5. P is the set of divisors of 12.

Q is the set of divisors of 9.

Using this information, copy and complete the Venn diagram.

Hence, state if P and Q are mutually exclusive. Justify your answer.

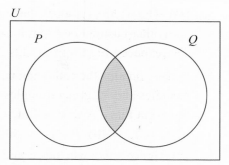

6. Carry out your own class survey and show your results on a Venn diagram for:

(i) Two events

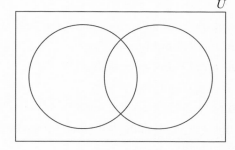

(ii) Three events

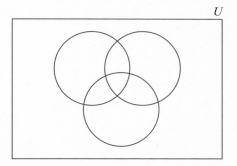

7. A restaurant owner carried out a survey to see if his customers liked wine or beer. He surveyed 135 customers. The Venn diagram shows his results.

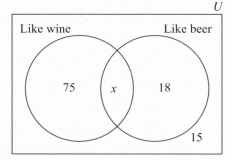

(i) Find the value for x.

(ii) What can you say about the customers in the region marked x?

(iii) If one customer is chosen at random, what is the probability they like neither wine nor beer?

(iv) One of the customers chosen at random liked wine. What is the probability that the customer also liked beer?

(v) The next month, the owner expects to serve 570 customers. Estimate how many of those customers he will expect to like beer. Explain your answer.

(vi) The waitress notices that customers who like wine only give much bigger tips than other customers. From the expected 570 customers, how many of them can the waitress expect a big tip from? Justify your answer.

8. A bag contains the following cardboards shapes: 8 red squares, 17 green squares, 8 red triangles and 12 green triangles. One of the shapes is drawn at random from the bag. E is the event that a square is drawn. F is the event that a red shape is drawn. Find:

    (i) $P(E)$ (ii) $P(F)$ (iii) $P(E \cup F)$ (iv) $P(E \cap F)$

    (v) Hence, state whether E and F are mutually exclusive.

9. A group of 100 students was asked if they had a presence on particular social networking websites A, B and C.

    24 students had a presence on A only, 40 had a presence on B and 50 had a presence on C.

    14 students had a presence on A and B but not on C.

    18 students had a presence on A and C but not on B.

    8 students had a presence on B and C but not on A.

    4 students stated that they did not have a presence on any of the websites.

    (i) Using x to represent the number of students who had a presence on all three websites, construct a Venn diagram and solve for x.

    (ii) Complete the Venn diagram.

    (iii) Hence, write down the following probabilities.

        (a) $P(A)$

        (b) $P(B')$

        (c) $P(B \cap C)$

        (d) $P(B \cup C)'$

        (e) $P(A \cup B \cup C)$

        (f) $P(A \cap B)'$

10. U is the universal set and P and Q are two subsets of U.

    $\#U = 20$

    $\#(P \cap Q) = x$

    $\#(P \setminus Q) = 2x$

    $\#((P \cup Q)') = 4$

    $\#Q = 2(\#P)$

    (i) Represent the above information on a Venn diagram and hence find $\#Q$.

    (ii) Find $P(Q)$, the probability of Q.

11. U is the universal set.

A, B and C are three subsets of U.

$\#(A \cap B \cap C) = 3x$

$\#(A \cap C) = 4x$

$\#((A \cap B) \setminus C) = y$

$\#(B \cap C) = 16$

$\#(C \setminus (A \cup B)) = 2y$

$\#(B \setminus (A \cup C)) = 11$

$\#A = 31$

 (i) Represent the above information on a Venn diagram.

 (ii) Given that $\#B = 32$ and $\#C = 29$, calculate the value of x and the value of y.

 (iii) Find $P(A \cap B \cap C)$.   (iv) Find $P(A \setminus B)$.

12. In a class of 56 students, each studies at least one of the subjects Biology, Chemistry, Physics. The Venn diagram shows the numbers of students studying the various combinations of subjects.

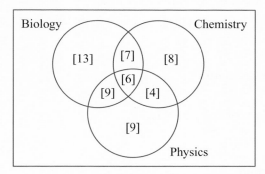

 (i) A student is picked at random from the whole class.
     Find the probability that the student does not study Biology.

 (ii) A student is picked at random from those who study at least two of the subjects. Find the probability that the student does not study Biology.

 (iii) Two students are picked at random from the whole class. Find the probability that they both study Physics.

Terminology and notation

A function is a rule that changes one number (input) into another number (output). Functions are often represented by the letters f, g, h or k. We can think of a function, f, as a number machine which changes an input, x, into an output, $f(x)$.

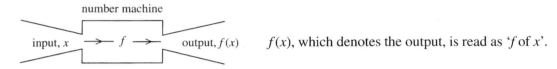

$f(x)$, which denotes the output, is read as 'f of x'.

For example, let's represent the function 'treble input and then subtract two' by the letter f. This can be written as:

$$f : x \rightarrow 3x - 2 \quad \text{or} \quad f(x) = 3x - 2 \quad \text{or} \quad y = 3x - 2$$
$$(\text{input, output}) = (x, f(x)) = (x, 3x - 2) = (x, y)$$

Note: A **function** is also called a '**mapping**' or simply a '**map**'.

One number is mapped onto another number.
In the above example, x is mapped onto $3x - 2$, usually written $f : x \rightarrow 3x - 2$.

Input number

If $f : x \rightarrow 3x - 2$, then $f(4)$ means input 4 into the function,
i.e. 'it is the result of applying the function f to the number 4'.

$$f(4) = 3(4) - 2 = 12 - 2 = 10 \quad (\text{input} = 4, \text{output} = 10)$$

$$(\text{input, output}) = (4, \ f(4)) = (4, 10)$$

Example ▼

The function f is defined as $f : x \to 7 - 3x$, $x \in \mathbf{R}$.

  (a)   Find   (i) $f(-2)$ (ii) $f(24)$.

  (b)   Find the number k such that $kf(-2) = f(24)$, $k \in \mathbf{R}$.

  (c)   Find the value of x for which $f(x) = -23$.

Solution:

$$f(x) = 7 - 3x$$

(a) **(i)**
$$
\begin{aligned}
f(-2) &= 7 - 3(-2) \\
&= 7 + 6 \\
&= 13
\end{aligned}
$$

(ii)
$$
\begin{aligned}
f(24) &= 7 - 3(24) \\
&= 7 - 72 \\
&= -65
\end{aligned}
$$

(b)
$$
\begin{aligned}
kf(-2) &= f(24) \\
k(13) &= -65 \\
13k &= -65 \\
k &= -5
\end{aligned}
$$

(c)
$$
\begin{aligned}
f(x) &= -23 \\
7 - 3x &= -23 \\
-3x &= -30 \\
3x &= 30 \\
x &= 10
\end{aligned}
$$

Example ▼

$f : x \to x^2 - 1$ and $g : x \to 1 - 2x$ are two functions defined on $\mathbf{R}$.

(i) Find $f(\sqrt{2})$ and $g(-3k)$ **(ii)** Find the values of x for which $3f(x) = 5g(x)$

Solution:

(i)
$$f(x) = x^2 - 1$$

$$
\begin{aligned}
f(\sqrt{2}) &= (\sqrt{2})^2 - 1 \\
&= 2 - 1 \\
&= 1
\end{aligned}
$$

$$g(x) = 1 - 2x$$

$$
\begin{aligned}
g(-3k) &= 1 - 2(-3k) \\
&= 1 + 6k
\end{aligned}
$$

(ii)
$$
\begin{aligned}
3f(x) &= 5g(x) \\
3(x^2 - 1) &= 5(1 - 2x) \\
3x^2 - 3 &= 5 - 10x \\
3x^2 + 10x - 8 &= 0 \\
(3x - 2)(x + 4) &= 0
\end{aligned}
$$

$3x - 2 = 0$ or $x + 4 = 0$

$3x = 2$ or $x = -4$

$x = \frac{2}{3}$ or $x = -4$

Example ▼

Let $h(x) = x(x - 2)$ for $x \in \mathbf{R}$.
Show that $h(1 + t) = h(1 - t)$ for $t \in \mathbf{R}$.

Solution:

$$h(x) = x(x - 2) = x^2 - 2x$$
$$h(x) = x^2 - 2x$$
$$h(1 + t) = (1 + t)^2 - 2(1 + t)$$
$$= 1 + 2t + t^2 - 2 - 2t$$
$$= t^2 - 1$$

$$h(x) = x^2 - 2x$$
$$h(1 - t) = (1 - t)^2 - 2(1 - t)$$
$$= 1 - 2t + t^2 - 2 + 2t$$
$$= t^2 - 1$$

$$\therefore \ h(1 + t) = h(1 - t)$$

Exercise 20.1 ▼

1. The function f is defined as $f : x \to 2x + 5, \quad x \in \mathbf{R}$.
   Find   **(i)** $f(3)$ **(ii)** $f(4)$ **(iii)** $f(1)$ **(iv)** $f(-2)$ **(v)** $f(-3)$

2. The function g is defined as $g : x \to x^2 + 3x, \quad x \in \mathbf{R}$.
   Find   **(i)** $f(3)$ **(ii)** $f(1)$ **(iii)** $f(0)$ **(iv)** $f(-2)$ **(v)** $3f(-4)$

3. The function f is defined as $f : x \to x(x + 2), \quad x \in \mathbf{R}$.
   Find   **(i)** $f(1)$ **(ii)** $f(-1)$ **(iii)** $f(2) + f(-2)$ **(iv)** $-2f(-3)$
   Find the two values of x for which $f(x) = 15$.

4. The function f is defined as $f : x \to x^2 + 2x - 1, \quad x \in \mathbf{R}$.
   Find the value of   **(i)** $f(0)$ **(ii)** $f(-1)$ **(iii)** $f(\tfrac{1}{2})$ **(iv)** $f(\tfrac{3}{5})$

5. The function g is defined as $g : x \to \dfrac{1}{x - 1}, \quad x \in \mathbf{R}, x \neq 1$.

   Evaluate   **(i)** $f(2)$ **(ii)** $f(0)$ **(iii)** $f(\tfrac{3}{2})$

6. The function h is defined as $h : x \to 2 - 3x, \quad x \in \mathbf{R}$.
   Solve each of the following:
   (i) $h(x) = -4$ **(ii)** $h(x) = x$ **(iii)** $xh(x) + 1 = 0$ **(iv)** $h(x) \geqslant -1$

7. The function g is defined as $g : x \to 2x - 5$.
   (a) Find the value of   **(i)** $g(3)$ **(ii)** $g(0)$ **(iii)** $g(-\tfrac{1}{2})$
   (b) Express, in terms of x,   **(i)** $g(3x)$ **(ii)** $g(x + 3)$
   Hence, find the value of x for which $g(3x) + g(x + 3) = g(x) + g(0)$.

8. The function f is defined as $f : x \to 4 - 3x, \quad x \in \mathbf{R}$.
   (a) Find   **(i)** $f(-2)$ **(ii)** $f(-\tfrac{1}{3})$
   (b) Find the number k such that $f(-2) = kf(-\tfrac{1}{3})$.

9. The function g is defined as $g : x \rightarrow 7 - 4x, \quad x \in \textbf{R}$.

 Find the number k such that $kf(-8) = f(-\frac{3}{2})$.

10. The function f is defined as $f : x \rightarrow x^2 - 1, \quad x \in \textbf{R}$.
 (a) find (i) $f(4)$ (ii) $f(-3)$ (iii) $f(2)$
 (b) for what value of $k \in \textbf{R}$ is $2k + 1 + f(4) = f(-3)$?
 (c) find the values of x for which $f(x) - f(2) = 0$
 (d) verify that $f(x - 1) = f(1 - x)$.

11. $f : x \rightarrow x^2 + 1$ and $g : x \rightarrow 2x$ are two functions defined on $\textbf{R}$.
 (i) find $f(\sqrt{3})$ and $g(1)$
 (ii) find the value of k for which $f(\sqrt{3}) = kg(1)$
 (iii) find the value of x for which $f(x) = g(x)$
 (iv) verify that $f(x + 2) = g(x^2 + 2x + 1) - f(x) + f(\sqrt{3})$.

12. $f : x \rightarrow 2x^2 + 1$ and $g : x \rightarrow 5x - 1$ are two functions defined on $\textbf{R}$.
 (i) find $f(\sqrt{5})$ and $g(2k + 3)$
 (ii) find the value of k for which $g(2k + 3) = f(\sqrt{5}) - 7$
 (iii) find the two values of m for which $f(m) - g(m) = 0$.

13. h and k are two functions defined by $h : x \rightarrow x^2 + 4$ and $k : x \rightarrow 2x + 1, \quad x \in \textbf{R}$.
 (i) find $k(4)$, $h(2x)$ and $k(3x + 2)$
 (ii) for what values of x is $h(2x) = k(3x + 2) + k(4)$?

14. $g : x \rightarrow (x - 1)^2$ is a function defined on $\textbf{R}$.
 (i) find $g(1)$ and $g(-1)$
 (ii) find the value of $t \in \textbf{R}$ for which $tg(-3) = g(9)$
 (iii) verify that $g(1 + k) = g(1 - k)$

15. The function f is defined as $f : x \rightarrow 2x + 5, \quad x \in \textbf{R}$.
 Find a function g for which $g(x) = f(2x + 3) - f(x)$.
 Hence, or otherwise, find the value of $g(3)$.

16. $f : x \rightarrow x^2 - 1$ and $g : x \rightarrow (x - 1)^2$ are two functions defined on $\textbf{R}$.
 (i) If $9f(x) + 8 = f(kx)$, find two values for $k \in \textbf{Z}$.
 (ii) Find a function h for which $g(x) = f(x) - 2h(x)$.
 (iii) Express $g(x + 1)$ in terms of $f(x)$.

Functions with missing coefficients

In some questions coefficients of the functions are missing and we are asked to find them. In this type of question we are given equations in disguise and by solving these equations we can calculate the missing coefficients.

Notation

$f(x) = y$

$f(2) = 3$ means when $x = 2$, $y = 3$ or the point $(2, 3)$ is on the graph of the function.

$f(-1) = 0$ means when $x = -1$, $y = 0$ or the point $(-1, 0)$ is on the graph of the function.

Example ▼

$f : x \rightarrow 5x + a$ and $g : x \rightarrow x^2 + bx - 3$ are two functions defined on **R**.
(i) If $f(2) = 7$, find the value of a.
(ii) If $g(-1) = -4$, find the value of b.

Solution:

(i) $\quad f(x) = 5x + a$

Given: $f(2) = 7$

$\therefore\ 5(2) + a = 7$

$10 + a = 7$

$a = 7 - 10$

$a = -3$

(ii) $\quad g(x) = x^2 + bx - 3$

Given: $\quad g(-1) = -4$

$\therefore\ (-1)^2 + b(-1) - 3 = -4$

$1 - b - 3 = -4$

$-b - 2 = -4$

$-b = -4 + 2$

$-b = -2$

$b = 2$

Example ▼

$g : x \rightarrow ax^2 + bx + 1$ is a function defined on **R**.
If $g(1) = 0$ and $g(2) = 3$, write down two equations in a and b.
Hence, calculate the value of a and the value of b.

Solution:

$$g(x) = ax^2 + bx + 1$$

Given: $g(1) = 0$

$\therefore\ a(1)^2 + b(1) + 1 = 0$

$a(1) + b(1) + 1 = 0$

$a + b + 1 = 0$

$a + b = -1 \quad$ ①

Given: $g(2) = 3$

$\therefore\ a(2)^2 + b(2) + 1 = 3$

$a(4) + b(2) + 1 = 3$

$4a + 2b + 1 = 3$

$4a + 2b = 2$

$2a + b = 1 \quad$ ②

We now solve between the equations ① and ②:

$$a + b = -1 \quad ①$$
$$\underline{2a + b = 1 \quad ②}$$
$$-a = -2 \quad \text{(subtract)}$$
$$a = 2$$

put in $a = 2$ into ① or ②
Thus, $a = 2$ and $b = -3$

$$a + b = -1 \quad ①$$
$$\downarrow$$
$$2 + b = -1$$
$$b = -1 - 2$$
$$b = -3$$

Example ▼

The graph of the quadratic function
$f: x \rightarrow x^2 + bx + c, \quad x \in \mathbf{R}$, is shown.
Find the value of b and the value of c.
Hence, find the value of k.

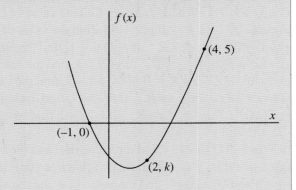

$f(x)$

•(4, 5)

x

(−1, 0)

(2, k)

Solution:

$$f(x) = x^2 + bx + c$$

The graph goes through the point $(-1, 0)$
$$\therefore f(-1) = 0$$
$$\therefore (-1)^2 + b(-1) + c = 0$$
$$1 - b + c = 0$$
$$-b + c = -1$$
$$b - c = 1 \quad ①$$

The graph goes through the point $(4, 5)$
$$\therefore f(4) = 5$$
$$\therefore (4)^2 + b(4) + c = 5$$
$$16 + 4b + c = 5$$
$$4b + c = -11 \quad ②$$

We now solve between equations ① and ②:

$$b - c = 1 \quad ①$$
$$\underline{4b + c = -11 \quad ②}$$
$$5b = -10 \quad \text{(add)}$$
$$b = -2$$

put in $b = -2$ into ① or ②

$$b - c = 1 \quad ①$$
$$\downarrow$$
$$-2 - c = 1$$
$$-c = 1 + 2$$
$$-c = 3$$
$$c = -3$$

Thus, $b = -2$ and $c = -3$
$$f(x) = x^2 + bx + c = x^2 - 2x - 3$$
The graph goes through the point $(2, k)$
$$\therefore \qquad f(2) = k$$
$$\therefore \qquad (2)^2 - 2(2) - 3 = k$$
$$4 - 4 - 3 = k$$
$$-3 = k$$

Thus, $k = -3$

Exercise 20.2 ▼

1. Let $f(x) = 3x + k$, $x \in R$. If $f(1) = 5$, find the value of k.
2. Let $g(x) = ax + 5$, $x \in R$. If $g(2) = 11$, find the value of a.
3. Let $f(x) = x^2 + 3x + h$, $x \in R$. If $f(1) = -1$, find the value of h.
4. Let $g(x) = 2x^2 + bx + 3$, $x \in R$. If $g(2) = 3$, find the value of b.
5. Let $h(x) = ax^2 + 3x$, $x \in R$. If $h(-1) = -5$, find the value of a.
6. Let $f(x) = (x + k)(x - 2)$, $x \in R$. If $f(3) = 7$, find the value of k.
7. Let $k(x) = (ax)^2 - 7ax + 6$, $x \in R$. If $k(2) = 0$, find two possible values of a.
8. $f : x \rightarrow 2x + a$ and $g : x \rightarrow 3x + b$
   If $f(2) = 7$ and $g(1) = -1$, find the value of a and the value of b.
9. $h : x \rightarrow 2x + a$ and $k : x \rightarrow b - 5x$ are two functions defined on R.
   If $h(1) = -5$ and $k(-1) = 4$, find the value of a and the value of b.
10. $f : x \rightarrow 3x + a$ and $g : x \rightarrow ax + b$ are two functions defined on R.
    If $f(2) = 8$ and $g(2) = 1$,
    (i) Find the value of a and the value of b.
    (ii) Find $f(-1)$ and $g(4)$.
    (iii) Using your values of a and b from (i), find the two values of x for which:
    $$ax^2 - (a - b)x + 2ab = 0$$
11. $h : x \rightarrow 2x - a$ and $k : x \rightarrow ax + b$ are two functions defined on R, where a and $b \in Z$.
    $h(3) = 1$ and $k(5) = 8$.
    (i) Find the value of a and the value of b.
    (ii) Hence, list the values of x for which $h(x) \geqslant k(x)$, $x \in N$.
12. $g : x \rightarrow ax^2 + bx + 1$ is a function defined on R.
    If $g(1) = 2$ and $g(-1) = 6$, write down two equations in a and b.
    Hence, calculate the value of a and the value of b.
13. $g : x \rightarrow px^2 + qx - 3$ is a function defined on R.
    If $g(1) = 4$ and $g(-1) = -6$, write down two equations in p and q.
    Hence, calculate the value of p and the value of q.
    Find the two values of x for which $px^2 + qx - 3 = 0$.

14. (i) $f(x) = ax^2 + bx - 8$, where a and b are real numbers.
If $f(1) = -9$ and $f(2) = 0$, find the value of a and the value of b.
  (ii) Using your values of a and b from **(i)**, find the two values of x for which
  $ax^2 + bx = bx^2 + ax$.

15. $f : x \rightarrow ax^2 + bx + c$, where a, b and c are real numbers.
If $f(0) = -3$, find the value of c.
If $f(-1) = 6$ and $f(2) = 3$, find the value of a and the value of b.

16. $h : x \rightarrow x^2 + x + q$ is a function defined on $\mathbf{R}$ where $q \in \mathbf{Z}$.
  (i) If $h(-3) = 0$, find the value of q.
  (ii) Hence, solve the equation $h(x + 5) = 0$.

17. The graph of the quadratic function
$f : x \rightarrow x^2 + bx + c$, $x \in \mathbf{R}$, is shown.
Find the values of b and c.
Hence, find the value of k.

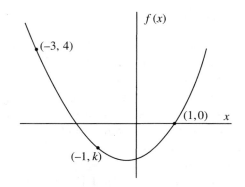

18. The graph of the quadratic function
$g : x \rightarrow ax^2 + bx - 3$, $x \in \mathbf{R}$, is shown.
Find the values of a and b.
Hence, calculate the value of h and k.

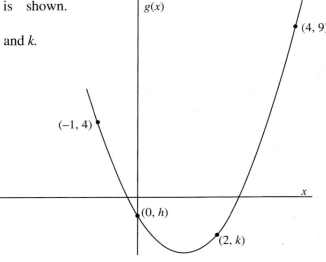

19. The graph of the quadratic function $h : x \to c + bx - x^2, \quad x \in \mathbf{R}$, is shown.
Find the value of b and c.
$k : x \to px + q$ is a function defined on $\mathbf{R}$.
If $k(0) = -1$ and $k(1) = 1$, find the value of p and the value of q.
Hence, find the two values of x for which $k(x) = h(x)$.

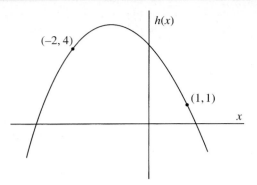

20. Let $f(x) = x^2 + bx + c, \quad x \in \mathbf{R}$.
The solutions of $f(x) = 0$ are -3 and 1.
Find the value of b and the value of c.
If $f(-1) = k$, find the value of k.
Solve the equation $f(x) - k = 0$.

21. Let $g(x) = x^2 + bx + c, \quad x \in \mathbf{R}$.
The solutions of $g(x) = 0$ are symmetrical about the line $x = 1$.
If $x = -3$ is one solution of $g(x) = 0$, find the other solution.
Find the value of b and the value of c.

CHAPTER 21

Notation

The notation $y = f(x)$ means 'the value of the output y depends on the value of the input x, according to some rule called f. Hence, y and $f(x)$ are interchangeable, and the y axis can also be called the $f(x)$ axis.

Note: It is very important not to draw a graph outside the given values of x.

Graphing linear functions

The first four letters in the word '**linear**' spell '**line**'. Therefore the graph of a linear function will be a straight line. A linear function is usually given in the form $f: x \rightarrow ax + b$, where $a \neq 0$ and a, b are constants. For example, $f: x \rightarrow 2x + 5$. As the graph is a straight line, two points are all that is needed to graph it. In the question, you will always be given a set of inputs, x, called the domain.

To graph a linear function do the following:

> **1.** Choose two suitable values of x, in the given domain.
>   (Two suitable values are the smallest and largest values of x.)
> **2.** Substitute these in the function to find the two corresponding values of y.
> **3.** Plot the points and draw the line through them.

Note: $-3 \leqslant x \leqslant 2$ means 'x is between -3 and 2, including -3 and 2'.

Example ▼

Graph the function $g : x \rightarrow 2x - 3$, in the domain $-2 \leqslant x \leqslant 3$, $x \in \mathbf{R}$.

Solution:

Let $y = g(x) \Rightarrow y = 2x - 3$

x	$2x - 3$	y
-2	$-4 - 3$	-7
3	$6 - 3$	3

Plot the points $(-2, -7)$ and $(3, 3)$ and join them with a straight line.

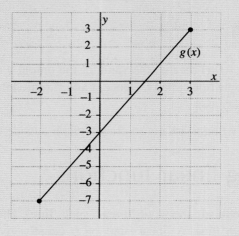

Exercise 21.1 ▼

Graph each of the following functions in the given domain:

1. $f : x \rightarrow 2x + 1$ in the domain $-2 \leqslant x \leqslant 3$, $x \in \mathbf{R}$
2. $g : x \rightarrow 3x + 2$ in the domain $-1 \leqslant x \leqslant 4$, $x \in \mathbf{R}$
3. $f : x \rightarrow 4x - 3$ in the domain $-3 \leqslant x \leqslant 3$, $x \in \mathbf{R}$
4. $g : x \rightarrow 2x - 5$ in the domain $-1 \leqslant x \leqslant 5$, $x \in \mathbf{R}$
5. $h : x \rightarrow x + 2$ in the domain $-5 \leqslant x \leqslant 3$, $x \in \mathbf{R}$
6. $f : x \rightarrow 3x - 1$ in the domain $-3 \leqslant x \leqslant 3$, $x \in \mathbf{R}$
7. $g : x \rightarrow 5x + 2$ in the domain $-2 \leqslant x \leqslant 4$, $x \in \mathbf{R}$
8. $k : x \rightarrow x$ in the domain $-3 \leqslant x \leqslant 3$, $x \in \mathbf{R}$
9. $f : x \rightarrow 2x$ in the domain $-2 \leqslant x \leqslant 2$, $x \in \mathbf{R}$
10. $g : x \rightarrow 3x$ in the domain $-3 \leqslant x \leqslant 2$, $x \in \mathbf{R}$
11. $f : x \rightarrow -x$ in the domain $-3 \leqslant x \leqslant 3$, $x \in \mathbf{R}$
12. $h : x \rightarrow 2 - x$ in the domain $-4 \leqslant x \leqslant 4$, $x \in \mathbf{R}$
13. $k : x \rightarrow 3 - 2x$ in the domain $-3 \leqslant x \leqslant 4$, $x \in \mathbf{R}$
14. $f : x \rightarrow 4 - 3x$ in the domain $-2 \leqslant x \leqslant 4$, $x \in \mathbf{R}$
15. $g : x \rightarrow -1 - x$ in the domain $-4 \leqslant x \leqslant 3$, $x \in \mathbf{R}$

Graphing quadratic functions

A **quadratic** function is usually given in the form $f : x \rightarrow ax^2 + bx + c$, $a \neq 0$, and a, b, c are constants. For example, $f : x \rightarrow 2x^2 - x + 3$. Because of its shape, quite a few points are needed to plot the graph of a quadratic function. In the question, you will always be given a set of inputs, x, called the domain. With these inputs, a table is used to find the corresponding set of outputs, y or $f(x)$, called the range. When the table is completed, plot the points and join them with a '**smooth curve**'.

Notes on making out the table

1. Work out each column separately, i.e. all the x^2 values first, then all the x values, and finally the constant. (Watch for patterns in the numbers.)
2. Work out each corresponding value of y.
3. The **only** column that changes sign is the x term (middle) column.
    If the given values of x contain 0, then the x term column will make one sign change, either from + to − or from − to +, where $x = 0$.
4. The other two columns **never** change sign. They remain either all pluses or all minuses. These columns keep the sign given in the question.

Note: Decide where to draw the x and y axes by looking at the table to see what the largest and smallest values of x and y are. In general, the units on the x axis are larger than the units on the y axis. Try to make sure that the graph extends almost the whole width and length of the page.

Example ▼

Using the same axes and scales, graph the functions:
$f : x \rightarrow 5 + 2x - x^2$, $g : x \rightarrow 2x - 1$, in the domain $-3 \leqslant x \leqslant 4$, $x \in \mathbf{R}$.

Solution:

Let $y = f(x) \implies y = -x^2 + 2x + 5$ Let $y = g(x) \implies y = 2x - 1$

x	$-x^2 + 2x + 5$	y
-3	$-9 - 6 + 5$	-10
-2	$-4 - 4 + 5$	-3
-1	$-1 - 2 + 5$	2
0	$-0 + 0 + 5$	5
1	$-1 + 2 + 5$	6
2	$-4 + 4 + 5$	5
3	$-9 + 6 + 5$	2
4	$-16 + 8 + 5$	-3

x	$2x - 1$	y
-3	$-6 - 1$	-7
4	$8 - 1$	7

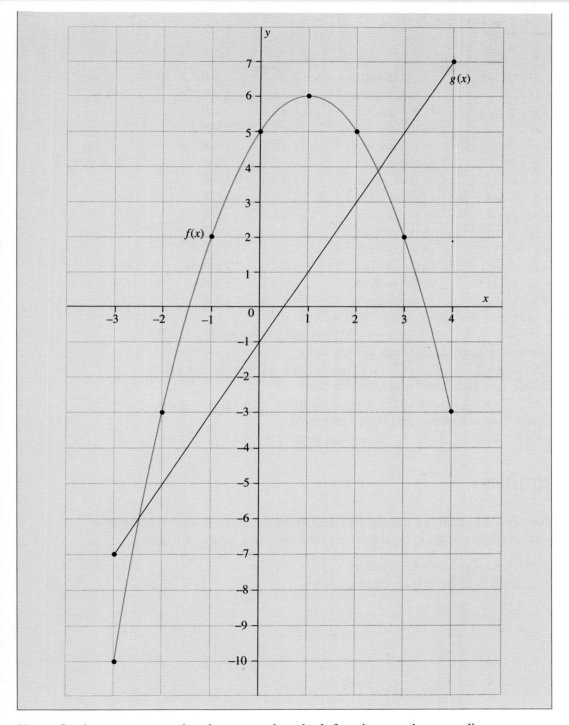

Note: On the same axes and scales means draw both functions on the same diagram.

Exercise 21.2 ▼

Graph each of the following functions in the given domain:

1. $f : x \to x^2 + 2x - 8$ in the domain $-5 \leqslant x \leqslant 3,$ $x \in R$
2. $f : x \to x^2 - 3x - 4$ in the domain $-2 \leqslant x \leqslant 5,$ $x \in R$
3. $f : x \to x^2 - 2x - 3$ in the domain $-2 \leqslant x \leqslant 4,$ $x \in R$
4. $f : x \to x^2 - x - 2$ in the domain $-2 \leqslant x \leqslant 3,$ $x \in R$
5. $f : x \to x^2 + 3x - 2$ in the domain $-5 \leqslant x \leqslant 2,$ $x \in R$
6. $f : x \to x^2 - 3x$ in the domain $-2 \leqslant x \leqslant 5,$ $x \in R$
7. $f : x \to 9 + x - x^2$ in the domain $-3 \leqslant x \leqslant 4,$ $x \in R$
8. $f : x \to 6 - x - x^2$ in the domain $-4 \leqslant x \leqslant 3,$ $x \in R$
9. $f : x \to 3 + 2x - x^2$ in the domain $-2 \leqslant x \leqslant 4,$ $x \in R$
10. $f : x \to 2x - x^2$ in the domain $-2 \leqslant x \leqslant 4,$ $x \in R$
11. $f : x \to 2x^2 + 3x - 2$ in the domain $-3 \leqslant x \leqslant 2,$ $x \in R$
12. $f : x \to 2x^2 - x - 1$ in the domain $-3 \leqslant x \leqslant 3,$ $x \in R$
13. $f : x \to 5 + x - 2x^2$ in the domain $-2 \leqslant x \leqslant 3,$ $x \in R$
14. $f : x \to 3 + 5x - 2x^2$ in the domain $-1 \leqslant x \leqslant 4,$ $x \in R$
15. On the same axes and scales, graph the functions:
$f : x \to x^2 - 2x - 4,$ $g : x \to 2x + 1$, in the domain $-3 \leqslant x \leqslant 5,$ $x \in R.$
16. On the same axes and scales, graph the functions:
$f : x \to 5 + 2x - x^2,$ $g : x \to 2 - x$, in the domain $-2 \leqslant x \leqslant 4,$ $x \in R.$
17. On the same axes and scales, graph the functions:
$f : x \to 2x^2 - 3x - 8,$ $g : x \to 3x - 2$, in the domain $-2 \leqslant x \leqslant 4,$ $x \in R.$
18. On the same axes and scales, graph the functions:
$f : x \to 6 + x - 2x^2,$ $g : x \to 1 - 2x$, in the domain $-2 \leqslant x \leqslant 3,$ $x \in R.$

Using graphs

Once we have drawn the graph, we are usually asked to use the graph to answer some questions. Below are examples of the general type of problems where graphs are used.

Notes: 1. $y = f(x)$, so $f(x)$ can be replaced by y.
       2. In general, if given x find y, and vice versa.

Examples of the main problems, once the graph is drawn:

1. **Find the values of x for which $f(x) = 0$.**
   This question is asking:
   'Where does the curve meet the x axis?'

   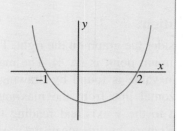

   Solution:
   Write down the values of x where the graph meets the
   x axis.
   From the graph: $x = -1$ or $x = 2$.

2. **Find the values of x for which $f(x) = 2$.**
   This question is asking:
   'When $y = 2$, what are the values of x?'

   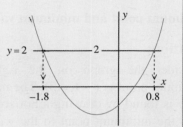

   Solution:
   Draw the line $y = 2$. Where this line meets the curve
   draw broken perpendicular lines onto the x axis.
   Write down the values of x where these broken lines
   meet the x axis.
   From the graph:
   When $y = 2$, $x = -1.8$ or $x = 0.8$.

3. **Find the value of $f(-1.5)$.**
   This question is asking:
   'When $x = -1.5$, what is the value of y?'

   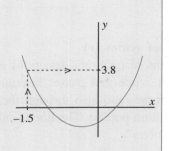

   Solution:
   From $x = -1.5$ on the x axis draw a broken perpendicular line to meet the curve. From this draw a broken horizontal line to meet the y axis. Write down
   the value of y where this line meets the y axis.
   From the graph:
   $f(-1.5) = 3.8$

4. **Maximum point and maximum value.**

   Solution:

   Consider the graph on the right. The maximum point is (2, 4). The maximum value is found by drawing a horizontal line from the maximum point to the y axis and reading the value where this line meets the y axis. The maximum value is 4 (the same as the y coordinate of the maximum point).

   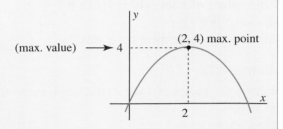

5. **Minimum point and minimum value.**

   Solution:

   Consider the graph on the right. The minimum point is $(-1, -3)$. The minimum value is found by drawing a horizontal line from the minimum point to the y axis and reading the value where this line meets the y axis.
   The minimum value is -3
   (the same as the y coordinate of the minimum point).

   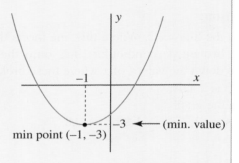

6. **Axis of symmetry**
   Graphs of quadratic functions are symmetrical about a line that passes through the middle of the curve (and also through the maximum and minimum points). The line is called the 'axis of symmetry'.

   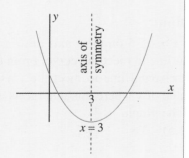

   Solution:

   From the graph:
   The equation of the axis of symmetry is $x = 3$.
   3 is where the line meets the x axis.

7. Increasing and decreasing

Graphs are read from left to right.

Increasing: $f(x)$ is increasing where the graph is **rising** as we go from left to right.

Decreasing: $f(x)$ is decreasing where the graph is **falling** as we go from left to right.

The diagram shows the graph of a quadratic function, $f(x)$ in the domain $-2 \leqslant x \leqslant 4$.
Find the values of x for which   **(i)** $f(x)$ is decreasing   **(ii)** $f(x)$ is increasing.

Solution:

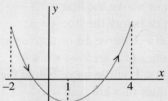

(i) $f(x)$ decreasing, graph falling from left to right.
The values of x are: $-2 \leqslant x < 1$

(ii) $f(x)$ increasing, graph rising from left to right.
The values of x are: $1 < x \leqslant 4$

Note: At $x = 1$, the graph is neither increasing nor decreasing.

8. Positive and negative

Positive, $f(x) > 0$: Where the graph is **above** the x axis.
Negative, $f(x) < 0$: Where the graph is **below** the x axis.

The diagram shows the graph of a quadratic function, $f(x)$, in the domain $-4 \leqslant x \leqslant 2$.
Find the values of x for which   **(i)** $f(x) > 0$ **(ii)** $f(x) < 0$.

Solution:

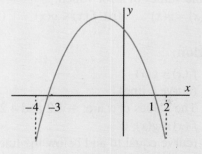

(i) $f(x) > 0$, curve **above** the x axis.
The values of x are: $-3 < x < 1$.

(ii) $f(x) < 0$, curve **below** the x axis.
The values of x are:
$-4 \leqslant x < -3$ and $1 < x \leqslant 2$.

Note: If the question uses $f(x) \geqslant 0$ or $f(x) \leqslant 0$, then the values of x where the graph meets the x axis must also be included.

9. **Graph above or below a constant value (an inequality)**
   The diagram shows the graph of a quadratic function, $f(x)$, in the domain $-2 \leqslant x \leqslant 5$.

   Find the values of x for which (i) $f(x) \geqslant 3$ (ii) $f(x) \leqslant 3$.
   These questions are asking:
   'What are the values of x for which the curve, $f(x)$, is (i) 3 or above (ii) 3 or below?'

   Solution:

   Draw the line $y = 3$.
   Write down the values of x for which the
   curve is:
   (i) on or above the line $y = 3$
   (ii) on or below the line $y = 3$.
   (i) $f(x) \geqslant 3$, curve on or above the line $y = 3$.
   The values of x are: $-1 \leqslant x \leqslant 4$
   (ii) $f(x) \leqslant 3$, curve on or below the line $y = 3$.
   The values of x are: $-2 \leqslant x \leqslant -1$ and $4 \leqslant x \leqslant 5$

   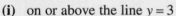

   Note: If the question uses $f(x) > 3$ or $f(x) < 3$, then the values of x where the curve meets the line $y = 3$ (-1 and 4) are not included.

10. **Two functions graphed on the same axes and scales**
    The diagram shows the graphs of the functions $f : x \rightarrow x^2 - x - 6$ and $g : x \rightarrow 2x - 1$
    in the domain $-3 \leqslant x \leqslant 5$.
    ($f(x)$ is a curve, $g(x)$ is a line)

    Find the values of x for which:
    (i) $f(x) = g(x)$ (ii) $f(x) \leqslant g(x)$ (iii) $f(x) \geqslant g(x)$

    Solution:

    (i) $f(x) = g(x)$
          (curve = line)
          The values of x are: -1.2 and 4.2
    (ii) $f(x) \leqslant g(x)$
          (curve equal to and below the line)
          The values of x are: $-1.2 \leqslant x \leqslant 4.2$
    (iii) $f(x) \geqslant g(x)$
          (curve equal to and above the line)
          The values of x are:
          $-3 \leqslant x \leqslant -1.2$ and $4.2 \leqslant x \leqslant 5$

    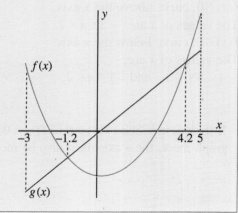

11. The number of times a graph meets the x axis gives the number of roots of its equation. Often we need to find a range of values of a constant, which shifts a graph up or down, giving a graph a certain number of roots, e.g.,

For what values of k does the equation $f(x) = k$ have two roots?

Solution:

The equation $f(x) = k$ will have two roots if the line $y = k$ cuts the graph twice.
So we have to draw lines parallel to the x axis that cut the graph twice.
The range of values of k will be in between the lowest and highest values on the y axis that the line $y = k$ cuts the graph twice.

On the right is a graph of the function

$f: x \rightarrow x^2 - 2x - 5$, in the domain $-3 \leqslant x \leqslant 4$, $x \in \mathbf{R}$.

Question: Find the range of values of k for which $f(x) = k$ has two roots.

Solution:

The range of values of k are found by finding the range of the equations of the lines, parallel to the x axis, which cut the graph twice.

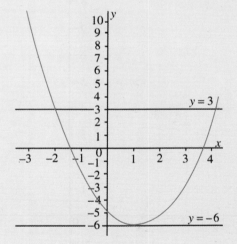

Any lines drawn parallel to the y axis between $y = -6$ and $y = 3$, will cut the graph twice.
∴ k will lie between -6 and 3.
∴ $f(x) = k$ will have two roots for $-6 < k \leqslant 3$ (at $k = -6$ there is only one root).

Example ▼

Graph the function $f: x \rightarrow 2x^2 - 3x - 5$ in the domain $-2 \leqslant x \leqslant 3$, $x \in \mathbf{R}$.
Use your graph to estimate:
(i) the values of x for which $f(x) = 0$
(ii) the value of $f(-1.6)$
(iii) the values of x for which $f(x) \geqslant -2$
(iv) the values of x for which $f(x) > 0$ and decreasing.

Solution:

Let $y = f(x)$ $\Rightarrow$ $y = 2x^2 - 3x - 5$

x	$2x^2 - 3x - 5$	y
-2	$8 + 6 - 5$	9
-1	$2 + 3 - 5$	0
0	$0 + 0 - 5$	-5
1	$2 - 3 - 5$	-6
2	$8 - 6 - 5$	-3
3	$18 - 9 - 5$	4

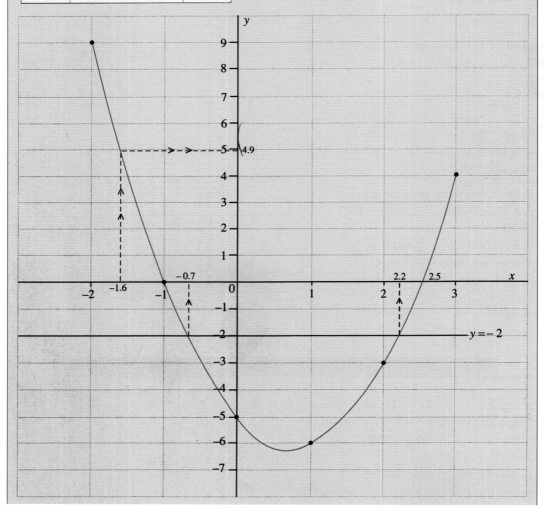

(i)   Values of x for which $f(x) = 0$

This question is asking, 'where does the curve meet the x axis?'.

The curve meets the x axis at -1 and 2.5.

Therefore, the values of x for which $f(x) = 0$, are -1 and 2.5.

Note: 'Find the values of x for which $2x^2 - 3x - 5 = 0$, is another way of asking the same question.

(ii)   The value of $f(-1.6)$

This question is asking, 'when $x = -1.6$, what is the value of y?'

From $x = -1.6$ on the x axis draw a broken perpendicular line to meet the curve.

From this draw a broken horizontal line to meet the y axis.

This line meets the y axis at 4.9.

Therefore $f(-1.6) = 4.9$.

(iii)   The values of x for which $f(x) \geqslant -2$

This question is asking, 'what are the values of x for which the curve is **on** or **above** the line $y = -2$?'.

Draw the line $y = -2$.

Where this line meets the curve draw broken perpendicular lines to meet the x axis.

These lines meet the x axis at -0.7 and 2.2.

From the graph, the curve is above the line $y = -2$ between -2 and -0.7 and between 2.2 and 3.

Therefore the values of x for which $f(x) \geqslant -2$ are $-2 \leqslant x \leqslant -0.7$ and $2.2 \leqslant x \leqslant 3$.

Note: 'Find the values of x for which $2x^2 - 3x - 5 \geqslant -2$' is another way of asking the same question.

(iv)   The values of x for which $f(x) > 0$ and decreasing.

This question is asking,

'where is the curve above the x axis and decreasing as we go from left to right?'.

From the graph, the curve is above the x axis and decreasing between -2 and -1.

Therefore, the values of x for which $f(x) > 0$ and decreasing are $-2 \leqslant x < -1$.

Note: $x = -1$ is not included because at $x = -1$, $f(x) = 0$ and is not decreasing.

1. Below is a graph of the function $f : x \rightarrow 2x^2 + x - 6$ in the domain $-3 \leqslant x \leqslant 2$, $x \in \mathbf{R}$.

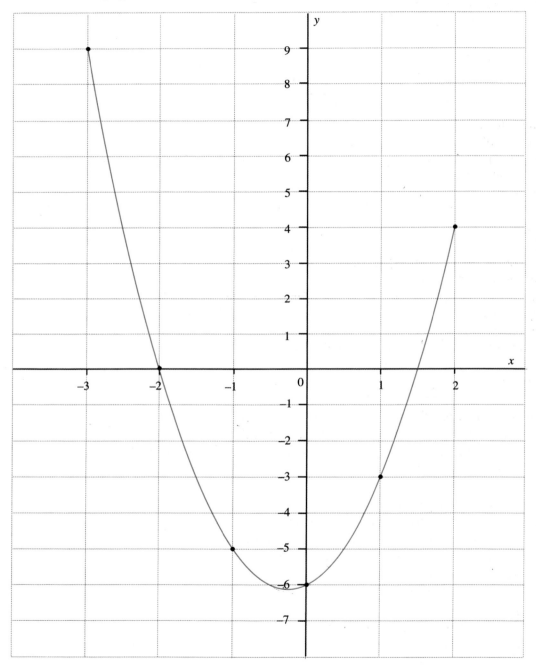

Use the graph to estimate:

(i) the values of x for which $f(x) = 0$

(ii) the minimum value of $f(x)$

(iii) the values of x for which $f(x) = -5$

(iv) the value of $f(-2.8)$

(v) the values of x for which $f(x) \leqslant 0$

(vi) the values of x for which $f(x) > 0$

(vii) the values of x for which $f(x) \leqslant -3$

(viii) the values of x for which $f(x) > 0$ and increasing

(ix) the values of x for which $2x^2 + x - 6 = 4$

(x) the value of k such that $f(k) = f(-2.25), \quad k \neq -2.25$

Draw the axis of symmetry of the graph of $f(x)$.

2. Draw the graph of the function $f : x \rightarrow x^2 + 2x - 3$ in the domain $-4 \leqslant x \leqslant 2, \ x \in \mathbf{R}$.
Use your graph to find:

(i) the values of x for which $f(x) = 0$

(ii) the values of x for which $f(x) = -3$

(iii) the minimum value

(iv) the minimum point

(v) the values of x for which $f(x) \leqslant 0$

(vi) the value of $f(-3.7)$

The equation of the axis of symmetry is $x = k$. Find the value of k.

3. Draw the graph of the function $f : x \rightarrow 4 + 3x - x^2$ in the domain $-2 \leqslant x \leqslant 5, \ x \in \mathbf{R}$.
Use your graph to:

(i) find the values of x for which $f(x) = 0$

(ii) find the values of x for which $f(x) = f(3)$

(iii) estimate $f(-1.6)$

(iv) estimate the maximum value of $f(x)$

(v) find the values of x for which $f(x) \leqslant 0$

(vi) find the value of k such that $f(k) = f(3.5), \quad k \neq 3.5$.

4. Draw the graph of the function $f : x \rightarrow 4x - x^2$ in the domain $-1 \leqslant x \leqslant 5, \ x \in \mathbf{R}$.
Use your graph to find:

(i) the maximum point

(ii) the values of x for which $f(x) \geqslant 3$

(iii) the values of x for which $f(x) \geqslant 0$ and increasing

(iv) the values of k for which $f(x) = k$ has two solutions.

5. Graph the function $f : x \rightarrow 3x^2 + 2x - 8$ in the domain $-3 \leqslant x \leqslant 2, \ x \in \mathbf{R}$.
From your graph estimate:

(i) the values of x for which $f(x) = 0$

(ii) the values of x for which $3x^2 + 2x - 8 \leqslant 0$

(iii) the values of x for which $3x^2 + 2x - 8 = 3$

(iv) the value of $f(1.8)$

(v) the minimum value of $f(x)$.

6. Graph the function $f : x \to 2x^2 - 4x - 5$ in the domain $-2 \leqslant x \leqslant 4, \ x \in \mathbf{R}$.
   Use your graph to find:
   (i)   the minimum point of $f(x)$
   (ii)   the roots of the equation $2x^2 - 4x - 5 = 1$
   (iii) the range of values of x for which $2x^2 - 4x - 5 \leqslant -5$
   (iv)   the range of values of x for which $f(x)$ is decreasing
   (v)   the value of k for which $f(x) = k$ has only one solution.

7. The function $f : x \to 3 + 2x - x^2$ is defined in the domain $-2 \leqslant x \leqslant 4, \ x \in \mathbf{R}$.
   (i)   Complete the table:

x	-2	-1	0	1	2	3	4
$f(x)$	-5				3		

   Graph the function f.
   Use your graph to find:
   (ii)   the maximum value of $f(x)$
   (iii) the maximum point of $f(x)$
   (iv)   the value of $f(3.6)$
   (v)   another value of x such that $f(x) = f(3.6)$
   (vi)   the values of $f(x)$ for which $-1 \leqslant x \leqslant 3$.

8. Graph the function $f : x \to 7 + 5x - 2x^2$ in the domain $-2 \leqslant x \leqslant 4, \ x \in \mathbf{R}$.
   Use your graph to estimate:
   (i)   the values of x for which $7 + 5x - 2x^2 = 0$
   (ii)   the values of x for which $f(x) = f(1) - f(3)$
   (iii) the maximum value of $f(x)$
   (iv)   the values of k for which $f(x) = k$ has no solutions.

Example ▼

Using the same axes and scales graph the functions:

$f : x \rightarrow 5 - x - 2x^2,$ $g : x \rightarrow 1 - 2x,$ in the domain $-3 \leqslant x \leqslant 2,$ $x \in \mathbf{R}.$

Use your graphs to estimate:

(i)   the maximum value of $f(x)$
(ii)   the values of x for which $f(x) = g(x)$
(iii) the values of x for which $f(x) > g(x)$

Solution:

Let $y = f(x) \Rightarrow y = -2x^2 - x + 5$

x	$-2x^2 - x + 5$	y
-3	$-18 + 3 + 5$	-10
-2	$-8 + 2 + 5$	-1
-1	$-2 + 1 + 5$	4
0	$-0 + 0 + 5$	5
1	$-2 - 1 + 5$	2
2	$-8 - 2 + 5$	-5

Let $y = g(x) \Rightarrow y = -2x + 1$

x	$-2x + 1$	y
-3	$6 + 1$	7
2	$-4 + 1$	-3

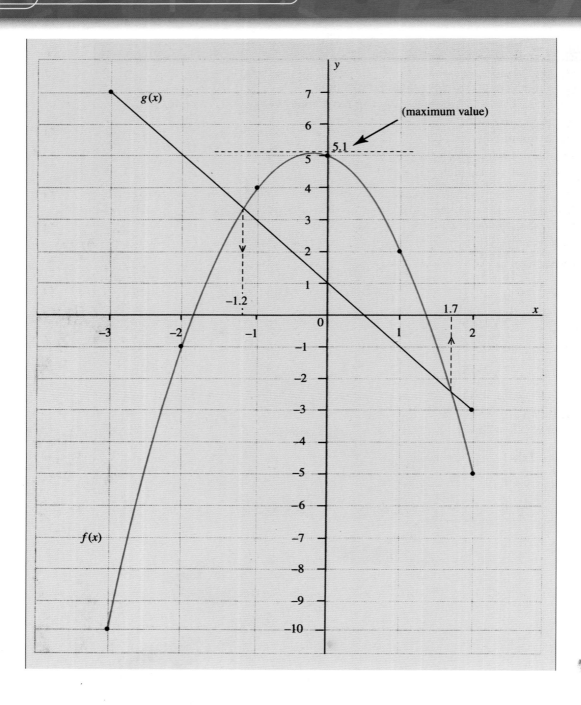

(i) **Maximum value**

This question is asking 'what is the greatest height reached by the curve?'.

Through the highest point on the graph draw a broken horizontal line to meet the y axis.

This line meets the y axis at 5.1.

Therefore, the maximum value of $f(x)$ is 5.1.

(ii) **Values of x for which $f(x) = g(x)$**

$f(x) = g(x)$,   (curve = line.)

This question is asking 'what are the values of x where the curve and line meet?'.

Where the curve and line meet, draw broken perpendicular lines to meet the x axis.

These lines meet the x axis at -1.2 and 1.7.

Therefore, the values of x for which $f(x) = g(x)$ are -1.2 and 1.7.

(iii) **Values of x for which $f(x) > g(x)$**

This question is asking 'what are the values of x where the curve is **above** the line?'

The curve equals the line at $x = -1.2$ and $x = 1.7$.

From the graphs, the curve is above the line between -1.2 and 1.7.

Therefore, the values of x for which $f(x) > g(x)$ are $-1.2 < x < 1.7$.

9. Below is a graph of the functions $f : x \rightarrow 8 - 2x - x^2$ and $g : x \rightarrow 6 - x$, in the domain $-5 \leqslant x \leqslant 3$, $x \in \mathbf{R}$.

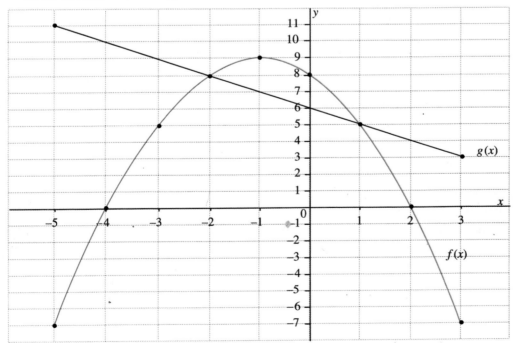

Use the graph to:

(i) find the maximum value of $f(x)$

(ii) find the coordinates of the maximum point of $f(x)$

(iii) find the values of x for which $f(x) = g(x)$

(iv) find the range of values of x for which $f(x) \geqslant g(x)$

(v) find the range of values of x for which $f(x) \leqslant g(x)$

(vi) find the values of x for which $f(x) = g(-2)$

(vii) estimate $f(-4.5)$

(viii) find the area of the rectangle that encloses the graphs of $f(x)$ and $g(x)$ in the domain $-5 \leqslant x \leqslant 3$

(ix) the roots of the equation $8 - 2x - x^2 = 5$

(x) the value of k such that $f(k) = f(1.6)$, $k \neq 1.6$

(xi) the value of x for which $g(x) = 9$

(xii) the equation of the axis of symmetry of $f(x)$ is $x = h$. Write down the value of h.

10. Using the same axes and scales, draw the graphs of:
$f : x \rightarrow x^2 - 2x - 3$, $g : x \rightarrow x - 3$, in the domain $-2 \leqslant x \leqslant 4$, $x \in \mathbf{R}$.
Use your graphs to find:

(i) the values of x for which $f(x) = 0$

(ii) the minimum point of $f(x)$

(iii) the values of x for which $f(x) = g(x)$

(iv) the values of x for which $g(x) \geqslant f(x)$

(v) the values of x for which $f(x) \geqslant g(x)$

(vi) the values of $f(x)$ for which $0 \leqslant x \leqslant 2$.

11. Using the same axes and scales, draw the graphs of:
$f : x \rightarrow x^2 + x - 2$, $g : x \rightarrow 2 - 2x$, in the domain $-4 \leqslant x \leqslant 3$, $x \in \mathbf{R}$.
Use your graphs to find:

(i) the values of x for which $f(x) \leqslant 0$

(ii) the value of x for which $g(x) = -4$

(iii) the values of x for which $f(x) = g(x)$

(iv) the values of x for which $f(x) \geqslant g(x)$

(v) the values of x for which $f(x) \leqslant g(x)$.

12. Using the same axes and scales, draw the graphs of:
$f : x \rightarrow 3 + x - 2x^2$, $g : x \rightarrow x + 1$, in the domain $-2 \leqslant x \leqslant 2$, $x \in \mathbf{R}$.
Use your graphs to estimate:

(i) the maximum value of $f(x)$

(ii) the values of x for which $f(x) = g(x)$

(iii) the values of x for which $f(x) \geqslant g(x)$

(iv) the values of x for which $g(x) \geqslant f(x)$ and $x > 0$.

13. Using the same axes and scales, draw the graphs of:
$f : x \rightarrow 9 - 3x - 2x^2$, $g : x \rightarrow -x$, in the domain $-4 \leqslant x \leqslant 2$, $x \in \mathbf{R}$.
Use your graphs to estimate:
(i) the values of x for which $f(x) = 0$
(ii) the maximum value of $f(x)$
(iii) the values of x for which $f(x) \geqslant g(x)$.

14. Using the same axes and scales, draw the graphs of:
$f : x \rightarrow 7 - x - 2x^2$, $g : x \rightarrow 3 - x$, in the domain $-3 \leqslant x \leqslant 2$, $x \in \mathbf{R}$.
Use your graphs to estimate:
(i) the values of x for which $f(x) = 0$
(ii) the values of x for which $f(x) \geqslant 4$
(iii) the values of x for which $f(x) \geqslant g(x)$.

15. Using the same axes and scales, graph the functions:
$f : x \rightarrow 9 - 4x - 2x^2$, $g : x \rightarrow 1 - 2x$, in the domain $-4 \leqslant x \leqslant 2$, $x \in \mathbf{R}$.
Use your graph to :
(i) estimate the values of x for which $f(x) = 0$
(ii) find the value of x for which $g(x) = 0$
(iii) find the values of x for which $f(x) \geqslant 9$
(iv) estimate the values of x for which $f(x) = g(x)$
(v) estimate the values of x for which $f(x) \geqslant g(x)$
(vi) estimate the values of x for which $f(x) > 0$ and decreasing
(vii) find the values of k for which $f(x) = k$ has no solution.

16. Using the same axes and scales, graph the functions:
$f : x \rightarrow 6x - x^2$, $g : x \rightarrow 12 + 3x - x^2$, in the domain $0 \leqslant x \leqslant 6$, $x \in \mathbf{R}$.
Use your graph to find:
(i) the maximum value of $f(x)$
(ii) the value of x for which $f(x) = g(x)$
(iii) the coordinates of the point of intersection of $f(x)$ and $g(x)$
(iv) the values of x for which $f(x) \geqslant g(x)$.

Using graphs to solve real-life problems

Example ▼

Using the same axes and the same scales, graph the two functions:

$f : x \rightarrow 10 + x - 2x^2,$ $\quad -2 \leqslant x \leqslant 3,$ $\quad x \in \mathbf{R}$

$g : x \rightarrow 3x - x^2,$ $\qquad 0 \leqslant x \leqslant 3,$ $\qquad x \in \mathbf{R}$

$f(x)$ is the height in km reached by an incoming missile launched at 05:00 ($x = -2$).

$g(x)$ is the height in km reached by an intercepting missile launched from the ground at 05:10 ($x = 0$).

Use your graphs to estimate:

(i) the maximum height reached by the incoming missile

(ii) the height at which the two missiles meet

(iii) the time at which the two missiles meet.

Solution:

$f(x)$

x	$-2x^2 + x + 10$	y
-2	$-8 - 2 + 10$	0
-1	$-2 - 1 + 10$	7
0	$-0 + 0 + 10$	10
1	$-2 + 1 + 10$	9
2	$-8 + 2 + 10$	4
3	$-18 + 3 + 10$	-5

$g(x)$

x	$-x^2 + 3x$	y
0	$-0 + 0$	0
1	$-1 + 3$	2
2	$-4 + 6$	2
3	$-9 + 9$	0

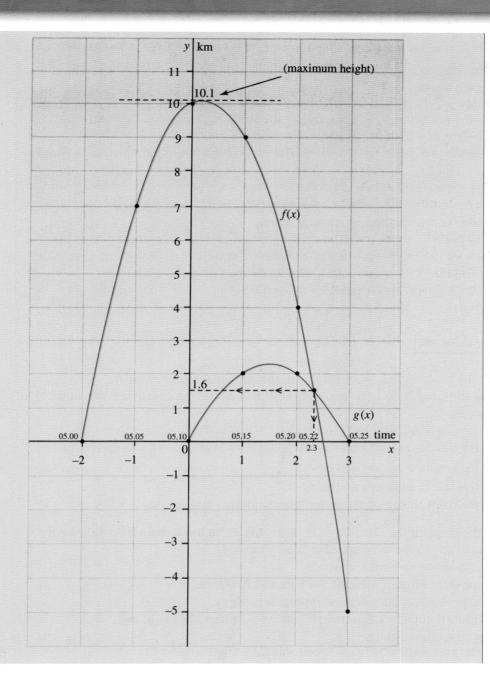

Note: The x axis, time axis, is marked in units of 5 minutes (given in the question)

(i) **the maximum height reached by the incoming missile**
Through the highest point on the graph of $f(x)$ draw a broken horizontal line to meet the y axis, (height axis). This line meets the y axis at 10.1.
Thus the maximum height reached by the incoming missile is 10.1 km.

(ii) **the height at which the two missiles meet**
Where the two curves meet draw a broken horizontal line to meet the y axis, (height axis).
This line meets the y axis at 1.6.
Thus the two missiles meet at a height of 1.6 km.

(iii) **the time at which the two missiles meet**
Where the two curves meet draw a broken vertical line to meet the x axis (time axis).
This line meets the x axis at 2.3 or 05.22 on the time axis.
Thus the two missiles meet at the time 05.22.

Exercise 21.4 ▼

1. Graph the function $f : x \to 3 + 2x$, in the domain $0 \leqslant x \leqslant 8$, $x \in \mathbf{R}$.
$f(x)$ is the cost, €C, of a taxi journey, the x axis representing the number of kilometres.
Use your graph to find:
(i) the cost to travel 5 km
(ii) the cost to travel $6\frac{1}{2}$ km
(iii) how far is a journey that costs €17
(iv) the fixed charge on the meter when a journey begins.

2. Draw the graph of the function $f : x \to x^2 - 6x + 9$ in the domain $0 \leqslant x \leqslant 6$, $x \in \mathbf{R}$.
The graph shows the wind speed at hourly intervals.
The x axis shows one-hour intervals:
for example, $x = 0$ means 12:00, $x = 1$ means 13:00, etc.
The y axis shows wind speed in kilometres per hour:
$y = 0$ means 0 km/h, $y = 1$ means 10 km/h, $y = 2$ means 20 km/h, etc.
Use your graph to estimate:
(i) the times when the wind speed was $22\frac{1}{2}$ km/h
(ii) the speed of the wind at 17:15
(iii) the time when there was calm.

3. Graph the function $f : x \rightarrow 7 + 5x - 2x^2$, in the domain $-1 \leqslant x \leqslant 4$, $x \in \mathbf{R}$.
Use your graph, or otherwise, to solve $7 + 5x - 2x^2 = 0$.
$f(x)$ is the height in metres reached by a particle fired from level ground at the point where $x = -1$, the x axis representing the level ground. From the time of firing until it hits the ground again, the particle was in flight for exactly 4.5 seconds.
Use your graph to estimate:
(i) the maximum height reached by the particle
(ii) the height reached by the particle after 1.5 seconds of flight
(iii) the number of seconds the particle is 4 m or more above the ground.

4. A ball is fired upwards from the top of a building.
The height, h metres, reached by the ball after t
seconds, is given by $h = 7 + 6t - t^2$.
Graph the function $f : t \rightarrow 7 + 6t - t^2$,
in the domain $0 \leqslant t \leqslant 7$, $t \in \mathbf{R}$.
Use your graph to find:

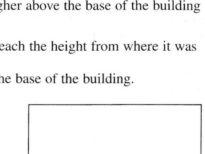

(i) the height of the building
(ii) the maximum height reached by the ball
(iii) the number of seconds taken for the ball to each a height of 15 m above the base of the building for the first time
(iv) the number of seconds the ball is 12 m or higher above the base of the building
(v) how high the ball is after $4\frac{1}{2}$ seconds
(vi) after how many seconds will the ball again reach the height from where it was fired
(vii) after how many seconds will the ball reach the base of the building.

5. The perimeter of a rectangle is 20 m
and the length of its base is x m.
Show that the width of the rectangle is $(10 - x)$ m.
Show that the area, A, of the rectangle
is given by $A = 10x - x^2$.
Graph the function $f : x \rightarrow 10x - x^2$
in the domain $0 \leqslant x \leqslant 10$, $x \in \mathbf{R}$.
Use your graph to find:
(i) the maximum area of the rectangle
(ii) the dimensions of the rectangle that gives this maximum
(iii) the area of the rectangle when the length is 4 m
(iv) the width of the rectangle when its length is 7 m
(v) the length of the rectangle when its area is 12.75 m^2.

6. A farmer has 12 metres of fencing which he uses to make a rectangular plot with a river on one side, as shown.
If the length is x m show that the width is given by $(12 - 2x)$ m.
Explain why the area, A, is given by $A = 12x - 2x^2$.

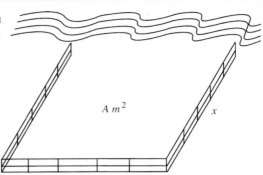

Copy and complete the table:

x	0	1	2	3	4	5	6
$A(x)$		10			16		

Graph the function $f : x \rightarrow A$ in the domain $0 \leqslant x \leqslant 6$.
Use your graph to find:
(i) the maximum area of the plot
(ii) the dimensions of the plot for this maximum
(iii) the length of the plot when the area is $10 \, \text{m}^2$
(iv) an estimate for the width when the area is $12 \, \text{m}^2$, correct to one decimal place
(v) the values of x for which the area is greater than or equal to $16 \, \text{m}^2$.

7. Using the same axes and scales, draw the functions:
$f : x \rightarrow 8x - x^2, \quad g : x \rightarrow x$, in the domain $0 \leqslant x \leqslant 8$.
$f(x)$ is the flight path of a projectile fired from a point o.
$g(x)$ is the side of a hill, (as shown).
r is the maximum point of the path.
s is directly beneath r and q is directly beneath p.
$x = 1$ represents $5 \, \text{m}$, $x = 2$ represents $10 \, \text{m}$, etc.
$y = 1$ represents $10 \, \text{m}$, $y = 2$ represents $20 \, \text{m}$, etc.
Use your graphs to find :

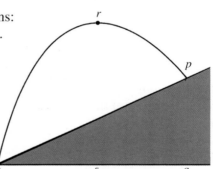

(i) the greatest height reached by the projectile, i.e. $|rs|$
(ii) the height of p above the horizontal, i.e. $|pq|$
(iii) the difference in height between the greatest height and the point p.
Express the distance $|op|$ in the form $a\sqrt{5}$.

Patterns 1

Much of mathematics is about patterns. Some are simple and numeric:

$$2, 4, 6, 8, 10, \ldots \qquad \frac{1}{2}, \frac{2}{3}, \frac{3}{4}, \frac{4}{5}, \ldots \qquad 10, 21, 32, 43, 54, \ldots$$

You should be able to write down the next three numbers in the list; you may even be able to predict the 10th number in the list *without* having to write out all the terms.

Other numeric patterns are more complicated:

$$1, 2, 4, 8, 16, \ldots \qquad 1, 0, 2, 0, 0, 3, 0, 0, 0, 4, \ldots \qquad 1, 2, 6, 24, 120, 720, \ldots$$

Even if you see a pattern and can write out the next number, it is much more difficult to predict what the 20th number or the 100th number in the list would be. If those numbers represented the population of the planet or the number of cancerous cells in a patient, then it would be very important to be able to predict future values.

Not all patterns are numeric. For example:

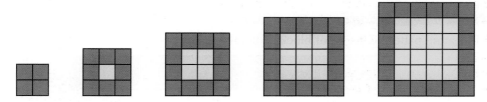

Is it possible to predict the number of squares in the 10th diagram? What about the number of yellow squares in the 10th diagram? What about the purple squares?

Many young children like to watch how tall they are growing and use some simple measuring techniques to record their growth. Is it possible to predict a child's height as each year passes?

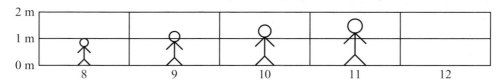

As an eight-year-old, Freddie was 1 m tall. By nine he was 1·25 m tall and by 10 he had reached 1·5 m. Could you use this information to calculate his height when he is 12 years old? What about when Freddie is 21? Do you see a problem?

Predicting the pattern

A pattern of repeating coloured blocks is easy enough to continue, but the challenge is to be able to predict what happens much further along.

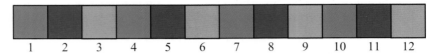

| 1 | 2 | 3 | 4 | 5 | 6 | 7 | 8 | 9 | 10 | 11 | 12 |

Looking at the orange blocks, there is an interesting pattern:

The 1st orange block is at position 3.	$3 = 3 \times 1$
The 2nd orange block is at position 6.	$6 = 3 \times 2$
The 3rd orange block is at position 9.	$9 = 3 \times 3$
The 4th orange block is at position 12.	$12 = 3 \times 4$

The 8th orange block should be at position $3 \times 8 = 24$.

We can predict that there will be another orange block at position $3 \times 9 = 27$. We can jump much further along and predict an orange block at position 99 (because $3 \times 33 = 99$).

So what about the 100th block? If the 99th is orange, then the 100th must be green and the 101st must be blue. To understand the sequence of this pattern, we need to find one sequence of colours which is easy to predict. From that we can deduce the positions of the other colours.

EXAMPLE

A repeating pattern consists of blocks coloured yellow, purple, green, yellow, . . . and so on.

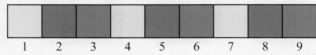

| 1 | 2 | 3 | 4 | 5 | 6 | 7 | 8 | 9 |

(i) Complete the table.

Block position	Colour
1	Yellow
2	
	Green
⋮	⋮

(ii) List the positions of the first three yellow blocks. Is there a pattern?

(iii) List the positions of the first three purple blocks. Is there a pattern?

(iv) List the positions of the first three green blocks. Is there a pattern?

  (v) What is the colour of the 48th block?
 (vi) What is the colour of the 50th block?
(vii) What is the colour of the 100th block?

Solution:

  (i) The completed table:

Block position	Colour
1	Yellow
2	Purple
3	Green
4	Yellow
5	Purple
6	Green
7	Yellow
8	Purple
9	Green

 (ii) Yellow blocks: 1, 4, 7, . . .
      Yes. Starting with 1 and adding 3 each time, the other positions can be found.
(iii) Purple blocks: 2, 5, 8, . . .
      Yes. Starting with 2 and adding 3 each time, the other positions can be found.
 (iv) Green blocks: 3, 6, 9, . . .
      Yes. Starting with 3 and adding 3 each time, the other positions can be found.
      Alternatively, the positions are multiples of 3, so the 1st green is at position $3 \times 1 = 3$,
      the 2nd green is at position $3 \times 2 = 6$, the 3rd green is at position $3 \times 3 = 9$ and so on.

  (v) As 48 is a multiple of 3 (48 can be divided exactly by 3), it must be a green block.

 (vi) Since the 48th block is green, the 50th must be purple.

(vii) Using a calculator, 100 is not a multiple of 3 (it divides in just over 33 times).
      $3 \times 33 = 99$ *is* a multiple of 3, so the 99th block must be green.

      The 100th block is therefore yellow.

Exercise 22.1

1. A repeating pattern consists of blocks coloured green, yellow, green, yellow, . . . and so on.

   (i) Complete the table.

Block position	Colour
1	Green
2	Yellow
⋮	⋮

   (ii) List the positions of the first three green blocks. Is there a pattern?

   (iii) List the positions of the first three yellow blocks. Is there a pattern?

   (iv) What is the colour of the 20th block?

   (v) What is the colour of the 33rd block?

   (vi) What is the colour of the 1,001st block?

2. A repeating pattern consists of blocks coloured red, white, blue, red, . . . and so on.

   (i) List the positions of the first three red blocks. Is there a pattern?

   (ii) List the positions of the first three white blocks. Is there a pattern?

   (iii) List the positions of the first three blue blocks. Is there a pattern?

   (iv) What is the colour of the 48th block?

   (v) What is the colour of the 50th block?

   (vi) What is the colour of the 100th block?

3. Players in a football competition are lined up in the following repeating sequence.

   (i) List the positions of the first four players in a blue shirt.

   (ii) List the positions of the first four players in an orange shirt.

   (iii) List the positions of the first four players in a yellow shirt.

   (iv) What is the colour of the shirt of the 15th player?

(v) What is the colour of the shirt of the 20th player?

(vi) Where in the line-up is the 8th player with an orange shirt?

(vii) Where in the line-up is the 10th player with a blue shirt?

4. As part of the opening ceremony of a hockey competition, the hockey players parade in the following repeating sequence.

(i) List the positions of the first three players in each colour.

(ii) What is the colour of the shirt of the 12th player?

(iii) What is the colour of the shirt of the 22nd player?

(iv) What is the colour of the shirt of the 23rd player?

(v) Where in the line-up is the 8th player with a green shirt?

(vi) Where in the line-up is the 10th player with a yellow shirt?

Sequences

A **sequence** is a set of numbers, separated by commas, in which each number after the first is formed by some definite rule.

Each number in a sequence is a **term** of that sequence. The first number is the **first term** and is denoted by T_1. Similarly, the second term is denoted by T_2 and so on.

3, 7, 11, 15, . . .

Each number after the first is obtained by adding 4 to the previous number. In this example, 3 is called the **first term**, 7 is the **second term** and so on.

1, 3, 9, 27, . . .

Each number after the first is obtained by multiplying the previous number by 3. In this example, 1 is called the **first term**, 3 is the **second term** and so on.

The general term, T_n

Very often a sequence is given by a **rule** which defines the **general term**. We use T_n to denote the general term of the sequence. T_n may be used to obtain any term of a sequence. T_1 will represent the first term, T_2 the second term and so on.

Notes:
1. The general term, T_n, is often called the nth term.
2. n used with this meaning must always be a positive whole number. It can never be fractional or negative.
3. A sequence is often called a progression.

Consider the sequence whose general term is $T_n = 3n + 2$.

We can find the value of any term of the sequence by putting in the appropriate value for n on both sides:

$$T_n = 3n + 2$$
$$T_1 = 3(1) + 2 = 3 + 2 = 5 \quad \text{(first term, put in 1 for } n)$$
$$T_2 = 3(2) + 2 = 6 + 2 = 8 \quad \text{(second term, put in 2 for } n)$$
$$T_5 = 3(5) + 2 = 15 + 2 = 17 \quad \text{(fifth term, put in 5 for } n)$$

In each case, n is replaced with the same number on both sides.

The notation $T_n = 3n + 2$ is very similar to function notation when n is the input and T_n is the output, i.e. (input, output) $= (n, T_n)$.

EXAMPLE

The nth term of a sequence is given by $T_n = n^2 + 3$.
  (i) Write down the first three terms of the sequence.
  (ii) Show that: (a) $\dfrac{T_5}{T_2} = T_1$ (b) $2T_4 = T_6 - 1$

Solution:
  (i) $T_n = n^2 + 3$
$$T_1 = 1^2 + 3 = 1 + 3 = 4 \quad \text{(put in 1 for } n)$$
$$T_2 = 2^2 + 3 = 4 + 3 = 7 \quad \text{(put in 2 for } n)$$
$$T_3 = 3^2 + 3 = 9 + 3 = 12 \quad \text{(put in 3 for } n)$$
Thus, the first three terms are 4, 7, 12.

  (ii) (a) From (i), $T_1 = 4$ and $T_2 = 7$.
$$T_5 = 5^2 + 3 = 25 + 3 = 28$$
$$\frac{T_5}{T_2} = \frac{28}{7} = 4$$
$$T_1 = 4$$
$$\therefore \frac{T_5}{T_2} = T_1$$

  (b) $T_4 = 4^2 + 3 = 16 + 3 = 19$
$$T_6 = 6^2 + 3 = 36 + 3 = 39$$
$$2T_4 = 2(19) = 38$$
$$T_6 - 1 = 39 - 1 = 38$$
$$\therefore 2T_4 = T_6 - 1$$

Exercise 22.2

In questions 1–8, write down the next four terms.

1. 1, 5, 9, 13, . . .
2. 40, 35, 30, 25, . . .
3. −11, −9, −7, −5, . . .
4. 13, 10, 7, 4, . . .
5. 2·5, 2·9, 3·3, 3·7, . . .
6. 2·8, 2·2, 1·6, 1, . . .
7. 1, 2, 4, 8, . . .
8. 2, 6, 18, 54, . . .

In questions 9–20, write down the first four terms of the sequence defined by the given nth term.

9. $T_n = 2n + 3$
10. $T_n = 3n + 1$
11. $T_n = 4n − 1$
12. $T_n = 5n − 3$
13. $T_n = 1 − 2n$
14. $T_n = 3 − 4n$
15. $T_n = n^2 + 5$
16. $T_n = n^2 + 2n$
17. $T_n = \dfrac{n + 1}{n}$
18. $T_n = \dfrac{2n}{n + 1}$
19. $T_n = 2^n$
20. $T_n = 3^n$

21. The nth term of a sequence is given by $T_n = 5n + 2$.

    (i) Write down the first three terms of the sequence.
    (ii) Show that: **(a)** $2T_5 = T_4 + T_6$ **(b)** $6(T_7 − 1) = T_2(T_3 + 1)$

22. The nth term of a sequence is given by $T_n = n^2 + 2$.

    (i) Write down the first three terms of the sequence.
    (ii) Show that: **(a)** $\dfrac{T_4}{T_2} = T_1$ **(b)** $\dfrac{T_6 − 2}{T_4} = \dfrac{T_2}{T_1}$

23. The nth term of a sequence is given by $T_n = \dfrac{n + 2}{n + 1}$.

    (i) Write down T_1, T_2 and T_3, the first, second and third terms.
    (ii) Show that $T_1 + T_2 > 2T_3$.

Differences 1

Some sequences can be understood better by investigating the differences between the terms. For example, the sequence 2, 5, 8, . . . has the same difference between consecutive terms. We can say that the difference between the terms is constant.

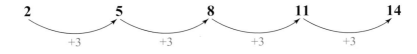

The differences are equal to 3 (which is a constant).

More complex sequences require us to check **the difference between the differences**. For example, the sequence 3, 6, 11, 18, 27, . . .

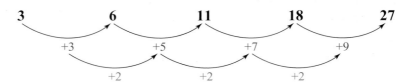

The first differences (3, 5, 7, . . .) are not constant, but the second differences are equal to 2 (which is a constant).

Exercise 22.3

In questions 1–6, find the first four terms and show that the difference between the terms is constant.

1. $T_n = 2n + 1$ 2. $T_n = 3n + 2$ 3. $T_n = 4n - 3$

4. $T_n = 5n + 2$ 5. $T_n = 3 - 2n$ 6. $T_n = 8 - 3n$

In questions 7–9, find the first four terms and show that the difference between the differences is constant.

7. $T_n = n^2 + 1$ 8. $T_n = n^2 - 2$ 9. $T_n = n^2 + n$

In questions 10–12, find the first four terms and show that the differences are such that this method of investigation will not produce a useful result.

10. $T_n = 2^n$ 11. $T_n = 3^n$ 12. $T_n = 3 + 2^n$

Linear sequence

Consider the sequence of numbers 3, 7, 11, 15, . . .

Each term, after the first, can be found by adding 4 to the previous term.

This is an example of an linear sequence.

> A sequence in which each term, after the first, is found by adding a constant number is called an **linear sequence**.

Note: A linear sequence is also called an **arithmetic sequence**.

Viewing the sequence as a graph

The patterns we look for are based on the relationship between two sets of values – the positions in a sequence and the values or terms in the sequence.

For example, the sequence 1, 3, 5, 7, 9, . . . can be represented in this table:

Position	1	2	3	4	5
Terms	1	3	5	7	9

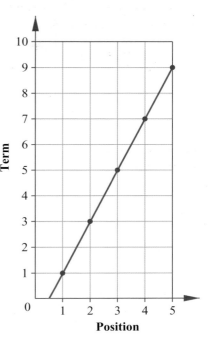

We can interpret the pairs (position, term) as points and plot (1, 1), (2, 3), (3, 5), (4, 7) and (5, 9).

The graph shows a line.

A line has a **constant rate of change**: positive if it is going up, negative if it is going down.

The **slope** of the line is equal to this rate of change.

Note: The first four letters of the word **linear** spell line. A graph is linear if all the points can be joined by one straight line.

Exercise 22.4

In questions 1–8, find the first five terms and show your results on a graph. State whether the graph is linear or not. Put the position along the horizontal axis.

1. $T_n = 2n$ 2. $T_n = 3n - 1$ 3. $T_n = 4n + 1$ 4. $T_n = n^2$

5. $T_n = n^2 - n$ 6. $T_n = n(n + 2)$ 7. $T_n = 2^n$ 8. $T_n = n^3 - n^2$

9. (i) Find the first four terms in the sequence defined by $T_n = 2n + 3$.
   (ii) By forming pairs of the form (position, term), plot the sequence on a graph.
   (iii) Using $x = 1, 2, 3$ and 4, find four points on the line $y = 2x + 3$. What do you notice?

10. (i) Find the first four terms in the sequence defined by $T_n = 3n - 2$.
    (ii) By forming pairs of the form (position, term), plot the sequence on a graph.
    (iii) Using $x = 1, 2, 3$ and 4, find four points on the line $y = 3x - 2$. What do you notice?
    (iv) What is the slope of the line in your graph?
    (v) What is the connection between the slope and the numbers in the original sequence?

11. Two sequences are defined as follows:

$$\text{Sequence A: } T_n = 2n + 7 \qquad \text{Sequence B: } T_n = 7n + 2$$

(i) In which sequence will the terms increase more rapidly? Explain your answer.

(ii) Verify your result by finding T_1 and T_5 of each sequence and compare your results.

(iii) Use your results from part (ii) to sketch a graph showing the two sequences as lines.

12. John receives a gift of a money box with €4 in it for his birthday. John decides he will save a further €2 a day each day after his birthday.

   (i) Draw a table showing the amount of money John saved for the first five days (his birthday being the first day).

   (ii) How much money will John have in his money box on the 10th day?

   (iii) How much money will John have in his money box on the 25th day?

   (iv) By looking at the pattern in this question, can you explain why the amount of money John has on day 10 is not twice the amount he has on day 5?

   (v) How much money does John have in his money box on day 100?

   (vi) How much money has John actually put in his money box after 10 days? Explain how you arrived at this amount.

   (vii) John wants to buy a new computer game. The game costs €39·99. What is the minimum number of days John will have to save so that he has enough money to buy the computer game?

13. Owen has a money box. He starts with €1 and adds €3 each day.

   (i) Draw a table showing the amount of money Owen has for the first 10 days.

   (ii) Draw a graph to show the amount of money Owen has saved each day. Put *Number of days* along the horizontal axis and *Amount of money* on the vertical axis.

   (iii) Why will the scale for the *Number of days* be different to the scale for the *Amount of money*?

14. Amy and Bill are discussing phone network offers. Amy says that she gets no free texts at the beginning of the month but that she receives five free texts each night. Bill says that on his network he begins each month with 30 free texts and receives three additional free texts each night.

   (i) Draw a table showing the start number of texts and the number of texts available for the first six days.

Day	Amy's texts	Bill's texts
Start (1)	0	30
Day 2	5	33
⋮		
Day 6		

   (ii) Who has the most free texts after six days?

   (iii) Using graph paper, draw a graph showing the number of texts for both Amy and Bill for the first 20 days. You should allow the vertical axis to reach 150 texts.

    (iv) Are the two graphs linear or something else?

    (v) At what point does Amy seem to have a better offer than Bill?

    (vi) Will Amy and Bill ever have the same number of texts on a particular day? If so, which day? If not, why not?

15. Lenny begins the month with 20 free texts and receives two additional free texts each night. Jane does not have any free texts at the beginning of the month but receives three free texts each night.

    (i) Draw a table showing the number of free texts for both Lenny and Jane for the first 10 days.

    (ii) Represent both sets of results on a graph.

    (iii) Will Lenny and Jane ever have the same number of free texts on a certain day? If so, which day? If not, why not?

    (iv) Who in your opinion has the better deal for free texts each month? Give a reason for your answer.

16. A yellow flower measured 5 cm high at the beginning of the week and grew 2 cm each week afterwards.

A red flower measured 8 cm high at the beginning of the same week but grew only 1·5 cm each week afterwards.

    (i) Calculate the heights of each plant for the first five weeks and plot your results on a graph.

    (ii) Which plant will be taller?

    (iii) Will the plants ever be the exact same height?

    (iv) Give some reasons why the growth suggested by the graph may be unreliable.

Differences 2

A sequence such as 2, 5, 8, 11, 14, . . . has the same difference between consecutive terms.

The differences are equal to 3 (which is a constant). This means that the sequence is linear and we can now look at finding the relationship between the term number (or position) and the value in the sequence. If the difference is 3, then each term can be approximated by multiplying the term number by 3.

Term number	1	2	3	4	5
Value	2	5	8	11	14

If we multiply each term number by 3, we get:

Term number	1	2	3	4	5
Difference × Term number	$3 \times 1 = 3$	$3 \times 2 = 6$	$3 \times 3 = 9$	$3 \times 4 = 12$	$3 \times 5 = 15$

This gives us the sequence 3, 6, 9, 12, 15, . . . but we want to arrive at 2, 5, 8, 11, 14, . . .

By inspection, we can see that if we subtracted 1 from each term in our new sequence, then we would have our original list.

Thus, the numbers in the sequence 2, 5, 8, 11, 14, . . . can be found by multiplying the term number by 3 and subtracting 1.

This can be written algebraically as $T_n = 3n - 1$.

EXAMPLE

  (i) Describe in words the relationship between the positions and the values in the sequence 5, 9, 13, 17, . . .

 (ii) Use this to find T_{50}.

(iii) Write an expression for T_n in the form $dn + v$.

(iv) Where in the sequence does the term 169 occur?

Solution:

 (i) First, we need to find the common difference.

    As the difference is 4, we need to multiply each position by 4 and then, by inspection, add or subtract a number.

Term number	1	2	3	4
Difference × Position	$4 \times 1 = 4$	$4 \times 2 = 8$	$4 \times 3 = 12$	$4 \times 4 = 16$

Original sequence	5	9	13	17

    By inspection, we can see we need to add 1.

    Thus, the numbers in the sequence 5, 9, 13, 17, . . . can be found by multiplying the position by 4 and adding 1.

 (ii) $T_{50} = 4(50) + 1 = 200 + 1 = 201$

(iii) $T_n = 4n + 1$

(iv) This is an equation in disguise as we know the **result** of using the formula.

$$T_n = 4n + 1 = 169$$
$$4n = 168 \quad \text{(subtract 1 from each side)}$$
$$n = 42 \quad \text{(divide each side by 4)}$$

Thus, the 42nd term is 169.

Exercise 22.5

In questions 1–9, find the common difference for the sequence and find, in terms of n, an expression for T_n, the nth term.

1. 1, 3, 5, . . .
2. 2, 5, 8, . . .
3. 3, 7, 11, . . .
4. 6, 11, 16, . . .
5. 9, 7, 5, . . .
6. 4, 1, −2, . . .
7. 8, 3, −2, . . .
8. 4, −2, −8, . . .
9. −5, −3, −1, . . .

10. The first three terms of a linear sequence are 1, 4, 7.

   (i) Find the common difference.

   (ii) Find, in terms of n, an expression for T_n, the nth term, and hence or otherwise, find T_{50}.

   (iii) Which term of the sequence is 88?

11. The first three terms of a linear sequence are 4, 9, 14.

   (i) Find the common difference.

   (ii) Find, in terms of n, an expression for T_n, the nth term, and hence or otherwise, find T_{45}.

   (iii) Which term of the sequence is equal to 249?

12. The first three terms of a linear sequence are 40, 36, 32.

   (i) Find the common difference.

   (ii) Find, in terms of n, an expression for T_n, the nth term, and hence or otherwise, find T_{15}.

   (iii) Which term of the sequence is 0?

13. The cost of visiting an exhibition is as follows.

Number of children	Price (€)
1	5
2	7
3	9
4	11

Number of adults	Price (€)
1	7
2	12
3	17
4	22

   (i) Find a formula to calculate the cost of n children visiting the exhibition.

   (ii) Verify that your formula works for three children.

   (iii) Find a formula to calculate the cost of *n* adults visiting the exhibition.

   (iv) Verify your formula works for four adults.

   (v) A group of six adults and 10 children are planning to visit the exhibition. How much will it cost?

14. A taxi charges €5 for a journey of 1 km, €8 for 2 km, €11 for 3 km and so on.

   (i) Write out a table showing the cost of journeys up to 6 km.

   (ii) Treating the costs as a linear sequence, find the common difference.

   (iii) The taxi fare is a fixed charge plus a rate per kilometre. What is **(a)** the fixed charge and **(b)** the rate per kilometre?

   (iv) How long a journey can be made with €100?

15. The instructions for cooking a chicken are 15 minutes per kg plus 20 minutes.

   (i) How long is needed to cook a 1 kg chicken?

   (ii) Write out a table showing the time needed to cook chickens weighing 1 kg, 2 kg, . . . , 6 kg.

   (iii) Find a formula which calculates the time, in minutes, to cook a chicken weighing *n* kg.

   (iv) Use your formula to find out how long it will take to cook a 9 kg chicken.

   (v) What is the heaviest chicken that can be cooked within 4 hours?

16. 5, 8, 11, . . . is a linear sequence. Which term of the sequence is 179?

17. 3, 8, 13, 18, . . . is a linear sequence. Which term of the sequence is 198?

18. Meriel's vocabulary was checked every two months beginning when she was 10 months old. At that time, she had a vocabulary of eight words. At 12 months she had a vocabulary of 11 words. By 14 months it was 14 words and by 16 months it was 17 words.

   (i) How old was she when the 10th check was made?

   (ii) Find a formula, in terms of *n*, which will calculate Meriel's age when the *n*th check is made.

   What's a vocabulary?

   (iii) Find a formula, in terms of *n*, which will calculate the vocabulary size when the *n*th check is made.

   (iv) At which check will Meriel know 500 words?

   (v) How old will Meriel be when she knows 500 words?

   (vi) Is it likely that a child will increase her vocabulary at the rate suggested?

Patterns 2

If we are asked to investigate pictures containing a mixture of colours or shapes, the first step is easy – number the diagrams! From this we can establish a connection between the diagram number and amount of colours or shapes in each one. This should lead us to a numeric pattern or sequence.

EXAMPLE

The diagram shows three shapes constructed using matchsticks.

  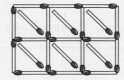

(i) If the pattern is continued, how many matchsticks will be needed for the 4th shape?

(ii) The amount of matchsticks used in the shapes form which type of sequence?

(iii) Find a formula, in terms of n, for the nth shape.

(iv) How many matchsticks will be needed for the 100th shape?

Solution:
Number the diagrams.

  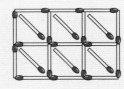

    1   2   3   4

Count the matchsticks in each diagram and put these in a table.

Shape	1	2	3	4
Number of matchsticks	9	16	23	?

(i) The difference between the number of matchsticks used is $16 - 9 = 7$ and $23 - 16 = 7$. As the differences are the same, we can easily predict the next number in the sequence. Therefore, the 4th shape will need $23 + 7 = 30$ matchsticks.

Alternatively, you could draw the new shape and simply count the matchsticks.

(ii) The numbers 9, 16, 23, . . . form a linear sequence, as the terms have a common difference of 7.

(iii)

Shape number	1	2	3	4
Difference × Position	$7 \times 1 = 7$	$7 \times 2 = 14$	$7 \times 3 = 21$	$7 \times 4 = 28$
Add/subtract	+2	+2	+2	+2
Sequence	9	16	23	30

Thus $T_n = 7n + 2$.

(iv)
$$T_n = 7n + 2$$
$$T_{100} = 7(100) + 2$$
$$= 702$$

Thus, 702 matchsticks will be needed for the 100th shape.

Exercise 22.6

1. These three diagrams were made using matches.

 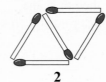 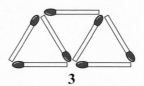

      1   2   3

  (i) If the pattern is continued, how many matches will be needed for the 4th, 5th and 6th diagrams?

  (ii) The amount of matches used in the diagrams form which type of sequence?

  (iii) Find a formula, in terms of n, for the nth diagram.

  (iv) How many matches will be needed for the 50th diagram?

  (v) Explain why there is no diagram with this pattern needing 200 matches.

2. The patterns shown are made from hexagonal tiles.

Pattern 1   Pattern 2   Pattern 3

 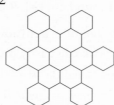 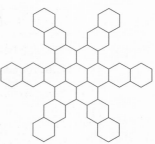

  (i) Construct a table showing the number of tiles for the first five patterns.

  (ii) Find a formula, in terms of n, for the number of tiles in the nth pattern.

  (iii) Which pattern is made from 253 tiles?

3. A series of shapes are made using matches.

    (i) How many matches will be needed for the 4th and 5th shapes?

   (ii) Find a formula, in terms of n, for the nth shape.

  (iii) Which shape will need 49 matches?

4. Orange and black discs are arranged in rectangular patterns as shown.

    (i) How many discs will be in the 10th rectangle?

   (ii) How many black discs will be in the 10th rectangle?

  (iii) Describe two methods of finding the number of orange discs in the 10th rectangle.

  (iv) Explain why there is no rectangle with this pattern needing 99 discs.

   (v) Explain why there is no rectangle with this pattern needing 50 discs.

5. Rectangles containing red and white squares form a sequence as shown.

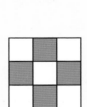 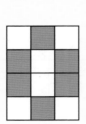 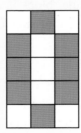

    (i) Copy and complete the table.

Rectangle	1	2	3	4	5	6
Number of white squares						
Number of red squares						
Total number of squares						

   (ii) Write down the number of white squares in the 10th rectangle.

  (iii) Write down the formula, in terms of n, for the number of white squares in the nth rectangle.

  (iv) Find a formula, in terms of n, for the number of red squares in the nth rectangle.

   (v) Use this formula to find the number of red squares in the 10th rectangle.

(vi) Deduce the total number of squares in the 10th rectangle.

(vii) Find a formula, in terms of n, for the total number of squares by using your answers from (iii) and (iv).

(viii) Verify your formula from (vii) by letting $n = 2$ and checking your table from (i).

6. The set of diagrams have been made from straws.

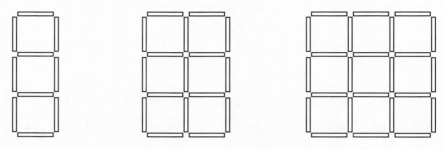

(i) How many straws will be needed for the 5th diagram?

(ii) Find a formula, in terms of n, for the nth diagram.

(iii) How many straws will be needed for the 20th diagram?

(iv) If $a : b$ is the ratio of the width to the height of the 1st diagram, find the value of a and the value of b.

(v) Which diagram has a ratio of its width to its height in the form $b : a$?

7. A long rectangular block is made using magnetic cubes. The sides are 1 cm. The diagram shows a block of four such cubes.

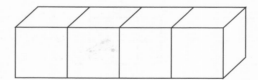

(i) How long is this block?

(ii) What is the surface area of this block?

(iii) If another block is attached to the end, what is the surface area?

(iv) What is the surface area of a block using 10 cubes?

(v) What is the surface area of a block using n cubes?

8. Patterns of dots are created as shown in this diagram.

(i) Draw the next two patterns.

(ii) Copy this table and complete it.

Diagram	1	2	3	4	5
Number of dots	5				

(iii) Find a formula, in terms of n, for the nth pattern.

(iv) Is it possible to predict from the table in **(i)** whether there is an even or an odd number of dots in the 50th diagram? Explain your answer.

(v) Is there an even or an odd number of dots in the 99th diagram?

(vi) Verify your predictions in **(iv)** and **(v)** by using the formula from **(ii)**.

9. A shop stacks two of its products as shown. The Economy brand is shown as a yellow square while the Deluxe brand is purple.

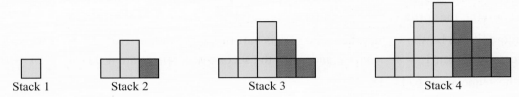

Stack 1   Stack 2   Stack 3   Stack 4

(i) Write out, as a sequence, the number of Economy products in the first four stacks.

(ii) Investigate whether the number of Economy products forms a linear sequence.

(iii) Write out, as a sequence, the number of Deluxe products in the first four stacks.

(iv) Investigate whether the number of Deluxe products forms a linear sequence.

10. A garden landscaper constructed small ponds of varying sizes. The diagram shows the three consecutive examples of a pond and the slabs that surround it.

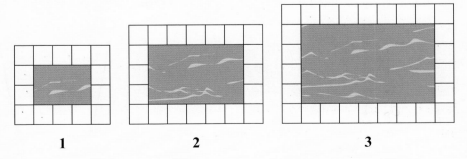

1   2   3

(i) Write out, as a sequence, the number of slabs needed for these three ponds.

(ii) Investigate whether the sequence forms a linear sequence. Explain your conclusion.

(iii) Find a formula, in terms of n, for the number of slabs needed to surround the nth pond.

(iv) Which pond would require 98 slabs to surround it?

(v) Write out, as a sequence, the width (shown vertically) as a number of slabs needed for these three ponds.

(vi) Find a formula, in terms of n, for the width of the nth pond.

(vii) What is the width and length of a pond which requires 98 slabs to surround it?

(viii) Draw the small pond that would precede the three shown and count the number of slabs needed. Verify that it fits in with the sequence you found earlier.

Differences 3

Earlier, we investigated differences between differences on some sequences. While these are not linear sequences, it is still possible to find an expression for T_n, the nth term. When it takes *two* differences to see a constant, the formula for T_n will be of the form $T_n = an^2 + bn + c$.

Furthermore, it can be shown that the value of a is half of the second differences. So if the second differences are 2 then $T_n = n^2 + bn + c$ and when the second differences are 4 then $T_n = 2n^2 + bn + c$.

Here is the sequence 3, 6, 11, 18, 27, . . .

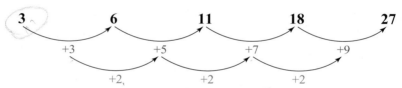

The general term of this sequence will be of the form $T_n = n^2 + bn + c$.

When the differences between the differences are negative, the graph will look like this:

When the differences between the differences are positive, the graph will look like this:

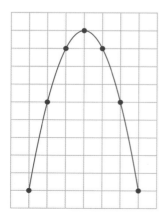

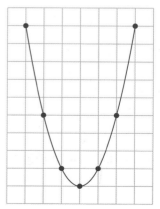

These are examples of quadratic graphs.

Find the general term, T_n, of the sequence 1, 5, 11, 19, 29, ...

Solution:

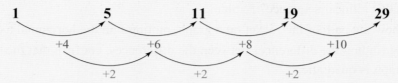

Because the second difference is 2, $T_n = n^2 + bn + c$. Now we need to find the value of b and the value of c.

We will use the first two terms to form two equations involving b and c and then use the method of simultaneous equations.

Given: $T_1 = 1$ and $T_2 = 5$

$T_n = n^2 + bn + c$	$-b - c = 0$ ① × -1
$T_1 = 1^2 + b(1) + c = 1$	$\underline{2b + c = 1 \qquad ②}$
$1 + b + c = 1$	$b = 1$
$b + c = 0$ ①	
	$b + c = 0$
$T_2 = 2^2 + b(2) + c = 5$	$1 + c = 0$
$4 + 2b + c = 5$	$c = -1$
$2b + c = 1$ ②	

Thus, $T_n = n^2 + 1n - 1 = n^2 + n - 1$.

Exercise 22.7

In questions 1–6, find an expression for T_n for the following sequences.

1. 3, 7, 13, 21, 31, . . .   2. 4, 9, 16, 25, 36, . . .

3. 2, 6, 12, 20, 30, . . .   4. 2, 5, 10, 17, 26, . . .

5. 0, 0, 2, 6, 12, . . .   6. 8, 15, 24, 35, 48, . . .

7. (i) Find T_n of the sequence 0, 4, 10, 18, 28, . . .
    (ii) Find T_{10}.
    (iii) Investigate whether T_{100} is less than or greater than 1,000.

8. A rocket is launched and its path is described by the formula $h = 10t - t^2$, where h is the height of the rocket in metres and t is the time in seconds after blast-off.

   (i) Find the height of the rocket after $t = 1, 2, \ldots , 6$ seconds.

   (ii) Is this a linear sequence? Explain.

   (iii) Show the path of the rocket on a graph, putting t on the horizontal axis.

   (iv) By finding the differences between the differences, confirm that the graph is quadratic.

   (v) Can you tell if the rocket has reached its maximum height? If so, what is this maximum height?

9. A missile is launched from ground level and its height is recorded each second after blast-off. The heights are 22 m, 36 m, 52 m, 70 m, . . .

   (i) Find T_n of the sequence.

   (ii) How high will the missile be after 10 seconds?

   (iii) How high will the missile be after 1 minute?

   (iv) Noting that the missile does not rise uniformly, give a reason why a missile would rise faster as time passes.

10. Mary is making rectangular patterns from counters. The length of each rectangle is one more than the width. The first three patterns are shown.

   (i) Each time, to get the next pattern, she increases the width by one more counter. Write an expression for the number of counters in the nth pattern.

   (ii) Mary notices that there is also a pattern in how many extra counters she needs each time to make the next pattern. How many extra counters does she need to make the $(n + 1)$th pattern from the nth pattern? Write your answer in the form $a(n + b)$.

11. (i) Copy and complete the following pattern up to the 6th term.

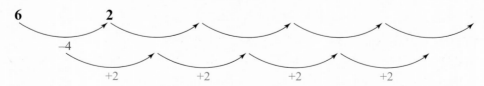

   (ii) Taking $T_1 = 6$, $T_2 = 2$ and so on, up to T_6, complete the list of six points $(1, 6), (2, 2), \ldots$.

   (iii) Show these points on a coordinated graph, labelling the axes with n and T_n, as appropriate.

   (iv) What type of graph is obtained by joining the points with a smooth curve?

Differences 4

Sometimes, the method of calculating differences does not work. Take the following sequence and its differences:

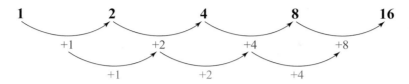

In this case the differences are repeating themselves. This sequence is a new type – an exponential sequence. If we look for a term-to-term rule, we find that it involves multiplying by 2. When terms are calculated by multiplying, the sequence is always exponential. There are other sequences which are also exponential.

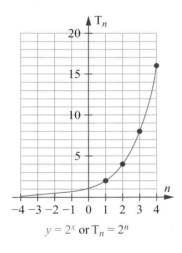

$y = 2^x$ or $T_n = 2^n$

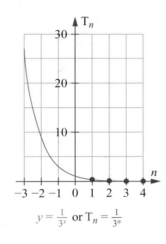

$y = \frac{1}{3^x}$ or $T_n = \frac{1}{3^n}$

Exponential graphs usually begin low and increase without limit or start off high and drop down towards a low level (often zero).

EXAMPLE

   (i)   Find the first four terms in the sequence defined by $T_n = 2^n$.

  (ii)   Show that the relationship between the position in the list is neither linear nor quadratic.

 (iii)   Show this relationship on a graph.

Solution:

(i) $T_n = 2^n$

$T_1 = 2^1 = 2$

$T_2 = 2^2 = 4$

$T_3 = 2^3 = 8$

$T_4 = 2^4 = 16$

(ii)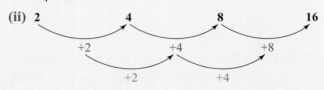

(iii)

The first differences are not equal, so the sequence is not linear.

The second differences are not equal, so the sequence is not quadratic.

Exercise 22.8

In questions 1–6, find the first four terms and show that the differences are not constant and that the differences between the differences are also not constant.

1. $T_n = 3^n$

2. $T_n = 3^n + 1$

3. $T_n = 3 + 2^n$

4. $T_n = 2(3^n)$

5. $T_n = 3(2^n)$

6. $T_n = 2(2^n + 1)$

7. A survey in a forest showed that there were eight pairs of red squirrels and three pairs of the larger grey variety. Further regular surveys showed that the number of red squirrels doubled each year, while the grey squirrels trebled in number.

   (i) Show the sequence of the numbers of each type of squirrel for the first four years.

   (ii) Draw a graph showing the numbers of each type over the four years.

   (iii) What notable event occurred after the third year?

Types and names of angles

Angles are named according to the amount of turning, or rotation, measured in degrees.

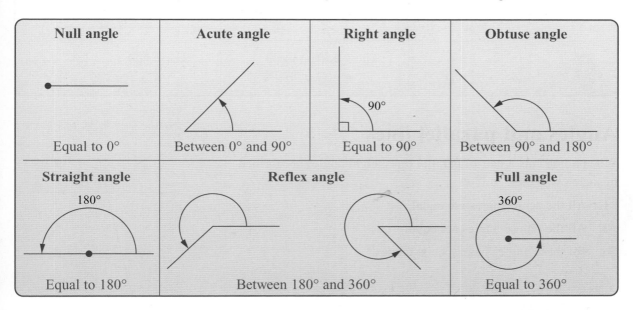

Null angle	**Acute angle**	**Right angle**	**Obtuse angle**
Equal to 0°	Between 0° and 90°	Equal to 90°	Between 90° and 180°

Straight angle	**Reflex angle**	**Full angle**
Equal to 180°	Between 180° and 360°	Equal to 360°

Ordinary angle

An **ordinary angle** is an angle between 0° and 180°. When naming an angle, it is **always** assumed that we are referring to the ordinary angle (non-reflex angle), unless the word **'reflex'** precedes or follows the naming of an angle. Consider the diagram.

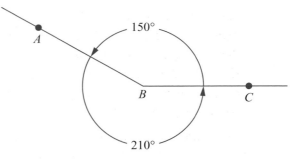

$|\angle ABC| = 150°$ (ordinary angle) $|\text{reflex } \angle ABC| = 210°$ (reflex angle)

Properties of angles

It is very important to know the following properties of angles.

Vertically opposite angles (angles formed by two lines)	Complementary angles (angles in a right angle)	Supplementary angles (angles in a straight line)
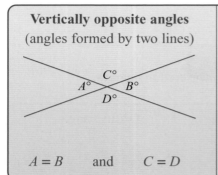	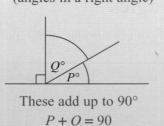 These add up to 90°	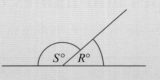 These add up to 180°
$A = B$ and $C = D$	$P + Q = 90$	$R + S = 180$

Angles and parallel lines

When a line cuts a pair of parallel lines, eight angles are formed in such a way that:

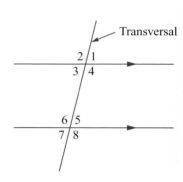

1. All the acute angles are equal.

2. All the obtuse angles are equal.

Some of these angles have special names.

Note: If you know one of these angles then you can work out all the others.

A line that intersects two or more lines is called a **transversal**, even if the lines are not parallel.

Corresponding angles

Corresponding angles are equal and occur in pairs. A pair of corresponding angles is marked on each of the diagrams. Corresponding angles are always on the **same** side of the transversal.

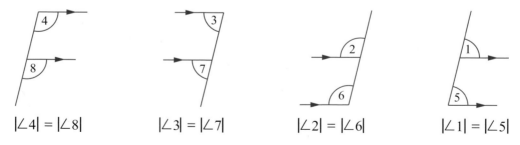

$|\angle 4| = |\angle 8|$ $|\angle 3| = |\angle 7|$ $|\angle 2| = |\angle 6|$ $|\angle 1| = |\angle 5|$

Looking for a ⌐, ⌐, ⌐ or ⌐ shape can help you to spot corresponding angles.

Alternate angles

Alternate angles are equal and occur in pairs. A pair of alternate angles is marked on each of the diagrams. Alternate angles are always on **opposite** sides of the transversal.

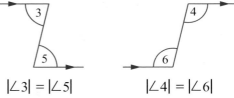

$$|\angle 3| = |\angle 5| \qquad |\angle 4| = |\angle 6|$$

Looking for a ⌐ or ⌐ shape can help you to spot alternate angles.

Interior angles

Interior angles add up to 180°. A pair of interior angles is marked on each of the diagrams. Interior angles are always on the **same** side of the transversal.

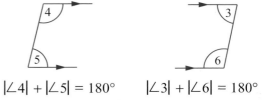

$$|\angle 4| + |\angle 5| = 180° \qquad |\angle 3| + |\angle 6| = 180°$$

Looking for a ⌐ or ⌐ shape can help you to spot interior angles.

In short: *comhthreagra*   *alterned*

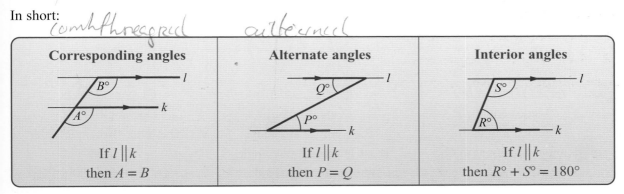

Corresponding angles	Alternate angles	Interior angles
If $l \parallel k$ then $A = B$	If $l \parallel k$ then $P = Q$	If $l \parallel k$ then $R° + S° = 180°$

The converses are also true:

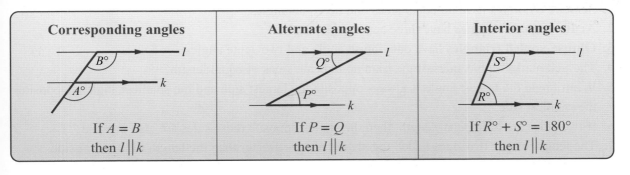

Corresponding angles	Alternate angles	Interior angles
If $A = B$ then $l \parallel k$	If $P = Q$ then $l \parallel k$	If $R° + S° = 180°$ then $l \parallel k$

Triangles

<table>
<tr><td colspan="1">Angle sum of a triangle</td><td>Exterior angle of a triangle</td></tr>
<tr><td>

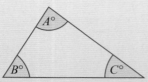

The three angles of a triangle add up to 180°.
$$A° + B° + C° = 180°$$

</td><td>

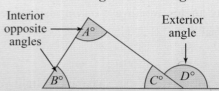

If one side is produced, the exterior angle is equal to the sum of the two interior opposite angles.
$$D° = A° + B°$$

</td></tr>
</table>

Special triangles

<table>
<tr><td>Equilateral triangle</td><td>Isosceles triangle</td><td>Right-angled triangle</td></tr>
<tr><td>

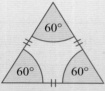

3 sides equal
3 equal angles
All angles are equal to 60°

</td><td>

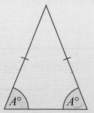

2 sides equal
Base angles are equal
(base angles are the angles opposite the equal sides)

</td><td>

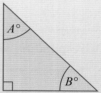

One angle is 90°
The other two angles add up to 90°
$$A° + B° = 90°$$

</td></tr>
</table>

Notes:

1. **Scalene triangles** have no equal sides and no equal angles.
2. **Acute-angled triangles** have three acute angles.
3. **Obtuse-angled triangles** have one obtuse angle and two acute angles.
4. The tick marks on the sides of the triangle indicate sides of equal length.
5. In a triangle the largest angle is always opposite the largest side and the smallest angle is opposite the smallest side.
6. If two sides are of unequal length, then the angles opposite these sides are also unequal.
7. The length of any two sides added together is always greater than the length of the third side.

Perpendicular bisector of a line segment

> Any point on the perpendicular bisector, m, of a line segment, $[AB]$, is equidistant from A and B.

The converse is also true.

> Any point equidistant from A and B lies on m, the perpendicular bisector of the line segment $[AB]$.

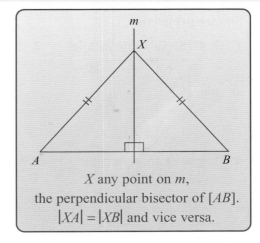

X any point on m,
the perpendicular bisector of $[AB]$.
$|XA| = |XB|$ and vice versa.

Note: The perpendicular bisector of a line segment is also called the mediator.

Bisector of an angle

> Any point on the bisector of an angle, b, is equidistant from the lines that form the angle.

The converse is also true.

> If a point is equidistant from two lines that form an angle, then the point is on the bisector, b, of the angle.

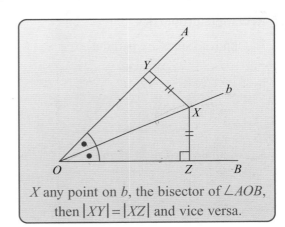

X any point on b, the bisector of $\angle AOB$,
then $|XY| = |XZ|$ and vice versa.

Quadrilaterals

A quadrilateral is a figure that has four sides and four vertices.
It has two diagonals that join the opposite vertices.

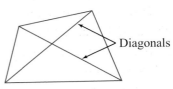

Diagonals

The four angles of a quadrilateral add up to $360°$.

$A° + B° + C° + D° = 360°$

(This is because a quadrilateral can be divided up into two triangles.)

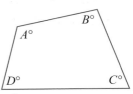

Note: A and C are called opposite angles and B and D are also called opposite angles.
   Some quadrilaterals have special names and special properties.

Square properties

1. Opposite sides are parallel.

2. All sides are equal.

3. All angles are right angles.

4. Diagonals are equal and bisect each other.

5. Diagonals intersect at right angles.

6. Diagonals bisect each angle.

Rectangle properties

1. Opposite sides are parallel.

2. Opposite sides are equal.

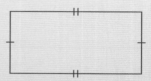

3. All angles are right angles.

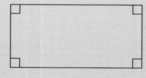

4. Diagonals are equal and bisect each other.

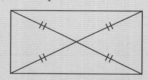

Parallelogram properties

1. Opposite sides are parallel.

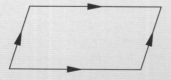

2. Opposite sides are equal.

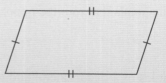

3. Opposite angles are equal.

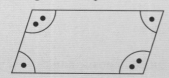

4. Diagonals bisect each other.

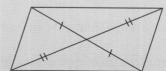

EXAMPLE

Calculate the value of x and the value of y.

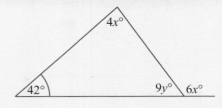

Solution:

$6x = 4x + 42$ (exterior angle)

$2x = 42$

$x = 21$

$6x + 9y = 180$ (straight angle)

$\downarrow$

$6(21) + 9y = 180$

$126 + 9y = 180$

$9y = 54$

$y = 6$

Alternatively, $4x + 9y + 42 = 180$ (three angles in a triangle)

and $6x + 9y = 180$ (straight angle)

Then solve these simultaneous equations to get $x = 21$ and $y = 6$.

Exercise 23.1

For questions 1–15, calculate the values of the letters representing the angles in each diagram.

1.

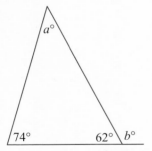

2.

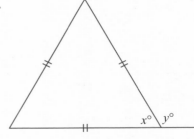

3.

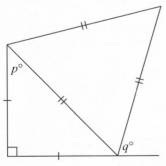

4.

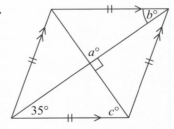

5.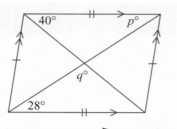

6.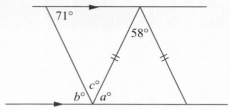

7.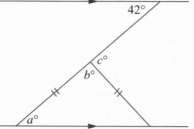

8.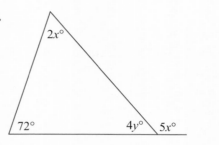

9.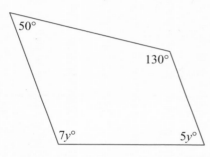

10.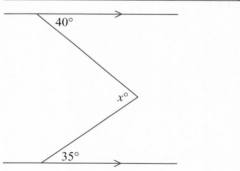

11.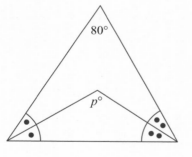

12.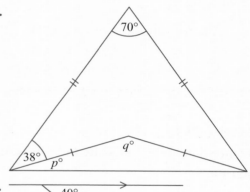

13.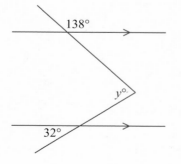

14.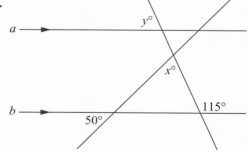

15.

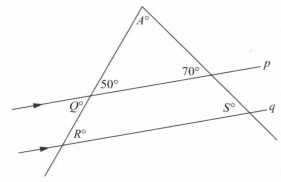

16. In the diagram, $|PQ| = |PR|$.
Find the value of:
(i) x **(ii)** y **(iii)** z
In each case, give a reason for your answer.

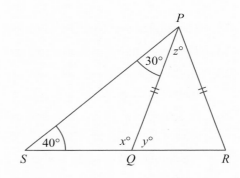

17. $|PR| = |QR| = |RS|$ and $|\angle PRQ| = 48°$.
Find: **(i)** $|\angle PQR|$ **(ii)** $|\angle PSR|$
In each case, give a reason for your answer.

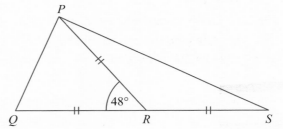

For questions 18–21, solve for x and y.

18.

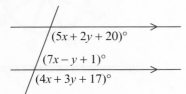

$(5x + 2y + 20)°$
$(7x - y + 1)°$
$(4x + 3y + 17)°$

19.

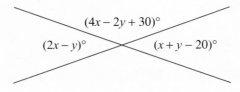

$(4x - 2y + 30)°$
$(2x - y)°$
$(x + y - 20)°$

20.

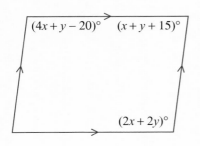

$(4x + y - 20)°$ $(x + y + 15)°$
$(2x + 2y)°$

21.

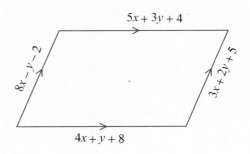

$5x + 3y + 4$
$8x - y - 2$
$3x + 2y + 5$
$4x + y + 8$

427

22. **(i)** What is an isosceles triangle?

    (ii) The diagram shows a triangle with sides of length x cm, $(3x - 8)$ cm and $(2x - 3)$ cm.

    Find the three values of x for which the triangle is isosceles.

    In each case, draw a rough sketch of the triangle.

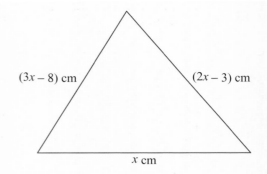

(3x – 8) cm (2x – 3) cm

x cm

23. The angles in a triangle are in the ratio $3\frac{1}{2} : 2 : \frac{1}{2}$. Calculate the measure of the three angles.

24. The four angles in a quadrilateral are $(3x + 10)°$, $x°$, $3x°$ and $(3x + 20)°$. Calculate x.

25. An isosceles triangle is always an obtuse-angled triangle. Is this statement true or false? Justify your answer.

26. In a right-angled triangle, one of the angles is obtuse. Is this statement true or false? Give a reason for your answer.

27. An equilateral triangle is also an acute-angled triangle. Is this statement true or false? Justify your answer.

28. A plumber uses connectors as shown. Explain why the connector shown is called a 30° connector.

150°

29. A paddle wheel has nine equally spaced arms, as shown. Showing all your work, calculate the angle between any two adjacent arms.

30. The diagram shows a side view of an ironing board.
    (i) If $A = 110°$, find the value of **(a)** B and **(b)** C.
    (ii) For health and safety reasons, A must be greater than or equal to 110°. Complete the following table, indicating whether the statement is correct (✓) or incorrect (✗) to satisfy the health and safety regulations.

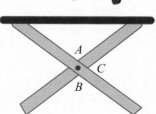

A
C
B

Statement	✓ or ✗	Reason
$C > 70°$		
$C \le 70°$		
$B > 110°$		
$(A + B) < 220°$		

31. Copy and complete the following table by placing a tick (✓) in any box where the given statement is true.

Statement	Square	Parallelogram	Rectangle
The diagonals are equal in length			
Opposite angles are equal			
Only one pair of opposite sides are parallel			
The diagonals are lines of symmetry			

32. In the triangle ABC, the sides AB, BC and CA are produced to E, F and D respectively, as shown.
  (i) Write down the value of $|\angle DAB| + |\angle BAC|$.
  (ii) Hence or otherwise, find the value of $|\angle DAB| + |\angle EBC| + |\angle FCA|$.

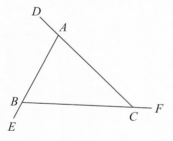

33. In the diagram, $|QR| = |QS| = |PS|$ and $|\angle PSQ| = x°$.
  Express in terms of x:
  (i) $|\angle PQS|$
  (ii) $|\angle SQR|$
  (iii) If $|PQ| = |PR|$, calculate the value of x.

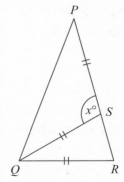

34. In the diagram, $|\angle RST| = 69°$, $|PQ| = |QS| = |SR|$ and $|\angle QRS| = a°$. Calculate the value of a.

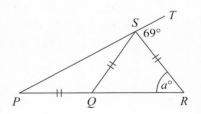

Transversal intersecting three parallel lines

> If three parallel lines cut off equal segments on some transversal, then they will cut off equal segments on any other transversal.

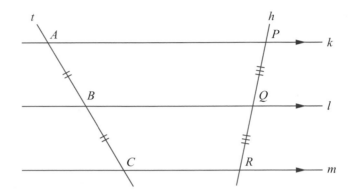

k, l and m are three parallel lines ($k \parallel l \parallel m$). t is a transversal that meets the lines k, l and m, respectively, at points A, B and C, such that $|AB| = |BC|$.

Draw any other transversal, h, to meet the lines k, l and m, respectively, at P, Q and R. $|PQ| = |QR|$.

This is true for any other transversal that meets the parallel lines k, l and m.

EXAMPLE

In the diagram, l, m and n are parallel lines that cut equal segments on the transversal, h. $|AB| = 10$, $|DE| = 12$ and $|EF| = 3x$.

(i) Find $|BC|$. Justify your answer.

(ii) Calculate x, giving a reason for your answer.

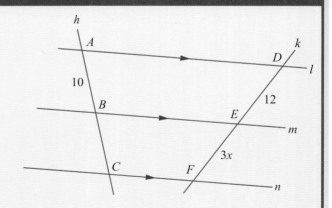

Solution:

(i) $|BC| = |AB|$ (given)
  but $|AB| = 10$
  $\therefore |BC| = 10$

(ii) $|EF| = |DE|$
  Equal segments are cut on any other transversal
  $\therefore 3x = 12$
  $x = 4$

Exercise 23.2

In the diagrams for questions 1–4, *l*, *m* and *n* are parallel lines. They each cut equal intercepts on the transversals. In each case, calculate the value of the variables *x*, *y*, *a* and *b*.

1.

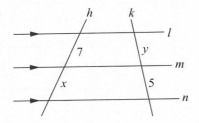

2.

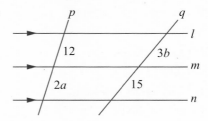

3.

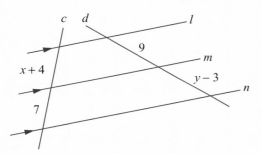

4.

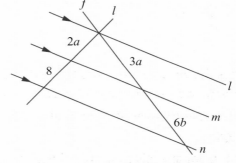

5. In the diagram, *l*, *m* and *n* are parallel lines. They make equal intercepts on the line *h*. $AB \parallel h$.
   (i) What are the lines *h* and *k* called?
   (ii) Giving a reason in each case, calculate:
      (a) $|AB|$ (b) $|AC|$

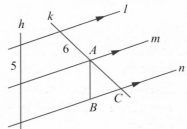

6. In the diagram, *p*, *q* and *r* are parallel lines. They make equal intercepts on the perpendicular transversal, *t*.
   (i) If $|AC| = 16$ cm, calculate $|AB|$.
   (ii) If $|AC| + |DF| = 38$ cm, calculate $|EF|$.
   (iii) *ACGD* is a rectangle. Indicate the point *G* on the diagram. Calculate the area of rectangle *ACGD* if $|AD| = |DF|$.

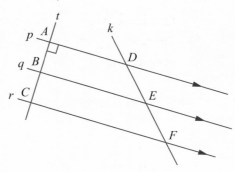

7. l, m and n are parallel lines. They cut equal intercepts on the line p, where $p \perp l$.

   (i) Describe the line p.

   (ii) Is $p \perp m$? Explain your answer.

   (iii) If $|XZ| = 20$ cm, calculate $|YZ|$.

   (iv) If $|XZ| + |DB| = 44$ cm, calculate $|FB|$.

   (v) If $|FG| = 30$ cm and $FB \parallel GH$, calculate the area of the parallelogram $BFGH$.

   (vi) Hence, calculate the perpendicular distance between the parallel lines FB and GH.

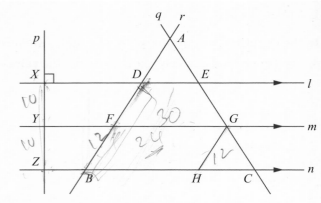

Proofs

A proof in geometry should consist of five steps:

1. **Diagram**

   Draw a clear diagram, if not given, from the information given in the question.

2. **Given**

   State what is given.

3. **To prove**

   State what is to be proved.

4. **Construction**

   If necessary, state any extra lines that have to be added to the diagram to help in the proof.

   Also at this stage, if necessary, it can simplify the work if the angles are labelled with a number.

5. **Proof**

   Set out each line of the proof, justifying each statement made.

EXAMPLE 1

The line m bisects $\angle ABD$ and the line k bisects $\angle CBD$. Prove that $m \perp k$.

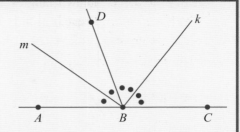

Solution

Given: Diagram as shown.

To prove: $m \perp k$

Construction: Label angles 1, 2, 3 and 4.
Prove $|\angle 2| + |\angle 3| = 90°$.

Proof:
$|\angle 1| + |\angle 2| + |\angle 3| + |\angle 4| = 180°$ (straight angle)
But $|\angle 1| = |\angle 2|$ and $|\angle 3| = |\angle 4|$ (given)
$\therefore 2|\angle 2| + 2|\angle 3| = 180°$
$\therefore |\angle 2| + |\angle 3| = 90°$
$\therefore m \perp k$

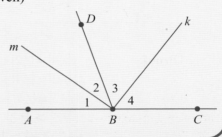

EXAMPLE 2

XYZ is an isosceles triangle with $|XY| = |XZ|$.
Prove that $|\angle XKZ| > |\angle XZK|$.

Solution

Given: Diagram as shown.

To prove: $|\angle XKZ| > |\angle XZK|$

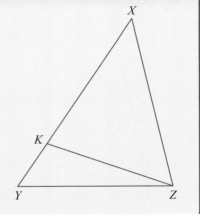

Construction: Label angles 1, 2, 3, 4 and 5.
Draw triangles XYZ and KYZ separately.
Prove $|\angle 3| > |\angle 2|$.

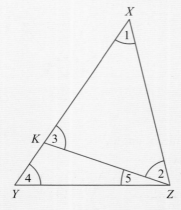 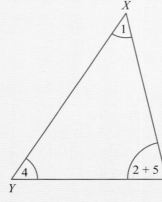 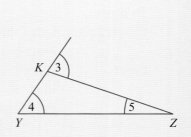

Proof:

$$|\angle 4| = |\angle 2| + |\angle 5|$$
$$\therefore |\angle 2| = |\angle 4| - |\angle 5|$$
$$|\angle 3| = |\angle 4| + |\angle 5|$$
$$\therefore |\angle 3| > |\angle 2|$$
$$\therefore |\angle XKZ| > |\angle XZK|$$

as $|XY| = |XZ|$

Exterior angle of $\triangle KYZ$
As $|\angle 4| + |\angle 5| > |\angle 4| - |\angle 5|$

Exercise 23.3

1. In the diagram,
   $PS \parallel QR$ and $|PQ| = |QR|$.
   Prove that PR bisects $\angle QPS$.

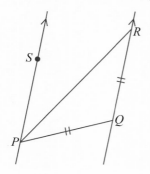

2. In the diagram,
   $PQ \perp QS$ and $ST \parallel PQ$.
   Prove that $|\angle QPR| = |\angle STR|$.

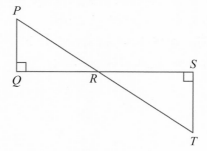

3. In the diagram,
    $PR \perp RQ$ and $UV \perp PQ$.
    Prove that $|\angle RPQ| = |\angle VUQ|$.

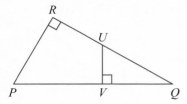

4. $m \parallel k$.
    $|\angle SPQ| = 48°$ and $|\angle TRQ| = 42°$.
    Prove that $PQ \perp QR$.

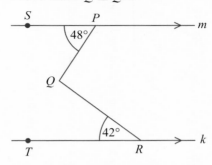

5. $PQRS$ is a parallelogram.
    ST bisects $\angle PSR$ and VQ bisects $\angle PQR$.
    Prove that: **(i)** $ST \parallel VQ$.
    (ii) $|PS| = |PT|$.

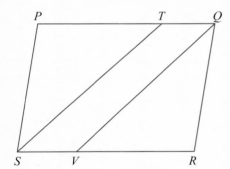

6. ABC is a triangle with the line BC
    containing the points D and E.
    Prove that:
    (i) $|\angle ACE| > |\angle ABC|$.
    (ii) $|\angle ABD| + |\angle ACE| > 180°$

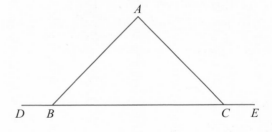

7. $ABCD$ is a quadrilateral and P, Q, R and S are four points as shown.
    (i) Prove that $|\angle ABC| + |\angle BCD| + |\angle CDA| + |\angle DAB| = 360°$.
    (ii) Evaluate $|\angle ABC| + |\angle CBQ|$.
    (iii) Prove that $|\angle PAB| + |\angle QBC| + |\angle RCD| + |\angle SDA| = 360°$.

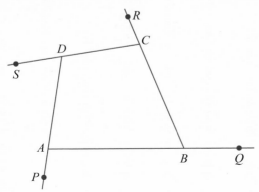

8. In the diagram,
$|\angle QPR| = 2x°$ and $|\angle PQR| = (90 - x)°$.
Prove that triangle PQR is isosceles.

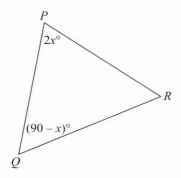

9. PQR is an isosceles triangle
with $|PQ| = |PR|$.
$|\angle SRQ| = 90°$ and SQ is a straight line.
Prove that triangle PSR is isosceles.

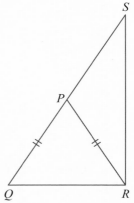

10. ABC is an isosceles triangle with $|AB| = |AC|$.
$[BA]$ is produced to D, so that $|AD| = |AB|$.
By joining D to C, prove that $|\angle BCD| = 90°$.

11. $m \parallel k$.
OA bisects $\angle PAB$.
OB bisects $\angle QBA$.
Prove that $|\angle AOB| = 90°$.

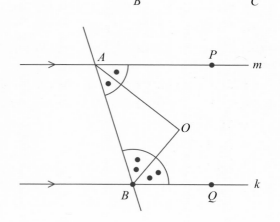

12. In the diagram, $QU \perp QP$
and $|\angle QUV| = |\angle KPZ| = 75°$.
Prove that $VW \perp KW$.

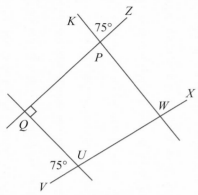

13. $ABCD$ is a rectangle in which
$|AD| = 2|AB|$ and
AE bisects $\angle BAD$.
Prove that E is the midpoint of $[BC]$.

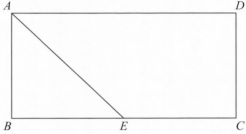

14. $PQRS$ is a parallelogram. k is the
perpendicular bisector of $[PQ]$. m is the
perpendicular bisector of $[QR]$. Prove that
$|PS| = |RS|$.

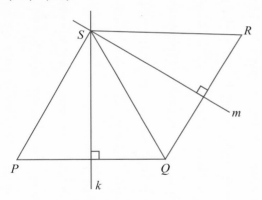

15. The two triangles PQR and ABC are
between parallel lines.
$|AC| = 4$ cm and $|PQ| = 12$ cm.

Prove $\dfrac{\text{area of } \triangle ABC}{\text{area of } \triangle PQR} = \dfrac{1}{3}$.

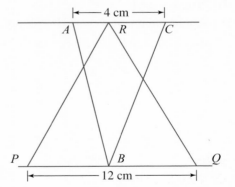

16. $ABCD$ is a parallelogram. The line BG bisects
$\angle ABC$. H is an element of the line CD and of the
line BG. Prove that:

  (i) $|AB| = |AG|$

  (ii) $|DG| = |DH|$

  (iii) $|AD| = |CH|$

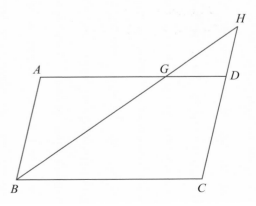

17. In the diagram,
$|\angle ACX| = |\angle AYC|$.

   (i) Prove that $|\angle YAC| = |\angle YCB|$.

   (ii) If $|AB| = |AC|$,
      prove that $|CY| = |CB|$.

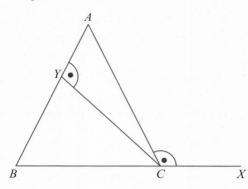

18. In the diagram,
$|AB| = |AD|$.

  Prove that $|\angle ABC| > |\angle ACB|$.

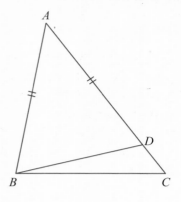

19. *ABC* is an isosceles triangle with $|AB| = |AC|$. $[BA]$ is
produced to *D*.

AE is parallel to *BC*.

  (i) Prove that $[AE]$ bisects $\angle DAC$.

  (ii) Would the result in part (i) still apply if $|AB|$ and $|AC|$
      were not equal? Give a reason for your answer.

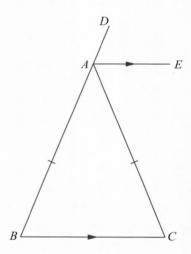

Congruent triangles

The word **'congruent'** means **'identical'**. Two triangles are said to be congruent if they have exactly the same size and shape. They have **equal lengths of sides, equal angles and equal areas**. One triangle could be placed on top of the other so as to cover it exactly. Sometimes it is necessary to turn one of the triangles over to get an exact copy. The symbol for congruence is $\equiv$. If $\triangle ABC$ is congruent to $\triangle XYZ$ then we write $\triangle ABC \equiv \triangle XYZ$. When naming congruent triangles, it is important that the order of the letters is correct when stating whether two triangles are congruent. In other words, the points ABC correspond to the points XYZ in that order.

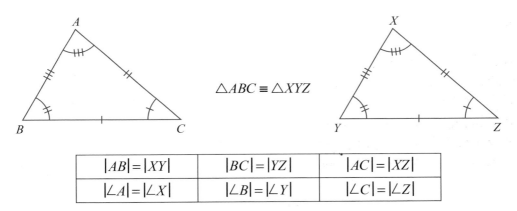

$$\triangle ABC \equiv \triangle XYZ$$

$|AB| = |XY|$	$|BC| = |YZ|$	$|AC| = |XZ|$
$|\angle A| = |\angle X|$	$|\angle B| = |\angle Y|$	$|\angle C| = |\angle Z|$

For two triangles to be congruent (identical), the three sides and three angles of one triangle must be equal to the three sides and three angles of the other triangle. However, it is not necessary to prove all six equalities to show that the two triangles are congruent. Any of the following four tests is sufficient to prove that two triangles are congruent.

Four tests for congruency

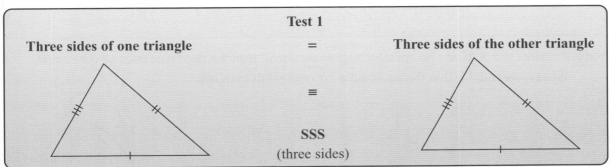

Test 1

Three sides of one triangle   =   **Three sides of the other triangle**

$\equiv$

SSS
(three sides)

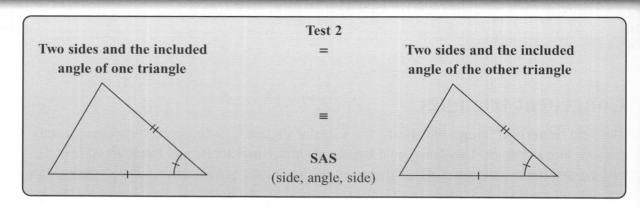

Test 2

Two sides and the included angle of one triangle

=

Two sides and the included angle of the other triangle

≡

SAS
(side, angle, side)

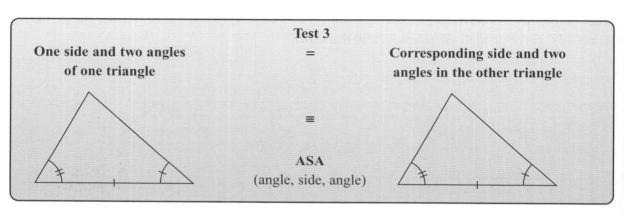

Test 3

One side and two angles of one triangle

=

Corresponding side and two angles in the other triangle

≡

ASA
(angle, side, angle)

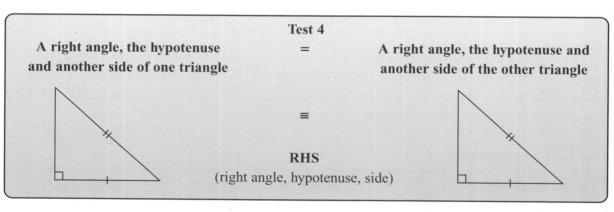

Test 4

A right angle, the hypotenuse and another side of one triangle

=

A right angle, the hypotenuse and another side of the other triangle

≡

RHS
(right angle, hypotenuse, side)

Note: Consider test 3. If any two pairs of angles are equal, then the third pair must also be equal. What is essential is that the equal sides correspond to each other.

A proof using congruent triangles contains three steps.

1. Identify the two triangles that are being used in the proof.
2. Name the three pairs of equal sides and/or angles.
   Always give reasons why the angles used are equal, e.g. alternate angles.
   Always give reasons why the lengths of the sides used are equal, e.g. opposite sides of a parallelogram.
3. Name the congruent triangles, in matching order.
   State the congruence test used, i.e. SSS, SAS, ASA or RHS.

If two triangles are congruent then all corresponding sides and angles are equal and the areas of both triangles are equal.

Many geometrical properties can be proved using the four cases of congruent triangles.

Always state which case of congruence is used, i.e. SSS, SAS, ASA or RHS.

Justify each statement made, e.g. common side, opposite sides.

State why angles used are equal, e.g. vertically opposite angles, and write down if you are given that two angles are equal or two sides are equal.

It can help to redraw the two triangles separately in a proof, but this is not necessary.

By convention, the sides or angles on the LHS (left-hand side) of the proof should belong to one triangle and the sides or angles on the RHS (right-hand side) should belong to the other triangle. It can also help in a test for congruency to label the angles used with a number.

Note: In many situations, more than one case of congruence can be used.

Congruent triangles and constructions
There is a link between congruent triangles and constructions. The four tests relate to given measurements from which exactly only one triangle can be constructed.

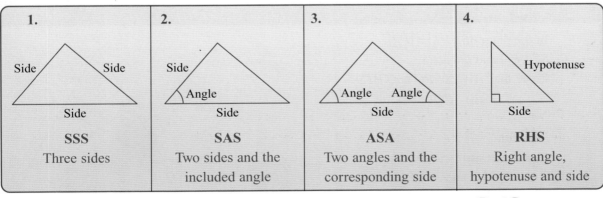

1.	2.	3.	4.
SSS Three sides	**SAS** Two sides and the included angle	**ASA** Two angles and the corresponding side	**RHS** Right angle, hypotenuse and side

DTS

Dromuillin, teobléçca
slio,

EXAMPLE 1

Given $\triangle XYZ$ with $|XY| = |XZ|$, prove that the bisector of $\angle YXZ$ bisects $[YZ]$ at right angles.

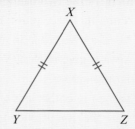

Solution:

Construction:

Draw $[XW]$, the bisector of $\angle YXZ$.

Draw $\triangle XYW$ and $\triangle XZW$ separately. Label angles 1, 2, 3, 4, 5 and 6 and indicate equal sides.

Note: We first have to prove that W bisects $[YZ]$ and *then* show that $[XW]$ is perpendicular to $[YZ]$.

Proof:

$|XY| = |XZ|$	(given)
$|\angle 1| = |\angle 2|$	(construction)
$|XW| = |XW|$	(common)
$\therefore \triangle XYW \equiv \triangle XZW$	(SAS)
$\therefore \ |YW| = |WZ|$	(corresponding sides)

Hence, W bisects $|YZ|$.

$|\angle 5| = |\angle 6|$	(corresponding angles)
But $|\angle 5| + |\angle 6| = 180°$	(straight angle)
$\therefore \ |\angle 5| = |\angle 6| = 90°$	

Hence, $[XW] \perp [YZ]$.

$\therefore [XW]$ bisects $[YZ]$ at right angles.

EXAMPLE 2

In the diagram, $|PT| = |PR|$, $ST \perp PQ$ and $QR \perp PS$.

Prove that: **(i)** $\triangle PRQ \equiv \triangle PTS$

(ii) $|PQ| = |PS|$

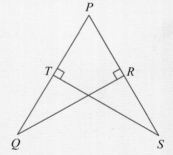

Solution:

Construction:

Draw $\triangle PRQ$ and $\triangle PTS$ separately.

Label angles 1, 2, 3 and 4 and indicate equal sides.

Proof:

$\lvert\angle 1\rvert = \lvert\angle 2\rvert$	(given as 90°)
$\lvert PR\rvert = \lvert PT\rvert$	(given)
$\lvert\angle 3\rvert = \lvert\angle 4\rvert$	(common)
$\therefore \triangle PRQ \equiv \triangle PTS$	(ASA)
$\therefore \lvert PQ\rvert = \lvert PS\rvert$	(corresponding sides)

In the next three examples the triangles are not drawn separately.

EXAMPLE 3

$ABCD$ is a parallelogram with M as the midpoint of $[AD]$.
BM produced meets CD produced at E.
Prove that $\lvert BM\rvert = \lvert ME\rvert$.

Solution:

Construction:

Label angles 1, 2, 3 and 4 and indicate equal sides.

Proof:

Consider $\triangle ABM$ and $\triangle DEM$.

$\lvert AM\rvert = \lvert MD\rvert$	(given)
$\lvert\angle 1\rvert = \lvert\angle 2\rvert$	(vertically opposite angles)
$\lvert\angle 3\rvert = \lvert\angle 4\rvert$	(alternate angles)
$\therefore \triangle ABM \equiv \triangle DEM$	(ASA)
$\therefore \lvert BM\rvert = \lvert ME\rvert$	(corresponding sides)

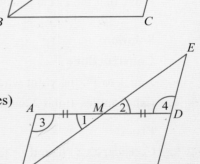

EXAMPLE 4

$PQRS$ is a parallelogram with diagonal $[QS]$.
PX bisects $\angle QPS$ and RY bisects $\angle SRQ$.
Prove that **(i)** $\triangle PQX \equiv \triangle RSY$
(ii) $\lvert PX\rvert = \lvert RY\rvert$

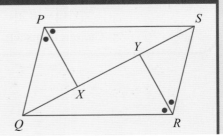

Solution:

Construction:

Label angles 1, 2, 3 and 4 and indicate equal sides.

Proof:

Consider $\triangle PQX$ and $\triangle RSY$.

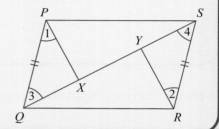

$$|PQ| = |RS| \qquad \text{(opposite sides)}$$
$$|\angle 1| = |\angle 2| \qquad \text{(given)}$$
$$|\angle 3| = |\angle 4| \qquad \text{(alternate angles)}$$
$$\therefore \ \triangle PQX \equiv \triangle RSY \qquad \text{(ASA)}$$
$$\therefore \quad |PX| = |RY| \qquad \text{(corresponding sides)}$$

EXAMPLE 5

A diameter of a circle is one of the equal sides of the isosceles $\triangle XYZ$ where $|XY| = |XZ|$.

Prove that the circle bisects $[YZ]$.

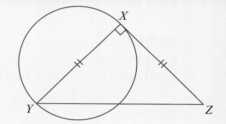

Solution:

Construction:

Join X to W, the point where $[YZ]$ meets the circle.

Label angles 1 and 2 and indicate equal sides.

Proof:

Consider $\triangle XYW$ and $\triangle XZW$.

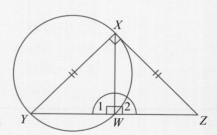

$$|XY| = |XZ| \qquad \text{(given)}$$
$$|XW| = |XW| \qquad \text{(common)}$$
$$|\angle 1| = 90° \qquad \text{(angle in a semicircle)}$$
$$\therefore \quad |\angle 2| = 90° \qquad \text{(as both add to 180°)}$$
$$\therefore \triangle XYW \equiv \triangle XZW \qquad \text{(RHS)}$$
$$\therefore \quad |YW| = |WZ| \qquad \text{(corresponding sides)}$$

$\therefore$ The circle bisects $[YZ]$.

Exercise 24.1

1. In the diagram, $|PR|=|RS|$ and $|QR|=|RT|$.

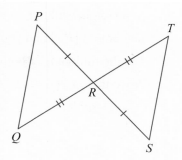

   (i) What type of angles are $\angle PRQ$ and $\angle SRT$?

   (ii) What type of angles are $\angle PQR$ and $\angle STR$?

   (iii) Prove that $\triangle PRQ \equiv \triangle SRT$.

   (iv) Prove that $PQST$ is a parallelogram.

2. In the diagram, $|AD|=|AE|$,
   $|\angle BAE|=|\angle CAD|$ and $|\angle ADE|=|\angle AED|$.

   Prove: **(i)** $\triangle ABD \equiv \triangle ACE$

   (ii) $|BD|=|CE|$

   (iii) $|BE|=|CD|$

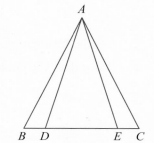

3. In the diagram, $|AB|=|AD|$,
   $AB \perp BC$ and $AD \perp DC$.

   Prove: **(i)** $\triangle ABC \equiv \triangle ADC$

   (ii) $|BC|=|DC|$

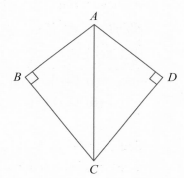

4. $PQRS$ is a square.

   TQR is an equilateral triangle inside the square.

   Prove that $|PT|=|ST|$.

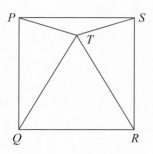

5. m is the perpendicular bisector of the line
   segment $[AB]$.

   C is a point on the line m.

   Prove that $|AC|=|BC|$.

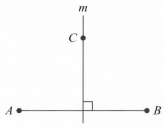

6. A person is walking on stilts that always remain parallel.
   The braces [PS] and [QR] are joined at T.
   T is the midpoint of both braces.
   Prove that $\triangle PQT \equiv \triangle SRT$.

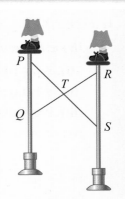

7. b is the bisector of $\angle AOB$ and X is a point on the line b.
   Prove that X is equidistant from OA and OB.

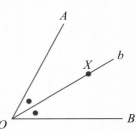

8. $ABCD$ is a parallelogram with diagonal [BD].
   $AP \perp BD \perp CQ$.

   Prove: **(i)** $|AP| = |CQ|$
   (ii) $|\angle DAP| = |\angle BCQ|$

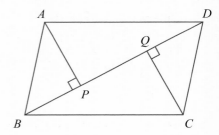

9. $PQRS$ is a parallelogram with diagonal [QS].
   PX bisects $\angle QPS$ and RY bisects $\angle SRQ$.

   Prove: **(i)** $\triangle PQX \equiv \triangle RSY$
   (ii) $|\angle PXQ| = |\angle RYS|$
   (iii) $|QY| = |SX|$

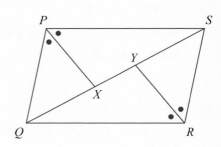

10. *ABCD* is a parallelogram with diagonal [*BD*].

Z is the midpoint of [*BD*].

Prove: **(i)** $|XZ| = |YZ|$

(ii) $|DX| = |BY|$

(iii) $|YC| = |XA|$

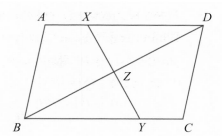

11. *SQ* is the bisector of $\angle PSR$ and $|PS| = |RS|$.

Prove: **(i)** $|PQ| = |RQ|$

(ii) *SQ* bisects $\angle PQR$

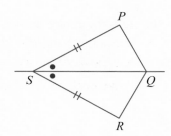

12. Given $\triangle XYZ$ and $|XY| = |XZ|$.

A, *B* and *C* are the midpoints of the sides, as shown.

Prove: **(i)** $|AC| = |BC|$

(ii) $|\angle YAC| = |\angle YXZ|$

(iii) If the area of $\triangle ABX = 10$, find the area of *YABZ*.

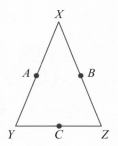

13. *ABCD* is a parallelogram with diagonal [*AC*].

X and *Y* are points on [*AC*] such that $|\angle ABX| = |\angle CDY|$.

Prove: **(i)** $\triangle ABX \equiv \triangle CDY$

(ii) *BXDY* is a parallelogram

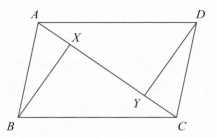

14. *PB* and *PC* bisect the angles shown.

(i) Prove that $|PX| = |PY| = |PZ|$.

(ii) If *P* is joined to *A*, prove that *PA* bisects $\angle BAC$.

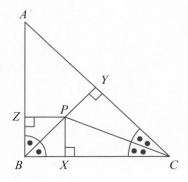

15. *PQRS* is a rectangle and *C* is the midpoint of [*PQ*].
With *C* as centre, arcs cut [*PS*] at *A* and [*QR*] at *B*.

Prove: (i) $|AP| = |BQ|$

(ii) $|AS| = |BR|$

(iii) $|AQ| = |PB|$

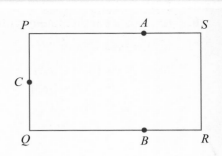

16. *O* is the centre of the circle and $|AB| = |CD|$.
Prove that $|\angle AOB| = |\angle COD|$.

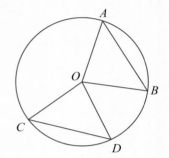

17. In $\triangle PQR$, $|PQ| = |PR|$ and $|QS| = |SR|$.
$SX \perp PQ$ and $SY \perp PR$.

Prove: (i) $|SX| = |SY|$

(ii) $|PX| = |PY|$

(iii) $|XQ| = |YR|$

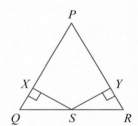

18. *WXYZ* is a parallelogram.
The diagonals intersect at *O*, such that $WY \perp XZ$.
Prove that *WXYZ* is a rhombus
(a parallelogram with four equal sides).

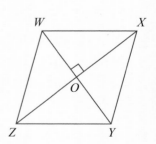

19. The diagram shows the end frame of a
child's swing. $|\angle ADF| = |\angle CDF|$ and
$|DE| = |DG|$.
Prove:

(i) $\triangle DEF \equiv \triangle DGF$

(ii) $|EF| = |GF|$

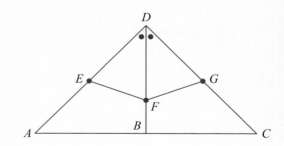

CIRCLE THEOREMS

Circle

The diagrams below show some of the terms we use when dealing with a circle.

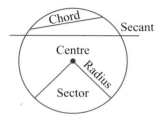

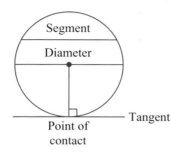

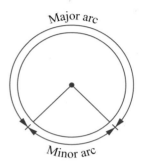

Circle theorems

1. Angle at the centre

The angle at the centre of a circle standing on a given arc is twice the angle at any point of the circle standing on the same arc.

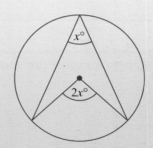

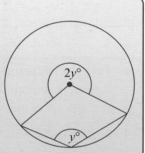

2. Angles on the same arc

All angles at points of a circle, standing on the same arc, are equal.

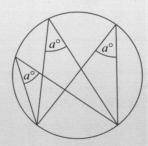

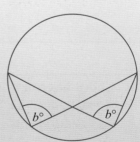

449

3. Angle in a semicircle

A diameter divides a circle into two semicircles.

Each angle in a semicircle is a right angle.

The converse is also true.

If the angle standing on a chord at a point on the circle is a right angle, then the chord is a diameter.

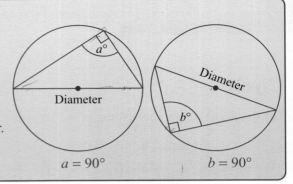

$a = 90°$

$b = 90°$

4. Cyclic quadrilateral

A cyclic quadrilateral has its four vertices on the circumference of a circle.

The sum of the opposite angles in a cyclic quadrilateral is $180°$.

$a° + c° = 180°$ and $b° + d° = 180°$

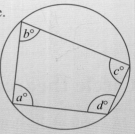

5. Tangent perpendicular to a radius (or diameter)

A tangent to a circle is perpendicular to a radius (or diameter) at the point of contact.

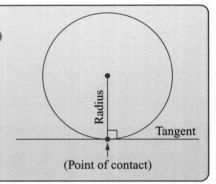

6. Chord bisector

A line through the centre of a circle perpendicular to a chord bisects the chord.

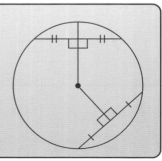

EXAMPLE 1

In the diagram, $PQRS$ is a cyclic quadrilateral.
O is the centre of the circle.
$|\angle QPS| = 61°$ and $|\angle OSR| = 72°$.
Find: (i) $|\angle QOS|$, where $\angle QOS$ is obtuse
   (ii) $|\angle SRQ|$
   (iii) $|\angle RQO|$

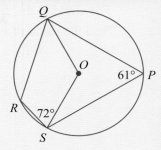

Solution:

(i) $|\angle QOS| = 2|\angle QPS|$ $\qquad \left(\begin{array}{c}\text{angle at centre} = \\ 2(\text{angle at circumference})\end{array}\right)$
$\qquad\quad = 2(61°)$
$\qquad\quad = 122°$

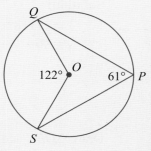

(ii) $|\angle SRQ| + |\angle QPS| = 180°$ $\qquad \left(\begin{array}{c}\text{opposite angles of} \\ \text{a cyclic quadrilateral}\end{array}\right)$
$\qquad |\angle SRQ| + 61° = 180°$
$\qquad\quad\; |\angle SRQ| = 119°$

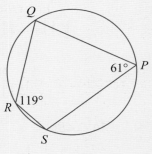

(iii) $|\angle RQO| + 119° + 72° + 122° = 360°$ $\quad \left(\begin{array}{c}\text{four angles in a} \\ \text{quadrilateral add to } 360°\end{array}\right)$
$\qquad\quad |\angle RQO| + 313° = 360°$
$\qquad\qquad\quad\; |\angle RQO| = 47°$

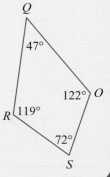

EXAMPLE 2

The circle in the diagram has centre O.
Find the value of x and the value of y.

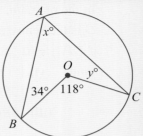

Solution:

$x = \frac{1}{2}(118°)$

$x = 59°$

$\left(\begin{array}{c} \text{angle at the circumference} \\ = \frac{1}{2} \text{ (angle at the centre)} \end{array} \right)$

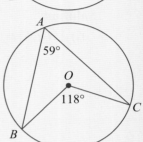

Draw $\triangle OBC$ and $\triangle ABC$ separately and label angles 1 and 2.

In $\triangle OBC$, $|OB| = |OC|$.　　　(both radii)

$|\angle 1| + |\angle 2| + 118° = 180°$　　(3 angles in a triangle)

$|\angle 1| + |\angle 2| = 62°$

but $|\angle 1| = |\angle 2|$　　(because $|OB| = |OC|$)

$\therefore |\angle 1| = |\angle 2| = 31°$

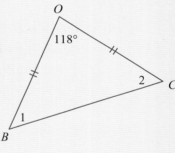

In $\triangle ABC$,

$y + 31° + 31° + 34° + 59° = 180°$　(3 angles in a triangle)

$y + 155° = 180°$

$y = 25°$

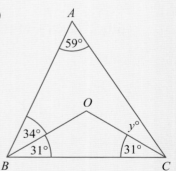

Exercise 25.1

For questions 1–30, find the value of the letter representing the angles in each of the circles.
Where necessary, the centre of the circle is indicated by O.

1.

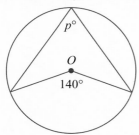

2.

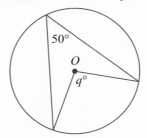

3.

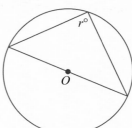

4.

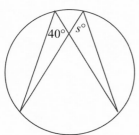

5.

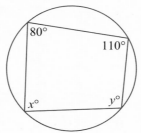

6.

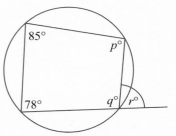

7.

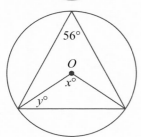

8.

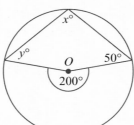

9.

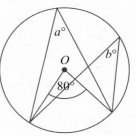

10.

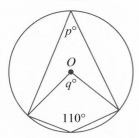

11.

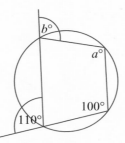

12.

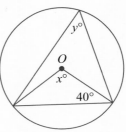

13.

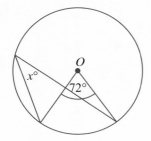

14.

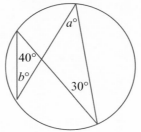

15.

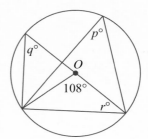

16.

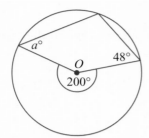

17.

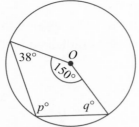

18.

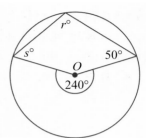

19.

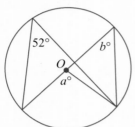

20.

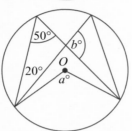

21.

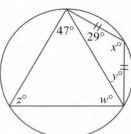

22.

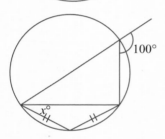

23.

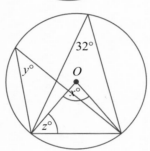

24.

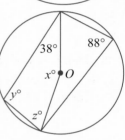

25.

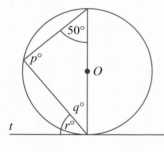

26.

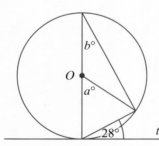

27.

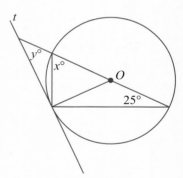

28.

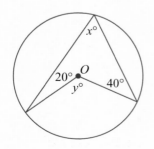

29.

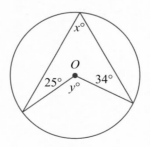

30.

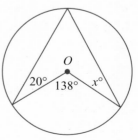

31. In the diagram, O is the centre of the circle.
    PT is a tangent, $|PQ| = |RQ|$ and
    $|\angle SPT| = 38°$.
    Calculate $|\angle QRS|$.

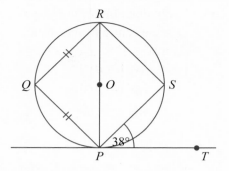

32. In a circle, centre O, OA is parallel to BC.
    If $|\angle ABC| = 23°$, find:
      (i) $|\angle AOC|$
      (ii) $|\angle OXB|$
      (iii) $|\angle OCA|$

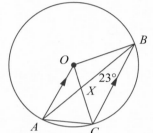

33. In the diagram, $|\angle XCB| = 54°$ and
    O is the centre of the circle.
    Calculate $|\angle BOD|$, where $\angle BOD$ is obtuse.

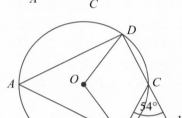

34. The centre of the circle is O.
    If $|\angle AOB| = 130°$ and $|\angle CAO| = 15°$,
    calculate $|\angle OBC|$.

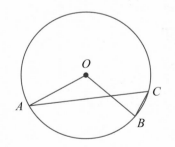

35. In the diagram, O is the centre of the circle.
    AB is a tangent and $|\angle BRQ| = 28°$.
    Calculate:
      (i) $|\angle SOQ|$, where $\angle SOQ$ is obtuse
      (ii) $|\angle SOQ|$, where $\angle SOQ$ is reflex
      (iii) $|\angle SRQ|$
      (iv) $|\angle SRA|$

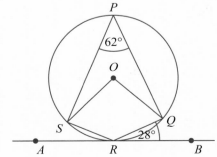

36. In the diagram, *PQRS* is a cyclic quadrilateral.
O is the centre of the circle.
$|\angle QOS| = 120°$ and $|\angle OSR| = 74°$.
Find: **(i)** $|\angle QPS|$
      (ii) $|\angle SRQ|$
      (iii) $|\angle RQO|$

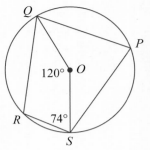

37. *R* is a point on a circle, centre *C*. $|\angle CPQ| = 40°$.
Calculate:
    (i) $|\angle PCQ|$
    (ii) $|\angle PRQ|$
    (iii) If $|\angle PCR| = 200°$, calculate $|\angle PRC|$.

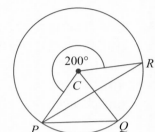

38. *AB* and *AC* are tangents to the
circle at *B* and *C*, respectively.
The centre of the circle is *O* and
D is a point on the circle.
If $|\angle BAC| = 30°$, find $|\angle BDC|$.

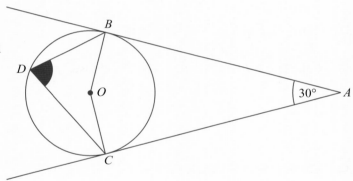

Proofs and the circle theorems

If a question says 'prove', 'verify' or 'show', then statements, but not necessarily deductions, made must be justified with a comment. Consider the next example.

EXAMPLE 1

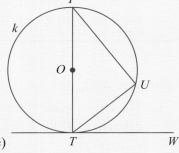

P, T and U are points on a circle k, centre O.

WT is the tangent at T.

$[PT]$ is a diameter.

Prove that $|\angle WTU| = |\angle TPU|$.

Solution:

Label angles 1, 2, 3 and 4.

$$|\angle 4| = 90°$$ (angle in a semicircle)

$\therefore \quad |\angle 1| + |\angle 2| = 90°$ (remaining angles in $\triangle PUT$)

$$|\angle 3| + |\angle 2| = 90°$$ (as WT is a tangent at T)

$\therefore \quad |\angle 3| + |\angle 2| = |\angle 1| + |\angle 2|$ (subtract $|\angle 2|$ from both sides)

$\therefore \qquad |\angle 3| = |\angle 1|$

i.e. $\quad |\angle WTU| = |\angle TPU|$

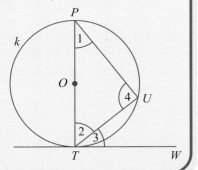

EXAMPLE 2

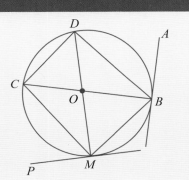

$[DM]$ and $[CB]$ are diameters of a circle, centre O.

AB and PM are tangents at B and M, respectively.

Show that $|\angle PMC| = |\angle ABD|$.

Solution:
Label angles 1, 2, 3 and 4.

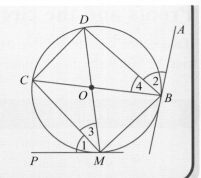

$$|\angle 1| + |\angle 3| = 90°$$ (as PM is a tangent at M)

and $|\angle 2| + |\angle 4| = 90°$ (as AB is a tangent at B)

$$\therefore \quad |\angle 1| + |\angle 3| = |\angle 2| + |\angle 4|$$

but $\quad |\angle 3| = |\angle 4|$ (both standing on arc CD)

$$\therefore \quad |\angle 1| = |\angle 2|$$

i.e. $\quad |\angle PMC| = |\angle ABD|$

Exercise 25.2

1. The circles h and k have diameters $[AB]$ and $[AC]$, respectively.
   Prove that EB is parallel to DC.

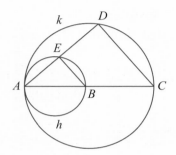

2. P, Q, R and S are points on a circle.
   If $PQ \parallel SR$, prove that $|\angle PSR| = |\angle QRS|$.

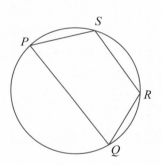

3. P, Q, R and S are four points on a circle.
   If $|\angle PSQ| = |\angle RSQ|$ and $|\angle PQS| = |\angle RQS|$,
   prove that $[SQ]$ is a diameter of the circle.

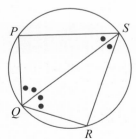

4. *ABCD* is a cyclic quadrilateral.
   O is the centre of the circle.
   AD is produced to *E*.
   Prove that $|\angle ABC| = |\angle CDE|$.

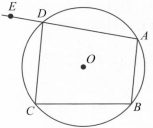

5. *ABCD* is a parallelogram and
   A, *B*, *Y*, *D* are points on the circle.
   Show that $|DY| = |DC|$.

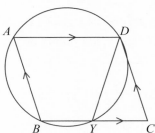

6. In the diagram, *PT* and *PS* are tangents
   to a circle of centre *O* at *T* and *S*, respectively.
   Prove:
   (i) $\triangle PSO \equiv \triangle PTO$
   (ii) $|\angle TPR| = 2\,|\angle TOP|$

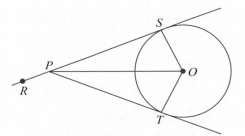

7. In the diagram, *KP* and *KQ* are tangents
   to a circle of centre *O*
   at *P* and *Q*, respectively.
   If $|\angle QKP| = 50°$,
   prove that $|\angle QKP| = 2|\angle RPS|$.

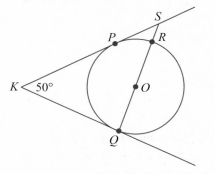

8. *ABCD* is a cyclic quadrilateral.
   $|\angle DAB| = 80°$ and $|\angle ACB| = 50°$.

   Prove that $|AD| = |AB|$.

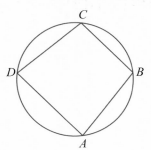

9. [AB] and [PQ] are two diameters of a circle, as in the diagram.

Prove: (i) $|\angle QAB| = |\angle QPB|$
(ii) $AQ \parallel PB$

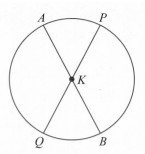

10. The diagram shows a circle, centre O. A, B, C, D and E are points on the circle such that $|\angle AOE| = 2|\angle EOD|$.

Prove that $|\angle ACD| = 3|\angle EBD|$.

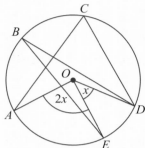

11. K is the centre of the given circle. $KP \perp BC$ and $|AB| = |AP|$.

Prove: (i) $|\angle PAB| = |\angle PAC|$
(ii) $|\angle ABC| = 22\frac{1}{2}^{\circ}$

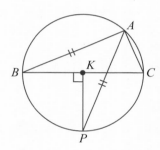

Similar triangles

Two triangles are similar if they have the same shape. One triangle can be obtained from the other by either an enlargement or a reduction (the reduction is also called an enlargement). The symbol for similarity is ||| or ~. If $\triangle ABC$ is similar to $\triangle XYZ$ then we write $\triangle ABC \,|||\, \triangle XYZ$.

Four tests for similarity of triangles

1. **If the lengths of matching sides are in proportion (same ratio), then the triangles are similar.**

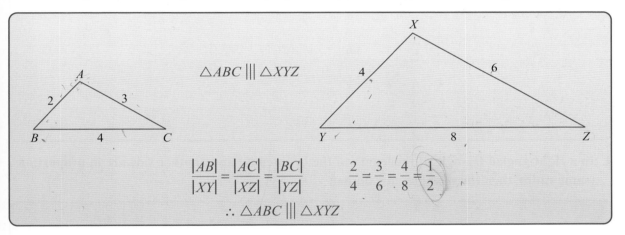

$$\triangle ABC \,|||\, \triangle XYZ$$

$$\frac{|AB|}{|XY|} = \frac{|AC|}{|XZ|} = \frac{|BC|}{|YZ|} \qquad \frac{2}{4} = \frac{3}{6} = \frac{4}{8} = \frac{1}{2}$$

$$\therefore \triangle ABC \,|||\, \triangle XYZ$$

2. **If two pairs of matching angles are equal, then the triangles are similar.**

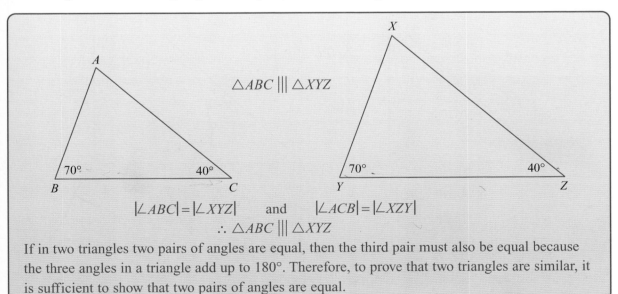

$$\triangle ABC \,|||\, \triangle XYZ$$

$$|\angle ABC| = |\angle XYZ| \qquad \text{and} \qquad |\angle ACB| = |\angle XZY|$$

$$\therefore \triangle ABC \,|||\, \triangle XYZ$$

If in two triangles two pairs of angles are equal, then the third pair must also be equal because the three angles in a triangle add up to 180°. Therefore, to prove that two triangles are similar, it is sufficient to show that two pairs of angles are equal.

3. **If the lengths of two sides are in proportion (same ratio) and the included angles are equal, then the triangles are similar.**

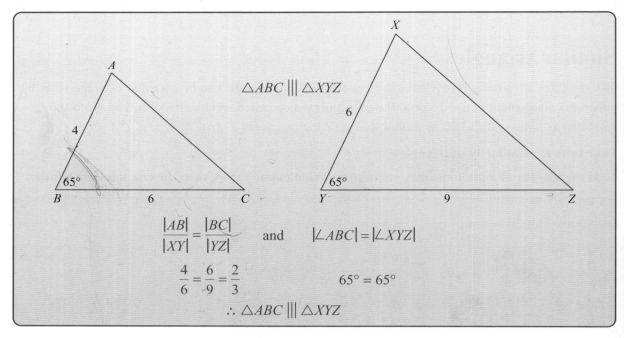

$\triangle ABC \,|||\, \triangle XYZ$

$$\frac{|AB|}{|XY|} = \frac{|BC|}{|YZ|} \quad \text{and} \quad |\angle ABC| = |\angle XYZ|$$

$$\frac{4}{6} = \frac{6}{9} = \frac{2}{3} \qquad\qquad 65° = 65°$$

$$\therefore \triangle ABC \,|||\, \triangle XYZ$$

4. **In a right-angled triangle, if the length of the hypotenuse and another side are in proportion (same ratio), then the triangles are similar.**

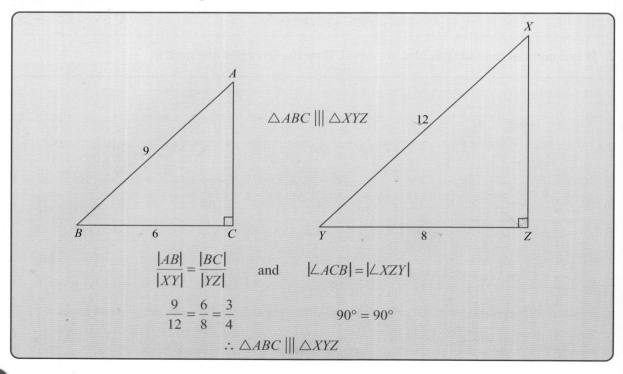

$\triangle ABC \,|||\, \triangle XYZ$

$$\frac{|AB|}{|XY|} = \frac{|BC|}{|YZ|} \quad \text{and} \quad |\angle ACB| = |\angle XZY|$$

$$\frac{9}{12} = \frac{6}{8} = \frac{3}{4} \qquad\qquad 90° = 90°$$

$$\therefore \triangle ABC \,|||\, \triangle XYZ$$

To prove that two triangles are similar, you only need to show one of the conditions for similarity. By convention, the abbreviations SSS, SAS, ASA and RHS are not used when tackling problems on similar triangles.

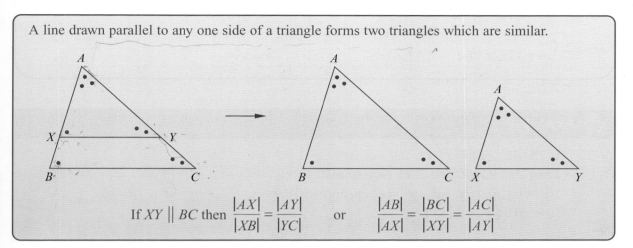

A line drawn parallel to any one side of a triangle forms two triangles which are similar.

$$\text{If } XY \parallel BC \text{ then } \frac{|AX|}{|XB|} = \frac{|AY|}{|YC|} \quad \text{or} \quad \frac{|AB|}{|AX|} = \frac{|BC|}{|XY|} = \frac{|AC|}{|AY|}$$

Note: It helps in solving problems on similar triangles if the two triangles are redrawn so that the corresponding sides, or angles, match each other. It is good practice to put the unknown length on the top of the first fraction.

EXAMPLE 1

Find the value of p and q, given the equal angles as shown.

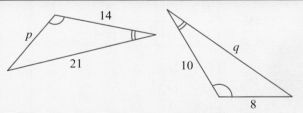

Solution:
As two pairs of angles are equal, the triangles are similar. Redraw both triangles so that corresponding angles match each other. Corresponding sides:

Large triangle	Small triangle
14	10
p	8
21	q

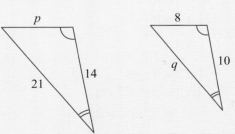

463

$$\frac{p}{8} = \frac{14}{10}$$

$$10p = 112$$

$$p = \frac{112}{10}$$

$$p = 11\tfrac{1}{5} \text{ or } 11\cdot2$$

$$\frac{q}{21} = \frac{10}{14}$$

$$14q = 210$$

$$q = \frac{210}{14}$$

$$q = 15$$

EXAMPLE 2

In $\triangle ABC$, $XY \parallel BC$.
Prove that $\triangle ABC$ and $\triangle AXY$ are similar.
If $|AX| = |BC| = 6$ cm, $|AY| = 5\tfrac{1}{2}$ cm and $|AB| = 9$ cm,
find **(i)** $|YC|$ **(ii)** $|XY|$.

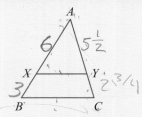

Solution:

Redraw $\triangle ABC$ and $\triangle AXY$ separately. Label angles 1, 2, 3 and 4 and put in known lengths.
As $XY \parallel BC$, $|\angle 1| = |\angle 2|$ and $|\angle 3| = |\angle 4|$ (corresponding angles).
$\therefore \triangle ABC$ and $\triangle AXY$ are similar.

Large triangle	Small triangle
9	6
$|AC|$	$5\tfrac{1}{2}$
6	$|xy|$

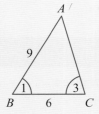 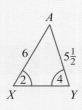

(i)
$$\frac{|AC|}{|AY|} = \frac{|AB|}{|AX|}$$

$$\frac{|AC|}{5\tfrac{1}{2}} = \frac{9}{6}$$

$$6|AC| = 49\cdot5$$

$$12|AC| = 99$$

$$|AC| = \frac{99}{12}$$

$$|AC| = 8\tfrac{1}{4} \text{ cm}$$

$$|YC| = |AC| - |AY|$$

$$= 8\tfrac{1}{4} - 5\tfrac{1}{2} = 2\tfrac{3}{4} \text{ cm}$$

(ii)
$$\frac{|XY|}{|BC|} = \frac{|AX|}{|AB|}$$

$$\frac{|XY|}{6} = \frac{6}{9}$$

$$9|XY| = 36$$

$$|XY| = 4 \text{ cm}$$

Exercise 26.1

1. In the diagram, $XY \parallel BC$.

    Prove that $\triangle ABC$ and $\triangle AXY$ are similar.

    Write down the following ratios in their simplest form:

    (i) $\dfrac{|AB|}{|AX|}$ (ii) $\dfrac{|XY|}{|BC|}$ (iii) $\dfrac{|YC|}{|AC|}$

    Verify: (iv) $\dfrac{|AB|}{|AX|} = \dfrac{|AC|}{|AY|} = \dfrac{|BC|}{|XY|}$

    (v) $\dfrac{|XY|^2}{|BC|^2} = \dfrac{|AY|^2}{|AC|^2}$

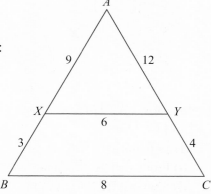

In questions 2–9 the triangles are similar, with equal angles marked. In each case, calculate the lengths p and q.

2.
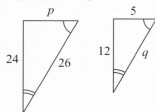

3.
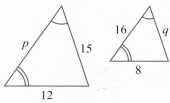

4.
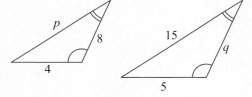

5.
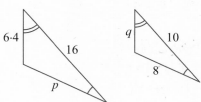

Note: It may help to redraw the triangles so that the positions of corresponding angles or sides match each other.

6.
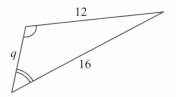

7.
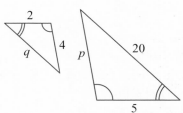

8.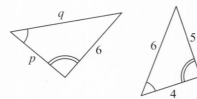

9.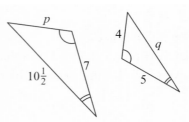

10. In $\triangle ABC$, $XY \parallel BC$.
$|AX| = 4$, $|XB| = 2$,
$|AY| = 6$ and $|BC| = 12$.
   (i) Prove that $\triangle ABC$ and $\triangle AXY$ are similar.
   (ii) Find **(a)** $|YC|$ **(b)** $|XY|$.

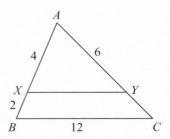

11. In $\triangle PQR$, $AB \parallel QR$.
$|PA| = 3$, $|PB| = 4$,
$|AB| = 6$ and $|QR| = 15$.
   Find: **(i)** $|PQ|$ **(ii)** $|AQ|$
            (iii) $|PR|$ **(iv)** $|BR|$

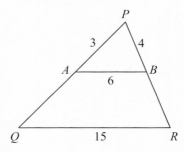

12. In $\triangle PQR$, $XY \parallel QR$.
$|PX| = 4$, $|PY| = 5$,
$|YQ| = 1{\cdot}25$ and $|QR| = 4{\cdot}5$.
   Calculate: **(i)** $|XR|$
             (ii) $|XY|$

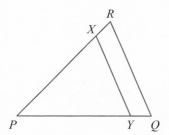

13. In $\triangle XYZ$, $AB \parallel XY$.
   (i) Explain why $\triangle XYZ$ and $\triangle ABZ$ are similar.
$|XZ| = 48$, $|YZ| = 36$,
$|BZ| = \frac{1}{3}|YZ|$ and $|XY| = 21$.
   (ii) Calculate: **(a)** $|AX|$ **(b)** $|AB|$

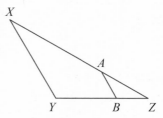

14. In $\triangle ABC$, $PQ \| AB$.
    If $|CP| = 4$, $|PA| = 2$ and
    $|CB| = 9$, find $|CQ|$.

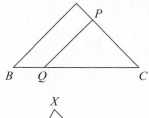

15. In $\triangle XYZ$, $AB \| YZ$.
    $|XA| = 12$, $|AB| = 9$
    and $|AY| = \frac{2}{3}|XA|$.

    Calculate $|YZ|$.

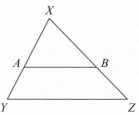

16. In $\triangle RST$, XY is parallel to ST.
    If $|XS| = 2$, $|YT| = 3$ and $|RS| = 10$,
    find $|RT|$.

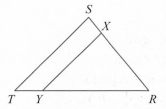

17. In $\triangle PQR$, $XY \| QR$ and $XT \| PR$.
    $|XT| = |TQ| = 5$ cm and $|XY| = 11$ cm.
    Find $|PR|$.

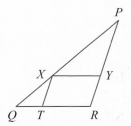

18. In the diagram, $PQ \| RS$.
    $|PQ| = 10$ cm, $|RS| = 8$ cm
    and $|ST| = 6$ cm.
    (i) Prove that $\triangle PQT$ and $\triangle SRT$ are similar.
    (ii) Which side in $\triangle SRT$ corresponds to $[PT]$?
    (iii) Calculate $|PT|$.

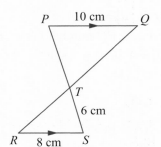

19. $ABCD$ is a parallelogram.
    AC intersects BX at Y, as shown.
    (i) Explain why $\triangle AXY$ and $\triangle CBY$ are similar.
    (ii) If $|AD| = 9$ cm, $|AY| = 4$ cm
        and $|YC| = 6$ cm, calculate $|AX|$.

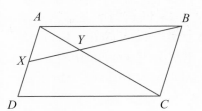

467

20. *PQRS* is a parallelogram.
$|PM| : |MS| = 4:3$.
(i) Prove that $\triangle PQM$ and $\triangle SNM$ are similar.
(ii) If $|PQ| = 24$ and $|MN| = 30$,
calculate (a) $|NS|$ (b) $|QM|$.

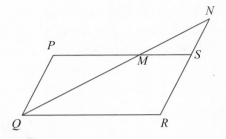

21. *ABC* is a right-angled triangle.
DEFB is a square of area 36 cm² and
the area of triangle *EFC* is also 36 cm².
Calculate:
(i) $|DE|$
(ii) $|FC|$
(iii) $|AD|$
(iv) Area of triangle *ADE*
(v) Area of triangle *ABC*

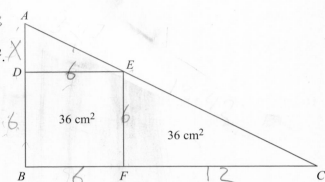

22. In the diagram, $|\angle PQR| = |\angle PST|$.
$|PQ| = 6, |QR| = 9$,
$|PS| = 8$ and $|PT| = 12$.
(i) Prove that $\triangle PQR$ and $\triangle PST$ are similar.
(ii) Calculate (a) $|ST|$ (b) $|PR|$.

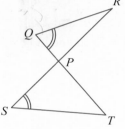

23. In $\triangle PQR$, *MN* is drawn
such that $|\angle PQR| = |\angle MNP|$.
(i) Prove that $\triangle PQR$ and $\triangle PNM$ are similar.
(ii) If $|PM| = 4, |PN| = 5$ and $|MQ| = 11$,
calculate $|NR|$.

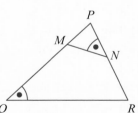

24. In $\triangle PQR$, *ST* is drawn
such that $|\angle PST| = |\angle QRP|$.
(i) Prove that $\triangle PTS$ and $\triangle PQR$ are similar.
(ii) $|PS| = 6$ cm, $|SQ| = 4$ cm,
$|QR| = 12$ cm and $|PR| = 8$ cm.
Calculate (a) $|ST|$ (b) $|TR|$.

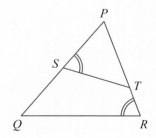

25. In △PQR, S is a point on [QR] such that |∠PQR| = |∠SPR|.
|PR| = 8 cm, |SR| = 4 cm and |PS| = 6 cm.
   (i) Show that △PQR and △SPR are similar.
   (ii) Verify that △PQS is isosceles.

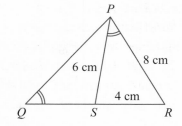

Using similar triangles to solve real-life problems

Similar triangles can be used to solve practical or real-life problems.

EXAMPLE

Helen wants to measure the height of a building. From the bottom of the building, she walks 25 m and places a pole in the ground 2 m vertically from the ground. She then walks another 5 m. She notices that from this point on the ground, the top of the building and the top of the pole are in line. Calculate the height of the building.

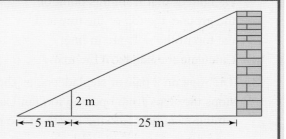

Solution:

Let the height of the building be h m and represent the situation with two similar triangles.

$$\frac{h}{2} = \frac{30}{5}$$

$$h = \frac{30 \times 2}{5} \qquad \text{(multiply both sides by 2)}$$

$$h = \frac{60}{5}$$

$$h = 12 \text{ m}$$

Thus, the height of the building is 12 m.

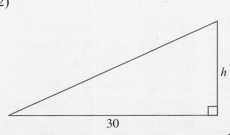

Exercise 26.2

1. A girl wants to measure the height of a building. From the bottom of the building, she walks 20 m and places a pole in the ground 3 m vertically from the ground. She then walks another 5 m. She notices that from this point on the ground, the top of the building and the top of the pole are in line. Calculate the height of the building.

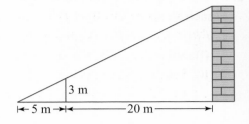

2. Jack wants to measure the height of a tree. From the bottom of the tree, he walks 15 m and places a pole in the ground 1·5 m vertically from the ground. He then walks another 3 m. He notices that from this point on the ground, the top of the tree and the top of the pole are in line. Calculate the height of the tree.

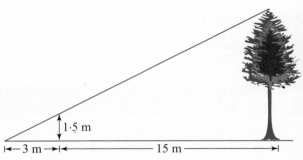

3. The rope on a pair of stepladders, as shown, stops the steps from opening too far. Using similar triangles, find the length of the rope.

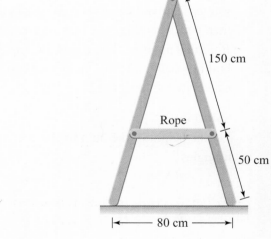

4. An escalator in a shopping centre is 48 m in length. When a man has travelled one-third the length of the escalator, he is 6 m vertically above the horizontal ground. Find the vertical height at the top of the escalator.

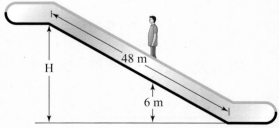

5. James estimated the width, *w* m, of a river by taking measurements as shown and then using similar triangles.

   (i) Find *w*.

   (ii) Explain why *w* is only an estimate.

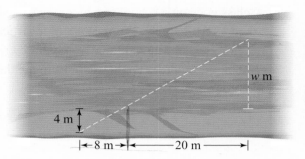

6. A 40 m swimming pool is being filled. Find the length, *L* m, of the surface of the water when the pool has been filled to a depth of 3 m.

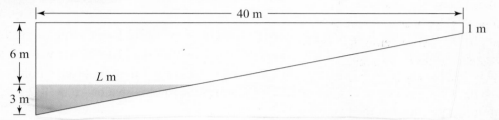

7. Find the value of the height, *h* m, in the following diagram at which the tennis ball must be hit so that it will just pass over the net and land 6 metres away from the base of the net.

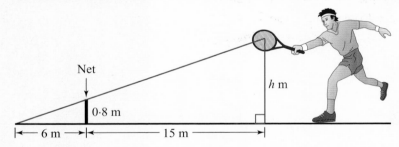

8. Ben looks in a mirror and sees the top of a building. His eyes are 1·2 m above ground level, as shown in the diagram.

   (i) If Ben is 1·5 m from the mirror and 181·5 m from the base of the building, how high is the building?

   (ii) In your opinion, which of the measurements was the most difficult to obtain? Explain your answer.

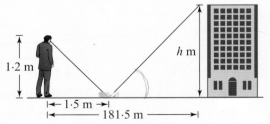

9. A class goes on a school trip to a monastic site. They are asked to estimate the height, *h* m, of a vertical round tower on level ground. Describe in your own words a method the students could use to estimate the height of the tower.

10. In Chapter 16 we met Jeff, who measured the height of the Eiffel Tower using trigonometry. Jeff later realised that he could have measured the height of the Eiffel Tower without the use of trigonometry. Jeff is 1·65 m tall and casts a shadow 0·7 m long. From a point directly under the centre of the tower, Jeff measures the tower's shadow to be 137·2 m. He carefully sketched out the two triangles:

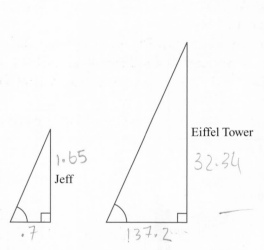

Eiffel Tower

32·34

   (i) What did he notice about the triangles?
  (ii) How many times longer is the tower's shadow compared to Jeff's?
 (iii) How did he now deduce the tower's height?
  (iv) What did Jeff find the height of the Eiffel Tower to be using this method?
   (v) Which method produced the more accurate result? Explain your reasoning.

11. A group of students was trying to find the distance between two trees on opposite sides of a river using pegs, a measuring tape and a large amount of string. They align the pegs in a particular way, take several measurements, and sketch this diagram. On the diagram, A and B are the trees and C, D and E are the pegs.

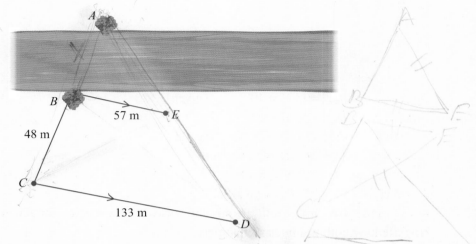

(i) In what way must the pegs and the trees be aligned if the students are to use these measurements to calculate $|AB|$?

(ii) Calculate the distance between the trees.

(iii) Another group of students repeats the activity. They have a similar diagram but different measurements. Their measurements are $|BE| = 40$ m and $|BC| = 9$ m. Based on the value of $|AB|$ that the first group got, what measurement will this second group have for $|CD|$?

(iv) Suggest how the group of students might have ensured that $[BE]$ was parallel to $[CD]$.

Proofs and similar triangles

$|\angle ABC| = |\angle RST| = 40°$.
$|\angle BCA| + |\angle STR| = 140°$.
(i) Show that $|\angle BAC| = |\angle STR|$.
(ii) Hence or otherwise, show that
$$\frac{|AB|}{|TS|} = \frac{|BC|}{|SR|}.$$

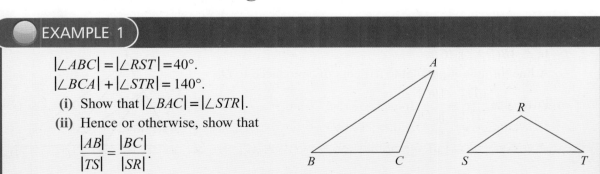

Solution:

(i) Label angles 1, 2, 3, 4, 5 and 6.

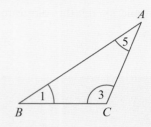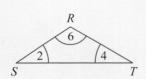

$$|\angle 1| = |\angle 2| = 40° \qquad \text{(given)}$$
$$\therefore \quad |\angle 3| + |\angle 5| = 140°$$
$$\text{but} \quad |\angle 3| + |\angle 4| = 140° \qquad \text{(given)}$$
$$\therefore \quad |\angle 3| + |\angle 5| = |\angle 3| + |\angle 4|$$
$$\therefore \quad |\angle 5| = |\angle 4|$$
$$\text{i.e.} \quad |\angle BAC| = |\angle STR|$$

$\therefore \triangle ABC$ and $\triangle RST$ are similar as two pairs of angles are equal.

(ii) Redraw both triangles so that corresponding angles or sides match each other.

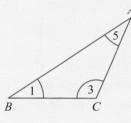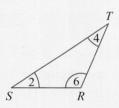

$$\therefore \quad \frac{|AB|}{|TS|} = \frac{|BC|}{|SR|}$$

EXAMPLE 2

In $\triangle ABC$, $XY \parallel AC$.

A line through A parallel to XC cuts BC, produced to D.

Prove that $\dfrac{|BY|}{|YC|} = \dfrac{|BC|}{|CD|}$.

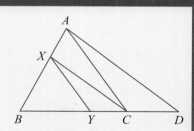

Solution:

Redraw so that corresponding parallel lines match each other.

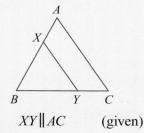

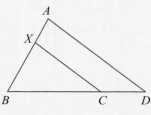

$$XY \| AC \quad \text{(given)} \qquad\qquad XC \| AD \quad \text{(given)}$$

$$\therefore \frac{|BX|}{|XA|} = \frac{|BY|}{|YC|} \qquad\qquad\qquad \therefore \frac{|BX|}{|XA|} = \frac{|BC|}{|CD|}$$

$$\therefore \frac{|BY|}{|YC|} = \frac{|BC|}{|CD|} \quad \left(\text{as both are equal to } \frac{|BX|}{|XA|}\right)$$

EXAMPLE 3

In the diagram, $|\angle YXZ| = 90°$ and $XW \perp YZ$.
Prove that $\triangle WYX$ and $\triangle WXZ$ are similar.
Deduce that $|XW|^2 = |YW| \times |ZW|$.

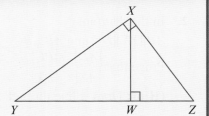

Solution:
Label angles 1, 2, 3, 4 and 5.

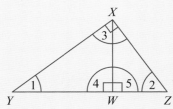

Redraw the three right-angled triangles separately so that corresponding angles or sides match each other.

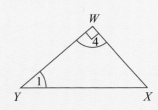
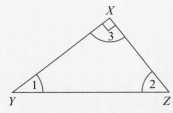
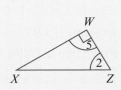

In $\triangle WYX$ and $\triangle XYZ$

$|\angle 1| = |\angle 1|$	(same angle)
$|\angle 4| = |\angle 3| = 90°$	(given)

$\therefore \triangle WYX$ and $\triangle XYZ$ are similar.

In $\triangle XYZ$ and $\triangle WXZ$

$|\angle 2| = |\angle 2|$	(same angle)
$|\angle 3| = |\angle 5| = 90°$	(given)

$\therefore \triangle XYZ$ and $\triangle WXZ$ are similar.

(i.e. all three triangles are similar)

$\therefore \triangle WYX$ and $\triangle WXZ$ are similar.

$$\therefore \frac{|XW|}{|ZW|} = \frac{|YW|}{|XW|} \qquad \text{(cross-multiply)}$$

$$\therefore |XW|^2 = |YW| \times |ZW|$$

Exercise 26.3

1. In $\triangle PQR$, MN is drawn
such that $|\angle PQR| = |\angle PNM|$.
   (i) Prove that $\triangle PQR$ and $\triangle PNM$ are similar.
   (ii) Prove that $\dfrac{|PQ|}{|PN|} = \dfrac{|PR|}{|PM|}$.

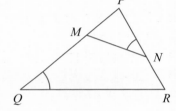

2. In the diagram,
$AB \parallel YX \parallel DC$ and $AB \perp BC$.
Prove that $\dfrac{|AD|}{|AY|} = \dfrac{|BC|}{|BX|}$.
   (**Hint:** Draw a line through A parallel to BC.)

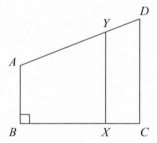

3. In $\triangle PQR$,
$BC \parallel QR$ and $AC \parallel BR$.
Prove that $\dfrac{|PB|}{|BQ|} = \dfrac{|PA|}{|AB|}$.

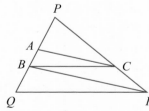

4. $|\angle PQR| = 50° = |\angle ABC|$ and
$|\angle QRP| + |\angle BAC| = 130°$.
   (i) Evaluate $|\angle QPR| + |\angle QRP|$.
   (ii) Prove that $|\angle QPR| = |\angle BAC|$.
   (iii) Hence or otherwise, show that $\dfrac{|PQ|}{|AB|} = \dfrac{|QR|}{|BC|}$.

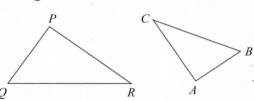

5. In $\triangle ABC$, $XY \| BC$ as shown,
   with $|\angle AYX| = |\angle XYB|$.
   (i) Prove that $|YC| = |YB|$.
   (ii) Hence, prove that $\dfrac{|AX|}{|AY|} = \dfrac{|BX|}{|BY|}$.

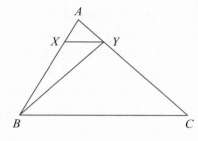

6. $ABCD$ is a rectangle.
   XY and RS intersect at Z, a point on AC.
   $XY \| BC$ and $RS \| DC$.
   (i) Prove that $|AX|:|XB| = |AR|:|RD|$.
   (ii) Prove that the rectangles $XBSZ$ and $RZYD$
   are equal in area.

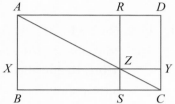

7. $ABDC$ is a rectangle. The lines BC and AC are
   produced to E and F, respectively,
   where $|\angle CEF| = 90°$.
   (i) Prove that $|AB|:|EF| = |BC|:|CE|$.
   (ii) DF intersects CE at the point G.
   $|DC| = 8$, $|CG| = 4$ and $|GE| = 1$.
   Find $|EF|$ and hence find $|BC|$.

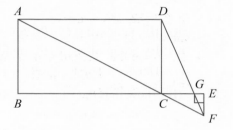

8. $ABCD$ is a parallelogram.
   (i) Prove that the triangles ADX and ABE
   are equiangular.
   (ii) If $|DX| = \frac{3}{4}|DC|$, show that $|BC| = \frac{3}{4}|BE|$.

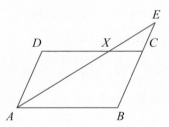

9. $\triangle PQR$ and $\triangle XYZ$ are similar.
   The perpendicular heights are 12 cm and
   9 cm, respectively.
   (i) If the area of $\triangle XYZ$ is $67\frac{1}{2}$ cm^2,
   prove that the area of $\triangle PQR$ is 120 cm^2.
   (ii) Hence or otherwise, verify that $\dfrac{\text{Area of } \triangle PQR}{\text{Area of } \triangle XYZ} = \dfrac{|PS|^2}{|XW|^2}$.

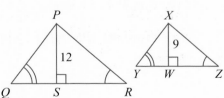

10. (i) $[PQ]$ is the diameter of circle $k1$.
   $[PS]$ is the diameter of circle $k2$.
   Explain why $|\angle PRQ| = |\angle PQS|$.
   (ii) Show that $\triangle PQR$ and $\triangle PSQ$ are similar.
   Redraw $\triangle PQR$ and $\triangle PSQ$ so that corresponding angles or sides match each other.
   (iii) Prove that $|PQ|^2 = |PR| \times |PS|$.

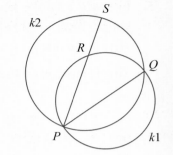

11. In $\triangle ABC$, $BA \perp AC$ and $AD \perp BC$.
   (i) Prove that $\triangle ABC$, $\triangle DBA$ and $\triangle DAC$ are similar.
   (**Hint:** Redraw the three triangles so that corresponding angles or sides match each other.)

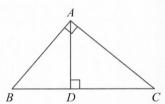

   (ii) By comparing $\triangle ABC$ and $\triangle DBA$, prove that $|AB|^2 = |BC| \times |BD|$.
   (iii) By comparing $\triangle ABC$ and $\triangle DAC$, prove that $|AC|^2 = |BC| \times |DC|$.
   (iv) Hence, prove that $|AB|^2 + |AC|^2 = |BC|^2$.

12. (i) Show that the triangles PBR and PAQ are equiangular (similar).
   (ii) Deduce that $|PA| \times |PB| = |PQ| \times |PR|$.

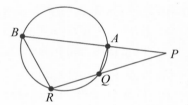

13. Two chords, PQ and RS, of a circle meet at T, such that $|\angle SRP| = |\angle QRT|$.
   Triangles SRP and QRT are equiangular.

   (i) Complete the ratio $\dfrac{|PR|}{|TR|} = \dfrac{|RT|}{|??|}$.

   (ii) Prove that $|PR| \times |RQ| = |RT|^2 + |PT| \times |TQ|$.

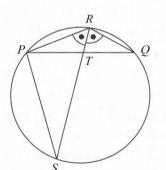

14. In the triangle ABC, $|\angle BAC| = 90°$ and $AD \perp BC$.
   (i) Using equiangular triangles or otherwise, prove that $|AB|^2 = |BD| \times |BC|$.
   (ii) Write down two ratios equal to $\dfrac{|AD|}{|BD|}$.
   (iii) If $|AC| = 2|AB|$ and $|AD| = 4$, find the value of $|AB|$.

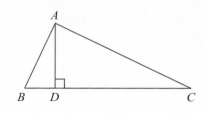

Pythagoras' theorem

The longest side of a right-angled triangle is always opposite the right angle
and is called the **hypotenuse**.

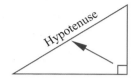

Pythagoras' theorem states that in a right-angled triangle:

The square on the hypotenuse is equal to the sum of the squares on
the other two sides.

$$(\text{hypotenuse})^2 = (\text{side 1})^2 + (\text{side 2})^2$$

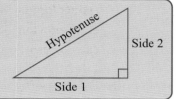

This equation can be written algebraically:

$$c^2 = a^2 + b^2$$

The converse (opposite) also applies:
If $c^2 = a^2 + b^2$, then the triangle must be right-angled.

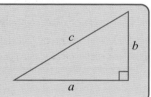

Note: Pythagoras' theorem applies only to right-angled triangles.

We can use Pythagoras' theorem to find the missing length of a side in a right-angled triangle if we
know the lengths of the other two sides.

Pythagoras' theorem can also be written:

$$|AB|^2 = |AC|^2 + |BC|^2$$

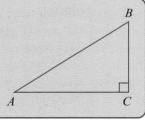

EXAMPLE 1

Find the value of x and y.

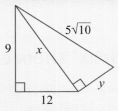

Solution:

Redraw both right-angled triangles separately and apply Pythagoras' theorem twice.

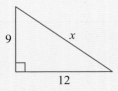

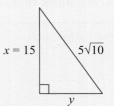

$$x^2 = 9^2 + 12^2$$
$$x^2 = 81 + 144$$
$$x^2 = 225$$
$$x = \sqrt{225}$$
$$x = 15$$

$$x^2 + y^2 = (5\sqrt{10})^2$$
$$15^2 + y^2 = (5\sqrt{10})^2$$
$$225 + y^2 = 250$$
$$y^2 = 25$$
$$y = \sqrt{25} = 5$$

EXAMPLE 2

Calculate the value of x.

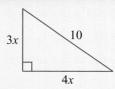

Solution:
$$(3x)^2 + (4x)^2 = (10)^2$$
$$9x^2 + 16x^2 = 100$$
$$25x^2 = 100$$
$$x^2 = 4$$
$$x = \sqrt{4} = 2$$

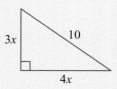

Note: $(\sqrt{a})^2 = a$. For example, $(\sqrt{20})^2 = 20$, $(\sqrt{35})^2 = 35$.

Exercise 27.1

1. Complete the table.

a	b	c	a^2	b^2	c^2
3	4				
	8	10			
8		17			
			144		169
			49	576	
		50		900	
	7		576		
				2·25	6·25

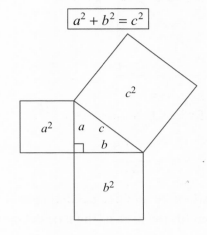

$$a^2 + b^2 = c^2$$

In questions 2–19, use Pythagoras' theorem to find the length of the sides indicated by a letter in each of the diagrams (answers in surd form when necessary).

2.
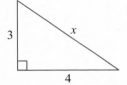

3.
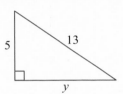

4.
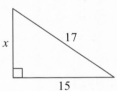

5.

6.
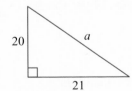

7.
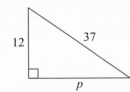

8.
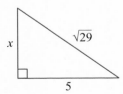

9.
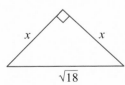

10.
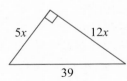

11.
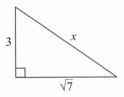

12.
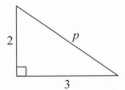

13.
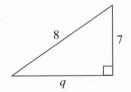

In questions 14–16, the diagrams represent squares.

14.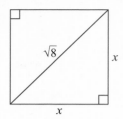

15.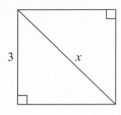

16.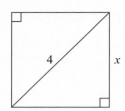

17.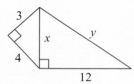

18.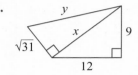

19.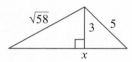

In questions 20 and 21, use Pythagoras' theorem (i) to find the perpendicular height, *h* cm, and then (ii) the area of the parallelogram.

20.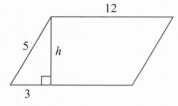

21.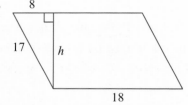

22. In $\triangle PQR$, $|\angle PQR| = 90°$.

    (i) Solve for *x*.

    (ii) Calculate the perimeter and area of the triangle.

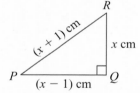

23. The centre of the circle is O, $|AB| = 6$ and $|BO| = 5$. Find $|BC|$.

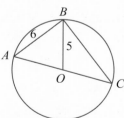

24. *PT* is a tangent to the circle at *T*.

    The centre of the circle is *O*.

    $|MO| = |NP|$.

    If $|PT| = 3$, find the radius of the circle.

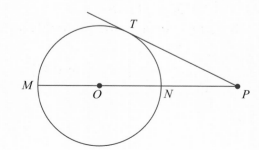

25. NT is a tangent to the circle at T.
    The centre of the circle is O.
    $|NT| = 12$ cm and $|MN| = 8$ cm.
    Find the radius of the circle.

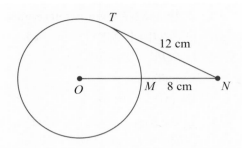

26. Find, in terms of π, the area of the circle inscribed in the
    square $PTWQ$, given that $|PR| = \sqrt{5}$ cm, $|QR| = 2$ cm and
    $|\angle QRP| = 90°$.

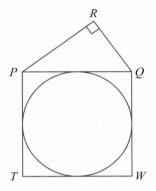

27. The lengths of the sides of a right-angled triangle are p, q and
    r, as shown.
    P, Q and R are semicircles with diameters of length p, q and r,
    respectively.
    (i) Express the area of P in terms of p and π.
    (ii) Prove that the area of P + area of Q = area of R.

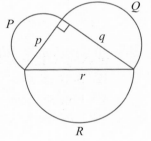

28. An equilateral triangle has sides of length 8 cm.
    The perpendicular height of the triangle is $a\sqrt{b}$ cm, where b is prime.
    Calculate: (i) The value of a and the value of b
                  (ii) The area of the triangle (leave your answer in surd form)

The following questions involve similar triangles.

29. ABC and LMN are right-angled triangles.
    $|\angle ACB| = |\angle LNM|$.
    $|AB| = 30$, $|BC| = 16$ and $|MN| = 8$.
    Calculate:
    (i) $|AC|$ (ii) $|LN|$ (iii) $|LM|$

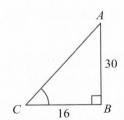

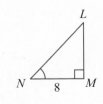

30. *PQR* and *STW* are two triangles.
$|\angle PRQ| = |\angle SWT| = 90°$ and
$|\angle PQR| = |\angle STW|$.
Calculate:
(i) $|SW|$ (ii) $|TS|$

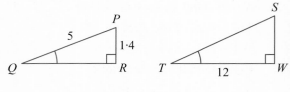

31. In the triangle *ABC*, $|\angle ABC| = 90°$,
$|AB| = 9$ cm and $|BC| = 12$ cm.
XY is parallel to *BC* and $|XY| = 8$ cm.
Calculate $|AY|$.

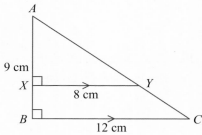

32. *ABC* is a right-angled triangle with $DE \parallel BC$.
$|AB| = 12$, $|BC| = 9$ and $|DE| = 3$.
Find $|AE|$.

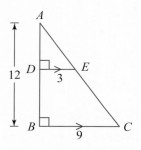

33. In the triangle *ABC*,
$$\frac{|AY|}{|YC|} = \frac{2}{3}.$$
$XY \parallel BC$ and $|\angle AYX| = 90°$.
Calculate the ratio $\dfrac{\text{Area } \triangle AXY}{\text{Area } \triangle ABC}$.

34. (i) In the triangle *PQR*, $PQ \perp QR$ and
$ST \parallel PQ$.
Calculate $|QT|$ if $|PQ| = 12$ cm,
$|ST| = 8$ cm and $|RT| = 6$ cm.
(ii) If $TW \perp PR$, calculate $|WR|$.

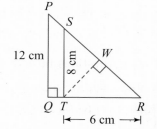

35. Three circles, *a*, *b* and *c*, have radii of 24 cm, 10 cm and
6 cm and centres *P*, *Q* and *R*, respectively. They also touch
each other externally, as shown. Show that $\triangle PQR$ is a
right-angled triangle.

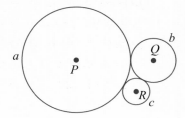

Using Pythagoras' theorem in real-world situations

Exercise 27.2

1. The diagram shows the side view of a ramp. Calculate the length, l, of the sloping part of the ramp.

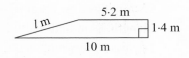

2. The top of a bucket has a diameter of 34 cm. The bottom of the bucket has a diameter of 20 cm. The sloping sides have a length of 25 cm. Calculate the depth, d, of the bucket.

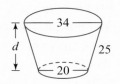

3. A vertical flagpole is held by four wires, as shown. Each wire is fixed to the pole at a height of 1·6 m above the ground and to the ground at 3 m from the foot of the pole.
   Calculate the total length of the wire used.

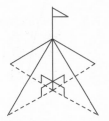

4. When selling a television a shop describes the size of the television by giving the measure of its diagonal. The diagram shows a television which has a height of 60 cm and a width of 91 cm.
   Calculate the size of this television.

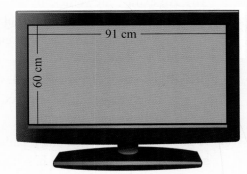

5. (i) The diagram shows a ladder, 6·5 m in length, leaning against a vertical wall. The foot of the ladder is on horizontal ground, 3·3 m from the wall.
   Calculate how far up the wall the ladder reaches.
   (ii) If the ladder must reach 6·3 m up the wall, how far should its base be from the foot of the wall?

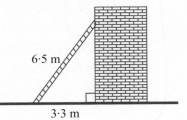

6. John needs to lay a piece of wood to act as a wheelchair ramp on a step. The height of the step is 50 cm and the ramp must be placed at a slope of $\frac{1}{3}$.
   Find the length of wood, to the nearest cm, needed to make this ramp.

7. Health and safety regulations state that a wheelchair ramp must be at a maximum slope of $\frac{1}{12}$. What is the minimum length of wood required to make a ramp that will go up a step 25 cm high?

8. Maria has a rectangular-shaped garden of length 48 m and width 28 m. There is an outdoor tap which is 3 m from one wall (as in the diagram).

    Maria needs to buy a hose that will reach to all corners of the garden.

    Would a 50 m or a 60 m hose suit her best?

    Give a reason for your answer.

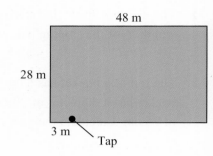

9. The diagram shows the cross-section of a road tunnel. The tunnel is part of a circle of radius 5 m. The width of the tunnel at road level is 9·6 m.

    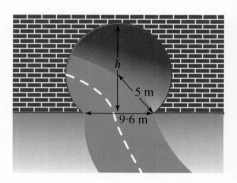

    (i) Calculate its height, h m.

    (ii) An extra-wide vehicle 6·8 m wide and 4·4 m high wants to enter the tunnel. Would this vehicle be able to enter the tunnel? Justify your answer.

    (iii) If this was a two-way tunnel, what precautions would be required for a wide vehicle to enter the tunnel?

10. A girl takes a shortcut along a path across a field from the gate to the bus stop.

    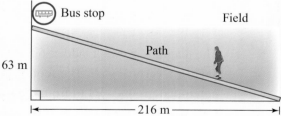

    (i) Calculate how much further she would have walked if she walked around the perimeter of the field.

    (ii) She can walk at 2 m/s on the perimeter of the field and 1·5 m/s across the field. Calculate the quickest route and the time saved.

11. In a boat race, the boats follow the triangular shape shown.

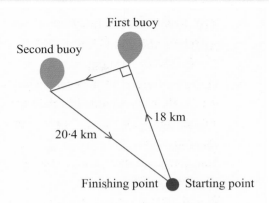

First buoy

Second buoy

18 km

20·4 km

Finishing point ● Starting point

   (i) Calculate:
      (a) The distance between the buoys
      (b) The length of the racecourse
   (ii) A boat can travel at an average speed of 8 m/s. How long will it take this boat to complete the race? Give your answer in:
      (a) Seconds (b) Minutes (c) Hours

12. Aisling and Brian are in the All-Ireland conkers competition in Freshford, Co. Kilkenny. Aisling's conker, C, is tied to the end of a string 34 cm in length. She pulls it back from its vertical position until it is 30 cm horizontal from its original position. Calculate h, the vertical distance that the conker has risen.

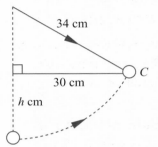

34 cm

30 cm C

h cm

13. $ABCD$ is a rectangular-shaped steel gate.
$AB \parallel PQ \parallel RS \parallel DC$ and
$|AP| = |PR| = |RD|$.
$|AB| = 2\cdot4$ m and $|BC| = 1\cdot8$.

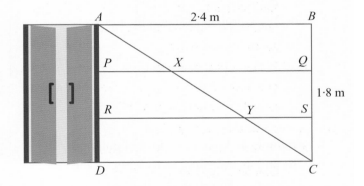

A 2·4 m B

P X Q

1·8 m

R Y S

D C

   (i) Calculate:
      (a) $|AP|$. Justify your answer.
      (b) $|XY|$. Give a reason for your answer.
   (ii) (a) $RAXZ$ is a parallelogram. Indicate the point Z on the diagram.
      (b) Calculate the area of the parallelogram $RAXZ$.

14. Mary is thinking of buying a new television. The television is advertised as having a 40-inch screen. This refers to the diagonal measurement of the screen. The *aspect ratio* of a television screen is the ratio of its width to its height. For this television, the aspect ratio is 16:9 (16 units wide for every nine units in height).

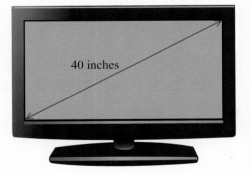

40 inches

    (i) Convert 40 inches to centimetres if 1 inch = 2·54 cm.

   (ii) Find the width and the height of the screen, in centimetres. Give your answers correct to the nearest cm.

  (iii) A different 40-inch television screen has an aspect ratio of 4:3. Which of the two television screens has the greatest area, and by how much?

15. A 4 m-wide crosswalk diagonally crosses a street, as shown. The curbs are 8 m apart. The crosswalk intersects the opposite curb with a 6 m displacement. Find the area of the crosswalk.

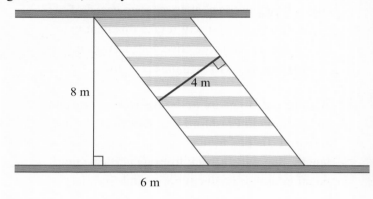

16. A team suspected that their pitch did not have 90° corners. Suggest a method that the team members could use to check the problem using only a metre stick.

17. A ship is 17 km due east of a lighthouse. The ship is travelling at 10 km/h, in the direction as shown in the diagram. After 1 hour 30 minutes it is as close to the lighthouse as possible.

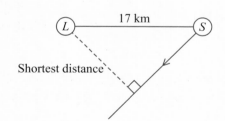

    (i) How far did the ship travel in the 1 hour 30 minutes?

   (ii) Calculate the shortest distance between the lighthouse and the ship.

  (iii) For how long, in minutes, is the ship within 10 km of the lighthouse?

18. At midday a ship is 31 km due north of a lighthouse. At 2 p.m. the ship is 31 km due east of the same lighthouse.

    (i) Draw a sketch of the motion of the ship.

    (ii) In what direction is the ship travelling?

    (iii) Find the distance travelled by the ship in the 2 hours, to the nearest km.

    (iv) Calculate the speed of the ship.

    (v) Find the point where the ship was closest to the lighthouse.

    (vi) At what time was the ship closest to the lighthouse?

    (vii) Find the shortest distance from the ship to the lighthouse.

Pythagoras' theorem and bisecting chords

You will recall that a line through the centre of a circle perpendicular to a chord bisects the chord.

Pythagoras' theorem can be used to solve problems involving lines through the centre of a circle which are perpendicular to a chord.

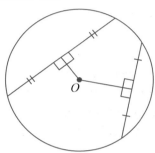

EXAMPLE

K is the centre of the circle.
If $|AB| = 9\cdot6$ cm and the distance from K to AB is $1\cdot4$ cm, calculate the length of the diameter of the circle.

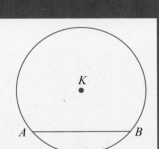

Solution:
Draw $KC \perp AB$. $\therefore |AC| = |CB|, |KC| = 1\cdot4$ cm,
$|AC| = \frac{1}{2}(9\cdot6) = 4\cdot8$ cm and $|AK| = $ radius.

Using Pythagoras' theorem:
$|AK|^2 = |AC|^2 + |CK|^2$
$|AK|^2 = (4\cdot8)^2 + (1\cdot4)^2$
$|AK|^2 = 23\cdot04 + 1\cdot96$
$|AK|^2 = 25$
  $|AK| = \sqrt{25} = 5$ cm
Diameter $= 2|AK| = 2(5) = 10$ cm.

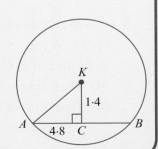

Exercise 27.3

1. K is the centre of the circle. If $|AB| = 30$ cm and the distance from K to AB is 8 cm, calculate the radius of the circle.

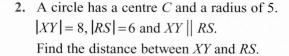

2. A circle has a centre C and a radius of 5.
$|XY| = 8$, $|RS| = 6$ and $XY \parallel RS$.
Find the distance between XY and RS.

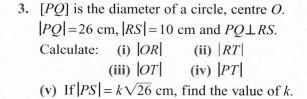

3. $[PQ]$ is the diameter of a circle, centre O.
$|PQ| = 26$ cm, $|RS| = 10$ cm and $PQ \perp RS$.
Calculate: **(i)** $|OR|$ **(ii)** $|RT|$
          (iii) $|OT|$ **(iv)** $|PT|$
(v) If $|PS| = k\sqrt{26}$ cm, find the value of k.

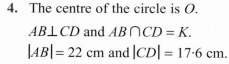

4. The centre of the circle is O.
$AB \perp CD$ and $AB \cap CD = K$.
$|AB| = 22$ cm and $|CD| = 17 \cdot 6$ cm.
Calculate: **(i)** $|OD|$ **(ii)** $|KD|$
          (iii) $|OK|$ **(iv)** $|KA|$

5. O is the centre of the circle.
$|AB| = 48$ cm.
If the area of $\triangle AOB$ is 168 cm^2, calculate:
(i) The distance from O to the line AB
(ii) The radius of the circle

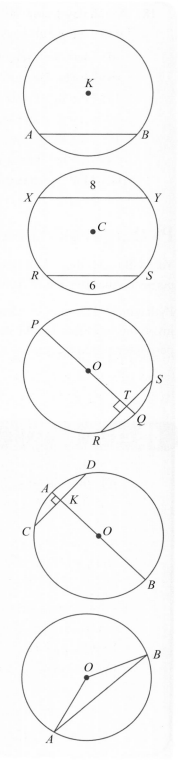

6. K is the centre of the circle.

   $|PQ| = 11$ cm.

   If the area of $\triangle PKQ$ is 72·6 cm^2,
   calculate the radius of the circle.

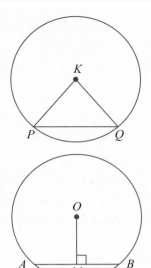

7. O is the centre of the circle and $[AB]$ is a chord. $OM \perp AB$.
   Prove that M is the midpoint of $[AB]$.

Proofs and Pythagoras' theorem

In many problems the diagram will contain two or more right-angled triangles.
It may help to draw the right-angled triangle separately and apply Pythagoras' theorem to each.
Isolating an algebraic expression for **common sides** can also help.

⬤ EXAMPLE

In $\triangle XYZ$, $|\angle XZY| = 90°$. K is a point on $[XZ]$.
Prove that $|XY|^2 + |KZ|^2 = |KY|^2 + |XZ|^2$.

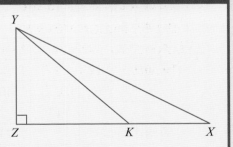

Solution:
Draw $\triangle XYZ$ and $\triangle KYZ$ separately and apply Pythagoras' theorem to each.
$[YZ]$ is a side common to both triangles.

Find two different algebraic expressions for $|YZ|$ and equate them.

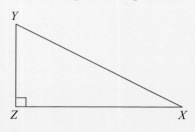
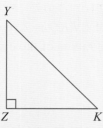

$$|YZ|^2 + |XZ|^2 = |XY|^2$$
$$|YZ|^2 = |XY|^2 - |XZ|^2$$

$$|YZ|^2 + |KZ|^2 = |KY|^2$$
$$|YZ|^2 = |KY|^2 - |KZ|^2$$

$$|YZ|^2 = |YZ|^2$$
$$\therefore |XY|^2 - |XZ|^2 = |KY|^2 - |KZ|^2$$
$$\therefore |XY|^2 + |KZ|^2 = |KY|^2 + |XZ|^2$$

Exercise 27.4

1. **(i)** Complete the following table.

a	b	$2ab$	$a^2 - b^2$	$a^2 + b^2$
2	1	4	3	5
3	1			
3	2			
4	1		15	
4	3			
5	2			
6		12		
6				40
7			13	
8				73

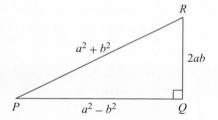

(ii) Show algebraically that
$$(a^2 - b^2)^2 + (2ab)^2 = (a^2 + b^2)^2.$$
What does this prove about $\triangle PQR$?

2. **(i)** $PQRS$ is a parallelogram, with $PR \perp QS$.
   Prove that $|PQ| = |PS|$.
   (ii) If $|PR| = 9{\cdot}6$ and $|QS| = 28$,
   calculate **(a)** $|PQ|$ **(b)** the area of the $\triangle PQR$.

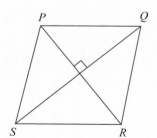

3. *ABCD* is a quadrilateral in which *AC* is perpendicular to *BD*.
   (i) Why is $|AB|^2 = |AM|^2 + |BM|^2$?
   (ii) Hence, prove that
   $$|AB|^2 + |CD|^2 = |AD|^2 + |BC|^2.$$

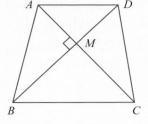

4. *PQRS* is a square.
   The diagonals meet at *T*.
   Prove that $|QR|^2 = 2|PT|^2$.

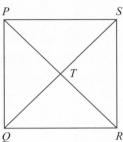

5. In $\triangle PQR$,
   $|PQ| = |PR| = |QR|$
   and $PQ \perp RS$.
   Prove: (i) $\triangle PRS \equiv \triangle QRS$
   (ii) $3|PR|^2 = 4|RS|^2$

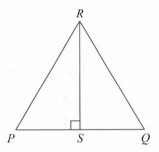

6. The diagram shows a square *PQRS* and another square *PRUV*.
   Prove $\dfrac{\text{area of square } PQRS}{\text{area of square } PRUV} = \dfrac{1}{2}$.

   (**Hint:** Let *x* = the length of a side of the smaller square.)

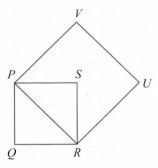

7. In the triangle *XYZ*, $XW \perp YZ$.
   Prove that
   $$|XY|^2 + |WZ|^2 = |YW|^2 + |XZ|^2.$$

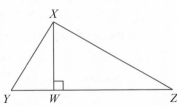

493

8. In the given diagram,
$|\angle PQR| = 90° = |\angle PRS|$.
$|PQ| = |QR| = 2|RS|$.
By letting $|RS| = x$ or otherwise,
prove that $|PS| = 3|RS|$.

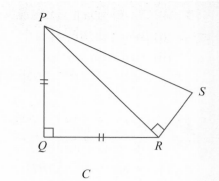

9. In $\triangle ABC, |\angle ACB| = 90°$,
$|AC| = |BC|$ and $AB \perp CD$.
Prove that $|AB| = 2|CD|$.

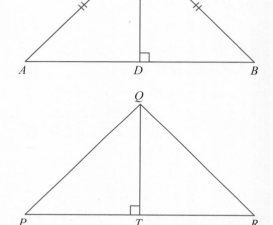

10. In $\triangle PQR$,
$|PQ|^2 = |PT|^2 + |TR|^2$ and $QT \perp PR$.
Prove that $|\angle QRT| = 45°$.

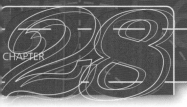

TRANSFORMATIONS

Transformations

The word '**transformation**' means change. The movement of a point or a shape from one position to another is called a **transformation**. In other words, a transformation changes the position of a shape.

Object and image

The original position of a shape is called the **object**. The new position of the shape is called the **image**. In other words, the image is where the object moves to. In mathematics we say that the object **maps onto** the image.

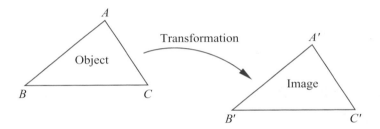

Often the images of points are indicated by primes. A' is pronounced 'A prime'. A and A' are called **corresponding** points because the point A' is the image of the point A. Figures have **critical** points that define its shape, usually its vertices (corners). When constructing an image, we usually only find the image of the critical points. In the triangle above, the critical points are A, B and C and their images are A', B' and C', respectively. Then we join the image points to construct the image of the object.

On our course we will meet three types of transformations:

1. Translation   **2.** Axial symmetry   **3.** Central symmetry

Each of these transformations changes the position of a shape but not its size or shape.

Translation

The diagram shows the movement of a child on a slide. She slides, in a straight line, from one position to another.

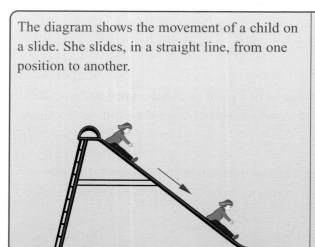

The diagram shows a person on an escalator. She moves, in a straight line, from one position to another.

In mathematics, movement in a straight line is called a **translation**.

Under a translation every point in the shape is moved the same distance in the same direction. It is often called a **slide**, since the shape appears to slide from one position to another. The shape does not turn or flip over. The object and its image are congruent (identical).

To describe a translation we need to give its direction and say by how much it has moved. A translation is often denoted by an arrow above two letters, for example $\overrightarrow{AB}$ or $\overrightarrow{AA'}$.

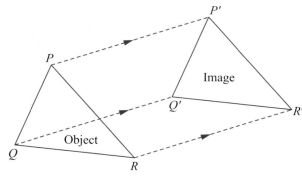

This translation could be described as $P \rightarrow P'$, written as $\overrightarrow{PP'}$.

The translation could also be written $\overrightarrow{QQ'}$ or $\overrightarrow{RR'}$. Under a translation, lengths and angles are preserved.

$|PQ| = |P'Q'|$, $\quad |PR| = |P'R'|$ $\quad$ and $\quad |QR| = |Q'R'|$.

$PQ \| P'Q'$, $\quad PR \| P'R'$ $\quad$ and $\quad QR \| Q'R'$.

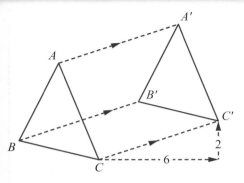

A translation is more easily described using a grid and indicating how far right (positive), left (negative) and how far up (positive) and down (negative) a figure is moved.

Each point on the object has moved 6 units to the right and 2 units up. To avoid using a sentence, this can also be described using a **column vector**. A column vector is written similar to coordinates, with the left or right (horizontal) displacement on top and the up or down (vertical) displacement on the bottom.

The translation can be written $\begin{pmatrix} 6 \\ 2 \end{pmatrix}$.

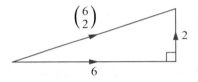

$\begin{pmatrix} 4 \\ -3 \end{pmatrix}$ is a translation of 4 units to the right and 3 units down.

$\begin{pmatrix} -2 \\ 5 \end{pmatrix}$ is a translation of 2 units to the left and 5 units up.

$\begin{pmatrix} -1 \\ -4 \end{pmatrix}$ is a translation of 1 unit to the left and 4 units down.

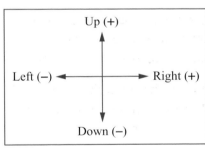

EXAMPLE 1

Construct the image of *ABCD* under the translation 5 units right and 1 unit down.

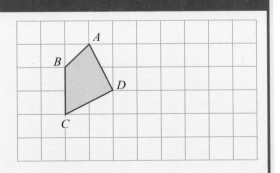

Solution:

Move the point A 5 units right and 1 unit down.
Label this point A'.
Construct B', C' and D', the images of B, C and
D, in the same way.
Join the points A', B', C' and D'.
$A'B'C'D'$ is the image of $ABCD$ under the
translation 5 units right and 1 unit down.

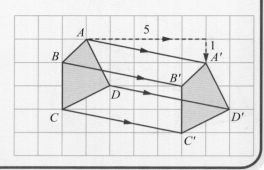

EXAMPLE 2

$ABCD$ and $ACED$ are parallelograms.
Under the translation $\overrightarrow{BC}$, write down the image of:

   (i) $\triangle ABC$ **(ii)** $[AC]$ **(iii)** $\angle BAC$

(iv) Name two other translations equal to $\overrightarrow{BC}$.

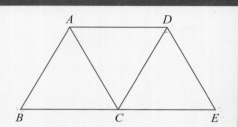

Solution:
The image of a point is where the point moves to after the transformation.
Under the translation $\overrightarrow{BC}$:

$A \rightarrow D$ (A moves to D)	**(i)** $\triangle ABC \rightarrow \triangle DCE$
$B \rightarrow C$ (B moves to C)	**(ii)** $[AC] \rightarrow [DE]$
$C \rightarrow E$ (C moves to E)	**(iii)** $\angle BAC \rightarrow \angle CDE$

(iv) Two other translations equal to $\overrightarrow{BC}$ are $\overrightarrow{AD}$ and $\overrightarrow{CE}$ (same length and direction).

Note: It is good practice, but not necessary, to keep the order of the images of points asked in the question.

Exercise 28.1

1. Describe the translation that
    maps the point:

      (i) A to B **(ii)** C to D

      (iii) E to F **(iv)** G to H

      (v) P to Q **(vi)** R to S

    Write your answers as a sentence
    or a column vector.

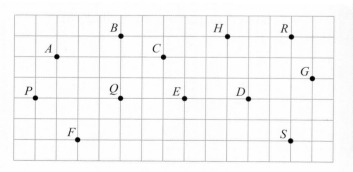

2. Describe the translation that maps the shape:

    (i) A to B

    (ii) C to D

    (iii) E to F

    (iv) G to H

Write each answer as a sentence or a column vector.

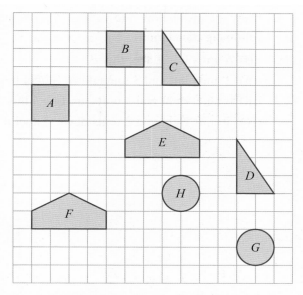

3. Copy the grid below into your copybook and construct the image of the triangle A under the following translations.

    (i) 2 units right and 3 units up. Label this B.   **(ii)** 4 units left and 1 unit up. Label this C.

    (iii) 5 units right. Label this D.   **(iv)** 4 units down. Label this E.

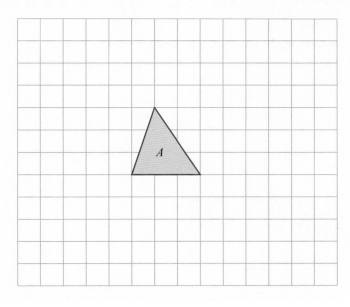

4. Copy the grid below into your copybook and construct the image of the shape *A* under the following translations.

   (i) 6 units left. Label this *B*.

   (ii) 2 units left and 3 units down. Label this *C*.

   (iii) 4 units right and 3 units up. Label this *D*.

   (iv) 5 units right and 2 units down. Label this *E*.

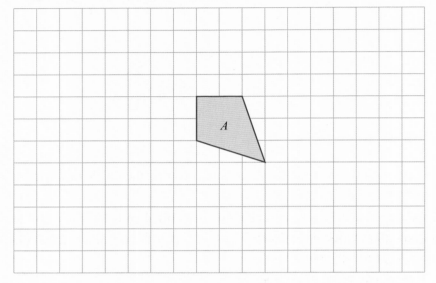

5. Describe fully the translation which maps figure *S* onto figure *S'*.

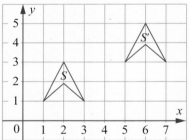

6. (i) Copy the grid into your copybook and construct the image *ABCDE* under the translation $\overrightarrow{AA'}$.

   (ii) Describe the translation.

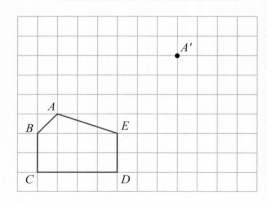

7. **(i)** Copy the grid into your copybook and construct the image of *ABCDE* under the translation $\overrightarrow{AA'}$.

    (ii) Describe the translation.

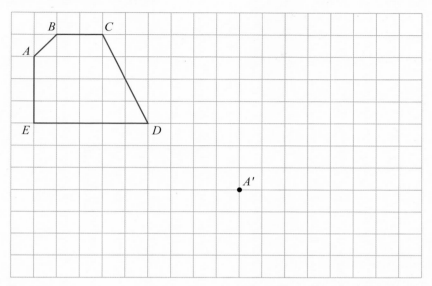

8. The diagram shows triangle *A*. Copy this grid into your copybook.

    (i) Construct the image of *A* under the translation 4 units right and 2 units up. Label this image *B*.

    (ii) Construct the image of *B* under the translation 3 units right and 5 units down. Label this image *C*.

    (iii) Describe the single translation that maps *A* onto *C*.

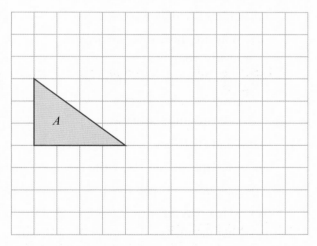

9. The diagram shows triangle *A*. Copy this grid into your copybook.

    (i) Construct the image of *A* under the translation 4 units up and 6 units to the left. Label this image *B*.

    (ii) Construct the image of *B* under the translation 3 units up and 10 units to the right. Label this image *C*.

(iii) Describe the single translation that maps *A* onto *C*.

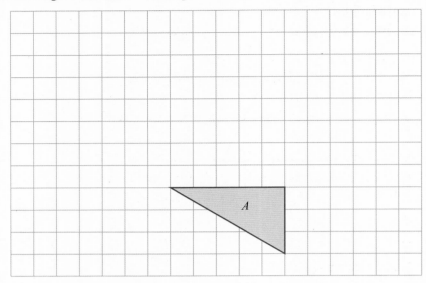

10. The diagram shows a translation. The arrows indicating the translations are drawn incorrectly.

    (i) Why are the arrows incorrect? Justify your answer.

    (ii) Using the diagram, draw an arrow which correctly indicates the translation.

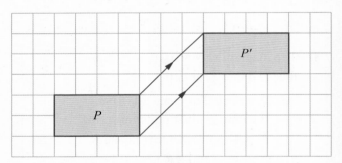

11. *PQRS* and *PRTS* are parallelograms.

    Under the translation $\overrightarrow{PS}$, write down the image of:

    (i) △*PQR*   **(ii)** [*QR*]   **(iii)** ∠*QPR*

    (iv) Name two other translations equal to $\overrightarrow{PS}$.
    (v) Find the image of *S* under the translation $\overrightarrow{RQ}$.

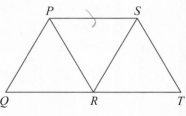

12. *RSTU* is a square and *USTV* is a parallelogram.
    Under the translation $\overrightarrow{ST}$, write down the image of:

    (i) △*RSU*   **(ii)** [*SU*]   **(iii)** ∠*SRU*

    Under the translation $\overrightarrow{UR}$, write down the image of:

    (iv) △*UVT*   **(v)** [*UT*]   **(vi)** ∠*TVU*

    Name one translation equal to:

    (vii) $\overrightarrow{SU}$ **(viii)** $\overrightarrow{VT}$ **(ix)** $\overrightarrow{TU}$

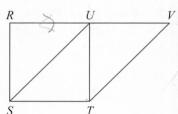

13. *PQRS* is a rectangle. The midpoint of [*QR*] is *Z*.
$|QZ| = |XY|$ and $|PX| = |YS|$.

Under the translation $\overrightarrow{QZ}$, write down the image of:

  (i) $\triangle XQZ$ **(ii)** [*XZ*]   **(iii)** $\angle QXZ$

  (iv) Name two parallelograms that are not rectangles.

  (v) Name two angles equal to $\angle XQZ$.

  (vi) If $|PQ| = 5$ cm and $|PX| = 2$ cm, calculate the area of the rectangle *PQRS*.

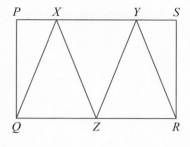

14. The diagram shows two identical squares, *ABCD* and *DCEF*, with their diagonals intersecting at *X* and *Y*, respectively. Under the translation $\overrightarrow{AD}$, write down the image of:

  (i) *C*   **(ii)** [*AB*]   **(iii)** $\triangle AXD$

  (iv) [*BX*]   **(v)** [*XD*]   **(vi)** $\angle XAD$

  (vii) Name another square.

If the area of $\triangle ABX$ is 4 cm^2, find the area of:

  (viii) $\triangle BAD$ **(ix)** $\triangle ACF$ **(x)** The rectangle *ABEF*

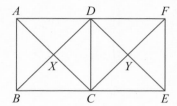

15. The diagram shows four equilateral triangles. Under the translation $\overrightarrow{QR}$, write down the image of:

  (i) *S*   **(ii)** [*QP*]   **(iii)** $\triangle PSR$ **(iv)** $\angle RPS$

  (v) Name a translation under which $\triangle PRS$ is the image of $\triangle SUV$.

  (vi) If the area of the parallelogram *PQUV* is 20 cm^2, what is the area of the parallelogram *PRUS*?

  (vii) Calculate $|\angle PRU|$.

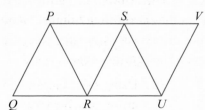

Axial symmetry

Axial symmetry is a reflection in a line. It involves reflecting points perpendicularly through a line.

| The diagram shows an **L** shape reflected in a mirror. | We can also draw the reflection without a mirror. The **object** is reflected in the mirror to give the **image**. The mirror becomes a line of symmetry. |

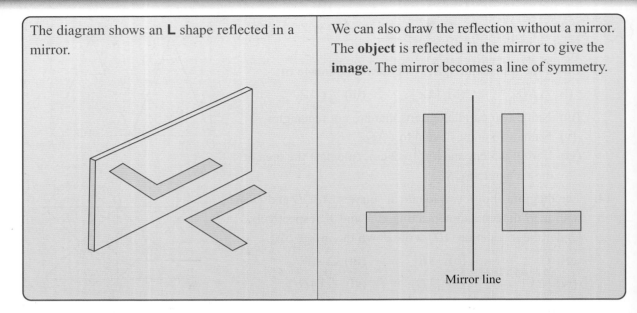

Mirror line

An object reflected in a mirror creates an image. A reflection in a line, an axial symmetry, gives an image that looks like a reflection in a mirror (sometimes called a mirror image). The line is called the **axis of reflection** or **line of reflection** or **mirror line**. The object and the image are symmetrical about the mirror line. In other words, any point and its image are the same perpendicular distance from the axis of symmetry. The object and the image are congruent. However, under a reflection in a line, a figure flips over.

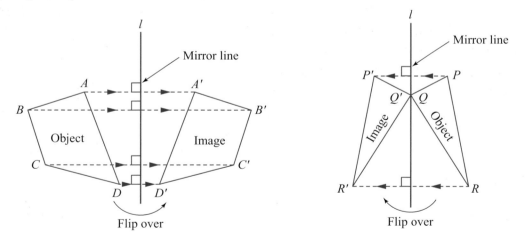

If a point is on the mirror line, its image is the same point. In the second diagram, the image of Q is still Q, i.e. $Q' = Q$. The line joining the corresponding points A and A' is perpendicular to the mirror line, i.e. $AA' \perp l$.

Note: Under an axial symmetry the order of the letters are reversed.

S_l denotes 'the axial symmetry in the line l'.

EXAMPLE 1

Draw the image of △*PQR* under an axial symmetry in the line *l*.

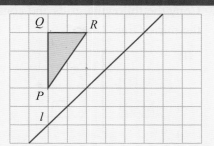

Solution
Draw a perpendicular broken line from *P* to the line *l*. Continue this broken line the same distance on the other side of *l*. Label this point *P'*.

Construct *Q'* and *R'*, the images of *Q* and *R*, respectively, in the same way.
Join the points *P'*, *Q'* and *R'*.

△*P'Q'R'* is the image of △*PQR* under an axial symmetry in the line *l*.

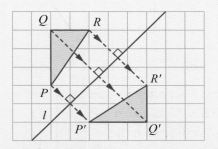

EXAMPLE 2

PQRS and *SRUV* are two squares with diagonals intersecting at *A* and *B*, respectively. Under the axial symmetry in *SR*, write down the image of:
(i) △*PQS*   **(ii)** [*PQ*]   **(iii)** ∠*APS*

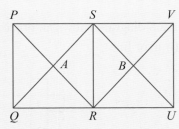

Solution:
Under the axial symmetry in *SR*:

$P \to V$
$Q \to U$
$S \to S$ (own image)
$A \to B$

  (i) △*PQS* → △*VUS*
  (ii) [*PQ*] → [*VU*]
  (iii) ∠*APS* → ∠*BVS*

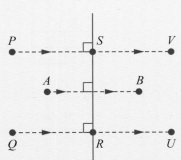

Exercise 28.2

1. Copy the following grids and construct the image of each figure under an axial symmetry in the mirror line, *l*.

   (i)

   (ii)

   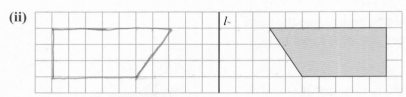

   (iii)   (iv)

   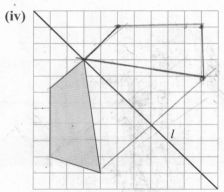

2. Each diagram shows an object and its image. In each case, draw the line of reflection (mirror line).

   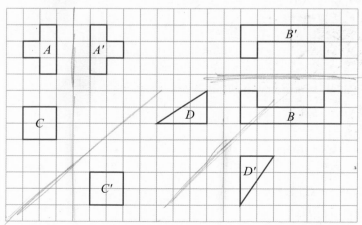

3. Copy the grid into your
copybook and construct the
image of *ABCD* under axial
symmetry in:
   (i) *l*   (ii) *k*

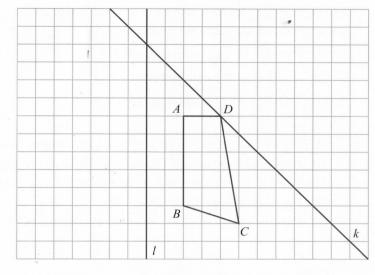

4. In each case, explain why *A'* is **not** the image of *A* under an axial symmetry in the line *l*.

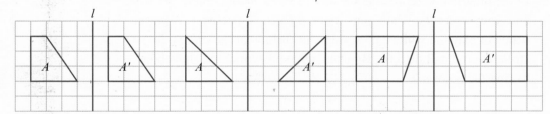

5. *PQRS* is a kite with diagonals intersecting at *O*. Under the axial
symmetry in *PR*, write down the image of:
   (i) *Q*   (ii) *S*   (iii) △*POS*   (iv) ∠*PSO*

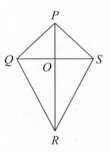

6. Sketch the image of △*ABC* under an axial symmetry in
the line *k*.

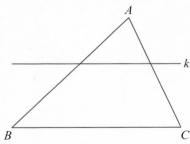

7. $[PQ]$ and $[RS]$ are two diameters of a circle that are perpendicular to each other. Write down the image of:

   (i) P under the axial symmetry in RS

   (ii) $[PO]$ under the axial symmetry in RS

   (iii) $\triangle QOR$ under the axial symmetry in PQ

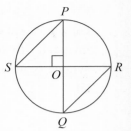

8. $ABCD$ is a parallelogram with diagonals intersecting at K and $AC \perp BD$.

   (i) Find the image of $\triangle BCK$ under the axial symmetry in BD.

   (ii) What is the image of $ABCD$ under the axial symmetry in AC?

   (iii) Name four isosceles triangles.

   (iv) Find the image of $[AB]$ under the translation $\overrightarrow{BD}$.

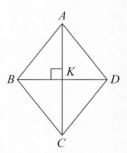

9. In the diagram, C represents the cushion of a snooker table. W, P and R represent the white, pink and red balls, respectively. A player wants to play the white ball against the cushion at the point q to strike the red ball directly. By using an axial symmetry, show how to find the point q.

10. X and Y represent two houses which require connection to a water main represented by the line m. By using an axial symmetry, determine the location of a common connection point on the main supply line (m) which will give the shortest length of pipe required.

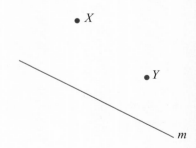

Axis of symmetry

A shape has an **axis of symmetry** or a **line of symmetry** when one half of the shape fits exactly over the other half when the shape is folded along that line. Shapes which are evenly balanced are said to be **symmetrical**. Some shapes have no axis of symmetry, some have only one axis of symmetry and others have more than one axis of symmetry.

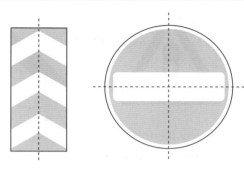

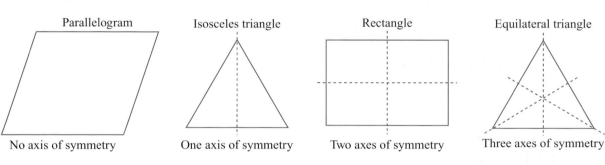

Parallelogram — No axis of symmetry

Isosceles triangle — One axis of symmetry

Rectangle — Two axes of symmetry

Equilateral triangle — Three axes of symmetry

Exercise 28.3

How many axes of symmetry has each of the following shapes in questions 1–16?

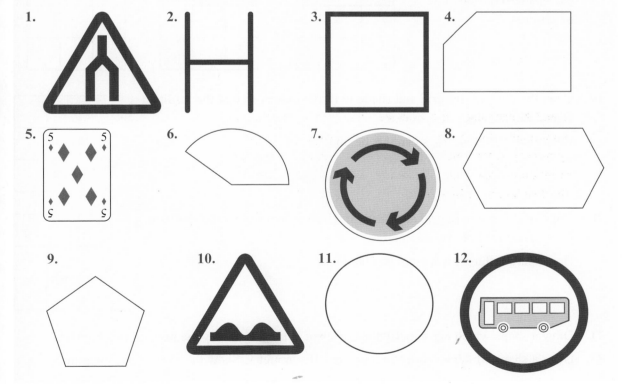

1.
2.
3.
4.
5.
6.
7.
8.
9.
10.
11.
12.

13. **14.** **15.** **16.**

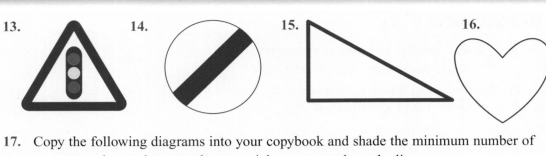

17. Copy the following diagrams into your copybook and shade the minimum number of squares so that each pattern has an axial symmetry about the lines.

(i) **(ii)** **(iii)**

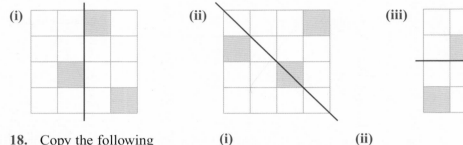

18. Copy the following diagrams into your copybook and shade in two more squares so that each pattern has one line of symmetry.

(i) **(ii)** **(iii)**

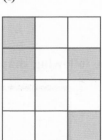 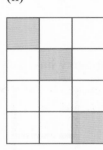 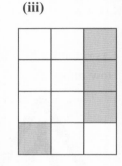

19. Copy the nine-square grid and shade in three squares so that the resultant figure has two lines of symmetry.

How many different ways can this be done?

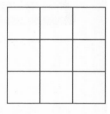

20. Copy the nine-square grid and shade in five squares so that the resultant figure has four lines of symmetry.

How many different ways can this be done?

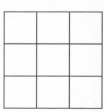

21. Draw a shape which has **exactly** three axes of symmetry. Show the axes on the diagram.

22. Draw a shape which has **exactly** four axes of symmetry. Show the axes on the diagram.

23. $\triangle ABC$ is mapped onto $\triangle A'B'C'$ under an axial symmetry in the y-axis.

    (i) Copy the graph and draw and label the image.

    (ii) Write down the coordinates of A', B' and C'.

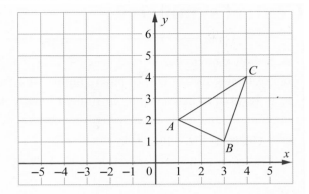

24. $PQRS$ is mapped onto $P'Q'R'S'$ under an axial symmetry in the line $y = x - 1$.

    (i) Copy the graph and draw and label the image.

    (ii) Write down the coordinates of P', Q', R' and S'.

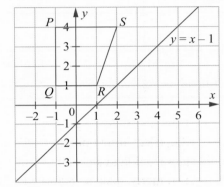

25.

Some words, written in upper case block form, have a horizontal line of symmetry. They also look the same after reflection at a horizontal line. For example, **KICK**.	Some words, written in upper case block form, have a vertical line of symmetry. They also look the same after reflection at a vertical line. For example, **TOT**.
-KICK- **KICK** ---------- **KICK**	**TOT** **T T / O O / T T**

   (i) Write down the four capital letters, in upper case block form, that have both horizontal and vertical symmetry.

   (ii) See how many words in the grid you can find with horizontal or vertical symmetry.

   (iii) Make up some words of your own that have horizontal or vertical symmetry.

H	O	B	B	O	Y
A	C	O	D	D	O
M	A	M	A	T	U
A	T	A	T	A	B
T	E	T	O	X	O
T	H	O	O	D	O
A	I	O	T	O	T
W	M	X	H	T	H

Central symmetry

A pinhole camera has a small hole cut in it and the opposite side has a piece of photographic film attached to it. Rays of light, travelling in straight lines, enter through the pinhole and form an image on the photographic film. The image on the film will be upside-down.

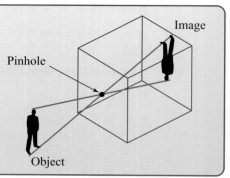

Central symmetry is a reflection in a point. The point is called the **centre of symmetry**. It involves reflecting points through the centre of symmetry to the same distance on the other side.

An object reflected in a point creates an image. Under a central symmetry any point and its image are equidistant from the centre of symmetry. The object and the image are congruent. However, under a central symmetry, a shape is turned over. Central symmetry is exactly the same as a rotation of 180° about the centre of symmetry.

Note: S_O denotes 'the central symmetry in the point O'.

EXAMPLE 1

Construct the image of $\triangle PQR$ under the central symmetry in the point O.

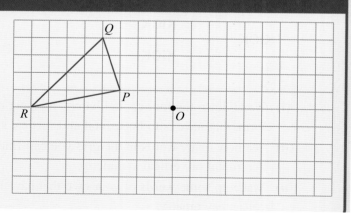

Solution:

Draw a straight line from P to O and continue the same distance on the other side of O. Label this point P'. Construct Q' and R', the images of Q and R, respectively, in the same way. Join the points P', Q' and R'.

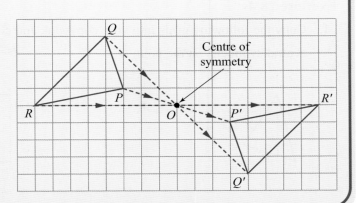

$\triangle P'Q'R'$ is the image of $\triangle PQR$ under a central symmetry in O.

EXAMPLE 2

$ABCD$ and $EDGF$ are two identical parallelograms with diagonals intersecting at P and Q, respectively. Under the central symmetry in D, write down the image of:

  (i) $\triangle APD$

  (ii) $[AB]$

  (iii) $\angle QFE$

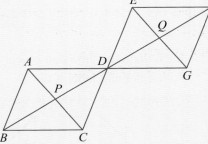

Solution:

Under the central symmetry in D:

  $A \rightarrow G$

  $P \rightarrow Q$

  $D \rightarrow D$ (own image)

  $B \rightarrow F$

  $Q \rightarrow P$

  $F \rightarrow B$

  $E \rightarrow C$

  (i) $\triangle APD \rightarrow \triangle GQD$

  (ii) $[AB] \rightarrow [GF]$

  (iii) $\angle QFE \rightarrow \angle PBC$

Exercise 28.4

1. Copy the following grids into your copybook and construct the image of each figure under a central symmetry in the point O.

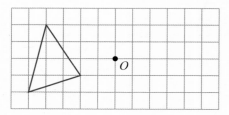 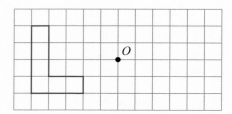

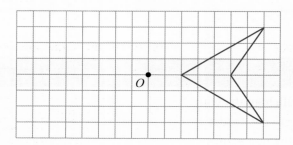 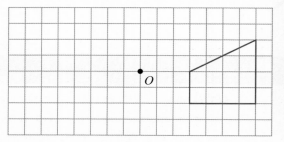

2. Each diagram shows an object and its image. In each case, indicate the centre of symmetry with a dot and label it O.

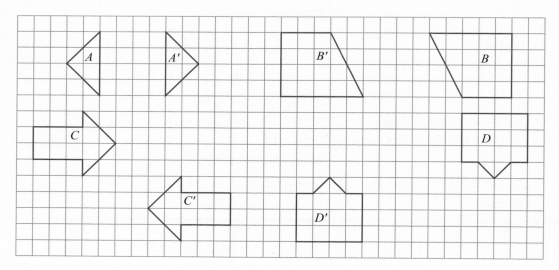

3. Copy the following grid into your copybook and construct the image of P under a central symmetry in the point (i) A and (ii) B.

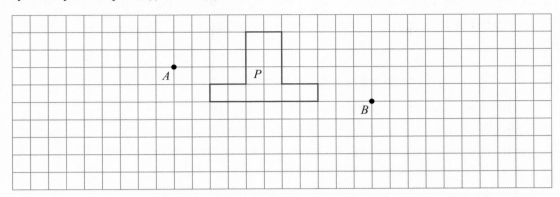

4. In each case, explain why A' is **not** the image of A under a central symmetry in the point O.

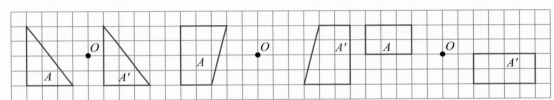

5. $ABCD$ is a parallelogram with diagonals intersecting at M.
Under the central symmetry in M, write down the image of:

   (i) A (ii) B (iii) $[DC]$
   (iv) $[AD]$ (v) $\triangle ABM$ (vi) $\angle BCM$

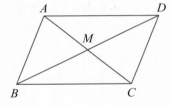

6. $PQRS$ is a square and $SQRT$ is a parallelogram with diagonals intersecting at X and Y, respectively.

   (i) Name four line segments equal in length to $[PS]$.

   Under the central symmetry in X, write down the image of:

   (ii) R (iii) Q (iv) $[PQ]$ (v) $\triangle PXS$

   Under the central symmetry in Y, write down the image of:

   (vi) R (vii) Q (viii) $[SQ]$ (ix) $\triangle STY$ (x) $\angle QRT$

   (xi) What is the image of $[PS]$ under the translation $\overrightarrow{QR}$?

   (xii) What is the image of P under the axial symmetry in SR?

   (xiii) If the area of $\triangle PSQ = 20$ cm^2, what is the area of the parallelogram $SQRT$?

7. *ABCD* is a rectangle. *ABDX* and *BYCD* are parallelograms.

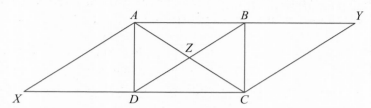

   (i) Name three line segments equal in length to [*DC*].
   (ii) What is the image of △*BCY* under the central symmetry in *Z*?
   (iii) What is the image of △*AXD* under the axial symmetry in the line *AD*?
   (iv) What is the image of [*AX*] under the translation $\overrightarrow{BY}$?
   (v) If |∠*AXD*| = 40°, write down the measure of |∠*ADZ*|.
   (vi) If the area of △*ADZ* = 8 cm², what is the area of the figure *AXCY*?

8. △*PQR* is mapped onto △*P′Q′R′* under central symmetry in the point *A*(2, 2).

   (i) Copy the graph and draw and label the image.
   (ii) Write down the coordinates of *P′*, *Q′* and *R′*.

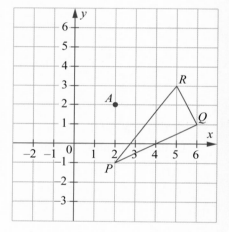

Centre of symmetry

Some shapes are symmetrical about a point. The point is called the **centre of symmetry** (sometimes called the point of symmetry). The following shapes have a centre of symmetry, indicated by *O*.

Circle

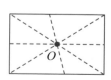

Rectangle

Square

Letter X

In each case, if any point is taken on the figure, its image under a central symmetry in the point O is **always** another point on the figure. To see if a figure has a centre of symmetry, rotate it by 180° (a half-turn). If the figure looks identical, then the figure has a centre of symmetry.

For example, consider the playing card, the 4 of clubs. Under a rotation of 180° (half-turn), the card looks identical. Every point P and Q on the card has a corresponding point P' and Q', respectively, on the card under a central symmetry in the point O. The point O is called the centre of symmetry. The centre of symmetry, point O, is the point of intersection of the lines PP' and QQ'.

Original position
(object)

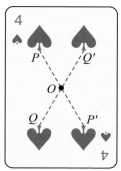

Rotation of 180°
(image)

Try the same thing with the playing card, the 5 of clubs. Does it have a centre of symmetry? Explain your answer.

Exercise 28.5
For each figure in questions 1–20, state whether it has a centre of symmetry and indicate where it is.

1.

2.

3.

4.

5.

6.

7.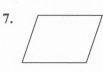

8.

9.

10.

11.

12.

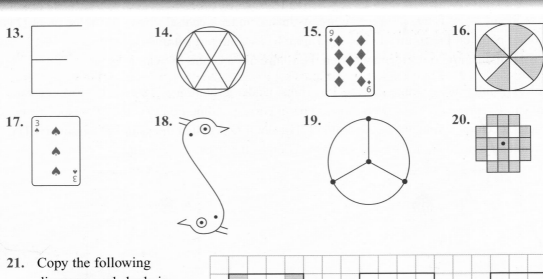

13.   14.   15.   16.

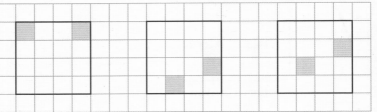

17.   18.   19.   20.

21. Copy the following diagrams and shade in two squares so that each pattern has a centre of symmetry.

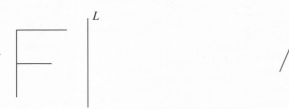

22. What letters, written in upper case block form, have a point of symmetry?

23. What letters, written in upper case block form, have a point of symmetry and have horizontal and vertical axes of symmetry?

24. No triangle has a centre of symmetry. Do you agree or disagree? Give a reason for your answer.

25. Copy the following diagrams and sketch the image of the capital letter *F* under:

   (i) Axial symmetry in the line *L*   **(ii)** Central symmetry in the point *P*

26. Copy the graph into your copybook.

    (i) Find the image of triangle A under axial symmetry in the line $x = 1$. Label this triangle B.

    (ii) Find the image of triangle B under axial symmetry in the line $y = 2$. Label this triangle C.

    (iii) Describe a single transformation that maps triangle A onto triangle C.

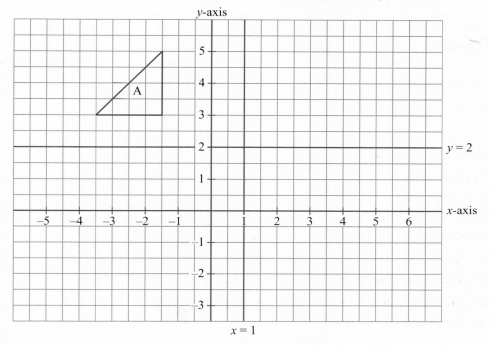

27. The diagram below shows a triangle A on the coordinate plane and its image under a number of transformations.

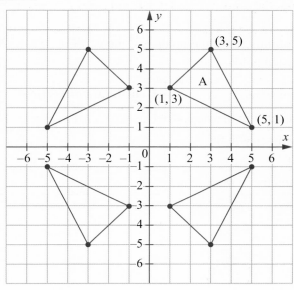

Write down the coordinates of the images of the vertices of A under each of the transformations listed below.

	Transformations	Coordinate of vertices
(i)	Axial symmetry in the y-axis	(,), (,), (,)
(ii)	Central symmetry in the point (0, 0)	
(iii)	Axial symmetry in the x-axis	

28. The diagram below shows a quadrilateral A on the coordinate plane and its image under a number of transformations.

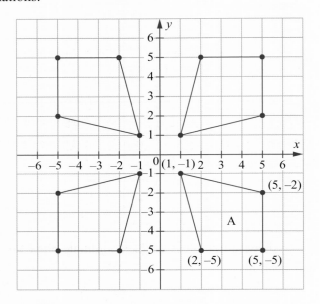

Write down the coordinates of the images of the vertices of A under each of the transformations listed below.

	Transformations	Coordinate of vertices
(i)	Axial symmetry in the y-axis	(,), (,), (,), (,)
(ii)	Central symmetry in the point (0, 0)	
(iii)	Axial symmetry in the x-axis	

29. Describe fully the single transformation that maps:

(i) A_1 onto A_2 (ii) A_1 onto A_3 (iii) A_1 onto A_4 (iv) A_2 onto A_3 (v) A_3 onto A_4

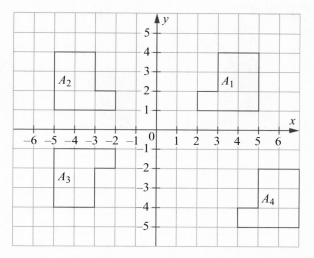

30. Each of the three figures labelled A, B and C shown below is the image of the figure X under a transformation. For each of A, B and C, state what the transformation is (translation, central symmetry or axial symmetry).

      X   A   B   C

31. Each of the three figures labelled A, B and C shown below is the image of the figure X under a transformation. For each of A, B and C, state what the transformation is (translation, central symmetry or axial symmetry).

      X   A   B   C

32. Each of the three figures labelled A, B and C shown below is the image of the figure X under a transformation. For each of A, B and C, state what the transformation is (translation, central symmetry or axial symmetry).

X   A   B   C

33. Each of the four diagrams A, B, C and D shows the object in Figure 1 and its image under a transformation. For each A, B, C and D, state one transformation (translation, axial symmetry or central symmetry) that will map the object onto that image.

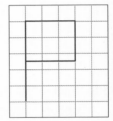

Figure 1

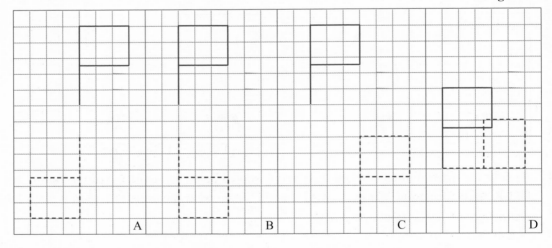

A   B   C   D

A	
B	
C	
D	

34. Each of the four diagrams A, B, C and D shows the object in Figure 1 and its image under a transformation. For each A, B, C and D, state one transformation (translation, axial symmetry or central symmetry) that will map the object onto that image.

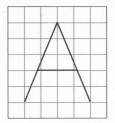

Figure 1

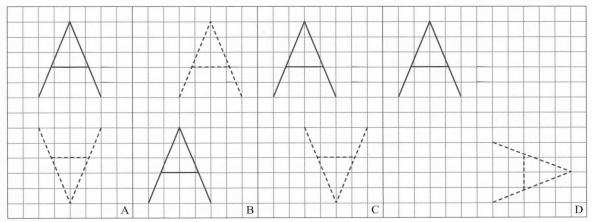

A	
B	
C	
D	

35. The diagram shows six square tiles which are arranged to produce a repeating pattern, as shown.

Describe fully the single transformation which maps:

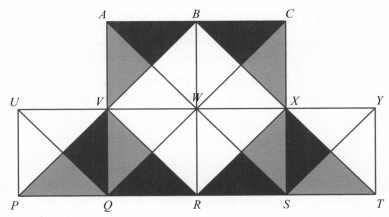

   (i) The tile *VWRQ* onto the tile *XWRS*

   (ii) The tile *ABWV* onto the tile *SRWX*

   (iii) The tile *UVQP* onto the tile *YXST*

   (iv) The tile *ACXV* onto the tile *QSXV*

PROOFS OF THEOREMS

Glossary of terms associated with theorems

Axiom:	An axiom is a statement which is assumed to be true and is used as a basis for developing a system. *Example: Axiom 1 - There is exactly one line through any two given points.*
Converse:	The converse of a theorem is formed by taking the conclusion as the starting point and having the starting point as the conclusion. *Example: The converse of Theorem 2 states 'If two angles are equal, then the triangle is isosceles'.*
Corollary:	A corollary follows after a theorem and is a proposition which must be true because of that theorem.
Implies:	Implies indicates a logical relationship between two statements, such that if the first is true then the second must be true.
Proof:	A proof is a sequence of statements (made up of axioms, assumption and arguments) leading to the establishment of the truth of one final statement.
Theorem:	A theorem is a statement which has been proved to be true.

You are required to know the following theorems and corollaries and be able to apply them in answering geometric questions.

Note: Theorems 7, 8, 16, 17 and 18 are **not** on this course.

*You are **only** required to be able to reproduce the proof for Theorems 4, 6, 9, 14 and 19.

Theorem 1:	Vertically opposite angles are equal in measure.
Theorem 2:	In an isosceles triangle the angles opposite the equal sides are equal. Conversely, if two angles are equal, then the triangle is isosceles.
Theorem 3:	If a transversal makes equal alternate angles on two lines then the lines are parallel (and converse).
Theorem 4:*	The three angles in any triangle add up to 180°.
Theorem 5:	Two lines are parallel if and only if, for any transversal, the corresponding angles are equal.
Theorem 6:*	Each exterior angle of a triangle is equal to the sum of the two interior opposite angles.
Theorem 9:*	In a parallelogram, opposite sides are equal and opposite angles are equal.

Theorem 10: The diagonals of a parallelogram bisect each other.

Corollary 1: A diagonal divides a parallelogram into two congruent triangles.

Theorem 11: If three parallel lines cut off equal segments on some transversal line, then they will cut off equal segments on any other transversal.

Theorem 12: Let ABC be a triangle. If a line l is parallel to BC and cuts $[AB]$ in the ratio $s:t$, then it also cuts $[AC]$ in the same ratio.

Theorem 13: If two triangles are similar, then their sides are proportional, in order.

Theorem 14:* Theorem of Pythagoras: In a right-angled triangle, the square of the hypotenuse is the sum of the squares of the other two sides.

Theorem 15: If the square of one side of a triangle is the sum of the squares of the other two sides, then the angle opposite the first side is a right angle.

Theorem 19:* The angle at the centre of a circle standing on a given arc is twice the angle at any point of the circle standing on the same arc.

Corollary 2: All angles at points of a circle, standing on the same arc, are equal.

Corollary 3: Each angle in a semicircle is a right angle.

Corollary 4: If the angle standing on a chord $[BC]$ at some point of the circle is a right angle, then $[BC]$ is a diameter.

Corollary 5: If $ABCD$ is a cyclic quadrilateral, then opposite angles sum to $180°$.

Theorem 4: The three angles in any triangle add to $180°$.

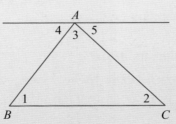

Given:	$\triangle ABC$ with angles 1, 2 and 3	
To prove:	$|\angle 1| + |\angle 2| + |\angle 3| = 180°$	
Construction:	Draw a line through A, parallel to BC.	
	Label angles 4 and 5.	
Proof:	$|\angle 1| = |\angle 4|$ and $|\angle 2| = |\angle 5|$	(alternate angles)
	$\therefore \ |\angle 1| + |\angle 2| + |\angle 3| = |\angle 4| + |\angle 5| + |\angle 3|$	
	but $|\angle 4| + |\angle 5| + |\angle 3| = 180°$	(straight angle)
	$\therefore \ |\angle 1| + |\angle 2| + |\angle 3| = 180°$	

Theorem 6: Each exterior angle of a triangle is equal to the sum of the two interior opposite angles.

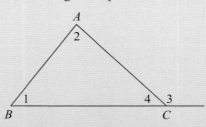

Given:	$\triangle ABC$ with interior opposite angles 1 and 2 and exterior angle 3
To prove:	$|\angle 1| + |\angle 2| = |\angle 3|$
Construction:	Label angle 4.
Proof:	$|\angle 1| + |\angle 2| + |\angle 4| = 180°$ (three angles in a triangle)

$|\angle 3| + |\angle 4| = 180°$ (straight angle)

$\therefore \quad |\angle 1| + |\angle 2| + |\angle 4| = |\angle 3| + |\angle 4|$

$\therefore \quad |\angle 1| + |\angle 2| = |\angle 3|$

Theorem 9: In a parallelogram, opposite sides are equal and opposite angles are equal.

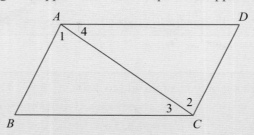

Given:	Parallelogram $ABCD$
To prove:	$|AB| = |DC|, |AD| = |BC|$
	$|\angle ABC| = |\angle ADC|, |\angle BAD| = |\angle BCD|$
Construction:	Join A to C.
	Label angles 1, 2, 3 and 4.
Proof:	Consider $\triangle ABC$ and $\triangle ADC$:

$|\angle 1| = |\angle 2|$ and $|\angle 3| = |\angle 4|$ (alternate angles)

$|AC| = |AC|$ (common side)

$\therefore \quad \triangle ABC = \triangle ADC$ (ASA) ~~Similar~~ $\triangle$'s

$\therefore \quad |AB| = |DC|$ and $|AD| = |BC|$ (corresponding sides)

and $|\angle ABC| = |\angle ADC|$.   (corresponding angles)

Similarly, $|\angle BAD| = |\angle BCD|$.

Theorem 14: Theorem of Pythagoras: In a right-angled triangle, the square of the hypotenuse is the sum of the squares of the other two sides.

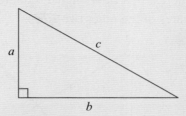

Given:	Right-angled triangle with length of sides a, b and c, as shown
To prove:	$a^2 + b^2 = c^2$
Construction:	Draw a square $PQRS$ with sides of length $a + b$.

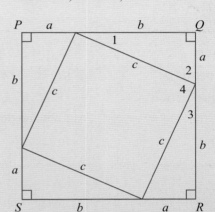

Draw four congruent right-angled triangles in the square with sides of length a and b and hypotenuse c, as shown.

Label angles 1, 2, 3 and 4.

Proof: Each of the four inscribed triangles is congruent to the original triangle (SAS).

∴ Each side of the inner quadrilateral has length c.

$|\angle 1| + |\angle 2| = 90°$ (remaining angles in the triangle)

$|\angle 1| = |\angle 3|$ (corresponding angles in congruent triangles)

∴ $|\angle 2| + |\angle 3| = 90°$

∴ $|\angle 4| = 90°$ (straight angle)

∴ The inscribed quadrilateral is a square.

Area of square $PQRS = 4$ (area of one triangle) + Area of inscribed square

$$(a + b)^2 = 4\left(\tfrac{1}{2}\,ab\right) + c^2$$
$$a^2 + 2ab + b^2 = 2ab + c^2$$
$$\therefore a^2 + b^2 = c^2 \qquad \text{(subtract } 2ab \text{ from both sides)}$$

Note: A difficulty with the proof is trying to draw the diagram. One way to do this is to let $a = 2$ cm, $b = 5$ cm and draw a square with each side 7 cm in length. Then simply mark off 2 cm on each side in a clockwise direction. Join these points to construct the smaller square.

Alternative proof for Theorem 14.

Theorem 14: Theorem of Pythagoras: In a right-angled triangle, the square of the hypotenuse is the sum of the squares of the other two sides.

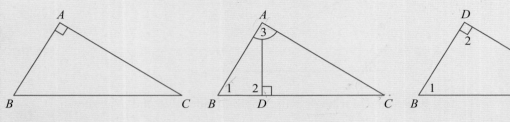

Given: $\triangle ABC$, $|\angle BAC| = 90°$

To prove: $|BC|^2 = |AB|^2 + |AC|^2$

Construction: Draw $AD \perp BC$.

Label angles 1, 2 and 3.

Proof: In $\triangle$s ABC and DBA

$|\angle 1| = |\angle 1|$ (common angle)

$|\angle 2| = |\angle 3| = 90°$ (construction)

∴ $\triangle ABC$ and $\triangle DBA$ are similar.

∴ $\dfrac{|AB|}{|BC|} = \dfrac{|BD|}{|AB|}$ (corresponding sides are in proportion)

∴ $|AB|^2 = |BC| \cdot |BD|$ ①   (cross-multiply)

Similarly, $\triangle ABC$ and $\triangle DAC$ are similar.

And $|AC|^2 = |BC| \cdot |DC|$ ②

Adding ① and ②:

$|AB|^2 + |AC|^2 = |BC| \cdot |BD| + |BC| \cdot |DC|$

$= |BC|(|BD| + |DC|)$ (factorise out $|BC|$)

$= |BC| \cdot |BC|$

$= |BC|^2$

∴ $|BC|^2 = |AB|^2 + |AC|^2$

$\dfrac{AC}{BC} = \dfrac{DC}{AC}$

$|AC|^2 = (BC)(DC)$

Theorem 19: The angle at the centre of a circle standing on a given arc is twice the angle at any point of the circle standing on the same arc.

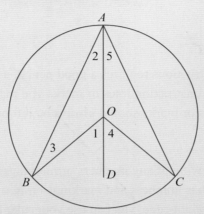

Given:	Circle, centre O, containing points A, B and C
To prove:	$\lvert \angle BOC \rvert = 2\lvert \angle BAC \rvert$
Construction:	Join A to O and continue to D.
	Label angles 1, 2, 3, 4 and 5.
Proof:	Consider $\triangle AOB$:

$\lvert \angle 1 \rvert = \lvert \angle 2 \rvert + \lvert \angle 3 \rvert$ (exterior angle of $\triangle AOB$)

But $\lvert \angle 2 \rvert = \lvert \angle 3 \rvert$ ($\lvert OA \rvert = \lvert OB \rvert$: both radii)

$\therefore$ $\lvert \angle 1 \rvert = 2\lvert \angle 2 \rvert$

Similarly, $\lvert \angle 4 \rvert = 2\lvert \angle 5 \rvert$

$\therefore$ $\lvert \angle 1 \rvert + \lvert \angle 4 \rvert = 2\lvert \angle 2 \rvert + 2\lvert \angle 5 \rvert$

$\therefore$ $\lvert \angle 1 \rvert + \lvert \angle 4 \rvert = 2(\lvert \angle 2 \rvert + \lvert \angle 5 \rvert)$

i.e. $\lvert \angle BOC \rvert = 2\lvert \angle BAC \rvert$

Constructions

Any work involving accurate constructions requires a good pencil, a compass, a ruler and a protractor. It is important not to rub out any construction lines or marks you make at any stage during a construction. All construction lines or marks should **always** be left on the diagram.

Notes:

- A straight edge is like a ruler without any numbers or markings.
- A ruler is a straight edge but has numbers and markings on it.
- When a question requires a straight edge, you can use your ruler but not the numbers or markings on it.

Locus

A locus is a set of points that obey a certain rule. For example:

A circle is the set of points that are the same distance from the centre.	The bisector of an angle is the set of points that are the same distance from the arms of the angle.	A point moves so that it is always the same distance from a line segment.

3ē Roimteoir

Bisector of an angle

Given the angle *ABC*.

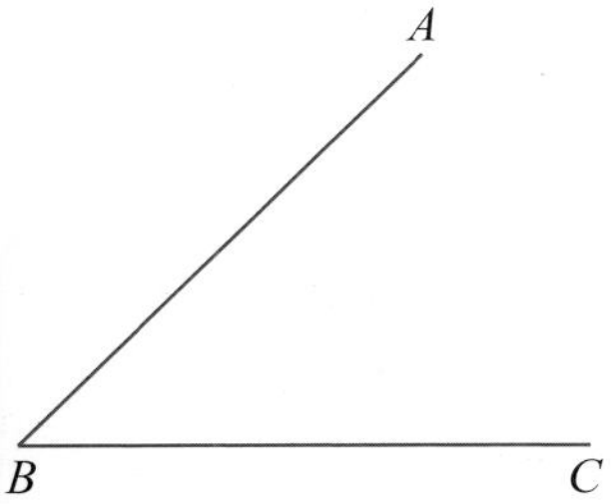

Steps to bisect any angle *ABC* (using only a compass and straight edge)

1. Set your compass to a sensible radius (not too large). Place the compass point on the vertex, *B*. Draw two arcs to intersect the arms at *X* and *Y*.

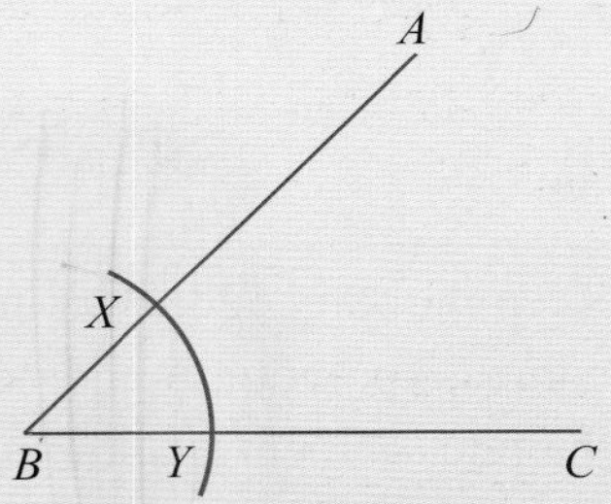

2. Place the compass point on *X* and draw an arc.
Keep the same radius.
Place the compass point on *Y* and draw an arc.
Where the arcs intersect, label the point *Z*.

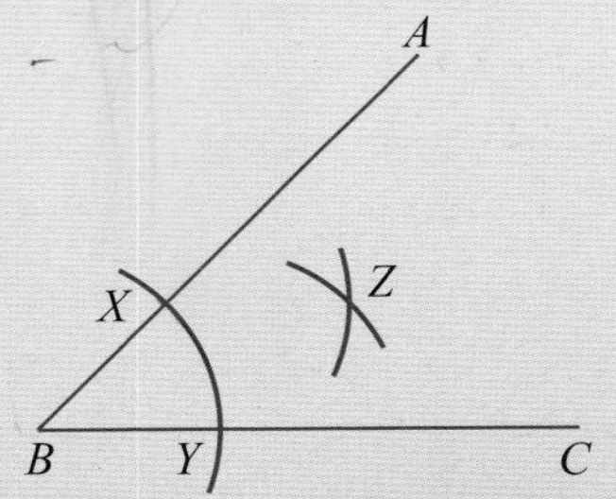

3. Draw a line from *B* through the point *Z*. The line *BZ* is the bisector of the angle *ABC*.

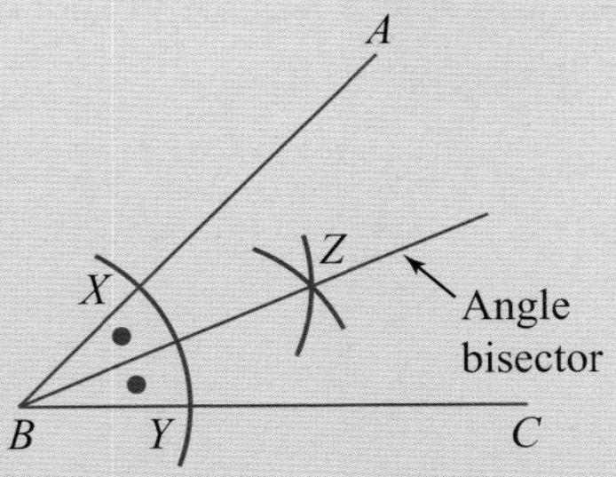

Any point on the bisector of an angle is equidistant (same distance) from the arms of the angle. The bisector of an acute or obtuse angle also bisects its related reflex angle.

Perpendicular bisector of a given line segment

Given a line segment [AB].

$A \text{———————} B$

Steps to bisect any line segment [AB] (using only a compass and straight edge)

1. Set the compass to a radius of about three-quarters of the length of the line segment [AB]. (Any radius above half the length of the line segment will do.) Place the compass point on A and draw arcs above and below the line segment.	
2. Keep the same radius as in step 1. Place the compass point on B and draw arcs above and below the line segment to intersect the other arcs. Where the arcs intersect, label the points X and Y.	 
3. Draw the line through X and Y. The line XY is the perpendicular bisector of the line segment [AB].	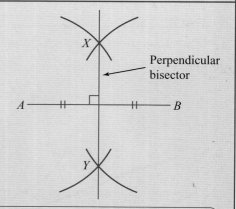

Any point on the perpendicular bisector of a line segment [AB] is equidistant (same distance) from the points A and B. The perpendicular bisector of the line segment [AB] is always at right angles to the line segment.

Line perpendicular to a given line *l*, passing through a given point not on *l*

Given a line *l* with a point *A* not on *l*.

Steps in drawing a line perpendicular to a given line *l*, passing through a given point not on *l* (using only a set square and ruler)

1. Place one of the **shorter** edges of the 45° set square on the line *l*. Place the ruler under the set square.	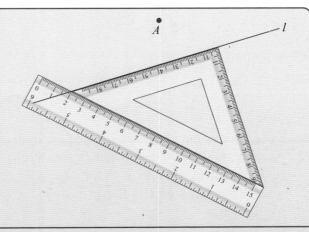
2. Keeping pressure on the ruler, slide the set square along the ruler until the edge meets the point *A*. Draw a line through the point *A* to meet the line *l*.	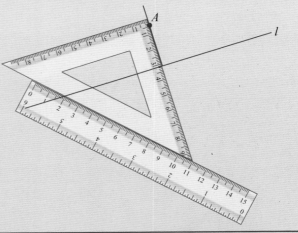
3. This line is perpendicular to *l* and passes through the point *A*.	Perpendicular line 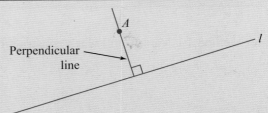

Line perpendicular to a given line *l*, passing through a point on *l*

Given line *l* and a point *A* on *l*.

Steps in drawing a line perpendicular to a given line *l*, passing through a point on *l*.
Method 1 (using a ruler and set square)

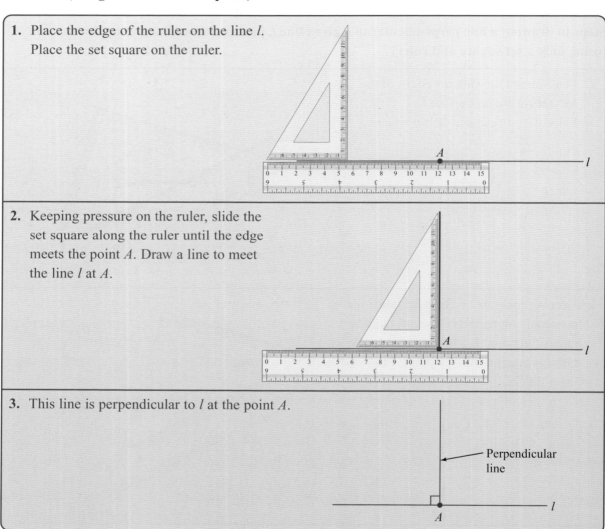

1. Place the edge of the ruler on the line *l*.
   Place the set square on the ruler.

2. Keeping pressure on the ruler, slide the set square along the ruler until the edge meets the point *A*. Draw a line to meet the line *l* at *A*.

3. This line is perpendicular to *l* at the point *A*.

   Perpendicular line

Note: Method 1 is very useful when constructing rectangles and right-angled triangles.

Method 2 (using a compass and straight edge)

1. With *A* as the centre and using the same radius, draw two arcs to intersect the line *l* at *X* and *Y*.	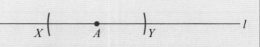
2. Place the compass point on *X* and draw an arc above the point *A*. Keep the same radius. Place the compass point on *Y* and draw an arc above the point *A* to intersect the other arc. Where the arcs intersect, label the point Z.	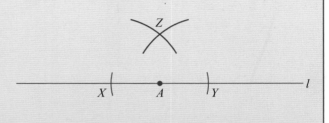
3. Draw the line from *A* through *Z*. The line *AZ* is perpendicular to *l* at the point *A*.	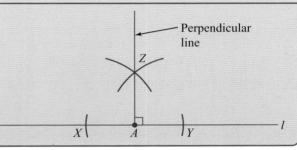

Line parallel to a given line *l*, passing through a point not on *l*

Given a line *l* and a point *A* not on *l*.

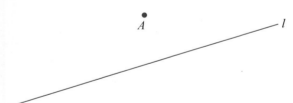

Steps in drawing a line parallel to a given line *l*, passing through a point *A* not on *l* (using only a ruler and set square)

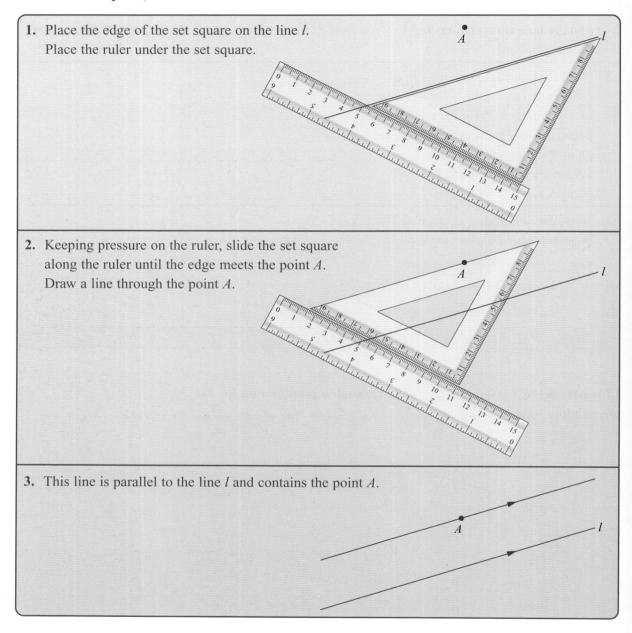

1. Place the edge of the set square on the line *l*.
   Place the ruler under the set square.

2. Keeping pressure on the ruler, slide the set square along the ruler until the edge meets the point *A*.
   Draw a line through the point *A*.

3. This line is parallel to the line *l* and contains the point *A*.

Division of a line segment into any number of equal parts (segments)

Note: This example shows how to divide a line segment into three equal parts. However, the method can also be used to divide a line segment into any number of equal parts. On your course, you can be asked to divide a line segment into any number of equal parts.

Given a line segment [AB].

A ——————————————— B

Steps to divide a line segment [AB] into three equal parts (using only a compass, straight edge and set square)

1. From A, draw a line at an acute angle to AB. Using your compass, mark off three equal spaces, 1, 2 and 3.	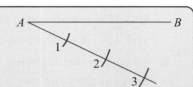
2. Join the last division, point 3, to B.	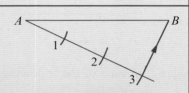
3. Draw lines parallel to 3B, from points 2 and 1. The line segment is now divided into three equal parts.	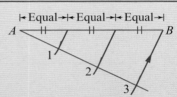

Exercise 30.1

1. Using only a compass and straight edge, construct the angle bisector of each of the following angles, showing all your construction lines. In each case, use your protractor to check your work.

(i)   (ii)   (iii)

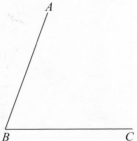
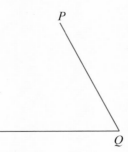
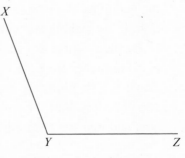

2. Construct each of the following line segments exactly. Using only a compass and straight edge, construct the perpendicular bisector of each line segment, showing all your construction lines. In each case, use your ruler to check your work.

   (i) |AB| = 8 cm   (ii) |PQ| = 7 cm   (iii) |XY| = 64 mm   (iv) |RS| = 85 mm

3. **(i)** Using a compass and straight edge only, construct the perpendicular bisector of the line segment [AB].
   (ii) Mark any point, C, on the perpendicular bisector. What is the relationship between the point C and the points A and B?
   (iii) If C is **not** a point on [AB], what type of triangle is △ABC?
   (iv) If C **is** a point on [AB], complete the following: |AC| + |CB| = | |.

4. In each of the following, draw a line through the given point, perpendicular to the line that contains the point.

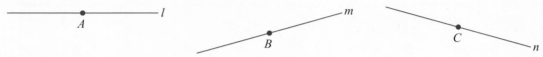

5. In each of the following, draw a line through the given point, not on the line, perpendicular to the line.

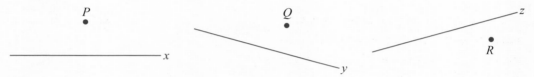

6. In each of the following, draw a line through the given point, not on the line, parallel to the line.

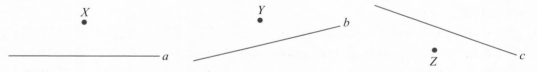

7. A boat sails from a harbour, H, on the mainland to a harbour, G, on an island. Throughout the journey the boat sails a course that remains at equal distances from the lighthouses R and S. Using only a compass and straight edge, draw the path of the boat and indicate on the diagram the locations of the harbours H and G.

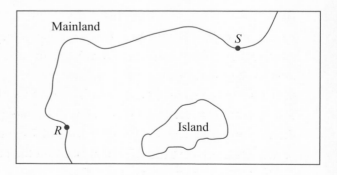

8. The diagram shows two fences that border a park that contains a circular garden, as shown. There is an entrance to the park where the two fences meet. A path is laid so that it is equidistant from each fence. Locate the point X on the circumference of the garden where that path meets the garden.

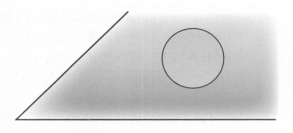

9. The diagram shows an island. There is treasure buried at the point T. T is equidistant from A and B and is also equidistant from C and D. Using only a compass and straight edge, locate the point T.

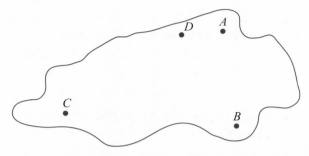

10. The diagram shows two straight roads connecting three towns A, B and C. A gas pipe was laid that is equidistant from towns B and C. Using a scale of 1 cm to 1 km, copy the diagram.

   (i) On your diagram, construct the path of the gas pipe.

   (ii) A new gas pipe is to be laid from town B that is to be equidistant from towns A and C. This new gas pipe is to connect to the older gas pipe at the point X. On your diagram, construct the path of the new gas pipeline and indicate the point X.

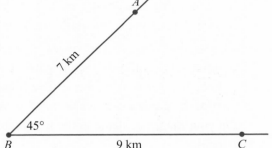

11. An electrical firm is asked to fit an outdoor spotlight in a rectangular garden measuring 16 m by 10 m. The light must be the same distance from the two corners, P and Q, of the back wall of the house, but also has to be the same distance from the fence RS at the end of the garden and the side of the garden, PS. Using a scale of 1 cm to 2 m, draw a scale drawing of the garden and find the position of the spotlight. Mark its position T.

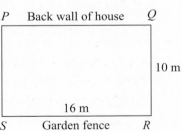

12. Construct each of the following line segments exactly. Using only a compass, straight edge and set square, show how to divide each of the line segments into three equal parts, showing all your construction lines. In each case, use your ruler to check your work.

A ————————— B   P ————————— Q   X ————————— Y
      9 cm $7\frac{1}{2}$ cm   63 mm

13. Draw the line segment [AB] such that |AB| = 10 cm. Using only a compass, straight edge and set square, show how to divide [AB] into four equal parts, showing all your construction lines.

14. A farmer wants to erect four more posts equally spaced between the posts A and B, as shown. Using a scale of 1 cm = 1 m, construct an accurate diagram for the farmer. Show all construction lines, using only a compass, straight edge and set square.

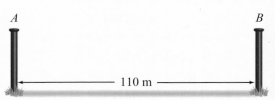

15. The diagram shows a rectangular garden, PQRS. Copy the diagram using a scale of 1 cm to 1 m. A concrete path is to be laid. The centre of the path runs diagonally from P to R.

The width of the concrete path is to be 1 m. On your diagram, shade in the concrete path. A circular flowerbed is to be planted in this garden. The flowerbed will cover the area of the garden that lies within 3 m from the point Q. On your diagram, shade in the region that the flowerbed occupies.

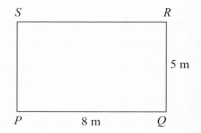

16. The diagram shows a circle with centre O and two chords, [PQ] and [RS]. Copy the diagram. Using only a compass and straight edge, construct the perpendicular bisectors of both chords. Show all your construction lines clearly. Comment on the point of intersection of the two chords.

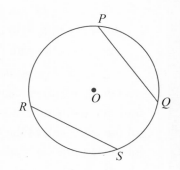

Constructing triangles and quadrilaterals

Triangles

The method used for drawing a triangle depends on the information you are given. We will look at four cases. A triangle can be drawn if you are given:

> 1. The length of the three sides (SSS).
>
> 2. The length of two sides and the angle between them (SAS).
>
> 3. The length of one side and two angles (ASA).
>
> 4. A right angle, the length of the hypotenuse and one other side (RHS).
>
> In each case, make a rough sketch at the beginning.

Note: If you know two angles in a triangle, it is possible to calculate the third angle. The four cases above are related to the **four cases of congruence**.

1. Given the length of the three sides (SSS)

Construct triangle ABC with $|AB| = 7$ cm, $|AC| = 6$ cm and $|BC| = 5$ cm.

Solution:

1. A rough sketch with the given information is shown on the right.

2. Using a ruler, draw a horizontal line segment 7 cm in length. Label the end points A and B.

3. Set your compass to a radius of 6 cm.
   Place the compass point on the point A.
   Draw an arc above the line segment.
   Set your compass to a radius of 5 cm.
   Place the compass point on the point B.
   Draw an arc above the line segment to meet the other arc.
   Label the point where the arcs meet C.

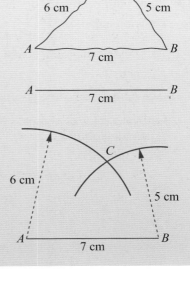

4. Using your ruler, join *A* to *C* and *B* to *C*.
The triangle *ABC* is now drawn as required.

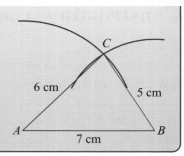

2. Given the length of two sides and the measure of the angle between them (SAS)

Construct triangle *PQR* with $|PQ| = 6$ cm, $|PR| = 5$ cm and $|\angle QPR| = 55°$.

Solution:

1. A rough sketch with the given information is shown on the right.

2. Using a ruler, draw a horizontal line segment 6 cm in length. Label the end points *P* and *Q*.

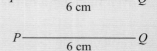

3. Place your protractor on the point *P*.
Draw an angle of 55°.

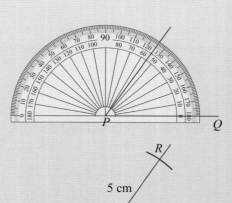

4. Use your ruler or compass to mark the point *R* such that $|PR| = 5$ cm.

5. Using your ruler, join *Q* to *R*.
Triangle *PQR* is now drawn as required.

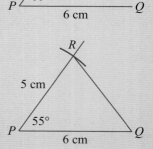

3. Given the length of one side and the measure of two angles (ASA)

Construct the triangle XYZ with $|XY| = 5$ cm, $|\angle YXZ| = 40°$ and $|\angle XYZ| = 70°$.

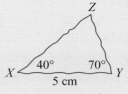

Solution:

1. A rough sketch with the given information is
   shown on the right.

2. Using a ruler, draw a horizontal line segment 5 cm in length.
   Label the end points X and Y.

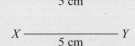

3. Place your protractor on the point X.
   Draw an angle of 40°.

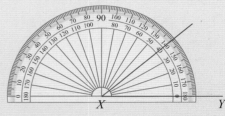

4. Place your protractor on the point Y.
   Draw an angle of 70°.

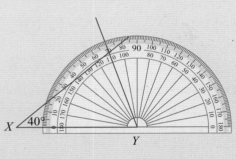

5. Where these two lines meet, label the point Z.
   The triangle XYZ is now drawn as required.

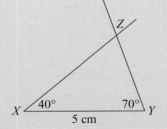

4. Given a right angle, length of the hypotenuse and the length of one other side (RHS)

Construct triangle ABC with $|\angle BAC| = 90°$, $|AB| = 7$ cm and $|BC| = 8$ cm.

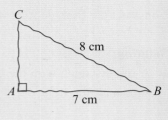

Solution:

1. A rough sketch with the given information is shown on the right.

2. Using a ruler, draw a horizontal line segment 7 cm in length. Label the end points A and B.

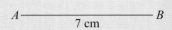

3. Using a set square or protractor, draw an angle of 90° at A.

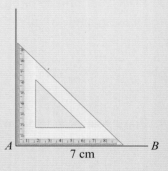

4. Set your compass to a radius of 8 cm. Place the compass point on the point B. Draw an arc to meet the vertical line. Label this point C.

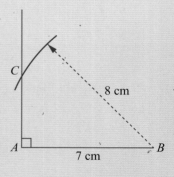

5. Using your ruler, join B to C. Triangle ABC is now drawn as required.

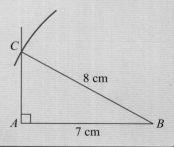

Quadrilaterals

As with triangles, always make a rough sketch at the begining.

Parallelogram

Construct parallelogram $ABCD$ such that $|AB| = 8$ cm, $|BC| = 5$ cm and $|\angle BAD| = 70°$.

1. A rough sketch with the given information is shown on the right.

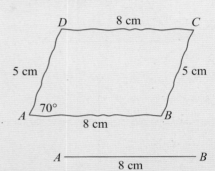

2. Using a ruler, draw a horizontal line segment 8 cm in length. Label the end points A and B.

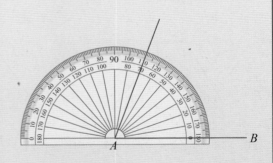

3. Place your protractor on the point A. Draw an angle of 70°.

4. Place your protractor on the point B. Draw an angle of 70°.

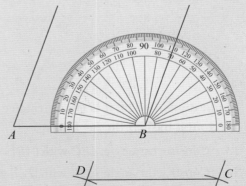

5. Use your ruler or compass to mark the points D and C such that $|AD| = 5$ cm and $|BC| = 5$ cm.
   Join D to C.
   Parallelogram $ABCD$ is now drawn.

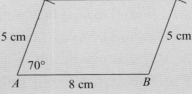

Exercise 30.2

Accurately construct each of the triangles in questions 1–20, with all dimensions in centimetres (the diagrams are not drawn to scale).

1.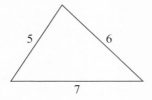

2.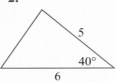

3.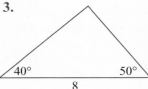

4.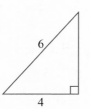

5.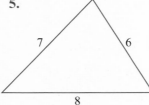

6.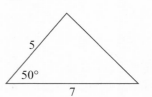

7.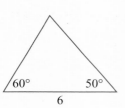

8.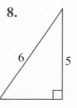

9.

10.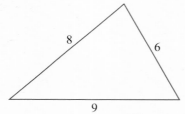

11.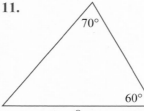

12.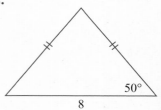

In questions 13–20, it is good practice to draw a rough sketch first and to draw one side as a horizontal base at the beginning.

13. Construct triangle ABC with $|AB| = 9$ cm, $|AC| = 8$ cm and $|BC| = 7$ cm.

14. Construct triangle PQR with $|PQ| = 8$ cm, $|QR| = 6$ cm and $|\angle PQR| = 30°$.

15. Construct triangle PQR with $|PQ| = 5$ cm, $|\angle RPQ| = 60°$ and $|\angle RQP| = 45°$.

16. Construct triangle XYZ with $|XY| = 8$ cm, $|XZ| = 6$ cm and $|\angle YXZ| = 90°$. Write down $|YZ|$.

17. Construct triangle ABC with $|AB| = 6$ cm, $|AC| = 5$ cm and $|BC| = 4$ cm.

18. Construct triangle PQR with $|PQ| = 7$ cm, $|\angle RPQ| = 80°$ and $|PR| = 6$ cm.

19. Construct triangle XYZ with $|\angle YXZ| = 90°$, $|XZ| = 6$ cm and $|\angle XYZ| = 35°$.

20. Construct triangle ABC with $|AB| = 8$ cm, $|\angle BAC| = 30°$ and $|\angle ABC| = 110°$.

21. Construct the following parallelograms.

(i)　　　　　　　　　　**(ii)**　　　　　　　　　　**(iii)**

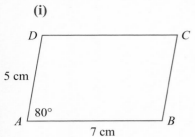　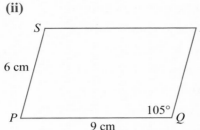　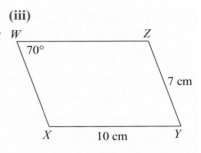

In questions 22–25, it is good practice to draw a rough sketch first and to draw one side as a horizontal base at the beginning.

22. Construct parallelogram $ABCD$ such that $|AB| = 6$ cm, $|\angle BAD| = 50°$ and $|AD| = 4$ cm.

23. Construct parallelogram $PQRS$ such that $|SR| = 8$ cm, $|\angle QPS| = 75°$ and $|QR| = 6$ cm.

24. Construct parallelogram $XYZW$ such that $|XY| = 9$ cm, $|YZ| = 7$ cm, $|\angle YXZ| = 30°$ and $|\angle XZY| = 35°$.

25. Construct parallelogram $PQRS$ such that $|PQ| = 12$ cm, $|QR| = 5$ cm and $|\angle PQR| = 90°$.

    (i) What type of parallelogram is $PQRS$?

    (ii) Using your ruler, find $|PR|$.

    (iii) Verify your answer by using Pythagoras' theorem.

26. In parallelogram $ABCD$, $|\angle BAD| = (3x + 5)°$ and $|\angle BCD| = (x + 45)°$.

    (i) Complete the statement:

      Opposite angles in a parallelogram are _____ in measure.

    (ii) Write down an equation in x.

    (iii) Solve your equation for x and calculate $|\angle BAD|$.

    (iv) $|AB| = 9$ cm and $|BC| = \frac{2}{3}|AB|$.

      Construct the parallelogram $ABCD$.

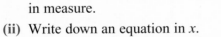

27. Construct the following quadrilaterals.

(i)

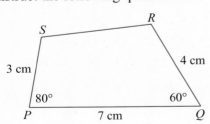

Measure and write down:

    (a) $|RS|$　　**(b)** $|\angle QRS|$

(ii)

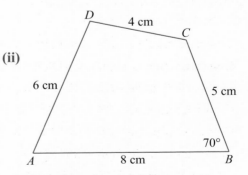

Measure and write down:

    (a) $|\angle ADC|$　　**(b)** $|\angle BCD|$

28. The diagram shows the sketch of a large office.

 (i) Construct an accurate scale drawing of the office. Use a scale of 1 cm to represent 10 m.

 (ii) A new printer is going to be installed in the office. The new printer must be same distance from A and B. Construct the set of points in the office equidistant from A and B.

 (iii) The printer must also be within 45 m of point C. Construct the set of points which are exactly 45 m from C.

 (iv) Show on your diagram all possible positions for the printer.

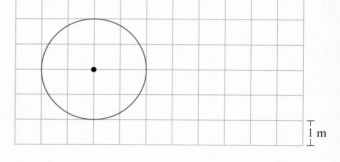

29. The diagram shows a rectangular lawn, 11 m by 6 m, containing a circular flowerbed of radius 2 m. A rose bush is to be planted in the garden. The rose bush is to be at least 1 m from the edge of the garden and at least 2 m from the flowerbed. On the diagram, shade in the region where the rose bush can be planted.

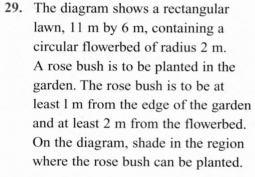

30. The diagram shows a rectangular garden, 24 m by 18 m. A tree is to be planted in the garden. The tree must be 12 m from P and the tree must be the same distance from SR and RQ. Copy the diagram using a scale of 1 cm to 3 m. Using only a compass and straight edge, construct the position of the tree.

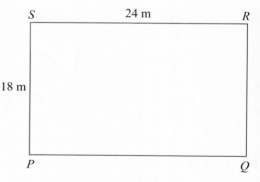

31. In a garden, a dog is on a lead that is 3 m in length. The lead is connected with a metal loop to a 10 m metal rail fixed horizontally to the ground so that the lead can slide easily along its length, as shown. Using a scale of 1 cm to 1 m, draw a diagram of the rail and shade the area of the garden that the dog can play on.

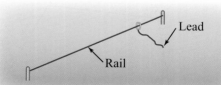

32. On a page indicate the point X. Construct an accurate diagram to indicate the set of all points such that each point is less than or equal to 5 cm from X.

33. On a page indicate the point Y. Construct an accurate diagram to indicate the set of all points such that each point is greater than or equal to 2 cm from Y and less than or equal to 6 cm from Y.

34. On a page draw two points A and B such that $|AB| = 6$ cm. Construct an accurate drawing to indicate the set of all points which are the same distance from A and B and also closer to A.

35. The two points P and Q are such that $|PQ| = 5$ cm. Construct the points. On your diagram, shade the region which contains all the points that satisfy both conditions:

  (i) The distance from P is less than or equal to 4 cm

  (ii) The distance from P is greater than or equal to the distance from Q

36. The diagram shows a seconds clock, not drawn to scale. The real length of the seconds arm is 5 cm. Make a copy of the clock using the correct scale. A small spider crawls at a constant speed along the seconds hand as it rotates. It starts at the centre when the hand is pointing to 60. It reaches the end of the hand 50 seconds later. By drawing lines from the centre to 5, 10, 15 and so on, find points on the spider's path and draw as accurately as you can the path (locus) of the spider's journey.

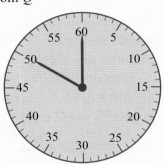

USING EQUATIONS TO SOLVE PROBLEMS

Forming expressions

Statements in words can be translated into algebraic expressions. It is common to let x represent the unknown number, usually the smallest, in a problem given in words. However, any other letter would do.

For example, if x represents an unknown number, then:

Words	Expression
5 more than the number	$(x + 5)$
2 less than the number	$(x - 2)$
3 times the number	$3x$
4 times the number, less 1	$(4x - 1)$
a third of the number	$\frac{1}{3}x$ or $\frac{x}{3}$
the number subtracted from 6	$6 - x$
the difference between two numbers is 8	x and $(x + 8)$
two numbers add up to 10	x and $(10 - x)$
the number plus 3, then divided by 4	$\dfrac{x + 3}{4}$

Steps in constructing an equation in solving a practical problem

A numerical problem given in words can often be translated into an equation. The solution of this equation will give the answer to the problem. To solve a practical problem by constructing an equation, do the following.

> **Step 1:** Read the question carefully a few times.
> **Step 2:** Let x equal the unknown number that is required.
> **Step 3:** Write each statement in the problem in terms of x. Use a diagram if necessary.
> **Step 4:** Use the information in the problem to link the parts in step 3 to form an equation. Make sure both sides are measured in the same units.
> **Step 5:** Solve the equation (find the unknown number).
> **Step 6:** Test your solution in the problem itself – **not in your equation**, as your equation may be wrong.

Note: If the problem requires simultaneous equations to be solved, then step 2 becomes 'Let x and y equal the unknown numbers that are required.'

When an equation is constructed from a problem given in words, it may lead to any one of three types of equation:

1. Simple linear equation   **2.** Simultaneous linear equations   **3.** Quadratic equation

Using simple equations to solve problems

EXAMPLE 1

The sum of three consecutive odd numbers is 87.

(i) If the smallest number is x, express the other two numbers in terms of x.

(ii) Write an equation in terms of x to represent this information and solve the equation to find the value of x.

(iii) Write down the three numbers.

Solution:

(i) $x =$ the smallest number.

The next number is 2 more than x, i.e. $(x + 2)$.

The next number is 4 more than x, i.e. $(x + 4)$.

(ii) **Link used to form the equation:**

Given: Sum of the three numbers is 87.

Equation: $x + (x + 2) + (x + 4) = 87$

$$x + x + 2 + x + 4 = 87$$
$$3x + 6 = 87$$
$$3x = 81$$
$$x = 27$$

(iii) $x = 27$ is the smallest number.

$x + 2 = 27 + 2 = 29$ is the next number.

$x + 4 = 27 + 4 = 31$ is the other number.

Check:

	LHS	RHS
	$x + (x + 2) + (x + 4)$	87
	$27 + (27 + 2) + (27 + 4)$	
	87	

$$\text{LHS} = \text{RHS}$$

Thus, the three numbers are 27, 29 and 31.

Note: If you are not told that the smallest number is x, then letting the three consecutive odd numbers be $(x - 2)$, x and $(x + 2)$ can simplify your equation.

EXAMPLE 2

The difference between two numbers is 5.
Half the larger number less one-third the smaller number is 4.
Find the numbers.

Solution:

Let x = smaller number.

Then $(x + 5)$ = the larger number.   (5 more than x)

Half the larger number $= \dfrac{(x + 5)}{2}$. $\left(\dfrac{\text{larger number}}{2} \right)$

One third the smaller number $= \dfrac{x}{3}$. $\left(\dfrac{\text{smaller number}}{3} \right)$

Link used to form an equation:

Given: (Half the larger number) − (one-third the smaller number) = 4

Equation: $\dfrac{(x + 5)}{2} - \dfrac{x}{3} = 4$

$\dfrac{6(x + 5)}{2} - \dfrac{6(x)}{3} = 6(4)$ (multiply both sides by 6)

$3(x + 5) - 2(x) = 24$ (divide the bottom into the top)

$3x + 15 - 2x = 24$ (remove the brackets)

$x + 15 = 24$ (simplify the left-hand side)

$x = 9$ (subtract 15 from both sides)

$x = 9$ is the smaller number.

$x + 5 = 9 + 5 = 14$ is the larger number.

Check:

LHS	RHS
$\dfrac{(x + 5)}{2} - \dfrac{x}{3}$	4
$\dfrac{14}{2} - \dfrac{9}{3}$	
$7 - 3$	
4	

LHS = RHS

Thus, the numbers are 9 and 14.

Note: This problem could have been solved using simultaneous equations.

Let x = the larger number and y = the smaller number.

Write two equations in x and y and solve these equations simultaneously.

Exercise 31.1

1. A certain number is multiplied by 5 and then 2 is taken away. The result is 18. Find the number.

2. When 6 is taken from four times a certain number, the answer is 22. Find the number.

3. A certain number is multiplied by 3 and then 4 is taken away. The result is the same as multiplying the number by 2 and then adding on 10. Find the number.

4. One number is 3 more than another number. If 10 times the smaller number is equal to 4 times the larger number, find the numbers.

5. One number is 4 more than another number. If five times the smaller number is equal to three times the larger number, find the numbers.

6. A bar of chocolate costs x cent.

   A bottle of orange juice costs 10 cent more than a bar of chocolate.
   Two bars of chocolate and one bottle of orange juice cost €2·50.

   (i) Write this information as an equation in x.

   (ii) Solve for x.

   (iii) What is the cost of a bottle of orange juice?

7. Find the value of x and y in each of the following parallelograms.

   (i)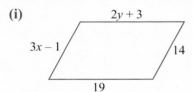

   (ii)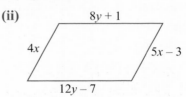

8. The length of a rectangle is 4 cm greater than its breadth, as shown.

   (i) Find, in terms of x, the perimeter of the rectangle.

   If the perimeter is 32 cm.

   (ii) Use this information to form an equation

   (iii) Solve the equation to find the value of x

9. The length of a rectangle is 3 cm longer than the breadth.

   If the breadth is x cm, write in terms of x:

   (i) The length of the rectangle

   (ii) The perimeter of the rectangle

If the perimeter of the rectangle is 26 cm:

(iii) Use this information to form an equation

(iv) Solve the equation to find the value of x

10. In a bag there are 44 discs, x of which are blue. There are four times as many red discs as blue and two more green than blue. Write down an equation in x to represent this information and solve it to calculate x.

11. **(i)** If x is an odd number, express, in terms of x, the next three odd numbers.

　　 (ii) If the sum of three consecutive odd numbers plus twice the next odd number is 73, find the four numbers.

12. Find three consecutive numbers that add up to 21.

13. Find three consecutive numbers that add up to 45.

14. **(i)** The difference between two numbers is 9. If the smaller number is x, express the larger number in terms of x.

　　 (ii) One-quarter of the larger number less two-thirds the smaller number is 1. Write down an equation in x to represent this information and solve it to calculate x.

　　 (iii) What is the larger number?

15. Two cylindrical buckets hold 18 litres and 6 litres of liquid, respectively. To each bucket are now added another $2x$ litres of liquid, so that the first one now holds twice as much as the second one.

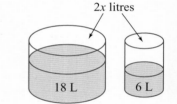

2x litres

18 L　　6 L

　　 (i) Express the volume of liquid in each bucket in terms of x.

　　 (ii) Form an equation in x.

　　 (iii) Solve the equation to find the value of x.

16. A woman's age this year is four times that of her son. In five years' time she will be three times as old as her son.

　　 (i) If the son's age is x years this year, find, in terms of x, his mother's age now.

　　 (ii) Write, in terms of x, their ages in five years' time.

　　 (iii) Form an equation in x.

　　 (iv) Solve the equation to find the value of x.

　　 (v) What age is each of them now?

17. Molly ate x sweets. Laura ate two sweets less than Molly. Janice ate three sweets more than Molly and Laura combined. If they ate 27 sweets altogether, how many sweets did each of the girls eat?

18. Adam receives €x pocket money each week. Ryan gets €1 less than Adam. Mark receives €2 less than Adam and Ryan combined. If they receive €16 altogether, how much pocket money does each boy receive?

19. A girl bought a coat for €$\frac{x}{3}$ and a dress for €$\frac{x}{5}$.

The total amount of money she spent was €112.

   (i) Use this information to form an equation in x.

  (ii) Solve the equation to find the value of x.

 (iii) Find the cost of her (a) coat (b) dress.

20.   (i) 1,500 people attended a concert when the price was €10 per ticket per person. Calculate the amount taken in by the venue.

  (ii) For another concert $(1,500 - x)$ people attended, but the price was €12 per ticket per person and the total income was €1,200 more. Form an equation in x to represent this information.

 (iii) Find the value of x.

21.   (i) A small firm employs 10 people, x of which are men. Express, in terms of x, the number of women.

  (ii) Each man earns €20 per hour and each woman earns €18 per hour. The total wages per hour amount to €192. Use this information to form an equation and use it to calculate x.

22.   (i) Express distance in terms of time and average speed.

  (ii) A car travels for 5 hours at an average speed of x km/h. Calculate, in terms of x, the distance travelled by the car.

 (iii) Two trains, one of which travels at an average speed of 10 km/h faster than the other, start towards each other at the same time from two places 320 km apart. They pass each other after two hours. The speed of the slower train is x km/h. Express in terms of x:

    (a) The speed of the faster train

    (b) The distance travelled by each train

    (c) Use this information to form an equation.

    (d) Solve the equation to find the value of x.

    (e) What is the average speed of the faster train?

23. A girl cycles from her home at an average speed of 15 km/h and immediately boards a train which then travels at an average speed of 45 km/h to her destination. The total distance travelled is 95 km and the total journey takes the girl 3 hours.

If the distance cycled by the girl was x km, express in terms of x:

(i) The distance travelled by the girl on the train

(ii) The time cycling

(iii) The time spent travelling on the train

(iv) Given that the total journey time is 3 hours, write down an equation in x to represent this information and use it to calculate x.

(v) How long, in hours and minutes, was the girl cycling?

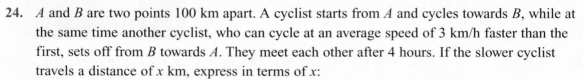

24. A and B are two points 100 km apart. A cyclist starts from A and cycles towards B, while at the same time another cyclist, who can cycle at an average speed of 3 km/h faster than the first, sets off from B towards A. They meet each other after 4 hours. If the slower cyclist travels a distance of x km, express in terms of x:

(i) The distance travelled by the faster cyclist

(ii) The average speed of the slower cyclist

(iii) The average speed of the faster cyclist

(iv) Form an equation in x to express the difference of their average speeds, and solve it to find the value of x.

(v) What is the average speed of the faster cyclist?

Using simultaneous equations to solve problems

Method:

> 1. Let x = one unknown number and y = the other unknown number.
> 2. Look for **two** facts that **link** x and y, and form two equations.
> 3. Solve these simultaneous equations.

EXAMPLE

300 people came to a school play, each adult paying €10 and each child paying €5. One of the organisers remarked that if each adult had been charged €12 and each child €4, there would have been an extra €240 taken in. How many adults and how many children came to the school play?

Solution:

Let x = number of adults and y = number of children.

First fact that links x and y:

Given: The total number of people who came was 300.

Equation: $x + y = 300$ ①

Second fact that links x and y:

Total money paid in: new situation: €$(12x + 4y)$

Total money paid in: old situation: €$(10x + 5y)$

Given: (Total money paid in new situation) − (Total money paid in old situation) = €240

Equation: $(12x + 4y) - (10x + 5y) = 240$
$$12x + 4y - 10x - 5y = 240$$
$$2x - y = 240 \quad ②$$

Now solve the simultaneous equations ① and ②.

$$
\begin{array}{ll}
x + y = 300 & ① \\
\underline{2x - y = 240} & ② \\
3x = 540 & \text{(adding the rows)} \\
x = 180
\end{array}
\qquad
\begin{array}{ll}
x + y = 300 & ① \\
180 + y = 300 & \\
y = 120 &
\end{array}
$$

Put $x = 180$ into ① or ②.

Check:

Equation ①	
LHS	**RHS**
$x + y$	300
$180 + 120$	
300	
LHS = RHS	

Equation ②	
LHS	**RHS**
$(12x + 4y) - (10x + 5y)$	240
$[12(180) + 4(120)] - [10(180) + 5(120)]$	
$2{,}640 - 2{,}400$	
240	
LHS = RHS	

Thus, the number of adults was 180 and the number of children was 120.

Note: This problem could have been solved using a single variable equation.

Let x = the number of adults, $\therefore (300 - x)$ = the number of children.

Then proceed to set up a single variable equation to find x.

Exercise 31.2

1. If x is a positive odd number and y is a positive even number, state which of the following can be true.

   (i) $2x = 14$ (ii) $2y = 18$ (iii) $3x = 24$

   (iv) $5y = 40$ (v) $2x = 21$ (vi) $x + y = 10$

   (vii) $2x + y = 20$ (viii) $x + y = 11$ (ix) $x + y - 10 = 6$

2. The sum of two numbers is 15. Their difference is 7.

   Let x = the larger number and y = the smaller number.

   (i) Write two equations in x and y to represent this information.

   (ii) Solve the simultaneous equations to find the numbers.

3. The difference between two numbers is 8. The sum of the two numbers is 20. Find the numbers.

4. The sum of four times one number and three times a second number is 61. If twice the first number less the second number is 13, find the numbers.

5. Five pens and two pencils cost €2·50. Three pens and two pencils are €1·70.

   (i) Write (a) €2·50 and   (b) €1·70 as cent.

   Let x cent be the price of a pen and y cent the price of a pencil.

   (ii) Write down an equation in x and y to show the price of

       (a) five pens and two pencils   (b) three pens and two pencils.

   (iii) Solve your two equations simultaneously.

   (iv) What is the price of (a) a pen   (b) a pencil?

6. Eight cans of cola and two packets of peanuts cost €5·30. Six cans of cola and two packets of peanuts cost €4·10.

   (i) Write (a) €5·30 and (b) €4·10 as cent

   Let x cent be the price of a can of cola and y cent the price of a packet of peanuts.

   (ii) Write down an equation in x and y to represent the data.

   (iii) Calculate the price of (a) a can of cola and   (b) a packet of peanuts.

7. A school bought 20 tickets for a show. Some were teachers' tickets, costing €8 each, and some were pupils' tickets, costing €5 each. The total price of the tickets was €118. Let x be the number of teachers' tickets bought and y be the number of pupils' tickets bought.

   (i) Write down an equation in x and y for the total number of tickets bought.

   (ii) Write down an equation in x and y for the total price of the tickets.

   (iii) Solve your two equations simultaneously.

   (iv) How many of each type of ticket did the school buy?

8. All 80 members of a club voted to elect the president of the club. There were only two candidates, Anne and Brian. Anne beat Brian by 20 votes.

   Let x be the number of votes Anne received and y the number of votes Brian received.
   - **(i)** Write an equation in x and y for the number of members in the club who voted.
   - **(ii)** Write an equation in x and y for the difference between the number of votes Anne received and the number of votes Brian received.
   - **(iii)** Solve your two equations simultaneously.
   - **(iv)** How many members of the club voted for Anne?

9. Two numbers are such that if 2 is added to the first the answer is twice the second. If 7 is subtracted from the first number, the answer is half the second.
   - **(i)** Write two equations to represent this information.
   - **(Hint:** Let x = the first number and y = the second number.)
   - **(ii)** Find the two numbers.

10. A bag contains 20 coins, all of them either 10c or 50c coins. If the value of coins in the bag is €7·60, how many of each coin does the bag contain?

    (Hint: Let x = the number of 10c coins and y = the number of 50c coins.)

11. The following diagram shows a pattern which continues:

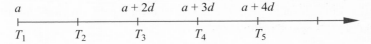

   - **(i)** Write an equation with a and d for the second term.
   - **(ii)** Write an equation with a and d for the seventh term.
   - **(iii)** If the second term, T_2, is 9 and the seventh term, T_7, is 49, solve the equations to find the values of a and d.
   - **(iv)** Hence find the tenth term, T_{10}.

12. A survey was carried out on Saturday night television viewing in a transition year group. The students were asked whether they watched *Match of the Day* (*M*) or *The X Factor* (*X*). The information is shown on the Venn diagram.
   - **(i)** Given 20 students watched *Match of the Day* (*M*), write this information in terms of p and q.
   - **(ii)** The total number of students surveyed was 75. Write an equation in terms of p and q to represent this information.
   - **(iii)** Hence, solve these equations for p and q.

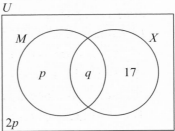

13. A firm exports two types of machine, P and Q. Type P occupies 2 m^3 of space and type Q occupies 4 m^3. Type P weighs 9 kg and type Q weighs 6 kg. The machines occupied 160 m^3 of space on a ship and their total weight was 360 kg.

Letting x = the number of type P exported and y = the number of type Q exported:

 (i) Write down an equation in x and y for the space occupied by the machines.

 (ii) Write down an equation in x and y for the weight of the machines.

 (iii) How many of each machine was exported?

14. During a certain day a factory produced two types of bicycles, racing bicycles and mountain bicycles.

The following table shows the cost and time requirement for each bicycle.

Type	Racing bicycle	Mountain bicycle
Cost of materials	€45	€30
Labour hours	5	4

 (i) The total amount of money spent on materials was €540 and the total labour time was 64 hours. Calculate the number of racing bicycles and the number of mountain bicycles produced.

 (**Hint:** Let x = the number of racing bicycles and y = the number of mountain bicycles produced.)

 (ii) If the profit on each racing bicycle is €60 and the profit on each mountain bicycle is €50, calculate the profit for the day.

15. A holiday campsite caters for caravans and tents. There are x caravans and y tents on the campsite. Each caravan accommodates eight people and each tent accommodates five people. On a particular evening each caravan and each tent is full, and the number of people on the campsite is 400. Each caravan is allotted 60 m^2 and each tent is allotted 50 m^2. The total area available is 3,600 m^2 and there is no more room left for a caravan or a tent.

 (i) Write two equations in x and y, one for the number of people on the campsite and the other for the area allotted to a caravan and a tent.

 (ii) How many caravans and how many tents are on the site?

 (iii) If the charges on the site are €30 for a caravan and €20 for a tent, calculate the income for the campsite owners for this particular evening.

16. **(i)** 7 is the mean of the six numbers 2, 4, x, y, $2x$, 13. Write this information in an equation with x and y.

    (ii) 6·5 is the median of 2, 4, x, y, $2x$, 13 written in ascending order. Use this information to write an equation with x and y.

    (iii) Hence, solve the equations for x and y.

17. The three numbers $x + y$, $2x - y$ and 18 are written in ascending order. The mean and median of the three numbers equals 13.

    (i) Write two equations in x and y to represent the information.

    (ii) Hence, solve the two equations for x and y.

18. The isosceles triangle has a perimeter of 18 cm. Solve for a and b.

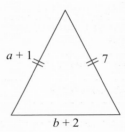

19. The given triangle has a hypotenuse of length 25 cm and perimeter of 53 cm.

    (i) Write down two equations in a and b.

    (ii) Hence, solve for a and b.

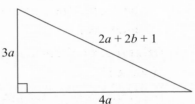

20. The following diagram shows a pie chart and a triangle.

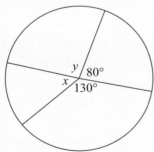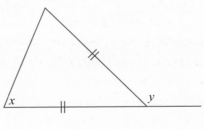

    (i) Use the given pie chart to write an equation in terms of x and y.

    (ii) Use the given triangle to write an equation in terms of x and y.

    (iii) Hence, solve for x and y.

21. The opposite sides in a parallelogram are equal in length. Use this information to calculate the values of x and y for the following parallelograms (all dimensions are in centimetres).

(i)

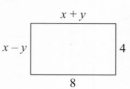

(ii)

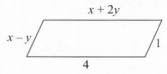

(iii)

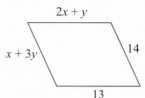

22. The opposite angles in a cyclic quadrilateral add up to $180°$. Use this information to calculate the value of x and y from the cyclic quadrilateral shown on the right.

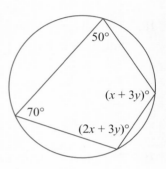

Using quadratic equations to solve problems

When we use an equation to solve a practical problem, the equation often turns out to be a quadratic equation. These equations usually have two solutions. If one of these makes no sense, for example producing a negative number of people, we reject it. Again, always look for the link in the question to set up the equation.

Note: The word 'product' means 'the result of multiplying'.

EXAMPLE

A rug is to fit in a room so that a border of consistent width is left on all four sides. If the room is 9 m by 25 m and the area of the rug is 57 m², how wide will the border be?

Solution:
Draw a diagram of the room and the rug.
• Let the width of the border be x.
• So the dimensions of the rug are:

$$\text{Length} = (25 - 2x)$$
$$\text{Width} = (9 - 2x)$$

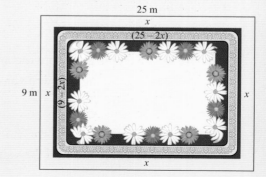

Area of the rug = (Length)(Width)

$$57 = (25 - 2x)(9 - 2x)$$
$$57 = 225 - 68x + 4x^2$$
$$0 = 4x^2 - 68x + 168 \qquad \text{(divide all parts by 4)}$$
$$0 = x^2 - 17x + 42$$
$$0 = (x - 3)(x - 14)$$
$$x - 3 = 0 \quad \text{or} \quad x - 14 = 0$$
$$x = 3 \quad \text{or} \qquad x = 14$$

We will reject $x = 14$ m, as this would be wider than the entire room.

Check:

LHS	RHS
57	$(25 - 2(3))(9 - 2(3))$
	$(25 - 6)(9 - 6)$
	$(19)(3)$
	57

LHS = RHS

Therefore, the border around the rug will be 3 m wide.

Exercise 31.3

1. When a number x is added to its square, the total is 30.
   Write down an equation in x to represent this information and solve it to calculate two possible values for x.

2. When a number x is subtracted from its square, the result is 12.
   Write down an equation in x to represent this information and solve it to calculate two possible values for x.

3. (i) A rectangle has a width of x m. Its length is 2 m longer than this. Write an expression in x for the area of the rectangle.

   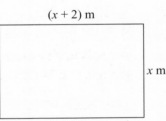

   If the area of the rectangle is 15 m²:

   (ii) Use this information to form an equation

   (iii) Solve the equation to find the value of x

4. A rectangle has a width of x m. Its length is 5 cm longer than this.

   (i) Sketch the rectangle, marking the length and width in terms of x.

   (ii) Write an expression in x for the area of the rectangle.

   If the area of the rectangle is 36 cm²:

   (iii) Use this information to form an equation

   (iv) Solve the equation to find the value of x

5. A square is altered so that one dimension is increased by 4, while the other dimension is decreased by 2. The area of the resulting rectangle is 55 cm^2.
   Find the area of the original square.

6. (i) A mug costs €$(x + 2)$ in a shop. A person bought x of these mugs at this price. Write, in terms of x, how much the person spent.

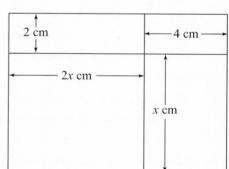

   If the person spent €80:

   (ii) Use the information to form an equation

   (iii) Solve the equation to find x

   (iv) What is the price of a mug?

7. (i) A man bought x articles at a price of €$(x - 2)$ each. Write an expression in x for the cost of the articles.

   If he spent €35 altogether:

   (ii) Use this information to form an equation

   (iii) Solve the equation to find the value of x

8. (i) A girl walked at an average speed of x km/h for $(x - 3)$ hours. Write, in terms of x, the distance walked by the girl.

   If the girl walked a distance of 18 km:

   (ii) Use the information to form an equation

   (iii) Solve the equation to find x

9. A rectangle of area 72 cm^2 is divided into four smaller rectangles. The lengths of the sides are as shown in the diagram.

   (i) Write down an equation in x to represent this information.

   (ii) Solve for x.

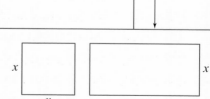

10. A square has a length of x cm.
    A rectangle has a length of 4 cm and a width of x cm.
    (i) Write, in terms of x, an expression for the area of
    (a) the square (b) the rectangle.

    If the area of the square added to the area of the rectangle is 12 cm^2:

    (ii) Use this information to form an equation

    (iii) Solve the equation to find x

11. A closed rectangular box has a square base of side x cm.
The height of the box is 5 cm.

The total surface area of the box is 288 cm^2.

Write down an equation in x to represent this
information and use it to calculate x.

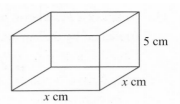

12. Four isosceles triangles of base x cm and height $(x + 2)$ cm are glued to the edges of a
square of side x cm. The tips of the triangles are brought to a point to make a pyramid. If
the total surface area of the pyramid, including the base, is 64 cm^2, find the value of x.

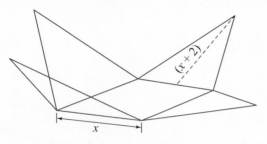

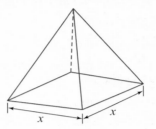

13. A farmer wants to fence off part of his garden.
He buys 18 metres of fencing and uses it to
make three sides of a rectangle, using trees
as the fourth side, as shown.

The length of one side of the rectangle is
x m and the length of the other side is
y m, where $x < y$.

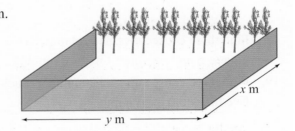

   (i) Write down an equation in x and y to represent this information.

   (ii) Express y in terms of x.

   (iii) If the area of the rectangle is 40 m^2, explain why $xy = 40$.

   (iv) Using your answer from part (ii), write down an equation in x only to represent the area
   of the rectangle and solve this equation to find the values of x and y.

14. One positive number is 2 greater than another positive number.

   (i) If the smaller number is x, write the larger number in terms of x.

   (ii) Write, in terms of x, an expression for the product of the two numbers.

   If the product is 8:

   (iii) Use this information to form an equation.

   (iv) Solve the equation to find x.

15. The profit P, in euro, gained by selling x laptops is modelled by the equation:

$$P = -5x^2 + 1,000x + 5,000$$

How many laptops must be sold to obtain a profit of €55,000?

16. An object is launched straight up into the air. Its height H, in metres, at t seconds is given by the equation $H = -16t^2 + 64t + 6$. Find the two times, t, for which the object is at a height of 54 metres off the ground.

17. A student opens a mathematics book to two facing pages. The product of the page numbers is 240. Find the page numbers.

18. Find three consecutive natural numbers such that the product of the first two numbers is two greater than four times the third number.

19. Find three consecutive even numbers such that the product of the first two is two less than five times the third number.

20. The three sides of a right triangle form three consecutive even numbers. Find the lengths of the three sides, measured in centimetres.

Exercise 1.1

1. $2x$ **2.** $4y$ **3.** $3x$ **4.** $3q$ **5.** 3 **6.** $2z$ **7.** 1 **8.** 1 **9.** $-2a$ **10.** $-2x$

11. $-y$ **12.** 2 **13.** $2x$ **14.** q **15.** $2a$ **16.** $3(x+y)$ **17.** $5(p-3q)$ **18.** $x(x+2)$

19. $2a(2a-1)$ **20.** $3p(p-2q)$ **21.** $-5p(q+2)$ **22.** $2xy(3x-2y)$ **23.** $-2x(x-3)$

24. $5(x+2)$ **25.** $p(q+r)$ **26.** $x(2+y)$ **27.** $x(x+5)$ **28.** $2x(2x+1)$ **29.** $a(a-3)$

30. $a(2-3b)$ **31.** $3a(b-2c)$ **32.** $x(x-1)$ **33.** $4x(2-3x)$ **34.** $x(x-6)$

35. $3c(5b-c)$ **36.** $4xy(x-2y)$ **37.** $ax(x+1)$ **38.** $5p(2-3q)$ **39.** $p(q+r+1)$

40. $ab(1-2a+3b)$ **41.** $4ab(2-3b+4a)$ **42. (i)** $36a(a-1) \neq 36a^2 - 12a$

(ii) $12a(3a-1)$ **43.** $(2x+1)$ cm **44.** $5x$ cm **45.** $x^2 - 4x; \ x(x-4)$

46. $3p^2 - 3pq; \ 3p(p-q)$ **47. (i) (a)** $6p(2q-1)$ **(b)** $3(2q-1)$ **(ii)** $2p$

Exercise 1.2

1. $(a+b)(c+d)$ **2.** $(p-q)(r-s)$ **3.** $(p+3q)(2x+y)$ **4.** $(x-2y)(3a-2b)$

5. $(x+y)(a+b)$ **6.** $(q+r)(p+x)$ **7.** $(m-n)(a+4)$ **8.** $(q+r)(p-3)$

9. $(x-3)(x+y)$ **10.** $(x-y)(x+z)$ **11.** $(p-2)(q+p)$ **12.** $(b-c)(a+c)$

13. $(2x-z)(3x+y)$ **14.** $(x-3y)(x+2a)$ **15.** $-3(p+q)$ **16.** $-5a(b+c)$

17. $-2x(x+1)$ **18.** $-2(p-q)$ **19.** $-x(x-3)$ **20.** $-x(3y-x)$ **21.** $1(a+b)$

22. $-1(y-x)$ **23.** $(b+c)(a-2)$ **24.** $(x+y)(x-3)$ **25.** $(p+q)(p-r)$

26. $(x+3)(p-q)$ **27.** $(a+b)(x+1)$ **28.** $(p+q)(x-1)$ **29.** $(x-y)(p-2)$

30. $(b-c)(a+1)$ **31.** $(x-2)(x-y)$ **32.** $(3-p)(p-q)$ **33.** $(p-q)(a+x)$

34. $(a-b)(5+2x)$ **35.** $(x-3y)(x-2a)$ **36.** $(x-y)(p-1)$ **37.** $(c+d)(a+b)$

38. $(q+r)(p+2)$ **39.** $(x+w)(y-z)$ **40.** $(x-y)(3-q)$ **41.** $(a+b)(2x-y)$

42. $(a+1)(b+2)$ **43.** $(a+b)(3-2a)$ **44.** $(p+3)(p-2q)$ **45.** $(a+b)(n-5)$

46. $(a-2b)(3x-2y)$ **47.** $(p+1)(p-2q)$ **48.** $(q+b)(q-2a)$ **49.** $(x-a)(x-b)$

50. $(a-b)(a-3)$ **51.** $(2p-q)(5r+p)$ **52.** $(a-y)(a-2x)$ **53.** $(a+b)$ cm

54. (i) $(x+y)$ and $(a+b)$ **55.**

$2ac$	$6ad$
bc	$3bd$

Exercise 1.3

1. $(2x+3)(x+1)$ **2.** $(3x+2)(x+3)$ **3.** $(2x-3)(x-2)$ **4.** $(3x+7)(x-1)$

5. $(2x+1)(x-5)$ **6.** $(3x-1)(x+3)$ **7.** $(5x+1)(x+3)$ **8.** $(5x-1)(x+2)$

9. $(7x - 2)(x + 1)$ **10.** $(2x - 5)(x + 2)$ **11.** $(3x + 5)(x - 2)$ **12.** $(3x + 2)(x - 1)$
13. $(2x + 1)(x - 3)$ **14.** $(x + 2)(x + 1)$ **15.** $(x + 3)(x + 4)$ **16.** $(x - 3)(x - 7)$
17. $(x - 5)(x + 3)$ **18.** $(x - 6)(x + 2)$ **19.** $(2x + 7)(x + 2)$ **20.** $(2x - 3)(x + 5)$
21. $(3x + 4)(x - 5)$ **22.** $(7x - 2)(x - 3)$ **23.** $(11x + 3)(x - 2)$ **24.** $(13x - 1)(x + 2)$
25. $(2x + 1)(2x + 3)$ **26.** $(3x + 1)(2x + 3)$ **27.** $(4x + 1)(x + 3)$ **28.** $(6x - 1)(x - 2)$
29. $(4x + 1)(x - 3)$ **30.** $(3x - 2)(2x + 1)$ **31.** $(4x + 5)(2x - 1)$ **32.** $(5x - 3)(2x + 1)$
33. $(9x - 7)(x + 1)$ **34.** $(6x + 5)(x - 2)$ **35.** $(4x - 3)(x + 2)$ **36.** $(3x + 4)(3x - 2)$
37. $(8x + 3)(x - 2)$ **38.** $(8x + 3)(3x - 1)$ **39.** $(5x - 4)(3x + 2)$ **40. (i)** 9   **(ii)** 18
41. $(2x - 5)(x + 3) = (ax + b)(cx + d)$ ∴ $a = 2, b = -5, c = 1$ and $d = 3$
42. (i) $(x + 5)$ cm   **(ii)** Length cannot be negative
43. (i) $a = 1, b = 14$ $a = 2, b = 7$

(ii)
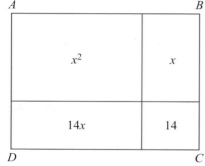 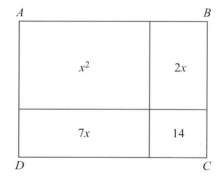

44. $(2x + 3)$ and $(x + 4)$ **45.**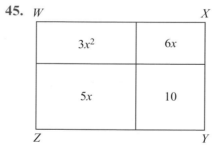

46. $2x^2 - x - 15; (2x + 5)(x - 3)$ **47.** $x^2 - 6x - 7; (x + 1)(x - 7)$
48. $2x^2 + 11x + 12; (2x + 3)(x + 4)$ **49.** $7x^2 + 15x + 8; (7x + 8)(x + 1)$
50. (i) 6   **(ii)** $2x^2 + 5x - 12; (2x - 3)(x + 4)$

Exercise 1.4

1. $(2a)^2$ **2.** $(3p)^2$ **3.** $(4b)^2$ **4.** $(6q)^2$ **5.** $(1)^2$ **6.** $(8x)^2$ **7.** $(9y)^2$ **8.** $(11p)^2$
9. $(12q)^2$ **10.** $(2p - 3q)(2p + 3q)$ **11.** $(4a - 5b)(4a + 5b)$ **12.** $(6x - 7y)(6x + 7y)$
13. $(8a - 9b)(8a + 9b)$ **14.** $(10 - 3a)(10 + 3a)$ **15.** $(1 - 5p)(1 + 5p)$

16. $(4x - 1)(4x + 1)$ **17.** $(5x - 2y)(5x + 2y)$ **18.** $(8q - 1)(8q + 1)$ **19.** $(q - 4)(q + 4)$

20. $(9a - 4b)(9a + 4b)$ **21.** $(x - 5)(x + 5)$ **22.** $(10 - a)(10 + a)$ **23.** $(5x - 4y)(5x + 4y)$

24. $(5a - 2)(5a + 2)$ **25.** $(7 - 10m)(7 + 10m)$ **26.** $(11x - 3y)(11x + 3y)$

27. $(12p - 5q)(12p + 5q)$ **28.** $(1 - 14x)(1 + 14x)$ **29.** $(10p - 9q)(10p + 9q)$

30. $(ab - 2c)(ab + 2c)$ **31.** $4x^2 - 9;\ (2x - 3)(2x + 3)$ **32.** $9x^2 - y^2;\ (3x - y)(3x + y)$

33. $49x^2 - 25y^2;\ (7x - 5y)(7x + 5y)$

Exercise 1.5

1. $3(x - y)(x + y)$ **2.** $2(x - 2y)(x + 2y)$ **3.** $3(2 - 3y)(2 + 3y)$ **4.** $5(x + 1)(x + 2)$

5. $3(x + 2)(x - 4)$ **6.** $4(x + 1)(x - 3)$ **7.** $3(a + b)(x + 2)$ **8.** $5(a + b)(2x - y)$

9. $2(a - b)(3 - q)$ **10.** $2a(3x - 5y)(3x + 5y)$ **11.** $6(2x + 1)(x + 3)$

12. $2q(3x - 2)(x + 4)$ **13.** $x(x + y)(x + 4)$ **14.** $5q(2p - 3q)(2p + 3q)$

15. $2ab(2p - q)(2p + q)$ **16.** $2p(q + r)(2p - 5)$ **17.** $3a(5a - 2b)(5a + 2b)$

18. $ab(2a - 5b)(2a + 5b)$ **19.** $3x(x - 2y)(x + 2y)$ **20.** $2a(5a - 7b)(5a + 7b)$

21. $2a(x + 5)(x - 3)$

22. **(i)** Yes. All products give $4x^2 - 4x - 8$.

(ii) If each term has a common factor other than ± 1. In this case, each term has a common factor of 4.

(iii) $4(x - 2)(x + 1)$; It has the HCF outside.

23. $25x^2 - 30x + 5;\ 5(5x - 1)(x - 1)$ **24.** $8x^2 - 18y^2;\ 2(2x - 3y)(2x + 3y)$

Exercise 2.1

1. $2x$ **2.** $3a$ **3.** $8b$ **4.** 2   **5.** 1   **6.** 3   **7.** 2   **8.** $\dfrac{3}{4}$ **9.** $\dfrac{5}{3}$ **10.** 2

11. $2x$ **12.** $2ab$ **13.** $x - 1$ **14.** $x + 3$ **15.** $3x$ **16.** $\dfrac{4}{x + 4}$ **17.** $\dfrac{1}{x - 2}$

18. $\dfrac{2}{x + 4}$ **19.** $\dfrac{x}{x + 3}$ **20.** $\dfrac{x + 3}{2x + 1}$ **21.** $\dfrac{3}{a + b}$ **22.** $\dfrac{2}{3}$ **23.** $\dfrac{2x}{3}$ **24.** 2   **25.** $\dfrac{x}{2}$

26. 2   **27.** $\dfrac{x}{y}$

Exercise 2.2

1. (i) $\dfrac{31}{45}$ **(ii)** $\dfrac{7}{30}$ **(iii)** $\dfrac{37}{60}$ **2. (i)** $\dfrac{11}{18}$ **(ii)** $-\dfrac{7}{18}$ **(iii)** $\dfrac{31}{18}$ **(iv)** $\dfrac{85}{18}$ **3. (i)** $\dfrac{47}{60}$ **(ii)** $\dfrac{9}{4}$

(iii) 2   **(iv)** $\dfrac{17}{20}$

Exercise 2.3

1. $\dfrac{17x}{12}$ 2. $\dfrac{13x}{6}$ 3. $\dfrac{x}{15}$ 4. $\dfrac{5x+13}{6}$ 5. $\dfrac{33x-17}{20}$ 6. $\dfrac{2-x}{21}$ 7. $\dfrac{x+5}{6}$ 8. $\dfrac{1}{12}$

9. $\dfrac{6x+1}{18}$ 10. $\dfrac{14x+11}{4}$ 11. $\dfrac{43}{12x}$ 12. $\dfrac{9}{20x}$ 13. $\dfrac{5x+7}{(x+1)(x+2)}$ 14. $\dfrac{5x+19}{(x+3)(x+5)}$

15. $\dfrac{3x}{(x+2)(x-4)}$ 16. $\dfrac{13x+14}{(2x+1)(3x+4)}$ 17. $\dfrac{18x-1}{(2x+1)(2x-1)}$ 18. $\dfrac{13x+4}{(3x-2)(2x+5)}$

19. $\dfrac{x+3}{2x(3x-1)}$ 20. $\dfrac{11x-29}{(2x-5)(x-3)}$ 21. $\dfrac{7-6x}{(3x-1)(2-3x)}$ 22. $\dfrac{3x+11}{x+3}$ 23. $\dfrac{5x+14}{3(x+4)}$

24. $\dfrac{2x+29}{6(2x-1)}$ 25. $\dfrac{x^2+3x+12}{4x(x+3)}$ 26. $\dfrac{x^2+10x+3}{3x(x+1)}$ 27. $\dfrac{x^2+4x-30}{3x(x-2)}$ 28. (i) $\dfrac{7}{12}$

(ii) $\dfrac{3}{14}$ 29. $\dfrac{11x-4}{30};\dfrac{3}{5}$ 30. $\dfrac{10x-1}{(2x+1)(2x-1)};3$ 31. 24   32. -1

33. (i) $\dfrac{13x-5}{10}$ (ii) $\dfrac{7a-1}{6}$ 34. (i) $p=2; q=3$ (ii) $a=7; b=-2$ 35. (i) $\dfrac{3}{x+2}$

(ii) $\dfrac{2}{2x-5}$ (iii) $\dfrac{-3}{3x-1}$ or $\dfrac{3}{1-3x}$ (iv) $\dfrac{1}{x-1}$ 36. (i) $\dfrac{2}{x-1}$ (ii) $\dfrac{3}{x-2}$ (iii) $\dfrac{10}{x-5}$

(iv) $\dfrac{8}{2x-3}$ (v) $\dfrac{5}{3x-1}$ (vi) $\dfrac{7}{2-5x}$ 37. (i) 0   (ii) 0   (iii) 1   (iv) 1

Exercise 3.1

1. x^2 2. $2x$ 3. $2x^2$ 4. 1   5. $4x$ 6. -2 7. $-2x$ 8. -1 9. -5

10. $-2x$ 11. $x+1$ 12. $x+3$ 13. $x+2$ 14. $x+4$ 15. $x+2$ 16. $x+5$

17. $x-3$ 18. $2x+5$ 19. x^2+3x+2 20. x^2+4x+3 21. x^2+3x+1

22. $2x^2+3x+1$ 23. x^2+2x+1 24. $2x^2+3x+4$ 25. x^2-2x-3 26. x^2+x-3

27. x^2-5x+6 28. x^2-3x-5 29. $2x^2+x-10$ 30. x^2-x-6 31. x^2+x-6

32. $x^2-2x-15$ 33. $2x^2-3x-5$ 34. $4x^2+3x-1$ 35. x^2-3x 36. $2x^2+10x$

37. x^2-x+2 38. $x^2+2x+15$ 39. x^2-4x+3 40. x^2-2x-1 41. $4x^2+8x+3$

42. $3x^2-8x+4$ 43. $x^2+3x+2; 24 \div 4 = 6$ 44. $x^2+x-2; 30 \div 3 = 10$

45. (i) $a=1, b=4, c=3$ (ii) (a) 6   (b) $(x+3)(x+1)$ 46. $(x-3)(x-2)$

47. (x^2+3x+3) cm   48. (i) (x^2+4x+4) cm^2 (ii) $(x+2)$ cm   (iii) Length be negative

49. x^2+4 50. x^2-5 51. $2x^2-7$ 52. x^2-4 53. x^2-2x+4 54. x^2+x-1

55. x^2+3x+9 56. $4x^2+10x+25$

Exercise 4.1

1. Not correct   2. Correct   3. Correct   4. Not correct   5. Not correct   6. Correct

7. Not correct   8. Not correct   9. Correct

Exercise 4.2

1. $x = 4$, $y = 3$ 2. $p = 6$, $q = 5$ 3. $x = 5$, $y = 4$ 4. $x = 4$, $y = 1$ 5. $x = 2$, $y = 1$

6. $x = 3$, $y = -1$ 7. $x = 3$, $y = 2$ 8. $p = -2$, $q = 5$ 9. $x = 1$, $y = -4$ 10. $x = 6$, $y = 1$

11. $g = 1$, $f = 4$ 12. $x = 5$, $y = 5$ 13. $x = 6$, $y = -3$ 14. $x = 1$, $y = 2$

15. $x = -2$, $y = 3$ 16. $x = -3$, $y = 5$ 17. $x = -1$, $y = 1$ 18. $f = 3$, $g = -2$

19. $x = 2$, $y = -3$ 20. $x = 10$, $y = 4$ 21. $x = 3$, $y = 3$ 22. $x = 15$, $y = 4$ 23. $x = 3$, $y = 4$

24. $x = -2$, $y = -1$ 25. $p = 2$, $q = -2$ 26. $m = 2$, $n = -2$ 27. $g = 1$, $f = 1$

28. $p = \dfrac{3}{2}$, $q = \dfrac{5}{2}$ 29. $f = 1$, $g = \dfrac{1}{3}$ 30. $x = \dfrac{3}{5}$, $y = \dfrac{4}{5}$ 31. $x = \dfrac{5}{2}$, $y = -\dfrac{5}{2}$

32. $x = 8$, $y = -\dfrac{2}{3}$ 33. $p = \dfrac{4}{5}$, $q = -\dfrac{3}{5}$ 34. 25   35. 34   36. (i) 3, 4   (ii) 5

37. (ii) 10, 25

Exercise 5.1

1.

Number	2·3	$\sqrt{3}$	$\sqrt{16}$	$3\dfrac{2}{5}$	32%	π	$\dfrac{-\sqrt{16}}{8}$	$\dfrac{\pi}{3}$	$-0{\cdot}625$	$\sqrt{7+9}$
Rational, $\mathbb{Q}$	$\dfrac{23}{10}$		$\dfrac{4}{1}$	$\dfrac{17}{5}$	$\dfrac{8}{25}$		$-\dfrac{1}{2}$		$-\dfrac{5}{8}$	$\dfrac{3}{1}$
Irrational, $\mathbb{R}\backslash\mathbb{Q}$		✓				✓		✓		

2. Yes. $-2\dfrac{1}{4} = -\dfrac{9}{4}$, can be written as a simple fraction.

3. True. All natural numbers can be written as a simple fraction. For example, $7 = \dfrac{7}{1}$.

4. False. For example, $\dfrac{2}{5}$ cannot be written as a positive or negative whole number.

Exercise 5.2

1. $2\sqrt{2}$ 2. $2\sqrt{5}$ 3. $3\sqrt{3}$ 4. $4\sqrt{2}$ 5. $2\sqrt{3}$ 6. $5\sqrt{2}$ 7. $10\sqrt{2}$ 8. $3\sqrt{5}$

9. $5\sqrt{5}$ 10. $2\sqrt{7}$ 11. $6\sqrt{2}$ 12. $7\sqrt{2}$ 13. $2\sqrt{6}$ 14. $8\sqrt{2}$ 15. $3\sqrt{7}$

16. $6\sqrt{5}$ 17. $2\sqrt{2}$ 18. Both equal $4\sqrt{3}$ 19. $\dfrac{2}{3}$ 20. $\dfrac{4}{5}$ 21. $\dfrac{9}{10}$ 22. $\dfrac{8}{7}$

23. $\dfrac{11}{9}$ 24. $\dfrac{1}{3}$ 25. $\dfrac{1}{5}$ 26. $\dfrac{3}{2}$ 27. $\dfrac{5}{4}$ 28. $\dfrac{8}{3}$ 29. $9\sqrt{2}$ 30. $6\sqrt{3}$ 31. $3\sqrt{5}$

32. $4\sqrt{3}$ 33. $4\sqrt{2}$ 34. $-2\sqrt{5}$ 35. $5\sqrt{2}$ 36. $6\sqrt{3}$ 37. $5\sqrt{2}$ 38. $9\sqrt{5}$

39. $3\sqrt{3}$ 40. $2\sqrt{2}$ 41. 6   42. $k = 12$; $\sqrt{12} = 2\sqrt{3}$ 43. $8\sqrt{2} + 2\sqrt{3}$ 44. $5\sqrt{5} - 2\sqrt{2}$

45. $\sqrt{\dfrac{49}{64}} = \dfrac{7}{8}$, which is a simple fraction and is therefore rational

Exercise 5.3

1. 2   2. 3   3. 5   4. 8   5. 4   6. 6   7. 6   8. 20   9. 20   10. 30   11. 60

12. 18   13. 1   14. 22   15. 7   16. −9   17. 2   18. 4   19. 41   20. 6

21. 6   22. (i) 18 (ii) 3   23. (i) 2 (ii) 4   24. 2   25. 5   26. $2\sqrt{2}$ 27. $17 + 5\sqrt{2}$

28. $1 + \sqrt{3}$ 29. $6 - 2\sqrt{5}$ 30. $7 + 4\sqrt{3}$ 31. $14 + 6\sqrt{5}$ 32. $27 - 10\sqrt{2}$ 33. $2 + \sqrt{2}$

34. $4 + 3\sqrt{2}$ 35. $4 + \sqrt{5}$ 36. $1 - \sqrt{5}$ 37. 1   38. 1   39. 1   40. 1   41. 2

42. Equals $\dfrac{3}{2}$, a simple fraction and is therefore rational   43. Equals $\dfrac{8}{3}$ 44. $33\sqrt{2} - 48$

45. $8 - 9\sqrt{2}$ 46. $4\sqrt{2}$ 47. $2\sqrt{3}$ 48. $4\sqrt{5}$ 49. $2\sqrt{2}$ 50. $3\sqrt{3}$ 51. $4\sqrt{2}$

52. (i) $3\sqrt{7}$ (ii) $2\sqrt{3}$ 53. $\dfrac{\sqrt{2}}{6}$ 54. Equals $\dfrac{5}{2}$, a simple fraction and is therefore rational

55. (i) $\sqrt{3} \times \dfrac{1}{\sqrt{3}} = 1$ (rational)   (ii) $(\sqrt{3} + 1)(\sqrt{3} - 1) = 2$ (rational)

Exercise 6.1

1. −4, 3   2. $-5, \dfrac{3}{2}$ 3. $-\dfrac{5}{2}, \dfrac{2}{3}$ 4. $0, \dfrac{3}{2}$ 5. −2, 0   6. $-\dfrac{2}{3}, \dfrac{2}{3}$ 7. $\dfrac{1}{2}, 5$

8. $-3, -\dfrac{1}{2}$ 9. $-\dfrac{5}{3}, 1$ 10. $-1, \dfrac{1}{5}$ 11. $-3, \dfrac{4}{3}$ 12. $-\dfrac{3}{2}, 1$ 13. $-4, -\dfrac{1}{7}$

14. $-4, \dfrac{2}{3}$ 15. $-1, \dfrac{2}{5}$ 16. −3, 7   17. −2, 8   18. −4, 6   19. −3, 0

20. 0, 2   21. 0, 5   22. $-\dfrac{5}{2}, 0$ 23. $0, \dfrac{2}{3}$ 24. $0, \dfrac{4}{5}$ 25. −2, 2   26. −5, 5

27. −1, 1   28. $-\dfrac{2}{3}, \dfrac{2}{3}$ 29. $-\dfrac{5}{2}, \dfrac{5}{2}$ 30. $-\dfrac{1}{2}, \dfrac{1}{2}$ 31. $-\dfrac{1}{4}, 3$ 32. $-\dfrac{5}{2}, \dfrac{1}{3}$

33. $\dfrac{1}{4}, \dfrac{3}{2}$ 34. 1, 1   35. $-\dfrac{1}{2}, -\dfrac{1}{2}$ 36. $\dfrac{2}{3}, \dfrac{2}{3}$ 37. $\dfrac{1}{4}, 7$ 38. $\dfrac{5}{6}, 4$ 39. $\dfrac{1}{2}, \dfrac{5}{2}$

40. $-2, -\dfrac{3}{2}$ 41. $\dfrac{2}{5}, \dfrac{1}{2}$ 42. −7, 0   43. $\dfrac{1}{2}, \dfrac{5}{2}$ 44. −1, 2   45. $-\dfrac{1}{4}, \dfrac{3}{2}$ 46. $-\dfrac{1}{3}$

47. −2, 3   48. −2, 2   49. −2, 6

Exercise 6.2

1. 1, 4   2. −6, −2   3. $-\dfrac{1}{2}, 2$ 4. $-3, \dfrac{4}{3}$ 5. $-\dfrac{2}{3}, 4$ 6. $-2, \dfrac{3}{5}$ 7. −1·27, 2·77

8. −7·41, 0·41   9. −2·35, 0·85   10. −0·26, 2·59   11. −2·57, 0·91   12. −1·58, 0·38

13. −0·64, 0·39   14. −1·84, 0·44   15. −1·35, 0·21   16. 0·39, 5·11   17. −2·87, −0·46

18. −1·40, 0·90

Exercise 6.3

1. $2\sqrt{3}$ **2.** $3\sqrt{2}$ **3.** $4\sqrt{2}$ **4.** $5\sqrt{2}$ **5.** $3\sqrt{3}$ **6.** $4\sqrt{5}$ **7.** $1 \pm \sqrt{5}$

8. $1 \pm \sqrt{3}$ **9.** $2 \pm \sqrt{3}$ **10.** $-3 \pm \sqrt{2}$ **11.** $-2 \pm 2\sqrt{3}$ **12.** $2 \pm 3\sqrt{2}$

13. $4 \pm 2\sqrt{3}$ **14.** $\dfrac{1 \pm \sqrt{3}}{2}$ **15.** $\dfrac{1 \pm \sqrt{5}}{4}$ **16.** $2 \pm 2\sqrt{3}$

Exercise 6.4

1. (i) $-2, 4$ (ii) $1, 7$ **2.** (i) $3, 5$ (ii) $2, 3$ **3.** (i) $-3, 7$ (ii) $-1, 1$ **4.** (i) $\dfrac{1}{2}, \dfrac{5}{2}$ (ii) $3, 7$

5. (i) $-\dfrac{3}{2}, 4$ (ii) $-5, 6$ **6.** (i) $2, 6$ (ii) $-3, -2, 1, 2$ **7.** (i) $-6, 14$ (ii) $-2, 2, 3, 7$

8. (i) $2, 5$ (ii) $-2, -1, 1, 2$ **9.** (i) $-2, 10$ (ii) $-2, 1, 2, 5$ **10.** (i) $-4.2, 1.2$ (ii) $-2.6, 0.1$

11. (i) $-0.55, 1.22$ (ii) $0.2, 1.1$ **12.** (i) $-0.9, 2.3$ (ii) $0.4, 1.4$ **13.** (i) $3, 8$ (ii) $-2, -1, 3, 4$

14. $\dfrac{2}{3}, 2$ **15.** $0.2, 1.3$

Exercise 6.5

1. $x^2 - 5x + 6 = 0$ **2.** $x^2 - x - 2 = 0$ **3.** $x^2 - 3x - 10 = 0$ **4.** $x^2 - 3x - 4 = 0$

5. $x^2 + 5x + 6 = 0$ **6.** $x^2 - 9x + 20 = 0$ **7.** $x^2 - x - 12 = 0$ **8.** $x^2 + 5x - 24 = 0$

9. $x^2 - 9 = 0$ **10.** $x^2 - 4x + 4 = 0$ **11.** $x^2 + 2x = 0$ **12.** $x^2 - 5x = 0$ **13.** $x^2 - 1 = 0$

14. $x^2 - 7x - 8 = 0$ **15.** $x^2 + 2x - 35 = 0$ **16.** $m = -2, n = -15$ **17.** (i) $k = -5$ (ii) $\dfrac{1}{2}$

Exercise 7.1

1. $x < 4$ **2.** $x > 2$ **3.** $x < 6$ **4.** $x \le -4$ **5.** $y \le -4$ **6.** $x \ge 4$ **7.** $x < -2$

8. $x \ge -4$ **9.** $x \le 6$ **10.** $t > -1.5$ **11.** $x \ge 2.5$ **12.** $x \le -4$ **13.** $-3 \le x \le 1$

14. $-3 < x < 5$ **15.** $-1 \le k < 4$ **16.** $-1 \le p \le 1$ **17.** $-3 \le x \le 1$ **18.** $-4 \le x \le -1$

19. $-1 < x \le 2$ **20.** $-1 < m < 4$ **21.** $5 > b \ge 1$ **22.** $2 > x > -1$ **23.** $-4 \le x < 3$

24. (i) $a = -2, b = 3$ (ii) 6 **25.** (i) $p = -1, q = 2$ (ii) $\dfrac{5}{2}$ **26.** (i) $1, 2, 3, 4$ (ii) 4

27. (i) (a) $x \ge 3$ (b) $x \le 5$ (ii) $3 \le (A \cap B) \le 5$ **28.** (i) (a) $x \le 4$ (b) $x \ge -1$

(ii) $-1 \le (H \cap K) \le 4$ **29.** (i) $t \le 1$ (ii) $t \ge -3$ (iii) $-3 \le (P \cap Q) \le 1$ **30.** (i) $x \le 2$

(ii) $x \ge -3.5$ (iii) $-3.5 \le (G \cap H) \le 2$ **31.** (i) $x \ge -2$ (ii) $x \le 5$ (iii) $a = -2, b = 5$

32. (i) $x < 4$ or $x \le 3, x \in \mathbb{N}$ (ii) $x < 5, x \in \mathbb{R}$ (iii) $x \ge -1$ or $x > -2, x \in \mathbb{Z}$ (iv) $x \ge 3, x \in \mathbb{R}$

33. (i) $2, 4$ (ii) 1 (iii) $1, 4, 9, 16$ (iv) $2, 3, 5, 7$ **34.** $n > 1$ **35.** $p > \dfrac{4}{3}$

36. (i) 5 cm (ii) 35 cm^2 **37.** (i) Since $x - 2 > 0$ (ii) $2(x - 2) + 2(4) > 4(x - 2)$; $x < 6$

38. (i) $9 < 2n + 3 < 21$ (ii) $3 < n < 9$ (iii) $4, 8$ (iv) $11, 19$ (v) No **39.** $(7, 8)$

40. (i) €$5,500 \le x \le$ €$12,500$ (ii) €$10,000 \le y \le$ €$17,000$

41. (i) €$22 \le x \le$ €55 (ii) €$30 \le y \le$ €63

Exercise 8.1

1. $\dfrac{z-y}{2}$ 2. $\dfrac{b+c}{3}$ 3. $\dfrac{s-r}{q}$ 4. $\dfrac{v-u}{a}$ 5. $\dfrac{3a+5c}{2}$ 6. $\dfrac{4p+2q}{3}$ 7. $\dfrac{2p+r}{2}$

8. $\dfrac{ac+d}{a}$ 9. $\dfrac{w-xz}{x}$ 10. $2q$ 11. $2z-2y$ 12. $3r-3s$ 13. $\dfrac{6c-2l}{3}$

14. $2r-p$ 15. $3w-s$ 16. $\dfrac{y-3x}{2}$ 17. $bd-ad$ 18. $\dfrac{sr-2pr}{3}$ 19. $3b+5c$

20. $\dfrac{p+r}{s}$ 21. $\dfrac{3a-2c}{d}$ 22. $\dfrac{2c-3b}{a}$ 23. $\dfrac{v^2-u^2}{2s}$ 24. $\dfrac{q-4p}{8}$ 25. $\dfrac{2s}{t^2}$ 26. $\dfrac{3v}{\pi r^2}$

27. $\dfrac{2s-2ut}{t^2}$ 28. $\dfrac{1}{r-t}$ 29. $\dfrac{t}{p+r}$ 30. $\dfrac{y}{w-x}$ or $-\dfrac{-y}{x-w}$ 31. $\dfrac{b^2}{a-bd}$ 32. $\dfrac{uv}{u+v}$

33. $\dfrac{ab}{4a-3b}$ or $\dfrac{-ab}{3b-4a}$ 34. $\dfrac{q^2+4q}{3q+14}$ 35. $\dfrac{pr-q}{s}$ 36. (i) $\dfrac{ac}{2a-c}$ (ii) 12 37. $\pm\sqrt{\dfrac{r}{q}}$

38. $\pm\sqrt{\dfrac{2s}{a}}$ 39. $\pm\sqrt{\dfrac{b}{c}}$ 40. y^2 41. $\dfrac{r^2}{q}$ 42. $\dfrac{p}{a^2}$ 43. $\dfrac{z^2}{9x}$ 44. $\dfrac{4s^2}{t}$ 45. $\dfrac{y^2+3}{2}$

46. $\dfrac{r+s^2}{q}$ 47. $\dfrac{gt^2}{k^2}$ 48. (i) $\dfrac{x+2t^2}{t^2}$ (ii) 3 49. (i) $\dfrac{2a}{a+b}$ (ii) 12 50. (i) $2l+2w$

(ii) $\dfrac{P-2l}{2}$ (iii) lw (iv) $\dfrac{A}{l}$ (v) $\dfrac{Pl-l^2}{2}$ 51. (i) $\pm\dfrac{1}{\sqrt{m^2+8p}}$ (ii) $\pm0\cdot2$ or $\pm\dfrac{1}{5}$

52. (i) $\dfrac{16t}{3}-3$ (ii) $\dfrac{9}{16}$ 53. (i) $2x-3$ (ii) x 54. (i) $3a-a^3$ (ii) 2

55. (i) $2a^2+a$ (ii) 0 or -2

Exercise 9.1

1. 2^7 2. 3^8 3. 3^6 4. -4^5 5. 4^1 6. 2^7 7. 7^2 8. 2^3 9. 3^3 10. 4^4

11. -9^2 12. -5^4 13. 2^6 14. 5^8 15. 8^{10} 16. 6^{20} 17. 7 18. 3 19. 4

20. 6 21. -6 22. 2 23. $\dfrac{5}{2}$ 24. 3 25. 5 26. 2 27. 11 28. 4 29. 5

30. 2 31. 3 32. 8 33. $4\cdot5$ 34. 77 35. 8 36. 8 37. 4 38. 125

39. 64 40. 25 41. 16 42. 4 43. 243 44. 32 45. $\dfrac{1}{2}$ 46. $\dfrac{1}{3}$ 47. $\dfrac{1}{9}$

48. $\dfrac{1}{16}$ 49. $\dfrac{2}{3}$ 50. $\dfrac{4}{25}$ 51. $\dfrac{16}{9}$ 52. $\dfrac{27}{64}$ 53. $\dfrac{1}{9}$ 54. $\dfrac{9}{8}$ 55. $\dfrac{4}{3}$ 56. $\dfrac{1}{32}$

57. $\dfrac{17}{72}$ 58. $\dfrac{7}{12}$ 59. 4^2 60. 3^4 61. 2^3 62. $2^{\frac{3}{2}}$ 63. $5^{\frac{5}{2}}$ 64. $2^{-\frac{5}{2}}$

66. (i) (a) 5 (b) 5^3 (ii) 5^{-3} 67. $3^{\frac{3}{2}}$ 68. 2^3 69. (i) x^2-x (ii) $x=-2, 3$

70. (i) (a) a (b) b (c) x (d) $(x+3)$ (ii) (a) $(x+1)^2$ (b) $(x+2)^2$ (iii) $2x+3$ (iv) $x=3$

71. $9^{-1}, 3^{-2}$ 72. (i) x^2+x (ii) $x^2+x=42; 6$

Exercise 9.2

1. 2^3 **2.** 3^2 **3.** 2^5 **4.** 3^3 **5.** 5^3 **6.** 3^4 **7.** 7^2 **8.** 4^3 **9.** 3^5 **10.** 2^7

11. 7^3 **12.** 2^{-4} **13.** 3^{-5} **14.** $3^{\frac{5}{2}}$ **15.** $5^{-\frac{3}{2}}$ **16.** 8 **17.** 5 **18.** 3 **19.** 2

20. 3 **21.** 5 **22.** 2 **23.** 1 **24.** $\dfrac{7}{2}$ **25.** $\dfrac{1}{4}$ **26.** -1 **27.** -3 **28.** $\dfrac{1}{2}$

29. $\dfrac{1}{4}$ **30.** 3 **31.** 2 **32.** 1 **33.** (i) 4^2 (ii) $\dfrac{3}{2}$ **34.** (i) 2^4 (ii) $x = 3$

35. $x = -1, 2$ **36.** (i) (a) $2^{\frac{1}{2}}$ (b) 2^3 (c) 2^4 (d) $2^{\frac{7}{2}}$ (ii) (a) 1 (b) $\dfrac{3}{2}$ (c) 2

37. (i) (a) $3^{\frac{1}{2}}$ (b) $3^{-\frac{1}{2}}$ (c) 3^4 (d) $3^{\frac{7}{2}}$ (ii) (a) $\dfrac{1}{4}$ (b) $\dfrac{1}{4}$ (c) $\dfrac{11}{2}$

38. (i) (a) 5^3 (b) $5^{\frac{1}{2}}$ (c) $5^{\frac{5}{2}}$ (d) 5^5 (ii) (a) $-\dfrac{1}{6}$ (b) $-\dfrac{1}{4}$ (c) 3

39. (i) $2x + y = 4, x - y = -1$ (ii) $x = 1, y = 2$ **40.** (i) $3x + 2y = -10, x + 4y = 0$ (ii) $x = -4, y = 1$

41. (i) $x + 1$ (ii) 4 **42.** (i) $\dfrac{1}{2}$ (Base) $\times$ (Height) (ii) (a) x^2 (b) 9

43. (i) 2^{k+2} (ii) (a) $k = 3$ (b) $k = \dfrac{1}{2}$

Exercise 9.3

1. 7×10^3 **2.** $8 \cdot 5 \times 10^4$ **3.** $4 \cdot 31 \times 10^5$ **4.** $5 \cdot 4 \times 10^2$ **5.** $6 \cdot 8 \times 10^3$ **6.** $3 \cdot 7 \times 10^6$

7. $4 \cdot 86 \times 10^2$ **8.** $4 \cdot 1 \times 10^1$ **9.** 4×10^{-3} **10.** 7×10^{-4} **11.** $8 \cdot 9 \times 10^{-2}$

12. $2 \cdot 83 \times 10^{-4}$ **13.** $2 \cdot 8 \times 10^3$ **14.** $5 \cdot 7 \times 10^5$ **15.** $3 \cdot 5 \times 10^{-2}$ **16.** $7 \cdot 3 \times 10^{-3}$

17. 2 **18.** 4 **19.** -3 **20.** $a = 3 \cdot 3, n = 4$ **21.** $a = 2 \cdot 7, n = 3$

Exercise 9.4

1. $3 \cdot 4 \times 10^3$ **2.** $2 \cdot 81 \times 10^5$ **3.** $6 \cdot 92 \times 10^4$ **4.** $-1 \cdot 837 \times 10^4$ **5.** 6×10^{-3}

6. $2 \cdot 94 \times 10^{-4}$ **7.** 7×10^7 **8.** $3 \cdot 45 \times 10^6$ **9.** $8 \cdot 64 \times 10^5$ **10.** $9 \cdot 54 \times 10^6$

11. $1 \cdot 9 \times 10^3$ **12.** 3×10^3 **13.** $9 \cdot 675 \times 10^8$ **14.** $1 \cdot 673 \times 10^4$ **15.** $7 \cdot 68 \times 10^8$

16. $2 \cdot 5 \times 10^3$ **17.** $5 \cdot 8 \times 10^3$ **18.** $9 \cdot 5 \times 10^6$ **19.** 3×10^4 **20.** 5×10^2

21. $1 \cdot 52 \times 10^2$ **22.** $2 \cdot 8 \times 10^3$ **23.** $0 \cdot 0723$; Less   **24.** $0 \cdot 2$; Greater   **25.** 20

26. $1,062 \cdot 5$ m   **27.** $5 \cdot 986 \times 10^{24}$ kg   **28.** $8 \cdot 75 \times 10^7$ **29.** 5×10^2 s   **30.** 15

31. $1 \cdot 25$ kg   **32.** (i) $1 \cdot 4 \times 10^3$ m^3 (ii) 140 mins

Exercise 9.5

1. $\dfrac{1}{2}$ **2.** $-\dfrac{1}{8}$ **3.** $\dfrac{1}{7}$ **4.** $-\dfrac{1}{6}$ **5.** $\dfrac{3}{2}$ **6.** $\dfrac{8}{5}$ **7.** -9 **8.** $-\dfrac{7}{4}$ **9.** 37

10. $-\dfrac{13}{7}$ **11.** $\dfrac{11}{12}$ **12.** $-\dfrac{7}{10}$ **13.** $\dfrac{3}{7}$ **14.** $\dfrac{4}{13}$ **15.** $\dfrac{7}{37}$ **16.** $\dfrac{9}{32}$ **17.** $0 \cdot 392$

18. $-0 \cdot 312$ **19.** $1 \cdot 923$ **20.** $0 \cdot 671$

Exercise 10.1

1. Queue 1 in 690 secs   2. (i) 90 km/h   (ii) 1,350 sec or $22\frac{1}{2}$ min   (iii) 189 km

3. $6\frac{1}{4}$ m/s   4. 60 km/h   5. (i) 5 m/s   (ii) 99 km/h   6. 81 km/h   7. 12:20

8. 1 hr 57 mins   9. (i) 60 km/h   (ii) 12:40   10. (i) 1,820 m   (ii) 635

11. (i) 17 s   (ii) 260 m   (iii) [AC] takes 19·5 s (A → B → C Quicker)

12. (i) 1 hr 4 mins   (ii) 60 km/h   13. 08:35   14. 5 hrs 12 mins   15. $3\frac{1}{2}$ hours

16. 7 km/h   17. (i) 1·5   (ii) 1·2   (iii) 0·3   (iv) 1·35   (v) 0·15   18. (i) 60   (ii) 90 km

(iii) Yes   19. $1·392 \times 10^8$

20.

Driver	Speed in km/h	Time for journey in hours	Fuel consumption km per l	Quantity of fuel required in l	Cost € to nearest cent
A	60	9	12	45	71·33
B	80	6·75	15	36	57.06
C	100	5·4	10	54	85·59
D	120	$4\frac{1}{2}$	8	67·5	106·99

21. (i) 243 km   (ii) $2\frac{1}{4}$ hours   (iii) 108 km/h   22. (i) (a) 4 hours   (b) 1 hour   (ii) 32 km/h

23. (i) (a) €5   (b) €8   (ii) (a) €20·60   (b) €25   (iii) 10 mins; €13·50   (iv) Whichever could come first or company h slightly cheaper   24. (i) (a) 24 mins   (b) 38 mins

(ii) (a) 5·5 km   (b) 15·2 km   (iii) (a) $\frac{1}{3}x$ (b) $\frac{10+x}{4}$ 25. (i) 12   (ii) 9

(iii) 12 km/l and 9 km/l, respectively   (iv) (a) 480 km   (b) 360 km   (v) (a) 4·4 hrs   (b) 2·8 hrs

(vi) At 110 km/h cost €111·02 is cheaper   26. (i) 200   (ii) 1,750   27. 18 km/h

28. (i) 43,332 km   (ii) 28,888 km/h

Exercise 11.1

1. Discrete numerical   2. Continuous numerical   3. Unordered categorical

4. Ordered categorical   5. Unordered categorical   6. Ordered categorical

7. Continuous numerical   8. Discrete numerical   9. Continuous numerical

10. Unordered categorical   11. Discrete numerical   12. Ordered categorical

13. Discrete numerical   14. Continuous numerical   15. Unordered categorical

16. Discrete numerical   17. Discrete numerical   18. Continuous numerical

19. Continuous numerical   20. Discrete numerical   21. Unordered categorical

22. Continuous numerical   23. Continuous numerical   24. Unordered categorical

25. (i) Colour of the car, red   (ii) Number of doors   (iii) Diameter of the wheels

26. (i) Country of origin, colour, first class or second class   (ii) Dimensions   (iii) Cost

27. Ordered categorical data. The data can be put in categories which can be ordered.

28. The lecturer is wrong as we can **count** the number of shoes even if they are half sizes.

29. (i) How many rooms in your house?   **(ii)** What height are you?
(iii) What is you favourite colour?   **(iv)** What year are you in school?

Exercise 11.2

Note: In many questions in this exercise there can be a few different answers. The answers below only give a selection of possible answers.

1. Primary data (first-hand data) are data that you collect yourself or are collected by someone under your direct supervision. Secondary data (second-hand data) are data that have already been collected and made available from an external source such as newspapers, government departments or the internet.

2. (i) Primary   **(ii)** Secondary   **(iii)** Secondary   **(iv)** Primary

3. A census is a collection of data from the whole population. A sample is a collection of data from a small part of the population.

4. Sample. Otherwise they would have no batteries to sell.

5. (i) Leading question as it forces an opinion on the person being interviewed   **(ii)** Overlapping boxes   **(iii)** Not enough response sections   **(iv)** Leading question as it forces an opinion on the person being interviewed that sweets are bad for you before they answer the question   **(v)** Biased question   **(vi)** Personal question

6. (i) Question is too vague. Does not give a time period, such as per week, per month or per year or what time of the year, school term or not school term.   **(ii)** During school term, how many times per month do you attend the cinema? Please tick one box.

7. (i) (a) Does not give a time period, such as per week, per month or per year or what time of the year   **(b)** Overlapping boxes   **(ii)** During school holidays, how many hours per week do you spend on the internet? Please tick one box.

8. Overlapping boxes; No 4 in the boxes; No zero for people who work at home

9. Overlapping boxes   **10. (i)** Overlapping boxes; No greater than €1,000 box
(ii) Question assumes that all people have a mortgage

11. (i) Biased sample because many of the people who use the train may not be interested in a road by-pass of the town; the first 50 people who leave the train in the town on a Friday in June would not be representative of the whole town   **(ii)** Ask the question in a few different places in the town, such as shops, schools or workplaces, and try to question people of different ages and genders (male or female)   **(iii)** Leading question which would lead to biased answers

12. (i) (a) These students' are already using the school canteen and would be a biased sample. She also needs to ask the question to students who do not use the school canteen.   **(b)** Leading question as it forces an opinion on the person being interviewed that the food prices are already overpriced
(ii) To find students' opinion of the price of food in the school canteen and to see if the price affects the number of students who use the school canteen   **(iii)** Pick 10 students at random from the school register from each of the six year groups

13. Mark out an even number of different sections of the same field with the same area. Plant the new Better Grow compost in half of these sections and plant its competitors' compost in the other half of the these sections. It would be a good idea to use a few different **independent** growers. Then record which compost helps seeds germinate more quickly

14. (i) No females interviewed and shop assistants on their own are not a representative sample of the store   **(ii)** 360

(iii)

	Shop assistants	Warehouse	Management	Security
Male	5	4	2	1
Female	15	7	1	1

15. (i) Primary   **(ii)** Discrete, as the number of hours to the nearest hour can be counted exactly **(iii)** There are no boys in her school and her school may not be representative of other all-girl schools, for example her school may be a fee-paying school **(iv)** Have the same number of boys and girls in the sample and survey students from a wide range of different schools

16. (i) No boys are given the old brand and no girls are given the new brand. No adults in the experiment. **(ii)** The dentist needs to randomly give the new brand of toothpaste to both boys, girls, men and women and also randomly give the old brand to the same number of boys, girls, men and women.

17. Collecting the data during rush hour only would give biased results, as the traffic would be going slower. Helen needs to collect the data at different times of the day and on different days of the week.
18. (i) Primary data, as he collects the data himself   **(ii)** Biased sample because most people entering a sports stadium would already have a positive opinion on sports events. Did not interview people who did not attend the sporting event.   **(iii)** He needs to ask people who do not attend sports events and try to get a good mixture of different ages and gender and also interview people attending stadiums playing different types of sport.

19. One advantage of face-to-face interviews is that the researcher can clarify any doubt and ensure that the responses are properly understood. A disadvantage is that face-to-face interviews can be costly. Also some people might feel uneasy about the lack of anonymity of their response. A better method would be to have a bar code on each ticket so that a machine could record the time they entered and the time they left.

20. For each question, please tick **one** box.

   1. Gender: Male ☐   Female ☐
   2. What year are you in?
       1 ☐   2 ☐   3 ☐   4 ☐   5 ☐   6 ☐
   3. What is your favourite type of music?
       Rock ☐   Pop ☐   Hip hop ☐   R&B ☐
       Trad ☐   Dance ☐   Classical ☐   Other ☐

21. (i)

Colour of cars						
Number						

(ii) For each question, please tick one box.

    1. Gender: Male ☐   Female ☐

    2. Which is your age group in years?

        Under 18   18–40   41–60   Over 60

          ☐   ☐   ☐   ☐

22. (i) Be clear about who is to complete the questionnaire. Be as clear as possible with the questions. Be clear how and where the responses are to be recorded.
(ii) (a) Relatively cheap and can ask many questions   **(b)** Poor response rate and no way of clarifying the questions

Exercise 12.1

1. 4, 3, 3, 5   **2.** 6, 4, 5, 10   **3.** $\dfrac{1}{2}, \dfrac{1}{3}, \dfrac{5}{12}, \dfrac{5}{12}$ **4.** 4·7, no mode, 4·35, 7·2

5. (i) 5·06 **(ii)** 5·15   **6.** 45   **7.** 9, 8   **8.** 2   **9. (i)** 40 **(ii)** 100   **10.** €168

11. 7   **12. (i) (a)** $3x$ **(b)** $2x$ **(c)** $4x + 1$ **(d)** $3x + 5$ **(ii)** 7   **13. (i)** 14 **(ii)** 2 **(iii)** 6
(iv) 4   **14. (i)** Two values **(ii)** 3   **15.** 16   **16.** 5, 5, 7, 9   **17.** 6   **18.** 45   **19.** 11
20. {11, 11, 11, 20, 31}   **21. (i)** 12 **(ii)** 8   **22. (i)** $x = 60$; $y = 144$ **(ii)** Q and P
(iii) R and Q **(iv)** Q **(v)** 11·1   **23. (i)** {−3, −2, −1, 0, 1, 2, 3} **(ii)** {14, 1, 0, 0, 0, 0, 0, 9}
24. r **25. (i)** 250 **(ii)** 240 **(iii)** 100 **(iv)** >250

Exercise 12.2

1. (i) 63 and 19 **(ii)** 62·75 and 78 **(iii)** Eileen is more consistent than Sean

2. (i) Company A: 50, 52, 22; Company B: 48, 52, 14 **(ii)** Company B: more reliable

3. (i) Brendan 3·5; Colm 3·6 **(ii)** Brendan 7; Colm 3 **(iii)** Brendan 3; Colm 3·5
(iv) Colm more consistent   **4. (i)** 24 **(ii)** 18 **(iii)** 14 **(iv)** 10   **5. (i)** All 7·4
(ii) Yousef 5; Lily 3; Stephen 7 **(iii)** Lily more consistent

6. (i)

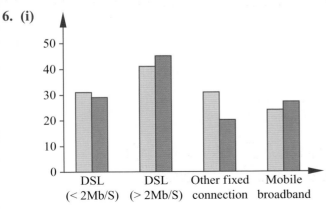

(ii) No change in broadband connection
DSL < 2 Mb/S slight decrease
DSL > 2 Mb/S slight increase
Other fixed connections major decrease
slight increase in mobile broadband

Exercise 12.3

1. (i) 3 (ii) 1 (iii) 2 (iv) 2 2. (i) 8 (ii) 6 (iii) 4 (iv) 4 3. (i) 4 (ii) 5 (iii) 6 (iv) 6·5 4. (i) 8 (ii) (a) 7 (b) 6·8 5. (i) 1 (ii) 2 6. (i) 25 (ii) 18 (iii) (a) 4 (b) 19 7. (i) (a) 2 (b) 3 (ii) (a) 4 (b) 3 (iii) The weight of parcels is continuous data 8. (i) 3, 5, 8, 8, 9, 4, 2, 1 (ii) 4 (iii) 4 (iv) 5 (v) 40% (vi) 200 (vii) 6

Exercise 12.4

1. 18; 15–25; 15–25 2. 3; 2–4; 0–2 3. 154; 140–160; 140–160 4. 20·5; 10–20; 20–35 5. 20; 15–25; 15–25 7. (i) 102 8. (i) 2, 28, 10, 6, 4 (ii) 20 m 9. (i) Collected directly is primary data (ii) Time is a continuous variable (iii) 41 (iv) 35–45 (v) 14 (vi) 30 10. (i) 70 (ii) 12–16 (iii) 16–20 (iv) 14·97 mins 11. (i) 36 (ii) 31 (iii) 90 (iv) 30–40 (v) 40–50

Exercise 13.1

1. (ii) 50 (iii) 24% 2. (i)

Marks	0	1	2	3	4	5	6	7	8	9	10
No. of pupils	3	2	0	3	4	6	5	4	2	3	4

(ii) 0 (iii) 9 (iv) 5 marks (v) 36 (vi) 5·5 (vii) $66\frac{2}{3}$% 3. (ii) 70,000,000 km^2 (iii) 47%

4. (i)

Score	1	2	3	4	5	6
Tally	||| ||||		||| |||		||| ||	|||	
Frequency	9	10	11	7	5	8

(iii) 25 times (iv) 40%

5. Mean = $\dfrac{20 + 25 + 20 + 50 + 40}{5}$ = 31 ≠ 46 on graph.

Or surplus above the dotted line should equal the deficit below the dotted line.

6. (i) Laura (ii) Nina (iii) Chris (iv) Ronan

7. (i)

Day	Mon	Tues	Wed	Thurs	Fri	Sat	Sun
Rebecca	2	3	4	3	5	3	2
Bren	1	0	2	2	3	5	8

(ii) Rebecca (22), which is more than Bren (21) (iii) (a) 3 (b) 8 (iv) 3 hours (v) (a) 3 (b) 2

Exercise 13.2

1. (ii) 4

2. (i)

Amount, in €	0	2	4	6	8	10
Tally	IIII I	IIII	IIII IIII	IIII I	IIII	II
No. of people	5	4	9	6	4	2

(iii) €4   (iv) €4·4

3.

No. of movies watched	0	1	2	3	4	5	6
No. of students	3	2	0	6	4	2	3

(i) One student who watched a certain number of movies   (ii) Mode, 3   (iii) 20   (iv) 3·2

4. (i) 6   (ii) 17   (iii) 40%   (v) May, June   5. (i) 28   (ii) Catagorical   (iii) Mode

Exercise 13.3

2. (i) 54   (iii) Bronze   (iv) Number of gold medals much lower than other medal types

3. (ii) 3   (iii) 20%   4. 36 : 72 : 108 : 144   5. (i) 16,030   (iii) 19%   6. (i) 75
(iii) 60,000–80,000   (iv) Mid-interval values times the number of employees gives €3,750,000.
∴ Answer given in question is too high.

Exercise 13.4

1. (i) 70°   (ii) 720   (iii) 140   2. (i) 64°   (ii) 432, 216, 192   (iii) 1,080   3. (i) 20°
(ii)

A	B	C	D	E
40	50	60	20	10

4. (i) 116°   (ii) (a) 1,044   (b) 3,240   5. 4

6. (i) $x = 300$, $y = 255$ (ii) 1,080   (iii) €28·75   7. (i) 6,265   (ii) 49,225

8. Higher Level St Bridget's $= \dfrac{100}{360}(420) = 116$ students

   Higher Level St Joseph's $= \dfrac{100}{360}(780) = 216$ students

   Disagree with Emily.

9. (i) 5   (ii) The 9 students (or none) who missed no days would not change
   (iii) Smallest possible 9, 7, 3, 4, 1, 0   (iv) 9, 2, 5, 4, 3, 1 and 1·7 days
        Largest possible 9, 2, 3, 4, 1, 5

Exercise 13.5

3. (i) 7   (iii) Continuous data not represented by a histogram   (iv) €10–€15   (v) €12·50
(vi) $12·50 \times 42 = €525$

4. (i)

Time in hours	0–4	4–8	8–12	12–16
Tally	卌 卌 I	卌 卌 III	卌 卌 I	卌
No. of students	11	13	11	5

(ii) 4–8   5. (i) $45 \le t \le 60$ (iii) 42 mins   (iv) €1,417,500   6. (ii) €460·80   (iii) €315
(iv) €3,494·40   (v) €3

Exercise 13.6

1. (i) $a = 2, b = 4$ (ii) Modal group $14 < x \le 16$ (iii) Mean 16 petals   2. (i) 2, 5, 8, 6, 3, 1
(ii) 25   (iii) 15   (v) 07:40–07:50   (vi) 28%   (vii) 15   (viii) No, cannot represent continuous
data on a bar chart   3. (i) 12, 30, 12, 27, 9, 3   (ii) €25   (iii) Not surprised as there are 3 people
who each gave more than €50   4. (i) 10, 15, 25, 50   (ii) 10–15 mins   (iii) 25
(iv) 100, everyone   5. (i) 16, 48, 80, 36, 20   (ii) 64   (iii) (a) 20   (b) 56
6. (i) 42, 10, 28, 18, 6   (ii) 104   (iii) (a) €96   (b) 33 kg   (iv) 1,440

Exercise 13.7

1. (i)
```
5 | 0 3
6 | 2 2 4
7 | 3 5 7
8 | 1
```
Key: 6|2 =
6·2 secs

(ii)
```
4 | 5 8
5 | 3 6
6 | 4 8 9
7 | 0 3 5 8
8 | 2 4 8
```
Key: 7|3 =
73 mins

(iii)
```
0 | 0 2 2 2 2 4 5 7 8 9
1 | 0 3 4 6 7 8 9
2 | 1 2 3 4 6 8 8
```
Key: 1|8 =
18 CDs

(iv)
```
15 | 3 4 9
16 | 4 4 5 7
17 | 2 2 3 4 5 7 9 9
18 | 0 2 5 5 5 6 6
19 | 4 5 8 9
20 | 3 5 5 9
```
Key: 18|5
= 185 cm

2. (ii) 31   (iii) 36   (iv) 4   3. (ii) (a) 34 *l*   (b) 26 *l*   (iii) 35 *l* is the only number in the list
twice   (iv) $26\frac{1}{2}$ *l*   (v) 10   4. (i) 20   (ii) 24 cm   (iii) 50%   5. (i) 5·9 mins   (ii) 0·59 m
(iii) 0·059 g

6. (i)

Stem	Leaf
1	9
2	4 5 9 9
3	2 2 3 3 3 5 6 7
4	2 5
5	6 8 9

(ii) (a) 1·9 secs **(b)** 5·9 secs **(iii)** 4·0 secs
(iv) 3·3 secs **(v)** 3·65 **(vi)** Increase **(vii)** 0·1 secs

7. (i) (a) 9 **(b)** 21 **(ii) (a)** 63 **(b)** 66 **(iii) (a)** 70 **(b)** 74 **(iv) (a)** 4 **(b)** 11
(v) Spanish, best in **(ii), (iii)** and **(iv)**

8. No key
Which side of plot is before race?
69 and 67 not in order
Short one piece of data on LHS
Two extra pieces of data on RHS

9. (i)

```
         Before        After
               8 | 4  |
       7 3 1 1 0 | 5  |
       9 9 6 6 4 | 6  | 9
     9 5 3 3 0 0 | 7  | 0 2 5 7 7
               1 | 8  | 0 0 4 4 4 6
   8 8 3 3 1 0 0 | 9  | 5 6 7
             5 0 | 10 | 4 4 4 6 8 9
           1 1 0 | 11 | 7
                 | 12 | 5
                 | 13 | 0 0 1 7 7
                 | 14 | 3 5
```

Key: 5 | 10 = 105 pulse rate before
Key: 11 | 7 = 117 pulse rate after

(ii) (a) 74 **(b)** 100·5
(iii) (a) 63 **(b)** 76
(iv) Pulse rate is raised after exercise
(v) Age of workers

11. (i)

```
          Test 2          Test 1
                   | 2 | 7 9
     9 9 8 8 7 3   | 3 | 3 6 7 7 8
 9 9 9 8 6 4 4 4 0 | 4 | 0 1 4 5 5 5 6 7 8 9
   9 8 2 2 1 1 0   | 5 | 1 1 2 2 3 9
             2 1   | 6 | 0
```

Key: 2 | 7 = 27 sit-ups

(ii) 24 **(iii)** Test 1: 63, Test 2: 29

(iv) Yes • General shift of data upwards
   • Median higher
   • Mean higher

(v) • Compared favourably. The class average improvement is 2·67. John's improvement is 3. He improved more than average.
   • Compared unfavourably. There were 8 people below him before the practice. There were only 7 people below him after the practice.

Exercise 13.8

1. First graph: Bars not same width; vertical axis not starting at zero.
   Second graph: Bars not same width, no scale on L.H.S.

2. Bars not same width. The vertical (number) axis does not start at zero. Do not know how many in each class.

3. Car B is much bigger than twice Car A

4. Number of trucks does not start at zero. Each box should be the same width.

5. Yes, because a clear majority get paid €40,000

6. It is impossible for ALL the measurements in any sample/survey to be above the average

7. Adds up to 109%. 50% business should occupy half the pie.

8. No, because the number scale does not start at zero and this makes the diagram misleading

9. Does not say the 10 cat owners were selected at random   **10.** (R)

Exercise 13.9

2. **(i)** Positively **(ii)** Negatively **(iii)** Symmetric   **3. (i)** Positively skewed with one outlier (at 9)
(ii) Symmetric with no outliers   **(iii)** Uniform with no outliers   **(iv)** Positively skewed
(v) Negatively skewed   **(vi)** Symmetric   **(vii)** Positively skewed, no outliers
(viii) Negatively skewed   **(ix)** Symmetric, no outliers   **(x)** Uniform distribution with one outlier

4. **(i)** Before game is negatively skewed.
      After game is positively skewed.
   (ii) Before game time interval is 60 mins.
      After game time interval is 20 mins.

5. **(ii)** Both plots are symmetric. The plots have different modes   **(iii)** Girl with height 149 cm

6. **(i)** 0, 3, 4, 6, 9 ⟹ positively skewed   **(ii)** 8, 6, 4, 3, 1 ⟹ negatively skewed
(iii) 5, 11, 6 ⟹ symmetric

7. **(ii)** Kerry has symmetric distribution, while Offaly has uniform distribution.
      Offaly has higher readings than Kerry.   **(iv)** 22·1 in Offaly is an outlier

8. (i)

Number	0–10	10–20	20–30	30–40	40–50	50–60
Frequency	3	5	8	7	5	2

(ii) 30   **(iii)** Symmetric

9. Group at scout camp have positively skewed ages.
Group at a party has symmetric shape.

Exercise 14.1

1. (i) True   **(ii)** True   **(iii)** True   **(iv)** False   **(v)** False   **(vi)** True   **(vii)** False   **(viii)** True
(ix) True   **(x)** True   **(xi)** False   **(xii)** True   **2. (i)** Double counting the common elements
(ii) $S \cap T = \varnothing$

Exercise 14.2

1. (i) 18   **(ii)** 45   **(iii)** 33   **(iv)** 20   **(v)** 42
2. (i) U

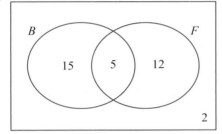

(ii) (a) 5   **(b)** 27   **(c)** 32   **3.** 50   **4. (i)** 7   **(ii)** 21

5. (i) 5   **(ii)** 4   **6. (i)** 21   **(ii)** 8   **(iii)** 47   **7. (i)** $x = 8$ **(ii) (a)** 15   **(b)** 7   **(c)** 22
8. (i) $x = 15$ **(ii)** 30   **(iii)** 45   **(iv)** 63   **(v)** 56   **9.** 12   **10.** 22   **11. (i)** 8   **(ii)** 15
12. (i) 9   **(ii)** 51   **13. (i)** 32   **(ii)** 20   **(iii)** 29   **14. (i)** 19   **(ii)** 11   **15. (i)** 1   **(ii)** 12
17. (i) $a = 20, b = 35, c = 0, d = 15$ **(ii)** 23

Exercise 14.3

1. (i) 5   **(ii)** 12   **(iii)** 46   **(iv)** 6   **(v)** 4   **(vi)** 23   **(vii)** 33   **(viii)** 9   **(ix)** 37   **(x)** 14   **(xi)** 19
2. (i) 38   **(ii)** 22   **(iii)** 19   **(iv)** 10   **(v)** 4   **(vi)** 22   **(vii)** 32   **(viii)** 6   **(ix)** 7   **(x)** 10
(xi) 5   **(xii)** 19
3. (i) U

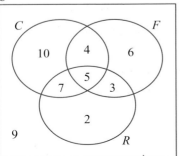

(ii) (a) 9   **(b)** 2   **(c)** 18   **(d)** 37   **(e)** 31   **(f)** 4

4. (i) U

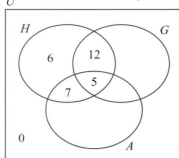

(ii) 12   **(iii)** 7   **(a)** $15 - x$ **(b)** $12 - x$

(c) U

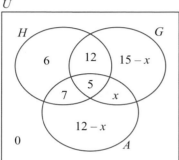

(d) $x = 11$

5. (i) U

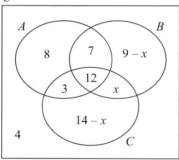

(a) $9 - x$ **(b)** $15 - x$ **(ii)** $x = 15$ **(iii) (a)** 4   **(b)** 9
(c) 15   **(d)** 27

6. (i) U

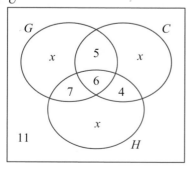

(ii) $x = 9$ **(iii)** 20

7. (i) $x = 3$ **(ii)** 9   **8. (i)** $x = 2$ **(ii)** 9

9. (i) (a) $9 - x$ **(b)** $6 - x$ **(c)** $7 - x$ **(d)** $8 + x$; $6 + x$; $3 + x$

(ii) 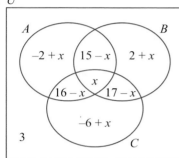 **(iii)** $x = 4$

10. (i) U **(ii)** $x = 10$

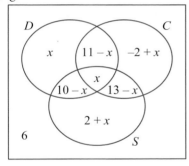

11. (i) U **(ii)** $x = 4$ **(iii) (a)** 14 **(b)** 26

12. (i) 4 **(ii)** 10 **(iii) (a)** 44 **(b)** 37 **(iv)** 5

13. (i) R ... W **(iii) (a)** 8 **(b)** 2 **(iv)** 42 **(v)** 6

14. *U*

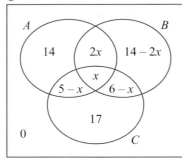

$x = 2$

15. (i) $x + y = 11$; $2x + 3y = 27$ **(ii)** $x = 6$; $y = 5$ **(iii) (a)** 6 **(b)** 23 **(c)** 21 **(d)** 5 **(e)** 4
(iv) 48

Exercise 14.4

1. (i) (a) *U* **(b)** *U* **(c)** *U* 2; 4; 8

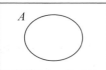 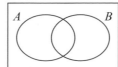 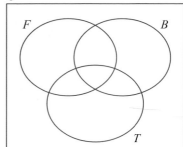

(ii) Yes: 16 **(iii)** Yes: 1 **(iv)** Greater than 1,000

2. (ii) 4 **(iv)** *U*   **3. (ii)** *U*   **(iii)** #*U* = 100%
                                                            (iv) 12 people

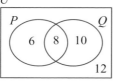 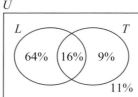

4. (i) *W* ... *E* **(ii) (a)** $\{s, p, i, d, e, r, m, a\}$ **(b)** $\{i, d, e, r, m, a, n\}$

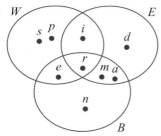

(iii) (a) $\{s, p, i, d, e, r, m, a, n\}$ **(b)** $\{s, p, i, d, e, r, m, a, n\}$ **(iv)** No. Only for these sets.

5. (iv) Yes

6. (i)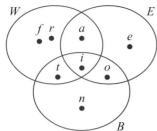

(ii) (a) {a, i} **(b)** {i, o}

(iii) (a) {i} **(b)** {i}   **(iv)** No. Only for these sets.

7. (iv) Yes

8. (i)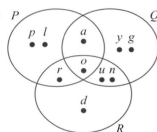

(ii) (a) {t, a} **(b)** {r, i}   **(iii) (a)** {t} **(b)** {t, a, n}

(iv) No. But proves that it is NOT associative.

9. (i)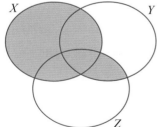

(ii) {o, u, n}   **(iii)** {p, l, a, r, o, u, n}

(iv) (a) {p, l, a, y, g, r, o, u, n}   **(b)** {p, l, a, r, o, u, n, d}

(v) {p, l, a, r, o, u, n}   **(vi)** It seems that set union is distributive over set intersection

10. (i)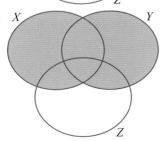

(ii) (a) 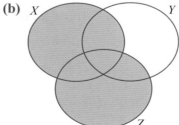 **(b)** 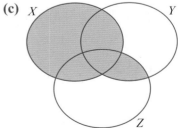 **(c)**

(iii) Set union is distributive over set intersection

589

11. (i)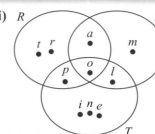

(ii) $\{a, m, p, o, l, i, n, e\}$ **(iii)** $\{a, p, o\}$
(iv) (a) $\{a, o\}$ **(b)** $\{p, o\}$ **(v)** $\{a, p, o\}$
(vi) It seems that set intersection is distributive over set union

12. (i)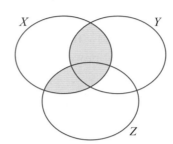

(iii) Set intersection is distributive over set union

Exercise 15.1

1. $(4, 3)$ **2.** $(5, 3)$ **3.** $(9, -3)$ **4.** $(-6, 5)$ **5.** $(-8, -3)$ **6.** $(-2, 2)$ **7.** $(3, 3)$

8. $(1, -1)$ **9.** $\left(\dfrac{7}{2}, -2\right)$ **10.** $(3, 1)$ **11.** $\left(2, -\dfrac{1}{2}\right)$ **12.** $\left(\dfrac{3}{2}, \dfrac{5}{2}\right)$

13. $(5, 2)$ **14.** $(-5, -1)$ **15.** $p = 10, q = -5$ **16.** $a = -2, b = 5$
17. $p = 6, q = -3$ **18.** $(4, 6), (6, 9), (8, 12)$

Exercise 15.2

1. 5   **2.** 10   **3.** $\sqrt{5}$ **4.** $\sqrt{65}$ **5.** 3   **6.** 6   **7.** $\sqrt{40}$ or $2\sqrt{10}$ **8.** $\sqrt{50}$ or $5\sqrt{2}$
9. $\sqrt{40}$ or $2\sqrt{10}$ **10.** $\sqrt{72}$ or $6\sqrt{2}$ **11.** $\sqrt{5}$ **12.** $\sqrt{10}$ **13.** $|AB| = |BC| = \sqrt{34}$
14. 5   **15. (i)** A **(ii)** B **17.** $M(3, 1)$ **18. (i)** $P(1, -1)$ **(ii)** $Q(5, -4)$
19. (ii) Parallelogram   **(iii)** $|AD| = \sqrt{18}$ or $3\sqrt{2}$; $|AB| = \sqrt{26}$; $|BC| = \sqrt{18}$ or $3\sqrt{2}$;
$|CD| = \sqrt{26}$; yes   **(iv)** $(5, 2)$ **21. (ii)** A-F-G-B   **(iii)** Yes. Move R one unit closer to Q.
22. (i) C1(4, 2), C2(4, 6), C3(1, 10), C4(1, 14), C5(6, 16), C6(5, 14), C7(5, 10), C8(8, 6), C9(8, 2)
(ii) $32 + 4\sqrt{2}$ or 37·7 units   **(iii)** 34 units

Exercise 15.3

1. (i) $\dfrac{2}{5}$ **(ii)** $\dfrac{1}{6}$ **(iii)** $-\dfrac{2}{3}$ **2. (i)** e and f **(ii)** c and d **(iii)** a and b **3.** 1   **4.** $\dfrac{3}{2}$

5. 1   **6.** $\dfrac{5}{3}$ **7.** -1 **8.** $-\dfrac{8}{11}$ **9.** -1 **10.** 10   **11.** -1 **12.** -2 **18.** $\dfrac{4}{3}$

19. $-\dfrac{3}{5}$ **20.** 3   **21.** -4 **22.** $\dfrac{1}{3}$ **23. (i)** $\dfrac{1}{2}$ m per year   **(ii)** 13 m

24. (ii) S1–S2: $\frac{1}{2}$, S2–S3: $\frac{1}{7}$, S3–S4: $\frac{1}{3}$, S4–S5: $\frac{3}{10}$, S5–S6: $-\frac{3}{10}$, S6–S7: $-\frac{2}{15}$,

S7–S8: $\frac{1}{4}$, S8–S9: $-\frac{4}{5}$ **(iii)** We measure slope from left to right **(iv)** Beginners: S2–S3, S4–S5,

S5–S6, S6–S7, S7–S8; Experienced: S1–S2, S3–S4; Expert: S8–S9

25. (ii) $\frac{5}{2}$, 1, $\frac{1}{2}$, $\frac{3}{4}$, $-\frac{4}{3}$, $-\frac{2}{3}$, $-\frac{1}{2}$, $-\frac{3}{5}$ **(iii)** The roads go down the hill **(iv)** Sections 2–4 and 6–8

26. Yes: London

Exercise 15.4
1. On **2.** On **3.** Not on **4.** On **5.** Not on **6.** On **7.** Not on **8.** Not on
9. On **10.** Not on **12.** 7 **13.** 2 **14.** 3 **15.** −5 **16.** 4

Exercise 15.5
1. $2x - y - 7 = 0$ **2.** $3x - y + 2 = 0$ **3.** $x + y + 2 = 0$ **4.** $5x + y - 22 = 0$
5. $4x - y = 0$ **6.** $3x - 5y - 47 = 0$ **7.** $4x + 3y + 15 = 0$ **8.** $5x - 4y - 30 = 0$
9. $x + 6y + 15 = 0$ **10.** $5x + 7y + 17 = 0$ **11.** $2x - 5y - 9 = 0$ **12.** $x + 2y + 1 = 0$
13. (i) 70 minutes **(ii)** 130 minutes **(iii)** $20x - y + 30 = 0$

(iv)
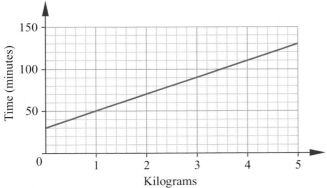

(v) (a) 90 mins **(b)** 110 mins
(c) 4·5 kg

Exercise 15.6
1. $x - y + 3 = 0$ **2.** $2x + y - 10 = 0$ **3.** $3x - y - 18 = 0$ **4.** $x - 2y + 1 = 0$
5. $5x + 7y - 19 = 0$ **6.** $3x - 5y + 13 = 0$ **7.** $x + 2y + 9 = 0$ **8.** $5x - 2y - 14 = 0$
9. $4x + 2y + 3 = 0$ **10. (i)** $4x - 3y - 18 = 0$ **(ii)** $3x + 4y - 1 = 0$
11. (i) $2x - y - 6 = 0$ **(ii)** $x + 2y + 2 = 0$ **12.** $2x + 3y - 7 = 0$ **13.** $3x - 2y + 14 = 0$
14. (iii) $15x - 2y + 100 = 0$ **15. (i)** $(4, 8)$, $(12, 12)$ **(ii)** $x - 2y + 12 = 0$
(iv) Fixed charge: €6; charge per km: €0·50

Exercise 15.7

1. $y = -\dfrac{2}{3}x + 3$ 2. $y = \dfrac{5}{2}x - 6$ 3. $y = \dfrac{3}{2}x - 4$ 4. $y = \dfrac{4}{3}x + 7$ 5. $y = 3x + 8$

6. $y = \dfrac{2}{3}x - 5$ 7. $y = -\dfrac{1}{2}x + 8$ 8. $y = -\dfrac{1}{2}x + 2$ 9. $y = -\dfrac{5}{2}x - 5$ 10. $3x - y + 7 = 0$

11. $2x + y - 11 = 0$ 12. $8x + y + 5 = 0$ 13. $2x - 3y + 3 = 0$ 14. $3x - 5y - 30 = 0$

15. $x - 3y + 9 = 0$ 16. $3x + 4y + 36 = 0$ 17. $2x + 3y + 6 = 0$ 18. $5x + 5y - 24 = 0$

Exercise 15.8

1. -2 2. 3 3. 2 4. -3 5. $-\dfrac{2}{3}$ 6. $\dfrac{4}{3}$ 7. $-\dfrac{1}{4}$ 8. $\dfrac{1}{3}$ 9. $\dfrac{4}{3}$

10. $\dfrac{5}{7}$ 11. $\dfrac{3}{2}$ 12. $\dfrac{7}{10}$ 16. 6 17. 5

Exercise 15.9

1. $2x - y - 3 = 0$ 2. $2x + 3y = 0$ 3. $5x + 4y + 21 = 0$ 4. $3x + 4y - 14 = 0$

5. $5x - 3y + 10 = 0$ 6. $x + 2y + 5 = 0$ 7. $5x - 2y - 13 = 0$

Exercise 15.10

1. $(2, 1)$ 2. $(3, 2)$ 3. $(1, 0)$ 4. $(-4, 3)$ 5. $(-3, -1)$ 6. $(0, -5)$ 7. $(1, 2)$

8. $(6, -1)$ 9. $(-3, 7)$ 10. $\left(\dfrac{3}{5}, \dfrac{4}{5}\right)$ 11. $\left(\dfrac{3}{2}, -\dfrac{3}{2}\right)$ 12. $\left(\dfrac{6}{5}, \dfrac{2}{5}\right)$ 13. $\left(\dfrac{4}{5}, \dfrac{6}{5}\right)$

14. $\left(\dfrac{5}{2}, \dfrac{1}{2}\right)$ 15. $\left(\dfrac{10}{3}, \dfrac{10}{3}\right)$ 16. $(-3, -3)$ 17. $(-2, -4)$

18. $A(2, 1)$; $B(1, -3)$; $4x - y - 7 = 0$

Exercise 15.11

26. $(0, -7)$ 27. 3 28. $y = 3x + 2$ 29. $y = -\dfrac{2}{3}x - 3$

Exercise 15.14

1. (i) €100 = CHF120   (ii) CHF48   (iii) €83   (iv) €75   (v) $y = 1{\cdot}2x$ or $6x - 5y = 0$ (vi) Jerry

2. (i) 1 cm   (ii) Check vertical axis for length of spring, go right to graph and drop to horizontal axis to read mass   (iii) $\dfrac{7}{4}$ (iv) $\dfrac{7}{4}$ cm or $1\dfrac{3}{4}$ cm   (v) 9·75 cm

(vi) $y = \dfrac{7}{4}x + 1$ or $7x - 4y + 4 = 0$ (vii) 9·75 cm   (ix) Small masses won't stretch the spring; very large masses would break it

3. (i)

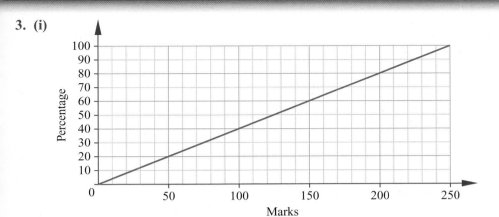

(ii) 175 marks   **(iii)** $\dfrac{2}{5}$ **(iv)** $y = \dfrac{2}{5}x$ or $2x - 5y = 0$ **4. (i)** $C(13, 17)$ **(iii)** $2x - y - 13 = 0$

(iv) $x + 2y - 34 = 0$ **(v)** $(12, 11)$ **(vi)** $\sqrt{125}$ or $11\cdot18$ units   **(vii)** 21,012 m   **(viii)** 2,592,000 m^2

5. (i) €350   **(ii)** $\dfrac{1}{2}$ **(iii)** Cost goes up by €$\dfrac{1}{2}$ per extra person; €100   **(iv)** $x - 2y + 200 = 0$

(v) Basic fee of €100   **6. (i)** $(10, 0)$ **(ii)** $(10, 5)$ **(iii)** 1,000 m or 1 km   **(iv)** $(4, 8)$ **(v)** $-\dfrac{1}{2}$

(vi) $x + 2y - 20 = 0$ **(vii) (a)** 1,342 m   **(b)** $\left(7, 6\dfrac{1}{2}\right)$ **(c)** Horizontal roads are on integral

y-coordinates   **(viii)** It is perpendicular

Exercise 16.1

1.

		sin A	cos A	tan A
	(i)	$\dfrac{4}{5}$	$\dfrac{3}{5}$	$\dfrac{4}{3}$
	(ii)	$\dfrac{15}{17}$	$\dfrac{8}{17}$	$\dfrac{15}{8}$
	(iii)	$\dfrac{\sqrt{3}}{2}$	$\dfrac{1}{2}$	$\dfrac{\sqrt{3}}{1} = \sqrt{3}$

		sin B	cos B	tan B
	(i)	$\dfrac{3}{5}$	$\dfrac{4}{5}$	$\dfrac{3}{4}$
	(ii)	$\dfrac{8}{17}$	$\dfrac{15}{17}$	$\dfrac{8}{15}$
	(iii)	$\dfrac{1}{2}$	$\dfrac{\sqrt{3}}{2}$	$\dfrac{1}{\sqrt{3}}$

2. (i) 25   **(ii)** 169   **(iii)** 100   **(iv)** 841   **(v)** 10   **(vi)** 4   **(vii)** 16   **(viii)** 25   **(ix)** 7   **(x)** 1
(xi) 9   **(xii)** 4   **3. (i)** 3, 4 and 5; 8, 15 and 17   **(ii)** 1, $\sqrt{3}$ and 2; 1, 2 and $\sqrt{5}$

4. (i) $x = 5;\ \dfrac{12}{13};\ \dfrac{5}{13};\ \dfrac{12}{5}$ **(ii)** $x = 21;\ \dfrac{20}{29};\ \dfrac{21}{29};\ \dfrac{20}{29}$ **(iii)** $x = 9;\ \dfrac{40}{41};\ \dfrac{9}{41};\ \dfrac{40}{9}$

(iv) $x = \sqrt{12};\ \dfrac{1}{\sqrt{13}};\ \dfrac{\sqrt{12}}{\sqrt{13}};\ \dfrac{1}{\sqrt{12}}$ **(v)** $x = \sqrt{7};\ \dfrac{\sqrt{7}}{4};\ \dfrac{3}{4};\ \dfrac{\sqrt{7}}{3}$ **(vi)** $x = \sqrt{13};\ \dfrac{3}{\sqrt{13}};\ \dfrac{2}{\sqrt{13}};\ \dfrac{3}{2}$

5. (i)

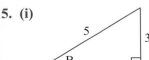

(ii) 4   **6. (i)**

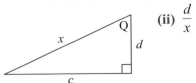

(ii) $\dfrac{d}{x}$

7. $a^2 > b^2 + c^2$ **8. (i)** Greater than   **(ii)** Equal to   **(iii)** Less than   **(iv)** Less than

9. (i) $\dfrac{24}{25}; \dfrac{7}{24}$ 10. 10   11. (ii) $\dfrac{4}{3}$ 12. (iii) $A < 90°$ 14. 17 cm   15. (i) 13 m
(ii) 1,265 cm   (iii) 566 cm   16. (i) 25 km   (ii) 10·6 km

Exercise 16.2

1. 0·7771   2. 0·2924   3. 1·0724   4. 0·9833   5. 0·8594   6. 0·6224

7. 0·7361   8. 0·4509   9. 0·6224   10. 0·2571   11. 0·9932   12. 0·4834

13. 4·6947   14. 31·6916   15. 173·1706   16. 78·5689   17. 39·1622   18. 149·9937

19. 17·9260   20. 12·1183   21. 19·6962   22. 259·6022   23. 3·3317   24. 1

25. −1   26. $\dfrac{1}{2}$ or 0·5   27. $-\dfrac{1}{2}$ or −0·5   28. $\dfrac{1}{4}$ or 0·25   29. 15   30. 35

Exercise 16.3

1. 42°   2. 55°   3. 7°   4. 17°   5. 63°   6. 53°   7. 44°   8. 18°   9. 38·42°

10. 67·82°   11. 40·75°   12. 19·47°   13. 66·42°   14. 78·69°   15. 36·87°

16. 11·54°   17. 48·19°   18. 18·43°   19. 40·89°   20. 19·11°   21. 17°27′

22. 69°31′   23. 56°19′   24. 40°22′   25. 81°15′   26. 12°4′   27. 60°   28. 30°

29. 45°   30. 9°   31. 42°   32. 9°   33. (i) $\dfrac{3}{5}; \dfrac{3}{4}$ (iii) 37°   34. (i) $\dfrac{8}{17}; \dfrac{15}{17}$ (iii) 28°

Exercise 16.4

1. 56°   2. 59°   3. 35°   4. 45°   5. 52°   6. 34°   7. 9·39   8. 28·84

9. 26·36   10. (i) 2·5   (ii) 37°   11. (i) 5   (ii) 39°   12. (i) 34   (ii) 64   (iii) 14°

Exercise 16.5

1. 4·85 m   2. 4·8 m   3. 11·64 m   4. (i) 3·5 m   (ii) 75°   5. 3·2 m   6. 1·9 m

7. (i) 47 m   8. (i) 18·5 cm   (ii) 57·1 cm   9. 15°   10. (i) 51 m   (ii) 20 m

11. (i) 12 m   (ii) 172 cm   12. (i) 26 m   (ii) 21 m   (iii) 33 m   13. (i) 30°   (ii) 2·5 m/s
(iii) 150 m   (iv) 1·5 m/s   14. 426 m   15. (i) 84 m   (ii) 19°   16. (i) 16 m   (ii) 24 m
(iii) 8 m   17. (i) 32 m   (ii) 61 m   (iii) 37 s   18. (i) 1 m 28 cm

19.

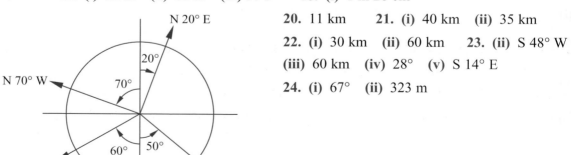

20. 11 km   21. (i) 40 km   (ii) 35 km
22. (i) 30 km   (ii) 60 km   23. (ii) S 48° W
(iii) 60 km   (iv) 28°   (v) S 14° E
24. (i) 67°   (ii) 323 m

Exercise 17.1

1. €28, €12   2. €36, €22·50   3. 34, 85, 119   4. €3,000

5. (i) 3 : 4   (ii) 5 : 4   (iii) 1 : 3   (iv) 6 : 3 : 4   (v) 3 : 2 : 4   6. 110 g : 132 g : 220 g

7. €252 : €168 : €126   8. (i) B (ii) $A = €40, B = €20, C = €80$

9. $A = €58, B = €116, C = €116, D = €203$ 10. €200   11. 4 : 6 : 7   12. 5 : 10 : 14

13. 6 : 5   14. 33   15. 343   16. 68 km/h   17. 112 km/h   18. €237·50

19. €60,000   20. (i) 475 ml   (ii) 30 ml   (iii) 149 : 11

21. No, because the ratio of their lengths changed   22. 3·2 kg in large and 0·8 kg in the small container

23. 6 hrs   24. 108 mins   25. $\dfrac{20}{9}$ mins   26. (i) 120 days   (ii) 8 days   (iii) 24 men

27. (i) 12 hours   (ii) 50   28. 21 mins   29. 3   30. 15

Exercise 17.2

1. (i) 30   (ii) 65·1   (iii) €24·05   (iv) €3·69   2. (i) 144   (ii) 28   3. €98·40

4. €361·60   5. 21%   6. 19%   7. €75   8. 1,260   9. €82   10. €6·75

11. €69   12. €1,476   13. (i) €850   (ii) €1,045·50   14. 700   15. €600,000

16. €200,000   17. 2·4 litres   18. €1,250   19. €28,000   20. €15,750

21. 351   22. 68,600   23. 160   24. 64   25. 16   26. $3x$ 27. $\dfrac{4}{5}y$ 28. 24

29. (i) €2,898   (ii) €3,999, €5,332   (iii) €5,418   30. (ii) €62   (iii) €68·82

31. (i) €145·20   (ii) €120   (iii) €1·67

Exercise 17.3

1. (i) $162   (ii) €850   2. €520   3. (i) ¥30,800   (ii) €450   4. Cheaper in South
Africa by €20   5. €2,556·25   6. (i) €21   (ii) 1·75%   7. $256   8. (i) R4,800
(ii) R160   9. 2·5%   10. €1 = R9·6   11. €515   12. THB 2,631,578·95
13. 45·6   14. 5·2

Exercise 17.4

1. €49·36   2. (i) €48·84   (ii) €60·12   3. €3,376·80   4. €33·10

5. (i) €51·21   (ii) €70·98   6. €36·17   7. €135·55

8. $A = 2,567, B = €205·36, C = €218·41, D = €30·58, E = €248·99$

9. $A = 6,552, B = €491·40, C = €509·37, D = €71·31, E = €580·68, F = €29·03, G = €551·65$

Exercise 17.5

1. (i) €40   (ii) $12\frac{1}{2}$%   2. (i) €25   (ii) 17·86%   3. €10,200   4. 20%   5. 8%

6. 2·5%   7. 17%   8. €17,205   9. €3,800   10. €1,200   11. €19,500   12. €214·62

Exercise 17.6

1. (i) 20% (ii) 16·67%   2. (i) 18·75% (ii) 15·79%   3. €8,625   4. €89·60

5. €200,000   6. €10,000   7. (i) €1,232·50 (ii) €1,545·45   8. (i) €413 (ii) €426·83

9. (i) €2,478 (ii) €2,838 (iii) €1,116   10. €14,340; €2,340   11. €12,465; €3,965

12. (i) £3·61 (ii) 39%

Exercise 17.7

1. €2,496   2. €1,738·80   3. €2,837·25   4. €4,775·40   5. €927·27   6. €2,497·28

7. €248·25   8. €306·04   9. €736   10. €1,755·52   11. €2,744·95   12. €30,767·56

13. €6,614·40   14. (i) €5,100 (ii) €5,222·40   15. €2,152   16. 8%   17. (i) 4% (ii) 6%

18. (i) €21,200 (ii) 3·5%   19. (i) €53,560 (ii) 2·5%   20. (i) 30,900 (ii) 4·5%

21. (i) 2% (ii) €2,060·45   22. (i) €1,805·44 (ii) €2,650·98

Exercise 17.8

1. (i) €6,240 (ii) 4·5%   2. €2,500   3. €10,000   4. €45,000   5. €22,000

6. (i) €22,472 (ii) €1,472   7. €11,600   8. €4,720   9. (i) €5,109·50 (ii) 5%

10. (i) €9,168·75 (ii) 4%   11. €5,000   12. €5,000   13. (i) €6,240 (ii) 4·5%

14. (i) €12,960 (ii) €160

Exercise 17.9

1. (i) €9,960 (ii) €7,470   2. (i) €11,398 (ii) €7,448   3. (i) €9,370 (ii) 1,290

(iii) €35,580   4. (i) €13,725 (ii) €9,575   5. (i) €9,070 (ii) €715 (iii) €28,815

6. €1,404·90   7. (i) €4,130 (ii) €4,626 (iii) €34,574   8. (i) €5,930 (ii) €6,460

(iii) 38,665   9. (i) €8,643 (ii) €30,275   10. (i) €8,438 (ii) €32,582

11. 20%   12. 18%   13. €3,500   14. (i) €19,000 (ii) €48,000

15. (i) €23,500 (ii) €52,000   16. (i) €26,450 (ii) €36,700   17. (i) €11,360 (ii) €51,000

18. (i) €37,520 (ii) €60,000

Exercise 18.1

1. (i) 64 cm (ii) 240 cm^2 2. (i) 60 cm (ii) 225 cm^2 3. (i) 24 cm (ii) 24 cm^2

4. (i) 94·2 cm (ii) 706·5 cm^2 5. (i) 52·56 cm (ii) 125·6 cm^2

6. (i) 56 cm (ii) 144 cm^2 7. (i) 23 cm (ii) 483 cm^2 8. 8 cm   9. 15 m

10. (i) B (ii) C   11. (i) 4·56 m (ii) 4·46 m^2 12. (i) 8 cm (ii) 96 cm

13. (i) 81 cm^2 (ii) 20 cm   14. (i) 8 cm (ii) 96 cm^2 15. 675 cm^2 16. 16 m; 8 m

17. 60 cm^2 18. 24 m^2 19. 276 m^2 20. 3,000 cm^2 21. (i) 12 cm (ii) 6 cm^2

22. (i) 364 cm^2 **(ii)** 80 cm **23. (i)** 80 cm^2 **(ii)** 16 cm^2 **(iii)** 32 cm^2 **24. (i)** $16\sqrt{3} \text{ cm}^2$

(ii) $96\sqrt{3} \text{ cm}^2$ **(iii)** 48 cm **25. (i)** 120 cm^2; 30 cm^2 **(ii)** $8 - x$; 6 cm **(iii)** 10 cm

26. (i) $\triangle ABC : 4 \text{ cm}^2$ **(ii) (a)** x^2 **(b)** $\dfrac{1}{2}(2 - x)(x) \text{ cm}^2$ **(c)** $\dfrac{1}{2}(4 - x)(x) \text{ cm}^2$ **(d)** $\dfrac{4}{3} \text{ cm}$

	π	Circumference	Area	Radius
27.	π	10π	25π	5
28.	π	$6\pi \text{ m}$	$9\pi \text{ m}^2$	3 m
29.	$3{\cdot}14$	$125{\cdot}6 \text{ m}$	$1{,}256 \text{ m}^2$	20 m
30.	π	$11\pi \text{ cm}$	$30{\cdot}25\pi \text{ cm}^2$	$5{\cdot}5 \text{ cm}$
31.	$\dfrac{22}{7}$	264 cm	$5{,}544 \text{ cm}^2$	42 cm

32. 21 cm **33.** $39\pi \text{ cm}^2$ **34.** 10 cm **35.** 6 cm **36. (i)** 616 cm^2 **(ii)** 88 cm

(iii) 98 cm^2 **(iv)** 56 cm^2 **(v)** 50 cm **37. (i)** 4 cm **(ii)** $4\pi \text{ cm}^2$ **38.** Square **39.** Square

40. $20{,}000 \text{ km}$ **41. (i)** 16 cm **(ii)** $128\pi \text{ cm}^2$ **(iii)** 50% **42. (i)** 400 m **(ii)** 44 m

43. (i) $4\pi \text{ cm}^2$ **(ii)** $d^2\pi \text{ cm}^2$ **(iii)** $(d + 4)(d) \text{ cm}^2$

Exercise 18.2

1. (i) 120 cm^3 **(ii)** 148 cm^2 **2. (i)** 576 m^3 **(ii)** 432 m^2 **3. (i)** $1{,}260 \text{ mm}^3$

(ii) 766 mm^2 **4. (i)** 5 cm **(ii)** 392 cm^2 **5.** 525 litres **6. (i)** 8 cm **(ii)** $1{,}720 \text{ cm}^2$

7. 576 **8.** 54 cm^2 **9.** 96 cm^2 **10.** 8 cm^3 **11.** 125 cm^3

12. $8 \text{ cm} \times 12 \text{ cm} \times 28 \text{ cm}$; $1{,}312 \text{ cm}^2$ **13. (i)** $8{\cdot}6 \text{ cm}$ **(ii)** 258 cm^2 **14. (i)** €$12{,}000$ **(ii)** 96

(iii) €$2{,}400$ **15. (i)** $1{\cdot}5 \text{ cm}$ **(ii)** 171 cm^2 **(iii)** 150 **16. (i)** $9{,}600 \text{ cm}^3$ **(ii)** 25%

(iii) $6{\cdot}96 \text{ cm}$ **17. (i)** $3{,}125{,}000 \text{ litres}$ **(ii)** $55{\cdot}9 \text{ m}$ **18.** $2\dfrac{1}{2} \text{ days}$

Exercise 18.3

1. 400 cm^3 **2.** $8{,}160 \text{ cm}^3$ **3.** $1{,}350 \text{ cm}^3$ **4.** $133{\cdot}2 \text{ cm}^3$ **5.** 121 cm^3 **6.** $93{\cdot}25 \text{ cm}^2$

7. (i) 300 cm^3 **(ii)** $0{\cdot}3 \, l$ **8. (i)** 240 cm^2 **(ii)** $96{,}000 \text{ cm}^3$ **9.** $1{\cdot}44 \text{ m}^3$ **10. (i)** $3{,}480 \text{ m}^3$

(ii) $5 \text{ hrs } 48 \text{ mins}$ **(iii)** €$4{,}176$ **11. (i) (a)** $6{\cdot}5 \text{ cm}$ **(b)** $4{\cdot}8 \text{ cm}$ **(c)** $2{\cdot}5 \text{ cm}$

(ii) 455 cm; 336 cm; 175 cm **(iii)** $19{\cdot}27 \text{ m}^2$ **(iv)** 159 m^3 **12. (i)** 6 cm^2 **(ii)** 20 cm

Exercise 18.4

	π	Radius	Height	Volume	CSA	TSA
1.	$\dfrac{22}{7}$	7 cm	12 cm	1,848 cm^3	528 cm^2	836 cm^2
2.	3·14	15 cm	40 cm	28,260 cm^3	3,768 cm^2	5,181 cm^2
3.	π	8 mm	11 mm	704π mm^3	176π mm^2	304π mm^2

	π	Radius	Volume	CSA
4.	$\dfrac{22}{7}$	21 cm	38,808 cm^3	5,544 cm^2
5.	3·14	9 m	3,052·08 m^3	1,017·36 m^2
6.	π	6 mm	288π mm^3	144π mm^2

	π	Radius	Volume	CSA	TSA
7.	π	15 mm	2,250π mm^3	450π mm^2	675π mm^2
8.	π	$1\dfrac{1}{2}$ cm	$\dfrac{9}{4}\pi$ cm^3	$\dfrac{9}{2}\pi$ cm^2	$\dfrac{27}{4}\pi$ cm^2
9.	$\dfrac{22}{7}$	42 cm	155,232 cm^3	11,088 cm^2	16,632 cm^2
10.	3·14	12 m	3,617·28 m^3	904·32 m^2	1,356·48 m^2

11. 24,492 cm^3 **12. (i)** 576 m^2 **(ii)** 2·4 m^2 **(iii)** 3·75% **13.** 9 **14. (i)** 19,800 cm^3

(ii) 4,851 cm^3 **(iii)** 14,949 cm^3 **15. (i)** $\dfrac{1,048,576}{3}\pi$ m^3 **(ii)** $\dfrac{131,072}{3}\pi$ m^3 **(iii)** $\dfrac{1}{8}$

16. (i) 439·5 cm^3 **(ii)** 246·2 cm^2 **17. (i)** 4·5π cm^3 **(ii) (a)** 1·5 cm; 12 cm **(b)** 27π cm^3

(c) $\dfrac{2}{3}$ **18. (i)** 4,620 m^3 **(ii)** 4,620,000 *l* **19. (ii)** €61,600 **20. (i)** 1,152,000π cm^3

(ii) 1 hour

Exercise 18.5

	π	Radius	Height	Slant height	Volume	CSA
1.	π	8 cm	6 cm	10 cm	128π cm^3	80π cm^2
2.	$\dfrac{22}{7}$	21 mm	20 mm	29 mm	9,240 mm^3	1,914 mm^2
3.	3·14	3 cm	4 cm	5 cm	37·68 cm^3	47·1 cm^2
4.	3·14	40 cm	9 cm	41 cm	15,072 cm^3	5,149·6 cm^2
5.	$\dfrac{22}{7}$	2·8 cm	4·5 cm	5·3 cm	36·96 cm^3	46·64 cm^2
6.	3·14	11 cm	60 cm	61 cm	7,598·8 cm^3	2,106·94 cm^2

7. 10,666·6π cm^3 **8. (i)** 4·5 cm   **(ii)** 170 cm^2 **9. (i)** 15 cm   **(ii)** 320π cm^3
(iii) 64π cm^2 **(iv)** 136π cm^2 **(v)** €7,536   **10. (i)** 105 cm   **(ii)** 360 cm   **(iii)** 375 cm
(iv) 4 m^3 **(v)** 16 m^2 **11. (i)** 9 cm   **(ii)** 40 cm   **(iii)** 41 cm   **(iv)** 369π cm^2
12. (i) $x^3\pi$ cm^3 **(ii)** 2 : 1   **13. (i)** 32π cm^3 **(ii)** 360 s   **14. (i)** 39·1 cm   **(ii)** 12·4 cm
(iii) 31·4 cm   **15. (i)** 125π cm^2 **(ii) (a)** 10 cm   **(b)** 7·5 cm   **(c)** 250π cm^3
16. (i) 31 cm   **(ii)** 1,950 cm^3 **17.** $\dfrac{7}{8}$

18.

Expression	$r + 2x$	$2xhl$	$\pi r(x + h)$	$\dfrac{r^2 h}{xl}$	$\dfrac{3xh}{7}$
Length, area or volume	length	volume	area	length	area

19. 2   **21. (i)** mistake   **(ii)** length   **(iii)** volume   **(iv)** area   **22. (i)** 47 m^2 **(ii)** 27
23. (i) 2·4 cm   **(ii)** 42·24 cm^3 **(iii)** 617·76 cm^3

Exercise 18.6

2. 108π mm^3 **3. (i)** 188·5 cm^2 **(ii)** 754 cm^3 **4. (i)** 8π cm^3 **(ii)** 3π cm^2
(iii) $(144 - 12\pi)$ cm^2 **5. (i)** 795·048 cm^3 **(ii)** 10·9 cm   **(iii)** 431·436 cm^2
6. (i) 180 l **(ii)** 270 l **(iii)** 90 l **7. (i)** 38,676 cm^3 **8. (i)** 350,000π m^3 **(ii)** 2,500π m^3
(iii) $\dfrac{5}{7}$%   **9. (i)** 280π cm^2 **(ii)** 427π cm^2

Exercise 18.7

1. (i) 20 cm   **(ii)** 260π cm^2 **2. (i)** 6 cm   **(ii)** 288π cm^3 **3.** 15 cm
4. (i) 3 cm   **(ii)** 36π cm^2 **5. (i)** 4 cm   **(ii)** 80π cm^2 **6. (i)** 20 cm   **(ii)** 1,570 cm^3
7. (i) 3·5 m   **(ii)** 34·1 m^2 **8. (i)** 10 cm   **(ii)** 96π cm^3 **9.** 10 cm
10. (i) 2 cm   **(ii)** 35·2 cm^2 **11. (i)** 4 m   **(ii)** 301·44 m^2 **12.** 45 cm

13. (i) 2·1 m **(ii)** 0·81π m^3 **(iii)** 0·096π m^3 **14.** 18 cm **15.** 3·2 m

16. 4 cm **17. (i)** $\dfrac{128}{3}\pi$ cm^3 **(ii)** $\dfrac{16}{3}\pi h$ cm^3 **(iii)** 16 cm **(iv)** 20 cm

18. (i) 1,543·5π cm^3 **(ii)** 42 cm

Exercise 18.8

1. 9 **2.** 2 **3.** 6 **4.** 18 **5.** 5 **6.** 7·5 **7.** 20 cm **8. (i)** 30,375π cm^3

(ii) 22·5 cm **9.** 8 cm **10. (i)** $\dfrac{32}{3}\pi$ cm^3 **(ii)** 150π cm^3 **(iii)** 0·43 cm

11. 400 **12. (i)** 3 cm **(ii)** 2 cm **13. (i)** 121·5π cm^3 **(ii)** 3·4 cm

14. (i) 300,000π cm^3 **(ii)** 28,125 **(iii)** 1 cm **15. (i)** 509 mm^3

(ii) (a) 48 mm **(b)** 18 mm **(c)** 20 mm **(iii)** 17,280 mm^3 **(iv)** 5,064 mm^3

16. (i) 66 cm^3 **(ii)** 52 **17. (i)** 3,920π cm^3 **(ii)** 144π cm^3 **(iii)** 9 cm **18.** 20 cm

19. (i) 1·75 m **(iii)** 9 m^3

Exercise 18.9

1. (1, C) (2, E) (3, A) (4, F) (5, B) (6, D) **4. (i)** 5 **(ii)** 6 **(iii) (a)** 312 **(b)** 288

5. (i) 2·64 m^2 **(ii) (a)** 378,000 cm^3 **(b)** 0·378 m^3 **(c)** 378 l

6. (ii) (a) 12,650 cm^2 **(b)** 1·265 m^2 **7. (i)** Square pyramid **(ii)** triangular prism

9. (i) 8 **(ii)** 5 **(iii)** 12 **(iv)** 96 cm **10.** triangular prism

11. (i) cylinder **(ii)** 10 cm **(iii)** 8 cm **(iv)** 62·8 cm **(v)** no

14. (i) square pyramid **(ii)** pentagon based prism

Exercise 19.1

1. 6 **2.** 12 **3.** 30 **4.** 18 **5.** 30 **6. (i)** 10 **(ii)** (H, P) (H, Q) (H, R) (H, S) (H, T)
(T, P) (T, Q) (T, R) (T, S) (T, T) **7. (i)** 18 **8. (ii)** None **(iii)** 2 **9. (i)** 234
(ii) For a class of 30 students where every student bought 1 ticket, there would be too many tickets, so not suitable in that case

10.

	Boys	Girls	Total
Late	4	3	7
Not late	9	12	21
Total	13	15	28

11. (i) 205 **(ii)** 49 **12. (i)** 239 **(ii)** 942 **13. (i)** 763 **(ii)** 203 **(iii)** 360

14. (i) 6 **(ii)** 10 **15. (i)** BACD, BCAD, BDAC BADC, BCDA, BDCA **(iii)** 24
(iv) BACD and CDBA and 12 **16. (i) (a)** 120 **(b)** 216 **(ii) (b)**

Exercise 19.2

1. (i) $\dfrac{3}{10}$ (ii) $\dfrac{4}{5}$ (iii) $\dfrac{7}{10}$ 2. (i) $\dfrac{1}{6}$ (ii) $\dfrac{1}{2}$ 3. (i) $\dfrac{1}{2}$ (ii) $\dfrac{1}{4}$ (iii) $\dfrac{1}{52}$ (iv) $\dfrac{1}{13}$

4. (i) Impossible (ii) Likely (iii) Unlikely   5. $\dfrac{7}{10}$ 6. (i) C (ii) A (iii) E (iv) B (v) D

7. (i) €20   8. (i) $\dfrac{2}{5}$ (ii) $\dfrac{3}{5}$ (iii) $\dfrac{1}{5}$ (iv) $\dfrac{7}{10}$ 9. (i) $\dfrac{1}{7}$ (ii) $\dfrac{2}{3}$ (iii) Unlikely

(iv) Likely   10. $\dfrac{1}{2}$ 11. $\dfrac{1}{7}$ 12. (i) $\dfrac{4}{5}$ (ii) $\dfrac{1}{5}$ (iv) Three

13. (i) Very unlikely (ii) Evens (iii) $\dfrac{3}{5}$ (iv) $\dfrac{1}{4}$ (v) Impossible (vi) Certain (vii) Very likely

14.

15. B (5 wins)

16. (i) 0·02 (ii) 0·07 (iii) $\dfrac{23}{25}$ and $\dfrac{21}{50}$ 17. (i) $\dfrac{5}{21}$ (ii) $\dfrac{11}{21}$ (iii) (a) $\dfrac{1}{7}$ (b) $\dfrac{1}{21}$

18. (i) 150 (ii) $\dfrac{3}{5}$ (iii) $\dfrac{1}{5}$

19.

21.

Colour	Number	Probability
Red	9	$\dfrac{3}{8}$
Blue	6	$\dfrac{1}{4}$
Yellow	9	$\dfrac{3}{8}$

22. (i) 106 (ii) $\dfrac{13}{14}$ (iii) 16 (iv) $\dfrac{2}{25}$ 23. (i) $\dfrac{1}{100}$ (ii) $\dfrac{1}{10}$ (iii) 0·84

(iv) O – can give blood to all groups

O – can only receive blood from other O people. This is only 8% of the population, therefore it is vital that this category donates blood.

Exercise 19.3

1. (ii) $\dfrac{1}{5}$ (iii) $\dfrac{3}{10}$ 2. (ii) $\dfrac{1}{6}$ 3. (ii) (a) $\dfrac{1}{5}$ (b) $\dfrac{3}{10}$ (c) $\dfrac{11}{20}$ (d) $\dfrac{1}{4}$

4. (ii) (a) $\dfrac{2}{15}$ (b) $\dfrac{2}{15}$ 5. (i) $\dfrac{1}{18}$ (ii) $\dfrac{1}{3}$ (iii) (a) 0·36 (b) Patricia

6. (i) $\dfrac{21}{100}$ (ii) $\dfrac{49}{100}$ (iii) $\dfrac{21}{50}$ (iv) $\dfrac{29}{50}$ 7. (ii) (a) $\dfrac{1}{4}$ (b) $\dfrac{1}{4}$

8. (ii) (a) $\dfrac{1}{40}$ (b) $\dfrac{27}{40}$ (c) $\dfrac{3}{10}$

9. (i) mmm, mmf, mfm, fmm, mff, fmf, ffm, fff   (ii) (a) $\frac{1}{8}$ (b) $\frac{3}{8}$ 10. (i) $\frac{4}{9}$ (ii) $\frac{2}{9}$ (iii) $\frac{5}{9}$

(iv) $\frac{4}{9}$ 11. (i) $\frac{25}{36}$ (ii) $\frac{5}{18}$ 12. (i) $\frac{1}{5}$ (ii) $\frac{3}{20}$ (iii) $\frac{3}{5}$ (iv) $\frac{1}{20}$ (v) $\frac{13}{20}$

13. (i) (a) $\frac{1}{4}$ (b) $\frac{1}{16}$ (c) $\frac{3}{16}$ (d) $\frac{3}{8}$ (ii) (a) $\frac{1}{18}$ (b) $\frac{7}{18}$

Exercise 19.4

1. $\frac{13}{20}$ 2. 200   3. Unfair, score 2 frequency very low, score 6 frequency very high

4. (i) $\frac{3}{10}$ (ii) Become $\frac{1}{4}$ 5. (i) Frequency 7, 8, 10, 9, 6   (ii) Spinner not biased

6. (i) $\frac{7}{50}; \frac{43}{100}; \frac{2}{25}; \frac{11}{50}; \frac{13}{100}$ (ii) 20   (iii) Not fair   7. 837   8. 7   9. (i) $\frac{3}{10}$ (ii) $\frac{3}{5}$

10. (i) $\frac{5}{6}$ (ii) 75   11. (i) 12   (ii) 9   12. (i) $\frac{4}{5}$ (ii) 288   13. (i) (a) $\frac{3}{5}$ (b) $\frac{7}{50}$

(ii) $\frac{2}{5}$ (iii) (a) 320   (b) 400   14. (i) 0·35   (ii) 140   15. (i) (a) 16   (b) 8   (ii) 3

(iii) (a) 496   (b) 248   (c) 93

17. (i)

	Frequency	Probability
Win	6	$\frac{3}{20}$
Lose	34	$\frac{17}{20}$

(ii) 54   (iii) You do not win €5, you win €4·50

18. (i) Elaina   (ii) 0·27   19. (i) Nell   (ii) Taras   20. (iii) is correct

21. (i) 20   (ii) (a) $\frac{1}{20}$ (b) $\frac{3}{10}$ (iii) Not fair

22. (i) 90   (ii) + (v)

Colour	Frequency	Relative frequency	Daily frequency (part (e) below)
Red	70	$\frac{70}{500}$ or 0·14	336
Blue	100	$\frac{100}{500}$ or 0·2	480
Yellow	45	$\frac{45}{500}$ or 0·09	216
White	55	$\frac{55}{500}$ or 0·11	264
Black	90	$\frac{90}{500}$ or 0·18	432
Silver	140	$\frac{140}{500} = 0·28$	672
Total	500	$\frac{500}{500}$ or 1	2,400

(iii) Sum of relative frequencies = 1 (or) 100%   **(iv)** 14% = 0.14

(v) No. A test is reliable if repeated runs of the test would give the same results. There is no reason to say that if this test was run again it would be different because of the sample not being random. The colour of a vehicle is random and running the test at different times of the day or on different days would not necessarily make the test any more reliable.

Exercise 19.5

1. (i) 1   **(ii)** $\dfrac{5}{23}$ **(iii)** $\dfrac{25}{46}$ **(iv)** $\dfrac{39}{46}$ **(v)** $\dfrac{9}{23}$ **(vi)** $\dfrac{18}{23}$ **(vii)** $\dfrac{11}{46}$ **(viii)** $\dfrac{9}{23}$

2. (i) $\dfrac{2}{5}$ **(ii)** $\dfrac{3}{40}$ **(iii)** $\dfrac{23}{40}$ **(iv)** $\dfrac{7}{20}$ **(v)** $\dfrac{1}{20}$ **(vi)** 360,000

3. (i) 70   **(ii)** $\dfrac{29}{35}$ **(iii)** $\dfrac{1}{14}$ **(iv)** $\dfrac{1}{10}$ **(v)** $\dfrac{4}{7}$

4. (i) $\dfrac{11}{20}$ **(ii)** $\dfrac{13}{40}$ **(iii)** $\dfrac{1}{100}$ **(iv)** $\dfrac{1}{50}$ **(v)** $\dfrac{193}{200}$ **(vi)** $\dfrac{129}{200}$

5. $P \cap Q = \{1, 3\} \neq \{ \ \}$. P and Q not mutually exclusive.

7. (i) 27   **(ii)** They liked both wine and beer   **(iii)** $\dfrac{1}{9}$ **(iv)** $\dfrac{9}{34}$ **(v)** 190   **(vi)** 316 or 317

8. (i) $\dfrac{5}{9}$ **(ii)** $\dfrac{16}{45}$ **(iii)** $\dfrac{11}{15}$ **(iv)** $\dfrac{8}{45}$

(v) Since $P(E \cap F) \neq 0$ we say E and F are not mutually exclusive

9. (i) 10   **(iii) (a)** $\dfrac{33}{50}$ **(b)** $\dfrac{3}{5}$ **(c)** $\dfrac{9}{50}$ **(d)** $\dfrac{19}{50}$ **(e)** $\dfrac{24}{25}$ **(f)** $\dfrac{19}{25}$

10. (i) 12   **(ii)** $\dfrac{3}{5}$ **11. (ii)** 3; 5   **(iii)** $\dfrac{9}{59}$ **(iv)** $\dfrac{17}{59}$ **12. (i)** $\dfrac{21}{56}$ **(ii)** $\dfrac{4}{26}$ **(iii)** $\dfrac{27}{110}$

Exercise 20.1

1. (i) 11   **(ii)** 13   **(iii)** 7   **(iv)** 1   **(v)** −1   **2. (i)** 18   **(ii)** 4   **(iii)** 0   **(iv)** −2   **(v)** 12

3. (i) 3   **(ii)** −1   **(iii)** 8   **(iv)** −6; −5, 3   **4. (i)** −1   **(ii)** −2   **(iii)** $\dfrac{1}{4}$ or 0·25   **(iv)** $\dfrac{14}{25}$ or 0·56

5. (i) 1   **(ii)** −1   **(iii)** 2   **6. (i)** $x = 2$ **(ii)** $x = \dfrac{1}{2}$ **(iii)** $x = -\dfrac{1}{3}$ or 1   **(iv)** $x \leq 1$

7. (a) (i) 1   **(ii)** −5   **(iii)** −6   **(b) (i)** $6x - 5$ **(ii)** $2x + 1$; −1   **8. (a) (i)** 10   **(ii)** 5
(b) $k = 2$ **9.** $k = 3$ **10. (a) (i)** 15   **(ii)** 8   **(iii)** 3   **(b)** $k = -4$ **(c)** $x = \pm 2$

11. (i) 4; 2   **(ii)** $k = 2$ **(iii)** 1   **12. (i)** 11; $10k + 14$ **(ii)** $k = -1$ **(iii)** $\dfrac{1}{2}, 2$

13. (i) 9; $4x^2 + 4$; $6x + 5$ **(ii)** $-1, \dfrac{5}{2}$ **14. (i)** 0; 4   **(ii)** 4   **15.** $g(x) = 2x + 6$; 12

16. (i) $k = \pm 3$ **(ii)** $h(x) = x - 1$ **(iii)** $f(x) + 1$

Exercise 20.2

1. $k = 2$ 2. $a = 3$ 3. $h = -5$ 4. $b = -4$ 5. -2 6. $k = 4$ 7. $\dfrac{1}{2}; 3$

8. $a = 3; b = -4$ 9. $a = -7; b = -1$ 10. (i) $a = 2; b = -3$ (ii) $-1; 5$ (iii) $-\dfrac{3}{2}; 4$

11. (i) $a = 5; b = -17$ (ii) $0, 1, 2, 3, 4$ 12. $a + b = 1; a - b = 5; a = 3; b = -2$

13. $p + q = 7; p - q = -3; p = 2; q = 5; -\dfrac{1}{2}, 3$ 14. (i) $a = 5; b = -6$ (ii) $0; 1$

15. $c = -3; a = 4; b = -5$ 16. (i) $q = -6$ (ii) $-8; -3$ 17. $b = 1; c = -2; k = -2$

18. $a = 2; b = -5; h = -3; k = -5$ 19. $b = -2; c = 4; p = 2; q = -1; -5; 1$

20. $b = 2; c = -3; k = -4; x = -1$ 21. $b = -2; c = -15$

Exercise 21.3

1. (i) $-2; 1\cdot5$ (ii) $-6\cdot1$ (iii) $-1; 0\cdot5$ (iv) 7 (v) $-2 \le x \le 1\cdot5$
(vi) $-3 \le x < -2$ and $1\cdot5 < x \le 2$ (vii) $-1\cdot5 \le x \le 1$ (viii) $1\cdot5 < x \le 2$ (ix) $-2\cdot5; 2$ (x) $1\cdot75$

2. (i) $-3; 1$ (ii) $-2; 0$ (iii) -4 (iv) $(-1, -4)$ (v) $-3 \le x \le 1$ (vi) $3\cdot3; k = -1$

3. (i) $-1; 4$ (ii) $0; 3$ (iii) $-3\cdot4$ (iv) $6\cdot25$ (v) $-2 \le x \le -1$ and $4 \le x \le 5$ (vi) $-0\cdot5$

4. (i) $(2, 4)$ (ii) $1 \le x \le 3$ (iii) $0 \le x \le 2$ (iv) $-5 \le k < 4$ 5. (i) $-2; 1\cdot3$
(ii) $-2 \le x \le 1\cdot3$ (iii) $-2\cdot25; 1\cdot6$ (iv) $5\cdot3$ (v) $-8\cdot3$ 6. (i) $(1, -7)$ (ii) $-1; 3$
(iii) $0 \le x \le 2$ (iv) $-2 \le x < 1$ (v) $k = -7$ 7. (ii) 4 (iii) $(1, 4)$ (iv) $-2\cdot75$ (v) $-1\cdot6$
(vi) $0 \le f(x) \le 4$ 8. (i) $-1; 3\cdot5$ (ii) $-0\cdot2; 2\cdot7$ (iii) $10\cdot1$ (iv) $k > 10\cdot1$ and $k < -11$

9. (i) 9 (ii) $(-1, 9)$ (iii) $-2; 1$ (iv) $-2 \le x \le 1$ (v) $-5 \le x \le -2$ and $1 \le x \le 3$ (vi) $-2; 0$
(vii) $-3\cdot25$ (viii) 144 (ix) $-3; 1$ (x) $-3\cdot6$ (xi) -3 (xii) $h = -1$ 10. (i) $-1; 3$
(ii) $(1, -4)$ (iii) $0; 3$ (iv) $0 \le x \le 3$ (v) $-2 \le x \le 0$ and $3 \le x \le 4$ (vi) $-4 \le f(x) \le -3$
11. (i) $-2 \le x \le 1$ (ii) 3 (iii) $-4; 1$ (iv) $1 \le x \le 3$ (v) $-4 \le x \le 1$
12. (i) $3\cdot1$ (ii) $-1; 1$ (iii) $-1 \le x \le 1$ (iv) $1 \le x \le 2$ 13. (i) $-3; 1\cdot5$ (ii) $10\cdot1$
(iii) $-2\cdot7 \le x \le 1\cdot7$ 14. (i) $-2\cdot1; 1\cdot6$ (ii) $-1\cdot5 \le x \le 1$ (iii) $-1\cdot4 \le x \le 1\cdot4$
15. (i) $-3\cdot3; 1\cdot3$ (ii) $0\cdot5$ (iii) $-2 \le x \le 0$ (iv) $-2\cdot6; 1\cdot6$ (v) $-2\cdot6 \le x \le 1\cdot6$
(vi) $-1 < x < 1\cdot3$ (vii) $k > 11$ 16. (i) 9 (ii) 4 (iii) $(4, 8)$ (iv) $4 \le x \le 6$

Exercise 21.4

1. (i) €13   (ii) €16   (iii) 7 km   (iv) €3   2. (i) $13{:}30$ and $16{:}30$ (ii) 50 km/h   (iii) $15{:}00$

3. $-1; 3\cdot5$ (i) $10\cdot1$ m   (ii) 9 m   (iii) $3\dfrac{1}{2}$ seconds   4. (i) 7 m   (ii) 16 m   (iii) 2 secs

(iv) 4 secs   (v) $13\cdot75$ m   (vi) 6 secs   (vii) 7 secs   5. (i) 25 m^2 (ii) 5 m by 5 m
(iii) 24 m^2 (iv) 3 m   (v) $8\cdot5$ m or $1\cdot5$ m   6. (i) 18 m^2 (ii) 6 m by 3 m   (iii) 1 m or 5 m
(iv) $2\cdot6$ m or $9\cdot4$ m   (v) $2 \le x \le 4$ 7. (i) 160 m   (ii) 70 m   (iii) 90 m; $35\sqrt{5}$

Exercise 22.1

1. (ii) 1, 3, 5; yes: odd numbers **(iii)** 2, 4, 6; yes: even numbers **(iv)** Yellow **(v)** Green
(vi) Green **2. (i)** 1, 4, 7 **(ii)** 2, 5, 8 **(iii)** 3, 6, 9 **(iv)** Blue **(v)** White **(vi)** Red
3. (i) 1, 4, 7, 10 **(ii)** 2, 5, 8, 11 **(iii)** 3, 6, 9, 12 **(iv)** Yellow **(v)** Orange **(vi)** 23 **(vii)** 28
4. (i) Yellow: 1, 5, 9; Purple: 2, 6, 10; Green: 3, 7, 11; Blue: 4, 8, 12 **(ii)** Blue **(iii)** Purple
(iv) Green **(v)** 31 **(vi)** 41

Exercise 22.2

1. 17, 21, 25, 29 **2.** 20, 15, 10, 5 **3.** −3, −1, 1, 3 **4.** 1, −2, −5, −8 **5.** 4·1, 4·5, 4·9, 5·3
6. 0·4, −0·2, −0·8, −1·4 **7.** 16, 32, 64, 128 **8.** 162, 486, 1,458, 4,374 **9.** 5, 7, 9, 11
10. 4, 7, 10, 13 **11.** 3, 7, 11, 15 **12.** 2, 7, 12, 17 **13.** −1, −3, −5, −7 **14.** −1, −5, −9, −13
15. 6, 9, 14, 21 **16.** 3, 8, 15, 24 **17.** $2, \frac{3}{2}, \frac{4}{3}, \frac{5}{4}$ **18.** $1, \frac{4}{3}, \frac{3}{2}, \frac{8}{5}$ **19.** 2, 4, 8, 16
20. 3, 9, 27, 81 **21. (i)** 7, 12, 17 **22. (i)** 3, 6, 11 **23. (i)** $\frac{3}{2}, \frac{4}{3}, \frac{5}{4}$

Exercise 22.3

1. 3, 5, 7, 9; 2 **2.** 5, 8, 11, 14; 3 **3.** 1, 5, 9, 13; 4 **4.** 7, 12, 17, 22; 5
5. 1, −1, −3, −5; −2 **6.** 5, 2, −1, −4; −3 **7.** 2, 5, 10, 17; 2 **8.** −1, 2, 7, 14; 2
9. 2, 6, 12, 20; 2 **10.** 2, 4, 8, 16 **11.** 3, 9, 27, 81 **12.** 5, 5, 11, 19

Exercise 22.4

1. 2, 4, 6, 8, 10; linear **2.** 2, 5, 8, 11, 14; linear **3.** 5, 9, 13, 17, 21; linear
4. 1, 4, 9, 16, 25; not linear **5.** 0, 2, 6, 12, 20; not linear **6.** 3, 8, 15, 24, 35; not linear
7. 2, 4, 8, 16, 32; not linear **8.** 0, 4, 18, 48, 100; not linear **9. (i)** 5, 7, 9, 11
10. (i) 1, 4, 7, 10, 13 **(iv)** 3 **11. (i)** Sequence B
12. (i)

Day	1	2	3	4	5
€	4	6	8	10	12

(ii) €22 **(iii)** €52 **(v)** €202 **(vi)** €18 **(vii)** 19 days

13. (i)

Day	1	2	3	...	10
€	1	4	7	...	28

(ii)

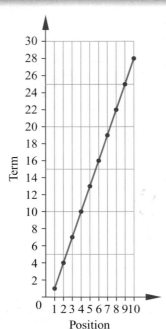

(iii) The values grow more quickly

14. (ii) Amy   **(iv)** Linear   **(v)** Day 18   **(vi)** No   **15. (iii)** Yes; day 21   **(iv)** Jane

16. (ii) Yellow flower   **(iii)** Yes

Exercise 22.5

1. 2; $T_n = 2n - 1$ **2.** 3; $T_n = 3n - 1$ **3.** 4; $T_n = 4n - 1$ **4.** 5; $T_n = 5n + 1$

5. -2; $T_n = 11 - 2n$ **6.** -3; $T_n = 7 - 3n$ **7.** -5; $T_n = 13 - 5n$ **8.** -6; $T_n = 10 - 6n$

9. 2; $T_n = 2n - 7$ **10. (i)** 3 **(ii)** $T_n = 3n - 2$; $T_{50} = 148$ **(iii)** T_{30}

11. (i) 5 **(ii)** $T_n = 5n - 1$; $T_{45} = 224$ **(iii)** T_{50} **12. (i)** -4 **(ii)** $T_n = 44 - 4n$; $T_{15} = -16$

(iii) T_{11} **13. (i)** $2n + 3$ **(iii)** $5n + 2$ **(v)** €55   **14. (ii)** $a = 5$, $d = 3$

(iii) (a) €2   **(b)** €3   **(iv)** $32\frac{2}{3}$ km   **15. (i)** 35 mins   **(iii)** $a = 35$, $d = 15$ **(iv)** $15n + 20$

(v) 155 mins   **(vi)** $14\frac{2}{3}$ kg   **16.** T_{59} **17.** T_{30} **18. (i)** 28 months   **(ii)** $2n + 8$

(iii) $3n + 5$ **(iv)** 338 months   **19.** $k = 3$; $5, 7, 9$ **20.** $k = 43$; $3, 7, 11$

21. $k = 11$; $17, 23, 29, 35$ **22. (i)** $k = 5$; $3, 11, 19, 27$ **(ii)** $T_n = 8n - 5$; $T_{21} = 168$ **(iii)** T_1

Exercise 22.6

1. (i) $9, 11, 13$ **(ii)** Arithmetic   **(iii)** $2n + 1$ **(iv)** 101

2. (i)

Pattern	1	2	3	4	5
No. of tiles	7	13	19	25	31

(ii) $6n + 1$ **(iii)** Pattern 42

3. (i) 17, 21   (ii) $4n + 1$ (iii) Shape 12   4. (i) 40   (ii) 10

5. (i)

Rectangle	1	2	3	4	5	6
Number of white squares	5	6	7	8	9	10
Number of red squares	4	6	8	10	12	14
Total number of squares	9	12	15	18	21	24

(ii) 14   (iii) $n + 4$ (iv) $2n + 2$ (v) 22   (vi) 36   (vii) $3n + 6$

6. (i) 38   (ii) $7n + 3$ (iii) 143   (iv) $a = 4, b = 3$ (v) 9th diagram

7. (i) 4 cm   (ii) 18 cm^2 (iii) 22 cm^2 (iv) 42 cm^2 (v) $(4n + 2) \text{ cm}^2$

8. (ii)

Diagram	1	2	3	4	5
Number of dots	5	8	11	14	17

(iii) $3n + 2$ (v) Odd

9. (i) 1, 3, 6, 10   (iii) 0, 1, 3, 6

10. (i) 14, 20, 26   (iii) $6n + 8$ (iv) Pond 15   (v) 4, 5, 6   (vi) $n + 3$ (vii) 18 slabs × 33 slabs

Exercise 22.7

1. $n^2 + n + 1$ 2. $n^2 + 2n + 1$ 3. $n^2 + n$ 4. $n^2 + 1$ 5. $n^2 - 3n + 2$ 6. $n^2 + 4n + 3$

7. (i) $n^2 + n - 2$ (ii) 108   (iii) Greater

8. (i) 9 m, 16 m, 21 m, 24 m, 25 m, 24 m   (ii) No. The differences are different.

(iii)   (v) Yes; 25 m

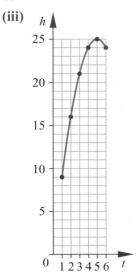

9. (i) $n^2 + 11n + 10$ (ii) 220 m   (iii) 4,270 m

10. (i) $n(n + 1)$ or $n^2 + n$ (ii) $2(n + 1)$

Exercise 22.8

1. 3, 9, 27, 81   **2.** 4, 10, 28, 82   **3.** 5, 7, 11, 19   **4.** 6, 18, 54, 162   **5.** 6, 12, 24, 48

6. 6, 10, 18, 34

7. (i) Red: 16, 32, 64, 128; Grey: 6, 18, 54, 162

(ii) **(iii)** The grey squirrels outnumbered the red ones

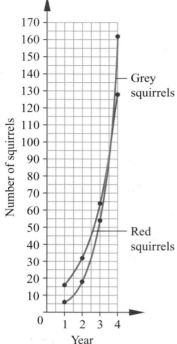

Year

Exercise 23.1

1. $a = 44; b = 118$ **2.** $x = 60; y = 120$ **3.** $p = 45; q = 75$ **4.** $a = 90; b = 35; c = 55$

5. $p = 28; q = 112$ **6.** $a = 61; b = 71; c = 48$ **7.** $a = 42; b = 96; c = 84$

8. $x = 24; y = 15$ **9.** $y = 15$ **10.** $p = 17; q = 146$ **11.** $p = 130$ **12.** $x = 75$

13. $y = 74$ **14.** $x = 65; y = 65$ **15.** $A = 60; Q = 50; R = 50; S = 70$ **16. (i)** 110

(ii) 70   **(iii)** 40   **17. (i)** 66°   **(ii)** 24°   **18.** $x = 12; y = 15$ **19.** $x = 40; y = 30$

20. $x = 25; y = 30$ **21.** $x = 2; y = 1$ **22. (ii)** 3, 4 or 5   **23.** 105°, 60°, 15°   **24.** 33

25. False   **26.** False   **27.** True   **29.** 40°   **30. (i) (a)** 110°   **(b)** 70°

32. (i) 180°   **(ii)** 360°   **33. (i)** $\dfrac{180 - x}{2}$ **(ii)** $2x - 180$ **(iii)** 108   **34.** 46°

Exercise 23.2

1. $x = 7; y = 5$ **2.** $a = 6; b = 5$ **3.** $x = 3; y = 12$ **4.** $a = 4; b = 2$

5. (i) Transversal   **(ii) (a)** 5   **(b)** 6   **6. (i)** 8 cm   **(ii)** 11 cm   **(iii)** 352 cm^2

7. (i) Perpendicular transversal   **(ii)** Yes   **(iii)** 10 cm   **(iv)** 12 cm   **(v)** 300 cm^2 **(vi)** 25 cm

Exercise 23.3

7. **(ii)** 180°

Exercise 24.1

1. **(i)** Vertically opposite   **(ii)** Alternate angles   12. **(iii)** 30

Exercise 25.1

1. $p = 70$ 2. $q = 100$ 3. $r = 90$ 4. $s = 40$ 5. $x = 70; y = 100$

6. $p = 102; q = 95; r = 85$ 7. $x = 112; y = 34$ 8. $x = 100; y = 50$ 9. $a = 40; b = 40$

10. $p = 70; q = 140$ 11. $a = 110; b = 100$ 12. $x = 100; y = 50$ 13. $x = 36$

14. $a = 40; b = 30$ 15. $p = 54; q = 54; r = 36$ 16. $a = 52$ 17. $p = 105; q = 67$

18. $r = 120; s = 70$ 19. $a = 104; b = 52$ 20. $a = 100; b = 110$

21. $w = 75; x = 122; y = 29; z = 58$ 22. $x = 40$ 23. $x = 64; y = 32; z = 58$

24. $x = 176; y = 92; z = 54$ 25. $p = 90; q = 40; r = 50$ 26. $a = 56; b = 28$

27. $x = 65; y = 40$ 28. $x = 60; y = 120$ 29. $x = 59; y = 118$ 30. $x = 49$

31. 83°   32. **(i)** 46° **(ii)** 69° **(iii)** 67°   33. 108°   34. 80°

35. **(i)** 124° **(ii)** 236° **(iii)** 118° **(iv)** 34°   36. **(i)** 60° **(ii)** 120° **(iii)** 46°

37. **(i)** 100° **(ii)** 50° **(iii)** 10°   38. 75°

Exercise 26.1

1. **(i)** $\frac{4}{3}$ **(ii)** $\frac{3}{4}$ **(iii)** $\frac{1}{4}$ 2. $p = 10; q = 13$ 3. $p = 24; q = 10$ 4. $p = 12; q = 10$

5. $p = 12.8; q = 4$ 6. $p = 6; q = 8$ 7. $p = 10; q = 8$ 8. $p = 4.8; q = 7.2$

9. $p = 5.6; q = 7.5$ 10. **(ii) (a)** 3 **(b)** 8   11. **(i)** 7.5 **(ii)** 4.5 **(iii)** 10 **(iv)** 6

12. **(i)** 1 **(ii)** 3.6   13. **(ii) (a)** 32 **(b)** 7   14. 6   15. 15   16. 15

17. 16   18. **(iii)** 7.5 cm   19. **(ii)** 6   20. **(ii) (a)** 18 **(b)** 40

21. **(i)** 6 cm **(ii)** 12 cm **(iii)** 3 cm **(iv)** 9 cm^2 **(v)** 81 cm^2 22. **(ii) (a)** 12 **(b)** 9

23. **(ii)** 7   24. **(ii) (a)** 9 **(b)** 0.5

Exercise 26.2

1. 15 m   2. 9 m   3. 60 cm   4. 18 m   5. **(i)** 10 m   6. 15 m   7. 2.8 m

8. **(i)** 144 m   10. **(i)** The triangles are similar **(ii)** 196 **(iv)** 323.4 m

11. **(i)** A, B and C must be collinear; A, E and D must be collinear; $[BE] \parallel [CD]$
(ii) 36 m **(iii)** 50 m **(iv)** Insert a peg X, such that $CBEX$ is a parallelogram where
$|CB| = |XE| = 48$ m and $|BE| = |CX| = 57$ m. Then produce CX to B.

Exercise 26.3

4. (i) 130°   **7.** (ii) 2; 20   **13.** (i) $|RQ|$ **14.** (iii) $2\sqrt{5}$

Exercise 27.1

1.

a	b	c	a^2	b^2	c^2
3	4	5	9	16	25
6	8	10	36	64	100
8	15	17	64	225	289
12	5	13	144	25	169
7	24	25	49	576	625
40	30	50	1600	900	2500
24	7	25	576	49	625
2	1·5	2·5	4	2·25	6·25

2. 5   **3.** 12   **4.** 8   **5.** 40   **6.** 29   **7.** 35   **8.** 2   **9.** 3   **10.** 3   **11.** 4
12. $\sqrt{13}$ **13.** $\sqrt{15}$ **14.** 2   **15.** $3\sqrt{2}$ or $\sqrt{18}$ **16.** $2\sqrt{2}$ or $\sqrt{8}$ **17.** $x = 5; y = 13$
18. $x = 15; y = 16$ **19.** $x = 11$ **20.** (i) 4 cm   (ii) 48 cm^2 **21.** (i) 15 cm
(ii) 270 cm^2 **22.** (i) 4   (ii) 12 cm; 6 cm^2 **23.** 8   **24.** $\sqrt{3}$ **25.** 5   **26.** $2·25\pi$ cm^2
27. (i) $\dfrac{p^2}{4}\pi$ **28.** (i) $a = 4; b = 3$ (ii) $16\sqrt{3}$ **29.** (i) 34   (ii) 17   (iii) 15   **30.** (i) 3·5
(ii) 12·5   **31.** 10 cm   **32.** 5   **33.** $\dfrac{4}{25}$ **34.** (i) 3   (ii) 3·6 cm

Exercise 27.2

1. 5 m   **2.** 24 cm   **3.** 3·4 m   **4.** 109 m   **5.** (i) 5·6 m   (ii) 1·6 m
6. $50\sqrt{10}$ cm or 158 cm   **7.** 301 m   **8.** 60 m; needs at least 53 m   **9.** (i) 6·4 m
10. (i) 54 m   (ii) Perimeter; 10·5 sec   **11.** (i) (a) 9·6 km   (b) 48 km   (ii) (a) 6,000 secs
(b) 100 min   (c) $\dfrac{5}{3}$ hrs   **12.** 18 cm   **13.** (i) (a) 0·6 m   (b) 1 m   (ii) (b) 0·96 m^2
14. (i) 101·6 cm   (ii) 89 cm, 50 cm   (iii) 4 : 3 screen by 505 cm^2 **15.** 40 m^2
17. (i) 15 km   (ii) 8 km   (iii) 72 min   **18.** (ii) South-east   (iii) 44 km   (iv) 22 km/h
(v) 22 km from start   (vi) 1 pm   (vii) 21·84 km

Exercise 27.3

1. 17 cm   **2.** 7   **3.** (i) 13 cm   (ii) 5 cm   (iii) 12 cm   (iv) 25 cm   (v) $k = 5$
4. (i) 11 cm   (ii) 8·8 cm   (iii) 6·6 cm   (iv) 4·4 cm   **5.** (i) 7 cm   (ii) 25 cm   **6.** 14·3 cm

Exercise 27.4

1. (i)

a	b	$2ab$	$a^2 - b^2$	$a^2 + b^2$
2	1	4	3	5
3	1	6	8	10
3	2	12	5	13
4	1	8	15	17
4	3	24	7	25
5	2	20	21	29
6	1	12	35	37
6	2	24	32	40
7	6	84	13	85
8	3	48	55	73

(ii) The table proves that $\triangle PQR$ is right angled.

2. (ii) (a) 14·8   **(b)** 134·4

Exercise 28.1

1. (i) $\begin{pmatrix} 3 \\ 1 \end{pmatrix}$ **(ii)** $\begin{pmatrix} 4 \\ -2 \end{pmatrix}$ **(iii)** $\begin{pmatrix} -5 \\ -2 \end{pmatrix}$ **(iv)** $\begin{pmatrix} -4 \\ 2 \end{pmatrix}$ **(v)** $\begin{pmatrix} 4 \\ 0 \end{pmatrix}$ **(vi)** $\begin{pmatrix} 0 \\ -5 \end{pmatrix}$

2. (i) $\begin{pmatrix} 4 \\ 3 \end{pmatrix}$ **(ii)** $\begin{pmatrix} 4 \\ -6 \end{pmatrix}$ **(iii)** $\begin{pmatrix} -5 \\ -4 \end{pmatrix}$ **(iv)** $\begin{pmatrix} -4 \\ 3 \end{pmatrix}$

5. 4 units to the right and 2 units up   **6. (ii)** 6 units to the right and 3 units up

7. (ii) 9 units to the right and 6 units down   **8. (iii)** 7 units to the right and 3 units down

9. (iii) 4 units to the right and 7 units up

11. (i) $\triangle SRT$ **(ii)** $[RT]$ **(iii)** $\angle RST$ **(iv)** $\overrightarrow{QR}, \overrightarrow{RT}$ **(v)** P

12. (i) $\triangle UTV$ **(ii)** $[TV]$ **(iii)** $\angle TUV$ **(iv)** $\triangle RUS$ **(v)** $[RS]$ **(vi)** $\angle SUR$

(vii) $\overrightarrow{TV}$ **(viii)** $\overrightarrow{US}$ **(ix)** $\overrightarrow{SR}$ **13. (i)** $\triangle YZR$ **(ii)** $[YR]$ **(iii)** $\angle ZYR$ **(iv)** $XYZQ, XYRZ$

(v) $\angle XZQ, \angle YZR, \angle YRZ, \angle QXP, \angle ZXY, \angle ZYX, \angle RYS$ **(vi)** 40 cm^2

14. (i) E **(ii)** $[DC]$ **(iii)** $\triangle DYF$ **(iv)** $[CY]$ **(v)** $[YF]$ **(vi)** $\angle YDF$ **(vii)** $XDYC$

(viii) 8 cm^2 **(ix)** 16 cm^2 **(x)** 32 cm^2 **15. (i)** V **(ii)** $[RS]$ **(iii)** $\triangle SVU$

(iv) $\angle USV$ **(v)** $\overrightarrow{SP}, \overrightarrow{VS}, \overrightarrow{UR}, \overrightarrow{RQ}$ **(vi)** 10 cm^2 **(vii)** 120°

Exercise 28.2

5. (i) S **(ii)** Q **(iii)** $\triangle POQ$ **(iv)** $\angle PQO$ **7. (i)** Q **(ii)** $[QO]$ **(iii)** $\triangle QOS$

8. (i) $\triangle BAK$ **(ii)** $ADCB$ **(iii)** $\triangle ABD, \triangle CBD, \triangle ADC, \triangle ABC$ **(iv)** $[DC]$

Exercise 28.3

1. 1　　**2.** 2　　**3.** 4　　**4.** 0　　**5.** 0　　**6.** 1　　**7.** 0　　**8.** 2　　**9.** 5　　**10.** 1

11. Limitless　　**12.** 0　　**13.** 1　　**14.** 2　　**15.** 0　　**16.** 1

23. (ii) $A' = (-1, 2)$, $B' = (-3, 1)$, $C' = (-4, 4)$　　**24. (ii)** $P' = (5, -2)$, $Q' = (2, -2)$,
$R' = (2, 0)$, $S' = (5, 1)$　　**25. (i)** H, O, I, X

Exercise 28.4

5. (i) C　**(ii)** D　**(iii)** $[BA]$　**(iv)** $[CB]$　**(v)** $\triangle CDM$　**(vi)** $\angle DAM$

6. (i) $[QR]$, $[PQ]$, $[RS]$, $[ST]$　**(ii)** P　**(iii)** S　**(iv)** $[RS]$　**(v)** $\triangle RXQ$　**(vi)** S　**(vii)** T
(viii) $[RT]$　**(ix)** $\triangle RQY$　**(x)** $\angle TSQ$　**(xi)** $[ST]$　**(xii)** T　**(xiii)** 40 cm^2

7. (i) $[AB]$, $[BY]$, $[XD]$　**(ii)** $\triangle DAX$　**(iii)** $\triangle ACD$　**(iv)** $[BD]$　**(v)** 50°　**(vi)** 64 cm^2

8. (ii) $P' = (2, 5)$　$Q' = (-2, 3)$　$R' = (-1, 1)$

Exercise 28.5

22. H, I, N, O, S, X, Z　　**23.** H, I, O, X　　**26. (iii)** Central symmetry in (1, 2)

27. (i) (−1, 3), (−3, 5), (−5, 1)　**(ii)** (−1, −3), (−3, −5), (−5, −1)　**(iii)** (1, −3), (3, −5), (5, −1)

28. (i) (−1, −1), (−5, −2), (−5, −5), (−2, −5)　**(ii)** (−1, 1), (−5, 2), (−5, 5), (−2, 5)
(iii) (1, 1), (5, 2), (5, 5), (2, 5)

29. (i) Axial symmetry in y-axis　**(ii)** Central symmetry in (0, 0)　**(iii)** 2 units right and 6 units down
(iv) Axial symmetry in x-axis　　**(v)** Central symmetry in (1, −3)　　**30.** A = central symmetry,
B = axial symmetry in the y-axis, C = translation

31. A = axial symmetry in the x-axis, B = translation, C = central symmetry

32. A = translation, B = central symmetry, C = axial symmetry in the y-axis

33. A : central symmetry, B : axial symmetry, C : translation, D : axial symmetry

34. A : axial symmetry, B : translation, C : central symmetry, D : axial symmetry

35. (i) Axial symmetry in $[RW]$　**(ii)** Central symmetry in W　**(iii)** Axial symmetry in $[RW]$
(iv) Axial symmetry in $[VX]$

Exercise 30.2

25. (i) Right-angled triangle　**(ii)** 13 cm　**(iii)** $5^2 + 12^2 = 13^2$

26. (i) Equal　**(ii)** $3x + 5 = x + 45$　**(iii)** $|\angle BAD| = 65°$

27. (i) (a) 4·5 cm　**(b)** 113°　**(ii) (a)** 100°　**(b)** 123°

Exercise 31.1

1. 4   **2.** 7   **3.** 14   **4.** 2, 5   **5.** 6, 10   **6. (i)** $2x + (x + 10) = 250$ **(ii)** $x = 80$ **(iii)** 90c

7. (i) $x = 5, y = 8$ **(ii)** $x = 3, y = 2$ **8. (i)** $P = 2(x + 4) + 2(x)$ **(ii)** $32 = 2(x + 4) + 2(x)$

(iii) $x = 6$ **9. (i)** $x + 3$ **(ii)** $P = 2(x + 3) + 2(x)$ **(iii)** $26 = 2(x + 3) + 2(x)$ **(iv)** $x = 5$

10. 7   **11. (ii)** 11, 13, 15, 17   **12.** 6, 7, 8   **13.** 14, 15, 16   **14. (i)** $x + 9$

(ii) $\frac{1}{4}(x + 9) - \frac{2}{3}(x) = 1$ **(iii)** 12   **15. (i)** $18 + 2x; 6 + 2x$ **(ii)** $18 + 2x = 2(6 + 2x)$ **(iii)** 3

16. (i) $4x$ **(ii)** $4x + 5; x + 5$ **(iii)** $4x + 5 = 3(x + 5)$ **(iv)** $x = 10$ **(v)** Son = 10, Mam = 40

17. Molly: 7, Laura: 5, Janice: 15   **18.** Adam: €5, Ryan: €4, Mark: €7   **19. (i)** $\frac{x}{3} + \frac{x}{5} = 112$

(ii) $x = 210$ **(iii) (a)** €70   **(b)** €42   **20. (i)** €15,000   **(ii)** $12(1,500 - x) = 15,000 + 1,200$

(iii) $x = 150$ **21. (i)** $10 - x$ **(ii)** $20x + 18(10 - x) = 192; x = 6$

22. (i) Distance = Speed × Time   **(ii)** $D = 5x$ **(iii) (a)** $x + 10$ **(b)** $2x, 2x + 20$

(c) $2x + (2x + 20) = 320$ **(d)** 75   **(e)** 85 km/h   **23. (i)** $95 - x$ **(ii)** $\frac{x}{15}$ **(iii)** $\frac{95 - x}{45}$

(iv) $x = 20$ **(v)** 1 hr 20 mins   **24. (i)** $100 - x$ **(ii)** $\frac{x}{4}$ **(iii)** $\frac{100 - x}{4}$ **(iv)** $\frac{x}{4} + 3 = \frac{100 - x}{4}$

(v) 14 km/h

Exercise 31.2

1. (i) T   **(ii)** F   **(iii)** F   **(iv)** T   **(v)** F   **(vi)** F   **(vii)** T   **(viii)** T   **(ix)** F

2. (i) $x + y = 15, x - y = 7$ **(ii)** $x = 11, y = 4$ **3.** 6, 14   **4.** 7, 10   **5. (i) (a)** 250c

(b) 170c   **(ii) (a)** $5x + 2y = 250$ **(b)** $3x + 2y = 170$ **(iii)** $x = 40, y = 25$

(iv) Pen = 40c, pencil = 25c   **6. (i) (a)** 530   **(b)** 410   **(ii)** $8x + 2y = 530, 6x + 2y = 410$

(iii) (a) 60c   **(b)** 25c   **7. (i)** $x + y = 20$ **(ii)** $8x + 5y = 118$ **(iii)** $x = 6, y = 14$

(iv) 6 teacher tickets, 14 student tickets   **8. (i)** $x + y = 80$ **(ii)** $x - y = 20$ **(iii)** $x = 50, y = 30$

(iv) 50   **9. (i)** $x + 2 = 2y, x - 7 = \frac{1}{2}y$ **(ii)** $x = 10, y = 6$ **10.** $x = 6, y = 14$

11. (i) $a + d$ **(ii)** $a + 6d$ **(iii)** $a = 1, d = 8$ **(iv)** $T_{10} = 73$ **12. (i)** $p + q = 20$

(ii) $p + q + 2p + 17 = 75$ **(iii)** $p = 19, q = 1$ **13. (i)** $2p + 4q = 160$ **(ii)** $9p + 6q = 360$

(iii) $p = 20, q = 30$ **14. (i)** 8 racing bicycles, 6 mountain bicycles   **(ii)** €780

15. (i) $8x + 5y = 400, 60x + 50y = 3,600$ **(ii)** Caravan = 20, tents = 48   **(iii)** €1,560

16. (i) $\frac{3x + y + 19}{6} = 7$ **(ii)** $\frac{x + y}{2} = 6 \cdot 5$ **(iii)** $x = 5, y = 8$

17. (i) $\frac{(x + y) + (2x - y) + (18)}{3} = 13, 2x - y = 13$ **(ii)** $x = 7, y = 1$ **18.** $a = 6, b = 2$

19. (i) $2a + 2b + 1 = 25, (3a) + (4a) + (2a + 2b + 1) = 53$ **(ii)** $a = 4, b = 8$

20. (i) $x + y + 210 = 360$ **(ii)** $2x = y$ **(iii)** $x = 50, y = 100$ **21. (i)** $x = 6, y = 2$

(ii) $x = 2, y = 1$ **(iii)** $x = 5, y = 3$ **22.** $x = 20, y = 30$

Exercise 31.3

1. $-6, 5$ 2. $-3, 4$ 3. (i) Area $= (x + 2)(x)$ (ii) $15 = x^2 + 2x$ (iii) $x = 3$

4. (ii) Area $= (x + 5)(x)$ (iii) $36 = x^2 + 5x$ (iv) $x = 4$ 5. 49 cm^2 6. (i) $x(x + 2)$
(ii) $x^2 + 2x = 80$ (iii) $x = -10, 8$ (iv) €10   7. (i) $x(x - 2)$ (ii) $x^2 - 2x = 35$ (iii) 7

8. (i) $x(x - 3)$ (ii) $x^2 - 3x = 18$ (iii) 6 9. (i) $(2x + 4)(x + 2) = 72$ (ii) $x = 4$

10. (i) (a) x^2 (b) $4x$ (ii) $x^2 + 4x = 12$ (iii) $x = 2$ 11. $2x^2 + 2(5x) + 2(5x) = 288; x = 8$

12. $4\left[\dfrac{1}{2}(x)(x + 4)\right] + x^2 = 64; x = 4$ 13. (i) $2x + y = 18$ (ii) $y = 18 - 2x$

(iv) $x(18 - 2x) = 40, x = 4, y = 10$ or $x = 5, y = 8$ 14. (i) $x + 2$ (ii) $x(x + 2)$ (iii) $x^2 + 2x = 8$
(iv) $x = 2$ 15. 100 16. $T = 1s, 3s$ 17. $15, 16$ 18. $5, 6, 7$ 19. $6, 8, 10$

20. $6, 8, 10$